PN 1993.5 .A1 R46 1985

Rhode, Eri

W9-DIW-723

A history of the cinema from
its orgins to 1970

DATE DUE

LEARNING RESOURCES CTR/NEW ENGLAND TECH.
GEN   PN1993.5.A1 R46 1985
Rhode, Eric,   A history of the cinema fr

3 0147 0001 0584 4

Eric Rhode: A HISTORY OF THE CINEMA FROM ITS ORIGINS TO 1970

NEW ENGLAND INSTITUTE
OF TECHNOLOGY
LEARNING RESOURCES CENTER

Eric Rhode: A HISTORY OF THE CINEMA
FROM ITS ORIGINS TO 1970

A DA CAPO PAPERBACK

11573301

Library of Congress Cataloging in Publication Data

Rhode, Eric, 1934–
  A history of the cinema from its origins to 1970.

  (A Da Capo paperback)
  Reprint. Originally published: New York: Hill and
Wang, 1976.
  Bibliography: p.
  Includes index.
  1. Moving-pictures — History. I. Title.
[PN1993.5.A1R46   1985   791.43'09   84-29263
ISBN 0-306-80233-3

This Da Capo Press paperback edition of A *History of the Cinema*
is an unabridged republication of the first edition published in
New York in 1976. It is reprinted by arrangement with Farrar,
Straus & Giroux, Inc.

Copyright © 1976 by Eric Rhode

Published by Da Capo Press, Inc.
A Subsidiary of Plenum Publishing Corporation
233 Spring Street, New York, N.Y. 10013

All Rights Reserved

Manufactured in the United States of America

Contents

List of Illustrations   *vii*

Part One: Before 1920
1. Inventions and Discoveries   *3*
2. Primitives   *29*
3. The Age of D. W. Griffith   *45*

Part Two: The 1920s
4. Aspects of the Soviet Cinema   *79*
5. The Influence of the French Avant-Garde   *117*
6. Weimar and Scandinavia   *157*
7. Hollywood in the Twenties   *217*

Part Three: The 1930s
8. Adapting to Sound   *267*
9. The Depression: The Media and Social Conscience   *285*
10. Utopianism and Despair   *335*

Part Four: 1940–1956
11. The Second World War   *369*
12. Neo-realism and the Cold War   *431*

Part Five: 1956–1970
13. Internationalism   *483*
14. The New Wave   *525*
15. Radical Compromise   *587*

Notes   *635*
Bibliography   *641*
Acknowledgements   *651*
Index   *653*

List of Illustrations

Page 2 Engraving of a photograph taken at 1/720 seconds by E. J. Marey.

6 A two-disc phenakistoscope.

11 Eadweard Muybridge: *The Cat.*

11 Eadweard Muybridge: *The Sulphur-Crested Cockatoo.*

12 E. J. Marey: part of the skeleton of a walking figure.

12 E. J. Marey: a man stepping out.

13 E. J. Marey: revolver photograph of a man walking slowly.

14 E. J. Marey: photographic revolver.

16 The Boulevard des Capucines: the Salon Indien.

17 A. Lumière et ses fils: advertisement.

18 A. Lumière ses fils: programme.

20 Lithograph of the Bazar de la Charité fire. (Coll. Viollet.)

21 Lumière: *The Treacherous Folding Bed.*

23 Lumière: *Le Déjeuner du chat.* (Coll. Cinémathèque Française.)

24 Filming a boxing-match inside Edison's Black Maria.

24 An Edison kinetoscope.

28 Edwin S. Porter: *The Great Train Robbery.*

35 Georges Méliès: *Le Voyage dans la lune.*

36 Georges Méliès: sketch for *Le Mélomane.*

37 Filming at Pathé studios.

42 Edwin S. Porter: *The Great Train Robbery.*

49 D. W. Griffith: *Judith of Bethulia.*

50 D. W. Griffith: *The Birth of a Nation.*

52 D. W. Griffith: *The Birth of a Nation.*

54 Part of the Babylon set from D. W. Griffith's *Intolerance.*

55 D. W. Griffith: *Intolerance.*

56 D. W. Griffith: *Isn't Life Wonderful?*

60 Mack Sennett: *Tillie's Punctured Romance.*

62 Charles Chaplin: *Kid Auto Races at Venice, California.*

64 Charles Chaplin: *The Champion.*

66 D. W. Griffith: *True-Heart Susie.* Lillian Gish and Robert Harron.

67 Marshall Neilan: *Rebecca of Sunnybrook Farm,* Mary Pickford.

68 Mary Pickford in *Daddy Long-Legs.*

69 Douglas Fairbanks in *His Majesty the American.*

74 D. W. Griffith: *Broken Blossoms.* Richard Barthelmess.

78 Dziga Vertov: *The Man with a Movie Camera.*

81 Nodding Head: an example of A. G. Bragaglia's Fotodinamismo.

83 Lunacharsky and Mayakovsky in 1918.

84 Alexander Rodchenko's design for a ciné-car, published in *Lef.*

84 Cinema carriage on an agit-prop train.

90 Lev Kuleshov: *Against the Law (Dura Lex).*

94 S. M. Eisenstein: *Strike.*

96 S. M. Eisenstein: *The Battleship Potemkin.*

Page 97 S. M. Eisenstein: *The Battleship Potemkin.*
98 Eisenstein during the filming of *The Battleship Potemkin.*
99 S. M. Eisenstein: *October.*
101 V. Pudovkin: *Mother.* Vera Baranovskaya.
102 V. Pudovkin: *Storm over Asia.*
106 Dziga Vertov: *The Man with a Movie Camera.*
109 S. M. Eisenstein: *The General Line.* On location.
110 V. Turin: *Turksib.*
111 V. Turin: *Turksib.*
113 A. Dovzhenko: *Earth.*
115 J. Protazanov: *Aelita.* (Coll. Cinémathèque Française.)
119 Louis Feuillade: *Fantômas.*
123 Louis Delluc: *Le Silence.*
125 Louis Delluc: *L'Inondation.* On location.
128 Jean Painlevé: *Crabes et crevettes.*
130 Jean Epstein: *Mor Vran*
131 Jean Epstein: *La Chute de la maison Usher.*
132 Jean Grémillon: *Gardiens de phare.*
133 Jean Renoir: *La Fille de l'eau.* Catherine Hessling.
135 Marcel L'Herbier: *L'Inhumaine.* (Coll. Cinémathèque Française.)
136 Marcel L'Herbier: *L'Inhumaine.* Jaque Catelain. (Coll. Cinémathèque Française.)
137 Marcel L'Herbier: *Feu Mathias Pascal.* Michel Simon.
138 Marcel L'Herbier: *Feu Mathias Pascal.*
140 Ivan Muzhukin: *Le Brasier ardent.*
141 Dmitri Kirsanov: *Ménilmontant.* Nadia Sibirskaya.
142 René Clair: *Le Voyage imaginaire.*
143 René Clair: *Les Deux Timides.*
144 Abel Gance: *J'accuse.*
145 Abel Gance: *J'accuse.*
147 Abel Gance: *La Roue.*
151 Jacques Feyder: *Les Nouveaux Messieurs.*
153 Luis Buñuel: *Un Chien andalou.*
154 Luis Buñuel: *Un Chien andalou.*
156 Fritz Lang: *Die Spinnen.*
158 Peter Urban Gad: *Afgrunden.* Asta Nielsen.
159 Peter Urban Gad: *Engelein.* Asta Nielsen.
161 Paul Davidson and Ernst Lubitsch.
162 Ernst Lubitsch: *Madame Dubarry.* Pola Negri.
164 Ernst Lubitsch: *The Doll.*
171 Fritz Lang: *Die Spinnen.*
173 Fritz Lang: *Die Nibelungen: Siegfried.*
173 Fritz Lang: *Die Nibelungen: Kriemhild's Revenge.*
175 Fritz Lang: *Dr Mabuse, the Gambler.*
182 F. W. Murnau: *Nosferatu.* (Coll. Prague Archives.)
183 F. W. Murnau: *The Last Laugh.*
186 F. W. Murnau: *Faust.* Emil Jannings.
189 G. W. Pabst: *Pandora's Box.* Louise Brooks and Francis Lederer.
191 G. W. Pabst: *The Love of Jeanne Ney.* Brigitte Helm.
193 Paul Czinner: *Dreaming Lips* (first version). Elisabeth Bergner.
195 Max Ophüls: *Leibelei.*
196 Arnold Fanck: *The White Hell of Pitz Palu.*
197 Arnold Fanck: *S.O.S. Iceberg.*
198 Leni Riefenstahl: *The Blue Light.*
199 G. W. Pabst: *The Threepenny Opera.* Lotte Lenya.

Page *200* Slatan Dudow: *Kuhle Wampe.*
201 Piel Jutzi: *Berlin Alexanderplatz.*
203 Fritz Lang: *Spione.*
205 Josef von Sternberg: *The Blue Angel.* Marlene Dietrich, Hans Albers, Emil Jannings.
207 Mauritz Stiller: *Arne's Treasure.*
207 Victor Sjöström: *Ingeborg Holm.*
209 Victor Sjöström: *Karin Ingmarsdotter.*
211 Mauritz Stiller: *Arne's Treasure.* Mary Johnson.
212 Mauritz Stiller: *Gunnar Hedes Saga.* Einar Hanssen.
216 Rex Ingram directing *The Four Horsemen of the Apocalypse.*
219 Josef von Sternberg: *The Last Command.* Emil Jannings.
225 Cecil B. DeMille: *The Ten Commandments.* On location.
227 The funeral of Rudolph Valentino.
231 Erich von Stroheim: *Greed.*
234 Charles Chaplin: *The Kid.* (Coll. Cinémathèque Française.)
235 Charles Chaplin: *A Woman of Paris.* Adolphe Menjou, Edna Purviance.
236 Charles Chaplin: *The Gold Rush.*
237 Charles Chaplin: *The Circus.*
240 Victor Schertzinger: *The Hired Man.* Charles Ray.
241 Henry King: *Tol'able David.* Ernest Torrance, Richard Barthelmess.
243 Buster Keaton: *Neighbors.*
245 Harold Lloyd: *Movie Crazy.*
248 Robert Flaherty: *Nanook of the North.*
252 John Ford: *The Iron Horse.*
253 John Ford: *The Iron Horse.*
254 King Vidor shooting the final scenes of *The Big Parade.*
256 William Wellman: *Wings.*
258 F. W. Murnau: *Sunrise.*
261 Alan Crosland: *The Jazz Singer.* Al Jolson.
263 Charts taken from F. D. Klingender and Stuart Legg: *Money Behind the Screen.*
266 King Vidor: *Hallelujah.*
269 Mervyn LeRoy: *Three on a Match.* Bette Davis, Joan Blondell, Ann Dvorak. —
273 Walt Disney: *Steamboat Willie.*
274 Universal's *The King of Jazz.* Paul Whiteman.
275 MGM's *Hollywood Revue of 1929.* Laurel and Hardy.
276 Ernst Lubitsch: *The Love Parade.*
279 Marcel Pagnol: *Marius.*
279 Marcel Pagnol: *Fanny.*
279 Marcel Pagnol: *César.* Pierre Fresnay, Orane Demazis.
281 René Clair: *Le Million.*
283 *Horse Feathers.* Harpo, Chico, Groucho and Zeppo Marx.
284 The *March of Time* series.
292 Henri Storck and Joris Ivens: *The Borinage.*
296 Lowell Sherman: *She Done Him Wrong.* Mae West.
300 Josef von Sternberg: *An American Tragedy.* Sylvia Sidney.
303 William Wellman: *The Public Enemy.*
307 William Wellman: *The Public Enemy.* James Cagney, Jean Harlow.
308 Howard Hawks: *Scarface.*
312 Erle C. Kenton: *Island of Lost Souls.* Charles Laughton.
316 Mervyn LeRoy: *I am a Fugitive from a Chain Gang.*
318 Mervyn LeRoy: *Hard to Handle.*
320 Busby Berkeley: *Dames.*
333 Jean Vigo: *Zéro de conduite.*

Page 334 Frank Capra directing Claudette Colbert and Clark Gable in *It Happened One Night.*
337 Joris Ivens and Hemingway in Spain.
337 Joris Ivens: *The Spanish Earth.*
340 Frank Capra: *Mr Deeds Goes to Town.* Gary Cooper.
341 Frank Capra: *Mr Smith Goes to Washington.* James Stewart.
345 Marcel Carné: *Hôtel du Nord.* Louis Jouvet.
347 Marcel Carné: *Le Jour se lève.*
347 Fritz Lang: *Fury.* Spencer Tracy, Sylvia Sidney.
352 Alfred Hitchcock filming the opening scenes of *The Man Who Knew Too Much.*
354 John Ford: *Young Mr Lincoln.* Henry Fonda.
356 John Ford: *Stagecoach.*
357 Victor Fleming: *Gone with the Wind.* Clark Gable.
362 Jean Renoir: *La Règle du jeu.* Jean Renoir, Roland Toutain.
365 Jean Renoir: *La Règle du jeu.*
368 Humphrey Jennings: *Fires were Started.*
370 Ministry of Information van carrying mobile projector and documentary films.
372 Harry Watt: *Target for Tonight.*
373 Pat Jackson: *Western Approaches.*
377 Humphrey Jennings: *London Can Take It.*
381 Charles Frend: *The Foreman Went to France.*
385 John Ford: *They were Expendable.*
386 Orson Welles: *The Magnificent Ambersons.* Agnes Moorehead, Tim Holt.
388 Orson Welles: *Citizen Kane.*
391 Preston Sturges: *The Lady Eve.* Henry Fonda, Barbara Stanwyck.
393 John Huston: *The Maltese Falcon.* Humphrey Bogart, Peter Lorre, Mary Astor.
399 Fritz Lang: *The Woman in the Window.* Edward G. Robinson.
400 Michael Curtiz: *Yankee Doodle Dandy.* James Cagney.
401 Arthur Freed and Busby Berkeley: *For Me and My Gal.* Gene Kelly, Judy Garland.
401 Busby Berkeley: *The Gang's All Here.*
403 Irving Rapper: *Now Voyager.* Bette Davis.
405 Mitchell Leisen: *Lady in the Dark.* Mischa Auer, Ginger Rogers.
407 Billy Wilder: *Double Indemnity.* Fred MacMurray, Barbara Stanwyck.
408 Michael Curtiz: *Mission to Moscow.*
409 Michael Curtiz filming *Casablanca.* Ingrid Bergman, Humphrey Bogart.
411 David Lean: *Brief Encounter.* Celia Johnson.
414 Leonid Varlamov: *Stalingrad.*
416 Walt Disney: *Victory through Air Power.*
417 John Ford: *The Grapes of Wrath.* Jane Darwell.
417 Mark Donskoi: *My Childhood.* Massalitinova.
419 William Wyler: *The Little Foxes.* Herbert Marshall, Bette Davis.
420 William Wyler: *The Best Years of Our Lives.*
421 William Wyler: *The Best Years of Our Lives.* Dana Andrews.
423 Jean Grémillon: *Lumière d'été.*
425 Claude Autant-Lara: *Douce.*
427 Marcel Carné: *Les Enfants du paradis.*
430 Roberto Rossellini: *Germania, anno zero.*
433 Alfred Hitchcock: *Notorious.* Cary Grant, Ingrid Bergman.
435 George Cukor: *A Star is Born.* James Mason.
440 Vittorio de Sica: *The Children are Watching Us.*
440 Vittorio de Sica: *Bicycle Thieves.*
444 Vittorio de Sica: *Umberto D.*
446 René Clement: *Jeux interdits.*
447 Georges Rouquier: *Farrebique.*

Page *448* Robert Flaherty: *Louisiana Story.*
449 Robert Flaherty: *Louisiana Story.*
451 Luis Buñuel: *Los Olvidados.*
454 Robert Bresson: *Un Condamné à mort s'est échappé.*
458 Roberto Rossellini: *Rome, Open City.*
461 Charles Crichton: *Hue and Cry.*
464 Jean Cocteau: *Orphée.*
466 Alain Resnais: *Nuit et brouillard.*
467 Alain Resnais: *Toute la mémoire du monde.*
469 Luchino Visconti: *Ossessione.*
474 Elia Kazan: *A Streetcar Named Desire.* Vivien Leigh.
474 Elia Kazan: *A Streetcar Named Desire.* Marlon Brando.
475 Elia Kazan: *Wild River.*
477 Robert Rossen: *Body and Soul.*
482 Akira Kurosawa: *Rashomon.* Machiko Kyo, Toshiro Mifune.
484 Ingmar Bergman: *Cries and Whispers.* Liv Ullmann.
489 Satyajit Ray: *Days and Nights in the Forest.*
491 Yasujiro Ozu: *Good Morning.*
492 Akira Kurosawa: filming at the studio-constructed Rasho gate.
493 Akira Kurosawa: *Living.*
500 Kenji Mizoguchi: *Sisters of the Gion.*
503 Kenji Mizoguchi: *The Story of the Last Chrysanthemums.*
506 Yasujiro Ozu: *Records of a Tenement Gentleman.*
506 Yasujiro Ozu: *What Did the Lady Forget?*
506 Yasujiro Ozu: *The Only Son.*
507 Yasujiro Ozu: *Early Summer.*
507 Yasujiro Ozu: *An Inn in Tokyo.*
507 Yasujiro Ozu: *Young Miss.*
509 Yasujiro Ozu: *The Brothers and Sisters of the Toda Family.*
512 Kon Ichikawa: *Conflagration.*
516 Nagisa Oshima: *Boy.*
517 Nagisa Oshima: *The Ceremony.*
518 Kenji Mizoguchi: *The Life of O-Haru.*
521 Akira Kurosawa: *Red Beard.*
523 Akira Kurosawa: *The Seven Samurai.*
524 Alain Jessua: *La Vie à l'envers.*
526 Elia Kazan: *East of Eden.* James Dean, Julie Harris.
527 Roger Vadim: *And God Created Woman.* Jean-Louis Trintignant, Brigitte Bardot.
531 Jean Rouch: *Chronique d'un été.*
535 Chris Marker: *La Jetée.*
536 Alain Resnais: *Hiroshima mon amour.* Eiji Okada, Emmanuele Riva.
537 Alain Resnais: *Muriel.* Delphine Seyrig.
539 François Truffaut: *Anne and Muriel.* Kika Markham, Jean-Pierre Léaud.
545 Jean-Luc Godard: *Les Carabiniers.*
547 Jean-Luc Godard: *Pierrot le fou.* Anna Karina.
548 Jean-Luc Godard: *Weekend.*
552 Claude Chabrol: *Le Beau Serge.* Gérard Blain, Jean-Claude Brialy.
553 Jacques Rivette: *Paris nous appartient.*
554 Jacques Rivette: *La Religieuse.* Anna Karina.
555 Jean Rouch: *Chronique d'un été.*
556 Joseph Strick: *The Savage Eye.*
560 Allan King: *Warrendale.*
562 Alfred Hitchcock: *Psycho.*
563 Billy Wilder: *The Apartment.* Jack Lemmon, Shirley MacLaine.

Page *564* Terry and Denis Sanders: *Crime and Punishment USA.* George Hamilton.
566 Ron Rice: *Chumlum.*
568 Francesco Rosi: *Salvatore Giuliano.*
574 Federico Fellini: *Juliet of the Spirits.*
576 Federico Fellini: *8½.*
577 Federico Fellini: *8½.*
578 Michelangelo Antonioni: *Cronaca di un amore.*
579 Michelangelo Antonioni: *The Red Desert.* Monica Vitti.
580 Michelangelo Antonioni: *The Eclipse.* Monica Vitti.
581 Michelangelo Antonioni: *Blow Up.*
582 Ermanno Olmi: *Il posto.*
584 Valerio Zurlini: *Cronaca familiare.*
586 Milos Forman: *Taking Off.*
589 Humberto Solas: *Lucia.*
592 Andrzej Wajda: *A Generation.*
595 Andrzej Wajda: *The Birch Wood.*
595 Wojcieck J. Has: *Farewells.*
597 Roman Polanski filming *Repulsion.*
598 Jerzy Skolimowski: *Le Départ.*
598 Dušan Makavejev: *The Switchboard Operator.*
601 Alexander Kluge: *Artists at the Top of the Big Top: Disorientated.*
601 Jiří Menzel: *Closely Observed Trains.*
604 Miklós Jancsó: *The Round Up.*
608 Lindsay Anderson: *Every Day except Christmas.*
608 Richard Lester: *Petulia.* George C. Scott, Julie Christie.
613 Stanley Kubrick: *The Killing.*
613 Stanley Kubrick: *A Clockwork Orange.*
615 George Dunning: *The Yellow Submarine.*
616 Ken Loach: *Kes.*
619 Martin Ritt: *Hud.* Paul Newman, Mervyn Douglas, Brandon de Wilde.
619 John Huston: *The Misfits.*
620 John Frankenheimer: *All Fall Down.* Brandon de Wilde, Warren Beatty.
621 John Frankenheimer: *The Manchurian Candidate.* Angela Lansbury, Laurence Harvey.
623 John Frankenheimer: *Seconds.*
626 Robert Rossen: *The Hustler.* Jackie Gleason, Paul Newman.
626 Robert Rossen: *Lilith.* Jean Seberg.
629 Arthur Penn: *The Chase.* Marlon Brando.
631 David Newman and Robert Benton: *Bad Company.*
631 Dennis Hopper: *Easy Rider.*
633 Francis Ford Coppola: *The Rain People.*

Of everything other than thought, there can be no history.

R. G. COLLINGWOOD, *The Idea of History*

**It is as if the outer world were woven into our mind
and were shaped
not through its own laws but by the acts of our attention.**

HUGO MÜNSTERBERG, writing about the cinema in 1916

Part One: Before 1920

Engraving of a photograph taken at 1/720 seconds by E. J. Marey.

1. Inventions and Discoveries

I had some glowing dreams about what the cinema could be made to do and ought to do in teaching the world things it needed to know — teaching it in a more vivid, direct way . . . When the industry began to specialize as a big amusement proposition I quit the game as an active producer. [1]

T. A. EDISON

My work has been directed towards scientific research. I have never engaged in what is termed 'production'. [2]

LOUIS LUMIÈRE

To try to chart the origins of the cinema in terms of its inventors and inventions opens up a maze of claims and counter-claims, of parallel discoveries and freakish anticipations. Even in the 1890s these claims were the source of a number of lawsuits over patents that make Dickens's celebrated case of Jarndyce versus Jarndyce, in *Bleak House*, seem by comparison a model of legal simplicity. Was it R. W. Paul in England or one of three sets of brothers — the Lathams in the United States, the Skladonovskys in Germany or the Lumières in France — who gave the first film show? Or was it any one of a dozen other claimants? How do we distinguish, in fact, between a projection of moving images which is interesting and no more, and one which marks a new stage in technology?

Watersheds, when looked at closely, become less and less distinctive. In 1888, Thomas Alva Edison, aided by W. K. L. Dickson, constructed the kinetoscope, a peep-show that ran fifty feet of moving film. Yet Edison's discovery was not isolated. It depended on the film roll promoted by the inventor of the Kodak, George Eastman; and Eastman in turn had profited from Hannibal Goodwin's recognition that celluloid would make a suitable base for the film strip. Who was the father of what, and where, and to whom?

Again and again events appear to be marked by coincidence. Why was it that in 1839, quite independently of each other, Daguerre announced his invention of the daguerreotype, Bayard of his paper positives and William Henry Fox Talbot of his calotypes; all of them, by the way, potentially excellent forms of photography? And why in 1832 should Plateau and Stampfer, also unknown to each other, have simultaneously invented the phenakistoscope and the stroboscope, laboratory models that gave the illusion of moving images; and why did many other devices of a similar kind appear at this time?

The civilized world was fascinated by movement and the recording of movement. Machines had at last undermined the assumption that movement was of necessity linked to nature, to the power of the horse or the wind. Science had already shaken the belief in some immutable social and natural order, the great chain of being; and the steam engine, an autonomous source of energy, disturbed it even further. A favourite hero among the Romantic poets, Prometheus, had stolen the secret of fire from the gods: but Prometheus had been punished appallingly for his theft. By inference, accordingly, it was thought that the new technology, and the new ideas about the social order associated with it, would exact a heavy price. If the French Revolution had aroused fears as well as hopes about the nature of change, Stephenson's *Rocket*, which was at first a cause for elation, shocked the country when, on its first run on the Liverpool— Birmingham line in 1830, it killed a Member of Parliament, William Huskisson. If Shelley in a long epic was to praise Prometheus' defiance, his wife was to give voice in her novel *Frankenstein* to a far less agreeable view of human progress.

In this way the fascination with movement was charged with deep feeling. Yet the motives for this fascination, and the uses to which it was put, could not have been more varied. With hindsight it is possible to see how Eadweard Muybridge's sequence photographs of the 1870s (which he and the painter Meissonier set in motion on the zoöpraxiscope) and Dr E. J. Marey's chronophotography of the 1880s anticipated the cinema. But neither men saw their work in this light; and to separate their discoveries from the motives that lay behind their discoveries would be to give a mystifying account of how the cinema came about.

Darwin might have been pleased at the intricacy of this evolution, and astonished by its speed; for its mutations occurred in a time span of less than a century. It was to become the most influential form of entertainment the world had known; yet the wishes of show-men played only a small part in its development.

Its momentum came from the Industrial Revolution. Bertrand Russell once said that the effect of this Revolution had been 'to make instruments to make other instruments, to make still other instruments *ad infinitum*'.[3] Edison modelled his kinetoscope on the phonograph—on the principle that a system which recorded and replayed images might be arrived at by imitating one which recorded and replayed sounds. (In fact, the analogy turned out to be misleading.) In the same way, the investigation of the chemical constituents of matter had laid the ground for the discoveries of those emulsions and fixatives necessary to photography. J. H. Schultz, followed by Tom Wedgwood, son of the famous potter, demonstrated that silver nitrate could register light and shade; John Herschel discovered (in 1819) that silver salts could be dissolved in hypo; Blanquet Evrard improved the quality of these salts with albumin. Yet there was an interaction throughout society that makes it too simple to say that the enunciation of theory led to its application which in turn led to its exploitation—though commercial urgency certainly concentrated the mind of inventors after Edison had more or less abandoned the kinetoscope, and showmen realized they could get round his inadequate patents.

Yet even if we stratify the various figures involved in this evolution as scientists, inventors and showmen, and even if we attempt to define their aims, and the perhaps haphazard cross-fertilizations between their differing interests, we shall miss the main source of pressure, which lay rather in a change of consciousness—a change that is related primarily to an understanding of visual experience. We can describe this change most dramatically by asking two questions: what was the missing link between Newton's work on optics and the emergence of the film camera; and why should Daguerre have painted Diorama backcloths that looked like photographs long before he had invented the kind of photography known as the daguerreotype?

The missing link was an old science given a new direction: physiology applied to the field of optics. In 1811 Charles Bell, in a pamphlet circulated among his colleagues, made an announcement which was to be confirmed publicly by Magendie in 1822 and which was to be known eventually as the Bell-Magendie law. Bell had discovered two kinds of nervous system: the sensory nerves which lead from the posterior roots of the spinal cord and the motor nerves which lead from the anterior roots of the spinal cord. 'This dichotomy of nervous action into sensory and motor', writes Edwin Boring, 'reminded the physiologists that the mind's sensations were as much their business as the muscles' movements.'[4] The work of such scientists as Hermann von Helmholtz in analysing these sensations prepared a base for the emergence, in the mid 1870s, of a new science: that of experimental psychology.

One of the problems which had exercised physiologists and opened the way to experimental psychology was the phenomenon of visual images persisting long after the light or colour stimulating the image has been removed. Such after-images had long been recognized: in one experiment, for instance, Newton had looked at the reflection of the sun in a mirror and then closed himself in a dark room to observe the fading optic image. But the physiologists who evolved various stroboscopic instruments to define the laws of retinal sensibility were soon inclined to induce that perception was located in the brain and not in some way in the eye. This postulate—that the mind understood movement where no movement existed—was to have a radical effect on theories of perception.

Literature on this subject was voluminous (a key paper being presented to the Royal Society in 1824 by P. M. Roget of *Thesaurus* fame), and the manufacture of all kinds of models to demonstrate it was extensive. Paris and Herschel produced the thaumotrope, and the thaumotrope was followed by Faraday's Wheel, Stampfer's stroboscope, Horner's Daedelum, and many other similar inventions. Toymakers recognized the commercial value of these models and sold copies of them in great numbers. It was soon common knowledge that some inherent disability in the human brain allowed visual images, when swiftly modified, to dissemble movement.

A two-disc phenakistoscope.

Probably the most persistent of the scientists engaged on this problem, and certainly among the more unfortunate, was the Belgian J. A. F. Plateau. Like Newton, Plateau experimented on himself and at the age of twenty-eight went blind from staring at the sun. After several agonizing months he partially recovered his sight, only to lapse permanently into blindness at the age of forty. Yet aided by his wife, Plateau continued to work on the problem of after-images until his death at the age of eighty-two. He invented the phenakisto-scope, another model which dissembled movement; but more importantly, he was the first scientist to use photographs in such a model and to devise a way by which these photographs could be projected onto a screen. Ironically, Edison was deaf when he invented the phonograph and Plateau blind when he created a rudimentary form of cinema.

In fact, the experience that we think of as cinematic had been fully realized, by complicated means, almost a century before Louis Lumière's first film show. The claim that Victorian novelists were using narrative devices similar to film technique long before the invention of the cinema can be well substantiated; but it can also be denied any suggestion of anticipation. The modes of perception later to be associated with the cinema were already well established by the end of the eighteenth century; technology, though it moved rapidly, lagged behind. If you look at a reproduction of Daguerre's painting of Holyrood Chapel (now in the Walker Gallery, Liverpool), your impression will probably be of a view so sharply defined that it seems more photographic than most photographs. In his painting Daguerre had not only foreshadowed the kind of sensibility required to respond to his silver copper-plate type of photograph known as the daguerreo-type, but also to that of the cinema, for he had based his painting on one of his Diorama screens; and the Diorama, which he had evolved in 1822, undoubtedly aroused sensations of a kind familiar to the filmgoer. It consisted of an auditorium which revolved its spectators slowly before two proscenium-like openings exhibiting gigantic paintings variously and varyingly illuminated from before and—they were partially translucent—from behind. By all accounts, audiences were thrilled by the size and depth of these images and underwent oceanic feelings similar to those we may feel today before the wide screen. Yet they appear to have accepted these photographic paintings as true to their observations of nature without any difficulty. (It is worth comparing their sophisticated acceptance of this convention to the inability of certain non-literate peoples to 'read' a photograph or film, such as Robert Flaherty encountered with natives of the South Sea Islands.)

Daguerre's audiences found the photographic convention unsurprising for a number of reasons, the most important one being their unquestioning belief in an aesthetic doctrine which, though unformulated at that time, already overshadowed a whole range of responses to art in the age of science. This doctrine, later to be categorized as naturalism, can be defined as an attempt to apply the quantifications of natural science to those processes of creation which may result in a work of art. Much as the physiologists were moving towards the science of experimental psychology through a rudimentary form of behaviourism, the supporters of naturalism in the arts viewed the world in terms of scientific models and measurements and assumed the mind of the artist to be machine-like.

During the late eighteenth century artists had made an increasing use of reproductive aids to achieve a likeness. One such device was the camera lucida, 'an instrument by which the rays of light from an object are reflected by a prism, and produce an image on paper placed beneath the instrument, which can be traced with a pencil' (O.E.D.). It usually took the form of a box in which the draughtsman could place a thin sheet of paper over a screen and trace the outline of a reflected landscape or whatever. In the eighteenth century an increase in middle-class wealth and leisure led to a demand for portraiture and topographical studies, so urgent that professional artists were at a loss to satisfy it; it was left to amateurs, with the camera lucida, to fulfil the need. 'Probably at no other period', claims Beaumont Newhall, 'were there so many amateur artists. This ineptitude fostered the development of many kinds of reproductive devices.'[5]

If the results were lifeless, they were so because the technique excluded feeling and because bad artists tend to be instinctive behaviourists, people who deny the existence of emotionality. Precursors of naturalism, these amateurs saw no objection in reducing their minds to the limitations of the camera lucida and in approaching the person or landscape they wished to depict as merely an appearance to be simulated: unlike the true artist, who, though he may be inarticulate about the creative process, usually approaches his subject as a motif which, perhaps unaccountably, stirs up memories and desires—an involvement with the subject that brings art to life. John Constable was conscious of this problem when he visited the Diorama in 1823 and wrote to his friend Archdeacon Fisher: 'It is in part a transparency. The spectator is in a dark chamber, and it is very pleasing and has great illusion. (Yet) it is without the pale of art, because the object is deception. Art pleases by *reminding*, not *deceiving*.'[6]

E. H. Gombrich has written of this letter: 'Had Constable written today, he would probably have used the word "suggesting". The artist cannot copy a sunlit lawn, but he can suggest it. Exactly how he does so in any particular instance is his secret, but the word of power which makes this possible is known to all artists—it is "relationships".'[7] It should be added that these relationships—of tone, colour and hue—are primarily regulated by the mental states that condition perception; and that when genuine artists have leant on reproductive aids (Vermeer allegedly resorted to the camera obscura), they have done so to give a fuller expression to these mental states.

Since a vast appetite for photography had been established before the invention of the daguerreotype and its equivalents—William Henry Fox Talbot, for instance, had begun his photographic researches as a keen but highly incompetent sketcher; he even failed to make efficient use of the camera lucida—it is hardly surprising that the photographic business, which began in a small backroom way, soon boomed into a major industry. In 1847, only eight years after its invention, over half a million photographic plates were sold in Paris; in 1862, over 105 million photographs were produced in Great Britain alone; and by 1900 (when the Kodak had been on sale for more than ten years) 'it was estimated that for each hundred persons passing through the turnstiles at the Paris International Exhibition, seventeen were armed with portable cameras. On days therefore when there were 300,000 visitors, 51,000 cameras were being used inside the exhibition ground.'[8]

This development had long before brought into question the idea that mechanical reproduction and art were identical. Portraitists had found their income threatened by the new market. Fear of unemployment drove many of them to attack this *foe-to-graphic* art, even though many of them relied surreptitiously on photography as a quick means to achieve a likeness. But some of the arguments raised against photography were less governed by self-interest. John Ruskin, who had at first welcomed the daguerreotype, believing it would encourage an understanding of 'true aerial perspective and chiaroscuro', had by the 1870s decided to condemn it as 'spoiled nature' and as contrary to his belief in art as 'human labour regulated by human design'.[9] Charles Baudelaire denounced an exhibition of photographs at the 1859 Salon on the grounds that photography would corrupt the meaning of art if it were not returned to its proper function—'which is to be a servant of the sciences and the arts . . . If it be allowed to encroach upon the domain of the impalpable and the imaginary, then it will be so much the worse for us.'[10]

Photography, then, edged artists into reconsidering the nature of the creative process; and its often accidental distortions opened up new models of perception. The blurred images and unexpected compositions of the Kodak stimulated Degas and Monet, and photography since then has influenced many artists, from members of the Post-

Impressionist movement to the present-day creators of various forms of assemblage and silk-screen print. But it was photography as 'a servant of science', and not as an art form, that had the most immediate bearing on the evolution of the cinema; as when on one light-hearted occasion Eadweard Muybridge, an English photographer working for a United States government agency, became a servant of science, and with an unexpected result.

In a perhaps apocryphal story, it is said that Leland Stanford, a governor of California and founder of Stanford University, had asked Muybridge to demonstrate whether at any moment a horse, when trotting, lifts all four legs off the ground. In Stanford's opinion, horses did become momentarily airborne, and he needed hard evidence to win a bet from a friend. It took Muybridge years to arrive at a solution to this problem—which proved Stanford right; and it was possibly not he, but a railroad engineer named John Isaacs who, in 1877, thought out an efficient way of analysing equestrian movement. Twenty-four cameras were placed side by side along a race track. Wires stretched from each of these cameras across the track to a sloping, sun-reflecting screen, white-painted and squared with black lines (it resembled a gigantic piece of graph paper). A horse tripping a wire would set off an electro-magnetic system which then released a camera shutter. The horse's silhouette against the graph-paper screen established its position exactly.

The success of this venture encouraged Stanford and Muybridge to photograph picture sequences on other subjects. Many of them were at first published in magazines; then, in 1887, 20,000 of them were brought together in an expensive collection of eleven folio volumes published under the title of *Animal Locomotion*. They created a considerable impression, stimulating Edison in his work on the kinetoscope and Degas in his studies of ballet-dancers in sequential poses, and deeply interesting scientists like Helmholtz and Huxley. It would not be improbable to say that by chance Muybridge had brought about a change in human consciousness. In much the same way as the telescope and microscope had done, his sequences opened up a world to the eye that the eye formerly had been unable to see. And when set in motion, they simulated in an extraordinary fashion an effect of movement.

But Auguste Rodin was to raise a telling argument against these sequences, when he was asked how he could sincerely continue with an interpretation of movement that was at odds with photographic veracity. 'It is photography that lies,' Rodin answered, 'for in reality time does not stop, and if the artist succeeds in producing the impression of a movement which takes several moments for accomplishment, his work is certainly far less conventional than the scientific

Eadweard Muybridge: *The Cat.* Breaking into a Gallop.
Time intervals: .031 seconds

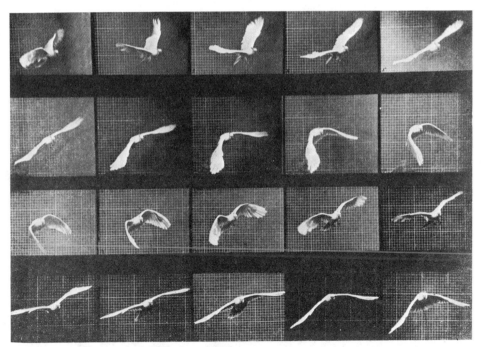

Eadweard Muybridge: *The Sulphur-Crested Cockatoo.*
One Flap of the Wings prior to Alighting. Time intervals: .017 seconds.

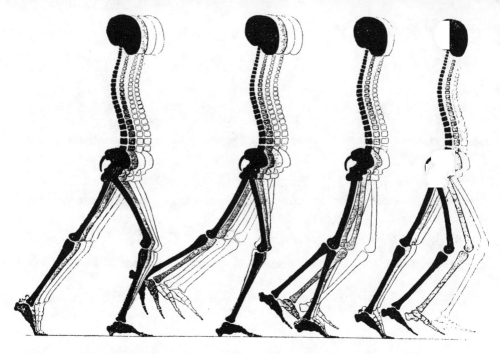

'Prefiguring time-and-motion studies . . .' E. J. Marey: *above*, part of the skeleton of a walking figure; *below*, a man stepping out; *opposite*, revolver photograph of a man walking slowly.

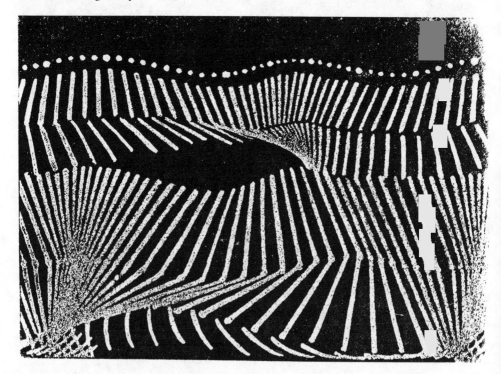

image, where time is abruptly suspended.'[11] For Rodin, as for Constable, truth in art often has to rely on suggestion.

The photo sequences in *Animal Locomotion* place together animals, crawling babies and naked men and women without regard for hierarchy: a returning of man to the animal kingdom that would have been inconceivable before the publication of Darwin's theory on evolution. But more than that, man had become dehumanized, an object for experiment. Francis Galton thought of imposing photographs of men on top of each other to see what their common denominator might be, and Ernst Mach, inspired by the projection of the Muybridge sequences, wished to arrange photographs of man—from infancy to old age—in a phenakistoscope in such a way that the whole life cycle would pass before the spectator within a matter of seconds. A recent film, setting in motion Muybridge's photo sequences of naked men and women, has retroactively shown them to be among the first examples of animated erotica. The camera seemed to confirm the behaviouristic interpretation of man as a machine-like object; and indeed certain forms of photography, such as the chronophotography of Dr E. J. Marey, complemented in an uncanny fashion fantasies about mass man that were already appearing in literature (as in Edgar Allan Poe's story *A Face in the Crowd*). In Marey's chronophotographs we find not only some of the most beautiful images ever revealed by the camera but also a prefiguring of time-and-motion studied man: of automata drilled to satisfy the needs of their masters.

*

E. J. Marey, one of the many scientists fascinated by Muybridge's publications, was a French physiologist who wished to discover a less laborious method than the recording instruments and statistics in use at his Physiological Station to chart the trajectory and oscillatory patterns of movement. He had begun to experiment with Muybridge's technique, but found it unsatisfactory when applied to random movement, since birds flying erratically were unlikely to trigger prearranged wires. Jules Janssen, a majestic colleague of Marey's (he appeared, incidentally, in one of the Lumière films), had tried to photograph the planet Venus as it passed across the sun in December 1874 and for this purpose had devised a photographic revolver – containing a revolving disc that notched up photographs at regular intervals. Marey adjusted this revolver to take photographs far more

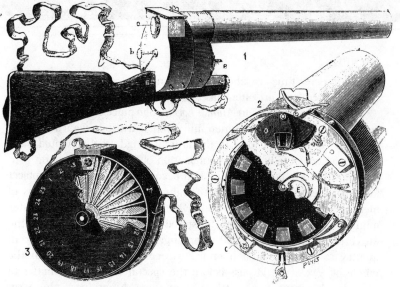

E. J. Marey: photographic revolver.

rapidly than Janssen's rate of one for every seventy seconds, and when in 1887 he abandoned gelatine plates sensitized with bromide of silver for paper roll-film, he was able to increase this speed to a hundred photographs a second. His camera carried a moving film as well as being portable (unlike Muybridge's cumbersome battalion on tripods), and Marey said that it was as much the forerunner of the cine-camera as the zoöpraxiscope was of the film projector. Duchamp's *Nude Descending a Staircase* and some of the work of the Futurist painters owe a debt to Marey's chronophotography, and the swirling draperies of art nouveau may derive something from it. But apart from Norman McLaren's *Pas de deux* (1968), where a slow-motion technique similar in impression gave two dancers the radiating splendours of a peacock's tail, its effect on the cinema has been less noticeable. And it was only accidentally related to aesthetic effect. Marey proudly claimed in his book *Le Mouvement* (published in 1894) that chronophotography had helped to clarify the diagnosis of cardiac and vascular diseases. The fact that its invention marked a crucial stage – *the* crucial stage – in the development of the film camera is one more example of how the cinema evolved as a by-product of other more urgent concerns.

Even the most decisive event in these early years, the first public showing of the *cinématographe*, was only accidentally related to the idea of film as an entertainment industry. Antoine Lumière, a successful photographer, and his eldest son, Louis, had invented a type of photographic plate that was greatly in demand. The family had prospered to such an extent that their factory at Lyons was to employ a staff of over three hundred people: it was second only to George Eastman's at Rochester N.Y. Recognizing the commercial value of the kinetoscope, Antoine was dismayed by the prohibitive charges Edison was making on the sale of film and asked Louis to invent something like it. Louis, in the event, came up with something better: a piece of equipment which was both camera and projector and had a novel claw-drive for moving the film strip.

Louis Lumière was modest about his achievement. 'What did I do? It was in the air. The work of Janssen, of Marey and his followers had one day or another to lead to its discovery.' (A generous tribute: one of Marey's assistants, Georges Demeny, unjustly sued the Lumières for having filched the idea of the *cinématographe* from his phonoscope.) At the same time Louis had no doubt about the importance of his invention: 'Other machines may have preceded mine. But they didn't work.'[12] Georges Sadoul has argued that it was Louis's care for detail which made him the true originator of the cinema. His camera (built by Charles Moisson) was a highly accomplished piece of engineering, and when fifty years later Georges Sadoul set it in motion once more he found that it functioned perfectly. Its stock of film, so supple and clear, might have just arrived from the laboratory. 'My brother,' said Auguste Lumière, 'invented the cinema in one night'[13] – a night in which Louis was suffering from disturbing dreams and a migraine.

Throughout 1895 the Lumières gave semi-private viewings; and then, at the end of the year, on 28 December, they opened a public auditorium in Paris. Their location was a basement to the Grand Café on the Boulevard des Capucines, the exotically decorated Salon Indien, reached by an awkward spiral staircase. Seats were priced at

The Boulevard des Capucines:
the Salon Indien is presumed to have been in the centre building.

one franc. During the first few days they aroused little attention; then they caught the public imagination and within weeks were a world-wide success. They had shrewdly anticipated this response and over the previous year built up their stock of machines. They had also trained a brigade of cameramen, capable of shooting films as well as projecting them, and sent off these men to foreign countries, where they had soon made a total of twelve hundred single-shot films on many subjects, including the Diamond Jubilee procession in London.

The Lumières recognized their novelty would be short-lived and went in for the quick kill. Their business acumen paid off. On 17 February they opened in London. April saw viewings in Vienna and Geneva; June, in Madrid, Belgrade and New York (where a team of twenty-one operators proved too small for the demand); July, in St Petersburg and Bucharest. During the latter part of the year their cameramen reached Egypt, India, Japan, Australia and many other places. Royalty, and celebrities of many kinds, flocked to their shows. Raff and Gammon, the company distributing Edison's kinetoscope, faced heavy losses.

The importance of this development in the history of communications cannot be overrated. Transcending differences of language and national custom, Lumière's *cinématographe* suddenly made the world a smaller and more ordinary place: the invention of faster forms of

Société Anonyme des Plaques et Papiers Photographiques

A. LUMIÈRE & SES FILS

CAPITAL TROIS MILLIONS

Usines à vapeur : **LYON-MONPLAISIR**

COURS GAMBETTA, RUES ST-VICTOR, ST-MAURICE ET DES TOURNELLES

NOTICE

SUR

LE CINÉMATOGRAPHE

AUGUSTE ET LOUIS LUMIÈRE

Imprimerie L. Decléris et fils, place Bellecour, 16, Lyon

— 1897 —

LE CINÉMATOGRAPHE

SALON INDIEN

GRAND CAFÉ

14, Boulevard des Capucines, 14

PARIS

Cet appareil, inventé par MM. Auguste et Louis Lumière, permet de recueillir, par des séries d'épreuves instantanées, tous les mouvements qui, pendant un temps donné, se sont succédé devant l'objectif, et, de reproduire ensuite ces mouvements en projetant, grandeur naturelle, devant une salle entière, leurs images sur un écran.

SUJETS ACTUELS

1	La Sortie de l'Usine LUMIÈRE à Lyon.	5.	Les Forgerons.
2.	La Voltige.	6.	Le Jardinier.
3.	La Pêche aux Poissons Rouges.	7.	Le Repas.
4.	Le Débarquement du Congrès de Photographie à Lyon.	8.	Le Saut à la Couverture.
		9.	La Place des Cordeliers à Lyon.
		10.	La Mer.

transport and of the radio—Marconi invented wireless telegraphy in 1895 and the Wright brothers first took flight in 1903—were never to have the same shocking, elating effect. In *The Moment of Cubism*, John Berger has written of how the new technology of the 1890s changed the consciousness of poets like Apollinaire and painters like Picasso and Braque. For a while at least it appeared as though mankind had become a Prometheus who could cheat the gods with impunity. Then came the First World War and put an end to that dream. But even in 1919 a poet like Blaise Cendrars could write about the cinema with an excitement that approached delirium—see, for example, his ciné-poem 'La Fin du monde'. Besides which, in shrinking the world, the *cinématographe* encouraged fashions and trends to spread with lightning speed, obliterating the idiosyncrasies of folk art. In 1909 the Bronco Billy Westerns began to enjoy a vogue in the United States; within months countries as far apart as Italy, Germany and Japan were manufacturing imitation Westerns by the hundred. The coming of the movies helped to undermine the notion of uniqueness, the magical fetishistic quality usually ascribed to visual works of art.

By 1896 Louis Lumière had begun to lose interest in his camera and was turning his mind to fresh problems. Over the next three decades he was to experiment with the idea of a giant screen—intended for the Paris International Exposition of 1900, but never realized—with wide-gauged film, with the Photorama (a screen encircling the audience), with stereoscopic effects. He also made a serious contribution to colour-plate photography. But he was unattracted to the cinema as an aspect of the entertainment business; and though the Lumière firm did produce fictions and subjects of a biblical nature, Louis had nothing to do with them.

In May 1897, a cinema fire at the Bazar de la Charité, at that time one of the most fashionable of annual events, frightened the public and brought the *cinématographe* into disrepute. An ether lamp, which provided light for the projector, went out of control, and within minutes a provisional auditorium of canvas and wood went up in flames, killing over a hundred people, including some leading society figures and a large number of children. It could be argued, very speculatively, that the sensational nature of this tragedy—it included the death of many aristocrats—was one of the reasons why the middle classes were to stay away from the cinema for over two decades and why it was to be known at first as a working-class entertainment. In 1900 the Lumière family sold off their camera rights to Charles Pathé. Louis Lumière died in 1948 at the age of eighty-four.

How do we account for the astounding popularity of the Lumière invention in 1896? The public had long been aware of moving photographs, of large screens and, in the theatre, of naturalistic detail taken to an absurd extreme. It took pleasure, certainly, in seeing movement of so fluid a kind and in recognizing certain shapes as, say, trembling leaves; but the main reason for its surprise, it could be argued, lay elsewhere.

In one of his films, *The Arrival of a Train*, Louis Lumière had seemingly contrived to break the screen surface so that a train appeared to rush out into the auditorium. This shock depended on catching the audience unawares and on transgressing a propriety in the arts: the distancing of the spectator from the object of his attention. Art, it had been assumed, could be admired if kept at arm's length—the gentleman separated from the players. But this conven-

Lithograph of the Bazar de la Charité fire. 'The Bazar de la Charité disaster led to one of the strangest quarrels of the period. The dandified Count Robert de Montesquiou, a scion of ancient French nobility, lost his wife in the fire. He was to achieve literary notoriety as the model for Huysmans's unregenerate aesthete, des Esseintes, in *A rebours* and for Proust's cultured and corrupt Baron de Charlus. It was rumoured after the Bazar fire that to identify his wife's body, Montesquiou insisted on using the tip of his cane to lift the coverings off the disfigured remains. At a reception in Baron de Rothschild's house the symbolist poet Henri de Régnier made insinuations about Montesquiou's sinister use of his cane and hinted (mistakenly) that the Count had fought his way out of the fire with it and left his wife behind. First the Count challenged Régnier, choosing pistols, with Maurice Barrès as one of his seconds. After an exchange of letters and *procès-verbaux* in the newspapers, the directions of the challenge reversed, with Régnier choosing swords. "Quite a few people came to watch the affair," Montesquiou wrote in his memoirs, "but nothing about it was uncomfortable, displeasing or ridiculous." He was wounded by Régnier, and the two participants refused to be reconciled.' (Roger Shattuck, *The Banquet Years*, New York, 1961, p. 13).

tion, and (related to it) the problem of aggression in the arts, was already being called into question. The Impressionist painters had drawn the spectator's attention to the picture plane (Henri Langlois thinks that Louis had a sense of composition similar to that of Auguste Renoir); and men of the theatre, like Strindberg and Antoine, had become sensitive to the convention of the 'fourth wall', which in 1896 the shrieks of Père Ubu, in Alfred Jarry's avant-garde play, were to bring tumbling down. Louis could easily have kept his images within the proscenium convention of the stage, but appar-

Lumière: *The Treacherous Folding Bed.*

ently did not wish to do so. He must have been conscious long before the Paris opening (which he did not attend) that the public would feel the arrival of the train at La Ciotat as an assault.

Another reason for its popularity is more perplexing. We take it for granted that the Victorians found all machines alienatory. In fact, as a writer in the *MacMillan Magazine* claimed in September 1871, their response to photography (and later to the cinema) was quite the opposite:

> Anyone who knows what the worth of family affection is among the lower classes, and who has seen the array of little portraits stuck over a labourer's fireplace, still gathering into one the 'Home' that life is always parting – the boy that has 'gone to Canada', the 'girl out at service', the little one with the golden hair that sleeps under the daisies, the old grandfather in the country – will perhaps feel with me that in counteracting the tendencies, social and industrial, which every day are sapping the healthier family affections, the sixpenny photograph is doing more for the poor than all the philanthropists in the world.

This insight has a human centrality that recalls Dickens. We may find it ironic that a class only recently touched by the hope of literacy should have been the first to give itself over to moving images; but the truth is that the cinema was to be a desperately needed consolation and source of knowledge to the poor, the illiterate and to immigrant communities (as in America) unable to speak the native language.

The *MacMillan Magazine* writer implies that photography can diminish distances of time and place: an astonishing prediction of the cinema's greatest power. He suggests, too, that since photography can redress the social and industrial tendencies of the age, which he equates with death, it has the power, in part, to conquer death. A journalist, writing in 1896 in *La Poste de Paris*, in one of the first reviews of a *cinématographe* show, makes this point more sharply: 'Now that we can photograph our loved ones, not only in stillness, but as they move, as they act, as they make familiar gestures, as they speak—death ceases to be absolute.'[14]

At the same time as the camera appeared to reinforce behaviourism, it confirmed the existence of mental states by shadowing forth images that resembled the images of the mind. Yet this contradiction was not new. While some of Muybridge's contemporaries had seen his sequence in *Animal Locomotion* as further evidence for equating man with the machine, Muybridge himself had consulted Edison in 1888 on the possibility of bringing together the photograph and the phonograph to 'reproduce simultaneously, in the presence of an audience, visible actions and audible words' so as to entertain the public 'long after the original participants shall have passed away'.[15] And Marey, for all his concern with time-and-motion studies, was to recognize the poignancy of passing time. 'Each of us', he wrote, 'has experienced the disastrous effect of time on memory. Who has not, on returning to a former place, been undisturbed by the false memory he has kept of it?'[16]

This desire to defy death and the erosions of time had its darker side. By 1861, claims Edgar Morin in *Le Cinéma ou l'homme imaginaire*, spiritualists and faith-healers had begun to use the photograph in place of wax figurines as a talisman for their spells and prognostics. And while Méliès, the conjuror, was soon to include film among the more amusing of his tricks, German directors just before the First World War were to reveal in certain screened images an inherently uncanny quality that was to be less innocent (cf. Chapter 6). There were other worlds, it had to be remembered, than the one posited by naturalistic doctrine, and not all of them were to be encouraging. Film opened the way to new nostalgias, modern sentimentalities and sophisticated forms of fetishism.

More positively, the fact that a well-known bustling street might be enshrined on celluloid without losing its vitality conferred an objective standing on the images of memory, as D. W. Griffith, more perhaps than any other director, was to realize. What had previously been seen only in the mind's eye—the dead friend, or the place long unvisited—was now no longer a private (and so perhaps delusive) experience. Marcel Proust, most extensive chronicler of consciousness of his time, within a few years was to begin writing his great novel

A la recherche du temps perdu; and it was no accident that this pro-longed essay in memory should have been woven with numerous tropes picked from the field of physiological optics, from stereoscopy and from a study of the magic lantern and the kaleidoscope. In a subterranean fashion, Louis Lumière confirmed the existence of psychic reality: how the projection of images could become an extension of the mind's eye. It was this confirmation, perhaps, that intuitively moved the first film audiences.

Lumière: *Le Déjeuner du chat.*

The first Lumière film performance has stood up well to the test of time. Formally simple (each consists of a single, well-composed static shot), at least four of them are intricate in content. *The Card Game,* Cézanne-like, has two men playing cards, another man opening a bottle and filling some glasses, and a capering waiter: a multiplicity of action that keeps the eye engaged and, in fact, offers the eye more than it can absorb at one viewing; it obliges the spectator to forget the camera and to become involved in the content of the film. In the 1930s by similar means, more fully developed, Jean Renoir was to create an impression of realism.

At least three other shorts made in 1895 challenge the spectator's powers of observation by concentrating on fast-moving crowds: workers leaving the Lumière factory, with not only hundreds of figures, but bicycles and a dog to hold his attention; members of a photographic congress (a fascinating variety of faces and clothes) disembarking at Neuville-sur-Saône, with Janssen in the lead; and the celebrated arrival of a train at La Ciotat station, with again a crowd of people, among them the hauntingly beautiful figure of a woman in a wide-brimmed hat. In discovering unexpected images in everyday experience, these films discovered a source often to be returned to at times of cinematic renewal, as in the Kino-Eye investigations, or neo-realism.

Their shortness (they last about a minute) and their pith give them the sharp memorability of certain dreams. Is it no more than a coincidence that Freud discovered the key to psychoanalysis in the year that Lumière created these films? *'The Interpretation of Dreams'*, Freud wrote to Wilhelm Fleiss, 'was finished in all essentials at the beginning of 1896.'[17] In psychoanalysis the crucial concept of transference, in which the patient 'projects' his fantasies onto what he feels to be the impersonal screen-like mind of the analyst, finds its analogy in the cinema and other nineteenth-century optical inventions to the same extent that psychoanalysis itself had developed out of experimental psychology.

If film humour originated in the music-hall gag, it did so perhaps because the films were so short; part of the pleasure of these gags lies in the tension of wondering whether the film will run out before the joke has been completed. The first one on record, rudimentary and rather feeble, was made at the studio Edison had built in the garden of his laboratory, a revolving, heliotropic prefabricated building that bore the nickname of 'Black Maria' (it looked like a police patrol wagon). Called *Fred Ott's Sneeze* this gag still delights audiences

Filming a boxing-match inside Edison's Black Maria (to the sound of an Edison phonograph). *Right*, an Edison kinetoscope.

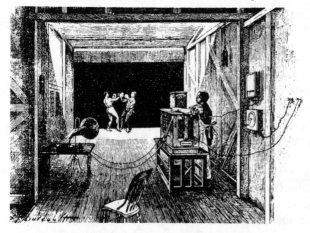

—in part, probably, because the build-up of the sneeze and its discharge is timed to fit the film's length. On the other hand, Louis's more sophisticated *L'Arroseur arrosé (Watering the Gardener)* continues beyond the gag—that is, of the boy stepping on the hose and the gardener having his face soaked: the spectator sees the gardener spank the boy and then return to his duties. Perhaps Louis did not want us to identify with the boy, as some of his successors (Zecca, Chaplin) might have wished. A rough sort of justice, you could say, brings stability back to the image.

The pioneers dwelt under the aegis of science. At the same time, many of the inventors were isolated men, unprotected by any kind of institution, lacking financial backing, often on the verge of despair. Their intuitions seldom had more than a random connection with theory. Edison, an autodidact, was obliged to employ a mathematician, Francis R. Upton, who had studied for a year under Helmholtz. (When Edison met Helmholtz they had little to say to each other.) Edison nicknamed Upton 'Culture'. He despised theory and scorned experiments that had no immediate application to industry.

But through his achievements he had, like the Lumières, built up material resources: a fine workshop at Menlo Park, a large staff, the provisional assistance of Wall Street bankers. Other pioneers lived a hand-to-mouth, lodging-house existence: William Friese-Greene, forever taking out patents, forever leaving his inventions unfinished, jailed for bankruptcy, dying at a film congress with less than two shillings in his pocket; the debonair Major Woodville Latham and his two sons, failed salesmen, failed businessmen, failed showmen—yet claimants to the Latham loop, still used on the modern projector; George Eastman, a multi-millionaire admittedly, who shot himself, leaving a note—'My work is done. Why wait?'; Emile Reynaud, who allegedly threw his machines into the Seine; Muybridge, impractical and a little mad, jailed briefly for murdering his wife's lover; Louis Le Prince, working on the same lines as the Lumières and perhaps the first to think of perforating the film strip, who mysteriously disappeared—perhaps in flight from his wife—while travelling by train from Dijon to Paris; Jean LeRoy, the original film entrepreneur, who founded a cinematograph company in New York and then vanished into obscurity. 'The cares and anxieties of being an inventor,' wrote Alexander Graham Bell, originator of the telephone, 'seem more than flesh and blood can stand.'[18] The tricksters, the fast talkers, the cranks, the defeated: all of them took part in the gold rush to invent the cinema. Yet for years the cinema was more likely to lose your fortune than to make it. It hovered between life and death in the nether world of the fairground, the second-class music hall, the beer garden, the penny arcades and the church social.

For many of the film-makers it was not (when compared to the restrictions imposed on many of their successors) an unsatisfactory life.
English pioneers, like Cecil Hepworth and R. W. Paul, established
cottage industries: would shoot a film in the garden, develop it in the
kitchen and have little trouble in hiring it out. 'There was nothing of
courage in what I did,' said Hepworth in 1948, 'it was always just a
lark for me.'[19] The zest carried over into his filming; as we can see,
for example, in his engaging one-reeler *The Revolving Table* (1903).

And now in the 1970s, with the waning of the big companies and
the growth of student audiences and club cinemas, and the foolproof
improvements in equipment, this way of working, which never died
out completely, appears to be on the increase. But between these two
periods of relative freedom we have the cinema as a great industry
and, at times, an art.

Rudolf Arnheim apart, most writers about film have neglected the
relationship between experimental psychology and the cinema. Yet
one of the first sustained inquiries into the qualities of film had been
of a psychological kind. The Harvard psychologist Hugo Münsterberg,
who had worked as a student with Wilhelm Wundt, was fascinated
by the movies; he believed they had brought a 'sharper accent' into
daily life and in *The Photoplay: A Psychological Study* (1916) tried to
define this pleasure. Like a number of other critics at the time of
the First World War—Pinthus in Germany, Lindsay in the United
States, Canudo and Delluc in France—he recognized that the cinema
had begun to attract members of every class and was no longer the
province of the uneducated (by 1915 box-office attendances in the
United States alone, he estimated, consisted of about ten million
tickets sold each day). He believed the time had come to address this
audience literately.

By considering the problem of after-images, or the ways in which
the camera can create an illusion of movement and space or the sort of
mental adjustments required to understand the close-up, he came to
the conclusion that films, by their nature, observe the laws of the
mind rather than those of the outer world. The most effective film
scripts, he thought, were created out of an association of ideas. They
'tell us the human story by overcoming the forms of the outer world,
namely space, time and causality, and by adjusting the events to the
forms of the inner world, namely attention, memory, imagination and
emotion'.[20] Although Münsterberg's conclusion sounds surprising,
coming as it does from someone who denied the existence of the unconscious and proclaimed himself anti-Freudian, the subsequent development of film technique has shown how right he was. Anyone
who has seen Fellini's $8\frac{1}{2}$ will acknowledge the permanent value of

his insights. 'Depth and movement alike come to us in the motion picture world not as hard facts but as a mixture of fact and symbol.'[21] 'It is as if the outer world were woven into our mind and were shaped not through its own laws but by the acts of our attention.'[22]

He wrote perceptively on a problem of primary concern to critics: that of the architectonics of screen space, or the meaning that certain camera movements can induce in our projection of depth onto the screened image. And he took care to show by what means film differs in creation of illusion from, say, the waxwork—means which allow it to be an art. At the same time, he dealt cursorily with another aspect of the film's effect on the mind: its reputation for corrupting the young. He had no sympathy for those moralists (always with us) who wish to spoil the pleasure of others by resorting to bogus statistics, such as that 'eighty-five per cent of the juvenile crime which has been investigated has been found traceable either directly or indirectly to motion pictures'.[23]

'A simple, primitive and universal language': Edwin S. Porter's *The Great Train Robbery*.

2. *Primitives*

So the cinema passed into the hands of small-time showmen – and within less than two decades had become a major industry and an art form. 'It was an extraordinary metamorphosis,' writes Edgar Morin. 'For it was not artists or educated men who brought about this transformation but rag merchants, autodidacts, conjurors and clowns.'[1] As European producers soon realized, the American market had begun to dominate the world by 1905, and in order to understand some of the tensions that underlay this expansion we need to enter a predominantly American debate.

One side in this debate depends on the belief that film narrative and sentiment derived principally from stage plays and stage productions; that even so cinematic a talent as Edwin S. Porter was heavily indebted to theatre technique. The other side to this debate concedes some influence from the theatre, but goes on to argue that the theatre, far from being a catalyst, was obstructive in its influence. The cinema was a self-generating activity; it had no model in the other arts; a virtually illiterate public created a new form of language by and for itself. (This notion of a 'film language' is no figure of speech: Vachel Lindsay, Abel Gance and others seriously compared film images to Egyptian hieroglyphs.) The immigrant communities of America had only one shared means of communication, suggests Terry Ramsaye, 'the simple, primitive and universal language of the pictures'; hence the warm demand for movies 'in the populous centres filled with polyglot populations':

> Pittsburgh, in the heart of the coal and iron country, with its vast numbers of poorly assimilated imported labourers, contained a wide array of differing linguistic groups. To these aliens the American theatre and the American arts in general were either unintelligible or without appeal. The motion picture offered no linguistic barriers. A story on the screen was a picture alike to Pole, Slovak, Russian, Magyar or Italian. And it was cheap, the price of a glass of beer.[2]

In this quotation Ramsaye raises at least two conflicting ideas. On the one side, there is the American theatre and arts in general, 'either unintelligible or without appeal', with the American middle classes, still enthralled by European culture, pretending snobbishly to enjoy the European imitation. On the other, you have 'a simple, primitive and universal language' suddenly emerging out of nowhere, like Elijah's cloud, an Old Testament vision that assumes America to be a void awaiting its own authentic culture. But Europeanized middle-class culture was neither more nor less alien to the United States than the cultures of the immigrant communities. The problem of America, in fact, was not an absence of culture—though the perception of a void waiting to be filled still captures the tourist—but an excess of conflicting cultures, ethnic and religious, some of them of great richness. The idea of the melting pot was for the most part a consoling fantasy, it would seem, and so was the dream of the primitive which infiltrates the sayings and makings of the first American film men (primitive, as well as being barbaric, carries the charge of 'vital', 'jagged', 'restless'—often desired attributes in the new craft).

Yet Ramsaye's argument does hint at an idea which needs to be grasped by anyone wishing to understand the unusual qualities of the new medium. To explain this idea we need to extrapolate two hypothetical polarities. Compare the theatre, that hothouse of artifice, with its painted actors and backcloths, its glut of words and its infusions of space and time, with the trajectories through landscape and timelessness of the Western—its rugged men and fresh-skinned women, its Homeric simplicities, its Homeric reliance on a few well-worn objects. Ideally, the action of the Western has the beauty and the vitality of the wild beast. Cage this beast, and you have the gangster movie, also truly cinematic, as the beast turns violently against its urban cage.

In the same way, styles imitate their content. *The film as play* tends to have inert camerawork, nondescript editing, an uneasy sense of location, grandiose actors who talk too much and call attention to their performance. *The film as an art* in itself has a probing yet tactful camera that creates tactile values (seemingly) out of space, and an articulated editing that sets up a new kind of rhythm and intonation. Its stars are charismatic, usually animal or childlike, untouched by apparent artifice. If you wish to find a model for this second kind of film, think of any muscular activity—the grace of the pugilist (boxing matches were a favourite subject in the early American movies) or of the racing horse.

Benjamin B. Hampton, writing about the formation of Paramount in 1913–14, elaborates on Ramsaye's theory. The public voted with its feet for better cinemas, extended runs, longer films. It alone gave actors the mixed blessings of stardom and refused to be intimidated by the great theatrical reputation. Hampton demonstrates these points with force. But his assumption that film audiences helped to create an entirely new culture is unfounded. Certainly, theatre people were diffident about working in the new profession until about 1915 when the prospect of high fees erased these doubts and, certainly, the film debuts of many stage eminences, including that of Sir Herbert Beerbohm Tree, were financially catastrophic and helped bring about the bankruptcy of the Mutual Company (though Beerbohm Tree, it should be said in his defence, tried to modify his oratorical delivery); but as soon as the one-reeler was replaced by lengthier narratives, the need for a consistent style of acting became imperative, and the stage was a ready source for this discipline.

European producers and distributors were not alone in successfully promoting filmed plays. The one-time furrier, Adolph Zukor, laid the ground for an accumulation of financial power that led to his near control of the American film industry in 1919 by rebuilding a New York theatre as a cinema with all the luxurious attributes of a theatre, and by choosing for his first programme there an imitation of the Société du Film d'Art style, *Queen Elizabeth* (1912), featuring Sarah Bernhardt and directed by Henri Desfontaines and Louis Mercanton.

The first star, Florence Lawrence, began her film career in a Shakespearean adaptation made for Vitagraph. And D. W. Griffith, who learnt a great deal from the Société du Film d'Art productions and may have been influenced by the operatic Italian film epics of Giovanni Pastrone and others, was a failed playwright, who (said he) never gave himself wholeheartedly to the cinema: theatrical in his derivation of ideas from Belasco and other talents of the American stage (which was flourishing at this time), theatrical also in his feeling for occasion, gesture, cadence. Yet Griffith had quickly grasped that he did not need to rely on the literalism of the filmed play in order to create a theatrical pathos in the new medium.

Hampton is also misleading when he argues that the demand for better pictures 'had to be devised and manufactured, not by intellectuals, but by mere businessmen',[3] although he had some reason for distrusting intellectuals. In part his defensiveness may have been forced on him.

Many thinking people were troubled by the cinema and spoke out against it. Writing about an education film on tuberculosis that blended 'stale romance and preachment in about the same proportion as the worst muck-raking novels', a young American intellectual, Randolph Bourne, stated in an article titled 'The Heart of the People', published in the *New Republic* of 3 July 1915, that

I feel even a certain unholy glee at the wholesale rejection of what our fathers reverenced as culture. But I don't feel any glee about what is substituted for it. We seem to be witnessing a lowbrow snobbery, in a thousand ways as tyrannical and arrogant as the other culture of universities and millionaires and museums . . . It looks as if we should have to resist the stale culture of the masses as we resist the stale culture of the aristocrat.

Others were more overtly hostile to the cinema: T. S. Eliot was to state in an essay on Marie Lloyd that 'With the decay of the music-hall, with the encroachment of the cheap and rapid-breeding cinema, the lower classes will tend to drop into the same state of protoplasm as the bourgeoisie.'[4] Eliot's statement is provocative, yet it does contain some truth. Screen images do tend to arouse a response both restless and addictive. At the same time, his argument fails to bear much thought and indeed the whole debate soon spirals into futility. The stage has a bad influence on the screen, the cinema destroys the values of the music hall: both views add up to a needless stratification.

The literate, it could be, were blinded by their literacy from understanding the language of the cinema; so it is not surprising that it needed a poet, Vachel Lindsay, to define the aesthetic of the silent film in terms that those versed in the idiom of traditional culture could understand. *The Art of the Moving Pictures* (1915; revised edition 1922), often a discursive and rhetorical book, contains a still effective appreciation of Griffith's achievement. It also adds a third argument to the American debate. Lindsay was little concerned with film as an immigrant's Esperanto or as an extension of stage techniques. He saw it, rather, as an antidote to the over-verbalization of Protestantism. The Founding Fathers had brought over books but had lacked baggage space for, say, the Elgin Marbles (though, by the time Lindsay came to write his book, the American rich had ransacked Europe for paintings and sculptures, cathedrals and castles). A society based on *laissez-faire* capitalism was liable to build monstrous cities and to ravage the countryside and perhaps the movies could alert audiences to this danger. The moment had come for America to visualize herself. Her hero should be the architect; her prophet, the film-maker.

Lindsay believed that the silent film might awaken audiences to a feeling for the architectural in landscape as well as in cities. He categorized its styles into three kinds—the dramatic, the lyric and the epic—and also, more pointedly, related its styles to various other kinds of visual art. The action picture should be like sculpture in motion. Thinking of Griffith's Assyrian commanders in *Judith of Bethulia*, he recalls Donatello's equestrian statute of Gattamelata and Verrocchio's Bartolommeo Colleoni. 'There is more action in them than in any of the cowboy hordes I have ever beheld zipping across the screen. Even in the simple chase picture, the speed must not destroy the chance to enjoy the modelling.'[5] Lindsay thinks of Griffith, and his view of American home life and young American women, when he likens the intimate picture to painting in motion; it should have the delicacy of certain Whistlers or of the minor Dutch masters. Finally, he saw the picture that aspired to splendour—

whether of a religious or patriotic nature, or concerned with the disposition of crowds—like architecture in motion. Even the fairy tale, he believed, although it may be about transformations or objects put to an unexpected use (as when the dish runs away with the spoon), is of this kind, and will imply, when ably filmed, an ordering of space and enclosure.

Lindsay can prefigure the Prohibition state of mind—the cinema keeps men out of beershops—and he can be cranky in other ways. But many of his predictions have been borne out: his guess, for instance, that the Japanese would create an outstanding tradition of film-making and that Lafcadio Hearn's *Kwaidan* would make an excellent movie script or (an allied thought) his wish that films should approach the clarity of Imagist poetry. He also thought that the attraction of the Western and, at that period, of stories about primeval man was bound up with the genius of this recent invention. 'There is a hunger in this nation for tales of fundamental life . . . The primitive is always a new and higher beginning to the man who understands it.'[6] As we shall see, Lindsay's insight into the American hunger for tales of fundamental life is central to an understanding of many American film-makers and stands in opposition to the glamour and illusion represented by the theatre.

By the time Vachel Lindsay came to write about it, the cinema had become relatively sophisticated and had passed through many stages of development. The imitators of Louis Lumière had been, quite literally, imitators. The technical possibilities of the camera were so unexpected that they seem to have inhibited the imagination. Everybody had turned out trains entering stations, babies at table, men at cards. The notion of film direction, of *mise en scène*, of using the actual to some other purpose than that of doggedly recording appearances in a single shot, was undiscovered; and so was the distinction between reportage and fiction. Even Georges Méliès began his career by running through the Lumière gamut, starting with a game of cards. The theatre was to provide him with a way out of this deadlock: but in his case the theatre was to be a trap as well as a liberation.

Méliès came from a wealthy family (his father manufactured high-quality footwear); and the young man had worked for a while in his father's factory, during which time he had incidentally become a proficient mechanic. In 1884 he was sent to London to scout out a possible shop site for the firm, and while there frequently went to see performances by the conjurors Maskelyne and Devant. Fascinated by them, he trained himself in their skills and on his return to Paris began to construct robots similar to those once used by the eminent illusionist Robert Houdin. He gave public performances and became acquainted with many professional magicians; and when, in 1888, the Robert-Houdin theatre came up for sale, he sold his share in the family business to his brother and bought the theatre. By the time the Lumières had opened their cinema in the Salon Indien he was well known in Paris as a scene designer, conjuror, theatre proprietor and cartoonist. He obtained a Bioscope and had soon cranked out about forty films, mostly of the Lumière kind—though he did demonstrate some conjuring tricks, recorded before an elaborately painted back-cloth in the Méliès's garden at Montreuil. Then in the spring of 1898, it is alleged, he discovered by chance the trick which was to open up the future to him. His camera stopped while he was filming in the Place de l'Opéra. Before he could set it in motion once more, one view of pedestrians and vehicles had been replaced by another. On the developed film women suddenly turned into men, a bus into a hearse. This trick—and the other tricks it suggested, like double ex-posure and superimposition—allowed him to appropriate photo-graphy and the visual world to the conjuror's sphere.

He was not the first to have recognized the possibilities of trick motion photography. One of the Lumière films has a wall being de-molished; then, the process reversed, the wall springing back into place. But the point of the Lumière experiment was to display the scope of the camera: it did not seek to create an autonomous world. The driving spirit behind the conjuror's art, on the other hand, is to seduce audiences away from nature and to enthrall them with another kind of order, in which the conjuror is the sole authority.

Méliès was the first film director in the sense that through his experience of the stage and through the accident of a jammed camera he was able to weave the fabric of screen fiction. Images could be removed from the flow of time and the flux of appearances; they could be studied and rearranged to enact mental states or intellectual chimeras. That he made so little of this discovery need not be ascribed to his theatricality (he employed actors and designed costumes and scenery), but to the poverty of his fantasies. It is for this reason that the Lumière films, ostensibly realistic, have the impact of certain dreams, while the Méliès fantasies, as inconsequential as some dreams, do not.

At first sight, his choice of subjects seems to cover a wide range of interests: fairy tale, legend (Don Quixote, Faust), history (Benvenuto Cellini), science fiction with trips to the moon and to the sea-bed, crime stories and newsreels both simulated and actual. In common with children, who will happily try to draw the most complicated of suggested ideas, Méliès seemed able to take on anything; yet there is an important difference between child art and his approach. Children, who are not inhibited, depend on their play with toys to work

'SF trips to the moon': backdrop for Georges Méliès's *Le Voyage dans la lune.*

through emotional difficulties and develop their range of symbolism by projecting their inner states onto these toys. In their drawings they may fall back onto a shorthand, but it is one vivified by these projections. In Méliès's settings, however, this shorthand remains both stereotype (because the feeling is defended against) and caricature (because the defended-against feelings tend to be persecutory). One familiar example: on the trip to the moon, the earth rocket lands in the moon's right eye. The moon's face is set in a terrible grimace: its left eye swells indignantly and the wounded eye drips from its socket. Méliès would seem to be touching on infantile feelings concerning sexual assault; at the same time his treatment, so mechanical, so slick, fails to acknowledge these or any other feelings.

His fairy stories lack the Vachel Lindsay splendour of architecture in motion. We are always conscious of watching a stage, an area pressed in by the splash and splatter of badly painted scenery. Themes borrowed from Gounod, Berlioz, Jules Verne and Edgar Allan Poe are shorn of their promise and made subordinate to a psychopathology. His symbolism tends to be so limited that if his films were longer they would have a mind-piercing monotony. A grimacing, decapitated head, usually his own, recurs as a motif, and as a form surely of genital displacement: as in *The Indiarubber Head* (1901), which has him, grinning furiously, pump up a head of himself to a vast size and then allow it to deflate. In another extravaganza, images of his head rise up and hang like quavers within a musical staff of telegraph wires.

'Images of his head hang like quavers within a musical staff of telegraph wires':
a Georges Méliès sketch for *Le Mélomane*.

He is often the animating spirit in these actions and liked to appear
as Mephisto. In common with many other film-makers of this time he
seemed unwilling to distinguish between newsreel and fabrication, and
he filmed *The Coronation of Edward VII* (1902) at Montreuil. Women
play a secondary role in these fantasies. They vanish inside boxes
or cones, and sometimes they reappear. Their heads twinkle inside
stars, or they sit on planets as though on swings; an idea given a
cornucopian plenty in the Italian epic *Dante's Inferno* (1909), which
had Virgil and Dante witness a night sky awash with floating, re-
cumbent, *fin-de-siècle* nudes. In taking the cinema into fiction Méliès
plunged it into kitsch – and put it on a level with peep-show taste and
the permitted, genteel pornography of his age.

The beginning of his fame is usually dated from 1899, when *Cinderella*
not only pleased the French, but was much in demand on the English
music-hall circuits and (a mark of success) pirated in the United
States. He filled the post-Lumière vacuum. More positively, his taste
for the fantastic amused audiences and later made him an admired
figure among the surrealists. But by 1906 the American public,
whose tastes were now all-powerful, had grown tired of whimsy; and
he was unable to adapt himself to new demands and techniques. In
1907 a slump on Wall Street coincided with a crisis of over-produc-
tion among the film-makers. The age of the manufacturer was over;
the age of the cartel had begun. In January 1908, Edison set up a

'The Pathé empire': photographing a number of films simultaneously at Pathé studios.

trust with the stronger companies to keep out the independent film-makers; and a congress aimed similarly to limit distribution rights (and also to stabilize the gauge and perforation systems on raw stock) was held in France in 1909. The trust and the congress treated Méliès fairly; but he was a manufacturer working on his own income, very different from industrialists like Charles Pathé and Léon Gaumont, and he was unable to meet the pressure of increased work. He drew up a contract with Pathé to hand over his distribution problems. In one clause of this ruinous agreement Pathé had Méliès mortgage his property to him, and then arranged for his manager, Ferdinand Zecca, to 'supervise' the Méliès output. Méliès, as was expected, lost heart at this interference and was eventually ousted.

It was, of course, unjust. But by 1909 the Pathé empire had turned to areas of interest quite unlike those that Méliès had opened up and he really had no place in it. As a director Zecca had plagiarized the semi-realistic techniques of British film-makers like Robert Paul and G. A. Smith and, although he was no longer to direct after 1906, his taste in down-to-earth comedies, *drames passionels* and historical subjects impressed itself on the directors he employed—among others Louis Gasnier (who supervised the serial *The Perils of Pauline* (1914), a Pathé co-production with various American companies, in part financed by William Randolph Hearst) and Albert Capellani, who later was to imitate the naturalism of the eminent stage producer Antoine. (Antoine also directed films for Pathé.) In 1911 Gérard

Bourgeois, the most important of these naturalistic directors, made *Les Victimes de l'alcoolisme and Le Roman d'une pauvre fille.*

But Pathé had also to contend with other trends, apart from American realism. In February 1908, the Lafitte brothers founded the Société du Film d'Art and invited the Comédie Française stage producer André Calmettes to direct *L'Assassinat du Duc de Guise*, a subject which had been filmed at least twice before. But the Film d'Art brought the prestige of the Comédie Française and of leading stage actors to its productions, and it attracted an audience which normally would have avoided the cinema. In 1908 alone the Société du Film d'Art produced among other films *La Tosca* with Sarah Bernhardt, *Oedipus Rex* and *The Kiss of Judas* with Mounet Sully and *Britannicus* with Mounet Sully and Réjane. It was all very different from the Méliès kind of pantomime, and in 1909 Pathé reformed his company into the Grand Société Cinématographique des Auteurs et Gens de Lettres in order to compete with the Film d'Art.

It is possible that Méliès would have been happier at the less powerful Gaumont studios. Yet under the various regimes of Alice Guy, Victorin Jasset and Louis Feuillade, Gaumont had moved into thriller serials and comedy series at a considerable remove from the Méliès interests. Feuillade himself strictly subordinated his sense of the magical to realistic expectations, while his two most prolific associates, Léonce Perret and Jean Durand, had long before absorbed the Méliès influence and gone beyond it in their serials and slapstick comedies. With the coming of the war, Méliès was not only out of fashion and bound by his Pathé contract; his Robert-Houdin theatre had been closed for the duration of the war and his brother Gaston had squandered a fortune setting up film productions in Japan. In 1923, after a prolonged lawsuit, Pathé was allowed to seize everything Méliès owned. For the remaining fifteen years of his life he was reduced (but quite happily, it seems) to selling confectionery and toys at a kiosk, owned by his second wife, on the Gare Montparnasse.

His downfall—though it has something self-willed about it—was typical of many men who invested in the booming, highly aggressive film market. In America, however, the trust companies did not have their own way so easily, and the tenacity and impudence of the independents has its exhilarating aspect. The law had virtually no control over the manufacture and showing of films, and there were many kinds of abuse: copyright legislation on the use of novels and plays, for instance, did not begin to be defined until the administrators of General Wallace's estate sued the makers of the 1907 *Ben Hur* and were given damages in 1911. But the main abuse related to camera patents. Edison had failed to secure his foreign rights on the kinetoscope, and any mechanic could get round the American patents by slightly modifying Edison's apparatus. In this way Thomas Armat and C. Francis Jenkins were able to put the vitascope on the market. There were many other kinds of modified kinetoscope. W. K. L. Dickson, a one-time Edison assistant who parted from his employer on bad terms, set up with Henry H. Marvin and others to form a company named after their camera: the Biograph. (More fully, the American Mutoscope and Biograph Company.) J. Stuart Blackton and Albert E. Smith, two out-of-work entertainers, hired equipment from Edison and then, in the usual way, cheated him out of his rental. By 1912–13 their company, Vitagraph (also named after a type of camera), had a gross income of between five and six million dollars a year.

Once you owned a camera and projector (the two being sometimes combined) it was easy to open a flea-pit anywhere and to shoot your own films. (The New York rooftop was a favourite studio location, providing both scenery and maximum sunlight.) In such a manner Marcus Loew, William Fox, Sigmund Lubin, Carl Laemmle, Adolph Zukor and many others separately began to make fortunes. George Spoor and G. M. ('Broncho Billy') Anderson used their initials (S and A) to name their Chicago company, Essanay; and George Kleine, Samuel Long and Frank Marion named Kalem on the same principle. 'Kalem', comments Lewis Jacobs, 'started in 1905 with a cash investment of only $600, by 1908 was clearing $5,000 a week profit. They were producing only two pictures a week at a cost of $200 each.'[7]

The function of producer and exhibitor was taking on some sort of definition; there now arose a third and, possibly, key figure in the growth of a future industry: the distributor. He, too, engaged in shady dealings, since there was no standard fee on rental or sales at the small, busy exchanges, often at the back of stores, where the commodity was traded. Sharp practices included the undercutting of prices, the running off of dupe prints and the breaking of licensing agreements—a familiar trick being to hire a film for one showing, then to have it secretly bicycled around to various theatres on the same evening.

At the turn of the century, American film-making had been lively but undistinguished, imitations mostly of Lumière, Méliès and Edison: gags, scenes of exotic places, prize fights, chases, news-shots. Apart from the occasional extravagance, such as Enoch Rector's 11,000 foot record of the Corbett-Fitzsimmons fight at Carson City, Nevada in 1897, dramas seldom exceeded four hundred feet in length and seldom resisted the social imperative to edify (the hostile pressure of religious and moral-minded organizations, already strong, continued to increase throughout the next three decades). But one Edison employee, a cameraman named Edwin S. Porter, found ways to bring these forms closer to sustained narrative. A. Nicholas Vardac has argued that Porter 'merely' translated the aims and methods of the naturalistic theatre into 'the idiom of the motion picture camera'.[8] Porter, indeed, drew on the resources of the theatre throughout his career—the film in which he radically transformed cinematic technique, *The Great Train Robbery*, was possibly based on a play by Scott Marble, first staged in New York in 1896—yet he slights Porter's importance by that 'merely', much as Lewis Jacobs over-estimates it when he claims that Porter discovered the principle of editing.

The historian may find it convenient to believe in such distinctions: that Porter, impressed by Méliès's way of recording stage scenes and then placing these scenes in sequence to make a casual narrative, decided to intercut scenes with each other (if for no other reason than to build up suspense). But the craft of editing signalled a much deeper process—which Porter quickened rather than precipitated. In *Jack and the Beanstalk* (1902) he proposed a refinement on Méliès's type of stage decor. In *Circular Panorama of Electric Tower* (1901) he enlarged the area to be viewed by placing his camera on a high building and panning it horizontally. Conversely, in *Gay Shoe Clerk* (1903) he emphasized a clerk's pleasure in a young woman's legs by a close-up of her feet as he placed a shoe on one of them. Porter gave a fuller expression to the naturalism of the nineteenth-century theatre by removing this naturalism from the conventions of the theatre. In doing so he took the risk, always entailed by naturalism, of assuming the observer to be similar to a machine in his perceptions and of reducing the observed person to a sum of experimental data. If the content of *Circular Panorama* resembles G. K. Chesterton's story *The Hammer of God*, in which a priest on a church tower feels no compunction in dropping a weighty object onto an insect-like person below, the technique of *Gay Shoe Clerk* comes close to dissociations and intensities of fetishism. In effect Porter was to acknowledge how the mobility of film could be used to increase impersonality and isolation (the loneliness of acts of sexual deviation), or how it could, by its wide-ranging linkages and containments of experience, increase an awareness of kinship.

In the 1920s Russian directors were to explore the social implications of editing. Now, many decades later, we have no way of knowing whether Méliès, Porter or even Griffith were more than intuitive in their insights. They were key figures in a general process which included many men. Méliès had begun to understand how a film image differs from the thing filmed. Porter, and others, went beyond Méliès in seeing that film might be cut and brought together in a way that—far from diminishing—enhances a sense of the actual.

In 1907, after months of struggle, Picasso completed *Les Demoiselles d'Avignon* and ushered painting and sculpture into the Cubist phase. Porter and other pioneers, in helping to release film from the bondage of consecutive time, freed it also from the tyranny of geographical space and unselfconsciously allied it with Cubism and with the many kinds of assemblage that resulted from Cubism. But they did more than that. Art traditionally has consisted of cult objects offered up for contemplation. Cinematic narrative, as Walter Benjamin has observed, escapes this reverential gaze. It assaults the audience with impressions; it raises and casts off metaphors so rapidly that the conscious mind may barely perceive them; it affects us like some agile yet penetrating notation.

Film-makers soon touched on its limitations. The mingling of four stories in Griffith's *Intolerance* bewildered the public and still overtaxes our powers of concentration on a first viewing. Griffith's theme—of intolerance—appears too intellectually tenuous for all this conflicting emotionality. (In its pre-release version, it is said, *Intolerance* was longer and more firmly structured and, for this reason, less fatiguing.) At the other end of the time scale, Eisenstein's conceits in *October*—Kerensky compared to Napoleon and to a peacock—appear too intellectually elaborate. Editors since then have tended to avoid these extremes of technique.

The two films on which Porter's reputation rests—he was to become Director General of Zukor's Famous Players Company and to continue as a leading figure in the industry until his retirement in 1915—are of varied achievement. *The Life of an American Fireman* (1902) fails to live up to the promise of its first shot: a fireman, asleep in his office, dreams (as shown in an inset) of a mother putting her baby to bed. Is this mother and child, already threatened by fire, the fire chief's own family? An identification has been suggested, and a fear aroused, and Porter does not emphasize it further. The ensuing race to save the mother and child heightens urgency and has at least one breath-stopping moment as prancing horses pull fire-wagons out of the engine station. But the burning house looks both within and without as though it were made of canvas and wood and the cluttered bedroom distracts our attention from the rescue. The billowing smoke gives no intimation of flame.

The Great Train Robbery (1903) creates a more substantial impression. Furnishings in the ticket office and in the interior of the express car are minimal and lit dramatically. We are conscious of the texture of wooden walls and floors. For the most part the Méliès bric-à-brac has been swept away, and a beautiful American efficiency takes its place. Settings and action function together, and the architectural sense is strong. A window in the ticket office and an open sliding door on the express train allow us to see an interior and its outside in a manner that enhances feelings of enclosure. The latter part of the

'Out into the open': Edwin S. Porter's *The Great Train Robbery*.

story, with its hold-up and chase, takes us out into the open: Porter's fluent camerawork and thoughtful, untheatrical set-ups extend this sense of openness further. Buffalo Bill's travelling circus had astonished the public with its spectacular fights between cowboys and Indians; and William Selig, and others, were toying with the format of the Western; but Porter on this occasion was really to tap the promise of the genre. Yet the openness of the final scenes may throw light on their confusing bittiness (for the film ends in a scramble): it is as though the vastness of America were too engulfing.

It could be argued that Porter's editing, and his Brechtian care in giving dimension to the railway engine and to rooms, were no more than procedures to raise suspense. Yet a radical difference exists between suspense intended to whip up thrills and suspense that touches on a genuine social anxiety. In *The Kleptomaniac* and *The Ex-Convict*, Porter was to reveal the humanitarian nature of his interests more boldly, by showing how an effective practice of parallel editing had to be bound up with an awareness of the social dialogue, an awareness that beneath the accepted classification of rich and poor, police and criminal, fireman and victim, men are members of the same species. As Dickens had understood years before, the distinctions between class and profession could not obliterate a much deeper web of binding relationships.

The popularity of *The Great Train Robbery*, and its many imitations, had an important side-effect. In June 1905 an experienced theatre manager, John P. Harris, and his brother-in-law, Harry Davis, converted a Pittsburgh store into a cinema, decorated it lavishly, brought in a pianist and (since tickets sold at five cents) called the place a nickelodeon. Their first programme included *The Great Train Robbery*, and this combination of relative comfort, continuous performances and at least one good story soon raised their receipts to a thousand dollars a week. A journalist, writing in 1907, said of the nickelodeons:

> Incredible as it may seem, over two million people on the average attend the nickelodeons *every day of the year*, and a third of these are children.
>
> The nickelodeon is usually a tiny theatre, containing 199 seats, giving twelve to eighteen performances a day, seven days a week. Its walls are painted red. The seats are ordinary kitchen chairs, not fastened. The only break in the red colour scheme is made by half a dozen signs, in black and white, *No Smoking, Hats Off* and sometimes, but not always, *Stay as Long as You Like*. Last year or the year before it was probably a second-hand clothier's, a pawnshop or cigar store. Now the counter has been ripped out, there's a ticket-seller's booth where the show-window was, an automatic musical barker somewhere up in the air thunders its noise down on the passer-by, and the little store has been converted into a theatrelet. Not a theatre, mind you, for theatres must take out theatrical licences at 500 dollars a year. Theatres seat two hundred or more people. Nickelodeons seat 199, and take out amusement licences.
>
> For some reason, young women from sixteen to thirty years old are rarely in evidence, but many middle-aged and old women are steady patrons, who never, when a new film is to be shown, miss the opening. In cosmopolitan city districts the foreigners attend in larger proportions than the English-speakers. As might be expected, the Latin races patronize the shows more consistently than Jews, Irish or Americans. Sailors of all races are devotees.[9]

By 1909, 8,000 nickelodeons—or nickelettes, as they were sometimes called—had opened up throughout the country, a figure shortly to be doubled. Exchanges proliferated. The legal battle over patents intensified with this expansion; all control seemed lost; and Edison, changing his strategy, organized a trust with the ten leading companies. The General Film Company, as the trust became to be known, announced that it would grade all theatres according to quality, fix a standard rental, determine both release dates and the choice of projectors and programmes. It also forced exhibitors to buy a licence at the cost of two dollars a week.

The independents, reacting furiously to this proposal, soon found means to evade it. The managers of General Film applied legal sanctions; and when these sanctions proved ineffective, as they often did, they resorted to violence. Anticipating the gangsterism of Prohibition days, thugs smashed cameras and raided illicit laboratories and machine shops.

Big business had been forming trusts for over twenty years, and anti-trust laws, such as the Sherman Act of 1890, had made little impact. (Theodore Roosevelt said that such acts were about as effective as a papal bull against a comet.) Yet by 1914 the General Film Company was demoralized, in part because the independents, taking advantage of America's size, were often able to slip out of their reach. One of these independents, William Selig, sent his company to Los Angeles (a short drive from Mexico, where American law had no jurisdiction) and soon received reports back East that the constant sunlight of California cut lighting and heating costs. He also learnt that its locations were ideal for the Western. His enthusiasm for the West Coast attracted other independents, and film companies began, in a sporadic way, to make the arduous trek from East Coast to West.

Even more damagingly, the trust had lost touch with public demand. It resisted the idea of the star system, of longer pictures—at first two- and three-reelers, then the feature-length story—and then of extended runs in luxury theatres: one-night stands had previously been the rule. The independents who backed these ideas prospered; and one of them, William Fox, won a law case against the Edison Company in 1912, which disheartened the trust further. By the time of the Great War, when Hollywood-centred producers were poised to take over a large part of the world market, four out of the ten companies that originally made up General Films—Edison, Biograph, Kalem and Méliès—had either gone bankrupt, been taken over, or closed down. The trust's battle against the independents was to be repeated more than once during the coming fifty years, with cautious distributors tending to block the way for the more imaginative filmmaker; and, indeed, it was only in the late 1950s, when public taste and box-office returns had become unpredictable, that the independents were once more to encroach on vested interests with some persistent gain.

3. The Age of D. W. Griffith

I, for one, am glad that I served my novitiate in a day when we could afford to be good fellows, and our hearts were young enough and happy enough to enjoy the gypsying way of things. [1]

LINDA ARVIDSON, for a while Mrs D. W. Griffith

The battle to control the film market was ruthless. Yet for a few years it had been possible for D. W. Griffith quietly to negotiate obstructions and to work in friendly surroundings. 'It was an easy matter in those days to get into the studio,' claims Mrs Griffith.

No cards of announcement were needed, no office-boy insulted you, no humiliation of waiting, as today. A ring of the bell and in you would go, and Bobbie Harron would greet you if he chanced to be near by. Otherwise, anyone of the actors would pass you the glad word. On an ordinary kitchen chair a bit to one side of the camera, Mr Griffith usually sat when directing. The actors when not working lingered about, either standing or enjoying the few other kitchen chairs. During rehearsals actors sat all over the cinema stand – it was at least six feet square – and as the actors were a rather chummy lot, the close and informal intimacy disturbed them not the least. [2]

From 1908 on, Griffith directed over 400 films for Biograph. But he left the company in 1913, when it declined to change its policy and release the four-reel *Judith of Bethulia,* even though the public had already shown its interest in five- and six-reel feature films. Together with Harry E. Aitken, a businessman, he formed Mutual and under various company names produced *The Birth of a Nation* (1915) and *Intolerance* (1916). But Mutual collapsed and so did Triangle, a corporation Aitken had set up with Kessel and Bauman and which employed Griffith, Mack Sennett and Thomas H. Ince as producer-directors. In 1919 Griffith joined with Douglas Fairbanks, Charlie Chaplin and Mary Pickford to found United Artists, so as to protect their interests against the encroachments of Adolph Zukor's ever-increasing empire. But Griffith, already constrained by his bankers and by debt, felt obliged to leave United Artists in 1924, and then lost most of his independence by signing a contract with Zukor at Para-

mount. It was the Méliès story once more. He found his work inter-
fered with; he began to drink too much. A return to United Artists
did not improve the situation. In 1931 he was edged out of the industry and remained in isolated though comfortable retirement until
his death in 1948.

Although changes in the industry played some part in bringing
about this decline, it would be wrong to leap to the conclusion, however, that the industry ousted him because it considered his ideas old-
fashioned. Throughout the 1920s other directors were to practise the
dreamlike idealization of women and landscape that had been one of
his concerns and were to prove again and again that the public welcomed this return to conventions considered outdated in the other
arts. One of Griffith's few box-office successes in the 1920s, indeed,
was an unrepentant screen version of a barnstorming relic, *Way
Down East* (1920).

Moreover, he was conscious of the social changes brought about
by the war and he was still open to new ideas. He anticipated the 'It'
girl with *The Girl who Stayed at Home* (1919), casting Clarine Seymour,
who died in 1920, as the cabaret performer Cutie Beautiful: in one
delightful sequence this attractive star dances to a record of 'Papa,
there's another Picture in Mama's Frame'. *In Hearts of the World*
(1917) he reworked in a somewhat stilted fashion parts of *The Birth
of a Nation* and yet went far beyond it in describing the cruelties and
monotonies of the battlefield; he himself risked his life filming on
location and appears to have felt deeply about the ways in which
mechanized warfare had given a new dimension to acts of atrocity. In
the remarkable *Isn't Life Wonderful?* (1924) he touched on the theme
of starvation in post-war Germany with a restraint and sense of the
actual that gives the film the appearance of having been made much
later in time than Pabst's *Joyless Street* (1925). But his epic *America*,
released in the same year as *Isn't Life Wonderful?*, suggests another
reason for his loss of authority. Its handsome production values and
polished style could not conceal a sense of exhaustion. He had lost
touch with his habitual sources of tension.

In his previous work his most distinctive tension—it appears quite
early on in his Biograph career—had consisted of an interplay between his sensitivity to the visual and his taste for the crudest types
of melodramatic plot. And in the same way as his delicate feeling for
painterly and sculptured effect can be associated with his intuitive
sympathy for the teenage girls whom he so often chose as the focus
for his interests, so his ability to harness film technique in the service
of narrative would seem to have been bound up with his taste in
melodrama and his need for plots containing brutish men who try to
destroy the girls. From his Biograph one-reelers to *True-Heart Susie*
and *Broken Blossoms*, both released in 1919, the contrast between a

capacity for appreciation and an appetite that approaches greed is reflected both in the content of his plots and in his style.

Through this tension, which seems to have touched many of his interests, he seems to have been able to resolve, at least temporarily, the debate between stage and screen: between the illusionism of the painted stage-like setting and the flexible wide-ranging possibilities of location shooting. *Intolerance*, for instance, is like a greenhouse in which it is possible to see how the Film d'Art flowered into the experimentalism of *The Cabinet of Dr Caligari*, *Aelita* and *L'Inhumaine* as well as into the artifices of Sternberg and Borzage, and in which it is possible to see how the more naturalistic and social interests of Porter could ramify into the kind of art practised by Pudovkin. The argument of screen versus stage and of location versus studio filming was to continue until the 1960s, largely on the false belief that cinematic renewal depends on a return, of the most simplistic kind, to the outward forms of nature; yet Stroheim and Eisenstein, who most closely observed the tradition of *Intolerance* in their bringing together of actuality material with the most theatrical sorts of device, demonstrate by their example that this question of convention is marginal to other concerns, such as the emotional nature of the film-maker's involvement in his subject, the process which Münsterberg had described as the weaving of the outer world into our minds.

Griffith was able to sustain this process by acting out a certain conception of himself. He claimed that he was a Southern gentleman and that his father had been Colonel Jacob Griffith, nicknamed 'Roaring Jake', a hero of the Civil War and a well-known Kentucky character. He moved uneasily among the Yankees. He preferred the culture and later—when he had become world-renowned—the company of European aristocrats. He often talked about his Kentucky upbringing, the manners of his father's generation, the poverty of his youth. Edward Wagenknecht, meeting him on the first night of *Orphans of the Storm* (1922), was struck by his egocentric loneliness. 'He took you in, and then he dropped you; you were not quite sure whether he heard what you were saying or not. As Henry James might say, you were all there for him but he was not all there for you.'[3] From him, even more than from Cecil B. DeMille, springs the legend of the Hollywood magnifico, devouring people and landscapes so as to manufacture images, inexhaustible in his appetite for retakes, vaster settings and larger casts. Yet in order to carry off this role he needed a supporting company for whom he rather selfconsciously could be seer and actor-manager. Once, when orating a prayer scene for his cast, a woman visiting the studio burst into laughter. Griffith smiled and said with a shrug, 'Well, do something like that, children,' and sat down.

His need for insulation was most apparent in his relationship with women. Billy Bitzer's mutoscope camera harshly exposed lines and wrinkles, and Griffith had to cast his heroines from girls in early adolescence: a state of affairs that he accepted with almost too much equanimity perhaps. Sharp-eyed Lillian Gish used to tease him on his liking for 'gaga babies', and she has described how in rehearsal, 'imitating a young girl, he would get up and hop about, shaking his balding head as if it had a wig of curls. A stranger would have thought him mad.'[4] He could be hard on these girls and, like the villains in some of his melodramas, appeared to enjoy his power over them. 'It once took six hours' solid work for Griffith to induce Carol Dempster to cry,' writes Kevin Brownlow in *The Parade's Gone By*. 'Refusing to resort to glycerine, Griffith had to work on her until she had achieved real tears.'[5] At the same time, he seems to have been more at his ease with them than with anyone else and savoured creating the playful tender atmosphere in which they worked best. He established the careers of Mary Pickford, the Gish sisters, Blanche Sweet, Bessie Love and Mae Marsh; and no one has equalled his ability to draw performances of such quicksilver grace and spontaneity out of young women. With Southern chivalry he idealized them in much the same way as he did the rural landscape, though this gallantry probably exacted its price. His two marriages lasted only briefly and he lived out most of his life in hotels. In his last years he seems to have been panic-stricken. The journalist Ezra Goodman could barely restrain his delight in describing an unhappy meeting with him in 1948, shortly before his death. 'The father of the American film sat in an easy chair in a hotel bedroom in the heart of Hollywood, guzzling gin out of a water glass and periodically grabbing at the blonde sitting on the sofa opposite him.'[6]

As with Keaton later, Griffith needed to be at the centre of a family nucleus to work well. The manner in which this protection affected the quality of his work is clear from his response to the technical challenge of *Judith of Bethulia* (1913). Apart from the difficulty of evoking an Old Testament atmosphere out of some inadequate studio scenery, and of keeping up this atmosphere over the unaccustomed length of four reels, he had to deal with the unusual subject (for him) of a sexually aggressive heroine: Judith, who decapitates Holofernes, oppressor of her people. To some degree he failed to meet the challenge: his settings resemble illustrations to a Victorian Bible: and he has Blanche Sweet play Judith as a child-vamp who kills Holofernes for having made a pass at her. Even so, family conditions encouraged a consistency in the acting and in the handling of the crowd scenes.

From the microcosm of the family Griffith sought to project the macrocosm of worlds both real and imaginary. But it would be wrong to take the title of *The Birth of a Nation* (1915) as literally celebrating

D. W. Griffith: *Judith of Bethulia*.

some familial act of birth. Even in its first part, which covers the events leading up to and including the Civil War, his interest in showing how the conflict, for all its destruction, brought out an underlying fraternity among the antagonists is secondary to his main concern: the isolation and virtual expulsion of the alien forces that he feels most threaten the family. From his opening titles in which he states that the 'bringing of the African to America sowed the first seed of disunion' to his concluding sequences in which the Ku Klux Klan ride to save some besieged whites, his aim is to show the Negro as the greatest danger to the values he most cherished. Iris Barry, in her monograph on him, has tried to extenuate his racism by seeing it as a consequence of his culture; after all, 'Lubin's *Coon Town Suffragettes* and Turner's *In Slavery Days*, which are more blatantly racist, have long since been forgotten.'[7] However, Griffith's masterwork has been remembered.

His racism comes over neither as some thoughtless reflection of views dinned into him since childhood nor as some imposed message that audiences can learn to disregard, but as a malevolence that suffuses the whole action; and allied as it is with his gift for persuasion, it results in a propaganda as noxious as the anti-semitism of the Nazi *Jew Süss*. 'In 1915 the Ku Klux Klan was unheard of,' wrote

H. L. Mencken in the mid-twenties. 'In 1925 it is one of the most powerful factors in American life.'[8] To a considerable extent, Griffith brought about this development; and the Payne Report of 1933 states that his racism continued to influence children until well into the 1930s.

Yet what were the grounds for his hostility to the Negro? *The Birth of a Nation* is a work of art, in the sense that it is as much about its director's mental states as about the condition of America, and like all genuine art, however much it may try to disseminate a lie, it cannot help but reveal to some degree the truth. It is probable that Griffith's blindness to the way others would react to his racism reflects not so much Southern obtuseness as a failure to recognize how internalized his feelings about the Negro were: in particular, how he thought of the Negro as a threat to his kind of studio family and to his playful relationships with young women. One shot in *The Birth of a Nation* has two lovers in the foreground involved in courtship, in the background Negroes picking cotton. For all his fear of the Negro, Griffith structures this shot in such a way as to allow us to infer that the idealized, even precious grace of his lovers, and the kind of civilization they represent, depend on the silent industry of the Negroes; or, to put it differently, that the lovers enact one kind of relationship between the sexes of a rather attenuated kind, while the Negroes, as they gather in the crop, enact another of a more productive sort.

D. W. Griffith: *The Birth of a Nation*. 'The idealized grace of his lovers.'

Griffith half-recognized that black labour supported the culture in which he imaginatively existed in the same way as parents support their children—a culture in which he was free to dramatize himself before his child actresses—but he declined to acknowledge the reason for his fear of the Negro, and in this respect he resembles certain jealous children who refuse to accept the sexuality of their parents and, in mind at least, keep them apart. He directs his rage in the main at the liberal senator Austin Stoneman—based on an actual senator, Thaddeus Stevens—whom he depicts as a dangerous man because he has taken a mulatto housekeeper as his natural wife. The mulatto housekeeper whispers evil liberal thoughts into the senator's ear and eventually is seen to go mad. Griffith goes so far as to suggest that this liaison is responsible for destroying the well-being of the country. The liberated Negroes take to drink, treat the whites with insolence and rape women. Griffith is so appalled at the prospect of adult sexuality that he exaggerates it into a species of self-destruction.

The Birth of a Nation provides the spectator with fluctuations in feelings of a fascinating variety as Griffith's mind engages, often subtly, with the symbolism of American history. (For all history is inference drawn from fragments of evidence, inferences that become part of the symbolism of our understanding.) If his anxiety is at its height in his handling of the Negro question, so intense indeed that it overrides the facts, it is almost wholly suppressed in his response to Abraham Lincoln. In spite of Joseph Henabery's acute impersonation, Griffith seems unable to give life to his conception of the President; he seems to have been unable to reconcile his dislike of the man who released the slaves with conventional pieties about the idea of the martyred hero. In *Abraham Lincoln* (1930) he gave this figure a partial vitality by imagining narcissistically that Ann Rutledge must have been a 'gaga baby'; on the whole, though, his dullness about the President stands in marked contrast to the rich ambivalence that John Ford brought to this figure in a succession of films.

But between the extremes of overwhelming anxiety and apathy, Griffith dramatized brilliantly a whole range of experiences. The remarkable sequence concerning the destruction of Atlanta, which opens with an iris shot of some troops marching through a valley, is like a boy's game with toy soldiers, but in its rhythms, camerawork and texturing by cloud and gunsmoke, a boy's game orchestrated with mature skill. Griffith lavished the admiration he excluded from his response to adult relationships onto the larger configuration of landscapes and groups and onto those pictorial and sculptural qualities that Vachel Lindsay so admired.

But how close did this controlling of response come to authoritarian modes of thought? One way of answering this question is to break it down into two parts and to consider it in terms of stage and

D. W. Griffith: *The Birth of a Nation.*
'A boy's game orchestrated with mature skill.'

screen: in terms of Griffith as actor-manager, creating histrionic effects in the manner of David Belasco, and of Griffith as the explorer of what he called the 'commonplace, undramatic event', using his camera analytically, as a scientist might.

The actor-manager

Although he admitted that he had been impressed and influenced by *L'Assassinat du Duc de Guise,* he denied that the Italian epics had played any part in his decision to make *Judith of Bethulia:* even so, the similarities between Italian film-making and his period reconstruction in *Judith* and *Intolerance* are so pressing that it is possible to assume a similar kind of spirit motivated both of them. By and large, the Italian epics fulfilled Lindsay's wish that space and crowd movement should be given an architectural presence. They concretely realized dimension, and they did so in part because, as Vernon Jarratt has suggested in his book *The Italian Cinema,* the aristocrats who managed the Italian film industry 'came from families going back with unbroken traditions into the Middle Ages. They lived, many of them, in the identical palaces in which the events they filmed had taken place centuries before, and they had been accustomed from childhood to live among the buildings, costumes, pictures, statuary and furniture of the past.'⁹ No doubt these producers found the epic useful in asserting the authority of lineage. But the traditions of opera with their grandiose staging, the quality of Italian light and the dream of ancient Rome also underlay this architectonic sense. Set designers on the Italian epics appear to have been impressed by the gigantic ruins of imperial Rome, ruins that raised the shadow of a heroic, phantasmal city. They, and the directors of these epics, often astutely evoked the fantasy of eminence and decay by the use of bold props, as in the great doors and massive fountain, with water spouting from a lion's mouth, in Giovanni Pastrone's *The Fall of Troy* (1910): by the use of light and shade that could, in Pastrone's *Cabiria* (1913), take on a considerable depth; and by slow-moving dolly shots that heightened the sense of monumentality. The screen no longer seemed a flat surface; it opened out into the vibrant measure of Mediterranean light. Holocausts and crowd conflicts would have confused the public without this inherent spatialism. The apocalyptic destructions of Mario Caserini's *The Last Days of Pompeii* (1913) and the battles in Enrico Guazzoni's *Quo Vadis?* depend for their narrative clarity on a choreography that seems to echo the stress and counter-stress of buttress and wall.

These skills, derived from Renaissance painting and sculpture, would have been pretentious if they had been less infused with the pleasures of showmanship. But they did portend a time when Mussolini would try to imitate ancient Roman pride and elevate similar fantasies into inflated myth. But this was to be later; few Italians took the cinema seriously before the First World War; and although the so-called father of Fascism, Gabriele d'Annunzio, wrote the script for *Cabiria* and sold the film rights on many of his plays, he was too snobbish about the craftsmen who worked in the industry to realize how he could use film for the purposes of propaganda. 'The one value of film', he said, 'is its power for metamorphosis. And Ovid is its poet.'¹⁰

For all his need to control experience, Griffith had no lineage to assert and no aristocratic position to consolidate; he merely had his dogmatic views of Southern superiority. In *The Birth of a Nation*, admittedly, he could call on first-hand evidence, and his cameraman, Billy Bitzer, could imitate the tones and textures of Mathew Brady's Civil War photographs. But he had little understanding of more than immediate history and his imagination could not make much of hierarchic societies remote in time and space from America. In *Intolerance* he was at a loss before the customs of Belshazzar's Babylon, Charles IX's Paris and Jerusalem at the time of Christ; and, the spirit escaping him, he relied too heavily on the letter. It was for this reason that he employed pedantic footnotes to warn his audiences that, for instance,

Part of the Babylon set, four years after *Intolerance* had been filmed.

certain shots would show a 'replica of Babylon's encircling walls, 300 feet in height and wide enough to let chariots pass'. If the ahistoricism and mobility of American society contributed to this too literal approach to the past, it also, just as probably, saved him from settling into authoritarian modes of thought.

The investigator of the commonplace undramatic event

He was more a visionary than a historian. In *Intolerance* he went against the records in asking for elephant sculptures on his Babylon set, and these sculptures are among the more striking features in this memorable scene. He was a visionary too in his development of film technique. Although he and his associates saw how the camera's fluency in movement, angling, close-up and deep focus could be given a narrative meaning through the craft of editing, and although they added the fade-out, iris and framed shots and new kinds of lighting to the repertoire of effects, Griffith did more than develop technique for its own sake. He recognized that the camera, more narrow in focus than the human eye, was an instrument of analysis engaged in a special form of exploration. He recognized that under its scrutiny people, landscapes and objects were of equal value and that, contrary to his wishes, it destroyed the mystique of the theatre, since editing annihilated the continuity of a stage performance. He was to say that the close-up had disclosed an unexplored terrain in the human face.

Strikers and . . .
Cyrus's army invading Babylon . . . D. W. Griffith's *Intolerance*.

His reported advice to actors sounds like the methods used by
Stanislavsky, though he probably knew nothing about Stanislavsky's
ideas. He wanted his actors to study the behaviour of ordinary people
and took them on visits to hospitals and asylums. 'I am trying', he
would cry, 'to make you *see!*' He evolved stories out of his actors'
personalities, basing one of them, for instance, on Lillian Gish's fear
of hurting animals; he improvised; and he discovered a leading
player in the Biograph office-boy, Robert Harron. Beginning with
'some commonplace undramatic event', he would impose tension on
it by such devices as parallel action, the race against time. But both
he and Stanislavsky (in his acting exercises) used to make a quite
gratuitous transition from observation to melodrama, as if they
understood the importance of observation without understanding
why observation might be important.

The early news-shots of Presidents McKinley and Theodore
Roosevelt and of the Diamond Jubilee processions in London had for
the first time in history shrunk the rulers of mankind to human size.
But the camera had not so much destroyed the idea of semi-divine
status as appropriated it for itself. Drunk on the possibilities of film,
Griffith had tried to incorporate more and more of the world into his
themes in order to illustrate general ideas: ideas often of a wild kind,
which his manner of investigation could neither confirm nor refute.

The misery of post-war Germany: D. W. Griffith's *Isn't Life Wonderful?*

Eisenstein was to say that he owed everything to Griffith, even though he rejected Griffith's politics. Yet Eisenstein was to follow Griffith in using a scientific instrument unscientifically to affirm political opinion. What he might have rejected to more effect was Griffith's manner of analysing experience. It is of secondary importance whether the spectator is more attracted to the racism of *The Birth of a Nation* or to the liberal sentiments of *Intolerance*, for Griffith's messianic technique leaves both of them on the level of mere assertion. Nothing is demonstrated, nothing proved.

Griffith justifiably wanted to record the commonplace undramatic event: but the divide between an art of the quotidian for and about ordinary people and an art of the quotidian for and about the masses is a narrow one. A universal access to intimacies opens the way—and Griffith was more than once tempted by it—to the controlling power of propaganda and the manic sweep of certain kinds of historical survey.

The immigrant communities of the United States sought a shared identity through stories about elemental living or the origins of mankind and thought it suitable that a pioneer industry should devote its newly discovered means of expression to 'the hunger for tales about fundamental life'. What did it mean to be an American? The Civil War provided one answer, the taming of the Wild West another. If the Civil War raised tragic complexities that could be by-passed by an appeal to patriotism, the Wild West aroused a fear of the unknown that could in part be assuaged by viewing the Western as a testing ground for moral value. The nickelodeon public was conscious of the harshness of daily life; the Labour movement was strong; and to say that this public was reassured by some easy picture of virtue triumphant would be to do it an injustice. It welcomed a series of topical films about the exploitation of women, the ill-treatment of children and the appalling conditions in most factories. It wanted to see things as they were. But the Western and all it represented was the greatest source of fascination, and not only in the United States.

For all the appeal to fundamental life, questions of social identity could only be tested in relation to living experience. Griffith had not been alone in failing to distinguish the remote past from myth, nor had he been alone in his confident evocation of recent American history. Old men were on hand who could talk fairly accurately about the Civil War, and old men, both white and Indian, could recall the taming of the West. Many film-makers took advantage of this knowledge, though none so thoroughly as one of Griffith's two other producer-director associates in the short-lived Triangle Corporation. In 1910 Thomas H. Ince had been an out-of-work stage actor who had taken on bit parts with Biograph and Carl Laemmle's Independent

Motion Picture Company (IMP) and had then tried his hand as a
director. Kessel and Bauman, two bookmakers who had moved into
the more profitable field of film production, hired him and sent him
out to Los Angeles to make Westerns. Freed from supervision, Ince
came into his own. By 1913 he was a manager of Kay-Bee, supervising an 18,000 acre estate of wild land near Santa Monica—it was
soon to be dubbed Inceville. 'He began with a small stage,' wrote W.
E. Wing in the *New York Dramatic Mirror* (December 1913). 'Since
that time he has extended construction throughout the mountains,
each colony laid in its suitable and logical location. With more than
seven hundred people on hand and an investment of $35,000 in
buildings, Ince is now the proud manager of an organisation as complete as a municipality. His shops construct everything from uniforms
and furniture to houses.'[11] In 1916 he laid out new studios at Culver
City; Kessel and Bauman were later to sell them to Goldwyn and in
1924 they were acquired by the newly formed MGM—appropriately,
perhaps, since Ince was among the first film-makers to adapt his
craft to the latest ideas in industrial management and to set up the
assembly-line type of production which MGM was to bring to the
highest peak of efficiency. By the end of 1913 Ince had stepped back
into a supervisory position, although of the strictest sort, and delegated the actual shooting of films to others.

Griffith had seldom, if ever, used a script: one reason why his projects tended to grow and grow in such a random and inspired manner.
Ince, on the other hand, had impeccably typed scripts that often included a detailed budget sheet, lengthy notes on how to obtain trick
effects and a shot-by-shot description of the action. Sometimes he
would stamp the injunction shoot as written' on the cover of these
scripts. He tightly controlled his productions at every stage and gave
himself the final say in their editing. He seldom gave screen credits
to his associate directors who during the Triangle period included
among others Reginald Barker, Lambert Hillyer and Raymond B. West
as well as the up-and-coming Frank Borzage and Allan Dwan. Many
French critics assumed that the vast Ince output had been filmed by
Ince himself; and even to this day many problems of attribution remain unsolved. Who directed which part of *Civilization* (1916), the
corporate mammoth attempt to enter the *Intolerance* league? But the
same sort of question might be asked of many later Hollywood
productions.

Impersonal in character, Ince however contributed more than narrative efficiency or editorial drive to the films which he had, without
question, directed himself earlier on in his career. *Custer's Last Stand*
(1912) has John Ford's brother, Francis, heavily whiskered in the title
role. A debt to Porter and Griffith is apparent, and yet absorbed; and
in his care for detail Ince imitated no one. Although Custer's office is

cluttered with objects, the clutter is such as to enhance composition and point action. In the same way Ince does not allow scenically picturesque surroundings to swamp the actors: during battle scenes his mastery over the relationship of figure and landscape is comparable to Griffith's *The Massacre* (1912). He knew the contours of his Inceville estate as well as a hand can know a glove and seems to have explored every gully, bush and hillside for its full dramatic potential. His multiple choreographies, moving on different planes of the landscape, still have the power to astonish, to such an extent that certain commentators—Cocteau, Paolella—have described his response to nature as pantheistic.

But his primary concern was with verisimilitude: in settings, in seeing that his actors had well-worn clothes, in qualities of light and atmosphere. George N. Fenin and William K. Everson (in their book *The Western*) have observed how the Griffith and Ince type of Western was enhanced by the true-to-life presence of dust. 'Dust was everywhere in the old West—behind men as they walked down streets, behind horses and coaches, in the air itself, wherever the wind blew. (It was) almost a symbol in itself of a land to be tamed. Because it was there, Griffith and Ince let the dust play its own role in their films.'[12] In his dour way, Ince was on good terms with the local Indians. He employed them at a fair wage and did not stereotype their characters on screen. In *The Pride of the Race* (1913), which tells of an Indian chieftain whose son (Sessue Hayakawa) is an alcoholic, he subordinates action to psychological nuance, perhaps regrettably; yet his sympathy for the Indian—his wish to show him as human and not to patronize his condition with a facile happy ending—brings its own distinction. In 1914 William S. Hart joined Ince as an actor and, on occasion, an uncredited director. Hart had been brought up in the West and in childhood had played with Sioux children; and though his association with Ince was an uneasy one, he was in agreement with Ince's aims. As an actor, Hart has been underrated. His upper lip may have been literally stiff but, contrary to legend, he was as little poker-faced as Buster Keaton. As a director, his work still awaits widespread appreciation.

Kessel and Bauman had joined with Griffith's sponsor and distributor at Mutual, Harry E. Aitken, to finance Triangle, and it was they who brought Mack Sennett of Keystone, as well as Thomas H. Ince, into the new organization. As producer-director, and third side to the triangle, Sennett used a technique as streamlined as Ince's, though to a different purpose—and by perverse contrast seemed to share areas of interest with D. W. Griffith. (It is possible to see the standard Keystone comedy, with its reductionism and shock effects, as inverting the delicacy of Griffith's imagination.) Put together, the work of both

Griffith and Sennett provides a composite picture of America at the time of the Kaiser's war. Griffith describes the dream and something of the reality, but Sennett's aggression provides a more despairing and farcical comment on free enterprise. His lavish waste of custard

Mack Sennett: *Tillie's Punctured Romance* (1915).
Marie Dressler and the Keystone Cops.

pies and Ford Ts satisfied a public already given to conspicuous consumption. The rest of the world warmed to this knockabout, if only at a distance; and the Dadaists, who had founded their anti-art movement in 1916 – in a Zürich café close to Lenin's lodgings – thought of it as a kind of testament.

Sennett, of course, did not wish for such meanings to be read into his entertainments and mocked critics who discovered 'cine-plastic' values in them. And certainly it was their energy and humour that captivated the Pittsburgh steelworkers. Lewis Jacobs has claimed that after the stock market crash of 1929, in which Sennett lost fifteen million dollars, the Disney cartoons supplanted them in the public affection; and it could be that their violence, distinctly of the silent screen, and softened down by Sennett in the early twenties, found a more satisfactory outlet in the gangster movie and in the comedy of Laurel and Hardy, W. C. Fields and the Marx Brothers.

Both Sennett and Griffith anticipate the future in different ways, yet both of them were members of a puritan industry which came closest to eroticism in the box-office draw *Traffic in Souls* (1913). The split between aggression and idealized romance, which together they represent, was a typically puritan defence against sexuality. Both of them steered clear of the sensuality of Asta Nielsen or of the Italian stars of that age (the Bathing Belles were no more than icing on the cake). Yet for all his polarity to Griffith, Sennett was indebted to him in most matters of technique.

Born Michael Sinnott in 1880, in the province of Quebec, Sennett was apprenticed as an iron foundry worker at the age of seventeen. His associates, he recalls in his autobiography, were 'the toughest, hardest men in the world'—their idea of a joke was to hurtle a ten-pound hammer at newcomers. But the youth wished to be an opera singer and moved to New York. Learning that he could not make a living from *bel canto*, he joined the Bowery Burlesque Theatre and took on the most ignominious of comedy roles, appearing as the back end to a pantomime horse. The five dollar a day fee offered by Biograph soon brought him to the brownstone mansion at 11 East Fourteenth Street, where for years he wrote scenarios, played bit parts and became Griffith's most devoted student: a devotion not untinged with competitive feeling. Eventually, with the backing of Kessel and Bauman, he was in a position to open the Keystone Studios, and at the beginning of 1912 arrived in Los Angeles with four other ex-Biograph employees: his sweetheart Mabel Normand; Henry 'Pathé' Lehrman, an eccentric ideas man from Austria who insisted that he had worked with Charles Pathé; and two comedians, Fred Mace and Ford Sterling.

Keystone knockabout derived from the routines of burlesque: yet even as Sennett and his troupe came out of Los Angeles station they began to scatter these routines across the pavement. A Shriners' parade was passing by, and Sennett sent Miss Normand and Ford Sterling to cavort before it. He then filmed their antics and the ensuing arrival of the police: these unhappy representatives of the law were to be the first Keystone Cops. Sennett used to work out script ideas while lying in a bath in a small room he had built at the top of a water tower; and though he found it hard to be articulate, he would force his gag men to sweat out ideas in detail. They were given little time: the demand for comedies was so fierce that Sennett began to run his organization like a newspaper. He relied on the opportunism of journalism, and like a good reporter made the whole city his raiding ground. If he heard that a building was to be demolished, or a lake drained, he would quickly incorporate it into one of his stories.

Many stage comics found their acts looked feeble when taken out into the open air. They had to adapt themselves to the new circumstances, and quite a number of them failed to do so. Others found the adaptation both painful and stimulating. Charlie Chaplin was one of those who suffered to good effect. His dandified appearance in *Making a Living* was too shrinking to make an impact, and it needed the improvised *Kid Auto Races at Venice, California* (1914), in which the grimacing, stick-twirling, camera-hogging tramp keeps butting into

Charles Chaplin: camera-hogging in *Kid Auto Races at Venice, California.*

an apparently straightforward newsreel shot, to give birth to his best-known screen character—although in later work he was to reincorporate some of the dandy traits in the figure of the tramp.

Sennett's flair lay mainly in his editing. He used to watch run-throughs in a rocking chair and when he stopped laughing and his chair stopped rocking his staff would mark down a cut. He was also shrewd about casting. At various times he employed, among the better-known, Harry Langdon, Fatty Arbuckle, Ben Turpin, Chester Conklin, W. C. Fields, Charlie Chaplin and Bing Crosby. Frank Capra was among his gag men. Few of these men remained with him long; he was always slow to re-negotiate fees.

Life was nasty, brutish and short for most working people at this time; and the cinema, bound to travelling fairs and beer-halls, had reflected this brutality from the start. In Ferdinand Zecca's production *The Well Washed House* (1907) a boy steals a hosepipe and directs a lusty spout of water through the ground-floor window of a house; it thrusts its way through ceilings, lifting tables and beds and terrifying the inhabitants of various rooms, until it bursts through the roof and cascades down through a similar number of rooms in the adjoining building. Everyone may have imitated *L'Arroseur arrosé*, but Zecca's version is not so much a caricature of Lumière's jape as a declension from it into the boyish wish to piss further than your neighbour: a return to the infantile that relates it, and the Sennett comedies, to the preoccupations of Alfred Jarry's Père Ubu. Sennett's skill lay in finding a style (principally through the speeding-up of action) which allowed these primitive eruptions to seem credible among the oil rigs and semi-urban desolation of Los Angeles.

If most jokes jolt us by their oblique revelation of unconscious motive, then Sennett's have the force of a kick. The assaults of black comedy begin with him, and set his comedians apart from at least two of their more celebrated predecessors; for in contrast to them, both gallant Max Linder and sweet, stout John Bunny, the D'Artagnan and the Pickwick of the screen, look like probable adults. Linder gave an observed portrayal of a suave, charming Paris rentier and founded his gags on more or less credible events, while the henpecked Bunny was usually involved in adventures (with Flora Finch) that could happen to anyone. The Sennett team, in contrast, could be as alarming as Sennett's animal menagerie, although the beauty among these beasts, the effervescent Mabel Normand, may be excepted. In one of the funniest of Sennett comedies, Miss Normand takes a lion for a walk through a film studio, thinking it a dog; then discovers her error and tries to placate the lion by waving a duster in its face.

'Though catastrophic rage isn't exactly unknown in Sennett,' claims Raymond Durgnat, 'still the name of Sennett recalls speed gone mad, fandangos of disintegrating flivvers, spraying Keystone Cops to right and left as they swerve between converging streetcars, of jallopies stuck on level crossings as expresses charge nearer at supersonic velocity, of a crazy world, of a ballistic nightmare.'[13] In its rapidity, this crazy world resembles a paranoid attack, as in the protracted ballet of the collapsing victim. 'The least he might do', writes James Agee,

was to straighten up stiff as a plank and roll over backward with such skill that his whole length seemed to slap the floor at the same instant. Or he might make a cadenza of it—look vague, smile like an angel, roll up his eyes, lace his fingers, thrust his hands palm downwards as far as they would go, hunch his shoulders, rise on tiptoe, prance ecstatically in narrowing circles until, with tallow knees, he sank down the vortex of dizziness on the floor, and there signified Nirvana by kicking his heels twice, like a swimming frog.[14]

Anal sadism and fecality abound in these comedies: in the splashings of pies and stiflings in dough, in explosions, bottom-kickings and gassings. The hunger for tales of fundamental life had many meanings, including fundament, and the wish to alleviate a little the toll of

Chaplin in *The Champion.*

poverty by joking about some of its nastier features. 'One of the charms of the Keystone Pictures', said Sennett, 'was the knockaboutness of the sets.' Or their dingy drabness. In them, and in many of the two-reelers Chaplin made for Mutual in 1916–17, such as *Easy Street* and *The Pawnbroker*, we can observe the squalor of slum life.

It was probably the qualities which we may now think of as defects which won Chaplin his public: the meanness of his settings, especially, and the ugliness of his actions—whoever thwarts the tramp's wishes, however slightly, tends to be rewarded with punches and kicks. His working-class audiences lived among similar degradations— and life in the trenches was no improvement. They must have found in these comedies an identification and release from resentment they could not have found elsewhere.

Chaplin raised his first laugh, as a boy in the English music-hall, by miming a dog with a cocked leg (he was tartly rebuked for his pains). The humour in his early shorts usually veers between a delight in fecal objects and a fastidious distaste for them—or, rather, a complicity with the audience in a *pretence* at distaste: watch him brandish an old sausage (in *The Champion*), sniff at it with a delicious quiver of of disgust, then offer it to his impassive bull-terrier. The energy and acrobatic skill, which Debussy was to praise and which at times, as in *The Cure* of 1917, takes on a ballerina's elegance, has its source in this kind of invention; a display that brought him both status and wealth. In 1916 he signed a contract with Mutual, for which he received a salary of ten thousand dollars a week and a starting bonus of $150,000. He soon broke this contract for a better one, and his earnings continued to rise steeply. He was not the first star to earn a fortune. Mutual and Triangle had begun this upward spiral in wealth when they had invited stage actors into the studios, although the main impetus to salaries had come from elsewhere, from the shrewdest partnership in the business: Mary Pickford and her mother.

Miss Pickford, like Chaplin, came from an Anglo-Irish family. She had known poverty and hardship in her earliest years and during her time as a child actor in stock companies. In 1909, aged sixteen, she had joined Biograph, and in 1911 Carl Laemmle had brought her to IMP. After a return to the stage (where she worked for David Belasco) and to Biograph, she joined Zukor's Famous Players Film Company.

Few producers have been so adroit in negotiation as Adolph Zukor, and Miss Pickford's financial sparrings with him over a period of six years deserve a footnote in any history of the suffragette movement. She usually got the better of him, for her guile and parsimony matched his, and she and her mother had quickly recognized her command at the box-office. But these business triumphs, and her off-putting legend as America's sweetheart, though strenuously won, should not be allowed to overshadow her ability. She was confined for most of her acting life—until well into her thirties—to child roles, and these of the most unattractive sort: good little girls who spread sweetness and light about them and who, like some of Dickens's heroines, become through death, or quasi-death, redeemers of stony-hearted mothers and aunts. Her public had a fetish about her curls and was unforgiving when she cut them off in 1925. Yet to see the films is to wipe away this varnish and to find oneself drawn into her legion of admirers.

She is almost as skilled a comedian as Chaplin, and like him often plays dispossessed characters who find themselves in oppressive situations. Unlike Chaplin, she can fight these pressures without a show of rancour or self-pity. She has the knack of accommodating herself to the whims of others in such a way as to make them recognize the folly of these whims—as when, in *Pollyanna* (1920), she lays down pieces of paper on the floor of her pernickety aunts' house and leaps from one to the other so as not to muddy the carpet. She can also be ironic about herself. She horrifies her aunts when she converts their barn into a circus and, strapped into a harness, circles above the other children like some superior angel. Acute observation lies behind much of her humour: the premeditated way in which she flicks a dead fly off a table, or the neatness with which she caps the malice of a priggish contemporary at the grand tea party in *The Poor*

Lillian Gish and Robert Harron: *True-Heart Susie*, directed by D. W. Griffith.

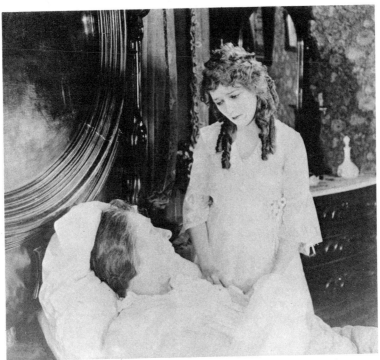

Mary Pickford: *Rebecca of Sunnybrook Farm*, directed by Marshall Neilan.

Little Rich Girl (1917) or the extraordinary high-wind mime with an umbrella in *Rebecca of Sunnybrook Farm* (1917).

She played a wide variety of girls of differing ages and characteristics, yet she gave most of them a likeness of guise: the wide-brimmed hats, the famous curls, the slight hunch, the gingham dresses and, above all, the deftness of foot movement. She often wears black stockings and full skirts that, intentionally or not, seem to accentuate the agility of her legs. Many of her gags depend on a dancer's grace: some of the best occur in *Through the Back Door* (1921), where she cleans the kitchen floor by skating over it with a pair of scrubbing brushes attached to her shoes. In *Pollyanna*, suitably, she has to pay for her altruism by what is, for her, the worst of fates: a car knocks her down as she tries to rescue a child from its path, and she loses the power of her legs.

The youthfulness of her face and the regularity of her features would be insipid without the spirit that animates them: the candour of her smile and the knowing twinkle in her eyes. Like all great stars, she can establish an intimacy with each spectator that each spectator will feel is his or hers alone. Many actors set up a complicity with audiences by implying that they share slightly shameful qualities or aspirations with them. Mary Pickford is unusual in that she captures attention by her straightforwardness. She would seem to recognize a core of likeability in everyone while remaining sharp-eyed enough not to be taken in by cant.

She worked hard to have first-class craftsmen around her and was well rewarded whenever Frances Marion took charge of her scripts or Charles Rosher her camerawork. One of the directors most associated with her career, Maurice Tourneur, was a distinguished craftsman, often praised for his 'pictorialism', and sometimes capable of creating really memorable images, such as the one in *The Poor Little Rich Girl* of the cossetted child's glimpse of street urchins skating on ice below its barred nursery window. But Miss Pickford's favourite director was the engaging Irishman Marshall Neilan. Neilan knew how to elicit unselfconscious behaviour in child actors, and his feeling for space, as in the way he used the high walls of an orphanage in *Daddy Long-Legs* (1919), is comparable in its architectonic sense to Fritz Lang's *Der Müde Tod*.

The Age of Innocence did not presuppose an absence of sexual tension. The courtly love affairs that enchanted Griffith contained a good deal of feeling; and elaborate courting rituals, by seeming to

Mary Pickford and the high-walled orphanage of *Daddy Long-Legs*.

curb sexuality, tended to heighten polarity between the sexes. Although the Pickford public only allowed her to retain the title of the world's sweetheart on condition that she concealed any evidence of adult sexuality on screen, they welcomed her marriage to Douglas Fairbanks, who had been voted the most popular male actor in 1920, and in no way saw this marriage as diminishing her box-office appeal. On the contrary, by general accord Douglas Fairbanks and Mary Pickford took on the status of King and Queen of the film industry, as they royally entertained royalty at their palatial villa 'Pickfair'.

Fairbanks was one of four brothers. His parents had separated shortly after his birth and his mother had scraped together a living by taking in lodgers. The self-sufficient masculinity projected by all his screen characters and his lifelong fascination with the Four Musketeers (reduced to three in one of his film versions of the Dumas novels) or with aristocratic fathers who come to the aid of their sons—Fairbanks playing both father and son—may owe something to this upbringing. After a successful stage career, and an interlude in which he bummed around and tried to break into other professions, he was signed up

Douglas Fairbanks appearing in *His Majesty the American* (1919).

by the Triangle Corporation at $2,000. Although he irritated Griffith by his exuberance and seemed unfitted for a screen career, his first role in *The Lamb*, directed by W. Christy Cabanne and supervised by Griffith, won him a public following.

In his admirable Museum of Modern Art monograph, *Douglas Fairbanks: The Making of a Screen Character*, Alistair Cooke admits his perplexity in trying to place an actor who produced 'a type of pleasure which is closer to old-time vaudeville or that of a jam-session than to an audience contemplating a painting or play'.[15] Considered an 'unfamiliar misfit' by the film industry, Cooke argues, Fairbanks was lucky to have made his mark on it before the emergence of the casting bureau and the star system. Even so, it is possible, with hindsight, to see his career as inevitable, as part of a widespread need among film people physically to master the world. In the same way as Griffith was moved through his increasing understanding of film technique and cosmic intentions to take in every aspect of human sensation, and Sennett to extend the routines of burlesque over the whole of Los Angeles, so Fairbanks was tempted to convert more and more of the world into a gymnasium in which he could exercise his seemingly effortless powers as an athlete. It is curious how at many points the formation of the cinema parallels the development of children. Fairbanks, perhaps more single-mindedly than any of his contemporaries, enacts the desire children often have during the latency period to control and master their environment. Photographs of him in rehearsal, working out his stunts, show that while he perfected the beauty of movement that Muybridge had sought to trace in his picture sequences, his spontaneity and capacity for last-minute improvisation saved him from being the logical successor to Muybridge's kind of analysis: the deliberate, Harold Lloyd type of time-and-motion studied man.

All the same, many present-day spectators react as blankly to him as they do to Mary Pickford. He is too debonair, too enthusiastic, too much the scout-masterly exponent of healthy living. The characters he plays are nearly always good to the point of being stereotypes, and in his historical romances he sometimes has to pretend to be bad to save the plot from insipidity. Unselfcritical if not unselfconscious, his demonstrations of strength have a touch of coercion about them, and it would be tempting to see him as an imperialist hero—he greatly admired Theodore Roosevelt—if his humour did not have the effect of undermining pretension. He wanted to be the good sport surrounded by an admiring crowd, the man President Harding might have coined the term 'normalcy' for. And, in a sense, he almost succeeded in this role. But it was play-acting of a kind, and perceptive Anita Loos, who was writing scripts with her husband John Emerson, found a way to capitalize on the strain beneath the *bonhomie*, the intimation that he was a misfit, by evolving a series of semi-satirical roles for him in which his slightly dissociated, slightly old-fashioned romantic personality could be contrasted with the war-time metropolitan excitement for trends and fads—an excitement that eventually was to erupt into the twenties' pursuit of Ballyhooism. Fairbanks took part in close on forty films of this sort and at the same time put his name to a number of books promoting 'inspirational philosophy' with titles like *Laugh and Live* and *Whistle and Hoe — Sing as We Go*.

In 1920 Fairbanks turned to historical romance and enjoyed such a success with *The Mark of Zorro* that he remained faithful to the genre to the end of his career. (*The Private Life of Don Juan* was made in England in 1934; he died in 1939.) As a director of United Artists he had the final say on these productions and saw to it that the finest designers, lighting cameramen and action directors worked with him. The virtuosity of his stunts needed the distancing provided by romance and the past to make it credible; yet in common with his ascetic virility and the unrelenting sunshine of his personality, the settings for these romances lack the shadowings of poetry. Although their inspiration may be derived from the historical spectacles of Lubitsch, they have little of the Reinhardt kind of fantasy, the interior of the castle in *Robin Hood* (1922) excepted. Fairbanks democratizes the past. He seems incapable of appreciating the solemnities of societies more hierarchic than the United States. In the characters he played he is without awe, a conquistador, a leading light of the free-enterprise system, a debunker of history in the manner of Mark Twain. Yet if he and his designers failed to achieve poetry, they often stumble onto incongruous effects that have some kinship to poetry. The miracle at the opening of *The Gaucho* (1927), with Mary Pickford appearing as the Virgin Mother beneath a whirling halo, though presented seriously, is bizarre in a way that prefigures Buñuel; and certain images in *The Black Pirate* (1926)—as when the screen pullulates with pirate heads or is filled with the intricate woodwork of a ship— have a dream-like uncanniness: an uncanniness to be sustained with deliberate artistry throughout Allan Dwan's *The Iron Mask* (1929). Dwan develops the fascination Griffith had shown for the twinkling similarity of the Gish sisters in *Orphans of the Storm* (1921) by having many of his characters—such as his four musketeers, or four nuns who carry off the dead Constance, or twin kings, one true, one false— reflect each other like mirror images.

Although stage producers can often camouflage the emotional shallowness of their actors, the microscopic scrutiny of the camera usually reveals it. But producers soon realized that immaturity could appeal to immaturity and began to exploit this appeal. (Fan magazines date back to at least 1912; they had a collective circulation of several millions by 1920.) At times their exploitation took an extreme form. The producer William Fox created a star by going to the furthest extreme from Pickfordian innocence and by imposing a parody of eroticism on poor Theda Bara, whose convolutions in an adaptation of the Kipling poem *A Fool There Was* (1914) introduced the word 'vamp' into film publicity and gave Fox the financial resources to set up his studio, among the most important in the 1920s. Actors had to face other pressures also. Pirandello once claimed that his interest in psychic alienation had been aroused by several visits to a film studio, and it is true that the actor has not only to contend with the superstitious dread of having his spirit robbed by the camera but must also face the more insidious possibility that skilful camerawork will fabricate a personality only marginally related to himself. Many performers have failed to distinguish between legend and fact, and although none perhaps was so lost in confusion as Norma Desmond (the faded star of Billy Wilder's *Sunset Boulevard*), the willingness with which publicists began to believe in their own copy, and promoters of the dream to see no difference between dream and reality, added to the difficulties of stardom.

But to Hollywood producers the problems of stardom were secondary to the sudden wealth and influence stardom had brought to certain actors. Conscious of how their bargaining power had been weakened, many producers wasted little time in trying to redress the balance by mergers, devious contracts and attempts to crush reputations. Ironically the company most sensitive to this issue was one whose production styles had been most conservatively modelled on the theatre. Adolph Zukor had founded the Famous Players Company at the time of his success with *Queen Elizabeth* and in 1916 had merged his company with Jesse Lasky's Feature Players, acting as president with Lasky as vice-president, Samuel Goldwyn as chairman and Cecil B. DeMille as director-general. They wished to give photoplays, as films were called, the prestige of a stage production and to capture the middle-class market with feature length five-reelers, good theatrical scripts, distinguished stage actors and high quality cinemas. They succeeded; and almost too well, perhaps, when they took on Mary Pickford. DeMille warned Zukor that the competitive inflation of actors' salaries would soon bankrupt everyone; Zukor thought otherwise. He believed that the star system allowed the established studios to control the industry by controlling public taste. By skilful business management, a series of takeovers and an eventual change in policy, his company managed to ride out the storm, but many others sank.

The industry had assumed its unique quality by taking over many of the attractions of the theatre. In 1913 Mitchell L. Mark built the Strand Theatre, a 3,000-seat cinema on Broadway, and established the taste for baroque picture palaces. The days of the nickelodeon were past; middle-class values had come to the fore; the cry was for 'Universal American Entertainment'. By 1919 Hollywood was everywhere recognized as the dream capital of the world although Los Angeles was still a small town. Nothing had existed like it before and, it seems probable, nothing will exist like it again. Tourists flocked to it in their thousands. The Press turned its glare on every policy announcement, on premieres and parties and on private lives. The conditions were ready for the exposure, or creation, of scandal.

1919 was a boom year in the American economy. In Hollywood the outlay in salaries alone reached twenty million dollars. Chaplin opened his own studio in that year, and Paramount and Fox extended theirs. Goldwyn, estranged from Zukor, moved from New York to Hollywood's Culver City. 'The price of admittance paid by moviegoers in the boom days of 1919–20 astonished the theatre owners,' writes Benjamin B. Hampton in his *History of the American Film Industry.* 'Either film had ceased to be a "poor man's show" or there were no poor men left in the United States. The movie ticket now encompassed nearly all city and town dwellers and the millions of motor cars being purchased by farmers and villagers made the screen easily accessible to the rural population.'[16]

In 1919 Zukor, operating from New York, had at last decided that power did not lie in the control of stars, but in the control of first-run cinemas. In 1917 he had edged out W. W. Hodkinson, chairman of Paramount, the distribution company which specialized in Famous Players-Lasky Corporation films. He now tried to take over the whole industry. In 1919 the gross annual return of the 15,000 principal American cinemas was eighty million dollars. Zukor began to buy up these theatres. He bought and bought, and where he could not buy, he built. He began to make serious inroads into the estates of his foremost competitor First National (a combine of theatre exhibitors) and, to raise capital, floated Paramount stock on the Wall Street market. Movies had become a large and, in many ways, a safe business. Wall Street financiers began to join the boards of certain film companies and to dictate policy.

Yet in 1919 there appeared an outstanding film which, in contrast to the fever of expansion, was intimate and sombre. (Admittedly, it did not have much appeal at the box-office.) D. W. Griffith's *Broken Blossoms,* based on Thomas Burke's collection of short stories, *Limehouse Nights,* tells of a Chinaman (Richard Barthelmess) who comes to London to preach the gospel of peace—with disastrous results. He opens an opium shop by the docks and befriends Lucy (Lillian Gish); but when her father (Donald Crisp), a boxer past his prime, learns of

D. W. Griffith: *Broken Blossoms*. Richard Barthelmess as the Chinaman.

her friendship, he beats her to death; and the Chinaman, disregarding his gospel of peace, shoots the father and kills himself. Griffith's feeling for this subject raises it above the limitations of its stilted origins. The father, a residual Satan, may be postured by Donald Crisp in a performance that is not so much weak as too strong, and the flagellation and murder of Lucy may be a cruelty too protracted; yet without this brutality, the opium shop idyll would have seemed too fragile. Griffith's tact and capacity for communicating intuitions is such that although he employed two photographers on the film, Bitzer and Sartov, he was able to unify their very different styles without a loss of nuance.

Without idealizing poverty, he at no point leans on actuality. His mistily-seen China and his fog-bound Limehouse are studio bound and exist only in the imagination. His use of masking and iris shots—few directors have been so adept at creating new forms of composition framing—and his orchestrations of pace harmonize with the stylized mode of playing he elicited from his two leading actors. With

Lillian Gish, the fantastic element lies in her choice of a crippled gait, a tartan bonnet and a touching smile; the reality lies in the presence of pain in her eyes and in such moments as her harrowing fit of claustrophobia when her father locks her in a cupboard (Miss Gish actually induced this fit). Richard Barthelmess's Chinaman is a white-faced pierrot from Cathay, oblique in glance, angular in movement. *Broken Blossoms* pre-dates the extreme stylizations of *The Cabinet of Dr Caligari* without making an ostentation of experiment. It is like *Madame Butterfly* (Belasco's American production of the stage play gave Puccini the idea for his opera), where a hint of cruelty also sharpens an inherent preciosity of theme. Yet in spite of its cruelty, *Broken Blossoms* demonstrates, in the spirit of the Woodrow Wilson age, a concern for the deprived and a wish for racial tolerance that seems surprising, and not only because Griffith was its director. It appeared on the eve of a racialist eruption and a backlash against Bolshevism that was to disturb the country deeply.

Part Two: The 1920s

Dziga Vertov: *The Man with a Movie Camera.*

4. Aspects of the Soviet Cinema

The Ancient World overlooked the invention of machines not through stupidity nor through superficiality. It turned them into playthings in order to avoid repugnance. [1]

HANNS SACHS. *The Creative Unconscious* (1942)

How many times we have seen upon the cheek of the person with whom we are talking the horse that was passing in the distance. Our bodies penetrate the sofas on which we sit, and the sofas penetrate our bodies, just as the tram that passes enters the houses, which in their turn throw themselves upon the tram and are merged with it. [2]

Futurist Manifesto (1910)

In 1909 F. T. Marinetti, an Italian out to conquer Paris (the cultural centre of his age) and intending to subdue the French with their own arguments, published his first Futurist manifesto in *Le Figaro*. The French poet Arthur Rimbaud had described the modern city as the perfect setting for a season in hell; Marinetti turned this idea on its head and welcomed glare and dissonance as the next best thing to paradise. But for all his startling vehemence, Marinetti did little more than add a loud voice to a well-established nineteenth-century debate on whether industrialization had a dehumanizing effect (he thought it did; and approved). His fervent identification with technology merely amplified the optimism of Jules Verne's science fiction, while his demand for an art modelled on the machine was similar to Joris-Karl Huysmans's cult of the unnatural in *A rebours* – a novel in which a languid character named des Esseintes enjoys an infatuation with two locomotives named Crampton and Engerth. Marinetti gave all this an anarchist tinge by insisting that the art of the past should be blown up to clear the way for an art of the future.

If he made an impression on the Parisians, he did so, maybe, because his defiance contained a grain of sense: technology had to be adjusted to in some way. And in challenging good taste, he did reveal how questions of taste could mask a fear of the new. Baudelaire had recoiled from the chaos of the metropolis: Marinetti welcomed its assault on the senses; both men were referring to cities that are now as lost to us as ancient Athens and as much wreathed in sentiment. On arriving in London in 1912 Marinetti had applauded, provocatively, its 'brilliant-hued motor-buses'.[3] He did not recognize that Futurism, and the objects of its admiration, would one day be numbered among the more popular kinds of antiquarianism.

The actress Eve Francis thought that he had the eyes of a rapist. He was less of a maniac, though, than a manic mechanic: an impresario gesticulating the role of machine-man, at times with enough sense of humour to realize his own ineffectuality. In his first manifesto, he describes a tremendous car-ride through the night which ends up in a ditch. He recalls the strivings of Père Ubu and anticipates Mack Sennett's comedians. Most of all, in his boasting *rentier* thoughtlessness and gusto for fast cars, he resembles Mr Toad in *The Wind in the Willows*.

He was to stimulate many artists: in Italy the painters Severini, Balla, Boccioni and Carrà, and the architects Sant'Elia and Chiattone — who were among the first to evolve high-rise apartments out of the conception of the building as a machine. His belief that music should incorporate industrial noises impressed Russolo, who made up noise symphonies, prototypes of *musique concrète*. And his view that the poet should freely dislocate syntax and resort to neologisms was also to be influential. In 1916 he launched a manifesto on the cinema, 'a new art, much more agile and vast than any other'.[4] But,

except for certain films on travel, hunting, wars, film-makers have done no more than inflict on us the most backward-looking dramas, great and small. The cinema is an autonomous art. The cinema must therefore never copy the stage. The cinema, being essentially visual, must above all fulfil the evolution of painting, detach itself from reality, from photography, from the graceful and solemn. It must become antigraceful, deforming, impressionistic, synthetic, dynamic, free-wording . . . Painting + sculpture + plastic dynamism + words-in freedom + composed noises + architecture + synthetic theatre = Futurist cinema.'[5]

The painter Robert Delaunay was soon to describe the Italian Futurists as 'cinematic'. He was hoping to insult them: yet the charge had some descriptive truth. Balla and Boccioni had derived some of their ideas from Marey's chronophotography, and one of the Futurist manifestos carries an aphorism which probably refers to a Marey graph. 'A racing horse does not have four legs; it has twenty, and their movements are triangular.'[6] In 1916 Marinetti and some of his colleagues took part in the now-lost film *Vita futuristica*, directed by Arnaldo Ginna. Ginna was to claim — *Bianco e Nero* (May–June 1965) — that he had used concave and convex mirrors to distort images of the actors in certain shots, while in others he had resorted to superimposition and split screen techniques, and had painted dots onto the film by hand. *Vita futuristica* consisted of several short scenes;

one of them showed Balla making love to a chair, another of them included 'a discussion between a foot, a hammer and an umbrella'.

But the most sustained Futurist activity in photography and the cinema was carried on by Anton Giulio Bragaglia, who later disclaimed any connection with the movement. In association with his brother Arturo, he worked out the technique of Fotodinamismo, a

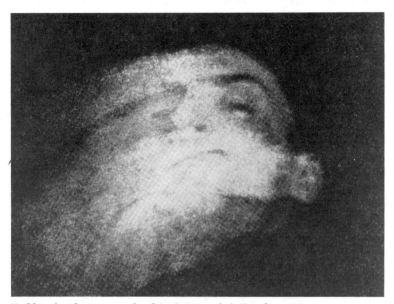

Nodding head: an example of A. G. Bragaglia's Fotodinamismo.

more sophisticated means of recording the impression of movement than Marey's chronophotography. He also directed two films in 1916, *Il perfido incanto* and *Thais* (with settings by the Futurist artist, Enrico Prampolini), for a long time thought to be the first avant-garde films. But in fact the Russian Futurists had anticipated the Italians in 1913 with *Drama of the Futurist Cabaret No 13*, directed by the painters Larionov and Goncharova, who also acted in it with Vladimir Mayakovsky and David and Nicolai Burliuk. The Great War blighted the growth of the Italian Futurists' interest in film, and the main Futurist activity in both the theatre and the cinema was to take place in Russia.

In this respect the October Revolution acted as little more than a catalyst to the modern movement. Many of the most important trends in the Russian arts of the 1920s had originated before the Great War. Kandinsky, Chagall, the Russian Cubists and Cubo-Futurists had formulated their doctrines long before 1914, much at the same time as the stage producer Meyerhold had abandoned both naturalism and the techniques of Stanislavsky's Moscow Art Theatre. 'In a revolutionary break in the life of society,' wrote Trotsky,

> there is no simultaneousness and no symmetry of processes either in the ideology of society, or in its economic structure. The premises which are needed for the revolution are formed before the revolution, and the most important deductions from the revolution only appear much later. It would be extremely flippant to establish by analogies and comparisons the identity of Futurism and Communism, and so deduce that Futurism is the art of the proletariat. Such pretensions must be rejected. But this does not signify a contemptuous attitude towards the work of the Futurists. In our opinion they are the necessary links in the forming of a new and great literature; but they will prove to be only a significant episode in its evolution.[7]

The Futurists were the first group of artists willing to cooperate with the Bolsheviks, and for this reason the Politburo was willing to accept their views as official policy. It supported their paper 'Art in the Commune' (1918–19) and it even allowed them to propose that art need not be intelligible to the masses. But the Futurists alienated many of their sympathizers by their aggressive dogmatism and in 1921, at the time of Lenin's New Economic Policy (NEP), many of the more traditional kinds of writers, known as 'fellow travellers', began to edge back into prominence. The Futurists tried to regain their former power by forming an alliance with the Constructivists, who had argued in 1920 that artists should apply their skills to the problems of factory production and modern life. Some of the leading figures in this alliance published their views in the magazine *Lef* (1923 – 5) and, for a while, in *Novy Lef*, which came into being in 1925. It is possible to discern a clear shift away from Futurism during the 1920s; its wildly fantastic thinking giving way to the Constructivist impulse, which in turn was superseded by the doctrine that the artist should concern himself wholly with fact. (A similar trend towards 'objectivity' and documentation also occurred in non-Socialist countries.)

Yet the leading Russian Futurist Vladimir Mayakovsky, and at least one of his followers, the film-maker Dziga Vertov, remained faithful in spirit to the original movement. In 1908 Mayakovsky had joined the Bolshevik party and in 1911 declared himself a Futurist. He had signed the Futurist Manifesto of 1912, and in 1913 wrote an article in *Kino-Journal* on 'Theatre, Cinema, Futurism'. 'The art of the actor, in its dynamic sense, is chained to the dead background of its setting. This absurd contradiction is abolished by the cinema which is firmly attached to the action of actuality.'[8]

He became, it is said, the incarnation of Futurism: in his demonstrations, in his choice and use of imagery and in his projection of verse, which he insisted on shouting at the top of his voice. He was all expression, and the Mayakovsky strain, wrote Boris Pasternak in *Safe*

Conduct, touched every gifted poet during the 1920s. 'Of all men he had the newness of the age climatically in his veins. He was through and through strange with all the but half-achieved strangeness of the epoch.'[9] He amazed and troubled his contemporaries. Trotsky was worried by his neglect of the inner life, his lack of measure and perspective, and Pasternak, who mourned his death, still felt inclined to describe him, in *An Essay in Autobiography*, as being like 'some minor Dostoyevsky character out of the provinces'.[10]

He was actively involved in the cinema from at least 1915. In 1918 he wrote scripts and acted in three films for an incompetent company named Neptune. He was so dismayed by this experience that when he attended a conference in Petrograd in 1919—chaired by his friend Anatoli Lunacharsky, the first People's Commissar for

Lunacharsky and Mayakovsky (*right*) in 1918: in the background, Leschenko.

Enlightenment—he denounced the Soviet film industry and demanded that it should be handed over to artists. 'It is conceivable', writes Jay Leyda in *Kino*, 'that the first distinctive form of revolutionary film was stirred to life by Mayakovsky's booming voice—the *agitka*—the film leaflet.'[11] Lenin had recognized the propaganda value of the cinema, and under his his directive Lunacharsky, a playwright and film director, founded State Schools of Cinematography in Petrograd and Moscow and organized the first agitational-propaganda train. In April 1919 Lenin appropriated the film industry, set up a network of producing companies and told Lunacharsky that 'of all the arts, for us the cinema is the most important'.[12] The gaily decorated agit-prop trains followed in the wake of the Red Army. The artists and technicians on board printed and distributed leaflets, drew and displayed scenes of war. They shot newsreel material, edited this material on

Alexander Rodchenko's design for a ciné-car, published in *Lef*. Rodchenko was a friend of Dziga Vertov's and designed titles and posters for *Kino Pravda*. He worked as an art director on a number of films, including Boris Barnet's *Moscow in October* (1927).

Cinema carriage on an agit-prop train. Film projector painted at one end of the carriage, a camera and reels of film at the other.

the train and arranged film shows. Among them was a Swede, Edward Tisse, shortly to become Eisenstein's cameraman, and the film editor and Mayakovsky disciple Dziga Vertov.

But this inspiration was not to last. In 1925 one of the Sovkino administrators tried to prohibit the foreign distribution of *The Battleship Potemkin*. Mayakovsky still had enough influence to have this decision changed; but he had already begun to lose his battle against the bureaucrats. Although he continued to write film scripts, only a few of them—ones he had intended for children—were accepted by the studios and even these were to be extensively reworked by other writers. (Yet he made a virtue out of failure by turning two of the rejected scripts into effective stage plays, *The Bed Bug* and *The Bath House*.) In 1927 he publicly denounced Sovkino for its conservatism, but his complaints fell on deaf ears. He committed suicide in 1930. Was he a victim of Stalinism, as Edward Crankshaw and others have suggested? 'His presentiment of tragedy was, as always, uncanny; the purges of the intelligentsia were at hand,'[13] writes Patricia Blake in an introduction to the Penguin edition of *The Bed Bug*.

Although there is some evidence that his motives might have been of a more intimate nature, it would be hard to dissociate his suicide from the deportation of Trotsky in 1928, the deposition of Lunacharsky in 1929 and the hardening of the Party line against any form of individuality in the arts: a tragedy that reached its denouement at the First Writers' Congress in 1934. At this conference, attended by many noted men of letters from abroad, Radek and Zhdanov flatly declared that Soviet authors would have to support the dogmas of Socialist Realism. From then on the Soviet artist, if not purged, was offered the choice of silence or of truly becoming a machine.

The strangeness which, in Pasternak's view, made Mayakovsky so typical of his epoch lay primarily in his savage, even injurious hacking out of icons for the new faith. The polemical intent of so much Soviet art at this time, especially in its films, should not be allowed to conceal the fact that the Revolution harnessed mysterious forces which the term 'propaganda' does not quite cover. These mysterious forces can be thought of as madness or as a form of possession; yet such considerations are ancillary to the general meaning of Mayakovsky's violent play with language, the excess of such images as: 'The street ice falls in, like a syphilitic's nose.'

The October Revolution had dramatized a change in consciousness; even the physical world, it seemed, had changed. The ecstasy of the young revolutionaries resembled a vertigo. Mankind's most fundamental awareness, that of space and time, appeared to have been disturbed. However, war and revolution had done no more than heighten this sense of disturbance: writers and painters in industrialized societies had been recording something like it since the 1830s. And even now, a walk down any crowded street will re-enact it. Wholeness seems to fragment into random and strident sensation. Under the impact of faces, vehicles, advertisements and shop-displays, one begins to feel that repetition and coincidence provide the only kind of consistency. Viewpoints become relative; an awareness of perspective diminishes.

But while the emergence of the metropolis had disturbed stable forms of perception, the discoveries of technology were to disturb them even further. To look from the window of a fast-moving car or of an aeroplane is to become conscious of how speed distorts space and seems to flatten the view, so that it begins to resemble the unfurling of a backcloth. Rendering landscape insubstantial and diminishing the human figure, such speed can arouse delusional feelings of control, a state of mind that the cinema was well suited to reinforce.

That Futurism should have flourished in Italy and Russia, two backward countries rapidly industrialized, was no coincidence. In Russia especially the onrush of industrialism was to be dramatic, and artists who owed little allegiance to the Futurist movement resorted to techniques of a Futurist kind to acknowledge this change. The opening paragraph of Isaac Babel's story 'My First Goose' provides a good example of this viewpoint:

Savitsky, Commander of the VI division, rose when he saw me, and I wondered at the beauty of his giant's body. He rose, the purple of his riding breeches and the crimson of his little tilted cap and the decorations stuck to his chest cleaving the hut as a standard cleaves the sky. A smell of scent and the sticky sweet freshness of soap emanated from him. His long legs were like girls sheathed to the neck in shining riding boots.[14]

The reader may feel in such extreme close-up to the Commander that his eyes lose focus. He seems to dissolve into the figure, like a cloud drifting into a mountain, or in turn seems to see into him. This kind of writing may owe some debt to Gogol both in its profusion and its fantastic internality (the hut contains a giant, whose legs contain girls); but in its absence of perspective and breakdown of experience into a series of shock effects it applies just as well to Eisenstein's close-ups on the Odessa Steps—in Russian jargon, significantly, a 'close-up' is known as a 'large scale': in particular, to the most telling image in the history of the cinema, that of the woman with the shattered pince-nez, who has been shot in the face. (Babel's Red Cavalry stories were published in 1926, The Battleship Potemkin was released in 1925.)

'For the Russians,' claims Camilla Gray in The Great Experiment, a study of Russian art during the period 1863–1922,

the machine came as a liberating force, liberating man from the tyranny of nature and giving him the possibility to create an entirely man-made world. This vision of the machine was one of the reasons for the joyful welcome given to the Bolshevik regime a few years later—a regime which promised a new society transformed by industrialization.[15]

It has been argued that this machine vision was largely harmful to the Soviet cinema, putting an emphasis on film technique as a form of engineering at the expense of more humane concerns. The American critic Robert Warshow has stated that this cinema represented 'a triumph over humanity'.

> It could be said that Eisenstein, Pudovkin and Dovzhenko were the real victims, ultimately betrayed by the revolution they celebrated; but that idea, if it is important at all, becomes important only on reflection. It is hard to feel the pathos of their lives when you see them playing with corpses; if they had got the chance, they would have made a handsome montage of my corpse too, and given it a meaning—their meaning, and not mine.[16]

Yet the impression conveyed by these often murderous lyrics is of a range of feeling wider than Warshow allows for. 'Neither my wife nor I will ever forget his shining eyes as he retailed to her stories illustrating Lenin's coolness and wisdom in revolutionary crises,'[17] writes Ivor Montagu of Pudovkin. And Pudovkin was not alone in his hope. Many Soviet artists had come to the understanding demonstrated by the *MacMillan Magazine* writer of 1871, who suggested that technology might lessen certain forms of alienation. Rodchenko's photomontages and Vertov's newsreels revealed how technology could diminish the distances between the vast and often inaccessible republics of the Soviet Union, and how the media could be used to filter a mass of information and experience. Although Vertov's first series of newsreels, the forty-two issues of *Kino Nedelya* begun in 1917, is agitational-propaganda, his second series, the twenty-three issues of *Kino Pravda* (1922–5), is for the most part unpolemical. Vertov tries to cover as many facets of Soviet life as possible. He visits the exotic peoples who live by the Caspian Sea; he shows children delighted by a Chinese conjuror; he records the arrival of an elephant at the Moscow zoo; and the patients in a mental hospital are obviously as pleased to see him as he them. 'Let us make the streets our brushes, the squares our palette,' hymned Mayakovsky. It was thought that technology could avoid dehumanization and could be more than a tool for commercial or political interests. For a while many artists believed that it would actually bring about a humanist utopia.

The Russian need for mysticism and absolute faith had now been channelled into a new cause: but how were these oceanic feelings to be used? It was a question recognized, and argued about, by painters and sculptors as well as by film-makers. The Constructivists (who included Tatlin and El Lissitzky) believed that art should be applied to the making of functional objects and to propaganda, the Suprematists (led by Malevich) that it should remain essentially useless, a vehicle for pure feeling. Yet whether one served the people or the spirit (and in a certain light, the people and the spirit might be thought of as the same), the involvement was intense. As the careers of Pudovkin and others were to exhibit, this intensity could lead to ambiguous and perhaps unexpected results.

Vsevolod Pudovkin had studied chemistry and physics at Moscow University, and after the Great War had unhappily worked for a while in an army laboratory. He was thinking of a career in the fine arts or the theatre, when a viewing of *Intolerance* at the age of twenty-seven convinced him that he should devote his future to the cinema. He went to the front as a newsreel cameraman, then joined Lev Kuleshov's workshop at the Moscow State School of Cinematography. From this training, and from his memories of *Intolerance*, he came to a belief, shared by many of his contemporaries, that the basis for any art the cinema might aspire to lay in editing. Stalin was to describe the artist as an engineer of the soul, and Kuleshov's theory of editing, known as montage, was modelled on the engineering techniques of car assemblage.

But why did Soviet directors place so much emphasis on montage? In the first place, necessity was the mother of invention. 'From 1918 onwards,' write Thorold Dickinson and Catherine de la Roche in *Soviet Cinema*,

working conditions in the Petrograd studio were appalling. Worn-out equipment (four lamps doing the job of forty), shortage of food, fuel and transport physically handicapped the workers. Cameramen could allow themselves only one 'take' or performance of any shot, using in their cameras the 'short ends' of old rolls of unexposed negative, which were sometimes reduced to less than twenty seconds of running time. In that winter the thermometer registered the equivalent of twenty degrees Fahrenheit.[18]

The studios remained busy even during the winter of 1920–21, which was intolerable not only at the front; the toll in civilian deaths was also appalling.

There were several reasons for the absence of film stock: many Russian film producers, supporters of the old regime, had fled the country taking their equipment with them, and an Italian agent commissioned to replace this loss had cheated the Soviet film industry out of a large amount of precious foreign capital by sending it a shipload of dud equipment. Whatever material was available was sent to the front line, although even there cameramen had to rely on used film, stripped of its emulsion and reprocessed. Kuleshov, a former painter, and his students had only one reel of raw stock between them to experiment with. For the rest, they had to work from a small library of archive and foreign films which they re-edited to illustrate the Marxist-Leninist view of reality in compilations sometimes so effective that at least one of the editors, Esfir Shub, developed a legendary reputation both at home and abroad.

The importance of compilation as practised by Esfir Shub can be emphasized by relating it to what Claude Lévi-Strauss, in writing about myth-making, has described as intellectual *bricolage*. In much the same way as Picasso assembled sculptures out of bric-à-brac or pieces of junk, so according to Lévi-Strauss the intellectual bricolist changes the meaning of certain ideas in one system of thought by using them as ideas in another system: one of the more productive ways in which ideas can be developed, and one of the ways in which film clips, fairly meaningless in themselves, can be given meaning. In *Fall of the Romanov Dynasty* (1927) Shub takes a few unrevealing shots of the Tsar and his family and cuts them together in such a way as to place them within the context of the Marxist view of history. She does not so much discover something new as confirm accepted opinion. Demonstrating great skill in bringing about this transformation, she reveals none of the imaginative thinking that Marx, say, brought to his reading of economic information. But propaganda apart, the technique of compilation was to be most valuable in forcing film-makers to question the nature of their art. Eisenstein, for instance, was to formulate his views on montage while re-editing Fritz Lang's *Dr Mabuse, the Gambler* for Soviet consumption.

In his manual *Film Technique* Pudovkin refers to various examples of Kuleshov's montage. Perhaps because Kuleshov was so restricted in film stock, these examples sound trite; yet the principles they enact were to be as serious in their significance as the principle of film metamorphosis that Méliès had uncovered when his camera had jammed in the Place de l'Opéra. In one experiment the White House in Washington was made to reappear in the centre of Moscow, and in another, 'solely by means of montage', writes Kuleshov, 'we showed a living girl, but one who did not actually exist, because we have filmed the lips of one woman, the legs of another, the back of a third, the eyes of a fourth.'[19]

Kuleshov had a passion for the United States and in his feature films was usually attracted to American stories. Yet his work as a director was not to be as striking as his experiments at the Moscow State School of Cinematography. In *The Extraordinary Adventures of Mr West in the Land of the Bolsheviks* (1924), an ingenious American falls in with a gang of Muscovite confidence tricksters. His arrival in Moscow and his drive through snowy deserted streets in a tall narrow taxi-cab are endearing as reportage, but as *Izvestia* remarked fairly at the time of its first showing: 'There is more in the film of the absurd and the improbable than is necessary and, at places, the farce seems burdened.'[20]

As played by Boris Barnet, Mr West in his stars-and-stripes socks appears to be modelled on Harold Lloyd, clearly a popular comedian in the Kuleshov circle. In Pudovkin's more amusing *Chess Fever* (1925) Vladimir Vogel, appearing as a chess fanatic wearing a check cap, check socks and waving a check handkerchief, also gives his role some Lloyd-like touches. The idea of industrial efficiency fascinated Soviet artists—the stage producer Vsevolod Meyerhold, for instance, had derived his theory of bio-mechanics, or grotesque acting, from Taylor's time-and-motion studies—and Harold Lloyd was thought to epitomize machine-man. But Kuleshov was to be known abroad not so much for his comedies as his serious *Against the Law* (1926), based

Lev Kuleshov: *Against the Law* (also known as *Dura Lex*).

on a Jack London story: a melodrama competently enough handled but in no way experimental in technique. He had been criticized for the 'formalism' of *The Death Ray*—which, as Jay Leyda says in *Kino*, employs 'the best tricks of the French and American serials'—and perhaps he restrained any wish he might have had to take risks.

Kuleshov was remarkable, and much-loved, as a teacher. His workshop resembled a research unit in some large industrial combine: but his students were free to experiment with film, and to evolve theories about it, in a way that would have been frowned on in a more commercially-minded organization. Griffith had always assumed that films should be modelled on stage action in the sense that they should be rooted in some experience of space and time. Soviet film-makers, testing out the meaning of film at their cutting-room tables, reverted to an earlier idea: that film was a kind of discourse, or language, whose images could be given a kind of order similar to the forms of lyric poetry or music. These images were more than a shorthand for the actual: they could symbolize processes of thought.

The practice of montage implies all sorts of elisions and suppressions. It did not need to relate figures to other figures or to any specific location and it could be even more cryptic than a dream. Audiences who attended the workshop previews were often baffled, and in his book *The Art of the Cinema* Kuleshov mentions one critic who approached him in horror and said: 'You must be completely mad Futurists. You show films made up of tiny pieces, and the tiny pieces chase each other so fast that no one can find out what's going on.'[21] Under other circumstances montage was too ponderous as a narrative technique, overemphasizing ideas that were in themselves banal or too much of the moment, or making the contrast between shots too calculated.

The theory, indeed, became a tyranny. Too many people believed that the art of film depended on montage, and that strips of film could only take on significance when related to other film strips. The coming of sound brought this tyranny to a crisis, for sound and montage together had the effect of duplicating each other, rendering one of them redundant. In Fyodor Ozep's *The Brothers Karamazov* (1931), allegedly edited by Pudovkin, the montage is so explicit in the analogies it draws that the use of sound appears superfluous, as though it had been added on merely as a novelty. At the same time, the conjunction of sound and montage could be effective when both of them were recognized as types of stylizations, as in Vertov's *Enthusiasm* (1930) and Nicolai Ekk's *The Road to Life* (1931). Nearly all Soviet films to this day, in fact, continue to bear some trace of the montage theory of editing.

The Russians have long been attracted by tragic grotesquerie; and Futurism, with its clowning and violent metaphors, set off a detonation in this echo-chamber. Vertov, applying its doctrines to the stuff of journalism, bared a disjunctive poetry in the newsreel, while Kuleshov, cutting at the roots of film construction, came upon chimeras like his hybrid woman. In Meyerhold's theatre, actors made up as machines gave a modern interpretation to such traditional figures as acrobats, clowns, puppets or the masked players of the Commedia dell'Arte. In 1921 Grigori Kozintsev (aged seventeen), who had worked on the agit-prop trains, joined up with Serge Yutkevitch (aged eighteen) and Leonid Trauberg (aged nineteen) to form FEKS, or the Factory of the Eccentric Actor, very much under the inspiration of Mayakovsky and Meyerhold. Their first production, as Kozintsev later recalled, was 'extremely bizarre, for our own period was reflected in it. The structure of the spectacle, an amalgam of circus, cabaret and cinema, was improvised. We were haunted by all sorts of vague notions which were immediately supplanted by others, still more fantastic, still more precise.'[22] During a Civil War in which every institution in the country was on the point of collapse and nearly everyone suffered terribly from intense cold and famine, these 'young artists felt life in all its richness and colour . . . In the middle of every kind of privation a sort of fair was going on.'[23] Kozintsev and Trauberg were given the opportunity to direct films. *The Adventures of Oktyabrina* (1924) 'was all rather disconnected but galloped along the screen, full of dizzying abridgements of the story and shock cuts.'[24] Their adaptation of Gogol's *The Overcoat* (1926) was less fevered and, in spite of one or two expressionistic touches, they were able to give its compositions the stability and beauty of certain Gordon Craig stage designs. They were to achieve an equally vibrant imagery with their *New Babylon* (1929), in which they use an emporium—in fact, a large shop resembling the stage of a music-hall—to represent Paris at the time of the 1870 Commune. During the opening sequences they imitate an agit-prop stage revue, satirizing the class conflicts prevalent in Paris before the Commune and relying on such familiar stage props as parasols, fans, grotesque faces and silhouettes to create some wonderfully cinematic effects. It could be argued, though, that they sometimes fail to relate these devices and symbols to the actual events of the Commune. Anyone knowing little of French history would be hard put to follow their narrative.

It was in this atmosphere that Sergei Eisenstein, who had trained as an architect and engineer in St Petersburg and during the October Revolution had watched insurgent crowds bearing down on the Winter Palace, began his career. While Eisenstein's debt to Futurism is present in all his stage productions and films of the 1920s, his wide-ranging interests, and curiosity about past cultures, transform the machine aesthetic into something quite different. Marinetti had wanted to destroy all evidence of the Italian Renaissance and to free Italians from their burdensome heritage so that they could create a new kind of art. Eisenstein, on the other hand, deeply respected the achievements of the Renaissance and wished to learn from them. The architect in him was inspired by Renaissance conceptions of space, and he made an almost superhuman effort to bridge the gap between these conceptions and the distorting of space induced by technology. One way in which he related the grotesque and apparently insane features of the modern experience back to the Renaissance was through his interest in the Commedia dell'Arte, another was through his study of Leonardo da Vinci—and Freud's interpretation of Leonardo's character. He tried to understand how the sensations of the machine age could be incorporated into the grand styles of the Renaissance and how the meaning of Marxist humanism might be traced back to the spirit of the Quattrocento.

While serving at the front during the Civil War he had taught himself Japanese; and in Japanese culture, especially in its theatre and the logic of ideogrammatic writing, he found techniques that helped him to define the sensations of the machine age. He was able to profit from the tensions set up by the contrast between the strident, contrapuntal rhythms of Japanese music and the serenity of the Noh actor, especially the impersonal dignity conferred by the Noh mask: a tension which he realized most fully at the end of his life in the two parts of the uncompleted trilogy, *Ivan the Terrible*. But he was as much engineer as architect, scholar or aesthete; and it is the engineer in him that dominates his films of the 1920s. His sense of composition is Futuristic in the sense that his shots often include harshly-stressed diagonal lines that press down on the human figures, while his plots resemble the gnashing cogs and wheels of the assembly line in some *Modern Times* type of factory as they inexorably work through nightmare situations in which groups of people are trapped and destroyed.

He is most the machine-man in his taste for polished surfaces, in his anti-feminism, in his liking for themes of a collective nature and actors used as types. In these moods he comes closest to Marinetti's denial of psychic reality, without realizing how such a denial may entail the wholesale projection of mental states onto the outside world. For all their machine-tooling, his films are among the most confessional, above all when they enact rigorous machine-like processes.

Much as Griffith had been torn between the appeal of the stage with its special kinds of effect and the appeal of techniques appropriate to the film, so Eisenstein was drawn both to the grotesque theatrical symbolism of Meyerhold and to the logic of film structure Vertov had developed from his Futurist interests. His 1923 stage production of Ostrovsky's *Much Simplicity in Every Wise Man* at the Proletkult Arena Theatre followed Meyerhold in its choice of a circus setting and scintillating effects derived from the circus, the Commedia dell'Arte and the ballet; but his production of *Gas Masks*, set in an actual factory, was allegedly less assured. His ideas seemed attenuated in relation to the grim reality of the factory itself, and he was forced to realize that he needed a mediating technique, that of film editing, to bring together his strikingly dramatic fantasies with locations that owed nothing to the illusionism of the theatre.

The clue to how he might achieve this feat of engineering came from Griffith's *Intolerance*. In much the same way as the theory of montage had evolved out of a series of accidents—a shortage of film stock, the existence of Kuleshov's workshop—so the sudden emergence of an *Intolerance* print in Moscow was to be fortuitous, almost a miracle. 'By one of the most extraordinary flukes in history,'[25] claims Jay Leyda in his book *Kino*, a copy of *Intolerance* had found its way through the White Army blockade of Moscow in 1919. Lenin so approved of Griffith's epic (presumably because of its strike scenes) that he arranged for it to be shown throughout the Soviet Union; and he invited Griffith to run the nationalized film industry. It equally impressed many Soviet film-makers. Their work was to take on a grandeur of statement comparable to that of the early American cinema, and not only because they lived in a country as vast in its spaces as the United States. *Intolerance* pointed out means by which this kind of statement could be made. For Eisenstein especially, who was to have a strike as the centrepiece of his first feature, this viewing must have been a momentous occasion, for it gave him a lead on how eclectic styles, both theatrical and realistic, could be brought together in such a way as to supplement each other.

A small boy polishing his father's boots: S. M. Eisenstein's *Strike*.

Without some experience of Mayakovsky's poetry or of Vertov's news-reels he would have probably been unable to make the bold step forward; and yet no Mayakovsky poem or Vertov newsreel excels *Strike* (1924) in its ferociously clever inventions, startling metaphors and unexpected lunges in all directions. Shooting in a factory, Eisenstein moves his camera in such a way that the machinery seems to come alive; working up an atmosphere of farce in other sequences, he appears to transform human beings into automata. It is as though he had applied the techniques of Mack Sennett to the tragic subject-matter of the factory sequences in Griffith's *Intolerance*, but without excluding touches of a more gentle humour (as when a small boy pauses for a moment while trying to polish his father's enormous boots, and sighs hugely). He fuses a semi-documentary about industrial conditions with what the present-day spectator may now think of as a document recording the circus and music-hall styles of fifty years ago.

Lenin had thought that electrification plus the Soviets would equal Communism, but by 1924 the Politburo, recognizing that technology alone would not save the new state from the inertia of its peoples, had already begun to direct its attention to agricultural planning. In this sense *Strike* reflects the mood of an earlier time, when Lenin had still been alive. There are sequences in the Thorndikes' compilation *The Russian Miracle* (1963) showing the Baku oil fields during the pre-revolutionary years, where conditions of labour were so harsh that men collapsed into senility before they were thirty—and compared to which Eisenstein's film, set in the same period, appears to be fantastic. His workers are boyish, bloody-minded and never seen to work; precursors of Vigo's schoolboys, successors to Chaplin's belligerent tramp of the pre-1920s. At home among the machines, these workers swing from girders like monkeys and seem hardly different from the police informers whom Eisenstein protractedly compares to various species of beast.

But the tone of this invention changes in the final part of the story, a change prefigured earlier in two scenes of violence: a group of workers trample on their foreman, a company of soldiers beat up a worker. At the end of the film, farce turns into tragedy, machine-man into Frankenstein's monster; one kind of dehumanization giving way to another. During the concluding strike sequences Eisenstein's powers as an editor are such that when the troops open fire-hoses on the insurgents, he physically conveys the impact of a drenching that kills; appropriating one of the oldest gags on film, that of Lumière's gardener, he steeps it in terror. The nightmare communicated—in which no man can claim mastery over events—owes nothing to Marxism, and yet its intensity brings about a fusion of eclectic techniques. The tenement catwalks, on which the mounted police trap and murder women and children, might have been derived from a Constructivist stage setting, while the cross-cutting between a massacre and the slaughter of a bull has the bravura of a Mayakovsky poster. At such moments terror combines the stuff of newsreels with devices of the utmost theatricality in a manner that Eisenstein had failed to achieve in *Gas Masks*. For *Strike* continues to have the impact of a wholly new work of art. In part, its vitality arises from Eisenstein's optimism about technology and the kind of socialism it would give shape to; in part, from a fear of the machine that is only half acknowledged; and, in part, from his engineering skill as an editor, based on an unusual theory.

He had come to the conclusion that montage should be a collision of images, so strongly contrasted that when they were joined together they would create a dynamic interaction greater than the sum of the individual parts. No one could call it an unobtrusive technique, least of all Eisenstein himself, who thought that anyone who tried to conceal a montage cut was wasting a glorious opportunity. Sometimes his collisions were intended to enact an idea, sometimes a sensation; but they were always exploratory, always a testing out of the power in film. He believed, moreover, that this largely aesthetic method of working reflected the 'laws' of dialectical materialism, especially the Marxist interpretation of history, and it was on these grounds that he tended to criticize his own work and the work of others. In spite of his admiration for *Intolerance*, he believed that its

S. M. Eisenstein: *The Battleship Potemkin.*

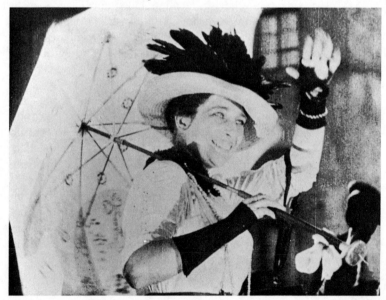

various stories did not hold together sufficiently because Griffith had failed to extract 'generalizing conclusions on historical phenomena from a wide variety of historical data'.[26] In fact, his own practice of montage owed little to Marxist historicism, and though based on socialist principles depended for the most part on a living out of socialism on the pulse, an exploration of consciousness through film that was sharply opposed to any cut-and-dried assertion of how consciousness should be experienced. It is not surprising that he should have soon come into conflict with the Party bureaucrats and dogmatists.

He was even less accurate in his use of facts than Griffith had been. *The Battleship Potemkin* (1925) is more a fiery emblem of the 1905 revolution than a systematic interpretation of the past, presenting the Potemkin mutiny as a series of flashpoints. Its most memorable sequence, the massacre on the Odessa steps, was dreamt up when Eisenstein first saw the steps while out looking for locations. Fascinated though he was by the ways in which men relate to their environment, his use of close-ups tended in a Futuristic manner to atomize his characters, almost to blow them up, representing them by a hand or foot or a pince-nez; or he dehumanized them by seeing them as types of members of some group or crowd.

The relationships that he evolved between these part-selves and their surroundings tended to be Futuristic also. The psychologist Hanns Sachs, drawing on clinical information about the anxieties

S. M. Eisenstein: *The Battleship Potemkin.*

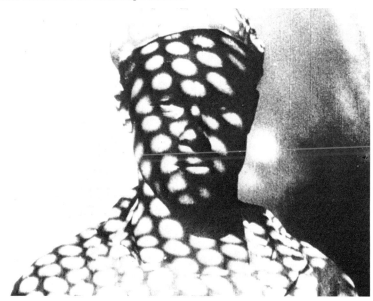

Eisenstein (fourth from right) during the filming of *The Battleship Potemkin.*

many people feel in relation to the relentless and impersonal quality of machines, had come to the conclusion that ancient Greeks and Romans had only used machines as toys in order to avoid feelings of repugnance. Eisenstein, like Marinetti, would have nothing of this view. He welcomed dissonance and glare and those explosions which might clear a way for the new. He felt compelled to see man's involvement with the world as a form of torture. In *October* (1927) a dead horse attached to a carriage and the corpse of a girl lie across the centre of a bridge. The authorities order the bridges to be raised; and as the bascules of this particular bridge rise up, the girl's hair slides sensuously across the widening gap, and the horse, held back by its carriage from falling into the river, dangles over the edge—until the bascules reach such a height that the harness snaps and the horse drops. Yet what is so striking about this episode is less the use of the girl and horse than the slow, vertical movement of girders as they move across the plane of the screen diagonally, an effect shortly to be echoed by the horizontal movement of girders on another bridge.

For Eisenstein, these bridges resemble torturers' racks. In *Strike* he had seen the tenement catwalks as a cage containing energies that exploded the moment an infant was dropped from a great height into the courtyard. Again and again he ascribes cruelty to the inanimate. In *The Battleship Potemkin* an abandoned pram, containing a baby,

'The bascules of the bridge rise up': S. M. Eisenstein's *October*.

bounces down the grandiose marmoreal steps. In *October* the baroque statues of St Petersburg seem to float in cold mockery over some crushed human beings. He conceives of these buildings and statues as persecutors that must be attacked and subdued. His 'collisions' often rely more on personal and very private hatreds than on political insight, and his exercise of them often appears disproportionate to the historical events he describes. *October* begins with a shot of the Tsar's statue, which is followed by a sequence of shots framed on various insignia of imperial power as they tumble off the statue. Finally, when there is nothing left on the pedestal, Eisenstein reverses these shots so that the statue is re-formed. It could be argued that this trick points up the hollowness of the Tsar's authority, or that Eisenstein was following the semi-scientific methods of his hero, Leonardo da Vinci, and investigating the structure of things. But these arguments sound like rationalizations of an impulse that could, in a protracted way, show soldiers thrusting their bayonets into the Tsarina's bed.

His view of events, then, was ahistorical, timeless, perhaps animistic. Trotsky's criticism of Mayakovsky's poetry, which applies just as well to montage by collision, defines the limitations of this view.

> The thing that is most lacking in his work is action. This may look like a paradox, for Futurism is entirely founded on action. But there enters the unimpeachable dialectics: an excess of violent imagery results in quiescence. Action must correspond to the mechanics of perception and to the rhythm of our feelings if it is to be perceived artistically, and even physically. A work of art must show the gradual growth of an image, of a mood, of a plot, or an intrigue to its climax, and must not throw the spectator about from one to another, no matter if it is done by the most skilful boxing blows of imagery. [27]

By alluding to action, rhythm, growth, Trotsky assumes that art should be modelled on the processes of nature, especially of human nature. He assumes that any theory of action and history must depend on this conception of nature. But Eisenstein wished to model art on the machine. He loathed nature, at least in its pastoral form, and would probably have admired Marinetti's denunciation of John Ruskin.

> With his sick dream of a primitive, pastoral life; with his nostalgia for Homeric cheeses and legendary spinning wheels; with his hatred of the machine, of steam and electricity, this maniac for antique simplicity resembles a man who in full maturity wants to sleep in his cot again and drink the breasts of a nurse who has grown old, in order to regain the carefree state of infancy. [28]

One of the most coherent arguments to counter Marinetti's position, interestingly enough, has come from a Marxist humanist, the Hungarian literary critic Georg Lukács. In contrast to Marinetti's distaste for 'Homeric cheeses and legendary spinning wheels', Lukács has seen in the Homeric epic a hopeful alternative to industrial alienation: a type of society in which human relationships and the relationship of men to the objects they use are of a kind that allow for personal integration and development.

Echoes of this debate can be heard in Pudovkin's many disagreements with Eisenstein. Although impressed by the machine aesthetic, Pudovkin came down in favour of an art modelled on the processes of nature. He proposed that montage should be a form of linkage, not collision, and that the actor should be given an almost idealized dignity. He set considerable store on the meaning of an actor's relationship to objects. 'The performance of an actor linked with an object, and built upon, will always be one of the most powerful methods of film construction. It is, as it were, a filmic monologue without words.' [29]

He was editing *Mechanics of the Brain*, a six-reel documentary about Pavlov and the nature of conditional reflexes, when he began to work on *Mother* in 1926; and it is possible to give a behavourist reading to this film version of Gorky's play, in the sense that the mother, brought into conflict with the forces of Tsarist oppression, is educated by a series of shocks into realizing the need for revolution. But in fact this machine-like view of human behaviour only has bearing on the treatment of the opening sequences, in which Pudovkin's filming of the heroic, muscular son and blockish, drunken father prefigures the stiffness of Socialist Realist sculpture (much as the rigged trial of the son foreshadows Stalinist justice). Pudovkin soon warms this stiffness into pliability by the performance he elicits from Vera Baranovskaya and by the quality of his editing. Baranovskaya appears as a listless nondescript peasant woman who on three occasions becomes the embodiment of incandescent passion: when the

Vera Baranovskaya, in the title role of V. Pudovkin's *Mother*.

police arrest her son, when she greets her son after his escape from prison and when, having witnessed his murder, she lifts the Red Flag and allows herself to be killed by the charging mounted police.

Through his editing, Pudovkin suggests that the mother becomes the spirit of the revolution. But he also implies—by her unintended part in bringing about the son's arrest and by the conjunction in the final sequences of her embrace and a gloved hand giving a signal for the first murderous police charge—that this spirit has to kill in order to give life. Through editing, his description of a workers' uprising carries within it a seemingly remote and cryptic description of how love may conquer egotism. He wrote about the ice-bound thawing river in Griffith's *Way Down East*—an image that in Russian literature has haunted many writers—as 'an impression of death'; yet the renowned sequence in which he edits together shots of the son in prison, of the workers in arms and of ice blocks sweeping down a river conveys more than an impression of death or of a growing revolutionary vigour that will break apart the frozen old order: on a far more generalized level, it represents an experience of the heart in thaw, of an emotional liberation.

By relating politics and history, through mental states, to changes in the seasons and landscape, he involves himself in a kind of symbolism familiar to poets, especially Romantic poets, in which metaphors assume a proliferating complexity of a type often known as 'organic'. He begins *Storm over Asia* (1928) with shots of mountains, hillsides, a huge rock bounding over the edge of a cliff, and for the first part of the film unfurls many events against an unending Mongolian plain, while placing later events against cliffs or on top of craggy promontories: a primordial background that recalls *Nanook of the North* and the Ince Westerns and, in the opening sequence at least, appears to underwrite the epic status of the whole enterprise by suggesting the world at its moment of creation. But this visionary ambition lends authority to a story that hardly lives up to such grandeur—as Pudovkin may have recognized. A general in the British expeditionary force in Russia at the time of the Civil War discovers that a Mongol trapper he has condemned to death is a descendant of Genghis Khan, and he sets up the trapper as a pawn ruler to consolidate imperial power in Mongolia. Pudovkin tries to build up the significance of this intrigue through a series of often overwrought

'An imperial mummy and British dupe': V. Pudovkin's *Storm over Asia*.

linkages: between British diplomacy and the religious customs of the Mongol community, and between the trapper and his precious white fox fur, as well as between the various characters and their surroundings. Even so, his editing, especially in the 1950 re-edited version of the film, is perhaps the most sustained example of the ways in which montage can transform the meaning of an image, unfolding like some rich tapestry of metaphor. A hand raised in protest, for instance, will become a hand raised before a firing squad. Invention touches its peak in the scenes where the Mongol trapper, apparently executed and left for dead, is hauled back to the British HQ, revived, bandaged and dressed in the robes of an emperor. He is resurrected to a living death, transformed into an imperial mummy and British dupe, barely able to move for bandages. Left alone for an instant and gasping for water, he drags himself across the room and accidentally knocks over a tank of fish, which lie gasping and wriggling on the floor. Complex meanings, however, are diminished by a poverty of sentiment. For all his magnanimity as an epic film maker, Pudovkin is mean as a propagandist, unable to see his characters as other than extremely good or bad.

The Soviet cinema of the 1920s had little influence in the West from about the time of the Spanish Civil War to the mid-sixties. Eisenstein, Pudovkin and their contemporaries were admired but seldom imitated; they had been relegated, it seemed, to the museums of high culture. But in the sixties the relationship between art and technology emerged once more as a central topic, though few artists now expected technology to be the key to socialism. Sad acquiescence, rather, was the governing mood. For Richard Hamilton, one of the founders of the Pop Art movement, the motor car was no longer Apollo's chariot, as it had been for Marinetti; it had become a shimmering container for both yearning and regret, associated—as in Hamilton's silk-screen prints of Marilyn Monroe—with evanescence. And while César's blocks of crushed car-metal in no way checked this disquiet about machines, the flirtations of kinetic sculpture suggested a return to the technology of the Ancient World as envisaged by Dr Sachs: the machine turned into a plaything to diminish its repugnance.

In movies the techniques of *The Battleship Potemkin* reappeared in Penn's *Bonnie and Clyde* and Peckinpah's *The Wild Bunch*, but their iconography of violence seemed counters merely to the irony of stoic despair. More optimistically, various film cooperatives, like the American group Newsreel, revived methods of filming and distribution that in their flexibility recall the agit-prop trains Lunacharsky had sent to the Soviet front. The time was ripe for the rediscovery of the activist tradition in the cinema; and it is not surprising, then, that through the researches of Georges Sadoul, various French film-

makers (including Jean Rouch and Jean-Luc Godard) welcomed enthusiastically any knowledge of Denis Kaufman, the student in
mathematics and neurophysiology who had taken on the nickname
of 'spinning top', or 'Dziga Vertov', in order to proclaim his allegiance to the idea of movement. Unlike his brother Boris Kaufman,
a leading cameraman in the French and American cinema, Vertov
was little more than a name in textbooks, his writings untranslated,
his compilations inaccessible. He was thought to be a figure standing
outside the mainstream of the Soviet cinema, eccentric and likeable,
possibly mad. Yet more than anyone else it was he who had consistently challenged the studio-bound theatrical conception of film-
making.

He had worked as an editor with Kuleshov, organized the teams
of cameramen who roamed the Soviet Union during the Civil War,
and operated a camera himself. 'In the foremost positions at the
Polish front, in the Crimea, with Budenny's cavalry, in the rear of the
Czechoslovaks, everywhere the cameraman was to be seen, actively
participating in military operations and battles,' wrote the cameraman Vladimir Nilsen in *The Cinema as a Graphic Art*. 'Already he was
far from the neutral position of the bourgeois newsreel reporter who
seeks sensational shots amid the circumstances of a fighting front. He
became an active agitator and propagandist, frequently changing his
camera for a rifle.'[30]

Writing in *Lef*, of which Mayakovsky and Osip Brik, the Constructivist theorist and *Storm over Asia* screenwriter, were leading editors,
and Eisenstein among the principal contributors, Vertov was also to
consider the rifle viewfinder and the camera as interchangeable; and
through this equation, it seems, eroticized the eye, equating it with
some brutal conception of the penis. Kuleshov had fabricated an
imaginary woman, but Vertov was to say: 'I am eye. I have created a
man more perfect than Adam.' He wrote of the other arts as 'cas-
trated' and ascribed a superhuman potency to Mayakovsky. 'He sees
what the eye does not.' In the same way, the camera might see what
the eye could not. 'We cannot make our eyes better than they are,
but the movie camera we can perfect forever.'[31]

He bridges the disagreement between Eisenstein and Pudovkin
both by endorsing the machine aesthetic and by seeing films as docu-
ments, loving compilations of every aspect of reality. He believed that
the principles of montage extended beyond film editing into every
choice made by the organizing mind. He saw connections everywhere, a potentially unified world bound by sympathy. His spry intelligence allowed him at the same time to be a committed Marxist
and to maintain a spontaneous impressionism. He could take up
official themes, like the nation's debt to Lenin, and infuse them with
all the boldness of discovery. Long after many of the other pioneers

had retreated into a sort of deadness, he was able to identify the more peculiar and urgent elements in his self with public policy, perhaps because his probing eye was blind to the increasing hostility of this policy to the freedom of the artist.

Even as late as 1934, he was able (in his *Three Songs of Lenin*) to touch on the familiar contrast between old and new forms of agriculture with a freshness and grace untinged by irony. His exotic choice of peoples to represent the Russian peasant in part accounts for this freshness—he drew a great deal of his material from newsreel film about life in the Muslim republics around the Caspian Sea—and so, in part, does his careful research work. He compiled his songs from a collection of 150 films and during his researches discovered at least ten previously unknown clips of Lenin. But even more moving than his concern for the film as history is his ability to convey the impression that Lenin and the Soviet Union in all its vastness were bound to each other by almost familial ties. He himself attended Lenin's funeral as a cameraman, but his eye for unusual detail saves the obsequies from being too obsequious. He notices how a Dostoyevskian strangeness informs the grief and how some of the mourners in fur coats look seedily vulpine.

His skill as an editor seems to have been largely intuitive, in spite of his elaborate theories, and it plays on an audience's intuition or not at all; and now, as well as then, many spectators react in bafflement to it. Eisenstein, who had studied with Vertov, directed one of the early Kino Pravdas and acknowledged his influence on *The Battleship Potemkin*, was yet impelled to describe *The Man with a Movie Camera* (1929) as being no more than 'formalist jackstraws and unmotivated camera mischief'.[32] Admittedly, a Marxist might criticize this Futurist account of a day in the life of a city adversely on the grounds that it does not attempt to define the centres of urban power, but then it could be argued with equal force that its intentions are not directly political. Its concern is with perception and technology and the ways in which technology can increase powers of perception, a self-reflexive investigation into means of investigation. It describes a film-maker's attitudes to his camera, to things seen on location, to rushes in the cutting-room and to the audience. With this film, Vertov bids farewell to the silent screen by pursuing its techniques as far as he can take them.

It begins in an auditorium where a film, *The Man with a Movie Camera*, is about to be shown. Rows of seats uncannily tip open in the empty auditorium, then the audience arrives and the film itself commences with a succession of seemingly arbitrary static shots that in technique prefigure the final sequence of Antonioni's *The Eclipse*: a window, street-lamps, a close-up of a hand lying on a bed, a park, a close-up on part of a woman's naked body lying on a bed, a man-

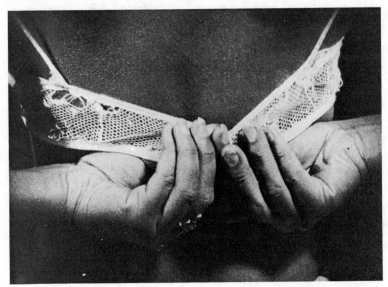

'Seemingly arbitrary, static shots': Dziga Vertov's *The Man with a Movie Camera.*

size beer bottle stranded in the park, another close-up on the sleeping woman, a tramp asleep on a park bench, a window, another window, a sleeping baby. Even more fixed shots of urban objects follow, their principal connection being an abstract one: similarities in shapes, contrasts in compositions. Vertov's response to the inanimate is quite different from Eisenstein's: he does not project his fantasies on to it; he observes, and in observing allows his intelligence to disclose connections. He cuts back and forth between some people lying on a railway track and the sleeping woman. A train runs over the people lying on the track, and in such a way as to raise the question whether the action is taking place in the mind of the sleeping woman or in the mind of the cameraman who imagines the woman's dream.

In the second section of the film, the camera assumes a more positive function as it moves through the city. The working day begins, and the immobile and mysterous shapes of the first section of the film are transformed into objects with a function. Contrasts and comparisons set up clever (yet perhaps inane) similarities, as when a pattern of weaving bobbins is related to water swirling forth from a dam. In the third and final section of the film, the action centres on a cutting-room, where an editor is slicing together shots of a wedding with those of a woman crying in a graveyard. The film-maker is seen to be a worker like any other. Perhaps Vertov in his enthusiasm includes too many trick devices in this panorama of human life—split screens, fast and slow motion, frozen shots and much else—and perhaps *The Man with a Movie Camera* eventually becomes blurred as an experiment; even so, it is a landmark in the exploration of the ways in which the camera can increase our powers of perception.

In Jean-Luc Godard's *La Chinoise* (1967) a painter named Kirilov sardonically claims that socialist art died in 1919, at the time of the Brest-Litovsk treaty. Although the days of international socialism were probably numbered when Lenin entered the field of conventional diplomacy and reinstated Tsarist bureaucrats to manage foreign policy, 1919 does seem a premature date to signal the end to socialist art. In *Kino* Jay Leyda is inclined to set the decline in Soviet film-making from 1927, exactly a decade after the October Revolution. He suggests that the first Five Year Plan of 1928 led to an industrialization of filming on the Hollywood model and to the opening of new studios in Moscow, Kiev and Tiflis, where a glossy kind of photography 'gave films an impersonal machine-like quality that characterizes most of the well-known films made in the last period of the Soviet silent film'.[33] Censorship, too, was increased, in the sense that government committees and groups of workers were invited to criticize films on the grounds of the most reductionist kind of propaganda and were given the right to block their release. But even so, certain directors continued to show the Soviet Union in a human and far from idealized way. Abram Room's *Bed and Sofa* (1926) is the most celebrated in a cycle of films that made public the moral licence of the years after the Revolution; and its description of a *ménage à trois*—a stonemason, his wife and former wartime buddy— in a small bed-sitting apartment has a twentyish insouciance of a Lubitsch kind. When the wife announces that she is pregnant, neither man will accept responsibility for the child, and they pack her off to an abortion clinic. She takes the train home to her father, and the two men, feeling abandoned, wonder whether they have enough food left for them in the apartment.

This casualness in relationships is reflected in a casualness about politics. 'Are you going to the Party meeting?' a worker asks the stonemason. 'No,' he answers, 'I prefer to go home.' Some commentators have seen *Bed and Sofa* as a protest against bad housing conditions and praised its kitchen-sink naturalism, but the quality that has helped it to endure is of a more subtle kind. Room's editing, in which a view of Moscow will be followed by a close-up of a soup tureen, has the effect of minimizing any difference between inside and outside the bed-sitting apartment, and in this way linking arbitrary relationships to the desolate urban vista. But if Room qualifies Soviet enthusiasm for the machine age, he does so reticently. *Bed and Sofa* is political only by implication—one of its saving graces.

In *The Non-Objective World*, his account of painting since Cézanne (published in 1927, but written well before that date), Kasimir Malevich places together three groups of photographs. In the first group, described as 'the environment which stimulates the Academician', he has four photographs, all of them taken in a rural setting: an alert pointer in a field, three horses on a dusty road, a soldier in a buggy playing an accordion (a cottage and peasant woman beside him) and a peasant family seated on a bench before a fenced-off orchard. As in the films of D. W. Griffith, these figures, animals and possessions are allowed to dominate the scene.

In the second group, 'the environment which stimulates the Futurist', there are twelve photographs so closely assembled that they look like a collage: they consist of dirigibles, battleships, locomotives, girders, skyscrapers, factory machinery and the criss-cross of searchlights against a night sky. Diagonal lines, strong yet restless, govern these photographs in much the same way as their massive industrial installations dwarf the few visible human beings.

In 'the environment which stimulates the Suprematist',[34] finally, Malevich places aerial photographs of docks, taken from high up, and of biplanes in flight, so far away that they are mere specks. Without any context to define them and so distanced that they lose any figurative meaning, the content of these photographs resembles Malevich's own abstract paintings. They seem to be journeys into both outer and inner space, trajectories of the self that are like the fluctuating ill-defined mental states induced by certain drugs.

These three modes of perceiving are present to some extent in every Soviet film of the 1920s, and the interaction between them is the main source of the tension that gives this cinema such power. In the 1930s, on the evidence of the incomplete *Que Viva Mexico* and *Bezhin Meadows*—as in his lingering over great tracts of sky—Eisenstein would appear to have been drifting towards the Suprematist kind of envelopment. But in the previous decade he had been engaged more immediately in politics and the Futurist aesthetic. The Politburo was concerned to develop an effective policy by which to mechanize agriculture, and opinion was divided on whether the kulaks—farmers who employed labourers—should be encouraged or suppressed. In 1924 Gorky had written: 'The fundamental obstacle in the path of Russia's progress towards Europeanisation and culture is the zoological individualism of the peasantry and its almost total lack of social feelings.'[35] The misfortune of Communism was that it had to prove itself with so backward a population. On a lesser scale, it was a misfortune that Sovkino should have asked Eisenstein to promote this theme.

He completed *The General Line* (also known as *Old and New*) in 1929, the year in which Stalin decreed the collectivization of agri-

S. M. Eisenstein: *The General Line*. On location.

culture. He was to develop some of its ideas far more persuasively in *Que Viva Mexico*—one image in *The General Line*, of bull-skulls against a twilight sky, foreshadows the extraordinary 'Cavalera' death-day pageant in *Que Viva Mexico*, and its key sequence, the priests' attempts to exorcise drought, was to be handled with far greater mobility in his treatment of the Virgin's Festival at Guadaloupe; but while he found Mexico and its people attractive, he seems to have thought his Russian subject unappealing and he fails to bring it to life. Apart from some splendid Renaissance heads, most of his characters are squalid, money-grubbing grotesques. Nature in its Russian guise distinctly repels him, and a wan resentment, which can take the form of facetiousness, is often present—as in the climactic scene of a prize bull being put out to mate. He presents fecundity in images which arrest any pleasure in living, as when he compares a vastly pregnant woman to some shivering, emaciated beast or arranges that a sow feeding its young should be of monstrous proportions. Although he seems to delight in the peasants' co-op, designed by the Constructivist architect Vesnin, and has a Marinetti-like tractor-driver sport dark goggles, his revulsion from nature appears more instinctive than Futuristically deliberate. Vertov had extolled male potency and, possibly, been fascinated by male brutality; but Eisenstein, faced by evidence of organic existence, takes flight into male graffiti. While his villagers greet the arrival of a milk separator with hostility, he responds to it with ponderous references to ejaculation.

Yet the theme of mechanization could be tractable. *Turksib*, released in the same year as *The General Line* and directed by Victor Turin, a Russian who had trained at the Massachusetts Institute of

Technology, brought a particularly Soviet interest to a subject that owed something to John Ford's *The Iron Horse*. Turin fully realizes the exotic promise of his subject—the laying of a railway track between Turkestan and Siberia—and systematically develops a contrast between deserts and icy wastes. But he is less concerned with incongruities—although he has one memorable shot of a camel nuzzling at

'Camel nuzzling the railway track': V. Turin's *Turksib*.

the track—than with the nature of process: the way in which rain is channelled down mountains into cotton fields, and the way in which the cotton, when grown, is made into thread, into linen and then into garments. He shows how men at work and the processes of industry imitate the cycles of nature, and it is to his credit that he neither hurries over the various stages of these transformations, nor feels obliged to energize them with a flashy display of technique, as Eisenstein was to do with his milk-separator sequence. Absorbed by the idea of a world at work, he builds up his film shot by shot as though he were laying brick upon brick. He demonstrates how a simoom, or desert wind, picks up force and how a close-up of sand, crumbling and spilling off a dune, can disclose a universe in microcosm. John Grierson was to add titles to *Turksib* for English-speaking audiences (according to Paul Rotha, he was also to tighten up its editing); and its technique may be seen as a model for the programme that Grierson imposed on the Empire Marketing Board documentary films of the 1930s.

But the theme of mechanization and the land could be more than tractable; it could be an inspiration, allowing Alexander Dovzhenko to bring together all of Malevich's categories: the Academic, the Futurist and the Suprematist. In *Earth* (1930) Dovzhenko's approach was to be Homeric, his technique as dissociated as Eisenstein's, yet his humanism was to be of a kind that could resolve the apparent

V. Turin: *Turksib.*

contradiction between art as modelled on either nature or the machine.

A native of the Ukraine, Dovzhenko entered films in 1926 at the late age of thirty-two, having fought on the Polish front, studied biology, economics and technology at the University, and made a living as a painter and political cartoonist. He first attracted public attention, and won the praise of Eisenstein and Pudovkin, with *Zvenigora* (1928), although many spectators, including Eisenstein, admitted they were bewildered by it. He seemed ill at ease with customary modes of narrative, did not signpost his intentions and thought in terms of unusual metaphors.

In *Zvenigora* Dovzhenko is so excited by the scope of film that he imposes little control over his range of associations. He holds audience interest by his contempt for orthodoxies, as he plunders stylistic devices from Méliès, Griffith, Sennett, Gance and Lang and mixes them together with little concern for consistency. An old man, seemingly as old as the legends he recounts, tells his grandson Pavlo a fairy tale about Zvenigora, a magic earthwork that contains treasure. The boy grows up to be a counter-revolutionary and swindles an audience of ghoulish émigrés by breaking his promise to commit suicide during a stage performance. Another grandson, Timochka, ignoring the old man's stories, becomes a Cossack who realizes that the ground of the Ukraine contains a different sort of treasure: its rich soil and mines. At the end of the film the grandfather unsuccessfully tries to derail a train; and swamped by this conclusion, the spectator may willingly clutch at the straw offered by Jay Leyda when he proposes that this train could well be viewed as a symbol for progress.

Two themes emerge in *Zvenigora*, which Dovzhenko was later to develop: one being a contrast between myth and actuality, superstition and materialism, the atemporal and the transient; the other, related to these contrasts, being his fascination with death, dramatically enacted in the scene of Pavlo's pretended suicide. He sees death as grotesque, terrifying or rending the mourner with grief. Yet he also tries to see it as a natural experience, bringing the one who dies, and the mourners, into touch with the fullness of existence.

Struggling to bring this theme to fruition in *Arsenal* (1929), he clearly had trouble in working it out coherently. At certain Futuristic moments—the scenes in which men rush by on horseback or in which a train is derailed—he angles shots oddly and to no apparent purpose and is barely able to place geographically his concluding sequence, a battle at a Kiev munitions factory, inchoate in its succession of close-ups; it is as though he were using the elations of Futurist technique to avoid forebodings about death. In contrast to this fever, he has certain other scenes made up of immobile shots containing monumental figures. In one such shot he shows three old men in the street of a Ukrainian village, where most of the young men have been killed in the Civil War. The image is informal and strange, as though the camera had picked it up by chance; it might be a still photograph, yet it has the vibrancy of film. The old men seem to have been caught in the interstices of time.

In another shot the camera looks down onto a ploughed field which fills the screen, its furrows drawing together at the top left hand corner of the screen. A woman in black, three of whose sons have died in the war, stands at this corner. She does not move and the shot is held. Dovzhenko likes to raise an illusion in which the seemingly dead, like the old men and the woman in black, are living, while the seemingly living—like mouths that appear to be laughing but are, in fact, mouths in the grimacing faces of corpses—are dead. In the concluding minutes of the film, Red soldiers are lined against a wall and shot. The rifles and bullets that kill them are never seen; the soldiers unaccountably jerk into a dance and then fall to the ground.

But one of them pulls open his shirt and moves forward, undeterred by the hail of bullets directed at him.

The subject of death, both anticipated and unexpected, dominates *Earth* (1930). Robert Conquest has calculated, in his book *The Great Terror*, that between five and six million people died because of Stalin's collectivization policy of 1929, many of them at the hands of the secret police, many more from famine. The most terrible of the conflicts over collectivization occurred in the Ukraine, Dovzhenko's birthplace and the setting of *Earth*; yet Dovzhenko presents the policy of collectivization as benign and his admiration for Stalin's regime as unqualified. Like *The Birth of a Nation, Earth* is a masterpiece built on an inhuman base, wide-reaching and rich in its quality of feeling, except in this fundamental blankness. It could be argued that he had no choice: better an *Earth* so flawed than no *Earth* at all.

Dovzhenko has his camera move no more than two or three times throughout the film, and movement within the image tends to be restricted. But his editing of these immobile shots has the cumulative effect of emphasizing both the relationship between things and their separateness. He begins his remarkable opening sequence, in which the old peasant Semyon dies, with six shots of a cornfield, a vast cloudy sky pressing down on it; he then follows with a shot of a young woman standing by a sunflower with six close-ups of branches weighed down by apples. The apples are huge, in full maturity, per-

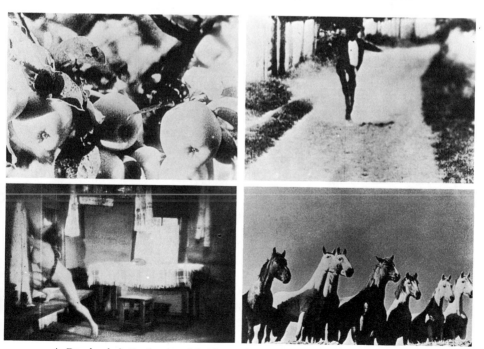

A. Dovzhenko's *Earth: above left,* 'the apples are huge, in full maturity, perfect'; *above right,* Vassil, dancing in the moonlight; *below left,* Vassil's wife beats her fists against the walls of their bedroom; *below right,* unbridled horses.

fect. Semyon lies on the ground, a mound of apples fills the background. Near by children eat a melon. A series of shots shows faces looking down on him in unruffled sadness. He says he is going to die. His middle-aged son asks him to return after death and tell them what the after-life is like. The old man sits up, sniffs appreciatively and claims to be hungry. One of his relatives hands him a pear, which he eats; then he says amiably that he is about to go, lies down once more and dies imperceptibly. This death, these apples, this sky, these children eating a melon are linked to each other as aspects of a beneficent nature, living out the axiom that each person and thing is part of nature and yet each is alone. Almost as a reduction to absurdity of this maxim, a relative puts his ear to Semyon's grave and asks: 'Are you there?'

Dovzhenko works out this idea of separateness within the commonalty of nature even more intricately in relation to another death. As leader of the village cooperative Semyon's grandson, Vassil, brings a tractor to the village. One night while walking home in the moonlight he begins to dance, then unaccountably stumbles and falls. His body is laid out on a bed, and it emerges that a kulak named Foma, who resented the arrival of the tractor, had killed him. Dovzhenko then weaves together six seemingly disconnected events that unite into a coherent impression: while Vassil's naked wife beats her fist against the walls of their bedroom, a priest, rejected by the village, kneels before a cross and curses all atheists; Foma, the murderer, runs wildly across a churchyard and buries his head in the earth; unbridled horses race across a field; a pregnant woman heaves in labour; and the villagers, singing revolutionary anthems, carry Vassil's body to its grave (a tracking shot, disturbing in its uniqueness, has branches of an apple tree brush across Vassil's face). Dovzhenko plays images of life at its most violent against images of death in a surprising yet harmonious manner. But then the structure of *Earth* itself is surprising. In part directed against kulak-type farming, it presents the kulaks as gallant and vigorous. In part directed against organized religion, it conveys a pantheistic vision of life. It incorporates the three modes of Soviet perception as described by Malevich. It is Futurist in its grain-separator sequence—derived, perhaps, from Fernand Léger's *Ballet mécanique*—'Academic' in its disposition of figures in a landscape, and yet Suprematist in its overwhelming feeling for envelopment. It may be said to contain all of Malevich's categories and, in doing so, to transcend them.

Well before the Revolution, the cinema had attracted Russian audiences from every class. The Tsar, who liked to make home movies, gave it his patronage, and writers of the calibre of Tolstoy, Gorky and Andreyev recognized its promise. Although the natives of Nizhny

Novgorod allegedly suspected witchcraft and burnt a *cinématographe*, Lumière's cameraman, Félix Mesguich, had been warmly welcomed everywhere else. From the earliest days foreign distributors – Pathé, Gaumont, Nordisk, Cinès – had set up profitable exchange centres in Russia, and the five local companies also thrived, their output ranging from Starevich's outstanding puppet films to adaptations from the classics, directed most notably by Khanzhonkov and Protazanov. The Russians greatly admired Asta Nielsen, and among their own actors Ivan Muzhukin acquired an international reputation.

At the time of the Revolution film companies in their entirety left Russia by way of the Crimea. Many artists and technicians settled in France. Kirsanov and Muzhukin and others were to play an important role in the progress of the French avant-garde, while the producer Alexander Kamenka, who set up his Société Albatros in Méliès's old studio at Montreuil, was to be one of its keenest supporters. But, as Thorold Dickinson and Catherine de la Roche point out in *Soviet Cinema*, the Russians were to be found everywhere in the French film industry. 'As late as 1925 the Billancourt studios (then under the control of Abel Gance) in the south-west of Paris were almost wholly staffed by Russian émigrés, some of whom had not troubled to learn more than a few words of French. High up on the wall of the main studio nearest the entrance was fixed an icon of the Greek Orthodox Church.'[36]

The movement was not all one way. Jacob Protazanov returned to the Soviet Union and in *Aelita* (1924) tried both to work out his mixed feelings concerning Bolshevism and to bring together the styles of the Russian and French avant-garde. Los, an engineer, is torn be-

J. Protazanov: *Aelita*. The workers who live underground.

tween dreams of the Russia he hopes will emerge from the machine age and dreams of a Martian kingdom which he believes is ruled over by the androgynous princess Aelita. He designs a spaceship to take him to this kingdom.

While unintentionally predicting the nightmare of the Soviet concentration camps, the luxurious, mysterious and oppressive kingdom of Mars is presumably intended to represent the capitalist West (in a Wellsian manner, Aelita forces her workers to live underground and sometimes puts them into hibernation by freezing them). Protazanov places Los during his Russian dream against a Futurist background of machines and building sites and, during his Martian dream, against remarkable Constructivist settings designed by Simov and Rabinovich. He cuts back and forth between Moscow and Mars in such a way that the spectator cannot be sure whether the kingdom of Mars actually exists or exists only in the engineer's mind: a type of ambiguity that many members of the French avant-garde were also to practise.

Los's hesitation in choosing between two kinds of society, which Protazanov himself at one time had shared, is acted out less equivocally by other characters. His alter ego Spiridonov (Nikolai Tseretelly plays both Los and Spiridonov) finds the hold of the past too strong on him and leaves Russia for the West, while Los's wife cannot resist Erlich, an amusing con-man involved in the black market, who takes her to a lavish illegal ball for Tsarist sympathizers. Los's jealousy of Erlich increases as his dream of Mars intensifies. Inner and outer worlds begin to mingle. Los believes that he murders his wife and travels in his spaceship to the dream planet; but when he kisses Aelita, she turns into his wife. He and his friends then liberate the Martian workers. Waking from this dream and finding his wife unharmed, he decides to destroy his plans for space travel and to devote his life to realizing the new Russia. One of the many fascinations of *Aelita* is that Protazanov is able both to symbolize a deeply Romantic impulse in the French manner and at the same time to qualify this impulse by a down-to-earth humour and some valuable newsreel filming of Moscow and Muscovite life in the early 1920s.

5. The Influence of the French Avant-Garde

No doubt the cinema is only one among many activities which have opened up the vast penumbras surrounding the bright islet of our conscious powers of reasoning. A host of techniques, from psychoanalysis to micro-physics, has begun to describe a universe where, to use Descartes's words, reason no longer always seems right. The cinema has an isolated position among these techniques, one often misunderstood, but primordial. Because it encourages us to think in a dreamlike way, to associate images with a lightness and subtlety that escape the constraints of syntax; because it reveals to us the mobility of all forms, all laws, all kinds of measurement, the cinema slowly but surely filters the most basic of doubts throughout society: that of questioning the value of all absolutes.

JEAN EPSTEIN (1953)

By the beginning of the Great War Charles Pathé, who had set up business in 1894 with a capital of 1,000 francs, had developed Pathé Frères into the largest company in the world. Valued at 30 million francs in 1912, this company was to be worth 45 million francs by 1923. Yet Charles Pathé was to be largely responsible for breaking up the French film industry. The Marxist historian Georges Sadoul has described him as the archetypal capitalist, and justly, even though Pathé had some feeling for the value of film in itself. In 1910 he had subsidized the micro-cinematographic studies of Dr Comandon, and he was to back Gance's *La Roue* financially. Rigid in character—in his autobiography *The Advice and Memories of an Upstart* he hectors parents on the need to bring up children strictly—he was supple in business. As chairman of his company, he set store by paying his shareholders handsome dividends—eventually at the expense of his film empire.

He lost his nerve when the war began to diminish his profits. The Americans were pouring films into France; the German invasion had diminished the home market; many of his more able employees were at the front. In 1917 Henri Diamant-Berger, a journalist and director of what was to be a highly popular version of *The Three Musketeers* (1921), wrote in the weekly magazine *Le Film*: 'British production is insignificant. Great Britain is no more than a colony to the American film industry. If we don't take warning at this example, we shall undergo the same fate.'¹ Pathé ordered his film-makers to adapt their subjects to the international market: then, as now, a decision of this kind was to be disastrous. He determined to stop film production. He closed down studios and diversified. His shareholders prospered; the film industry collapsed. 'In 1914,' wrote Léon Moussinac, '90 per cent of the films shown throughout the world were French; by 1928, 85 per cent of them were American.'²

But the war, which helped to destroy an industry, also helped to create an informed opinion about a new art. 'The war was the time when men of my generation discovered the cinema,' claimed Alexandre Arnoux in the *Revue de cinéma*. 'Perhaps in breaking down our assumptions and habits and our very lives, the war made us more responsive to the power of images and silence, to those barbarous, taciturn and concretely-realized dreams, which gradually were to be modified and refined.'³ A few artists and intellectuals had begun to discover the cinema before the war. In 1913 Guillaume Apollinaire had reviewed Westerns seriously in *Les Soirées de Paris*. He and others were to be enthusiastic about both American serials and their French derivative *Fantômas* (1913–14), which was not so much a serial as five loosely-connected episodes drawn from some best-selling novels by Pierre Souvestre and Marcel Allain. Max Jacob and Apollinaire founded La Société des Amis du *Fantômas*, of which in truth they were the only members. Louis Aragon, Philippe Soupault, Paul Eluard and André Breton, who were awaiting their mobilization papers, were also to be fascinated by it, and so was Pablo Picasso. Soupault began to contribute ciné-poems to avant-garde magazines and Aragon's first publication was to be *Les Décors du cinéma*.

Louis Feuillade, who directed *Fantômas*, had been a discovery of Léon Gaumont's assistant, the first woman director Alice Guy-Blaché. By temperament antipathetic to the biblical or classical tragedy type of presentation, Feuillade had been responsible for the semi-realistic Bébé comedies and then (admittedly because Gaumont wanted to economize) the semi-documentary series *La Vie telle qu'elle est*. Although he loathed the Film d'Art type of production, he appears to have been influenced by it; and the memorable incongruities of *Fantômas* depend on a fusion of contemporary and fairly realistic thriller themes with the histrionics of the Film d'Art style. Part of the fascination of his bowler-hatted detectives is that they should move with the gravity of tragedians, and that René Navarre's Fantômas, selfconsciously noble in profile and gesture, should be as other-worldly in his criminal activities as some angel of destruction. By directing the film mostly in long shot, placing chairs and tables face on to the screen, Feuillade (perhaps deliberately) increased the stiff-

Louis Feuillade: *Fantômas.*

ness of his compositions and by contrast heightened the startling effects of certain events; as when, for instance, Fantômas pierces a white wall and blood gushes out of it, or when five men in identical masks and black tights pursue each other at a ball. This matter-of-fact recognition of the bizarre has since become so inseparable from the paintings of René Magritte and other surrealists—although many of the qualities they admired in it were, perhaps, accidental to Feuillade's purpose—that it may be impossible to dissociate *Fantômas* from the sensibility that has evolved out of it. In 1913 many of the future surrealists were in a state of disequilibrium induced by the prospect of war. They had begun to see their surroundings in a quite new way, as though they had never seen them before, and they were to recognize how *Fantômas* appeared to confirm this sense of the uncanny, how the fantastic behaviour of Feuillade's characters complemented and even highlighted the shadowy atmosphere of his Paris locations: villas on the outskirts of the city, dawn streets, sombre theatres.

In 1963 Georges Franju, a founder member of the Cinémathèque Française and a long-standing surrealist, made *Judex*, an affectionate tribute to Feuillade's 1916 serial of that name. In doing so, he tried to recapture this experience of disequilibrium. Each generation presumes that the interlocking styles, fashions and manners of its age represent by their consistency some rational norm; and yet, in the same way as a visitor from outer space might see them as convoluted growths from the depths of the mind, an intricate surfacing that has sprung into existence by no apparent logic, so Franju, bringing a self-consciousness to the Feuillade style that Feuillade did not have, unmasks a world in which Art Nouveau stair-railings, the thoughts of a financier and the costumes at a masked ball seem no less disconcerting in their consistent strangeness than an 'unreal' plot crammed with secular resurrections, coincidences and miracles.

Yet this assumption that the fantastic story in some way echoed the metropolitan mind and its conflicts was not new even in Feuillade's day; it goes back at least to Charles Baudelaire and his interpretation of the Edgar Allan Poe stories. And it could bypass Feuillade. Louis Delluc, who laid the ground for a truly French kind of film-making and who struggled, after Pathé's abdication, to encourage this style at whatever cost (and it included through ill-health his own death) repeatedly attacks Feuillade's *Judex* in his collection of essays *Cinéma et cie*. But Delluc came to film with tastes already developed elsewhere, and indeed only began to dedicate himself to the cinema after a period of hostility to it.

Born in 1890 in the Dordogne and brought to Paris in 1903, Delluc went to a school where his closest friend was Léon Moussinac, also to be a film critic. At the age of twenty he joined the staff of the stage magazine *Comœdia illustré* and began to frequent a circle of people who idolized the actor Edouard de Max. One of them was the Belgian actress Eve Francis, later to be his wife, who tried to interest him in the movies. He showed little interest. She took him to Ince Westerns and praised them as romantic documentaries that owed nothing to the theatre. He would answer that their imagery was of interest to people with no imagination and on their outings usually persuaded her to go to the circus instead.

He was absorbed in the symbolist aesthetic of that time, with an art that could formulate spiritual mysteries. He admired greatly Maurice Maeterlinck, so much a hero of that age that he received a ticker-tape welcome when he went to New York. 'In some strange way,' wrote Maeterlinck,

we devalue things as soon as we give utterance to them. We believe we have dived to the uttermost depth of the abyss, and yet when we return to the surface the drop of water on our pallid finger-tips no longer resembles the sea from which it came. We think we have discovered a hoard of wonderful treasure-trove, yet when we emerge again into the light of day we see that all we have brought back with us is false stones and chips of glass. But for all this, the treasure goes on glimmering in the darkness, unchanged.[4]

In the light (or darkness) of this vision Delluc was as fascinated as were many of his contemporaries with the Ballet Russe, *Parsifal*, Ida Rubinstein, Debussy's music and the plays of Paul Claudel, which often had Eve Francis in the leading role. He preferred Gordon Craig's designs to Antoine's naturalism. And when he came at last to appreciate the power of the cinema it was in terms of the symbolist aesthetic. He was to establish the tradition of the *film noir*: yet it would be inaccurate to believe that his concern with depressed situations or working-class settings of the poorest sort had primarily a social or political motive, as it had with some of his followers. He was intent, rather, in transposing to the screen the three-o'clock-in-the-morning mood and aspirations of the most distinguished of symbolist poets, Charles Baudelaire, and as a critic his achievement—a major one— was to redefine the Baudelairian point of view in a manner that acknowledged the capacities of the new medium.

The moment of insight came in 1916. 'Audiences, stretched for months on a nightmare, in a Paris dead to pleasure and vowed to silence and the anguish of war, relaxed before a captivating, exotic drama admirably motivated by a new spirit, a sharper pace, an unexpected dynamism,' writes Eve Francis in her memoirs, *Temps héroïques*. 'Delluc, sitting beside me, was trembling. For the first time ever on the screen, objects bore witness.'[5] In French this film was titled *Forfaiture*; in English, *The Cheat* (1915). Its director was Cecil B. DeMille.

Delluc was later to write temperately of it as 'the *Tosca* of the American cinema'[6]—a view which tactfully does justice to the refined sadism of its plot—and he was to limit his praise to the subtly impassive acting of Sessue Hayakawa as the Japanese villain who tries to blackmail a young woman (Fanny Ward) into becoming his lover and then, when she resists him, brands her on the back. Although DeMille brought his usual expertise to this production, and his costumes, settings and Rembrandtesque lighting were impeccable, the one quality his technique appears devoid of was any sense of the spiritual. At best, *The Cheat* could be seen as an unintended satire on capitalism in the sense that the villain misunderstands the American passion for property, but this justification will not do. And DeMille's xenophobia, which was to pour forth in his anti-German films of this period, is scarcely veiled.

The Parisians had seen little or nothing of D. W. Griffith at this time and for Delluc the great American masters of the cinema were to be (at least until about 1919) Thomas H. Ince and Chaplin. It would seem, then, that the French appreciation of *Forfaiture* was based on one of those fruitful misunderstandings that so often happen when the French write about the American cinema. At one time Delluc applied his highest term of praise to it, when he described it as 'photo-genic'. Quite what he meant by this word, which Daguerre had first used, is open to interpretation, but one meaning was suggested by Edgar Morin in *Le Cinéma ou l'homme imaginaire* (1956) when he argued that the Lumière audiences were less astonished by the fact of a train pulling into a station or workers leaving a factory—after all, a visit to a station or a factory would have been just as satisfying—than by the *image* of these events. The image on a screen can reveal a perhaps unexpected poetry in the quotidian. It can transcend the limitations of language and give form to the verbally inexpressible, to a poetry of silence. At such times it becomes photogenic.

Delluc was opposed to the laboriously constructed script. Mallarmé had wanted a poetry without a subject; Delluc was moving in this direction when he stated that film-making should begin in some lyric impulse, some movement of the inner life that casts a radiance on the experience of ordinary things. He believed this impulse would crystal-lize into 'some sentiment or thought centred on an individual who is, in presence or not, the principal factor in the drama'.[7] The photo-genic, in other words, was the potential in photography that can make everyday objects witness to interior truth. 'There is a great actor in *L'Atlantide*,' he once wrote, 'it is sand.'[8] He acknowledged the value of cadence and lighting, especially in the work of Sjöström and Stiller, and recognized the expressiveness of the human face as the director's most valuable property. At times he fell into excess, as when he praised the photogenic possibilities of the telephone receiver; yet it could be argued that his theory is among the most important statements ever made on the kind of sensibility which distinguishes the film-maker from the hopeless aspirant.

He inspired a tradition which still has force. As with many later French directors and critics, his response to American movies seems based on a sexual polarity, as though his sensibility had to be stimu-lated by the unselfconscious Western or adventure story before it could give birth to insight. He was one of the precursors of the Pop Art movement, although his tenderness is remote from the desperate ironies of its recent practitioners. His desire to give popular culture an honourable pedigree lends his writings a warmth and at times a straining after effect which readers of *Cahiers du cinéma* will still find familiar. In his monograph on Chaplin he compares the clown in a matter of pages to Molière, Nijinsky and 'those portrait painters whose slender conceptions illuminate the small rooms of the Louvre: Henry III, Francis I, and what else besides?'[9]

But such lapses were exceptional and in no way overshadow his definition of how photography could be a vehicle for thought: of how film, in effect, could be an art. And he was more than a brilliant theorist. He wrote for two specialist magazines, which he edited, and a weekly article for the more widely read *Paris-Midi*. He was probably the first reviewer to achieve an informed yet unsnobbish style. But his wish to reach the general public brought him into conflict with Ricciotto Canudo, an Italian-born poet, who has some claim to be the first among many spokesmen for the avant-garde film. Canudo coined the term *écraniste* for anyone artistically involved in film-making. Delluc rejected this word as a barbarous coinage and proposed *cinéaste*. Canudo called the movies the seventh art and started the high-flown Club des Amis du Septième Art (CASA); Delluc called them the fifth art and, on the model of the Touring Clubs, founded with Léon Moussinac the less modish Ciné Clubs of France (with which, after Canudo's early death in 1923, CASA was merged). These clubs, and the vociferous screenings, polemics and lectures they were host to, stimulated a vitality in the cinema unequalled in any other country. During the 1920s, writes Alexandre Arnoux, three Paris cinemas were noted for their avant-garde programmes: Studio 28, which premiered *Un Chien andalou*, *L'Age d'or* and *Le Sang d'un poète*; the Vieux-Colombier, a theatre formerly run by Jacques Copeau and still patronized by the Copeau public, left-wing, Gidean-Calvinist, vegetarian and sharply intelligent; and the Studio des Ursulines, where the audience tended to wear exotic clothes and an excellent band

Louis Delluc: *Le Silence*, with Signoret. 'Faire d'un visage un masque. c'est actuellement le plus sûr moyen d'obtenir d'un talent toute sa forte expression'. (Delluc, *Photogénie*).

played blues derived from Debussy's *Pelléas et Mélisande*. Moussinac, a Marxist, brought *The Battleship Potemkin* to Paris and wrote one of the first books on the Soviet cinema. His club, *Les Amis de Spartacus*, had 20,000 members in Paris alone: the police, worried by such enthusiasm, had it closed after six months. Delluc introduced the French public to *The Cabinet of Dr Caligari* and to the Swedish cinema.

Between 1919 and 1923 Delluc wrote and directed six films and provided scripts for two others. Some of them are at present untraceable; by many accounts, the most grievous loss being *Le Silence* (1920). Jean Epstein commended it for the way in which Delluc used objects to convey the mental state of his central character: a man alone in his apartment reflecting on a murder he has committed and awaiting the arrival of the woman who precipitated this crime. Apparently Delluc here initiated the technique which achieved its fullest expression in the 1960s, in Buñuel's *Belle de jour* and Resnais's *Last Year in Marienbad*, in which thoughts are presented in so undifferentiated a way from actuality that the ambiguity of who is thinking what event is left unresolved. Of his still available films, *La Femme de nulle part* (1922) gives the perhaps false impression that his talent as a director was no match for the interest of his ideas. A mysterious woman in black (Eve Francis) appears at an Italian villa near Genoa and tells its owners, an unhappily married couple, that she had once lived there. At moments Delluc implies that she had been happy during her time at the villa and has Eve Francis touch furnishings and moon through gardens with an expression of anguished ecstasy (she tends to grimace; perhaps in compensation for her surroundings, which largely fail to exemplify Delluc's photogenic theory). Yet at other moments he implies that she had been far from happy, and has her encourage the young wife to leave her husband for a lover, on the grounds that she herself had never regretted once making such a decision. But if she had been so unhappy at the villa, why has she been so eager to return to it? Delluc neither raises this question nor accounts for her unattractive wish to break up the young wife's marriage—which, in fact, the presence of a child averts. For all its interiority, Delluc's treatment is confused in its analysis of motive.

Even so, his imagery is powerful and his technique potentially effective: a potential which he was largely to realize in his last film, *L'Inondation* (1922). He had been impressed by river sequences in the films of Sjöström and Stiller; and he manages to use some documentary footage, of the Rhône flooding its banks and partly engulfing a village, both as a spectacle in its own right and as a convincing metaphor for his heroine's infatuation with a landowner. Germaine, his heroine, is once more played by Eve Francis, in the role of a mysterious woman who returns home to her dotty father, clerk to the

Louis Delluc: *L'Inondation*. On location.

village mayor and (to Germaine's distress) held in ridicule by most of the villagers. Margot, the landowner's fiancée, is drowned in the river, or so it seems; it later emerges that she had been murdered by Germaine's father. The treatment of the story deliberately raises an ambiguity as to whether the events take place in actuality or in Germaine's imagination. Yet for all its implications, Delluc's style is one of selective realism, economic in its portrayal of provincial life, both in its characterization of the villagers and of the place itself: its stone walls, bare rooms and windswept trees over shining water. In contrast to *La Femme de nulle part*, Eve Francis's performance is restrained, and although Delluc uses a trick effect when he has her look at a magazine photograph of a woman in a wedding dress and then transposes an image of her into the photograph, his filming tends to have something of her repose. If his treatment of the flood lacks the complexity that Pudovkin gave to the melting ice floes in *Mother* or the grandeur that Griffith discovered in the river sequences of *Way Down East*, this limitation can be accounted for on grounds other than that of lesser talent; it was important that the flood scenes should not overwhelm the intimate and domestic tone that predominates in so many scenes.

In *Intolerance* Griffith had anticipated most of the directions film-makers were to take in the 1920s; without seeing *Intolerance*, Delluc had recognized two of the possibilities open to the French cinema. One was an urban realism touched with Baudelairian melancholy, fatalistic, stoical and concerned with dispossessed characters, most vividly represented by the *films noirs* of the 1930s and 1940s. The other was an obligation to analyse or enact mental states or to transcribe thought in a manner that Astruc was to define in his 1948 essay on the *camera-stylo*: a style that transcends questions of time and therefore cannot technically be described as using flashbacks, since thought of its nature exists in the present. This second kind of film-making could rely on painted scenery or be given all the appearances of realism; it could evoke the processes of thought through an imitation of the Joycean stream of consciousness or through the incongruous juxtapositions of surrealism. But the governing attitude of the French avant-garde when filming an impression of mental states was to resort to selfconscious experiment, using superimposition, speeded-up images or other forms of trick effect, as though dominated by the spirit of the neglected and virtually forgotten Méliès. This avant-garde was defiantly cinematic in a way that its contemporaries in Germany and the Soviet Union, more confident in their audiences, had no need to be.

Germaine Dulac, who had filmed Delluc's script *La Fête espagnole* in 1919, and not entirely to his satisfaction, was to show how well his kind of impressionism could be adapted to other kinds of statement. Born in 1882, Miss Dulac directed over twenty films from 1916 on; and then, with the coming of sound and the diminution of experimental filming, turned to supervising newsreels for Pathé and Gaumont. She died in 1942. *La Souriante Madame Beudet* (1922), adapted from an André Obey play, discloses how Madame Beudet's thoughts, when filmed, take on a different form from the technique of flashback which film directors often desperately seize on in order to open out the action of stage plays. Madame Beudet's wish to murder her husband is conceived of in terms of the objects in her apartment, as when, out of her imaginings, a tennis-player phantasmally leaps out of the pages of a magazine to swipe at him: a conception that has the paradoxical effect of heightening the oppressive nature of her surroundings. When she reads a poem, the images she conjures up from it offer no release; they enclose her even more within her mental prison. As one of the titles states, '*Et toujours les mêmes horizons*'. Her thoughts, as visualized, have no resonance; they become as solid and predictable as the chairs and tables around her. Anyone concerned with the emancipation of women will have observed that Dulac's picture of Madame Beudet differs radically from Delluc's fantasies about the characters played by Eve Francis. While Dulac sees her heroine as trapped by domesticity and marriage, Delluc tends to see women from a male viewpoint, as mysterious and in some sense free. The only way Madame Beudet can mobilize her state of non-being is by an imagined act of murder; either way, she cannot escape dehumanization.

Dulac continued to be fascinated by extreme mental states, although she had moved away from impressionism by the time she came to direct *The Seashell and the Clergyman* (1928). The freely associated fantasies that Antonin Artaud's script idea ascribes to the sexually frustrated clergyman have usually been taken to be surrealist in character. But Artaud and Dulac have little insight into the clergyman's anguish and for the most part see him as a figure of fun. The train of thought they allow him is shallow, and their exercise soon appears to be protracted. To conceal this weakness, Dulac abandons herself to an excess of trick effects that, for all its panache, tends to be uncommunicative.

She was very much at the centre of a debate at this time on whether films should be based on scenarios or not: a controversy that did not so much centre on the question of improvisation, as it was to in the 1930s, as on the need for 'pure' filming. She and her associates were attracted to the abstract aspect of film-making: the plasticity of the image, the rhythmic possibilities of editing; interests derived from the other arts. André Breton had attacked the narrative logic of most novels in his first surrealist manifesto of 1924 and Picasso's revival of neo-classicism was to challenge many painters into asking whether art should be figurative or not: a question that also fascinated the avant-garde film-makers.

In order to make a living, some of them took on more commercial commissions. They were only able to infiltrate their experimental ideas into these commissions with some difficulty. But in this, perhaps, they were fortunate, since too often those trick effects that their friends most applauded in the 1920s are the ones that have weathered least well with the passing of time. Too much the product of theory, of a *willed* idea about the nature of film, they bear all the marks of faded fashion and of mechanical trickery. The avant-garde tended to confuse originality with novelty, and indeed was most bold when least consciously experimental; when its output was indistinguishable in kind, if not in quality, from anyone else's. For instance, Dulac's *La Mort du soleil* (1921), a semi-documentary on tuberculosis, has a rigour of style absent from her more experimental exercises, while her plot—in which, among other complications, a laboratory worker leaves her husband to become a scientist honoured throughout the world—is far more explicit in its feminism, and more sociologically complex, than *La Souriante Madame Beudet*.

Although many of the avant-garde ideas were less futile in theory and practice than this account suggests, they could lead into an increasing poverty of invention. This happened to Jean Epstein: yet Epstein, as both film-maker and critic, is a figure of major importance. Trained as a doctor, his scientific interests were evident in the reconstruction of Pasteur's life with which he began his career as a director, and in his belief that avant-garde activity was a 'mode of intelligence'. He believed that like the microscope or the telescope, the camera had opened up a fascinating area for investigation which the emergence of the star system had largely obscured and which he proposed once more to bring into the open: an appeal to the scientific spirit that places him in a tradition that had begun with E. J. Marey, was continued by two pioneers in micro-cinematography, Pathé's Dr Comandon and the Englishman Percy Smith (who made over fifty films in *The World before Your Eyes* series before the First World War) and eventually reached its maturity with Jean Painlevé. In this tradi-

Jean Painlevé: *Crabes et crevettes*.

tion art and science unite and the word 'experiment' takes on its fullest meaning, in terms both of film technique and richness of content.

In such studies as *La Daphnie* (made in 1925, the year of his first film), *Caprelles* (1931) or *L'Hippocampe* (1933), Painlevé's micro-cinematographic view of life under water creates images that substantiate the doctrines of both 'pure' filming and surrealism. New

worlds of the imagination, as amazing and suggestive as any panoramic sweep of the cosmos, are disclosed as the *daphnies*, magnified
to the power of 150,000, totter like ambulatory towers along the
water bed, or as the *caprelles* bow like gallants dancing a minuet.
Epstein subscribed to this scientific kind of impulse, as he subscribed
to the documentary, but his thought also contained a good deal of
mysticism. In common with Dulac, he wished to reject the constraints of dramatic narrative. He felt that life consisted of events
without beginning or end and that film-making, in imitating it,
should be like a train journey into a land of surprises: a sense of
the open-ended that one of his commercial ventures, *La Glace à trois
faces* (1927), admirably implies. But he also believed, going beyond
Delluc's photogenic theory, that 'there is no still life on the screen.
Objects take up attitudes. Trees make gestures. Mountains have
meanings. Each accessory becomes an actor. Backgrounds fragment,
and each fragment assumes a unique expression. An astonishing
pantheism is renewed in the world and fills it to breaking point.'[10]

In writing in this way, he describes the dance of the universe, a
traditional conception of *amor dei*; his own work, however, illuminates a secular love, the universe in harmony with human sensation. In *Cœur fidèle* (1923) his sense of composition, editing and use
of locations – the Brittany seashore, the austere furnishings of a fisher-
man's bar – all enhance a spiritual experience. A young woman is
terrorized by her husband, her lover waits for her by a quay: Epstein
visualizes the feelings in these situations with the minimum of effects
and with an assurance that can allow him justifiably to impose an
image of the girl's face onto an image of the sea and to have her lover
stretch out his hand to this extraordinary vision. Corot-like compositions of a wine bottle and two glasses on a table, or a shot of the
lovers sitting on a rock, create a vibrant stillness. But Epstein's first
audiences were less impressed by the strength of these images than
by the virtuosity of the fairground sequence with its rapid cutting and
expressionistic agitation: they wanted an overtly experimental
technique.

For the rest of his life, and whenever his finances permitted,
Epstein returned to Brittany and the Ushant and filmed there. It
would be false, however, to see him as trying to evolve a proletarian
cinema concerned with working-class subjects in the way that
Antoine, a famous stage producer who made over half a dozen films,
had allegedly tried to do, for his choice of these fishermen and these
locations was primarily aesthetic. Lumière's shot of a rowing-boat
caught up in the waves at the mouth of a harbour had revealed the
plasticity of the sea as an image; and Epstein, too, appears to have
been impressed by the way water can fragment light. Yet his aestheticism lacked some anchorage, and in his later work he was seldom

able to recapture the tension of *Cœur fidèle*. By the time he came to direct *Finis terrae* (1929) his compositions had become beautiful to the point of excess, his concern with the texture of worn wood and pebbles and with the movement of the sea tending to overwhelm the presence of his actors. Yet he was to continue with this kind of art photography in *Mor Vran* (1931) and *L'Or des mers* (1933).

His influence over others was to be widespread. In *La Belle Nivernaise* (1924) he initiated a cycle of films about life on barges that reaches its highest point with Vigo's *L'Atalante*. In *La Chute de la*

Jean Epstein: *Mor Vran; opposite, La Chute de la maison Usher.*

maison Usher (1928), with its tight close-ups in large rooms, he evoked a persuasive interpretation of Edgar Allan Poe's story, a key text for the Symbolists. Many of its ideas – the billowing curtains or the magical effects imitative of *The Golem*, such as flames creeping up through floorboards – gave Cocteau the inspiration for *La Belle et la bête* (1946) and bolstered his confidence in a symbolist type of film-making.

But Epstein's celebration of nature in all its aspects most impressed his immediate contemporaries. Indeed, the French cinema of the 1920s so reflects his fascination with Brittany and with barge owners

and fishermen, rivers and the sea that it as good as became his spiritual kingdom. One of his more outstanding disciples was to be Jean Grémillon—who had already begun his professional association with the cameraman Georges Périnal and made a number of short films and *Un Tour au large* (1926) before he came to direct his first feature *Maldone* (1927). The opening scenes of *Maldone* project a sense of space comparable in impact to the shock that a city dweller might feel on his return to the countryside after a long period of living among high buildings. Trees mass against the over-arching sky, a dark accent that releases the light of the sky seemingly into infinity. Grémillon's sense of the gravity and ethereality possible in composition is distinguished, and no one, apart from Jean Renoir in the final sequence of *Boudu sauvé des eaux*, has conveyed so effectively the manner in which a boat rests on water or the manner in which slow travelling shots can open up the qualities of a landscape on a sleepy day. A woman peels potatoes, a dog dozes, smoke from a barge chimney barely has the energy to dissipate itself. 'Les jours ressemblent aux jours.' But the mood is not held: German expressionism is evoked, and a scene in which Maldone, a divided soul, shatters his reflection in a mirror explicitly associates him with Henrik Galeen's student of Prague.

The conflict between mood-making and plot-building is just as apparent in Grémillon's *Gardiens de phare* (1928) with its script by Jacques Feyder. Like Epstein's *Finis terrae* its contrived situation—in which a sick man has to be transported to hospital from a lighthouse—seems disproportionate to its director's gift for discovering painterly images. In many shots the sea stretches like a thread at the base of the screen, giving generous dimensions to the sky. In

Jean Grémillon: *Gardiens de phare.*

other shots, Breton women seem to rest their chins on the base of the screen as though it were a sill, while their head-dresses, framed by the sky, rise elaborately above them: an impressionism soon marred by an agitated section that invites the spectator to see the waves as a metaphor, in Dellucian fashion, for the sick man's fever. Grémillon's thinking was, perhaps, over-determined by symphonic forms; in this case the requirement that slow movements should be followed by fast ones.

In common with so many of his contemporaries, he was too bound by theoretical preconception and felt obliged to interrupt his sensuous, almost pantheistic appreciation of nature with tricks intended to please his only public, the ciné-club audiences. The same is true of Jean Renoir, whose waywardness in style during the 1920s hardly anticipates his steadily increasing mastery during the next decade. But among his films of the twenties there are a few that are not wayward in style, and *La Fille de l'eau* (1924) must be included among them. Two brothers manage a barge: one of them drowns, and the other tyrannizes over his brother's daughter (Catherine Hessling), who runs away. Renoir concentrates on moments of heightened perception. Conscious of how films consist of light and nothing but light, he plays one cluster of images of water and its reflections against another, which takes in varieties of flame, moving from bonfires and a burning caravan to gentle sunlight. His manner of lingering over events looks forward to his mature style, although his liking for moments of charm and pretty touches remains as yet unchecked by the abrasive influence of Stroheim. At one point the water-girl falls asleep and dreams that she is dancing—in slow

Jean Renoir: *La Fille de l'eau*. Catherine Hessling as the sleeping water-girl.

motion—across a blitzed landscape in a wedding dress, a phantom resembling the angels of Mons. And the dream is studded with other camera tricks.

'During this period,' Renoir said of *La Petite Marchande d'allumettes* (1928), 'I was more interested in camera tricks than in anything else.'[11] In 1927 he had tried to tantalize the ciné-clubs with

Charleston, a science-fiction caprice in which a Negro travels by balloon to Europa Deserta and discovers the ruins of a city overlooked by a lopsided Eiffel Tower. He meets a wild girl, who dances for him, and he recognizes her dance to be the Charleston. Renoir forces this idea to the point of exhaustion. He usually needed the inspiration of nature, whether in the form of landscape or well-rounded human beings, to convert his apparent lack of concentration, and even diffidence, into a merit; as in *La Fille de l'eau*, where, largely ignoring the mechanics of plot, he allows his camera eye to wander over sunny garden walls and courtyards: divagations, in fact, that give his style concision in the spectator's memory.

Of *Nana* (1926), which was adapted from the Zola novel, he later said: 'It was the first film in which I learnt that one should not copy nature so much as reconstruct it.'[12] Reconstructing nature in the light of Stroheim's *Foolish Wives*, he emphasizes the fascinating ugliness of certain faces and of certain details, such as Nana's comb thick with strands of hair. But there is an element of autobiographical pain in his treatment of Nana's affairs with self-destructive aristocrats that modifies caricature and bitterness in a manner owing more to Sternberg's *The Blue Angel* than to anything by Stroheim; and with the pain goes a generous humour that is inimitably Renoir. Certain scenes in the Bois de Boulogne point out one way in which he reconstructed nature—they resemble paintings by Manet and Auguste Renoir. Other scenes, filmed at Les Variétés, reveal other means by which he brought about this reconstruction: through a pleasure in theatricality. Admittedly the actors in *Nana* are an unattractive group of people, yet the atmosphere of their lives, and their milieu, clearly appeal to him. Few other directors have shown so much respect for the actor as a being in his own right—or for the lore of acting technique, ranging from naturalistic improvisation at the one extreme to the formalized pantomime of Commedia dell'Arte at the other. The seeming paradox that nature can be reconstructed by these artificial means is very much at the heart of *Nana*.

The set designer Alberto Cavalcanti turned to direction in 1925. His training as an architect saved him from dully imitating *Cœur fidèle* in *En rade* (1928), and certain decorative features, such as his steaming washtubs and bottles lining a corridor, touch his compositions with some distinction. He had begun his career with *Rien que les heures* (1926), one of the first 'city' films, yet lacking in the substantiality or meaningful contrasts of Ruttmann's *Berlin*. For all his piling on of camera tricks, Cavalcanti seemed unable to take pleasure in them; and an atmosphere of chic devalues the few images that appear to be felt, rendering trivial his genuine sympathy for the clochards of Paris.

If Renoir and Cavalcanti thought in terms of the ciné-clubs, Marcel L'Herbier thought in terms of the *haute bourgeoisie*. Yet L'Herbier had more than snobbish intentions: he wanted to capture an audience that usually held the cinema in contempt. A theatre critic before the First World War, he had served in an army film unit, directed his first feature in 1917 and achieved a certain renown with *El Dorado* (1921). In spite of his claims to originality and wish to improve the standards of film-making—in 1943 he helped found the Institut des Hautes Etudes Cinématographiques (IDHEC)—he was more interested in appropriating the researches of others in order to scandalize the bourgeoisie than in exploring themes of a personal urgency.

His most ambitious attempt to bring about such a scandal was *L'Inhumaine* (1924). With Cavalcanti as his principal art director, he commissioned Claude Autant-Lara to design its garden scenes. Robert Mallet-Stevens the exterior to the scientist's laboratory and Fernand Léger its interior. Léger's genius, especially, demonstrates how Caligarism was not so much a fluke as a development of the Film

Marcel L'Herbier: *L'Inhumaine*.

d'Art style. Actors had once orated before painted backdrops; now they appeared, with expressionist gesture, before scenery of an aggressively Cubist inspiration. L'Herbier took pains to relate his machine age settings to the style of such objects as a suave sports car and a rudimentary television set—perhaps the first to play any part in a film. Yet the fashionable public had long since become accustomed to the shocks of modernism (though it did not like *L'Inhumaine*, which did badly at the box-office), and the main features of Cubism had long since dwindled into a style favoured by advertisers and interior

Marcel L'Herbier: *L'Inhumaine*. Jaque Catelain.

decorators. The main present-day attraction of *L'Inhumaine* is its period charm. It illustrates perfectly the fashion for art deco, a fashion widely popularized by the Paris Exhibition of Decorative Arts in 1925.

In spite of this timeliness, L'Herbier chose a story so old-fashioned that it might have been conjured up by Feuillade. Claire, a singer and *femme fatale*, is courted by a Swedish scientist, a rajah and a number of business tycoons. When the scientist pretends to commit suicide to test out her feelings for him, she is blamed for his presumed death and howled down at a society concert. Eventually, she and the scientist are reconciled; the angry rajah arranges for a snake to bite her; and the scientist brings her out of her coma in an experiment°

Marcel L'Herbier: *Feu Mathias Pascal*. Michel Simon.

that anticipates the rituals of Cocteau's *Orphée*. Alain Resnais was to declare—in an interview published in *Sight and Sound* (Summer 1969)—that sophisticated directors like L'Herbier used pulp-novel subjects as a means of entering the public unconscious; but such an idea is not borne out by *L'Inhumaine*, which is consciously *willed* to the point of being ridiculous. And L'Herbier's casting of Maeterlinck's first wife, Georgette Leblanc, as Claire and of Jaque Catelain as the scientist is disastrous: Georgette Leblanc has none of the magnetism of the *femme fatale*, and she and the doll-like Jaque Catelain look as though they loathed each other. Perhaps L'Herbier thought of her role as dramatizing his own condition as an artist, coldly or inhumanly trying to hold on to as many admirers as possible.

His talent was less strained by *Feu Mathias Pascal* (1925), adapted from Pirandello's novel about a man, presumed dead, who realizes that posthumous existence is less liberating than he had expected. L'Herbier appears to have been primarily interested in finding a photogenic equivalent for Pirandello's metaphysical realism—which he does effectively—and in drawing out excellent performances from Ivan Muzhukin as Mathias and Michel Simon (in his first leading film role) as a kindly country cousin. But he could not resist trying to cut a fine figure, and to damaging effect, as in his lavish *L'Argent* (1928). He barely warms up this frigid interpretation of a Zola novel with his picturesque long shots of stockbrokers milling around within the Paris bourse, and his tendency to make unsubtle comparisons—between, for example, the crash of a stockmarket and an aeroplane—appears to have blinded him to the opportunities provided by his production—the way in which he wastes the remarkable abilities of the actress Brigitte Helm being one instance. He was primarily a designer, or rather someone who could inspire his art directors, as in the San Gimignano settings which he and Cavalcanti worked out for *Feu Mathias Pascal*.

Marcel L'Herbier: *Feu Mathias Pascal.* Cavalcanti's San Gimignano.

Charles Pathé's withdrawal from the film industry had threatened it with collapse, and it was largely to be kept buoyant by the emergence of two new companies. In 1921 Jean Sapène, proprietor of the newspaper *Le Matin*, was so dismayed by the effect of a slump which kept audiences away from cinemas in France as well as in other countries, that he decided to enter the film business himself. Appointing the one-time Film d'Art producer Louis Nalpas as his artistic director, he proposed to film the fiction serials he ran in his paper, and to publish these *feuilletons* and to release their screen adaptations concurrently. The policy was successful enough for the Société de Ciné-Romans to branch out into feature-length production. Many of its serials and features, including Fescourt's *Les Misérables* and L'Herbier's *L'Argent*, expensively banked on hopes for an international distribution. Sapène also branched out into other fields: he financed some of Painlevé's first experiments in micro-cinematography.

Russian émigrés directed two of his most outstanding Ciné-Roman productions. Tourjansky's *Michel Strogoff* (1926) had a pace that rivals the Jules Verne novel from which it was drawn, a splendid sense of Russian landscape (it was, in fact, shot in Latvia) and an elaborately choreographed fight on a river-raft worthy of Fairbanks and Dwan at their best. Ivan Muzhukin played the title role, as he did in Alexander Volkov's *Casanova* (1927), which is even more dashing. Although Volkov appears to have been influenced by Lang's *Der Müde Tod* and its studied tableaux, he brought a Gancian *élan* to his filming that lightens the spectacle. *Casanova* is a fine example of how the risks in style taken by more imaginative directors could be absorbed into the more accessible form of an erotic adventure story.

The other new company, the Société Albatros, managed by the Russian expatriate Alexander Kamenka, had a policy that fitted in more closely with the interests of the avant-garde. (Jean Epstein was to have a long association with it.) Kamenka, for instance, produced *Le Brasier ardent* (1923), a unique experiment which cannot be placed in any genre. Directed by Muzhukin (with some help from Volkov) it begins with an erotic dream sequence in which a number of women pursue Muzhukin, who appears to them in various guises. Although this opening sequence prefigures the erotic wit of the surrealists, the rest of the film operates within a different convention, one that brings together something of Feuillade's romantic realism with the gentle earthiness of Lubitsch's earliest comedies. The dreamer awakes, and one of the reasons for her dream is evident from a magazine lying on her bed; it contains the photograph of a world-famous detective (played, of course, by Muzhukin). Her husband, suspecting from her wild behaviour that she has taken a lover, calls in a world-famous detective and in this way precipitates a genuine crisis in their marriage. But Muzhukin, as director, minimizes the resonance of this scenario by his inability to work it through, and he imposes a number of ideas on it which, though excellent in themselves, add little to the action. The wife's bed is so mechanized that when she presses a

Ivan Muzhukin: *Le Brasier ardent.*

button, trays and chutes open beside her, supplying her with most of her needs. The husband, abducted by the Agence Trouve Tout, finds himself confronted by a number of detectives who remove their disguises to reveal identical faces: altogether an intriguing fantasy, yet presented with not enough insight into its meaning.

Melodramatic episodes distract insight in a different way in the Albatros production *Ménilmontant* (1924), directed by Dmitri Kirsanov. A woman is brutally murdered. Her two daughters come to the Parisian suburb of Ménilmontant: one of them is abandoned by her lover and becomes the mother of an illegitimate child; the other drifts into prostitution; while the madam of a brothel kills the lover in a murder that recalls the startling opening to the film. Following the male *Schadenfreude* of Griffith and anticipating that of Pabst, Kirsanov appears to believe that beauty by its nature is continuously under threat: this, anyway, is implied by the furious plot and the presence in its leading role of his beautiful wife, Nadia Sibirskaya. Kirsanov shrouds her in Chekhovian moods and atmospheres. His Parisian suburb is all empty sunlit alleys, bare winter trees by a river, cobbles glistening in the rain. In the musicality of its editing, sensitivity and abrupt movement into expressionistic effects, *Ménilmontant* must rank with *Cœur fidèle* as among the finest examples of avant-garde filming.

Kirsanov's career as a director never recovered from the box-office failure of his sound film *Rapt* (1933). Another Albatros member of the avant-garde, however, was to find sound a liberation, even

Dmitri Kirsanov: *Ménilmontant*. Nadia Sibirskaya.

though he had predicted that its advent would bring to an end the art of the film. René Clair had been a journalist, actor and film editor before he made *Paris qui dort* (1924). Members of the surrealist movement—Robert Desnos in particular—who loathed the avant-garde for their selfconscious experimentalism and the often sickly kind of sentiment that went with it, welcomed Clair's gift for integrating fantasy into narrative and compared him to Buster Keaton, on the grounds that someone watching either *Paris qui dort* or *Sherlock Junior* will be so absorbed by its story that he will probably fail to recognize the extent to which it depends on a boldly unusual technique. And, indeed, it is possible to sit through *Paris qui dort*—a Sleeping Beauty kind of comedy about a scientist who invents a ray that can paralyse people in mid-action—without recognizing how ingeniously Clair has played on the intrinsic nature of film: its power to stop and start movement at will, or to show a highly-populated city as deserted. Where he really differs from Delluc and Epstein, though, is in his affection for stage farces, the music-hall and film comedians. He can allude to these pleasures with a great deal of skill and charm. In *Le Voyage imaginaire* (1925) Jean, a timid clerk, dreams that he has been transformed into a dog. He finds himself in the Musée Grevin and persecuted by its wax figures; only the gallant intervention of Chaplin's tramp saves him from Robespierre's guillotine.

Clair's populism often seems to be a means of expressing *bonhomie* and an attempt to conceal some defect in feeling. Unlike Jacques Prévert, whose imagination was also quickened by the Méliès tradi-

René Clair: *Le Voyage imaginaire.*

tion, he seems unable to relate the fantastic to some centrality in himself—such as can be found in Prévert's screenplay for Jean Renoir's *Le Crime de Monsieur Lange* (1935), where M. Lange's vocation as a writer of romances set in the Wild West is placed in a social context that illuminates the disconnected nature of his fantasies. Clair keeps returning to themes that haunt him: his fascination with pickpockets, the figure of the timid male lover, the power of money (as when in *Paris qui dort* two men with billboards interlock like stags as they both bend down to pick up a hundred-franc note). But intellectual brilliance distracts him from the meaning of these themes so that they remain on the level of gags, insufficiently related to each other.

He was at his most detached in *Entr'acte* (1924), which he and Francis Picabia devised as a section of Picabia's ballet *Relâche* for Rolf de Maré's Swedish Ballet: an extended skit remarkable only in its reputation as an avant-garde classic. It offers few attractions: some compelling images—a camel-drawn hearse, a bearded dancer (Erik Satie) in a tutu, a huntsman on the rooftops—and the mild pleasure of spotting Marcel Duchamp and other celebrities among its cast. And

René Clair: *Les Deux timides.*

Clair concentrates less on content than on a ballet-like action in his two adaptations from Labiche: the pace of farce in *Un Chapeau de paille d'Italie* (1927), a split-screen technique in *Les Deux Timides* (1928). In his evocation of Paris, he was fortunate in usually having as his art director Lazare Meerson, a Polish expatriate who had assisted Cavalcanti on *Feu Mathias Pascal.* During the late twenties and early thirties, Meerson covered a wide range of atmospheres. His settings for the contemporary Paris of Clair's *Sous les toits de Paris* and the *fin-de-siècle* Paris of *Un Chapeau de paille d'Italie* are as unlike each other in style as they are both dissimilar to the Paris settings he organized for Jacques Feyder's *Les Nouveaux Messieurs.* (He worked almost exclusively for these two directors.) In Clair's *Le Million* he placed furniture and bric-à-brac behind gauze so that they looked like delicate frescoes painted on the walls of rooms. No one has used different kinds of chairs to such effect as he has. He was to die in London in 1938 at the age of thirty-eight, but not before he had handed on some of his knowledge to his one-time assistant, Alexander Trauner, who was to design most of the principal Marcel Carné films of the 1930s and 40s, including *Les Enfants du paradis.*

*

Abel Gance: *J'accuse.*

Abel Gance, for all his experimentation, represents something quite distinct from the theorist cinema of the avant-garde. His disordered, over-abundant imagination recalls Jean Cocteau's remark that Victor Hugo's madness lay in thinking he was Victor Hugo—his work usually bears the strain of someone trying to act out the role of a primordial creator. Forcefully energetic in his editing and choice of images, he could be blunt to a wide variety of experience. But not always. In *J'accuse* he was to make a war film exceptional among war films of this period in its generosity to the enemy; it is possible that the awesome nature of his subject, the Great War, tempered his grandiosity.

Gance, in fact, directs one's attention away from the enemy. He firmly centres his conflict on the French themselves, seeing the war as originating in crowd psychology and the essential animality of mankind. An opening sequence makes this point with (for him) unusual subtlety. He shows villagers dancing a farandole—a way of representing the communal spirit that he was to use again in *La Roue* and that was to be much employed by other directors during the populist thirties. But he had no illusions about the emotional stability of these sunny dancers and relates them both to the mob that looted Paris in 1789 and to the animal kingdom of owls, stags, and dogs.

He interprets the habitual conflict in everyone as being between brute and angel, specifically in terms of the tension between a hunts-

Abel Gance: *J'accuse.*

man François and a poet Jean. François, married to unhappy Edith, is jealous over Jean's attention to her; a tension that erupts into violence when the two men meet at the front. Gance is able to use an inflated manner of acting and the techniques of melodrama in a way that enriches the meaning of the film, as when Edith, presumed to have been raped by a German, becomes mother to an illegitimate child – a stock situation in wartime propaganda – and allows the child to arrive at Jean's home shortly after the death of his mother. Not only does Gance assert by this coincidence that in the midst of death we are in life – the spectator may infer that Jean is the father of the child – but he characteristically takes this scene as far as it can go by allowing the child to crawl over the mother's bed and to babble over her corpse.

On the whole, he handles the relationship between domestic events and the war scenes adroitly and manages to parallel the tensions at home with those of the front by withholding battlefield atrocities until he reaches the last years of the war. It seems at first that he avoids images of the mutilated dead out of respect for a public shaken by recent memories, but this initial restraint not only allows him to imitate the increasing fury of the war itself but also to heighten the impact of the Passchendaele sequences. Against this destruction he raises his hope in Art (very much with a capital A) as typified by the poet Jean; a comparison that hardly raises the spirits, perhaps, yet does allow him to predict – through the blinding of the poet and his subsequent madness – the irrationality of much post-war art. His own art, in the meanwhile, remains in control. For interior sequences he often places his actors against dark backgrounds and models their faces with a chiaroscuro that gives his compositions some resemblance to the paintings of Georges de la Tour. For exteriors, in contrast, he often begins a scene with a slowly opening iris shot, the bleached light of day only gradually swallowing up the surrounding darkness.

He is most distinctive, though, in the way he sets up waves of energy by his rapid cutting – 'an art in itself', claims Kevin Brownlow in *The Parade's Gone By*. 'Basically, the style takes the form of sustained sequences in which strong images are intercut rhythmically at great speed. The impact is intensely dramatic and since rapid-cut shots range from two feet to one frame, the impact is also physical. For the flashing light from the screen activates the optic nerve and excites the brain.'[13] Although Hollywood directors were to reject this technique, finding it too obtrusive, many members of the French avant-garde were to welcome it. Germaine Dulac wrote of *La Roue*: 'Rails, locomotives, boilers, wheels, levers, smoke, tunnels: a new kind of drama, made up of abrupt energies and unfurling lines, surged into being. The art of movement, at last rationally understood, claimed its rights and led us magnificently towards the symphonic poem based on images.'[14] And Gance's editing was to be as much a model for the French commercial cinema as for the avant-garde — as in Volkov's handling of Muzhukin's drunken dance in *Kean* (1923). But occasionally his flamboyance was so great that it could override any other consideration. He embarked on *La Roue* (1923) at a time when he knew that the woman he loved was dying and, indeed, for her health's sake rewrote the scenario during shooting so that he could take her up into the Alps: an anxiety, however, that hardly accounts for the ferocity of his treatment. His state of mind is suggested in the two major sequences, both of train disasters; it is possible to see his railway engines, as they leap off the tracks, as emblems for an imagination at the moment when it loses control.

Similar in plot to *J'accuse*, *La Roue* tells of a jealous conflict between a brutish train driver and his angelic son, a maker of violins, both of them in love with Norma (Ivy Close), whom the train driver had adopted as a child. But for all its elaboration, the significance of this conflict is tokenly presented. In content, its precedents are literary, owing something to Balzac and Zola. In choice of imagery and technique, it remains harder to locate, suggesting that Gance was an isolated talent. *La Roue* impressed both Eisenstein and Pudovkin, and in many ways Gance foreshadowed Soviet ambition. In common with Vertov, he was fascinated by machines and a peculiar conception of the hero that appears to occur in minds infatuated by the machine.

Sisif, dying, sits at a window. Abel Gance: *La Roue*.

Vertov had been awed by Mayakovsky's eyes and read an almost supernatural meaning into them; and Gance, too, places an unexpected emphasis on eyes. When Sisif, the train driver, goes blind, his eye-sockets take on the stony glare of a Roman sculpted head. Loss of sight enhances, contradictorily, his sense of presence as, dying, he sits at a window with a miniature railway-engine in his hands. It is possible to surmise some displaced genital activity in this equation of eyes, machines and a rapid cutting that 'activates the optical nerve and excites the brain': a fantasy that gives substance to the figure of the mutilated father. Such fantasies were noticeable in the German as well as the Soviet cinema of the 1920s and probably owed something to the war and the changes it brought about in the popular conception of heroism and authority. The erotic meaning of this fantasy is very much present in Georges Bataille's writings, in the blind waxwork model of Robespierre in René Clair's *Voyage imaginaire*, and in the bleeding faces and fetishes of Luis Buñuel's *Un Chien andalou* and Jean Cocteau's *Le Sang d'un poète*.

Gance's view of heroism helps to illuminate the often vague political aspirations of the 1920s, aspirations which were to harden into Fascist certainties in the next decade. Although he was to think of Napoleon as the greatest of heroes (in Albert Dieudonné's performance, a hero with basilisk eyes), the title of his *Napoléon vu par Abel Gance* (1927) implies that Gance stares as much at his hero as his hero stares back at him. The pity is that Gance's boy-eyed view of Napoleon can only make sense of Napoleon as a boy, identifying him with an eagle—as much a representation of mania as the derailed trains of *La Roue*—and failing to show him responding to problems as an adult. He probably preferred to think of Napoleon's emotional life as oceanic, as a force of nature conquering the world, in much the same way as he wanted his camera to be cosmic in its agility. 'The German studios had put the camera on wheels,' writes Kevin Brownlow. 'Gance put it on wings. To this extraordinary man, a tripod was a set of crutches for a lame imagination. His aim was to free the camera, to hurl it into the middle of the action, to force the audience from being mere spectators into participants.'[15]

Stendhal, who idolized Napoleon, used to defend his idealization by saying that he only admired the young Republican up to the time when he first entered Italy as a conqueror. Gance, too, ends his four-hour film on this premature note of exaltation. The length of the film, and the brief part of the career it describes, intimate that Gance lost control over the project and was carried away by an impulse to evolve sensational effects, such as his symphonic contrast between the revolutionary convention in an uproar and a storm at sea. The opening scenes of the film, evoking Napoleon's childhood, make all the points; subsequent scenes elaborate on them with little further insight.

As a Romantic, Gance believed that the child was father to the man; and the compactness of his filming depends on a gift for concentrating into a few images the sum of experience, an accretion of whatever the growing mind perceives at each stage of its life. The snowball fight in the grounds of the military academy at Brienne tells the spectator all he needs to know about Napoleon's genius as a commander and also brings out the cost of genius in a boy, how it isolates him from his companions and turns him into an object of dread. At such moments Gance seems able both to glorify Napoleon and to be aware of the tragedy in his condition. In *Zéro de conduite* Vigo was to quote from Gance's dormitory sequence and at his best was to show the same ability in bringing together the fantastic and the real within the span of an image. Gance's limitation was that though he understood how the child might be father to the man, he failed to recognize how the man is more than just father to the child.

Too robust and non-intellectual to be considered a member of the avant-garde and too unusual to be thought of as a commercial director, Gance is similar in this to Jacques Feyder, a Belgian who mainly worked in France. Feyder was cool in temperament and too conscious of the film market to take wild risks, yet he was highly intelligent and even in his most routine commissions able to bring out the human meaning in the most banal of stories. And at least two of his films—*Crainquebille* and *Thérèse Raquin*—were to be important in the development of the major French tradition.

At one time an actor who had worked for Feuillade, Feyder had been invited by Léon Gaumont to direct a number of short films, few of them (reputedly) of high quality. But he must have shown promise, for he was entrusted with *L'Atlantide* (released in 1921), an expensive project successfully designed to give the French a place once more in foreign markets. Based on Pierre Benoit's novel, which August Blom (1913), Pabst (1932), Edgar G. Ulmer (1948) and George Pal (1961) were to find stimulating, *L'Atlantide* tells of the lost kingdom of Atlantis located somewhere in the North African desert, and of its Queen, Antinea, a *femme fatale* who drives her husbands mad through love and then galvanizes them into metal dummies. Feyder's instinct was to demythologize this romance. He shot its exterior scenes at great expense on location and in a manner recalling the Ince productions. He played down mystery, adopted an ironic tone, and showed no interest in seeing the journey into the desert as a *voyage imaginaire*. He did not see women as Medusas; and his *Carmen* (1926) and (perhaps) *Thérèse Raquin* (1928) suggest that he was interested in discovering why men needed to make such monsters of them. But in *L'Atlantide* he failed to throw light on this need. He tried to diminish the impossible demands made on Stasia Napierkovska, in the role of Antinea, by placing her in settings of a luxury that recalls the pre-war Italian epics. In fact, these settings tend to overwhelm her presence.

He was happier with *Crainquebille* (1922), adapted from an Anatole France story about a vegetable seller (played with total absorption by the veteran character actor, Féraudy), who wheels his barrow around Les Halles. 'I have seen,' said D. W. Griffith, 'a film that for me symbolizes Paris,'[16] and certainly Feyder evokes the vivacity of life in Parisian streets. Other films at this time were concerned with prole-tarian themes: but while Griffith imposed a tasteful beauty on poverty in *Isn't Life Wonderful?* and Delluc and certain German directors were to be evasively abstract about poverty, Feyder disciplined any ten-dency to read middle-class preoccupations into the behaviour of his working-class characters. His narrative skill was such that it could pass unnoticed, and indeed spectators of an avant-garde inclination thought more highly of the expressionistic sequence at Crainquebille's trial for contempt, a sequence that Feyder deals with competently enough, although its stylistic tricks go against the grain of his talent.

He later directed with his usual sensitivity the Swiss production *Visages d'enfants*—a study of the impact on two children of their mother's death and their father's remarriage. But a far more import-ant project was to be a satire commissioned by Albatros, *Les Nouveaux Messieurs* (1928). Feyder brings to it all the sense of ad-venture of Soviet filming at its finest: his editing, his use of close-ups and his capacity for manoeuvring groups—a *corps de ballet*, a chamber of deputies in furious session, strikers in arms, a pompous official parade—convey an excitement similar to *October*. Yet far from being progressive, Feyder is bitingly ironic and defeatist. A ballet dancer (Gaby Morlay), mistress to a rich gentleman (Henri Roussel)—elderly and a minister in the government—falls in love with a young radical (Albert Préjean), who also becomes a minister and allows himself to be corrupted. At the end of the film the dancer marries her elderly protector: she feels his kindness and worldliness to be her one protection in an unstable society.

Feyder appears to have accepted the venality of the radical mini-ster and, indeed, of ministers in general as a fact of life in the Third Republic, and the same was true of his public—Charles Spaak's script was taken from an old and popular boulevard play. Interestingly, *Les Nouveaux Messieurs* was banned (and eventually released after some cuts had been made), but not because it called into question the integrity of parliamentary deputies—which it does—but because it showed them fighting with each other in an undignified manner.

Jacques Feyder: *Les Nouveaux Messieurs.*

Unusual in the sense that it takes up a political position opposed to Communism—it could be seen as the culmination of White Russian thinking at Albatros—while maintaining this position with a Soviet vibrancy, it is also typical of French life in the late 1920s in its concern with *le sport*, social customs and *art deco* interiors.

One reason why so many French directors of the 1920s were interested in materiality and in conveying the view that the world is most obviously made up of concrete things was, paradoxically, their desire to find a photogenic equivalent for thought and feeling. The nature of photography is such, however, that although a director may wish to present an image of the sea as a symbol of infinity, he cannot distract the spectator from noticing the play of light or breeze on water. Admittedly, Delluc and his followers did not try to curtail symbolism in this way; they merely observed how certain objects, when photographed, took on a mysterious power.

These efforts to represent thought and feeling also emphasized the essence of things in another way. Anyone accustomed to the story conventions which the Hollywood studios had evolved out of the so-called 'well-made' play will find the narrative wayward in French movies of this period. In general, Hollywood films proposed an adventure, reiterated moral principles of a copybook kind and found means to enshrine the star as a personality. Landscape and decor were at most furnishings to this intent; the very notion of 'pictorialism' implies how far the filming of nature and man-made objects was thought to be little more than a glossy addition. The waywardness of the French film, on the other hand, draws the spectator away from its narrative; he becomes an observer—and an observer of seemingly irrelevant details; his mind is freely allowed to linger over the scene as though he were standing before a painting. Plot, when it comes to the forefront, is quite often dissociated from the director's main concern, tending to be strident and theatrical.

It may seem, then, that the attempts by Delluc and others to symbolize extreme feeling brings a large portion of the French cinema into the orbit of surrealism, even though many of the surrealists were hostile to the avant-garde, despised L'Herbier and loathed Gance. One of the values of surrealist film criticism has been to categorize a different kind of sensibility and to point out the charm of the fantastic. It has emphasized, for instance, the importance of the often bizarre Onésime comedies directed by Jean Durand between 1912 and 1914: an assessment that helps to illuminate the early work of Luis Buñuel, the only major director to have been involved in the surrealist movement. One of Jean Durand's gags, for instance, consists of a cow lying on a bed (cows, Durand believed, symbolize mothers-in-law), and he was among the first employers of Gaston Madot, leading man in Buñuel's L'Age d'or, where a similar cow gag recurs. And Buñuel himself has admitted that he determined to become a film director after seeing Lang's symbolist Der Müde Tod. He was to be Jean Epstein's assistant on La Chute de la maison Usher, and it could arguably be said that L'Age d'or derives as much from Epstein's symbolist aesthetic as from surrealism.

It is not an argument that would appeal to Buñuel, or to the surrealists in general, for they have always been superb publicists and made world-conquering claims for themselves. In Le Surréalisme au cinéma, Ado Kyrou defines their importance so widely that few screen incongruities, whether intentional or not, escape his net. But it would be misleading to give surrealism a centrality in film history that it does not deserve. Many of the works the surrealists have claimed for themselves owe more to other movements (though, admittedly, these movements overlap): Clair's Entr'acte and Man Ray's light-hearted experiments Emak Bakia (1927) and L'Etoile de mer

(1928) are more dadaist than surrealist, while Fernand Léger's beautiful, almost kinetic *Ballet mécanique* (1924), Clair's *La Tour* (1928) and Vigo's *A propos de Nice* (1929) are demonstrably Futurist in subject-matter and technique. And, in general, the free association technique and Freudian references central to surrealist practice (cf. my discussion of *The Seashell and the Clergyman*, p. 127) have had a deleterious effect on the cinema.

The principal patron of surrealism was the Vicomte de Noailles, who financed a considerable body of films and whose modish attitude to the arts can be felt in the Ray experiments, in the Buñuel and Dali collaboration *Un Chien andalou* and in Cocteau's *Le Sang d'un poète*, though less so in Buñuel's *L'Age d'or*. Buñuel described *L'Age d'or* (1930) as 'a desperate and passionate appeal to murder',[17] a remark that applies equally well to the more overtly surrealist *Un Chien andalou* (1928). Both are ferocious lyrics celebrating intense yet frustrated (and often comically so) love affairs, in which the man at most gets round to kneading the woman's body. Buñuel implies that these *amours fous* have the power to disrupt social conventions and to unseat civilizations. He describes the erotic history of his characters in such a way as to imply that their involvement entails both an emotional regression and, at the same time, a transcendence of regression. *Un Chien andalou* concerns itself almost wholly with intimate feints of a polymorphous perverse kind; allusions to an androgynous figure who holds up the traffic and pokes at a severed hand with

Luis Buñuel: *Un Chien andalou.*

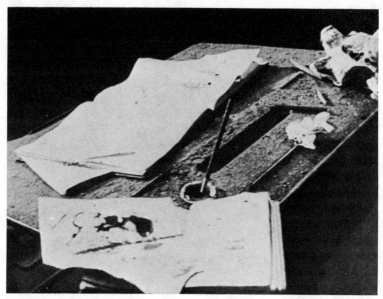

Luis Buñuel: *Un Chien andalou.*

its walking stick, or to the hero's schooldays, can be seen as analogues to the lovers' experience. In a Dellucian fashion, Buñuel suggests that both these films might be reveries about an actual love affair, although whether one or both the lovers are dreaming it, or indeed Buñuel himself, is never disclosed.

The imagery of *Un Chien andalou* includes hands and armpits covered by ants, soiled bodies, an emphasis on buttocks and the usual apparatus of sadistic practice. Less brittle and more wide-ranging than its predecessor, *L'Age d'or* brings this anality even more into the open: lovers roll ecstatically in mud beneath the shocked gaze of some dignitaries: later the woman dreams about her lover as she sits on the lavatory. From its opening sequence—a documentary in the manner of Painlevé about the death rites of scorpions—to its concluding quotation from de Sade's *140 Days in Sodom*, in which various noblemen dressed in robes imitative of figures from the past, including Christ, totter from their debauchery into the snow, *L'Age d'or* extends caustically over many notions of civilization and style, including the manners of polite society, the corruption and suicide of a minister and even the founding of Rome.

By comparison the lovers' passion renders the formality of bourgeois society ridiculous and yet, like Groucho's attacks on the characters played by Margaret Dumont, which have the effect of increasing rather than diminishing a liking for this formidable lady, Buñuel's attack on the bourgeoisie communicates a sneaking regard for its indomitability. A tumbril moves through the drawing-room; the guests continue to drink and chatter. Buñuel's mocking respect for this class has scarcely been modified over the years; the principal difference between *L'Age d'or* and *The Discreet Charm of the Bourgeoisie* (1972) being that by the sixties he had come to acknowledge that its clandestine activities were, unintentionally, among the wilder sources of surrealist fun.

If Buñuel does justify the incongruities of surrealism, he does so as an extreme form of lyricism. His editing follows Eisenstein's views on montage and yet goes far beyond anything Eisenstein had envisaged, for his 'collisions' are neither moralistic nor didactic, nor is he sanctimonious (as Eisenstein could be) about its origins in aggression. Yet he is serious, and his seriousness often converts absurdity into a Rimbaudesque poetry. And for all his aggression, many of his inventions evoke an eerie serenity; as when Lya Lys, as the beloved, shoos the infamous cow off her bed and to the sound of its tinkling pastoral bell sits before a mirror reflecting a cloudy sky. As she thinks of her lover, a breeze from the mirror blows back her hair. The mystery of *L'Age d'or* is that, despite the hermeticism of its images and associations, we should still find it powerful even after many viewings.

Fritz Lang: *Die Spinnen.*

6. Weimar and Scandinavia

1. Weimar

In 1906 Ole Olsen, a one-time acrobat, circus manager and casino owner, founded the Danish distribution company, Nordisk. Soon afterwards he entered production—brief newsreels in the Pathé manner and imitations of the Film d'Art—and in 1910, looking for a less constricted market, began to open up cinema circuits abroad, mostly in Germany. In 1910, also, the stage producer Peter Urban Gad directed for Olsen *Afgrunden* (The Abyss), his first film, and chose as his leading actress a singer from the chorus of a Danish opera company, an actress whom he was to marry in 1912: Asta Nielsen. *Afgrunden* was very popular, especially in Germany, and established Asta Nielsen as perhaps the only international star of the pre-war years. Largely on her appeal, Nordisk, with an output of 370 films a year, had become by 1913 second only to Pathé in the world league of film companies.

Afgrunden is still effective. A young woman nightly slips away from her middle-class home to the Circus Fortuna. Infatuated with a cowboy in the company, she elopes with him and when he takes up with another performer she attacks the girl on stage. Later in a fit of jealousy she kills the cowboy and the police arrest her. In summary trite, this plot however contains a serious intention, being part of a liberationist movement which includes plays like Ibsen's *A Doll's House* and a cycle of Danish films dealing with the rights of women. Urban Gad shot it on location, contrasting a country house with a tawdry theatre and sunny streets with a depressed lodging-house, and he minimizes its excesses by surrounding Nielsen with people—among them beer-drinkers at a bar, cyclists, and a plump, nondescript waiter, whose behaviour only tangentially relates to her. In *Afgrunden* the Lumière kind of cinema begins to come of age.

Audiences accustomed to the Biograph kind of heroine were startled by Asta Nielsen's physicality; and even now the vividness of *Afgrunden* depends on the sexual intensity of her acting. She was to be known throughout her career for the care she took in charting the emotional changes of the women she played and in choosing the right prop or costume to dramatize her characters. Both she and

Urban Gad, it would seem, were influenced by the clinical precision
that such playwrights as Schnitzler and Wedekind had brought to
the analysis of passion. In this, they foreshadow many German film
directors of the 1920s.

The fictional studies in prostitution of Pabst, Rahn and Mittler,
and the delicate portraits in femininity of Czinner and Ophüls, all
relate to *Afgrunden* in the sense that their directors, however unlike
in temperament, tended to share certain attitudes to society and sex.

Peter Urban Gad: *Afgrunden*. Asta Nielsen.

All of them assumed, as had the director of *Afgrunden*, that passion is
arbitrary in its choice of love-object and often bound to a wish for self-
destruction; that such a notion of the arbitrary arises in some manner from the haphazard nature of urban life; and that one of the denials
of this uncertainty, the complacency of bourgeois life, so dissociates
the middle classes from the precarious yet imaginatively richer community of artists that any attempt to bring together these two modes
of being must strain plots to the point of incredibility.

Often convincing in their picture of middle-class domesticity, many
of these directors tended to be confused about the supposed freedom
of the artist. They seldom moved beyond a state of adolescent be-

musement. Yet from the start many of them had been enchanted by this supposed freedom. The Skladonovsky brothers, who had been the first to make films in Germany, had turned their cameras not on arriving trains or babies but on music-hall performers; and later directors were to be enthralled by the theatre, the music-hall and the fairground in the same way as they were to be dazzled by the idea of woman as a will-o'-the-wisp, leading her admirers to fulfilment or annihilation. They seem to have viewed the careers of artists, enter-

Peter Urban Gad: *Engelein*. Asta Nielsen.

tainers and prostitutes indistinguishably (insofar as their fantasies about them had political overtones) as both the epitome of capitalist economics and its one redeeming alternative. The perhaps over-emphatically named Circus Fortuna of *Afgrunden* anticipates the phantasmagorias created by the German film-makers of the 1920s, in which confused and often extreme states of feeling were given an appropriate setting.

In 1912 Paul Davidson, a Jewish garment manufacturer who had entered the film industry as an exhibitor and then turned producer, brought Urban Gad and Asta Nielsen to Germany. *Engelein,* one of their earliest successes, has Nielsen as a schoolgirl in Pickford curls, a *Mädchen in Uniform* unable to keep her hands off men, denounced by a spying headmistress as degenerate. This unromantic romance, in which the little angel wins the love of her rich guardian by pretend-ing to drown herself, shows off Nielsen as a comedienne: a pencil-licking terror with sprayed-out hair, of a winning awfulness.

But Davidson was interested in more than money-spinning com-edies. Like Lasky and Zukor in the United States, he wished to increase the prestige of the film industry and to this end founded a guild with the stage producer Max Reinhardt in order to bring together stage and screen actors and to establish a system of contracts between the two professions. Although this agreement led to a number of reputedly dull films, two of them directed by Reinhardt himself, it did have the positive effect of alerting stage actors and producers to the promise of film and of diminishing their snobbery. The expertise of these stage people and their willingness to explore the new craft proved inval-uable in dealing with the technical problems brought into being by the development of feature length narratives. The quality of German film-making in the early twenties owes a great deal to this swift integration of old and new forms of culture.

In *The Haunted Screen* Lotte H. Eisner has pointed out the part played by Max Reinhardt in this development. Reinhardt had fol-lowed Gordon Craig and Adolphe Appia in demanding that stage sets should be as functional and strong in design as modern architecture. He had a gift for suggesting space by the use of light and for de-fining character by a mere silhouette. But his views were definite only in aesthetic matters. He believed that stage producers should in-volve themselves not so much in the ideological underpinning to plays as in mood and gesture, mastering every kind of statement without committing themselves to any one of them. He transformed the Deutsches Theater into a secular kind of cathedral by his incan-tatory spectacles, ritualized movement and highly choreographed crowd scenes; and, reciprocally, when he took *The Miracle* on tour, he transformed cathedrals into theatres. At the other extreme, he staged Ibsen, Strindberg and their followers in the most intimate manner possible at a small theatre known as Die Kammerspiele; and these chamber-play, or *Kammerspiel*, types of staging were to impress film-makers just as much as his grandiose productions.

His actors acquired a characteristic Reinhardt style, hard to define, that appears to incorporate the courtly elegance promoted by the Duke of Saxe-Meiningen's troupe with the introspective, studied techniques of Stanislavsky. If this style was to become a hallmark of the German cinema, it did so because many of its principal actors – among them Emil Jannings, Werner Krauss, Conrad Veidt, Fritz Kortner, Ernst Deutsch and Albert Bassermann – had worked for Reinhardt. Reinhardt also inspired F. W. Murnau, a leading director in this cinema, and, indirectly, a number of its designers; all of whom recognized the value to film of Reinhardt's discoveries in stage lighting. But at first two of his actors were to have the more immediate impact.

One of these actors, Ernst Lubitsch, had been limited by his diminutive size to comic roles and character parts. Son of a garment manufacturer in Berlin, Lubitsch had struck up a friendship with Paul

Paul Davidson (left) and Ernst Lubitsch.

Davidson, entered the movies and after acting in a number of slapstick comedies, won a considerable reputation in Germany as the director of *Schuhpalast Pinkus* (1915). But he was to become internationally known and, in the United States, to be considered the foremost European director through his historical romances *Carmen* (1918), *Madame Dubarry* (1919) and *Anne Boleyn* (1920), the first two of which starred another Reinhardt discovery, the Polish actress Barbara Appolonia Chapulek, known professionally as Pola Negri.

In *Madame Dubarry* (retitled *Passion* in the United States) Lubitsch counters the pretensions of the Italian film epics by relating large-scale actions to intimate relationships. 'I gave the same value to nuance as to crowd movements,' he said, 'and tried to fuse these elements.'[1] The war, it is probable, had prevented him from seeing Griffith's *The Birth of a Nation* with its demonstration of the means by which the impersonal forces of history shape the fate of individuals. In *Madame Dubarry*, at least, he interprets events according

Ernst Lubitsch: *Madame Dubarry*. Pola Negri (left).

to the quite opposite hole-in-a-bucket theory, which presumes that trivial, even comic incidents can momentously change the world. Uncertain as to which lover she should visit (proletarian poet or marquis), his heroine makes up her mind by counting the buttons on her dress. She visits the marquis, as it happens, and conceals herself behind a screen when a friend calls—none other than Monsieur Dubarry, who sees her reflection in a mirror as she signals to the marquis, understands this invitation as directed at him, takes her up and soon has married her. In this random manner, Madame Dubarry climbs up the various levels of society until she reaches the king's bed and then, in a similar fashion, slides down it to the guillotine: a game of snakes and ladders that owes more to the calculations of Lubitsch and his screenwriters, perhaps, than to the consequences of passion. Yet Lubitsch managed to bring together an epic sweep of a kind that Reinhardt had achieved at the Deutsches Theater with the more subtle techniques that Reinhardt had evolved at Die Kammerspiele. Hampered by Pola Negri's limited talent as an actress —a panther-like elegance in movement hardly compensates for an in-expressive face—he benefited from Emil Jannings's performance as Louis XV, genial and plump, playing blind man's bluff or remaining at the dining-table when his councillors need him, poignant on his deathbed as he calls for Madame Dubarry. Jannings was to become a star through this role, which Lubitsch had been reluctant to cast him in. The financier and newspaper tycoon Dr Alfred Hugenberg, who in 1927 was to take over the presidency of UFA and later to be elected leader of the German National Party—which supported the Nazis—welcomed *Madame Dubarry* as a satire on French decadence. It is possible that Lubitsch felt uneasy about the subtlety of French manners (and so, perhaps, tried to be too stylish), but there is no evidence to suggest that he wished to score points off the French. At most, a Berliner's scepticism about the loftiness of human motive informs his tone.

But historical themes cannot avoid some tinge of grandiosity, and Lubitsch was temperamentally happier with comedy. He created a mordant fairy tale out of *The Oyster Princess* (1919), which Dr Hugenberg, as usual misguidedly, interpreted as aggressively anti-American. Title-crazy Ossi, daughter of an American millionaire known as the oyster king, believes that she has married Prince Nukki, but in fact has accidentally married a froglike emissary of the prince; though all, of course, comes out well in the end. Lubitsch resorts to the familiar comic device of showing everything in excess and brings to it his own immediately recognizable brand of gentle fantasy: a platoon of flunkies attends to every need of the millionaire, Mr Quaker, and a team of typists takes down every word he says. Lubitsch feels most sympathy, however, for the emissary, unable to move around Mr Quaker's palace without a map or, bored while waiting for an audience with him, playing a solitary game of hopscotch on the vast chequered floor of Mr Quaker's entrance hall. At the wedding ban-quet, prepared and served by a host of cooks and servants, the emis-sary mildly surprises his bride by having eyes for nothing but the mountains of food. ('I've never been so happy.') Meanwhile the guests dance foxtrots and downstairs, in the kitchen, the cooks also dance to the music arm-in-arm. Lubitsch is playful in these sequences with-out ever being less than clear-eyed about the role of money and class in society.

In his opinion, *The Doll* (1919), taken from the E. T. A. Hoffmann story, was the most ingenious of his early comedies. It opens with the director himself building up a toy set of a house on a hill. Placing a pair of dolls in this house, he allows the male doll in the pair to roll down the hill and fall into a pond. Paper clouds roll back from the sun; and steam rises off the clothes of the actor now standing in for the doll. Lubitsch keeps up this interaction between dolls and actors, artifice and reality—representing a love affair by a paper heart or a horse by two men in a skin—with an insistence that in the hands of most other directors would have appeared facetious. In fact he manages beguilingly to control the play between these two styles.

Hoffmann's story touches on an anxiety of peculiar appeal to German film-makers. Sexually frightened by an aggressive woman, a young man retires to a monastery, only to come out of seclusion in order to fulfil the condition of a legacy: that he should marry. He gets around his difficulty by commissioning a toymaker to construct a lifelike doll as his bride; but the dollmaker's daughter breaks the doll and takes its place. In connivance with the monks, the young man

Ernst Lubitsch: *The Doll.*

prepares to spend his feigned honeymoon at the monastery. He delights them by showing off the verisimilitude of his doll and carelessly uses it as a hatstand. When he learns that in fact it is real, his dismay soon turns to delight and he willingly joins his bride in a monastic bed.

In his book *From Caligari to Hitler*, Siegfried Kracauer passes over the Lubitsch comedies with little comment in order to argue his point that German film-makers of the 1920s encouraged the rise of National Socialism, whether intentionally or not. Yet *The Doll* has a plot very similar to Kracauer's key film, *The Cabinet of Doctor Caligari* (1920), which is also about the relationship between a master and his uncontrollable automaton, though to darker purpose: the insane psychiatrist Dr Caligari exhibits one of his patients, the somnambulist Cesare, at fairgrounds and during this time directs him to carry out a series of murders. 'Caligari,' writes Dr Kracauer, 'exposes the soul wavering between tyranny and chaos . . . [It] spreads an all-pervading atmosphere of horror.'[2] Yet it enjoyed no more than a *succès d'estime* in Germany and its producer, Erich Pommer, was to admit later that it had been primarily intended for the export market; while *The Doll* was a huge success in Germany itself. In much the same way Lubitsch's *Kohlhiesal's Daughters* (1920), which plays a variation on the story of *The Taming of the Shrew* and has the much-admired Henny Porten in the double role of pretty Gretl and homely Liesl, can be compared to Stellan Rye's *The Student of Prague* (1913), another of Kracauer's key films, in which Paul Wegener takes on the double role of the student and his alter ego, a reflection in a mirror. Both films were popular enough to be remade later; it seems tendentious to argue, then, that while the theme of the double in *Kohlhiesal's Daughters* should demonstrate that happiness need not be the prerogative of beautiful people, the same theme in *The Student of Prague* should assert, by its very existence, some national psychosis. Nazism established its first foothold in Bavaria, the location for *Kohlhiesal's Daughters*. The conviviality of Lubitsch's actors throws light on another side of the German character.

Paul Wegener, the other Reinhardt actor to have an immediate impact on the formation of the German cinema, was unusual among members of his profession in recognizing the unique attributes of film. He seems to have understood intuitively an idea later to be articulated by Edgar Morin: that films are uncanny because they invoke visual memories with such fidelity that they seem to have robbed the world of its appearances. The student's pledging of his mirror reflection to the Devil—for the right to win a woman he loves—depends very much on this idea; even more so, the way in which he is pursued by this reflection. Like any horror film, the intention is to chill the spectator, but also to explore both the nature of film and an unusual compulsion.

Wegener was fascinated by Prague, only two hundred miles or so from Berlin, yet through its mysterious history and heritage of occult scholarship completely unlike it in atmosphere. He was not to be alone in this fascination; other German directors were to recognize its appeal but not necessarily as a form of chauvinistic splitting—between, say, Berlin as the city of sweetness and light and Prague as the city of irrationality and evil, or, more particularly, between Aryan enlightenment and Jewish mysticism (though German directors were to recognize the importance of the Jewish ghetto and of Jewish legends in their response to Prague). At this stage in time, anti-semitism was unusual in the German film industry and, far from being nationalistic, its studios employed talents of every race and religion. True, Hans Heinz Ewers, who wrote the script for *The Student of Prague*, was German, but his assistant was Czech (this assistant, Henrik Galeen, was to direct Wegener a number of times and to be responsible for the technically more deft 1926 version of *The Student of Prague*), the director Stellan Rye was Danish, while the leading actress (and Wegener's wife) Lyda Salmonova was also Czech. Moreover, Rye makes no attempt to see Prague as horrific or alien; he films it in a realistic Danish manner; and if his film strains credibility now, it does so because some of its trick photography looks unconvincing and Wegener too old and plump for his role. The intrusion of such marginal figures as the gypsy woman, who totters into as many shots as possible bringing auguries of woe, also seems needlessly grotesque.

The central character in *The Student of Prague* is similar to Asta Nielsen's young woman in *Afgrunden*, in the sense that he is exactly the sort of adolescent who would be bemused by the psychology of such a woman and exactly the sort of adolescent that the German cinema of the 1920s was to look to for its audience. And like the young woman in *Afgrunden*, he is a precursor in other ways. He has no productive role in society. He lives in the realms of possibility—like Faust, who wandered through empires of the mind and forfeited his soul to give these empires substance. The German cinema of the 1920s also lived in the realms of possibility, though its attempts at magic depended more on Aladdin's lamp than on a diabolical pact. As Wegener was soon to realize, the main difficulty lay in finding means to make credible the visions of this lamp. After a number of less than successful ventures into the uncanny, he and Galeen were to find such means in their second attempt to film *The Golem* (1920).

On the occasion of his first visit to Prague to scout out locations for *The Student of Prague*, Wegener had been intrigued by a legend concerning the medieval astrologer and magician Rabbi Löw, who had foreseen a pogrom in his reading of the stars and tried to protect the Jewish ghetto by bringing to life a juggernaut of a statue known as the Golem. Eventually Wegener determined to play the Golem role himself. His art director, Hans Poelzig, created settings that would not look flimsy in relation to the figure of the Golem, arranging that the studio-built ghetto should consist of architecturally massive buildings, their presence relieved by fantastic leaning walls and rooftops like half-melted candles. The Rabbi's workshop seemed as though carved out of rock; its staircase resembled a metal cone warped by fire. Poelzig would probably have been unable to achieve these powerful settings without the distinguished contribution of Karl Freund and Guido Seeber as lighting cameramen—who heightened his contrasts of mass and insubstantiality. They also gave their close-ups of the Rabbi some resemblance to Julia Margaret Cameron's photographs of the Victorian astronomer Sir John Herschel.

The contrast between weight and lightness is strongest in the sequence where the Rabbi evokes, like a film show, visions of the Jewish past—he hopes to dissuade the Christian emperor and his court from carrying out the pogrom—and then banishes these apparitions when they are greeted with ridicule, and brings the building crashing down on Christian heads; indeed, the Christians are only saved from death by the Golem, who holds up the ceiling on his shoulders. Wegener's interest in airiness and gravity takes on an ironic tone when the Golem, who has gone wild, meets some small girls, nymphs dancing with flowers in their hair: an image from an Arnold Böcklin painting that Fritz Lang was also to appropriate. One of these girls, lovingly held in his large hands, immobilizes him by removing a life-giving amulet from his chest. He falls to the ground, and the girls settle down on him like starlings on a park bench.

In the previous year Griffith had created an ethereal fog-bound Limehouse by shooting *Broken Blossoms* in a studio. *The Golem* was to be part of a trend towards studio-bound films set in fantastic places. The rapid evolution of cameras, film stock and lighting had opened up the prospect of almost any illusion being created in the studio— and the German cinema was to profit by this evolution, the boldness of its art direction often compensating for otherwise dull treatments, as in the case of Arthur Robinson's *Schatten* (1923). The mainstay of good design was so strong that even a minor master like Arthur von Gerlach could achieve atmospheres of startling yet effortless beauty in *Die Chronik von Grieshuus* (1925).

It seems all the more surprising, then, that the best-known of these fantasy films, *The Cabinet of Dr Caligari* (1920), should have relied on stridently painted scenery for its settings. In fact, its producer, Erich Pommer, had intended this jarring effect. Up to that time Pommer had worked mainly on film serials; then one day Carl Mayer and Hans

Janowitz brought him the screenplay for *The Cabinet of Dr Caligari*; and, recognizing that this intriguing thriller might appeal to the more intellectual theatre-going public, Pommer invited Alfred Kubin, most eminent of expressionist illustrators, to be its art director. In the event, Kubin was unable to accept the invitation and Hermann Warm, Walter Reimann and Walter Roehrig were asked to design sets that imitated the expressionist manner. It was a backward step, a return to the Film d'Art both in its theatricality and in its intention to sell culture to the public. But its fame was to be so considerable that even now many people believe that the German cinema of the 1920s was primarily expressionistic in style. John Willett has written of it in *Expressionism*: 'Nothing was more influential in bringing the movement to the notice of the outside world, or in deciding how we now use the term.'[3] He observes that expressionism was already a dying force in the post-war arts and had virtually spent itself by 1923. At no time could *The Cabinet of Dr Caligari*, which is hardly a cry from the soul, be considered a serious contribution to it. It was, rather, an attempt to popularize the complexities of genuine art: Pommer's most astute detective story, which cast the audience as detective and left it lost among a host of ambiguous clues.

It still continues to be problematic in ways that Pommer had probably not intended. On one level. there is the open question whether it should be thought of as a hallucination in the mind of Francis, a mental patient, in which case Dr Caligari and the somnambulist Cesare might possibly be benign figures distorted by Francis's thoughts. On another level, the association of a Die Brücke type of expressionism (see Willett) with insanity raises the doubt whether any psychotic has ever seen the world in this angular way. Dr Kracauer thought that the film played some part in preparing the climate for Hitler's rise to power. In the sense that it supports the view that modern art and insanity are inseparably linked, Dr Kracauer may be right. But in another sense it stood for much that the Nazis feared, and indeed they were to include examples of Caligarism in the 1937 Exhibition of Degenerate Art.

In November 1918 the Social Democrat leader Philipp Scheidemann proclaimed the republic at Weimar. Berlin was in the throes of a Communist revolution, Bavaria had already been established as a socialist republic and other towns and states were on the verge of an uprising. It took no more than a few months to put down this insurgence; yet Scheidemann and his colleagues had recognized how immediate the threat had been. They had chosen Weimar for their first constitutional assembly primarily as a matter of urgency, and only secondarily out of a wish to change the world's view of Germany —replacing belligerence by an image of enlightenment, as represented by Weimar's most illustrious son, Goethe.

These two events—the suppression of a revolution and the basing of a constitution on an idealized view of the past—were to exercise some influence over German film-makers, if only obliquely. Fritz Lang has said (in a conversation with the author) that during the twenties he dissociated himself from politics and was unaware of the political implications of his films. The meaning of the Spartaeist revolution and the later collapse of the monetary system impinged on him minimally. He was like a sleepwalker, he claims, moved by forces and images he had little or no control over. Only with Hitler's coming to power did he become aware of how important politics could be.

Lang's change of mind was not unusual. Bertolt Brecht, who for the most part lived outside the *Filmwelt*, and Thomas Mann, who lived outside it entirely, went through similar experiences. They only gradually awoke to the significance of politics. Some artists awoke much too late. The film director G. W. Pabst, though swayed back and forth by the cross-currents of politics, remained curiously insulated from the meaning of these shifts in position. At the beginning of the 1930s he moved close to Communism; yet within a brief time he was working for a film industry controlled by the Nazis. Until the dreadful awakening of 1945, he seems to have been in some way blind to the nature of his decisions.

The suppression of the Spartacist revolution, above all, marked the ending of a certain kind of hope. Yet it would be misleading to idealize the revolution. The Communists were totalitarian, opposed to elections of any kind and committed to subverting the Weimar republic. 'All that the Communists achieved was to increase the unscrupulousness of German political life, and to prepare the way for the rule of the truly ruthless and unprincipled,'[4] claims A. J. P. Taylor in *The Course of German History*. It would be equally misleading to idealize the republic. Its judiciary was often less than impartial, its universities run by authoritarians, and its constitution defective. One clause, especially, was to provide the loophole for Hitler's seizure of power: Article 48 stated that the President could dissolve the Reichstag, dismiss the Chancellor and take charge 'if public security and order are seriously disrupted or endangered'. The public declined to take the republic seriously. Many intellectuals, writes Peter Gay in *Weimar Culture*, if not bored by democracy, held it in contempt. Parliamentary debates had 'a curious air of unreality about them . . . Cabinet crisis followed cabinet crisis; in less than fifteen years of Weimar, there were seventeen governments.'[5]

The protected nature of the film industry also accounted for the political blindness of its artists. At the end of 1917 General Ludendorff had ordered a merger of German film companies under a secret state ownership, so that propaganda for the war effort might be concentrated. 'It must not be known', wrote Ludendorff to the War Ministry, 'that the state is the buyer.'[6] A combine known as the Universum Film Aktiengesellschaft, or UFA, came into existence. Far from being disbanded at the end of the war, UFA continued to take over companies; President Hindenburg, among others, believed that only a monolithic film industry would have the resources to restore Germany's reputation abroad and to deal with the threat of Soviet propaganda. Primarily financed by the Deutsche Bank and such companies as Krupp, AEG and IG Farben, UFA bought up the film studios of Joe May, Oskar Messter (most notable of the German film pioneers), Paul Davidson's Union-Film and Nordisk. With Nordisk it obtained a hold on cinema circuits abroad: a policy of foreign expansion which it continued to pursue vigorously.

During the 1920s UFA was the only film organization in the world able to compete seriously with Hollywood for foreign markets. Its growth was rapid and it soon had to move its headquarters from some studios at Tempelhof to a newly-built complex of studios at Neubabelsberg near Potsdam. Even so, the extent of its power can be, and has been, overrated. During the 1920s, at least, it was mainly a distribution company. Officially registered as a production company in 1924, it was responsible for only twelve of the 185 films produced by the German film industry in 1926, only fifteen of the films out of the 222 produced in 1927 (though it distributed 105 of them), only sixteen out of the 224 produced in 1928 (distributing eighteen) and thirteen out of the 183 produced in 1929 (distributing sixty-eight). And although its expansion continued until 1926 (in 1923, for instance, its chiefs took over Erich Pommer's company Decla-Bioscop and appointed Pommer head of production) it then entered a period of severe financial difficulty. Apparently little affected by the slump of 1923—like other companies it profitably dumped films on foreign markets and benefited from the movie-going public's reluctance to save money at a time of inflation—it was hit by the introduction of a new monetary system to stabilize the currency. The Retenmark could not be used to finance foreign trade and thereby cut off UFA from its vital export market. Paramount and Metro-Goldwyn-Mayer seized this opportunity to cripple their principal European competitor by signing contracts with it which, in exchange for various painless concessions, gave them the power to direct UFA policy and to intensify their appropriation of its leading talents. A loan of four million dollars at 7.5 per cent interest almost brought UFA to ruin. It was saved by a right-wing consortium led by Dr Alfred Hugenberg, who eventually managed to buy out the American companies and to lighten UFA's debts with the Deutsche Bank. Hugenberg's influence was to be felt at once on UFA newsreels.

When the Nazis came to power they found at their disposal a propaganda machine with outlets throughout Europe. But the Nazi propaganda minister, Dr Josef Goebbels, had the greatest difficulty in subordinating this machine to his will. Nazi propaganda films flopped at the box-office, actors and directors admired by the public often declined to respond to even the most careful wooing, while the attempt to oust Jews from the film industry was only to some extent effective. Goebbels's intrusions into the industry eventually alienated its members, many of whom had been lukewarm in their support for National Socialism, and in 1942 he was obliged to reorganize it under a holding company, UFA-Film GmbH.

The political blindness of the *Filmwelt* in the 1920s was also induced by the traditional German response to the artist as a superior being —as a magician who gives substance to reverie and who brings together the learning of Faust with the power of Mephistopheles. It was a response that fitted in well with wishful thinking about the republic. On this level, the Prague of Rabbi Löw, or the city where Dr Caligari committed his crimes, or the *Jugendstil* fantasy of the settings for Lubitsch's *The Mountain Cat* (1921) were all consequences of a fascination with magical possibility. Films that allowed their directors to

Fritz Lang: *Die Spinnen.*

contrast different styles illustrated this fascination most clearly. Fritz Lang's *Der Müde Tod* (1921) tells of a girl who bargains with a stranger, representing Death or Fate, for the life of her lover: an allegory that offers Lang the opportunity to link together three fables set in Islam, Renaissance Italy and ancient China respectively. But the meaning of this comparative technique remains uncertain.

Intolerance may have contributed something to the high tone of *Der Müde Tod*, but its form probably came from a less portentous source. Lang had a flair for composing awesome images and creating sardonic effects, while his wife Thea von Harbou, who wrote all his scripts at this time, had a gift for thinking up sequence upon sequence of bizarre situations. Together they were well suited to the fantastic adventure or detective story: genres which the German director Joe May, in serials like *Stuart Webbs* (1914), *Joe Deebs* (1915–16) and *Harry Higgs* (1917), had emphasized as an antidote to the grimness of war. Lang was to write scripts for May and to direct for him the two-part serial *Die Spinnen* (1919–20). In *Der Müde Tod* he uses a form analogous to the serial, but he also lays claim to a more elevated reputation by curbing his sense of humour and restraining his exuberance.

Paul Leni's triptych *Waxworks* (1924), although less inventive than Lang's film, brings out more clearly the nature of this comparative technique. A poet (William Dieterle) visits a waxworks booth at a fairground and sees the models of three tyrants: Haroun al Raschid, Ivan the Terrible and Jack the Ripper. Attracted by the girl who works at the booth, he falls asleep and dreams that he fights for the girl with each of these tyrants (played by Emil Jannings, Conrad Veidt and Werner Krauss). Like the student of Prague, the poet realizes his wishes through dreams that enact typically adolescent conflicts; yet interestingly none of the tyrants is German, and none of them has the kind of association that stirs guilt. The fantasies are distanced, and the very fact that they are contrasted tends to minimize uncritical identification: they are merely possibilities. And because Leni and Lang are so open about the erotic expediency (or, in the case of *Der Müde Tod*, the erotic anxiety) underlying these fantasies, they tend to defuse their power.

Indeed, it becomes hard to see what their involvement in these fantasies might be: a problem that becomes acute in relation to the two parts of Lang's *Die Nibelungen* (1924). Lubitsch had interpreted the rise and fall of Madame Dubarry in terms of chance—as a comic view of history. Lang raises momentous consequences out of trivial acts and, it would appear, wishes the spectator to see the workings of fate as tragic. But he links together the various episodes in his legend so arbitrarily that his theme never emerges. In *Siegfried*, the first part of *Die Nibelungen*, he occupies himself with architectural effects,

Fritz Lang: *Die Nibelungen: Siegfried.*

reducing his characters to miniature proportions by his use of long
shot—and increasing sensations of space by having dark silhouettes
in the foreground, an intensity of light in the middle distance and
remote faded shapes in the background: a manner of working that
may owe something to Gordon Craig and his insight into how one
vertical line, one flight of steps, or one cluster of trees can suggest
a cosmos. But what does all this pageantry add up to, if anything?

In the second part of *Die Nibelungen* gentle Kriemhild, embittered
by the murder of Siegfried, becomes the very embodiment of revenge.

Fritz Lang: *Die Nibelungen: Kriemhild's Revenge.*

Various analogues to her ruling passion—the killing of Attila's child and the burning of his castle, or the sack of Rome—may be intended to refer to the disastrous state of Germany in 1918. But Lang builds up his tableaux with such an overriding concern for monumental effect that he dissipates any pathos his characters might have had. He is unable to bridge the gap between the grandeur of his treatment and the mean futility of their acts.

Lang presents both Kriemhild and the Queen of Iceland as totemic. They stare out at the audience with glazed eyes. They move slowly, their gestures are measured, they are dressed in heavy pieces of armour. But Lang shows them to be passionate, and he underlines the contrast with a series of knowing allusions. Through the vulvar and phallic shapes of his settings, Siegfried's play with his sword and Walter Ruttman's semi-abstract animated cartoon of Kriemhild's 'hawk' dream—an example of twenties Freudianism at its smartest— Lang invites the spectator to patronize chaste Kriemhild, who presumably does not recognize the erotic significance of her dream.

Mockery of this kind suggests that Lang himself, recoiling baffled before the meaning of his subject, was projecting his bewilderment onto Kriemhild. In the same way, his attempts at mystification in *Dr Mabuse, the Gambler* (1922) suggest that he was looking for some escape from perplexity by imposing a perplexity on his audience. The society he describes in this two-part thriller is devoured by greed; and he and von Harbou work out this theme in terms of gambling, with Mabuse—the criminal of protean identity—as the winner who takes all. Lang has since said that his thriller was about the hysteria that seized the middle classes during the period of inflation; but he seems to be less concerned with describing this hysteria than defending himself against it. He shows us how a gambler can avoid feelings of despair at the chancy nature of capitalism, or of fate, by retreating into megalomania. At times he comes close to the satire of Brecht's *The Threepenny Opera*. But his Mabuse is a more metaphysical character than Brecht's MacHeath, beginning as a master of disguise, then evolving into a vampire-like predator and ending up as a devil with the power to possess souls. But when money can buy anything, magic of the Mabuse kind becomes no more than an extension of the advertiser's skill: a reductionism that levels everything, even the vocation of film director. For at moments Mabuse resembles a film director, as in the scene where he presents himself as 'Sandor Weltman, psychologist' and summons up (in the manner of Rabbi Löw) a vision of the desert. In an age of technology, all that such visions require to be realized is a considerable budget.

However, there was a productive side to this wishful thinking. In the 1920s Berlin had become an international centre for ideas as well as for brutal ideologies and crackpot fancies. Living in the realms of possibility, artists and thinkers were challenged to make a critique of relativity, Einstein being a key figure in this respect. Walter Gropius, who had founded the Bauhaus in 1919, wanted his students to be as open-minded in their response to technology as, ideally, scientists

Fritz Lang: *Dr Mabuse, the Gambler:*
above, 'the winner who takes all'; *below,* 'Sandor Weltman, psychologist'.

should be: to achieve a consistent Bauhaus style, he believed, would be tantamount to a retreat into academicism. The guild-like organization of the Bauhaus was to be found also in the film studios. At the Warburg Library, Erwin Panofsky and other scholars, following Aby Warburg, continued to investigate the problems of iconography, while Ernst Cassirer, who worked for a time in the Warburg Library, tried to demarcate levels of thinking, and the kinds of symbolism of which thought consists, in the three volumes of his *Philosophy of Symbolic Form*. Members of the Berlin Psychoanalytic Institute were charting the development of the mental structures out of which adult thought is formed and making some of the most important advances in this field since the days of Freud's earliest discoveries.

German film-makers of this time were also curious about the mind's ability to realize itself. And their interest in every kind of style, however alien this style might seem to be, stands in vivid contrast to Nazi bigotry. The Nazis were to draw those elements from these styles that most suited their purpose, but contrary to received opinion, these elements resided less in the Gothic or expressionistic aspects of German film-making in the 1920s than in its striving for a classical order. Wishing to corrupt the greatest good, they perceived this good to lie in the vision of classicism that the founders of the Weimar republic had ascribed to Goethe.

A German scholar, J. J. Winckelmann, had started the Hellenic revival of the late eighteenth century, and Germans were to be among the first connoisseurs of Greek art. Any visitor to the Pergamon Museum in East Berlin will be struck by the extent to which the settings for many German films of the 1920s recall its remarkable collection of Greek art. Hitler's Chancellery and the architectural plans and street models designed by Albert Speer for post-war Berlin—to be seen in the Sven Noldan film documentary *Das Wort aus Stein* (1939)—reveal how the totalitarian mind can reduce a classical inspiration into an experience of the most life-denying sort. The Weimar film-makers seldom took up classical legends or themes; but they did in certain productions, such as *Die Nibelungen*, try to achieve a classical measure. In the next decade this measure would be transformed either into an incantation to energy, as in Leni Riefenstahl's *Olympiad* (1938), or into an impersonal form of craftsmanship: the Greek sculptures in the UFA musical *Amphytrion* (1935), for instance, look as though they had been modelled in plastic.

The German film-makers of the 1920s also unintentionally anticipated the Nazis in their Faustian ambition to conquer all worlds. 'The camera should not remain immobile,' said the poet and screenwriter Carl Mayer, 'it must be everywhere. It must come close to things and it must above all come close to human beings; it must spy on their sorrows and joys, the sweat on their brows, their sighs of relief.'[7] In common with Gance and Vertov, Mayer exulted in the apparently all-embracing scope of his craft, an optimism about technology untempered by the war. He had the boldest imagination in the German industry. Few scripts so closely approximate to Imagist poetry as do his, or are so wide-leaping in their capacity for association, and yet manage to be so practicable, describing in detail camera placements or how certain scenes should be lit.

An Austrian Jew who from earliest youth had been obliged to support his younger brothers, Mayer had been initiated into scriptwriting by his friend Hans Janowitz, a Czech who had contributed stories—much as Kafka had done—to the Prague magazine *Arcadia*. Attracted as they were to allegorical, fantastic subjects, of which *The Cabinet of Dr Caligari* was to be the most eminent example, Mayer was drawn at the same time in the contrary direction, towards the spare chamber dramas produced by Reinhardt at Die Kammerspiele, and he was to write two *kammerspiel* scripts, *Scherben* (1921) and *Sylvester* (1923), for the Rumanian-born director Lupu Pick.

Scherben (Fragments) concerns a railway signalman and his family living in an isolated, snowbound mountain district. A railway inspector, staying overnight, seduces the daughter of the house; her mother, horrified by this news, goes to pray at a mountain shrine and dies of exposure, while her equally horrified father kills the inspector and then stops a train to confess his crime. Passengers in the dining-car, however, are more interested in their food than in him. The significance of this catastrophe is obscure; it may have something to do with the belief that those who respect the law too rigidly tend to be the first to crack up under stress, or that the bourgeoisie are by nature inclined to ignore the suffering of others. The main interest, however, lies elsewhere: in Lupu Pick's dramatization of the commonplace. He describes the daughter at her household duties, the father's inspection of the railway track or the lodger's shaving rituals before a mirror with a Chardinesque sense of composition and makes a great deal of moving lamps and shifting shadows. But his actors fail to discover a style applicable to this contrived intimacy. As the father Werner Krauss, who was later to show himself adept at restraining intensity, over-semaphores his reactions to the news of the seduction.

The failings of *Scherben* reflect an uncertainty about the taste of post-war audiences. Its snowscapes are too calculatedly beautiful, its interiors filmic without being photogenic. It is above all too abstract, too refined, too awkwardly stylized; its view of the poor more willed than felt. It allows us to understand why Chaplin's *The Kid*, made in the same year, should have been thought a work of genius. While *The Kid* must have seemed natural, *Scherben* must have seemed as much of an art film as *The Cabinet of Dr Caligari*.

In 1921 also, Mayer wrote a similar kind of script for the distinguished stage director Leopold Jessner; and *Hintertreppe* (or *Backstairs*) was to be even more theatrically derivative than *Scherben*. In its opening captions, its makers apologize for the humble nature of the emotions described and point out the extent to which their view of working-class life is cinematically pioneering. In fact, they add nothing to what Flaubert and the Goncourt brothers, in the novel, or Gerhart Hauptmann, in the drama, had revealed decades before. A maid (played by Henny Porten, longest-established of German stars) goes through her daily chores. Her lover is in hospital; a jealous postman (Fritz Kortner) intercepts the lover's letters and eventually murders him when he realizes that he cannot win the maid. The primary value of this theme was that it released Jessner from a decorum about style that he would have felt obliged to observe with a middle-class subject; he feels free to choose unusual angles and unorthodox compositions, while relying on theatrical devices. Following Ibsen, he merely implies the presence of the owners of the house and their guests by showing their silhouettes cast on the frosted glass panels of a dining-room door, or using the progress of their dinner party as a metaphor for the maid's thoughts: the disorder left by the guests, for instance, providing a suitable background for her despair.

But if Jessner is at his best when at his most theatrical (a case in point being his use of steps and stairs), Mayer more adventurously uses the working-class aspect of his theme to develop film narrative. His characters being inarticulate, for example, he is pretty well able to dispense with titles. He sets himself the task of discovering a visual wit in the most banal of daily events, suggesting the ringing of an alarm-clock by a close-up on the winding mechanism, or having the maid put back the clock by five minutes so that she can catch up on her sleep. He had also observed that since working-class people were forced to live in uncomfortable houses, many of them tended to spend as much time as possible in streets or courtyards: an insight that was to be thought forceful enough to stimulate a cycle of 'street films'.

Mayer contributed to a number of them and in doing so came up against a major problem in form. In recording his fascination with the trivia that make up the larger part of anyone's day, he must have realized that he was likely to end up with a shapeless piece of reportage. He was able to give this arbitrary behaviour a semblance of form by modelling it not on drama but on music and lyric poetry and he was to give it some semblance of universality by heightening any hint of repetition in the events described. But in achieving this rudimentary type of universalism, he began to move away from the individual to the group, and the logic of this process soon required him to doubt the typicality, in universal terms, of group behaviour. For if the behaviour of groups appears arbitrary when compared to the multiple events of a metropolis, then the patterns of urban behaviour will appear arbitrary when compared to a nation's behaviour and, in turn, the patterns of a nation's behaviour will appear arbitrary when compared to activities throughout the world. Mayer was in a position to recognize (though whether he recognized it or not is unverified) that the processes of naturalistic art have the effect of cancelling out meaning; however large the assemblage of facts, they remain a mere assemblage of facts. Within such procedures, meaning can only be imposed: by assuming such concepts as destiny or will, or by assuming that the existence of a nation is meaningful by the very fact of its existence.

In 1925 Mayer decided that it was once more time to take film-making out of the studio and to extend his sociological observation of the individual to a whole city. Various cameramen under the supervision of Karl Freund went out into the streets of Berlin with concealed cameras and filmed whatever they thought to be typical of Berlin life. It is not known whether Mayer had a clear idea of how the various aspects of these typical experiences were to be edited, but it is known that he disapproved of the way in which Walter Ruttmann, a gifted musician and architect who had been making animation films since 1918, edited Freund's rushes. In common with Cavalcanti, who was working on *Rien que les heures* at this time, Ruttmann derived many of his techniques from the avant-garde cinema without acknowledging how these techniques had emerged in the first place out of some necessity. His contrasts in pace and visual patterns are sometimes so mannered that the spectator may wish he had abandoned all claims to form.

But *Berlin: Symphony of a Great City* (1927) is reprieved from failure by its photography. For Karl Freund and his fellow cameramen managed to solve the problem of filming the typical without lapsing into either the banal or the picturesque—a problem that at this time exercised many film-makers, including King Vidor—by their sensitivity to tonality and their flair in using a high-speed film stock that had been especially developed for this production. Through their feeling for texture and shadow, they celebrated a city so assured that it appeared to be indestructible. From its massive doorways, restaurants and offices down to the details carved on to its street clocks, this Berlin reveals itself as the product of many craftsmen; even its vagrants have that three-dimensional clarity of presence that Brecht was later to aspire to in his stage productions. Yet in one important respect the impression created by this photography differs from the impression created by a Brecht production. It creates in the spectator a delusory sense of control over the world, of a complacent satisfaction similar to the one that a good meal can arouse, so that he may feel this world exists primarily to satisfy his needs. Audiences, unnerved by the precarious condition of the monetary system, must have felt reassured by *Berlin: Symphony of a Great City*; yet if the film has power now, it has power as the record of a city that was almost wholly destroyed in 1945.

Walter Ruttmann was himself to direct studies of Cologne and Düsseldorf modelled on Mayer's *Berlin*, but he was to feel in time the pressures inherent in naturalism and to extend his observation beyond such limited entities as cities. The extent of his ambition is implied by the title of *Melody of the World* (1929). Intended to advertise the superiority of the Tri-Ergon recording system over any other, which it does effectively through a medley of sound effects— though Ruttmann overplays his hand with some over-emphatic background music—*Melody of the World* resembles one of those 1950s travelogues intended to promote Cinerama. Ruttmann uses the story of a sailor's trip around the world as a framework for some film clips shot on location; they include an interview with Bernard Shaw in England and some valuable Far East sequences, taken at a time when its cultures were less homogenized than now. It is not so bad when he imposes a coherence on the world by drawing parallels between the shapes of windows in a cathedral and a mosque while ignoring the different functions of these buildings; but when—without satirical intent—he brings out the similarity in pattern between the rituals at a Fascist parade, the raising of the American flag, and the Pope at prayer, the subordination of meaning to impressionism becomes tendentious. *Melody of the World* offers no mediating intelligence between the spectator and its global loot; all mind has gone into its technique.

Ruttmann is reputed to have been a generous and unworldly man, impractical about money and the nature of politics. Yet the meaning of his fascination with the purely technical aspects of his universal themes was to become apparent in Leni Riefenstahl's *Olympiad*, on which Ruttmann acted as both adviser and senior editor. Perhaps because of his professional association with Riefenstahl (she and Goebbels were at loggerheads), he was not employed by UFA at the outbreak of the war. He was sent to the Eastern front as a cameraman, where he was killed in 1941. The progress of his career as a director illustrates how a sense of design, when put to the service of power, can lead to a blank-minded inhumanity. Although no racist, his omniscient technique was to lock in tightly with the promotion of racist beliefs: an insensitivity that is with us still in the comfortably contrasted vistas of abroad opened up by the package tour.

It would oversimplify Carl Mayer's position to say that by the mid-1920s he had come to recognize the extent to which the avant-garde impulse had been exhausted and turned to naturalism and the cult of the fact; it would be more true to say he had come to recognize, as had many artists, that the process crucial to avant-garde thought had been the juxtaposition of diverse and often conflicting elements and that he now thought this process might be more richly .applied to affirming the actuality of the world and of art than to eliciting strident, dissociated states of mind. The so-called neo-classical period of Picasso and Stravinsky, for instance, is not so much a retreat from experiment as an attempt to apply this process of collage, or editing, to the great art of the past.

In 1925 G. F. Hartlaub, director of the Mannheim Kunsthalle, organized a large exhibition called *Neue Sachlichkeit*, the new objectivity or matter-of-factness, which John Willett characterizes in *Expressionism* as 'a non-utopian even rather prosaic concern with clarity, accuracy and economy of means, biased towards the collective rather than the personal, and informed by a realistic social analysis'.[8] It is possible that the model for this objectivity was the kind of newspaper in which reports on events, often of a violent nature, are incongruously placed side by side without comment. Among film-makers G. W. Pabst practises an impersonality that in certain ways resembles such a treatment, clipping off shots or sequences at the moment when the feeling contained in them appears on the point of welling up. But Pabst's objectivity is not so much a denial of fantasy as a seemingly detached way of presenting such fantasies. There is no evidence that Carl Mayer ever worked for Pabst; indeed, this hardboiled manner is alien to his way of thinking; and although in *Berlin* he reveals that he had felt the attraction of the *Neue Sachlichkeit*, his long-standing professional association with F. W. Murnau, for whom he wrote six screenplays, suggests that he did not wish his talent to be confined by it.

Little is known of at least twelve of Murnau's films, all of them lost, although Lotte H. Eisner has tried to reconstruct their history in her detailed analysis of Murnau's career. An almost complete print of *Der Gang in die Nacht* (1920) in the East German archives, however, shows that by his seventh film he had discovered the means by which he could use location shooting to present unusual states of mind in an unforced manner. In its opening sequences camera set-ups have little of his later assurance, and the cluttered art direction of his scenes backstage and in a consulting room are no improvement. But the quality of his talent becomes apparent as soon as he takes his camera out of these studio settings onto location.

An actress pretends to sprain her ankle to gain the attention of an eye-surgeon. They marry and go to live in a small village, where a blind painter lives. It is possible that Carl Mayer wanted Conrad Veidt, who plays the blind painter, to allude to his performance as Cesare in *The Cabinet of Dr Caligari* and thereby to suggest a different interpretation of the somnambulist figure, not as murderer but as visionary. Clearly moved by this character, Murnau seems to be liberated by the scenes on the painter's island. But while these scenes reveal how impressed he had been by the Scandinavian cinema, they also reveal the strength of his unique talent. In a quite extraordinary way, certain landscapes and buildings, indifferent in themselves, become linked in the spectator's mind as Murnau landscapes and buildings.

Seemingly without effort, Murnau was able to solve a problem that had defeated Lupu Pick: that of harmonizing theatrical techniques with the seemingly uncontrollable expenses of location shooting. Few things are more incongruous than actors in exotic costumes and heavy make-up in the light of day, but Murnau was so skilful in his choice of locations and lighting that he was able to bring together coherently the artificial and the natural, a skill which he tested to its utmost in *Nosferatu* (1922), Henrik Galeen's adaptation of Bram Stoker's novel *Dracula*. The sequence in which Hutter, the estate-agent's assistant, rides through the Carpathian mountains to Count Orlok's castle is an outstanding example of how Murnau could project a mood that belies the apparent content of each of his shots. Its succession of landscape shots, photographed by Fritz Arno Wagner, recalls the tones of Fox Talbot's calotypes. Murnau presents them without calculated distortion, yet by their juxtaposition arouses an anticipation of menace in the spectator that reaches its culmination as Hutter arrives at the vampire's castle. Just as impressive is the way

F. W. Murnau: *Nosferatu.* Count Orlok's castle.

in which Murnau relates the grotesque and wholly theatrical figure of the vampire count to these natural locations so that he appears to be a distillation of their spirit. When he emerges high on the edge of a horizon, or framed in a doorway, or walking the deck of a ship, he seems to take possession of these places and to rob them of their identity. Coffins and doorways become apt niches for his emaciated body, and bare fields seem to distend from his gnarled form.

Murnau achieves this interaction between actors and their surroundings with little or no camera movement. In *The Last Laugh* (1924) he was to master space and the objects it contains by mobilizing his camera. It could be argued that the vehicle he chose for this demonstration was inappropriate. Carl Mayer had wanted *The Last Laugh* to be included with *Scherben* and *Sylvester* in a trilogy, the final stage in his search for a visual language that could imply, without titles, the thoughts and feelings of inarticulate people. But he and Lupu Pick had quarrelled, and Murnau took over the project and expanded it to such an extent that he concealed its origins in *Kammerspiel*. Robert Herlth and Walter Roehrig designed some studio settings for its hotel and neighbouring streets of so lavish a kind that they banished all hopes of intimacy; and the sentimentalities in Mayer's plot, which might have been less noticeable in a small-scale production, were magnified.

This plot has a number of implausibilities, one of which, as Fritz Lang has pointed out, is that the senior doorman at a grand hotel should be expected to act as a porter. When this doorman has a

F. W. Murnau: *The Last Laugh.*

heart attack while shifting a trunk, the manager of the hotel (also implausibly) demotes him to being a lavatory attendant, an experience so mortifying that the old man becomes senile. In other hands, this study in vanity might have elicited a comic treatment; and the sardonically happy ending, which Murnau tacked on to placate the public, and which most critics deplore, does suggest this. But on the evidence of his other *Kammerspiel* scenarios, Mayer had been aiming for the quite contrary effect, of a pathos tinged with *Schadenfreude*, an effect entirely lost by Murnau and Emil Jannings, who go all out for tragic grandiosity. Jannings wrings such an excess of emotion from his role that he eliminates any typicality it might have had.

Yet *The Last Laugh* enjoyed a world-wide fame; and rightly so, for in overriding Mayer's intentions, Murnau discovered an entirely new kind of cinematic form. He dissolves the obdurate actual world into an experience of light and movement so that it seems to become an aquarium. The camera drifts among the moving actors in such a way that it sometimes makes them loom forward, sometimes shrink back against their background: a subaquatic ballet where even walls and buildings may distend and shrink. By disrupting any sense of scale, Murnau encourages his audience to identify with the disequilibrium of his central character.

He did not discover the so-called subjective camera, as some critics have suggested. His camera records sensations; it cannot (as no camera can) have feelings. The opening shot of *The Last Laugh*, in which it descends in a glass elevator and (strapped by Karl Freund onto a bicycle) moves across the hotel lobby and scans the street through glass revolving doors, as though looking for a leading player eminent enough for this *mise en scène*, was thrilling enough in itself to capture Hollywood's attention. But Murnau stilled his camera for his remaining two German films and relied on editing for his main source of narrative energy, and it was left to E. A. Dupont to profit most immediately from his discoveries.

Perhaps more than any other film, Dupont's *Variety* (1926) depends for its brilliance on the period when it was made. Its ostentatious camerawork would have been inconceivable without Murnau's discoveries, and its melodramatic plot, unfolded in images as theatrical as paste diamonds, would have seemed excessive a few years later with the coming of sound. Dupont presents dressing-rooms, bars, fairgrounds, caravans and Berlin streets at night so vividly that he can afford to imitate the theatricality of his subject: a *tour de force* that achieves its greatest power in the circus sequences set in the Berlin Wintergarten; an arena so vast that, as in Leni Riefenstahl's filming of the Nuremberg Rally, an audience of thousands seems to be dwarfed. The camera, like the acrobats, swings through the air. Many of Dupont's effects depend on optical illusions or on abrupt cutting from long shot to close-up, often to Rouault-like heads seen hugely. The circus and the music-hall, as he shows them, are no different in meaning from the Circus Fortuna in *Afgrunden;* indeed, *Variety* has an important place in the tradition that extends from *Afgrunden* to Ophüls's *Lola Montès.*

But Dupont's talent was slight, and although he managed to co-ordinate subject and treatment in *Variety* in a way that Murnau had failed to do in *The Last Laugh,* he did not begin to have Murnau's grasp of the possible connections between images. It was to be the high point of his career and he was to lose all prestige with the coming of sound; hardly surprisingly in the light of his *Atlantic* (1929), one of the first British sound films, and so inept that it must rate as one of the worst films directed by an eminent director. Murnau, in the meanwhile, continued to test out his gifts with two of the most difficult projects imaginable.

In *Tartuffe* (1925), for instance, he engineered a relationship between two conceptions of style, each entailing a different kind of deftness; one of them being French elegance, the other a German sensitivity to the monumental in people and things. Carl Mayer's script encloses a version of Molière's play within a modern story in which a young man saves his grandfather and his own inheritance from a predatory housekeeper by screening a film of Molière's *Tartuffe:* a device that allows Mayer to trim Molière's intrigue and to propose the questionable view that films have the power to put hypocrites to rout.

In the modern story the settings for the grandfather's apartment (designed by Herlth and Roehrig) are furnished so sparsely that every object takes on a certain dramatic gravity. Karl Freund's lighting heightens this feeling for dimension in everything, from the wizened faces of the grandfather and his housekeeper to a pair of crusty boots. In general, Murnau shoots in close-up or tight two-shot and, until the grandson appears, leaves the spectator in doubt of the period in which the story takes place, an uncertainty that prepares the ground for a leap backwards in time to the seventeenth century. The style of the film within the film, on the other hand, has a graceful flimsiness in its reliance on the silhouettes of costumes, wrought-iron lamps and balustrades. Apart from *A Midsummer Night's Dream,* which Reinhardt co-directed with William Dieterle for Warner Brothers in 1935, it is the subtlest record on film of Reinhardt's ambition to realize character through gesture or to open up a confined space by having actors make great use of lamps on stairs. Nor is there a subtler record on film of the ways in which thoughts can be visualized. Tartuffe, attempting to seduce Orgon's wife (Lil Dagover), sees Orgon peeping at him from behind a curtain as a distorted reflection on a silver coffee pot and swiftly brings out his Bible. Jannings presumably modelled his Tartuffe on Luther and makes him a frighteningly massive presence, his nose usually stuck in a holy book, his eyes greedily watching everyone.

In one scene he sits on a terrace overlooking Orgon's estate and demolishes a meal while taking in the view. He appears to be gobbling up the estate as well as the food, and in much the same way as he attempts to ingest Orgon's wife and fortune. Although no more than a metaphor in *Tartuffe*, Murnau was to use this idea of the self's invasion of others as a theme in *Faust* (1926) and in doing so to relate himself to Goethe, hero of the republic, who had tried to understand the meaning underlying dreams of universal conquest, and to Reinhardt, who had tried to stage the apparently unstageable second part of Goethe's *Faust*. With larger sources of illusion at their disposal than Reinhardt ever had, Murnau and Mayer see the poem in terms of light, darkness, flame, smoke and water; images that are more architectonic than architectural. They create illusions of an incomparable grandeur, as when Mephistopheles draws his cloak across the sky and plunges a town into darkness—or takes Faust on a magic-carpet trip around the world, Murnau allowing the camera to float with them like an airship.

Tartuffe had been a brilliant exercise in style; *Faust* is both this and something more. The scenes in which a mother dies of the plague and a young woman, cast out into the snow, watches her baby freeze to death are as poignant as any 'street film' about the demoralization of 1923. But if the age of Faust provided an apt image for

F. W. Murnau: *Faust*. Emil Jannings as Mephistopheles.

such a despair, then the clear-cut choice it offered between Christ and Satan must have appealed just as much to many citizens of the republic, who also hankered for some ideology as all-embracing as medieval Christianity. For when Faust surveys the world from the wilderness of a mountain top, he begins to resemble the heroes of Arnold Fanck's popular mountaineering films of the 1920s, who risk their lives and the lives of others for no reasonable end and believe their compulsion to be inspired. And when he gains the magical power that allows him to banish the plague, he describes a ritual that the Nazis were to think analogous to Hitler's purging of the state — although Nazi schoolbooks tended to praise not Faust, with his demonic taint, but another medieval healer, the central figure in G. W. Pabst's technically outstanding film of 1943, *Paracelsus*.

While Pabst and the Nazis idealized Paracelsus, however, Mayer and Murnau expose Faust as a crypto-saviour by placing him to his disadvantage in relation to Christian iconography. Murnau fills the sky with what appears to be the furnishings of some baroque Bavarian church: an angel sunk into a feathery cope of wings, a sun radiating beams like the spokes of a wheel, a scroll bearing the word 'love'. He gives substance to the convention of seeing the sky as God's movie-screen — which arose from the discovery that shots of humans could be superimposed to ghostly effect on the sky — by avoiding superimposition and by resorting to extreme accents in lighting and acutely-angled shots to shadow forth an impressive angel and devil.

In spite of his interest in the theme of male enthralment — Nosferatu and Hutter, Tartuffe and Orgon, Mephistopheles and Faust — or of male degradation in *The Last Laugh*, Murnau clearly made an effort to hide his physical sympathies, at least until he came to direct his last film *Tabu* (1930). How far this restraint can be ascribed to his feelings of guilt about homosexuality, or to more general post-war tensions in society, remains an open question. G. W. Pabst, who seems to have thought of film-making as a form of erotic confession, still managed to be just as cryptic as Murnau; although he was to be cryptic in a different way and about different inclinations.

Pabst's camera haunts beautiful women, an attraction that he seems unable to separate from the theme of power and destruction. He views these women, if not as prostitutes, then as commodities, and at the same time as representing nearly all that he found dangerous, challenging and unpredictable in post-war life. 'We belong', he once said, 'to a lost generation, cut in two, for whom the rhythm of life has been broken, a generation faced by a fracture, an abyss, within itself.'[9]

More than any other German director, he was drawn to the pre-war Wilhelmine world of bourgeois solidity. A painstaking craftsman, his craft both recalls the unbroken rhythm of life in former times and points up the fractures in the present. Its perfection is chilling, an icy rebuff to the feminine distress he enacts, and yet, while cutting his heroines down, it is incomparable in eliciting their sexual appeal. The tension between the eroticist and the craftsman in him is most evident in *Pandora's Box* (1928), his conflation of Frank Wedekind's plays *Lulu* and *Earth Spirit*, which the expressionists had admired (Jessner had filmed *Earth Spirit* in 1923 with Asta Nielsen as Lulu) and from which he banished any trace of expressionism.

He presents Lulu as an attractive 1920s girl who cannot say no, who drives some of her lovers into a frenzy of self-destruction because they cannot possess her as they possess the seemingly imperishable things about them; he then heightens her volatility by contrast, by bringing out the grid system inherent in most of his compositions: a criss-cross of lines, consisting of doorways, windows and venetian blinds, that frames bodies and faces and points up the softness of the human form. Seldom moving his camera, he sharpens audience awareness not only of the rectangular shapes within the cinema screen but of the rectangular screen itself. His images are spare. When he includes some detail in furnishing, such as the ornate taps in Lulu's bathroom, he uses it boldly as a basic point of definition in the structure of the image. He appears to have experienced the spatial field in his compositions in a quite physical way, as though the objects contained in it were related to each other by the degree of their density or weight. In one typical shot, for instance, he has Lulu in a white wedding gown standing in the background to the left of the screen and framed by a doorway, while in the foreground to one side he balances her figure with a heavy dark vase on a balustrade.

He was careful to duplicate this tension in Lulu herself, by casting in the role an actress sufficiently ambiguous to suggest such a tension. Although Louise Brooks's intelligent modern face appears to epitomize twenties womanhood, and her hair style, costumes and coltish grace in movement appear to be almost an extension in style of her *art decoratif* apartment, his austere close-ups and his fascination with the contours of her neck and shoulders—in at least one shot they take on the muscularity of a Michelangelo carving—gives such a permanence to the transient that he could be said to have discovered an indestructible gravity in a fugitive style.

Through his desire for a classical harmony, for the Goethean ideal, he was a man of his age. But through his conflicting wish for both danger and security, he was to be a man of his age in a less lofty way. It was typical of him that he should have been attracted to reform in politics and at the same time shied away from radicalism in any but its vaguest forms, or that he should have been fascinated by the Soviet cinema and yet transformed the meaning of its films

G. W. Pabst: *Pandora's Box*. Louise Brooks, Francis Lederer.

into something far less provocative. Appropriating Pudovkin's kind of montage, a technique intended to awaken the political consciousness of the spectator, he made of it as fluent and undemanding a narrative style as Hollywood might admire, developing such a skill in cutting on a movement within the shot (so as to conceal the cut) that in *The Love of Jeanne Ney* (1927) he was able to maintain an unassuming flow even in one brief sequence of forty shots. But it would be misleading to say that he wished to adapt an intentionally disturbing technique for bourgeois consumption; his interests were more anxious than that. He liked to flirt with danger without actually taking risks.

The extent to which he was attracted to the idea of exposing the self to extremes and yet was unable to give up the desire for consolation—and not only in technique—is evident in the final episodes of *Pandora's Box*, in which Jack the Ripper murders Lulu in a dime-novel London of garrets and fogs. Although he creates effects in these scenes as anguished as any in the 'street films', he weakens them by measuring the Ripper's despair in terms of his exlusion from the spirit of Christmas. He has his killer, looking like some down-at-heel intellectual, peer at a Christmas tree in a parlour window, hold mistletoe over Lulu before kissing her and drop a coin in the collection

box of an attractive Salvation Army girl. The defiance of this outlaw—
consider what Brecht would have made of him—is seen as no different
from the negativity of Scrooge.

Born in Austria in 1885, Pabst had worked as an actor in Switzerland, Austria and Germany before the First World War and then after
the war as a stage producer. He had entered films in 1921, becoming
actor, scriptwriter and assistant director in turn, and in 1923 directing his first feature, *Der Schatz (The Treasure)*.

At first sight, *Der Schatz* seems remote from his later, more contemporary interests, a grave romance in the manner of *Der Müde Tod*
and *The Golem*, with solidly-built sets and sombre lighting. But it contains at least two of his obsessions. Through the figure of a bellfounder's assistant (Werner Krauss), who believes that he can win
the love of the bellfounder's daughter if only he can discover a hoard
of gold hidden in the cavernous smithy, Pabst introduces the spectator
to his fascination with the ways in which emotional and financial
values can be confused. And he reveals his concern with the idea of
suffocation, a phobia that haunts many of his films. Yet neither
here nor later does he investigate the meaning of his interest in
prostitution or his fear at the prospect of suffocation. He is the most
impassive of directors, the cold surface of his films being about as
yielding as the monocled eye of a Junker officer. He remains enigmatic
at every level; and whether or not he intended to be so, or was in fact
ingenuous, is part of the Pabst enigma.

In *The Love of Jeanne Ney*, for instance, he would appear to draw
a contrast between the ruined cities and desolate plains of Russia at
the time of the civil war with the trim motorcars, luxury apartment
blocks and tranquil countryside of France in the 1920s: a contrast
summarized by two key images, that of a shattered mirror in Russia
and of a monumental safe in France, belonging to the miserly detective Raymond Ney. A Marxist critic, recognizing that the script of this
film was derived from a novel by Ilya Ehrenberg, might be tempted to
think that the shattering of the mirror symbolized the ending of narcissism and the beginning of a more communal spirit in the Soviet
Union while the presence of the safe and its violation by robbery
represented a Marxist response to *petit bourgeois* greed. But Pabst
blocks such a response by the sympathy he shows for French comfort
and by other emphases in his story. He allows the spectator to infer
that nothing is inviolable without ever explaining quite what he
understands by the idea of violation or by the complementary imagery of the self as intruder and the self as victim of its own intrusions, suffocated or buried by the places it has intruded into.

Or so it may seem. But in spite of his apparent sophistication, his
feelings are often transparent, especially his feelings about women.

G. W. Pabst: *The Love of Jeanne Ney*. Brigitte Helm.

C. A. Lejeune likened him to a heartless surgeon, in the sense that he tends to cut off scenes or shots in such a way as to break off the spectator's identification with the subject: but this technique cannot obscure the fact that he is dealing in fantasies, not reportage, and that his fantasies are usually degrading. His objectivity, in fact, is often a form of brutality, and the heartless surgeon, or editor, or Jack the Ripper can be seen as the same men under different guises. In *Joyless Street* (1925), set in Vienna at the time when the inflation was at its height, he describes the careers of two women, one of them (Asta Nielsen) being induced into prostitution and committing a murder, the other (Greta Garbo) being saved from a similar fate at the last moment. He tries to present this story as a study in social conditions, but he has no insight into the psychology of his two prostitutes and, for all his lingering over their clothes, he is only able to use Garbo's fur coat and Nielsen's pearl collar as picturesque adornments. His imagination appears to be excited by two aspects of this story: the geographical relationship of a fur coat shop, a night-club and a butcher's shop—as in *Pandora's Box*, his fantasies find their most complete outlet in his conceptions of space—and the idea that both his heroines should be forced to sleep with older men whom they find repulsive. More than any other German director, he appears to be consoled by the delusion that women necessarily think older men unattractive and sleep with them only for money.

He presents this delusion unselfcritically, even though he had some reason to understand its significance. In the same way that Pudovkin had tried to describe the behaviourist psychology of Pavlov in *Mechanics of the Brain*, he was to try to film the methods of psychoanalysis in *Secrets of a Soul* (1926). Advised by Karl Abraham, a leading psychoanalyst at the Berlin Institute, he sought means by which to project onto film the dreams and compulsive thoughts of a scientist suffering from impotence (Werner Krauss). It is worth noticing how many of the scientist's dream images reflect Pabst's own abiding concern with intrusion and burial. Yet he seems to have been unaware of this connection; and his account of how the scientist recovers his potency is over-schematic, as though he were unable to feel through the meaning of this recovery. As always, his interest lay primarily in matters of technique, in finding ways of filming the scientist's dreams and his associations in thought. Freed from the pressures of story-telling, he was able to develop a more elliptical kind of editing, the benefit showing in the rich mosaic of his later work. He did not use psychoanalysis as an instrument to deepen insight; if anything, he used it to obscure insight. It was just another way of dramatizing the conflict between dangerous and comfortable situations, the erupting of nightmare in a domestic interior.

He never really accepted responsibility for these nightmares. In *Diary of a Lost Girl* (1929) relatives of the seduced lost girl send her to a reform school, where two supervisors bully young women. One of these supervisors beats a gong while the girls eat their meals, and seems to be excited by this cruelty, her face resembling in close-up one of the faces on the Odessa steps in Eisenstein's *The Battleship Potemkin*. But Pabst is not interested in presenting the conflicts of history, however caricatured, nor is he interested in 'psychology' in the sense that many Hollywood films of the 1940s were, nor in the terrible predicament of the lost girl (Louise Brooks). Lurid emblems attract him, fuel for a middle-aged director's *Schadenfreude* dream. It is possible, then, to redefine his impersonality as a take-it-or-leave-it manner of presenting atrocities; his only warmth lying in his fascination with actresses, his tact in drawing out and contrasting their temperaments: the diffidence of Greta Garbo with the nobility of Asta Nielsen, the sensitivity of Brigitte Helm with the brilliance of Edith Jehanne. He takes advantage of Louise Brooks's inexperience as an actress by effectively contrasting her American looks and nervous modern grace with the over-projecting, over-deliberate German actors who surround her.

As with so many of his contemporaries in the German cinema, his response to these actresses contains the assumption that women should be set apart; that however brutal the character they must play or the fate they must endure, they should be seen as fragile. He was never able to achieve the relaxed sense of humour that arises in Jean Renoir's relationship with Catherine Hessling in *La Fille de l'eau*, a humour implicit in the belief that women may be as informal as men and take part in work as naturally as they do. For Pabst, on the other hand, if a woman works, she must be shown as drudge or villain. If she enjoys herself, she must go through a number of routines to signal that she is enjoying herself. At all costs her behaviour must be guarded.

Of all the Weimar directors, Paul Czinner was to take this hermeticism to an extreme. The alternative title of his *Nju* (1924) is *Husband or Lover*, and it encapsulates a dilemma which the character Elisabeth Bergner plays—and was to play in other Czinner productions—had

Paul Czinner: *Dreaming Lips* (first version). Elisabeth Bergner.

continually to face. Like Anna Karenina, Nju finds her protective husband unattractive; and both Czinner and Jannings, as the husband, provide the ground for this irritability with a Tolstoyan accuracy. Nju takes a lover (Conrad Veidt) and, when he abandons her, commits suicide. 'I cannot live without complete adoration. I am moody and capricious,' she writes in a love letter. Elisabeth Bergner's charm is considerable enough to make such a demand sound reasonable. She projects remarkable qualities of being, as poignant in their modulation as passages in certain Mozart arias; an allusion deliberately fostered by Czinner, who isolates her beauty in a sensitive, even precious manner. He brings out the comparison with Mozart's music explicitly in *Arianne* (1931).

Both *Nju* and *Arianne* are products of a society in which the ideas of value in art and value in society are related through the assumption that only an aristocracy of the wealthy and cultivated has the time to devote itself to the appreciation of art: an appreciation that insists on the timeless, as though questions of value in the arts ('good taste') were immutable. But now that this society has vanished, it is possible to see how far Czinner, for one, confused the notion of high culture with the tastes of the upper middle class of Berlin and Vienna in the 1920s. When he and Elisabeth Bergner, now his wife, emigrated to England in the 1930s they were unable to recreate this taste, although their remake of *Dreaming Lips* (1937) had the formal society of London at that time as its subject and a producer, Alexander Korda, who shared some of their assumptions. *Dreaming Lips* demonstrates, in fact, how easily an elitist equation of art and society can lapse into an uncalculated snobbery.

While Czinner evokes the porcelain virtues of a leisured society, Max Ophüls records—as in *Liebelei* (1932)—a repertoire of styles, a light dry kind of playing that, though it now belongs to the past, is given a modern resonance by Ophüls's treatment. Ophüls directed *Liebelei* at a time when he and everyone else must have recognized that the Weimar republic was on the point of collapse, and his filming is suffused with a sense of catastrophe. But as he mourns the passing of an idealized Vienna and realizes the mutability of all fortunes—the play is set in the capital of the Austro-Hungarian empire just before the First World War—he also mourns the passing of a certain kind of lyricism, a purity of statement that Mozart and Schubert had captured in some of their love songs, a statement that conjures up a world which, it may be, exists in the minds of poets alone. In *Liebelei* Ophüls shadows forth an elegy to candour as well as to his two dead lovers, an openness of feeling which present times will allow him only to hint at. He gives form to Schiller's well-known distinction between the naïve and the sentimental, between an ideal of natural feeling and a talent that can only be self-conscious and ironic.

And because this ideal of natural feeling can only be hinted at, Ophüls employs circuitous means to evoke it. Like Czinner, he constructs his style around his leading actress Magda Schneider (as Christine); and in order to isolate her qualities he places her in a milieu that echoes to the sound of late eighteenth-century music. But he isolates her not so much to bring out her uniqueness as someone beloved as to give her the radiance of a cherished memory. Czinner's portraits of Elisabeth Berner are sealed off, autonomous, bound up with specific social conditions that no longer exist. Ophüls's portrait of Christine is more in the nature of a poet's reflection on beauty: perennially modern because like all true reflections, and like most modern art, it is open-ended. His convoluted self-qualifying camera movements throw into relief the simplicity of Arthur Schnitzler's play, in which a young lieutenant falls in love with Christine, accepts a challenge to fight a duel with the deathly cold and sexually ambiguous Baron (Gustaf Grundgens) and dies in a snowladen field. In the final sequence, after Christine has thrown herself out of a window, the camera retraces the snowy path where the lovers had formerly ridden in a sledge, and on the soundtrack their voices, as in a memory, pledge eternal love. In other hands, this conclusion would make too easy a demand on the spectator's sympathy, but the ebb and flow of Ophüls's camera movements, like a succession of qualifying clauses, allow an impression of both purity and mutability to emerge by its very hesitation, so that the spectator now associates snow not with death and the frigid Baron but with a fresh beginning.

Max Ophüls: *Liebelei.*

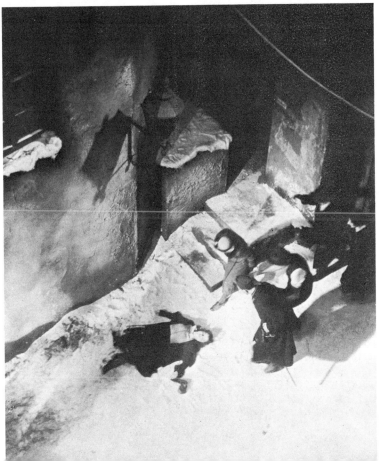

Arnold Fanck: *The White Hell of Pitz Palu*.

It is tempting to see many of the films made in the shadow of the Nazi accession to power as political texts either for or against National Socialism; indeed, under such anxious scrutiny premonitions will appear everywhere. Siegfried Kracauer, placing Ophüls on the side of the angels, claims that *Liebelei* is 'strongly antimilitaristic',[10] –hardly a point that would occur to anyone viewing the film. Dr Arnold Fanck's 'mountain films', on the other hand, encourage circumspection, even though they seem at first sight to be innocent celebrations of the 1920s passion for sport. The most renowned of them. *The White Hell of Pitz Palu* (1929), which Dr Fanck co-directed with Pabst, had Leni Riefenstahl as its star. Its principal cameraman, Sepp Algeier, was to supervise the camera teams working on Riefenstahl's *Triumph of the Will*.

The story's claims to plausibility rest on its tentative significance as myth. Rather incredibly, a young husband and wife climb mountains while on their honeymoon. A stranger, Dr Krafft, comes to their hut and tells them that five years before he had lost his wife while also climbing on a honeymoon and now spends his time haunting the peaks in search of her. The newly-weds incite him to spend the night with them and somewhat unusually sleep side by side with him. On the climb next day all three are stranded; Dr Krafft risks his

Arnold Fanck: *S.O.S. Iceberg* (1933).

life to save the husband from death and then, selfconsciously joining his dead wife, allows himself to freeze to death.

In his doom-laden quest, Dr Krafft could be seen as a Siegfried in contemporary guise; even so, it would require some straining of this story's meaning to see it as a Nazi myth. Where it does anticipate the Nazi cinema, though, and at the same time look back to Fritz Lang's *Siegfried*, is in the technique by which it projects a sense of the transcendental. Arnold Fanck was unusual among German film-makers of the 1920s in preferring to work on location, and the manner in which he angles some of his mountain shots or places small figures in relation to these sublime vistas prefigures Leni Riefenstahl's handling of the Nuremberg Rally. Fanck was to influence Riefenstahl in quite specific ways—his use of magnesium flares in the scene where the villagers search for the climbers by night, their torches illuminating snowy cliffs and icy grottoes, was to provide her with one of the best effects in *Triumph of the Will*—but it would be too far-fetched to see these influences as ideological, and even on the level of sensibility Riefenstahl made them over into an experience entirely personal to herself. A born film-maker, whatever one may think of the way she applied her talent, Riefenstahl gave evidence of a completely formed sensibility on even her first feature, *The Blue Light* (1932). She had an instinct for discovering unusual patterns—in crystal formations and frost marks on a window, in the physical interaction

Leni Riefenstahl: *The Blue Light.*

between the shape of a Gothic church and the edge of a crag. It would be as difficult to predict her later allegiance to Hitler from *The Blue Light* as it would be to anticipate the rise of National Socialism from *The White Hell of Pitz Palu*, where even the death-defying swoops of the veteran First World War pilot Ernst Udet, as he drops messages to the forlorn mountaineers from his aeroplane, are about as premonitory of totalitarian thought as the acrobatics of *Variety*. If the elegance of Udet's flying can be related to the Hellenic displays of physical power in Riefenstahl's *Olympiad*, it can be related in its elegance alone. Udet was a convivial figure and there was nothing of the intended superman about his performance.

The White Hell of Pitz Palu looks apolitical when compared to Pabst's film version of Brecht's *Threepenny Opera* (1931). Although Brecht sued Pabst for transposing sections of the play—and lost his lawsuit—

the film in fact realizes the meaning of Brecht's plot with a clarity unobtainable on stage. Pabst's sympathy for Brechtian restraint is most striking in the final image of the film in which various members of the dispossessed walk into a dark doorway while a voice refers 'to those who live by night'; it could appear overstated, but by his timing Pabst makes it look gravely appropriate. In other scenes, too, he manages to add to Brecht's ideas in a way that complements them, enhancing the impression of Mackie's power over London by showing

G. W. Pabst: *The Threepenny Opera*. Lotte Lenya.

the Queen's parade and augmenting Brecht's sobriety through his taste for rectangular shapes, as when Mackie makes love to Polly behind the panes of a beer-cellar window. Andreyev's setting for the wedding, a warehouse by the London docks filled with a jumble of stolen furniture and dominated by a chair riddled with bullet holes, is an extravagantly appropriate invention. Like Ophüls's *Liebelei*, Pabst's version of *The Threepenny Opera* is a permanent record of acting styles that no longer exist: Ernst Busch as the ballad singer, Lotte Lenya as Jenny and Carola Neher as Polly have a Brechtian edge to their playing usually missed by later actors in these parts, while Rudolf Forster as Mackie and Fritz Rasp as Peachum play these scoundrels neither for sympathy nor as grotesques.

Pabst's richness in response to populist themes is all the more marked in comparison with the imaginative poverty of most of his overtly radical contemporaries. Whatever direction German film-making might have taken if the country had not turned to totalitarian government, it is unlikely that it would have produced a socialist cinema of any force; its directors of radical inclination simply did not have the talent. Brecht contributed a script and Hans Eisler some incidental music to *Kuhle Wampe* (1932), gifted enough to expose, rather unfairly, its lack-lustre direction by Slatan Dudow. Friedrich Zelnick's *The Weavers* (1927) dully records Gerhard Hauptmann's play, doing little more than dwell on a contrast between the rich,

Slatan Dudow: *Kuhle Wampe*.

Piel Jutzi: *Berlin Alexanderplatz.*

their tables groaning with food, and the starving picturesque poor, while Piel Jutzi's *Mother Krausen's Journey to Happiness* (1929) and *Berlin Alexanderplatz* (1931), based on the Arthur Döblin novel, follow in the wake of Ruttmann's *Berlin* and are further illustrations of how a complacent naturalism usually results in an inert technique. In commenting on the shallow nature of their response to the problems of the proletariat, Lotte H. Eisner suggests that in terms of style *Berlin Alexanderplatz* is not far away from the Nazi propaganda film *Hitlerjunge Quex* (1938).

On the occasions when this naturalism was less complacent, when directors and their scriptwriters had the insight to see that its doctrines depend for their realization on a belief in chance, the quality of filming usually improved. Leo Mittler's *Jenseits der Strasse* (1929), which derives its plot from random connections between a beggar who finds a pearl necklace, a prostitute and an out-of-work dockhand who becomes her lover, makes a virtue of chance by having the camera casually pick up and drop characters and by exercising almost lazily its pleasure in the cranes, barges and iron foundries that make up the port of Hamburg. Some skilful editing brings vitality to this technique, yet Vigo was to discover a far more satisfactory form for this kind of sensibility in *L'Atalante*—and the outstanding set designer turned film director, Ernö Metzner, had already demonstrated a far more ingenious use of chance in his short film *Polizeibericht: Ueberfall* (1928).

Metzner saw how the techniques of montage, the contingencies of city life and the haphazard nature of the economic system could be brought together illuminatingly. He begins *Ueberfall* with a medium close-up shot of a coin lying in the road; a man picks up the coin and is knocked down by a car; another man uses the coin to win a fortune at a betting shop and becomes the victim of thieves and a pimp. The limitation of this kind of game is that once the spectator knows the rules he can predict the outcome of the story, though not perhaps the way in which it will be presented. Metzner moves into trick effects to heighten this unpredictability, but his attempt to evoke the hallucinations of the beaten-up gambler by distorted images is tantamount to admitting defeat.

The influence of Ruttmann's *Berlin* is as marked in *Ueberfall* as it is in *Menschen am Sonntag* (1929), a Sunday movie made by an experienced cameraman, Eugen Shüfftan, and some young men intent on establishing themselves in the film industry—and indeed Robert Siodmak and Edgar G. Ulmer, its directors, and Billy Wilder, who did a day's work on the script, were all to become distinguished figures in Hollywood. It would be tempting to describe *Menschen am Sonntag* as one of the precursors of Italian neo-realism (cf. Emmer's *Domenica d'Agosto*), except that such attempts to docket it fail to do justice to its exuberance. A taxi-driver quarrels with his wife and spends a day with a friend and two girls by the Berlin lakes: an incident treated with a down-to-earth Berliner humour that comes as a relief after the portentousness of much of the work from the German studios. Its directors avoid *imposing* political preconceptions on their characters— the bane of radical film-making at this time.

The main trouble with the doctrinal approach was that it reduced individuals to mere members of their class and failed to acknowledge the often strange corporate fantasies that most evoke the life of a community. Fritz Lang was no Marxist, but his genuine interest in the tabloid press, thrillers, science fiction and exotic tales of exploration put him in touch with populist sentiment. Although he was as much impressed by Brecht's technique as Pabst had been—by its dry manner of acting and anchoring of fantastic ideas to a social commentary in such a way that they became imaginative—Lang used them differently from Brecht. The collusion of criminals and the police force in *M* (1931) to hunt down a child murderer may owe something to the beggars' syndicate in *The Threepenny Opera*, but Lang uses it to draw a non-Brechtian inference about social psychology: that criminals tend to be more repressive about sex crimes than members of the police and more cruelly smug than even the bourgeoisie. In other words, the lawless should be primarily feared for their sense of propriety.

Lang plays a foxy game with totalitarian thought, much as Brecht does. Perhaps he was not too conscious of this game and indeed in later years was to say how slow he had been in recognizing why certain Nazi officials had tried to stop him filming *M*, at that time titled *Murderer Among Us*, or in failing to see why the Nazis had good reason to distrust him. In the opening sequences the murderer (Peter Lorre), though as yet unseen, unnerves the city sufficiently to become the stuff of legend like Jack the Ripper or Adolf Hitler. But then his function in the dynamics of plot is reversed as the underworld and the police separately begin to search him out. He becomes a scapegoat for communal anxieties, an alien presence that society must eradicate; and Lang shows him as an object of sympathy. In retrospect, it is possible to see how unconsciously prescient Lang was in having said all that needs to be said about the Nazi accession to power within the narrow field of hunter and hunted, crime and punishment.

But the principal appeal of *M* lies in Lang's precise use of detail and his capacity for relating the most immediate fact to metaphysics, so that on one level the murderer appears to be some immanent god who conditions the behaviour of everyone in the city. Throughout his years in Germany, Lang's development as a director depended on his ability to switch back and forth between a releasing of his imagination in fantastic subjects and a curbing of his imagination in subjects that obliged him to test the fantastic against the facts of daily life. For instance, in *Dr Mabuse, the Gambler* he had inflated his central figure to demonic proportions, in *Spione* (1927) he replaced him with a more probable financial buccaneer, Max Haghi, whose takeovers and political schemes reflect the flux of what Hannah Arendt has called 'the Imperialist maelstrom of unending expansion'.[11] In *Spione* he diminishes the metaphysical vision of *Dr Mabuse, the Gambler* by making everything clear, and at every level. Settings are pale, functional and so sharply lit that everyone has a razor-edged

Fritz Lang: *Spione*.

silhouette; even such minor figures as the Spanish cad, with his raffish sideburns, cigarette-holder and crocodile-skin tie, present themselves in diamond-hard detail. But in achieving such a clarity, Lang denied himself the challenge of the problematic, and it was typical of him that he should have preceded and followed *Spione* with the utopian fantasies of *Metropolis* (1926) and *The Woman on the Moon* (1928). His vision of a future city and a master-mind's control over its inhabitants in *Metropolis* is of a kind that overwhelms the quotidian theme of labour relations to such an extent that he was hard pressed to resolve this theme at the end of the film and fell back onto a schematic, ambiguous solution that apparently pleased Hitler. The strain put on his talent by these two utopian productions had its release in *M*, which was such a success that if he had wished he could have followed it with some kind of imitation.

In fact he preferred to strike out once more into metaphysical outer space with *The Testament of Dr Mabuse* (1933). He begins it with one of his most extravagant inventions, in which the insane Dr Mabuse, confined to an asylum, litters the floor of his cell with a pile of sketched plans for world domination and then, after his death, transmigrates into the mind of his psychiatrist. In *Nosferatu* Murnau had shot an uncanny tale on location in the hope not only that his choice of landscapes would bring a degree of verisimilitude to his tale, but also that these landscapes would allow the spectator to see how, on one level of his mind, a fear of phantoms was bound up with his response to certain kinds of place or building. Lang had a similar intention. His emphasis on settings and objects strengthens whatever plausibility his story may have but, more importantly, allows the spectator to realize that a sense of mystery may reside in his perception of the most mundane things: a sense of mystery implicit in the contrast Lang draws between Mabuse's small cell and his dreams of infinite power. But while Lang wished to demonstrate the impossibility of experiencing either the transcendental or the real separately, the Nazis saw his film in a simpler light—as an allegory and judgement on their intentions—and Goebbels had it banned.

A word about *The Blue Angel* (1930). Often thought to represent more completely than any other film the spirit of Germany during the last years of the Weimar republic, it was in fact directed by an American, Josef von Sternberg, on loan to UFA as part of the deal UFA had made with MGM and Paramount. According to one interpretation, its story supports the theory that the Nazis directly profited from the supposed sexual decadence of the Weimar citizens. A middle-aged schoolmaster becomes infatuated with a *chanteuse*, marries her and allows himself to be degraded as her stage partner; in other words, a wicked woman destroys the professor's authority. But such an interpretation

Josef von Sternberg: *The Blue Angel.*
Marlene Dietrich, Hans Albers, Emil Jannings.

fails to do justice to this double-edged film. Although the professor's relationship with Lola-Lola has a sado-masochistic side to it, it also shows his development from a state of prolonged childhood into adolescent feeling; and Sternberg sees more in the Heinrich Mann novel, on which the film is based, than simply the example of a cunning woman trapping a stupid man.

'Falling in love again,' sings Lola-Lola, 'what am I to do? Can't help it.' Sternberg begins the film by drawing a parallel between the two lovers. The professor somewhat buffoonishly sits on a platform before his class of regimented boys, while Lola-Lola also sits on a stage, a centre of attraction at the Blue Angel beer-cellar. The professor, in moving from the classroom to the beer-cellar, loses his bearings, enters a state of confusion and feels attacked by mockery; all parts of the experience, perhaps, of falling in love. Sternberg, who was falling in love with Marlene Dietrich at the time, must have been aware of how far the delusive mirrors and maze-like draperies of the beer-cellar, like some jumble of props in a film studio, could fittingly describe the sensations of a proud man in love making a fool of himself. In his subsequent six films with Dietrich, he was never really to escape from the atmosphere of the Blue Angel beer-cellar, plunging ever more deeply into it, and with each film heightening all the delusional possibilities that lighting and props could afford. While a class-conscious European will notice that the professor takes up with a *demi-mondaine* and thereby forfeits his status in society, an American is more likely to observe that the professor seizes on the opportunity of living out his adolescence before it is too late. In the concluding reel he makes himself up as a clown, allows eggs to be broken on his head and agonizingly crows like a cock. Is it possible to see this sequence as marking his degradation or, more obliquely, as a picture of a proud man recognizing both the animality in his nature and the extent of his jealousy? The professor, in fact, finds the condition of loving intolerable and retreats from it; he returns to his classroom and dies at his desk. Perhaps *The Blue Angel* has less bearing on the atmosphere of the Weimar republic at its decline than on the central preoccupations of the young Ingmar Bergman, whose script for Söberg's *Frenzy* (1944) uses much the same subject.

2. *Scandinavia*

The perfunctory mention of Nordisk at the beginning of the Weimar chapter does no justice to the Scandinavian film industry in general; yet the Swedish achievement, especially, had been considerable. In Charles Magnusson Sweden had a producer comparable in flair to Denmark's Ole Olsen. As a young man Magnusson bought a camera and for his own pleasure shot newsreel-type films in the manner of the Lumières. His hobby became so all-absorbing that he set up as a film exhibitor, and in 1909 he was invited to be manager of a newly formed company, Svenska-Bio. He hired Julius, Henrik and Hugo Jaenzon as his photographers: and these three talented brothers were to be responsible for the camerawork on most outstanding Swedish films of the silent period. Magnusson also recognized the very different qualities of Victor Sjöström and Mauritz Stiller and invited these two actors to join him as film directors in 1912.

Sjöström was to claim that he had known little of the cinema when he joined Magnusson, although he admitted that he had been impressed by the *Scenes from True Life* series (produced by Vitagraph) and by the restrained acting of Vitagraph's Maurice Costello. Yet within a year of joining Magnusson the main attributes of his style as director had been formed. His assurance in making *Ingeborg Holm* (1913) is authoritative, not least in the ease with which he sustains a 2,000-metre-length narrative or holds shots for a much longer time

Mauritz Stiller: *Arne's Treasure*. On location.

than was usual at this period—allowing the spectator to take in every detail of the setting and to observe how the players relate to their surroundings. He also has a taste for deep-focus shots and for heightening the illusion of perspective by placing tables, fences and roads at an angle of ninety degrees to the camera, so that they seem to extend away into the distance. In effect, Sjöström discovered a

Victor Sjöström: *Ingeborg Holm*.

new kind of filming, a natural development of the Lumière kind of cinema, that parallels the realism of Ince and Griffith.

His story concerns the enforcement of an unjust poor law, by which a young widow, Ingeborg Holm, is separated from her children. It is of a kind that invites a sentimental treatment, yet his choice of technique allows him to bring out its pathos without over-emphasis, as in the scene where he shows the children playing in an adjacent room while close to the camera their father dies of a haemorrhage. He does not intrude on this scene by isolating figures from their setting. Nor does his sense of composition distract us from the *feeling* of the scene, although this sense of composition is deliberate —as in the way he integrates the image by setting up a connection between the white pillows on the deathbed and the white tablecloth in the adjacent room.

Sjöström's technique was original enough to impress many film-makers. He had a momentous influence on Louis Delluc, not only on Delluc's work as a director (the recurring view of the dusty road that appears to stretch to infinity in *La Femme de nulle part* is, I suspect, a good example of how Delluc adapted Sjöström's technique to the needs of his own sensibility) but also on his work as a theorist. For Sjöström's career anticipates all that Delluc thought exemplary in a film-maker. He avoids the blandness of the international style and concentrates on the intricacies of local custom, the idiosyncrasies of feeling and on the unique qualities of places. He is concerned to celebrate nature—and to such an extent that in *Terje Vigen* (1916) his seascape has a role as central to the action as any of his characters. Like many of the French avant-garde directors, he recognizes the photogenic possibilities of the sea and tends to read a pantheistic meaning into it: the sea rules over his Värmlanders like some god. Värmland, his favourite location, bears some resemblance, in its atmosphere and configurations, to Jean Epstein's Brittany.

Delluc described *Berg-Ejvind och Hans Hustru* (1917) as 'le premier chant d'amour *entendu* au cinéma'.[12] Berg-Ejvind, played by Sjöström himself, might be one of Ince's doomed, restless hunters. Yet he lives in a climate far more harsh than Ince's Wild West and he has a Calvinist selfconsciousness that Ince's heroes knew nothing of. The landscape of rock and snow appears to be immersed in time, the isolated Värmland communities to have long clung to this terrain. The inextricability of man and nature is like the close-knit relationship between the different generations of Värmlanders. Sjöström's care for circumstantial detail in *Karin Ingmarsdotter* (1919) brings out the nature of long-standing family tensions and of immemorial village customs in a manner that no other style could have done; while his steady sense of pace and architectural sympathy for the ways in which a narrative can be structured reinforce this harmony of sub-

Victor Sjöström: *Karin Ingmarsdotter.*

ject-matter and treatment. (*Karin Ingmarsdotter* was the second film in a Sjöström trilogy drawn from a novel by Selma Lagerlöf, whose writings were a source of inspiration to many Swedish film-makers.)

It is perhaps unfortunate that Sjöström was to be best known abroad at this time for *Korkarlen* (*The Phantom Carriage*, 1920), a *tour de force* in its complex dovetailing of flashbacks and skilful double-exposure photography by Julius Jaenzon, yet an anomaly in his total output. Its trick effects, though handled deftly, go against the grain of his ruminative talent and yield up little in the way of insight – perhaps because they require a virtuosity that would have been better suited to the temperament of someone like Mauritz Stiller.

A Russian Jew who had been brought up in Finland, Mauritz Stiller had a flair for every kind of dramatic effect and cinematic possibility. Though in likelihood more variously gifted than Sjöström, he was without Sjöström's coherence of feeling or his emotional commitment to certain themes and places. His magpie imagination relied – and very effectively too – on its exceptional capacity for wit. In *Thomas Graal's Best Film* (1917), an amusing comedy about the making of a film, with Sjöström in the leading role of the lazy Thomas Graal, he compares the comfortable high living of his film people with their wish to achieve tragic intensities. Bessie (Karin Molander), a girl from a well-to-do home, amazes the family cook by her posturings in an empty room. 'Knowing nothing about acting,' someone remarks, 'she naturally wants to play all the great tragic roles.' In *Erotikon* (1920), a comedy admired by Lubitsch and a precursor of Ingmar Bergman's *Smiles of a Summer Night*, he contrasts the amatory adventures of an entomologist's wife (Tora Teje) with scenes in a theatre, playing the artifice of his comedy style against the different grace of the Swedish ballet. Through Lubitsch, in fact, Stiller's dry elegance and humour were to have an important influence on Hollywood film comedy of the twenties.

Somewhat cold in temperament, Stiller seems to have been mainly interested in finding subjects that could test his agility as a film-maker. His technical skill was outstanding. F. W. Murnau once said to the film historian Jean Mitry that he thought Stiller's *Arne's Treasure* (1919) came as close to perfection as any film could and that he had modelled *Sunrise* on it. And indeed *Arne's Treasure* does have an icy completeness about it: a perfection that is closer to pastiche, though, than to any statement existing in its own right. It is as though Stiller were trying to show Sjöström how he (Stiller) could handle Sjöström's kind of subject with an incomparable brilliance. In this he succeeds. Yet brilliance is beside the point with this kind of subject and tends to have a hollow ring about it. From the opening prison sequence with its audacious and arresting tracking shot, through the scenes of a vividly-composed banquet at Arne's house (perhaps modelled on a painting in the Stockholm National Museum, Rembrandt's *The Batavians' Oath of Allegiance to Claudius Civilis*), to the tightly-edited scene of a sleigh ride across ice, it unfurls a dazzling series of impressions. Some of its images – of a spectral ship locked in a frozen sound, or of a funeral procession that Eisenstein seems to have recollected when shooting the final moments of *Ivan the Terrible*, Part One – deserve a place in any film anthology. But for all its splendour, *Arne's Treasure* cannot banish the thought that Sjöström would probably have warmed to its events with far more insight. Three Scottish mercenaries, escaping from prison, loot Arne's home and murder his family and retainers. Prevented by the frozen sea from fleeing the country, they wait restlessly at an inn; and one of them falls in love with a girl (Mary Johnson), who turns out to be Arne's niece. Stiller can see this love affair as no more than a pretext for romantic gesturing. Like Eisenstein (and unlike Sjöström), he is hesitant in filming the more tender emotions. If he does find an emotional centre in his story, he finds it in moments of epic action, such as the scenes in which Arne's house is burnt down and the three mercenaries flee with the treasure across the ice: scenes that he was

Mauritz Stiller: *Arne's Treasure*. Mary Johnson.

to repeat, though with less *éclat*, in his better-known *Gösta Berlings Saga* (1924).

His darting imagination might have led him into incoherence if his wit had been less sure. In fact, he turned this darting quality to his advantage by creating metaphors that in other, less adept hands would have appeared far-fetched. A case in point is the structure he gave to *Gunnar Hedes Saga* (1923). He had already decided to direct a film based on the Selma Lagerlöf novel *En Herrgårdssägen*, when he saw a documentary about reindeer which so impressed him that he determined to incorporate some of its footage into his original story. He begins the film with this documentary material. His hero, Nils, is told as a child how his grandfather had acquired the family fortune (now lost) by capturing reindeer, and he sees in his mind's eye herds of reindeer stream across snow wastes. As a young man, Nils decides to restore the family fortune by imitating his grandfather. However, he is less lucky than his grandfather. The reindeer prove untameable, and one of them drags him across the wastes in such a way that he is

Nils (Einar Hanssen) dragged across the ice, Mauritz Stiller: *Gunnar Hedes Saga*.

severely hurt and loses his memory. Stiller places these visionary events within the context of another story, just as dreamlike, yet more gentle. Before the reindeer hunt, Nils had met two grotesque acrobats and fallen in love with their daughter—and now, at the conclusion of the film, the daughter helps him to recover his memory by re-enacting their first meeting. The mystery of this process and of the scenes in which Stiller films the fragmented nightmares that haunt Nils during his period of amnesia are anticipated by his juxtaposition of the reindeer documentary footage and the story of the acrobats: the spectator has already begun to accept a narrative convention in which incongruous events and styles seem compatible. It could be argued that Stiller's inability to become emotionally involved in his subject-matter gave him the distance to see how inherently strange certain fragments of filmed experience might be, and how these fragments might be edited together in ways that at this time only certain Soviet theoreticians, such as Kuleshov, were beginning to be aware of.

Apart from Sjöström and Stiller, a considerable number of distinguished film-makers were working in Scandinavia at this time, among them J. W. Brunius, Rune Carlstein and Ivan Hedquvist in Sweden and Benjamin Christensen and Holger Madsen in Denmark. The best known of them internationally, and perhaps the most outstanding, was a Dane: the journalist, screenplay writer and film editor Carl Dreyer. *Prästänken (The Parson's Widow,* 1920), one of Dreyer's earliest films, was made in Sweden and—at first sight at least—seems to have been untouched by his taste for those ceremoniously cruel touches that characterize his later work.

Its comedy pivots on the existence of an archaic Swedish custom, as a consequence of which a virile young preacher learns that in order to obtain the former parson's living he must marry the parson's widow, a formidable octogenarian who has already buried three husbands. Submitting to this chaste ordeal, he then tries to kill off his elderly wife by various means; but she either sees through his plans (as when he hovers over her bed dressed as a devil) or misconstrues his attacks, thinking them to be some form of sexual advance. But in time her kindness touches his heart; and when she dies naturally, he grieves over her death.

Dreyer approaches this peculiar story in a painterly fashion. He is fascinated by the leathery face of the old woman, and likes to place tall figures in small rooms so that they take on an oppressive monumentality—an optical trick pushed to an extreme in his last film, *Gertrud* (1964). His jewel-bright imagery has some kinship to certain Flemish paintings of the fifteenth century. But the tone of *Prästänken* is the most characteristic quality of his talent. Here, and in many of his subsequent films, he was to marry a stately sense of respectability with a predilection for weird and even obscene events.

In the early 1920s the Swedish film industry lost most of its impetus. Bengt Idestam Almquist has suggested various reasons for this failure in his monograph on Sjöström.[13] As a result of Swedish neutrality, the economy had boomed during the war years; but it had then entered a slump, with unfortunate consequences for film exhibitors. The public was less able to go to the movies, and when it did go tended to prefer Hollywood or Berlin comedies to local productions. Charles Magnusson, whose financial achievements during the war years had been such that he had been able to absorb most rival companies (his own organization was eventually re-formed into the Svensk Filmindustri in 1920), became less interested in films of social or aesthetic importance. The state of the industry was such that Sjöström, Stiller and two actors whose careers had been promoted by Stiller—Greta Garbo and Lars Hansen—were obliged to accept Hollywood contracts. Garbo, of course, achieved a legendary reputation in the United States, but Stiller failed to make an impact and returned to

Sweden in 1928, where he died shortly afterwards.

In the meanwhile, Sjöström was to enjoy a *succès d'estime* with *The Wind* (1928), which he directed with Lillian Gish in the leading role. Hitchcock's *The Birds* apart, no one has conveyed as well as Sjöström a foreigner's first shocked awareness of the American landscape—its obliterating sense of majesty, danger and indifference. A young woman travels from Kentucky to stay with relatives some-where on the Texas plains. A great wind blows ceaselessly in this arid place, whipping up dust and on luckless days bringing tornadoes or cyclones in its train. The impress of this wind lies on every scene in the film, giving the treatment its principal coherence: it kneads the actors' bodies so that their movements often resemble a fantastic mime; and it becomes a convincing metaphor for the young woman's confused thoughts about passion and mental break-down. Sjöström links together his images with a plasticity of expres-sion comparable to the wind itself; and the means by which he relates the wind to his heroine's feelings—and to the significance she finds in a side of beef or in the omnipresent dust—is remarkable for its psychological subtlety.

Carl Dreyer never worked in Hollywood, but he did go to France to direct *The Passion of Joan of Arc* (1928). In the opinion of many it is a masterpiece. Oscar Wilde once said that it was shallow not to judge a man by his face; and Dreyer goes beyond Wilde in his appa-rent belief that the history of mankind can be described through the human face, in this case through a contrast between the incandes-cent Joan and her devious accusers. *The Passion of Joan of Arc* con-sists largely of close-ups—twenty minutes have to pass during the opening courtroom scenes before the courtroom itself is seen in an establishing shot. Rudolf Maté's camera does not move as it looks up at Joan, as though it were as steadfast as she. It glides among her accusers; so that they appear to loom up before its lens like deep-sea monsters. At times they seem to glide past it like some corporate lizard, a shuddering and wrought mass of slithering darkness sil-houetted against the white walls of the courtroom. Although Dreyer is fascinated by the tormented and bewildered spirituality of his Belsen-cropped Joan, he appears to be even more compelled by the gnarled features of her accusers: the mean eyes of one of the judges, the different kinds of blandness exuded by various types of hypocrite. The way in which he keeps up narrative momentum with such a rigorous, excluding technique, and the consistency with which he forced his actors to maintain this unrelenting atmosphere, does help to explain why many of his admirers think that he took the silent film to its summit as an art. Yet if *The Passion of Joan of Arc* is a major work, it is one of a most callous kind. Like Pabst, Dreyer appears to have an attachment to the subject of degraded women (and indeed

Joan is seen to be broken when brought before the torture instruments). His wish to translate this attachment into art is presumably based on a curious belief in art as something both frigid and complete that avoids most of the more attractive, if confused, aspects of human experience. It results in an unwitting impression of male smugness: an impression which becomes even more forcible in his intolerably painful *Day of Wrath* (1943).

Rex Ingram directing *The Four Horsemen of the Apocalypse*.

7. Hollywood in the Twenties

California. *Los Angeles, its largest city, is run by Christian business men. Any visitor suspected of harbouring radical economic views is clubbed by the police and sent to jail. The courts of California are the worst of the United States. Just outside pious Los Angeles is Hollywood, a colony of picture stars. Its morals are those of Port Said.*[1]

H. L. MENCKEN

It might be a wooden shack, or it might be a palace decorated in red plush; but nearly every Western, at one time or another, takes the spectator into a saloon. In the grander ones, mirrors are a noticeable part of the furnishings, to be removed as guns are drawn. Men come here to lose themselves in drink and to triumph over each other at the gaming tables. The saloon usually has, if only by implication, a brothel upstairs.

Hollywood in the twenties severely tests the theme of this book: that some insight might be gained by relating movies, and the people who make them, to the culture of their society. Cultures are created out of sacrifice: 'And grave by grave we civilise the ground,'[2] wrote the poet Louis Simpson, speaking for the American pioneers. But Los Angeles was a boom town; it had no past. And the film industry sprawled about it had hardly evolved through the challenge of experience. Its major administrative problem during the twenties—that of gauging post-war mass taste and of gearing a factory system to it— had no precedent and no built-in predictability. It was, wholly, a gambling situation.

Los Angeles stood at the end of the trail, at the point where the frontier gave way to the Pacific. The pioneers had believed that beyond the frontier lay either paradise or the desert. Los Angeles was both the paradise and the desert. Its perennially blue, pre-smog skies and richness of crop at first pleased, then satiated. Its film studios provided wealth, power and fame for some: a slaking of greed and then, quite swiftly, feelings of desolation; feelings compounded by an awareness that fame and power were based on the precarious asset of the projected image. To the unsuccessful, the wish to be rich, powerful and famous was probably more painful, if no less delusive.

But too much emphasis can be put on childish motive. Jan and Cora Gordon, who visited Hollywood in the late twenties and wrote about their visit in *Stardust in Hollywood* (1930), were impressed by its hard-working professionalism and found its famous parties dull. The days of spontaneous carnival had ended in 1923, with the arrival of Will H. Hays. Even so, the sense of unreality persisted; and visitors to Hollywood tended to come away from it with either one of two theories about it. According to one theory, the visitor imagines Hollywood as realizing, in a scarcely veiled fashion, secret desires and tyrannies. (*Hollywood Babylon*, a book published in 1959, gives this fantasy its fullest expression; and Kenneth Anger, its author, is a key figure in the American underground cinema, whose unstated aim has been to create a mirror image of the Hollywood cinema, where secret desires and tyrannies can be explicitly enacted.) According to the other theory, the visitor to Los Angeles tends to see it as a slide area, a haunted, phantom city as provisional as a film set.

These two theories describe aspects of the same delusional state, in which phantoms are a consequence of greed. From the start, Hollywood executives have tried to present themselves as purveyors of wholesome entertainment—they have generally succeeded—and no doubt these two theories are tinged with envy; yet they do contain an element of truth. For the only social structure analogous to Hollywood in its function is the brothel-saloon. Both of them operate, as it were, in a void; both cater in mass entertainment, in glamour, in a narcissistic titillation of the customer which ends in feelings of dissatisfaction; both trade in the decorative and in fantasies of disguise; and both, in attempting to appease phantoms of desire, create a thousand more.

It should be enervating; but fortunately throughout the twenties nearly all the major film-makers tried to resist the lure of the saloon and to return to the testings of the trail—to what Vachel Lindsay had called the hunger for tales of fundamental life. If the sense of unreality which many of them reflected in their work came from a denial of the damage done by greed, then the craving for tales of fundamental life was, possibly, an attempt to propitiate this guilt, a wish to uncover some touchstone or trace of conviction in themselves and their audience. Yet even within the confines of the mirror-reflecting saloon, an art was possible. It is possible to see how by looking at a remarkable film from the end of the silent era.

The Last Command (1928), Josef von Sternberg's fifth film, starring Emil Jannings, contains most of the principal trends of the 1920s cinema. Its title, the name of its leading actor, a summary of its plot,

Josef von Sternberg: *The Last Command*. Emil Jannings.

point to an imitation of Murnau's *The Last Laugh*, while its treatment and locations recall other styles of filming. An autocratic Hollywood director (William Powell) typecasts from photographs the subsidiary role of a White general for some forthcoming epic on the Russian Civil War. Extras, squabbling and miserable, queue for costumes. Among them is Jannings, a vagrant who is cast as a general and claims once to have been such a person. No one believes him; he might be mad.

Then Sternberg throws away this card—the best in his pack—and reveals that the extra was the Tsar's most trusted general. He shows Hollywood and the old regime to be in essentials much the same thing. Both of them, indeed, are created on the same Paramount lot and both of them are dominated by people who wish to keep up appearances: a concern for display so pervasive that it undermines any grasp on reality. A caption announces that Hollywood has become 'the Mecca of the world'; and the whole world, it would seem, mirrors Hollywood's tyranny. Sternberg describes this reflection through many kinds of visual parallel and irony. The general, for instance, has to summon men back from the front, at a moment when the White Army is under attack, so as to reassure the Tsar with a military inspection. His whole life is an act, not least when he has to interrogate two stage actors, a man and a woman suspected of being Bolsheviks. Brutally contemptuous of the man (whom we recognize as his future Hollywood employer), he struts before the woman, displaying his finery and power; while she, hoping to save her friend's life, pretends to respond to these advances.

Sternberg provides no alternative to the hollowness of this display. He is as hostile to Bolshevism and as reluctant to contemplate the idea of poverty as any White Russian might be. He lights Evelyn Brent (as the actress) and dresses her in such a way as to give her beauty an uncanny quality. Like her, the general wears a fur coat; but unlike the doorman in *The Last Laugh* his authority does not depend on the trappings of office. In his courage he outwits the actress and wins her love. He makes a similar conquest as an extra in Hollywood. The vindictive director orders him to play a general who leads his troops in a last charge. Seized by the power of memory, he rises to the occasion; but the excitement brings on a heart attack and he dies. The director, impressed by his authority, drapes his corpse with a (prop) Russian flag.

The Last Command is saturated with references to various styles of filming. It would be hard to think of these references as parodies or plagiarisms. Parody implies a response to something substantial and so, in most cases, does plagiarism. The baseless fabric of metaphor and irony built up by Sternberg exclude the likelihood of such a substance. The artifice of the settings, so finely realized, reflects a Hollywood pleasure in production values, but given an ironic edge. Styles for Sternberg are like the skins on an onion: peel them away and you are left with nothing. It would be misleading to think of the film as being in some way confessional, though Sternberg was as much of an exotic tyrant in his professional role as are his general and director. But it is always possible that he was putting on an act to impress his actors and to provide copy for Paramount's press office.

Born in Vienna and brought to the United States as a boy, he was plain Joe Sternberg until someone embellished his name for the credits of a 1924 movie on which he was an assistant director. His success with *The Blue Angel* and his long professional association with Marlene Dietrich then sealed the legend that he was a high-born German. The unreality of Hollywood entered the lives of its inhabitants at many levels. Faked genealogies changed names and improbable biographies were all grist to its mill. In such a confusion of identity, some sort of paternity was often called for, and Hollywood producers and directors often listed their pedigree at length in their memoirs, as though they were Old Testament patriarchs. *The Last Command* absorbs all influences like a sponge and neutralizes them. Hollywood operated in much the same way. By its importation of foreign talent and its careful remodelling of this talent so that even its foreignness looked synthetic, Hollywood represented the idea of a melting-pot society in its most extreme form. Even so, its unreality cannot be entirely accounted for in terms of this process or in terms of its liking for masquerade. The principal reason for it lay in the society to which it had become a Mecca.

'The war has set back the people by a generation,' said Hiram Johnson, an ex-presidential candidate in 1920. 'They have bowed to a hundred repressive acts. They have become the slaves to government. They are frightened at the excesses in Russia . . . The interests which control the Republican party will make the most of their docility. In the end of course there will be a revolution, but it will not come in my time.'[3]

The government had assumed emergency powers; and after the war, as Woodrow Wilson lay sick and incapacitated in the White House, a hysterical attorney general, A. Mitchell Palmer, had used these powers repressively. He had seen 'the blaze of revolution' sweep over America; and on New Year's Day 1920 ordered raids on radical centres throughout the country. Over six thousand people were rounded up. In the same year, two Italian immigrants of anarchist persuasion were arrested for the alleged murder of a paymaster in South Braintree, Massachusetts. Liberals were outraged by the unjust and protracted progress of their trial, but their demonstrations had no influence. Sacco and Vanzetti were executed in 1927.

A succession of Republican governments under Harding, Coolidge and Hoover encouraged business enterprises at the expense of social reform and economic planning. The notion of politics was lost in that of profit. A phantasmal situation came into being. 'Throughout the decade, profits rose over eighty per cent as a whole, or twice as much as productivity; the profits of financial institutions rose a fantastic 150 per cent,' states Arthur M. Schlesinger Jnr. 'As the Twenties proceeded, the stock markets sucked off an increased share of the undistributed gains of industrial efficiency.'[4]

And not only industry was damaged. As the rich grew richer, the poor grew poorer, especially the agricultural poor. The 1920 Census disclosed for the first time in American history that more people were living in cities than in the countryside. The neglect of the farming communities, especially of the migrant worker, was a question returned to again and again by film-makers from the 1930s on, but with little or no legislative influence. By 1929, writes Schlesinger, 'the 60,000 families in the nation with the highest incomes saved almost as much as the bottom 25 million. The mass of the population lacked the increase in purchasing power to enable them to absorb the increase in goods.'[5] It was to be a contributing factor to the stock market crash of 1929.

It was the age of advertising and ballyhoo. It was the age of the tabloids. 'There was more than a coincidence that as they [the tabloids] rose, radicalism fell,' claims Frederick Lewis Allen in Only Yesterday. 'They presented American life not as a political and economic struggle, but as a three-ring circus of sport, crime and sex.'[6] It was an age of hypocrisy. As often before, and since, selfishness masked itself as self-righteousness and greed concealed itself in religious cant. It was an age of moralists, some of them well-meaning, many of them less so. The Volstead Act of 1919, which brought in Prohibition and by doing so made fortunes for the bootleggers and raised the Mafia to eminence, was typical of this humbug. And so in his term of office as Coolidge's secretary to the Treasury was the career of Andrew Mellon, a multi-millionaire, who believed that government was 'just a business, and can and should be run on business principles'.[7] Mellon pleaded with the public to pay its taxes and, meanwhile, used numerous means (on secret information provided by the Commissioners of Internal Revenue) for avoiding tax himself. By 1926, reported the New York Times, members of his family had made $300m on the post-war market.

Hollywood, which had never shown itself averse to greed, was not immune from this spirit. Zukor had led the way into Wall Street, and the main companies were now reliant on either stock market quotation or corporate investment. A slump in 1920–21 cut down production in the film industry as elsewhere. The country was strike-bound; and the government insisted that film producers should enter the fight against Bolshevism: that they should show how America had helped the immigrant communities and how the poor could become rich. So the producers kept off the subject of poverty; they had already, in 1919, initiated a cycle of anti-Red movies. Other forces were at work. 'Under the inspiration of "making the world safe for democracy", Americans had surrendered nearly all their rights of personal liberty,' states Benjamin B. Hampton. 'The Federal government had supplied the most delightful opportunities to professional reformers and fanatics that these gentry had known since their ancestors gave up the pleasant sport of burning witches. After the excitement of the war days died down, these patriots had to find new fields of endeavour, or lose the emoluments and glory of their position.'[8] The cry was for film censorship. Mary Pickford's divorce from Owen Moore and marriage to Douglas Fairbanks, Roscoe Arbuckle's supposed manslaughter of Virginia Rappe, the murder of the director William Desmond Taylor and the death by drugs of Wallace Reid were inflated by the tabloids into national scandals. Finally in 1922, after a good deal of hesitation, some of the leading figures in the industry formed the Motion Picture Producers and Distributors of America Inc. to protect their interests. They invited Will H. Hays, postmaster-general to the Harding administration, to be president.

Hays used his influence to raise the standard of reporting on Hollywood a little (which is not to say much). He propitiated some of Hollywood's more aggressive critics. And he placed film employment on a more organized basis by setting up the Central Casting Agency. (Its licensing system at least discouraged prostitutes from posing as actresses when booked by the police.) But he also felt obliged to regulate the private lives of Hollywood personalities and to impose back-room pressure on the studios' choice of scripts. His interference unnerved an already timorous industry and was a further encouragement to hypocrisy. His views were finally charted in the Hays Office Code of 1930, a bizarre document that remained in force until 1966.

But the reformers of the early twenties had been aroused by more than Hollywood scandals. They had wished to protest at the kind of splendidly profligate behaviour represented in particular by Gloria Swanson on and off screen. In *Stardom* Alexander Walker writes: 'It was largely due to Cecil B. DeMille that she (Gloria Swanson) was projected as a way of life for people to follow with fascination, as well as a personality for them to pay to see in a DeMille film.'[9] Describing her ritualized *levée* at the beginning of *Male and Female* (1919), the first in a series of motion pictures in which DeMille glamorized the new licence, Walker refers to the various means by which DeMille presents his slumbering heroine as a prelude to the famous bathroom scene. 'The still invisible Swanson has the way prepared for her by maids getting the tub and douche ready, busily displaying outsize bottles of bath-crystals, king-size powder puffs, etc . . . Now Gloria rises. She lets the bed-wrap slide off her shoulders while the maids raise a towel to exclude the intervening gap of bare flesh.'[10]

Apart from William Randolph Hearst, who as a part-time film producer had employed the prestigious designer Joseph Urban and lavished a fortune on decorating films intended to promote the career of Marion Davies, DeMille did more than anyone to heighten a certain kind of production value—the kind that brought movies close to the values of the then rapidly-expanding advertising industry. He took painstaking care over fashions in dress, jewellery and hairstyling, in evolving new types of lighting—such as the so-called

Rembrandt lighting of *The Warrens of Virginia* (1915)—and in employing a top set designer (a childhood friend who had worked for
Belasco), Wilfred Buckland. For box-office reasons, his flair for luxurious effect became especially useful in the post-war years. Paramount needed some attraction to compete with the newly-formed
distributors' alliance First National, and Adolph Zukor was fully to
support DeMille's intentions.

Even so, the bathroom scene in *Male and Female* is not incompatible with DeMille as a latter-day Victorian moralist, for its imagery
might be derived from a painting by the Victorian academic painter
Alma-Tadema. The film itself is a straightforward, trenchant screen
transcription of J. M. Barrie's play *The Admirable Crichton*. Its bathroom sequence is no more than a brief interpolation into this play,
and so is Swanson's Babylonian dream (crueller than anything in
Intolerance). In hotting up the property, DeMille elaborates on it in
ways true to him. Barrie's story of how the social order is upturned
when some aristocrats and their servants are wrecked on a desert
island, and Crichton the butler is recognized as a natural leader,
becomes for DeMille an opportunity to describe (with some humour)
the virtues of fundamental life. At the end of the film he has Crichton
and the Tweeny find the classbound society of London intolerable
and depart for the United States. They are last seen as settlers, tending
their homestead, as enterprising as the kind of character Buster
Keaton was shortly to play.

It is less than amazing, then, that DeMille should have switched
from sophisticated comedy to religious epic. By 1922 public interest
in his type of comedy had waned; and he was to be disappointed
by the box-office returns on *Adam's Rib*. Soliciting photoplay ideas
through a newspaper competition, he was impressed by the suggestion that he should film *The Ten Commandments* (1923). In the event,
the treatment owed little to conventional views of the Bible. Its opening hour dramatizes Moses' conflict with Pharaoh, the flight from
Egypt, the parallel action of Moses' vision of the tablets and the building of the Golden Calf. Theatricality is on the grandest scale, with
masterly lighting and art direction sustaining large gestures; a succession of sharply etched and seemingly three-dimensional compositions suspend disbelief; while some of the miracles, such as the parting of the Red Sea, remain among the most impressive ever filmed.

In the second part of *The Ten Commandments* DeMille links, by often
ingenious parallels, a modern story to the events in Egypt; and his
involvement in this second part is intense enough to belie the argument that he took on this film to profit from the puritan backlash. His
father had been a dramatist and his mother a powerful Broadway
agent, and he and his brother William had been brought up as men
of the theatre. But the move west had developed another side to his

Cecil B. DeMille: *The Ten Commandments*. On location.

character: his manner of dress, his camping trips, his first Westerns and his country retreat named Paradise suggest that it nurtured in him the fantasy that he was a pioneer from the same mould as Moses. His mother died shortly before he began filming *The Ten Commandments*; and although his distress is evident, it assumed an unusual form. In the modern story Mrs McTavish, a fundamentalist, argues furiously against the progressive views of her sons. She pits the ten commandments against their belief in Elinor Glyn's ideas on sex — whose Hollywood career was promoted by DeMille. Mrs McTavish throws out her unregenerate son Dan, who becomes a master architect, an epic designer like DeMille. He jerry-builds a cathedral, which collapses, crushing his mother. Eventually he dies, infected by a disease caught from a Chinese girl, politely described as leprosy. The imaginative vitality DeMille brings to this subject, as in the collapse of the cathedral with its slowly-spreading cracks and shower of tainted money, and the circumstantial feel to his humour — Dan locks a portrait of his mother with her Bible in his drinks cupboard — demonstrates how immersed he was in a conflict between repressive piety and sado-masochistic eroticism.

Many of his critics have found this conflict distasteful and have tried to account for their distaste by calling him a hypocrite and mere showman; and in so doing have condemned, in a blanket fashion, a whole culture. For his conflict is basic to an understanding of Los Angeles and its film industry at almost any time in their history. Reyner Banham has remarked in his study of the city how

The first wave of immigration came from Kansas City on excursion tickets after 1885; later they came in second-hand cars out of the dust bowl. In one unnervingly true sense, Los Angeles is the Middle West raised to flashpoint, the authoritarian dogmas of the Bible Belt and the perennial revolt against them colliding at critical mass under the palm trees . . . Miraculously the city's extremes include an excessive tolerance.[11]

Such was the city where the hot gospeller Aimee Semple MacPherson had a box-office appeal comparable to DeMille's, a city which yet had, according to H. L. Mencken, the morals of Port Said. But there was no conflict in this contrast. The nonconformist puritanism of New England and the Middle West continued to flourish under the sun in the form of freakish cults and doctrinaire experiments in living. *The Ten Commandments* is the first West Coast epic. Sunbaked and bizarre, clinging over-tenaciously to fragments of European culture, it reveals by contrast how far *The Birth of a Nation* and *Intolerance* were imbued with the moral attitudes of the East Coast and the South.

The morality of both Griffith and DeMille had been sharpened by the casualties of the Great War. In Griffith it led to the messianic liberalism of *Intolerance*, in DeMille to an identification both with the permissive society engendered by the war and with a prudish belief in war as God's retribution for Europe's past sins: a belief in expiation that commanded the attention of more than the Hollywood visionaries and accounts for the appeal of one of Metro's great successes.

Scripted and for the most part produced by June Mathis, and directed by Rex Ingram, *The Four Horsemen of the Apocalypse* (1921) describes pre-war Paris and the exotic adventures of Julio, darling of the tango halls (Rudolph Valentino), with an expensive care that vies with that of DeMille; and then, with equal care, mounts battle scenes to destroy this luxury. Ingram and his associates were too close to the war to focus on it convincingly. They see everything in terms of excess. Like the earthquake in *San Francisco*, the war is seen to be God's punishment; at the same time, the Boche are shown to be satanic, like stereotypes from the wartime cartoons. Religious allegory —the stranger who might be Christ, the Dürer-like horsemen wavering across the skies—mutes any hint of sexuality.

The Four Horsemen conveys something of war's desolation. But it lacks any feeling for the fate of ordinary people. Trading in exoticism, it shields its audiences from any close sympathy with its subject. Valentino has to play a dream figure, Latin lover transformed into doomed hero. His sincerity and humour temper some of the improbabilities of his role, and he became a star. But for the few remaining years of his life he was shackled to this unreal type of characterization and to parlourmaid fantasies, such as *The Sheik* and *The Son of the Sheik*, based on Edith M. Hull novelettes, in which sexuality

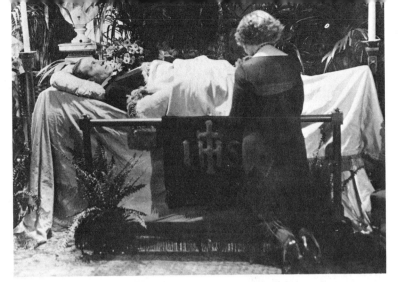

World-wide hysteria at the death of a star: Rudolph Valentino lying in state at the Campbell Funeral Parlour, New York; Pola Negri leaving Campbell's Funeral Church; mourners; the funeral procession moving up Broadway.

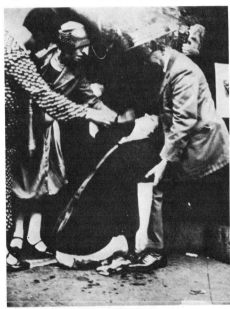

and pleasurable thoughts about death and flagellation were combined in a genteel fashion.

For in the Hays years, Hollywood films were far less frank than the novel or theatre, the press or popular psychiatry in describing intimate relationships. They continued to depict them in terms of spiritualized romance long after the temper of society had changed. Frank Borzage's *Seventh Heaven* (1927) conveys the tenderness of a love affair; it won three Oscars at the first Academy Award ceremony in 1928; yet though it was set in Paris, where screen convention allowed sexual taboos to be broken, it remained in sentiment as mystical and exquisite as *Broken Blossoms*. 'I work in the sewers but live near the stars,' says Charles Farrell of the garret he shares with Janet Gaynor—a slogan that converts the factory life of millions into a dream of the infinite. The corporeal nature of experience could only be implied. Hollywood favoured coyness; it seldom avoided some hint of prurience; and it welcomed Elinor Glyn as a godsend.

Lasky brought her, and a contingent of European writers including Edward Knoblock, Maurice Maeterlinck and Somerset Maugham, to Paramount in 1920 to bolster an exhausted script department. Since 1917, he and Zukor had been obliged to provide a turnover of 104 films a year to keep their cinema circuits busy, and though they had bought up the theatrical agency of Charles Frohman and the estate of J. M. Barrie, they had run short of stories. Elinor Glyn was the only member of the European contingent to remain any length of time in Hollywood. She stayed nine years and was responsible for the scenarios of ten films, many of them very popular.

Vain and dotty in appearance, Lord Curzon's former playmate charmed anglophile Hollywood by her knowledge of Edwardian upper-class life, and she shrewdly advertised sex in a manner acceptable to the American public. 'Her name is synonymous with the discovery of sex-appeal in the cinema,'[12] said Sam Goldwyn, recognizing her contribution to the consumer society. Her theory of sex was based on enthralment: seductive and tyrannical, its appeal to Hollywood was obvious. 'To have "It" the fortunate possessor must have that strange magnetism which attracts both sexes. There must be physical attraction but beauty is unnecessary.'[13] Fortunately Hollywood did not take Miss Glyn too seriously: she was part of the fun of the twenties, and Mae West guyed her ideas on stage. In Clarence Badger's *It* (1927), Miss Glyn herself appears, looking like some shady fortune-teller, and explains her ideas to guests in a nightclub. But most of the action is devoted to Clara Bow, as a shopgirl vivaciously flirting with her stuffy boss (Antonio Moreno), a Latin dressed like an Edwardian gentleman. In fact, *It* had nothing to do with free love— the boss rejects the shopgirl when misinformed that she has an illegitimate baby—and everything to do with trapping men in marriage. Clara Bow is so likeable an actress that she makes this intrigue appear natural, and the worship of muscle amusing.

If Elinor Glyn presented sexual sophistication in the guise of an Edwardian hostess, Erich von Stroheim presented it in the guise of a Prussian officer. Yet Stroheim's claim to stature is based not on his satirical comedies with their brutal, witty descriptions of the strange forms desire can take— not even on *Foolish Wives* (1922), the best of them—but on his excursion into a fundamental tale to end all fundamental tales, *Greed* (1923–4).

The unfortunate fate of this film is inseparable from Stroheim's conflict with the producer Irving Thalberg. The success of Stroheim's first feature as a director, *Blind Husbands* (1919), had made him excessively self-assured and he had become a tyrant on the Universal lot. His relationship with Carl Laemmle was friendly: but Laemmle had taken onto his staff a nephew, Irving Thalberg (who had contracted rheumatic fever at the age of seventeen and was to remain a semi-invalid until his death in 1936 at the age of thirty-seven), and Laemmle had been so impressed by Thalberg's gifts that he used to go off on business trips to Europe leaving the youth in charge of Universal City. Although fascinated by Stroheim's talent, Thalberg decided to curb his extravagance on *Foolish Wives* and to sack him as the director of *Merry-Go-Round* (1923). Stroheim moved over to Goldwyn, where he began shooting *Greed*. In the meanwhile, Marcus Loew, an exhibitor who by 1919 had partial or entire control over fifty-six theatres (whose programmes combined movies with vaudeville acts), had decided to move into production. He bought up Metro in 1920 and in 1924 took over Goldwyn, run by Frank Godsol, a sharp operator who had commissioned *Greed*—Sam Goldwyn, who had founded the company in 1917, had quit the previous year—and also Louis B. Mayer Pictures. Loew and Nicholas M. Schenk ran the financial side of the newly formed Metro-Goldwyn-Mayer from New York; Louis B. Mayer was senior executive at Culver City, formerly the Ince studios; and Mayer invited Thalberg to be his assistant chief.

It was a fortunate appointment. Thalberg was tactful, serious, quietly spoken. He knew how to deal with Mayer's unstable, perhaps psychotic personality. 'Next to D. W. Griffith, Thalberg was the greatest man in pictures,' said Anita Loos. 'If a picture proved a failure in the studio, he knew how to fix it.'[14] The studios had not taken kindly to time-and-motion studies, or to the well-paid advice of East Coast intellectuals and critics. Thalberg found ways, within limits, to organize this temperamental industry. He geared MGM to mass production of a high standard and largely he alone defined the characteristic MGM film with its team of stars, its sharp lighting and pace, its black and white clear-edged costumes supervised by Adrian and elegant settings supervised by Cedric Gibbons. But it is unlikely that Thalberg's talent extended beyond a feeling for timing, gloss and production values; unlikely that this mother's boy was sensitive to more than conventional good taste. Commercial considerations alone do not explain his failure to sympathize with the beautiful talent of Keaton, or with the obsessional insights of Stroheim, both of whom he broke; and he helped milk the danger out of the Marx Brothers' humour when they moved over to MGM in 1934. The industry grieved his death; he was the dutiful son prematurely lost; even so MGM's 'memorial' to him, The Good Earth (1937), could almost be a parody of his limitations. It takes up Depression themes explored by Warner Brothers in the early thirties and inflates them with production values and handsome landscape photography. Paul Muni and Luise Rainer give impeccably composed 'star' performances. For all that, it remains carbon-copy; it loses the rawness, edge and much of the vitality that other studios had discovered in these themes.

But Thalberg had some reason for preferring blandness and order to rude creativity. MGM had inherited two vastly expensive and unmanageable projects at the time of the merger: the epic Ben Hur, on location in Italy, and the twenty-four (already cut from forty-two) reels of Greed. Between 1914 and 1924 the cost of the average feature had risen from \$20,000 to \$300,000. Star salaries took up a sizeable part of this increased budget; overshooting and mismanagement accounted for too much of the rest. After months in Italy the Ben Hur unit had sent back rushes of a quality so mediocre that they had to be scrapped. Mayer sacked the director and some of the staff. He recalled the unit to Hollywood, where the project was completed by the end of 1925. From then on, Mayer insisted that productions should be kept within the studios, and he appointed supervisors to report on the behaviour of directors: a harsh, effective system. He delegated the problem of Greed to Thalberg, who fired Stroheim once more and cut the film to ten reels. Then MGM hired Stroheim to direct The Merry Widow (1925); he was under contract, short of money—and they needed his name. But again he could not curb his extravagance, and the production rocked under the threat, subsequently revoked, of his dismissal. His remaining work as a director took place far from Culver City. Gloria Swanson and Joseph Kennedy largely backed Queen Kelly (1928), while The Wedding March (1927) was backed by Paramount and Walking Down Broadway (1933) by Fox.

Greed runs for two hours, even in its ten-reel form. Thomas Mann claimed in the preface to The Magic Mountain that only the exhaustive is truly interesting; Stroheim also appears to have believed in the naturalistic doctrine that truth resides in covering the totality of events that make up a subject. He respected Frank Norris's novel *McTeague* and wished to adapt it as fully as possible. He also wished, like some muckraking journalist, to dig up all the facts, however unpleasant, about its characters and their environment. He enjoyed defying complacency and rubbing the nose of the American public in dirt: it was one way of breaking through social hypocrisy and reasserting the corporality of experience. In *Queen Kelly* Kitty, the convent girl, throws her panties into the face of Prince Wolfram, who takes this gesture as an invitation. In *Walking Down Broadway* a wind machine at a fairground excites two young women by blowing up their skirts. But Stroheim's ribaldry is often gentle. In common with Freud, he sees in sexuality something both higher and lower than the common understanding of it; typically so, in the scene where McTeague, the miner turned dentist, first recognizes his desire for Trina, while she lies in his dentist's chair, under anaesthetic, and coiffed like a nun. He is about to inflict pain on her; he could rape her; yet he kisses her tenderly.

Stroheim usually includes an unexpected surprise in his choice of incongruities. Trina's family might have stepped out of a Li'l Abner comic strip: Papa Sieppe wears *Lederhosen* and a small flag in his hunting cap; Mama is a monstrous Frau; and one of their twin sons is a bespectacled brat who wants to urinate at the least appropriate moments. But while at first the oddity of this family seems merely intended to amuse, another intention becomes plain when Stroheim films the wedding breakfast. He traps the spectator inside the vista of

Erich von Stroheim: *Greed*. The wedding breakfast.

family life and raises in him once more a child's panic at this prospect, while bringing to it an American sense of humour and openness, as well as all the rabid emphasis that German expressionism could muster.

Griffith, Ince and DeMille had used the epic to describe lofty national dreams and the behaviour of heroes. Stroheim reaches out for a different kind of totality; he turns epic into a compendium of the anti-heroic, devoting his encyclopedic attention to the manners of one section of the lower middle class and recording the unself-conscious garishness of a certain kind of popular taste. He was among the first knowing celebrators of kitsch. But his wish to take in the totality of experience became impossible when that totality included, as it did, the wilder forms of American landscape. He took on this extremity of experience when he shot the Death Valley sequences of *Greed*. He carried a pistol. The temperature wavered between 125 and 135 degrees fahrenheit. Two trucks were on hand to carry away the sun-struck and the heat-exhausted. 'Here we are, without law, without order and without restraint; in a state of nature, amid the confusing revolving fragments of elementary society,'[15] wrote Lansford W. Hastings in *The Emigrants' Guide to California and Oregon* in 1845. Stroheim captures such an awareness on film.

The Mormons, it is said, unloaded Victorian furniture from their wagons as they moved westward towards Utah, marking their passage across the desert with gigantic wardrobes and chests of drawers. In the same way, Stroheim's Death Valley locations could be seen to act as a criticism of the overstuffed sofas and kickshaws of the Sieppe home, as though one hell were burning out another. Fighting like prehistoric monsters in its wastes, McTeague and Marcus can achieve only one end: self-extinction. The desert proposes one totality, that of death. Compared to it, the gargantuan appetite of naturalism appears slight.

Stroheim's pursuit of totality depends on a power to make connections. Residues of his long apprenticeship with Griffith intrude at times. He turns Trina, less a victim of greed than of avarice, into Avarice, skeleton hands playing with a pile of hoarded gold. And with a Griffith kind of abstraction go touches of Griffith sentimentality: the kissing of a crushed bird is more appropriate to Lillian Gish than to his McTeague, Gibson Gowland, while the film's dedication 'To My Mother' is strange enough, considering the subject, to suggest a parody of Griffith. Another means by which he makes connections is more forward-looking as a technique: that of the deep-focus shot. He uses such shots to relate the interior of rooms to streets outside. McTeague's wedding in the Sieppe home takes place before an open window and the view of a passing funeral.

*

Greed comes from the same period as T. S. Eliot's *The Waste Land*, the first surrealist manifesto, Eisenstein's *Strike* and Chaplin's *A Woman of Paris*. The techniques of vaudeville, the squib and the cartoon, which poets had resorted to before the war to invoke the triumphs of technology, were now used to register disharmony. The centres of authority had shifted. Many conventions were to be called into doubt, new areas of experience to become available for exploration. If Stroheim thought the lower middle class worthy of epic attention, Eisenstein thought the same was true of factory workers and Chaplin of the proletariat. We need only look at the opening shots of Chaplin in *The Kid* (1920) to see why so many people thought this clown pointed the way to a new form of art.

As a founder member of United Artists, Chaplin was in a position by the twenties to script, produce and direct his own films; one of the few people in the industry to enjoy such autonomy. His work was to be self-regarding, and viewed as a totality it resembles a hall of mirrors reflecting only one image, that of Chaplin himself. Yet he was to be thought of as a social commentator and critic: a contradiction that resolves itself when we consider some of the factors contributing to his egotism. His slum childhood in Kennington had been appalling even by Victorian standards. He and his brother had been abandoned by their dipsomaniac father. Their mother had been periodically insane. The years in the halls (where his sensitivity was thought eccentric) and the swift rise to fame and wealth increased his egotism. Yet his talent depended on these experiences. The shock of poverty had provided him with a unique touchstone. (It is an assumption of our times that 'ultimate experiences' — of being in the concentration camps, facing death or living in the lower depths — provide a measure of all other experiences; much as in other times poets would gauge the truth of their sensations in relation to some concept of 'nature'.) Admirers were to think of Chaplin's art as being as much of a source book as nature itself; yet few of them had endured his suffering as a child, and when they tried to imitate him, they seldom achieved more than a mimicry.

The experience of poverty gave Chaplin an unusual insight into states of extreme wealth, and a number of his ideas depend on a comparison between his childhood past and his equally unbelievable present, as in the two contrasted plots of *The Kid*, co-directed by Chuck Reisner. One of these plots has a mother abandon her baby and then search for it in sequences that look as though they had been filmed in the more affluent suburbs of Los Angeles. The other has the tramp discover the baby and bring it up in locations that recall London slums of the worst kind. The quality of Chaplin's imagination, as he elaborates on the tramp's upbringing of the child, has nothing forced about it. The gags appear to be the product of loving rumination. They contain traces of wishful thinking, obviously, in the scenes where the tramp discards the baby and then retrieves it, yet this wishful element in no way softens a distressing situation. If Chaplin had been less schooled in the ways of extreme poverty, he would probably have been so shocked by them that he would never have thought of using them as a background to comedy. But he appears to have taken pleasure in recalling details of his miserable past. As a child, he had hungered after fame and recognition; as a rich and famous man, he looks back almost yearningly to the deprivation of his Kennington days.

A Dog's Life (1918), which is a prototype of *The Kid*, demonstrates how the natural flow of his invention depends on an eagerness to hold on to painful incidents evoked from memory. Its theme is starvation. The tramp fights a dog for scraps of food. It bites him; and he adopts it. Affection increases with hardship: impossibly, he tries to use the dog as a pillow. The tramp's hunt for food—it could be a horrific theme—has a cockney wit and vitality about it as he tries to jump a queue, escape from the police, rob a stall-holder or challenge propriety. At a dance-hall he places the dog in his trousers, then registers mock embarrassment as its tail, hanging out, thumps a drum. *The Kid* puts more weight on the horror of poverty. At his first appearance, the tramp looks grim-faced. Someone throws garbage at him. We see a close-up of his hands wearing torn gloves; in a genteel fashion, the

Charles Chaplin: *The Kid.*

hands open a tin containing cigarette butts. The lighting is harsh. Most of the objects are cast-offs: a worn-down pair of boots, ancient chairs, dilapidated prams, dustbins, rubbish. The tramp's lodgings, the street corner, the church mission and the dosshouse are all oppressive; and brick walls spread everywhere as though the district were a prison. Inventions subsist on threadbare surroundings, and their energy depends on an economy of means. The kid breaks windows, the tramp follows in his footsteps as a glazier. Chaplin's wit transforms the world without changing it. When the tramp dreams, his dream resembles a Victorian oleograph. Bewinged children, dressed in gauze, fly about like pantomime angels; yet they remain trapped within brick walls.

The tramp plays both father and mother to the kid, much as Chaplin had done with his younger brother. And the tramp's pleasure in bringing up the child is placed in contrast to the mother's anxious search for it, as though his pleasure were derived from her anxiety. His encounters with women remain distant; he is as courteous as a gentleman, as delicate as the Gish sisters. He idealizes prostitutes and turns little girls into angels. It was all very different from Chaplin's own past. Middle-class gentility had little sway in Kennington. Sexuality in all its forms, especially child prostitution, was a salient feature of working-class London in the nineteenth century.

Chaplin had modelled the tramp on Pierrot, the unrequited, pining lover, and he was probably afraid to disturb audiences too much by breaking away from this convention, though it reflected only one part of his personality. But he was to find a temporary release from the tramp when he wrote and directed *A Woman of Paris* (1923),

Charles Chaplin: *A Woman of Paris*. Adolphe Menjou. Edna Purviance.

which concerns itself with prostitution and which has, as its protagonist, a philanderer who could not be more unlike the tramp. Rich and upper-class, the philanderer sees women as sexual objects. Ruthlessly active in his relationships (whereas the tramp tends to be passive), he conquers and discards women at will. He remains triumphant throughout the action. In the forties, Chaplin shocked audiences when he played the part of Monsieur Verdoux, an extreme variant of the philanderer type. It would probably have ended his career if he had taken on this kind of role in the twenties; as it was, *A Woman of Paris* made a star of Adolphe Menjou.

In the meanwhile, the convention of the tramp's sexual innocence could only be maintained by removing him from the real world. *The Gold Rush* (1924) takes place in one of the most abstracted locations imaginable: a Pudovkin kind of hut in the Arctic wastes. It was as though Chaplin had taken the slum apartment of *The Kid* and literally wiped out the city around it, leaving nothing but a snowy white screen. In *The Kid* the tramp had been like an elder brother to

Charles Chaplin: *The Gold Rush*. The tramp, left at base of picture.

the child. In *The Gold Rush*, Chaplin reverts to the pre-1918 two-reelers and has the tramp terrorized by a bad big brother. The theme of starvation inspires him. He draws just about every analogy possible out of the scene where the tramp cooks and eats an old boot. At times, his interest in food looks like a displacement of other emotions. The tramp cooks a meal for a girl, as though he were a girl trying to impress a beau. Seeking to impress her, he sticks forks into bread rolls and has them dance like two feet.

By the time he came to direct *The Circus* (1928), Chaplin had moved entirely into psychological symbolism. He no longer wears shabby clothes; his garments are beautifully tailored. The tramp has become a Platonic idea, a transcendental tramp, and the events in the circus an allegory for the agonies suffered by an artist. As the silent period came to an end, Chaplin's procedures began to resemble those of Sternberg and Murnau: content becomes schematic and surfaces highly wrought.

*

Charles Chaplin: *The Circus.*

Film historians (Huff, Weinberg and others) have stated that the allusive style of *A Woman of Paris* transformed Hollywood comedy. The passing of time has blurred this distinction: it now appears less of a novelty than part of a trend. In 1920 William DeMille had pre-figured its shrewd ironies in *Conrad in Quest of His Youth*, a semi-parody of Paramount's favourite playwright, J. M. Barrie. Conrad back from the war invites four childhood friends down to his English country house to relive their nursery games. But the beautiful girl he had once loved has grown into a plump matron; and she and the other guests, who have also lost their childish appeal, flee after a dismal night. The narrative dexterity of *Conrad* is precocious for its date; where it appears immature, compared to *A Woman of Paris*, is in its Barrie whimsicality. Conrad, a Peter Pan plunged into the adult world, invites a woman to his bedroom and falls asleep while waiting for her.

A Woman of Paris has more in common with certain Soviet films than with most Hollywood comedies. Chaplin places little weight on the plot's central contrast between the quality of life in rural and metropolitan communities and stresses its implied contrast between poverty and riches. A Pudovkin hardness enters into the scene where Marie Saint-Clair (Edna Purviance) quarrels with her protector, Pierre Revel (Adolphe Menjou) and throws a string of pearls he has given her out of the window, then rushes down into the street to seize it from a passing tramp. And the insistent references to swaddled bodies—the transvestite at a party wrapping himself tightly in a woman's gown, Marie cocooned in a masseur's sheet or swathed in complicated garments and hats—foreshadow one strand of imagery in *Storm over Asia*. Yet, typically, Chaplin describes wealth—and sexuality—in terms of food. The nature of Marie's and Pierre's relationship first emerges at an expensive restaurant, where some of the patrons are gigolos and most of the waiters are snobs; its end is signalled by the scene where Pierre eats chocolates without offering one to Marie. Chaplin's distrust of pleasure only relaxes momentarily. His Paris is as febrile as the film colony. Everything is precarious. One scene, in which a young man commits suicide at a party/orgy, is perhaps revealing of Hollywood at the time of the pre-Hays scandals.

Henri d'Abbadie d'Arrast, one of Chaplin's assistants on *A Woman of Paris* and *The Gold Rush*, conjured up a more recognizable French capital in *A Gentleman of Paris* (1927). No wilderness beats at its door and, apart from the obligatory happy ending, no Hollywood anxiety about moral impropriety disturbs its tone. Its plot gives a fresh twist to the tale of Don Juan: a butler serves his philandering master, a marquis, faithfully until the day when he learns that the marquis has seduced his wife; he then has his master drummed out of society by framing him as a cheat at cards. Candid about duplicity and grave about escapades, d'Arrast does not attitudinize. His matter-of-fact filming avoids the innuendoes of Lubitsch's *So This is Paris* (1926). Characteristic of his tone, which depends on glances and implications, is the scene where a prospective father-in-law meets the marquis for the first time, recognizes him as a philanderer and accepts the situation in a worldly manner, while making it plain that these adventures must stop once the marquis has married.

Hollywood and its audiences put Paris and London in the same category as Griffith's Babylon, finding in them a notion of civilization (or, rather, of sophistication masking itself as civilization) both to be desired and condemned. Like Aaron's Gold Calf in *The Ten Commandments* or the saloon brothels of the Wild West, Paris and London were self-destructive as well as seducing. They bred social graces, certainly, but these graces bred in turn an effeminacy and hypocrisy of a fineness to be envied. Ultimately, the European metropolis, as Hollywood saw it, was a mirror image of Hollywood itself. Chaplin's identification with the underdog and Griffith's sympathy for the starving Germans of 1918 implied an alternative. Yet the Hollywood studios never drew the most striking factual comparison of all: between the economic condition of the cities and the country.

With reason. Few American farmers profited from the boom years; indeed, rural poverty grew worse during the decade. Hollywood in the early twenties had no time for the depressed subject. Perhaps farmers had no time for it either. They were almost the last sector of the public to be converted to film-going. The cheap, mass-produced Ford T allowed them and their families to drive into town for an evening at the cinema: machine locomotion supporting machine entertainment. In 1919 they would have seen, in Griffith's *True Heart Susie* and the Charles Ray parables, as idealized an image of themselves as the one DeMille was presenting of the urban upper middle class.

Yet the country qualities idealized were the civilizing virtues of honesty and renunciation, not consumer greed. *The Hired Man*, an Ince Production of 1919 directed by Victor Schertzinger (who later turned to Paramount musicals), has Charles Ray as Ezry Hollins, a desperately poor, good youth working for a rich farmer so as to save up enough money to go to the State Agricultural School. Ezry is the kind of hero who will not appear in American movies again until the Depression: worried-looking, skimpily clothed and embarrassed by poverty. He falls in love with the farmer's daughter and attracts the spite of the farmer's son. Schertzinger's shaping of the story as an Old Testament fable, and Charles Ray's modesty, give the advantage to puritan virtue. The biblical allusions—to Jacob and Esau and, in the final fire sequence, to the tribulations of Shadrach, Meshach and

Victor Schertzinger: *The Hired Man*. Charles Ray (left).

Abednego—are not overstressed: rural audiences, brought up on the Bible, would have picked them out without difficulty. Nor are they forced. The hardness of existence, the intensity of family life, the patriarchal father, the sense of adventure give substance to moral austerities of a copybook kind, while the well-photographed openness and spare light of Wyatt County appear in keeping with an Old Testament view of nature as a test of the human spirit.

By 1921 this idea of nature had mellowed. Henry King, director of *Tol'able David*, looks on the Virginian landscape of his youth with eyes adjusted to the abrupt sensations of city streets and sees it as idyll. He draws a pilgrim's progress out of country life, as Schertzinger had done, yet ignores the hard grind of farming routine. Joseph Hergesheimer's story describes an adolescent crisis of universal and therefore vague application. David might be a tourist, or dryad, removed from the specific circumstances of the labourer. Ezry had wished to improve his condition so as to escape from the drudgery of being a hired man, David merely wishes to prove himself without the slightest idea of how to do so. ('You're not a man yet, David—just tol'able, just tol'able'.) Providentially, three convicts break into the farm owned by his family and give him the chance to recognize his own strength. But his struggle with them seems to be a shallow piece of theatricality in comparison with the rest.

King creates a pastoral atmosphere with a skill that Pudovkin admired (and described inaccurately); it has the effulgence of happy

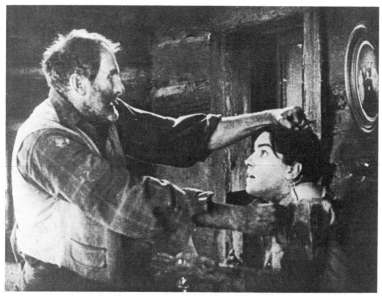

Henry King: *Tol'able David*. Ernest Torrance, Richard Barthelmess.

memory. At the same time he encouraged the process of converting images of the countryside into an advertiser's dream: even the biblical recall (in a title) of David's battle with Goliath is like the slogan to an advertisement. Richard Barthelmess's performance as David adds to this impression. Swinging on a six-barred gate, fooling with his dog Rocket or playing with his straw hat, he conveys spiritual radiance. But he has too much the presence of a star. However barefooted he may be, he looks in no way pinched by poverty; and his Ivy League face seems less suitable to a hick than to a Scott Fitzgerald character. He bodies forth an American myth about the pastoral swain, or flower-power child, based more on Leatherstocking legends than on observation: a myth that became fact, however, when it was acted out in the sixties.

Buster Keaton was to fit into this pastoral role more easily; its implicit comicality and humour suited his temperament. Very much the good son, he was devoted to his father, and the quality of this relationship underlies a good deal of his inspiration. In memory he was to recall the hard childhood years touring in vaudeville as happy ones, and perhaps his later interests as a film-maker in trains and dreams of a secure homestead were shaped while on the road. Like most comedians, Keaton derives humour from playing out childish misconceptions within an adult frame. But his humour also depends on a cool nostalgia for an America he had never known. *Our Hospitality* (1923) begins in New York, no more than a huddle of sunlit shacks in 1831, while *The General* (1926) disposes excellently of the furnishings and manners of the Civil War. His unusual approach to familiar problems suggests the initiative of the first American settlers, even when the action takes place in the present. He recognizes how similar are the perplexities that confront the pioneer and the small boy faced by a new range of experiences. And he knows how to realize the charming idiocy of the solemnly one-tracked person, so engaged by one problem that he misses other, more urgent concerns: the young man in *The General* is so busy chopping wood on the train fuel carriage that he fails to notice he is riding into the enemy lines. His humour often has an Alice-in-Wonderland logic about it, as though lunatic problems always required lunatic solutions. Rollo Treadway, the millionaire in *The Navigator* (1924), is like a helpless infant until he and his girlfriend are left stranded and alone on a vast liner. He rises to the challenge. By the time he has finished opening a can of meat he has reduced it to pulp; when he tries to boil two eggs in a pan fit to cook two hundred, he fumbles, breaks the eggs and burns his hand. He refuses to accept defeat, or to arrange the kitchen to suit his needs: instead of discarding the gigantic pan for a smaller one, he teaches himself to remove eggs with a claw made up of two spoons attached to a complicated system of ropes and pulleys. He opens cans of meat with a handsaw gently set in motion by the two stone wheels of a corngrinder, which he operates with a foot pedal.

The kitchen might have been built for voracious giants. Yet Keaton is never frightened by it. In one scene he and the girl think there are ghosts on board, but the humour is reassuring. Machines are seldom experienced as menacing in his films. He responds to the unexpected as though it were inevitable. A cyclone whirls him through a deserted town in *Steamboat Bill Junior* (1928). No father or girl friend stand by to help as a hospital bed carries him along. Horses neigh over his head; a tree lifts him over swollen waters; ponderous doors, pushed open with difficulty, turn out to be parts of fragmented, collapsing façades. He accepts it all in a matter-of-fact manner. Buildings frequently tumble when he is around. He sometimes can be seen pinned against Kafkaesque walls pocked with blank windows. Objects take on an unpredictable life, as though warmed by a juggler's hand. None is more appealing than the first American steam-engine in *Our Hospitality*, with its fragile chimney, vast wheels and carriages like Cinderella stage-coaches, thinned, it would seem, to fit the narrow gauge.

His nostalgia for the past usually has a contemporary reference. It avoids whimsicality. New York in 1831 has a traffic jam. Keaton, in a White Rabbit top-hat, footing along on a wooden bicycle without pedals, has to stop at a crossroad, while a sheriff grandly signals a

Buster Keaton (centre): *Neighbors* (1920).

cart to pass by. Sennett's team had been hectic about man's involvement with technology. Keaton engages with the same theme steadily. His stability marks him out. He has a wide-ranging attachment to the natural order of things: a dependence that illuminates his motto 'make it real'. He was determined not to fake gags, even though he often risked his life in carrying them out. Like Griffith, he tried to be accurate in reconstructing the past. When asked why *The General* gave a more convincing picture of the Civil War than did *Gone with the Wind*, he answered: 'Well, you see, they based their film on the novel. I went back to the history books.' On the whole, he imitated the Griffith of *The Birth of a Nation*, not *Intolerance*. When he parodied the structure of *Intolerance* in *Three Ages* (1923) his principal joke did not hinge on its obvious failings, but on changing conceptions of marriage: the Stone Age and Roman heroes end up with a trail of children, modern man and his wife with a terrier.

An idea of the family and its identifications lies behind his wish to make it real. *Sherlock Junior* (1924), for instance, proposes a guide to how security may be found in an agitated industrial society. Keaton appears as a film projectionist, who models himself unsuccessfully on the great detective. Estranged from his girl friend, he falls asleep while at work and dreams that he enters the film on view. Eventually he manages to master the rhythm of its changing locations and outbids Holmes in a bravura chase. His girl friend wakes him and he kisses her, taking a lead from lovers on the screen.

Perhaps Keaton placed too great a reliance on the idea of the family. At the time of the original American pioneers, a man could integrate himself within the tightly-knit community: an opportunity less available in vaudeville, and even less so in the distrustful atmosphere of big business in the twenties. Remarkably, Keaton had such an opportunity. In 1920, backed by Joseph Schenck, he opened his own studio (Metro and United Artists handled his releases). He was able to create a family situation in which he could coordinate his powers. As an actor, he had an athlete's grace: his timing and his acrobatic leaps and falls were perfect. As a director, he had a gift for seeing how the camera could relate harmoniously people, objects and landscape. For a while at least, the good son had reason to believe he could trust his paternal surrogate, benevolent Joseph Schenck. But in 1928 Schenck was induced to hive him off to his brother Nicholas at MGM, and Keaton was faced by a different kind of paternalism. He had some bruising encounters with Thalberg and the MGM supervisors. Projects were blocked or so tampered with that they lost all quality. In a sense he had been betrayed: by Schenck, and also by his wife, who left him as his fortunes declined. His drinking bouts and his collapse, as reported by his biographer Rudi Blech, are painful to read about. At the end of his life his achievement was to be recognized; but the damage done, and the years lost, were irreparable.

Obviously, corporations, bureaucracies and industries tend to dehumanize their employees. Keaton's retreat into the smaller community of the family was both a temperamental and necessary expedient. In the twenties, studio policy-makers were probably right in believing that the public was blind to the brutalizing nature of a technological society. King Vidor had great trouble in selling the scenario of The Crowd (1928); his producers thought no one would understand this study in dehumanization.

Certain intellectuals, admittedly, were articulate about the theme of alienation. Harold Lloyd (who joined the producer Hal Roach in 1915 and stayed with him until 1925, when he branched out as an independent) may seem to have agreed with them. His locations are usually urban. His humour relates to the anxieties of a mechanized society, and he appears to have been less wild in his feelings about technology than the Sennett team. But his pallid, bespectacled face is really the mask of organization man. He lives in a seemingly dan-

Harold Lloyd: *Movie Crazy* (1932).

gerous environment of skyscrapers, ladders balanced on fulcrums, cars, trains and trams—which, in fact, he controls and manipulates coldly. He uses machines functionally, seldom enjoying or demonstrating their beauty. He is often safe when he seems to be in despair, as when he cries for help as he dangles from a ground-floor window. He may win the girl in the end, but it is the winning and not the girl who matters. Going abroad in *Why Worry?* (1922), he looks like a gullible tourist, yet it is he who organizes the revolution and shows up the natives as foolish. A perfect example of the time-and-motion studies man, he discovers a geometry, and virtue, in absurd behaviour. By accommodating himself to the machine, he becomes the machine.

Tales of fundamental life were the alternative to this machine art. Yet no American film-maker appeared willing, or capable, of bringing together these alternatives. It has been argued, for instance, that Robert Flaherty's picture of the generous, enterprising Eskimo in *Nanook of the North* (1922) was intended to imply a criticism of Western civilization. But Flaherty did not have this bent of mind. He spent most of his life far away from urban stress, and in the twenties his criticism of technology is implicit to the point of being invisible. John Grierson, who coined the term 'documentary' for Flaherty's second feature *Moana* (1926), wanted him to turn to the problems of industrialism; Flaherty was unable to see his filming in this way. Eventually, in *The Land* (1940), he was to consider the problem of land erosion, the bleak landscape of the dust-bowl. But he was unable to edit his rushes into a formally coherent statement. His work during the twenties contains tensions that had not been defined. Grierson felt undefined tensions of a perhaps different sort. He wanted documentary to be a lyrical re-creation of pre-industrial life and, at the same time, a kind of hard-fact journalism: a contradiction that was to become pressing in the thirties, when poets wished to commemorate the supposedly organic societies that technology was destroying and at the same time to celebrate industrial and utilitarian virtue.

Flaherty was born in Michigan in 1884. His father had worked for various corporations as manager of an iron-ore mine and prospector, and it was one of his father's employers, Sir William Mackenzie of Mackenzie and Mann, who first sent young Bob in 1910 to explore for iron-ore on the east coast of Hudson Bay. He made a number of hazardous journeys to this part of the world and came to know well the Arctic coastline and the people who lived there. At Sir William's suggestion, he took a camera with him on these expeditions and eventually assembled his rushes into what has become known as the Harvard print. Perhaps fortunately, the negative of this print was destroyed in a fire: it could not be duplicated; and Flaherty soon learnt from showings of his one remaining print (which has since been lost) that his friends thought his outsider's view of the Eskimoes uninforming. He recognized that if he wished his subject to take on its own life, he would have to negate his preconceptions about it. He decided to return to the North and to set up a feature film about the Eskimoes, in which the Eskimoes would take an active part as makers as well as actors.

It was an expensive way of working. Without conscious prescription, Flaherty would film anything that captured his imagination, then screen his rushes many times until he began to observe a form in them. The process was slow and anguished and must have been especially difficult for his cutting-room assistants. One of them, John Goldman, who edited *Man of Aran* (1934), has written: 'His feeling was always for the camera. This wanting to do it all and through the camera was one of the main causes of his great expenditure of film — so often he was trying to do what could *not* in fact be done.'[16]

Flaherty saw himself as the servant of his material; he declined to be a God-like creator. He said of the Eskimoes: 'I have been dependent on these people.'[17] They showed him how to live under intolerable conditions; they saved his life; and, on a lesser level, one of them was able to repair his stills camera after he had dismantled it and left the pieces in despair. *Nanook of the North* was among the first films made by a cooperative, an urgent game played by Flaherty and his Eskimo friends to re-create the spirit of the Arctic. His 'participatory camera', stated Jean Rouch in a lecture at the British National Film Theatre, was very similar to Dziga Vertov's use of the camera, though probably neither of them knew of the other's work.

The notion of fabrication is essential. Nanook had to build a uniquely large, unroofed igloo to light the interior scenes. He and his family had to discard their everyday Western clothes for authentic Eskimo costumes. And as certain critics pointed out at the time, the seal Nanook pulls up through a hole in the ice had clearly been dead for days. On such grounds many of them dismissed the film as a fake. But they missed the point. Flaherty was not trying to compile an anthropologist's case history. He was not trying to be the clinical and detached observer. He was trying to show how filming was something else than the record of fact (Grierson called documentary 'the creative use of actuality')[18]: how it needed to include the fantasies and poetry which suffuse experience and give it meaning. He was trying to project a beauty which was more than scenic; a beauty to be found in the generosity and courage which certain men reveal under stress; and this beauty had to be reconstructed. The making of *Nanook* was in itself a struggle for survival and an exhibiton of such virtues. It may not be a film about film-making, but it does enact the duress of its own coming into being.

This making involves us on different levels. There is Nanook's complicity with the camera, both with us and with Flaherty. At moments he and his family deliberately try to entertain us. Eskimo upon Eskimo improbably climb out of a kayak; a Sennett gag revivified by its exotic surroundings. The family ribs us for having assumed that Eskimoes must be naïve. When Nanook bites into a gramophone record, or his son swallows castor-oil with an amused grimace, the joke is gently on us. These capers establish Nanook as real to the audience. (And he became widely loved; during the twenties you could buy a 'Nanuck' soap.) We are probably more influenced by bio-

Robert Flaherty: *Nanook of the North*.

graphical information about screen favourites than we would like to admit. *Nanook's* open structure invites this sort of knowledge; it is a becoming; it enters our time-stream; and part of this knowledge is the poignant fact that Nanook died of starvation two years after the film's completion.

Flaherty's camera does not watch him from a near view throughout. We see him afar in the fishing scene, a small dark shape against the white vastness. By establishing Nanook's personal warmth, Flaherty is able to have us feel his isolation. By emphasizing his ceaseless making of objects, he brings out the more strongly his lack of material resources. We may be fascinated by Nanook's skill in assembling an igloo. At the same time we recognize that this apparently solid building is one of the most transient imaginable. As the final scene shows, the only permanence in these wastes is the destructive power of nature. Nanook and his family are caught in a storm and retire into a deserted igloo for the night. A wind picks up and deposits snow on the reclining huskies, until finally they are no more than a grave-like mound.

Nanook of the North opened on Broadway in June 1922 and was so popular that Jesse L. Lasky invited Flaherty to direct a South Seas feature on similar lines. Flaherty worked on *Moana* for three years. He found it hard to modify his presumptions about Samoan life; kept changing his intentions; threw away a good deal of his filming as bogus—and made discoveries. Up to that time everybody had used orthochromatic stock, a black and white film insensitive to certain colour tonalities. Film-makers considered panchromatic stock, which registered these tonalities, too unstable for general use and relied on it for sky shots alone. Experimenting with this stock, Flaherty saw that it defined the texture of the dense Samoan foliage and brought out the modelling of semi-naked bodies. He used it throughout the film, and the richness of his panchromatic photography led, in turn, to its adoption throughout the world.

Moana, like *Nanook*, concentrates on man as a maker and hunter, absorbing the spectator in a sustained long shot of the boy Pe'a's dangerous climb up a coconut-tree and finely edited close-ups of women preparing meals or shredding bark into thread. Like *Nanook*, it reveals an understanding of the sympathy between hunter and hunted and, at its best, moves into semi-abstract imagery: divers glimpsed beneath limpid yet wrinkled sea water, an outrigger canoe swaying against towering, slowly falling waves. But *Moana* has all the marks of a transitional film. Its pot-hole sequence looks like a sketch for the storm in *Man of Aran* and its panning shots over foliage for the water-lily sequence in *Louisiana Story*. Its style is soft-edged, like a poem whose only cohesion is the poet's temperament. It remains tantalizingly elusive about the islanders, their customs and the way they run their community. Its large Gauguinesque close-ups on Moana's face fail to strike up any intimacy with this remote personality. The climactic sequence shows his being tattooed and initiated into tribal manhood, yet it does not bear the thematic weight Flaherty intended for it.

Partly through bad promotion, *Moana* grossed only $150,000. Flaherty's association with Hollywood was almost over. He worked with Thalberg on a project that came to nothing. He joined Murnau on *Tabu*, but his contribution to it was slight. In 1930, he and his wife left for Europe. He had disappointed Lasky commercially, though Lasky had been interested in his work from more than a commercial point of view. The ex-vaudeville showman had, when young, taken part in the Alaskan gold rush and often joined up with DeMille on trips into the wilds during their early Hollywood days. The pioneer way of life held little appeal at the box-office in the early twenties; it was an experience which the public wished to escape from. Yet Lasky clearly thought of himself as a pioneer—which, so far as Hollywood was concerned, he was—and, as well as supporting Flaherty, boldly sponsored the feature travelogue *Grass* (1925). Earlier he had backed James Cruze in making the first Western epic *The Covered Wagon* (1923), at a time when interest in the Western had been on the wane.

Grass, directed by the explorer Merian C. Cooper and photographed by Ernest Schoedsack (the team responsible for *King Kong*), was a success and travelogues—which Martin Johnson had been compiling since 1912—became a vogue. (Cooper and Schoedsack produced *Chang* in 1927 and *Rango* in 1931.) Its principal interest now lies in its perhaps unconscious echoes of *The Covered Wagon*. The forgotten tribe's trek eastward in search of grass (verdure, not drugs) reverses the journey westward of Cruze's pioneers, while the crossing of the Karun river on goat bladders competes, as a spectacle, with Cruze's wagons as they plunge through water.

The Covered Wagon is also concerned with actualities and facts, though William S. Hart was to complain about its inaccuracies. He thought some of its errors—a wagon train corralled in a blind box-canyon in hostile Indian country, its cattle neck-yoked as it swam across a river—were so serious that they 'would make a Western man refuse to speak to his own brother'.[19] The present-day moviegoer will probably think that its locations had been chosen to stir the historical imagination. Some of its props, like the walnut bureau discarded before a river crossing or the tripod frying-pan, have been used since, but seldom so evocatively.

James Cruze must have come into contact at one time or another with people who had known the first settlers. (He was born in Utah of Danish parents.) But *The Covered Wagon* looks like an antiquarian reconstruction of the West, intended to appeal to the city dweller. Ince and his company had worked within the frontier atmosphere and their Westerns gave a concrete, partial report on it. Now such a West was lost; it could only be revived in spirit. 'It was looked upon, for the first time, as a totality cut off from the present; and therefore, as an ideal to be longed for instead of a reality to be utilised and feared,'[20] writes Erwin Panofsky, describing the change from the medieval to the Renaissance view of ancient Rome. *The Covered Wagon* marks a similar change in consciousness. It has defects: too much time spent over a love triangle, with the girl dressed to the nines, and a promised battle with the Indians that turns out to be disappointing. Even so, projecting an image of the West that has none of the strained ingenuity of some later variations, it presents a myth potently and with grandeur: the wagon line stretching across the dusty plains, the lonely scout with his two Indian wives at Fort Bridger, the Indians massing for a charge, the feeling for different terrains as the pioneers move 'from Kansas to Oregon across to Wyoming' and then up into the snowy Rockies. Its largely non-professional cast adds to this sense of verisimilitude.

By 1927 Cruze was the highest-paid director in Hollywood, earning $7,000 a week. Yet he was never again to enjoy the success of *The Covered Wagon*. And its impact was to be overshadowed by that of another Western epic, John Ford's *The Iron Horse* (1924).

Born in 1895, Sean O'Feeney, alias John Ford, had come to Hollywood in 1913 to work with his brother Francis as a general dogsbody at Ince's studios. He was appointed a director shortly afterwards, his name appearing on the credits as Jack Ford. *Straight Shooting* (1917), his first feature, shows how he had learnt everything that could be learnt from Ince and Griffith (he had been one of the Klansmen in *The Birth of a Nation*): a mastery of melodrama and of the documentary type of Western, an ability to place figures in a landscape so that neither overwhelms the other, a sense of composition that can be picturesque and yet generate momentum. Ince had ordered his directors to follow the script meticulously, Griffith at most had worked from notes. Ford usually compromised between these two methods. He observed his scripts to the letter (necessarily so, in Hollywood), yet he directed sequence upon sequence that no printed word could suggest.

He bridged the difference between these two methods by excavating the basic situations that recur in most scripts, so that his fairly inflexible response to homesteads, heroes, bar-room clowns, the history of America or the relationship between senior and junior ranks emerges whatever the subject. Audience pleasure depends greatly on recognizing these Fordian traits. At such moments, though, he appears to expect the spectator to enter unquestioningly into his Flaherty-like reveries. His disregard of any fact that might weaken his fantasies about Ireland or the pioneering American spirit has carried him through a fifty years' period of achievement almost unparalleled in the most interfering of film industries.

Four qualities—all of them present in *Straight Shooting*—save him from emotional rigidity. At times, his sense of humour becomes a folksy kind of horseplay that so disturbs the convention of his stories that they have to be seen as mixed genres like Irish kitchen comedy; yet at times it can be gentle enough to dissolve any trace of the obsessional. During the silent period *Three Bad Men* (1926) gave this sense of humour its most free rein, though *Straight Shooting* has its moments—as when, for example, Cheyenne Harry (Harry Carey), a wanted man, peers out of a tree-bole on which a notice for his arrest has been nailed. An elegiac strain in his temperament also softens hardness. Many of his films pivot on a scene of mourning. Cheyenne Harry steps out of a wood into a burial-ground where an old man is bent over the grave of his only son. Harry's eyes fill with tears: an effect which Ford registers in one shot, startlingly, by blurring the lens of the camera.

His awareness of grief is bound up with his unequivocal and childlike admiration for heroes. But the characteristic which most marks him out from his predecessors is his ability to dramatize the easy-going. Ford understood how film could register better than any other means the bar-room pleasure of observing faces disinterestedly and of enjoying the passing moment for its own sake.

On the evidence of *Just Pals* (1920), which resembles *The Hired Man* and Borzage's *Lazybones*, and is not half as good as either, his work in the early twenties was uneven. With *The Iron Horse*, though, he rises to the challenge of a majestic subject: the building of the Union and Central Pacific Railway, America's first transcontinental railroad.

John Ford: *The Iron Horse.*

It sings of progress, power and the subjugation of an alien landscape and an alien people, the Indian. Yet typically, Ford qualifies enthusiasm with memories of grief. Many years before, Dave, the leading engineer on the enterprise, had buried his father, murdered by the Indians while surveying for the railway. Ford gives this theme of the dead father a national stature by pointing out how Lincoln had ratified the railroad contract shortly before his assassination. Both the father and Lincoln are like Christs sacrificed to save mankind: the father's blood sanctifies the building of the railroad, as Lincoln's blood had sanctified the union of the States. Lincoln's presence was to brood over many of Ford's films until the time when he made *They Were Expendable* (1945), when it was replaced, if only temporarily, by another kind of tutelary deity, General MacArthur. But Ford has never played down the fearsome side to Lincoln's character, the iron man of destiny, and he does not conceal the brutality required to tame the land and the Indians.

Like Cruze, he loses momentum with his love story, a predictable rivalry between two men over a girl. And like Cruze, he quickens

John Ford: *The Iron Horse.*

interest whenever he brings in historically accurate information, as when he alludes to the different ethnic types among the navvies or refers to the herds of cattle brought 800 miles to feed them. More importantly, he excels Cruze in the sensitivity of his imagery (George Schneiderman and Burnett Guffey were his cameramen), especially in his dynamic comparisons between man-made objects and landscape. His railroad track stretching out to the horizon is a motif so strong that it seems to tame nature in many of the compositions. He composes his images more tightly than Cruze. One shot has a solitary telegraph pole rising out of the desert, a geometric form that stands in contrast to the irregular shapes of nature and, like the incomplete church tower in *My Darling Clementine* (1946), foreshadows the civilization that will populate this barren space.

Ford takes possession of this alien landscape more suggestively than Mack Sennett or Douglas Fairbanks had done. He does not use his actors as acrobats or see the whole world as a circus. He remains true to the restraints of Ince and Hart. The swashbuckling tradition entered the Western with Tom Mix, whose gear and manner have only an attenuated connection with actual cowboys. Yet Mix had his virtues. In Lewis Seiler's *The Great K & A Train Robbery* (1926), cliffs tower over a seemingly miniature train as it steams through the Royal Gorge, Colorado, in a manner that Ford might have appreciated. Mix exploits the dimensions of the gorge with a verve more appropriate to Buffalo Bill's touring two-ring circus. He belongs to a tradition, central to the silent screen, that includes Douglas Fairbanks Senior, the Biograph neck-to-neck chases and the gags of the more athletic comedians.

Like a growing child, it would seem, the American cinema had to exhibit its mastery over the physical world before it could begin to approach problems of a more subtle kind. The movement into epic was at first a movement into extended adventure story, melodrama or romances concerning heroes of noble birth: claims rendered more complex by King Vidor's *The Big Parade* (1925), an epic about American soldiers in France during the First World War. Vidor recognizes how a uniform can depersonalize. He views the soldiers in Laurence Stallings's story as a group and brings out the representa-

King Vidor directing the final scenes of *The Big Parade*.

tive nature of his central character, Jim Apperson (John Gilbert). At the same time he runs head on into all the difficulties that attend any attempt to realize that hypothetical entity, democratic man. He fails to dramatize the idea of democracy, for his generalizations are too imprecise to be other than bland.

He emphasizes his generalizing intentions by, on the whole, limiting his camerawork to middle-distance and long shots. Yet this allows him to sustain a sweet and slow-moving lyricism and a low-keyed humour exemplified by the scenes in which Jim first sees his French girl friend from inside a barrel, or woos her with the help of a pocket dictionary, or receives a cake from home so stale that he virtually cannot saw it apart. In place of a marked rhythm in editing, Vidor substitutes, with some success, the inflection of rhythm within the shot: the tempo of men scrubbing shirts by a stream, shovelling, sweeping out a courtyard and, above all, the metronomic beat implied by their silent marching. The final battle scenes, which Thalberg had reshot in as spectacular a style as possible, reveal night panoramas of luminescent smoke, spiralling flares and a syncopation of shell-bursts that phantasmally conveys the din in the fields of death. Perhaps Vidor underplays the cost of war—Jim escapes from it with no more than the loss of a leg—but he did establish a manner of treating the subject that reappears in Milestone's *All Quiet on the Western Front* (1930), Hawks's *Sergeant York* (1941) and even his own *War and Peace* (1956).

Perhaps the most impressive of these silent war films was William Wellman's *Wings* (1927). Wellman had flown with the Lafayette Flying Corps during the war and later had acted with Douglas Fairbanks. A brief episode in *Wings*, the death of Cadet White (Gary Cooper, in a minute role that brought him to stardom), reveals how his feeling for the physical could gather to it the power of myth. The shadow of a plane passes over the airforce camp: a few scenes later we learn of the cadet's death in flight. The plane's shadow prefigures death; a plane actually brings about death; and yet, as the story suggests, this recent invention fulfils the cadet's youthful potential. His last flight embodies the Greek definition of action: it perfects his life as well as ends it.

One of the titles in *Wings* refers to 'the dreams of youth'. In the twenties Hollywood titles often referred to the dreams of youth, but Wellman's understanding of dream has nothing to do with the ethereality of Hollywood romance. He understood, at least intuitively, how adult life can interfuse with the experience of childhood. David (Richard Arlen), about to go to war, enters his parents' sitting-room. He picks up a small teddy-bear, a childhood toy which is now a mascot, from the floor. The camera pans upward to disclose that

William Wellman: *Wings.*

David's father is confined to a wheelchair. Wellman contrasts the crippled father with the athletic son, but by the teddy-bear suggests that David's skills as a pilot are rooted in his earliest relationships. Later Jack (Charles Rodgers), David's rival for the favours of Mary (Clara Bow), accidentally kills him in air battle. David's parents face Jack like judges as he brings them back the teddy-bear. Wellman's tactful recognition of our inability to escape from our past gives his flying sequences a poignancy lacking, say, in the more spectacular dogfights of Howard Hughes's *Hell's Angels* (1930). Leaving the virtue of machines untarnished, Wellman shows the aggression to lie elsewhere.

*

In 1926 F. W. Murnau came to Hollywood. He made *Sunrise* (1927) for William Fox, returned briefly to Germany and then signed a five-year contract with Fox, which was ended prematurely by a quarrel. Yet before his death in a car accident, Murnau had managed to direct *City Girl* (1928, not released until 1930) and *Four Devils* (1928), both at Fox, and *Tabu* (1931) at Paramount. *Sunrise* and *City Girl* can be seen as a diptych. Murnau was fortunate in having Carl Mayer as his screenplay writer and Charles Rosher as his cameraman on both projects. The way in which the films mirror each other largely depends on the creative give-and-take of this team.

Both plots depend on the bold thought that you virtually have to murder your lover before coming to realize the extent of your love. Both rely on a comparison between the country and the city. 'To equate good with rural life, evil with the urban, was by now a nostalgic exercise,' wrote Eileen Bowser in a programme note on *Sunrise*; and she mentions how, at its New York premiere in the Times Square Theatre, 'there was shown one of the early Movietone News shorts, in which Benito Mussolini made a speech to America.' With Mussolini and the gangsters around, allegories about good and evil were liable to seem attenuated.

Although Murnau was by inclination a city dweller who had dissociated himself from his peasant origins, and although his style tended towards the representative rather than the specific, he was hesitant about drawing any schematic moral comparison between the city and the country. The studio-built Chicago of *City Girl* has more in common with the streets of an UFA production than with the trading centre of the Middle West, and the remarkable city in *Sunrise*, set in some unnamed European country—it is, presumably, the Tilsit of Hermann Sudermann's story *A Trip to Tilsit*, on which the film is based—owes more to the imagination of its designer, Rochus Gliese, than to any actual place. Murnau was not interested in criticizing social conditions. If this Chicago is dirty, overcrowded and disconcerting in the sameness of its mass-produced goods, he shows it to be so in order to establish the loneliness of the lovers before their first meeting. The city girl, a waitress, works in a cafeteria where food is prepared with conveyor-belt impersonality. At home overhead trains thunder past her bedroom window; she tends a wilting plant on the sill. And though she is freed in certain ways by her journey to the Oregon plains, she discovers that life there also has its limitations. In different ways she is threatened by her in-laws and by the local farm workers.

In *Sunrise* Murnau may begin his story by equating 'good with the rural life, evil with the urban'—he shows the countryside at its most idyllic and describes the means by which a city vamp (Margaret Livingston) almost breaks up a happy rural marriage—but he soon

F. W. Murnau: the opening scene of *Sunrise*.

turns the equation on its head. The husband (George O'Brien) tries to murder his wife (Janet Gaynor) by drowning her; the plan misfires; she runs away, and he follows her onto a trolley-car that climbs a hill by the lake. In no more than ten shots, Murnau describes the husband's change of heart by placing the couple before the trolley-car windows and through the windows showing the lake, with a boat on it, swayingly give way to the sky. It is one of the most ecstatic sequences ever recorded; and Murnau sustains his lyricism into the next sequence by abruptly plunging his couple into the bewilderment of a fabulous city. The city girl had found Chicago intolerable; the *Sunrise* couple, on the contrary, rediscover happiness through the dazzling enchantments of the metropolis.

In design, this city resembles certain Bauhaus projects, but the feelings Murnau derives from it depend on at least two other models. One of them, familiar from UFA productions—and *Sunrise* has some claim to represent the ultimate refinement of the *Caligari* style—is the fairground. The lovers visit a fairground at night, where miniature planes pivot above them and a roller-coaster seems to float on air. These abrupt sensations and mingled movements carry over onto other locations: the whirl of traffic and the bustle of crowds in streets, the spatially immeasurable tea-room with its mirrored walls or the glass-domed railway station. In certain scenes Murnau includes dwarfs among his extras—they might be straight out of the fairground—to increase the illusion of perspective.

The other reference is to nature which, as Murnau envisages the countryside—with a huge Caspar David Friedrich sun, reflections in the lake and dissolving, dreamlike water—arouses sensations similar to the fairground aspect of the city. But with one important difference: whereas the city had dramatized the lovers' sentiments by echoing their mood, the countryside counterpoints their feeling by contrast. The benign nature of the troubled opening scenes, in which the husband plans the murder of his wife, capriciously changes its temper as the lovers, at peace with each other, return home. A storm whips up on the lake and almost succeeds in fulfilling the husband's abandoned wish to drown his wife. Like Chaplin's *City Lights*, *Sunrise* has the power to grow in the memory because the often sacramental typicality of its symbols—flowers, water jugs, etc., which Murnau in a church scene relates to the symbolism of the wedding service—carries beneath it a complexity of allusion and antithesis.

The highly selective realism of many Hollywood silent films in the late twenties, which included Chaplin's abstraction, Murnau's illusionism based on the principles of movement and Sternberg's shrouding of the image in layer upon layer of light and shade, could not have been achieved without the streamlining of the studio system in all its departments; and a mention needs to be made of all the craftsmen behind the camera who brought contrivance to such a peak of sophistication. Hollywood costumiers had the difficult task of anticipating public taste (often by years) as well as of creating clothes that would look striking within flamboyant sets; and the departments run by Howard Greer, Travis Banton and especially Edith Head at Paramount, or by Gilbert Adrian, a New Yorker at MGM noted for his designs of sharply silhouetted black and white gowns, contributed greatly to the glamour which the public had come to expect of major Hollywood productions. Their flair was equalled by the superb art direction supervised by Hans Dreier at Paramount, Cedric Gibbons at MGM and William Cameron Menzies at United Artists. High standards existed in every department of the leading studios: in lighting, editing, quality of prints and, not least, in the skills of make-up, which the firm of Max Factor had perfected. Hollywood had become like H. G. Wells's fantasy London of the future, domed against the vagaries of weather. All roughness and pain could be smoothed away, and almost any dream realized.

Until 1926, box-office figures suggested that audiences were satisfied by the standard feature; and though there was an increasing elaboration in the treatment of stories, no one appeared to want a dramatic change. Even the architecture of cinemas remained much the same. The New York Roxy, principal new cinema of the period, completed in 1927, owned by William Fox and managed by an astute promoter, Sam Rothapfel, differed only from its decade-old prototype in luxury, the Strand, in being larger and more ornate in its furnishings. Many important technical advances appeared at this time, which in subsequent years were to transform the movies; but during most of the 1920s, studio executives and the public alike thought of them as no more than isolated novelties. In 1915 Herbert Kalmus and his associates founded the Technicolor Motion Picture Corporation. In 1918, however, DeMille claimed that no one would wish to strain their eyes either watching or making feature-length films in bright colour (as opposed to having their prints coloured by tinting, toning and other gentler means); and although a number of two-process colour films were produced, the best-known of them being Douglas Fairbanks's *The Black Pirate*, they remained exceptions. The importance of colour remained unappreciated, and many of its difficulties left unresolved, until Walt Disney began to apply it systematically to his animated cartoons in the early 1930s. Del Riccio at Paramount and other inventors had evolved CinemaScope and Cinerama, but as so often with technical discoveries in the cinema it needed a crisis, the 1949 box-office panic over television, to encourage the studios to incorporate different widths of screen and different kinds of camera and projector lens into their schedules.

Experiments in colour and wide-screen viewing go back at least to Edison and Lumière, and so do attempts to marry sight and sound. Lee de Forest's silenium tube, invented before the Kaiser's war, provided one solution to the problem of amplification, and his phonofilm of 1923 demonstrated how light waves could synchronize sound and image. Many engineers and electrical companies were working within this area of research. The Germans evolved Tri-Ergon, the best recording system of all; and if their movie industry had been less recurrently hit by slump, could have produced quality sound films early in the decade. As it was, a number of films ran sound sequences, and Griffith's *Dream Street* of 1921 contained some recorded songs. William Fox bought the patents on Tri-Ergon and on an American recording system, Case, and in April 1927 launched Fox Movietone News ('movietone' being a type of sound film). Warner Brothers, who owned a Los Angeles radio station, were associated with Bell Telephone in developing the Vitaphone record system, and in August 1926 released *Don Juan*, starring John Barrymore, with Vitaphone sound effects and music score. But these experiments aroused little more than curiosity. Why then did Warners' *The Jazz Singer*, with its handful of songs and few snatches of incidentally recorded conversation, cause such a furore in October 1927?

Based on a play by Samson Raphaelson, *The Jazz Singer* sets out to assault its audiences' emotions—which it did, and which it still does.

Jakie Rabinowitz is intensely attached to his mother and he rebels against his cantor father by singing popular songs in a public bar. After repeated strappings by his father, the boy runs away. A few years later, as Jack Robin, a leading vaudeville performer, he returns home to share his success with his mother, only to have his father drive him out once more. But they are reconciled at his father's deathbed, and Jack gives up a first-night appearance to stand in for his father at the Passover service. *The Jazz Singer* is too much of a good thing: it drives the spectator through an Oedipal situation, the pangs of self-assertion, the bitter-sweet consequences of success, the anguish of stage loyalties and the difficulties of ethnic assimilation (Jack not only abandons orthodox Jewry but appears on stage with a blackened face). It universalizes its themes by levelling them down to show business values; and, in retrospect, audiences may feel tempted to agree with the reviewer in *Picture Play* (January 1928) who described it as 'second rate'. But in the face of its attack, critical gradings of any sort seem irrelevant.

The welcome extended to sound was related to a change in taste. The public was becoming jaded; it wanted movies with some edge to them. DeMille had amused it with the promise of sex and luxury. Now it wanted something stronger. In the thirties, Warner Brothers were to be best known for their gangster films and musicals: genres that trade in urban grit and demotic fantasies and appeal to audiences by their verve. The emotional attack of *The Jazz Singer* relies on its use of sound; but it is unlikely that audiences would have come round to the view that soundless movies were in some important respect disabled if its theme had been less aggressive.

It shifts between old and new expectations. During the sound scenes it is hard not to feel that its settings—the threadbare

Alan Crosland: *The Jazz Singer*. Al Jolson.

Rabinowitz apartment, the seedy dressing-room, the tawdry streets, locations remote in feeling from DeMille's dreamy bagnios—focus suddenly into a new conception of realism. We do not need to look far to understand why, at moments, it seems to prefigure the sadness and honesty of the Depression movie, for its music, though a synthetic jazz, puts us in touch with the voice of Negro anguish, a voice that was to break into the cinema the next year in *St Louis Blues*, through the tormented pure tones of Bessie Smith. Al Jolson's Jack Robin embodies a similar immediacy. With his blazing eyes and pallid face (when blackened it becomes in negative, as it were, the traditional clown's mask, concealing heartbreak) and—above all—fervent voice, he slams over his role with an intensity that annihilates scepticism. Few would argue that *My Mammy*, or *Toot, Toot, Tootsie, Goodbye*, or even Irving Berlin's *Blue Skies* were consummate examples of the songwriter's art, but in Jolson's rendering of them they might be the quintessence of the lyric spirit.

Throughout the twenties the four Warner brothers—Harry, Sam, Albert and Jack—had been hampered by a lack of capital. Their credits were not dishonourable. In 1924, for instance, they had produced *Main Street, Babbit, The Marriage Circle, Kiss Me Again* and *Beau Brummel* with John Barrymore in the leading role. But according to Jack Warner, animal performers alone saved them from bankruptcy: gorillas, tigers, chimpanzees—and Rin Tin Tin. The public demand for sound aroused by *The Jazz Singer* and their all-talkie *Lights of New York* (1928) brought them such wealth and gave them such an advantage over their competitors, who had not anticipated the need for expensive recording and amplifying equipment, that they swiftly became one of Hollywood's leading studios and were in a position to buy up a large number of the cinemas on the First National circuit.

Their competitors followed them as quickly as possible in adapting their studios and cinemas to sound, and by 1929 the change-over had virtually been completed. Warners fortunately had raised a loan to cover the cost of installing new equipment during the time of the Wall Street boom that had preceded the stock market crash. Their competitors, on the other hand, had to buy themselves into a market that had already attracted the more financially secure corporations of Wall Street, many of whom indirectly controlled the patents on the equipment the studios most needed. They were forced, in particular, at a time of scarce money to obtain equipment from the two companies most interested in taking over the film industry: Western Electric, a subsidiary of the American Telephone and Telegraph Company, almost entirely controlled by the J. P. Morgan group and holding assets of $30 billion, and RCA Photophone, a subsidiary of RCA of America largely controlled by the Rockefeller empire through the Chase National Bank.

INDIRECT DEPENDENCE THROUGH SOUND EQUIPMENT CONTROL

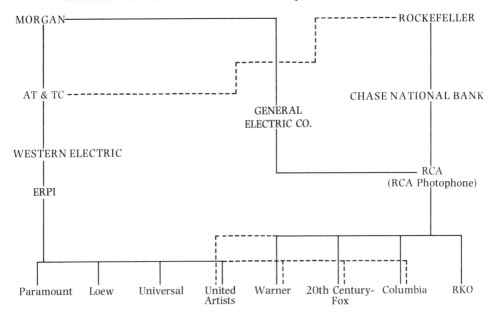

DIRECT FINANCIAL CONTROL OR BACKING, 1936

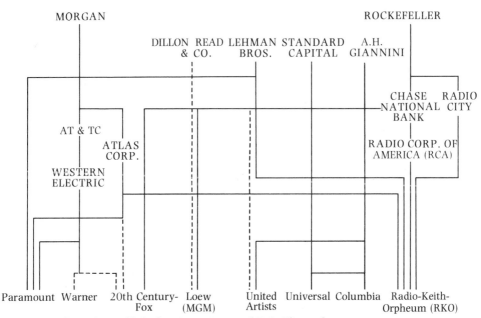

Charts first published in Stuart Legg and F. R. Klingender, *Money behind the Screen* (1937).

The decade-old struggle between RCA and AT&T over radio had now moved into the field of the cinema. RCA joined forces with Joseph P. Kennedy, father of a future president, to form the new film company Radio-Keith-Orpheum (RKO), while AT&T joined forces with William Fox to sell their sound-on-film system to MGM, Paramount, United Artists and First National. 'The adoption of sound led to the emergence – after violent struggles – of a new patents monopoly very nearly as complete in fact, if not in form, as the old patents trust of the pre-war years,'[21] state F. D. Klingender and Stuart Legg in their 1937 report on the structure of the film industry, *Money Behind the Screen*. By 1929 'all the pioneer executives, except William Fox and Carl Laemmle, had allowed the financial control of their enterprises to slip out of their hands into those of their backers. As yet, however, the latter were recruited in the main from the leading investment and merchant banking houses and did not include, except indirectly, the peak figures in the American financial oligarchy.'

Upton Sinclair Presents William Fox, one of the few books to lift the veil on the financial dealings of Hollywood and the East Coast business corporations, brings to life the bitter significance of this struggle for power and property. Admittedly Sinclair, a disgruntled Marxist, has his axe to grind and wastes no opportunity in pointing out the uglier side to Wall Street practices, compared to which the smart operating of the Hollywood tycoons looks ingenuous; even so, his chronicle is circumstantial enough to ring true.

Fox's picture-making policy had been shrewd. By 1929 his company was valued at $200m and his chain of cinemas at $50m: wealth enough to attract the attention of predators. Sinclair does not hesitate to suggest that his bankers and part-backers, Halsey, Stuart and Co., engaged in a conspiracy with AT&T to strip his wealth.

Marcus Loew had died in 1927, and Mrs Loew wished to sell her $50m block of shares in Loew Inc., the holding company which included Metro-Goldwyn-Mayer and 200 theatres among its assets. Encouraged to make this purchase, Fox only later learnt that it covered no more than a third of the voting rights in Loew Inc., and he was impelled to raise another $20m to buy a more substantial vote in the company. The prospect of gaining an empire – Loew Inc. not only owned MGM but had a stake in Paramount – seems to have gone to his head, for on the promise of financial support by AT&T he invested a further $20m in a take-over of British Gaumont with its chain of 300 cinemas. He was up to his neck in liabilities. His enemies now revoked their promises to underwrite him and, with support from the Rockefeller empire, had all the banks closed against him. Fox was divested of his company in 1930, went bankrupt in 1936 and was gaoled in 1942, allegedly for having tried to bribe a judge. He died in 1952.

Part Three: The 1930s

8. *Adapting to Sound*

The Symbolists, who had played such a strident role in the aesthetic debates at the end of the nineteenth century, had fought a rear-guard action to secularize religious awe. They had tried to give the integrating function ascribed to religion some meaning in an age of dissociation by seeing art as sacred, its practitioners as seers, and its products as icons veiling some mystic truth. The cinema challenged these attitudes. It communicated by technological means. It attracted the attention of a mass public; it throve on movement; it assaulted the sensibility. Each of its narrative developments—editing, camera movement and, above all, the close-up—carried with it an increase in shock.

But within twenty years everything had changed. Cultivated spectators, conditioned to the aggression of film narrative, tried to justify their pleasure in it by giving it prestige. In much the same way as Marinetti had built a shrine round the machine, so these spectators attempted to appropriate the values of 'art', or secularized religion, for the movies. They were willingly assisted in this activity by the pretensions of film-makers: the competition between Pathé and Gaumont to excel each other in grandiose enactments of Christ's life, the Film d'Art productions, the 'artistic' Italian epics, the cloudy handling of humanist themes by D. W. Griffith, the temple-like picture-palaces built on Broadway. From the start, too, film-makers had been unable to avoid the conventions of traditional art—Henri Langlois has observed that Louis Lumière's sense of composition has the same kind of instinctive coordination as the paintings of Auguste Renoir. They were compelled to filter the elements of actuality at their disposal into accepted forms; and the limitations of the silent screen stimulated this kind of refinement. When Iris Barry argued that the cinema should have begun with the talkies and then evolved into an art of silence, she was voicing a widespread opinion about the ways in which the cinema could be allied to an accepted understanding of art.

By the end of the silent era the feature film had developed into a form so sophisticated that present-day filmgoers are liable to think

King Vidor: *Hallelujah*.

of its types of narrative as bewildering. The paradoxical need to tell stories without speech forced story-tellers into an extreme stylization. Screen actors trained themselves in a sign language as flexible and yet as unlike ordinary behaviour as the styles of the Kabuki theatre. Captions seldom reported dialogue and, like the narrative sections in an idyll by Tennyson, were usually descriptive; they acted as a mediation, or chorus, between the audience and the images. The structure of this story-telling, in spite of its wholesale borrowings from the theatre, was closer to the ballad, the epic poem and the fairy-tale than to drama.

Strikingly, those parts of its syntax which had formerly given the most shock were among the first to be rendered into a convention. Editing, camera movement and the close-up were seen to be, by the originality of their effect, the essence of film narrative: those elements which separated it from other forms of expression. In exploring the implications of this syntax, the film-maker began to give it the sort of hieratic purity that the Symbolists had once demanded from art. The close-up, probably the richest discovery of the silent screen, reached its most impressive use as the silent age ended, in Carl Dreyer's lingering scrutiny of Falconetti's face. And Falconetti, of course, was playing Saint Joan: the approximation to the icon could come no nearer.

But as the coming of sound soon revealed, the remoteness of the silent screen mostly arose from its inability to dramatize huge tracts of recent public experience. The Hollywood film of the twenties only occasionally touched on the contemporary pulse of the United States. In the early years of the new decade, some of the studios tried to put this right. Sound allowed them to employ talented people whose gifts had previously been unusable, and who had built reputations in the theatre or on radio: comedians like Mae West, W. C. Fields and the Marx Brothers; singers and dancers like Ruby Keeler, Joan Blondell, Eddie Cantor and Fred Astaire; straight actors like Bette Davis, Katharine Hepburn, James Cagney and Spencer Tracy; directors and choreographers like Rouben Mamoulian, James Whale and Busby Berkeley. Many of the films that now seem to define aspects of the thirties had been popular novels or plays of the previous decade.

But this dependence on the past had a more intimate meaning. Again and again the more vital of the thirties movies had, as a mainspring, the theme of a return to the past. Mervyn LeRoy's *Three on a Match* (1932), typical of this surge in retrospection, examines the ways in which the success and failure of three women in their adult relationships and professions is related not only to childhood circumstances but also to the idiom of the twenties. An opening sequence of newsreel and headline shots, intercut with scenes of the

Mervyn LeRoy: *Three on a Match*. Bette Davis, Joan Blondell, Ann Dvorak.

women as girls, suggests that LeRoy and his associates, though they felt it intensely, were unable to give this connexion a logical explanation. They seem to have been aware that they were handling experiences new to the screen, experiences that had never been articulated before. Having no precedents, they had to work largely from intuition. And also, perhaps, with a sense of foreboding. As the title of the film implies, with its reference to a wartime superstition, the fate of the three women is bound up in some indefinable yet nagging way with the events and outcome of the 1914–18 war.

One of the most remarkable features of the early Warner Brothers sound movies is that they released energies that had been long repressed. The First World War had stirred up aggressions both murderous and, in the case of the suffragette and labour movements, constructive. The political conservatism of the 1920s had, for the most part, curbed these aggressions, so that greed and guilt had taken on the bizarre forms of Prohibition. bootlegging and the rise of organized crime. LeRoy's *Little Caesar* (1930), for one, opened up this area of psychic disturbance. Its exceptional popularity demonstrates the relief it brought to the public; and yet, like the amnesiac who recovers his powers of memory too quickly, its release of suppressed material probably gave more trouble than had been anticipated. The material was volatile, and no recognized genre or technique existed by which it could be contained.

In Raoul Walsh's *The Roaring Twenties* we can see how film-makers, even as late as 1939, were straining to find some form or convention for this theme. An opening sequence attempts to relate the leading heroes and villains of the pre-war years—Roosevelt, Mussolini, Hitler—with the Kaiser's war, Woodrow Wilson's signing of the peace treaty in 1919, and the bootleggers of the twenties. But the meaning of these connections, though deeply enough felt, is never defined. A contrast between James Cagney as the good gangster and Humphrey Bogart as a vicious one implies by its very nature that gangsterism, when backed by loyalty and frankness, can be condoned, if not praised. The spectator is left in doubt about whether he should view gangsterism as heroic, futile or comic. Walsh's attitude to his material is volatile. He seems to have sensed that there was no clear mode by which it could be channelled, that it was continually in a process of self-transformation; for though his ostensible aim is to review the twenties through the career of one bootlegger, his real theme is to recall, in the minutest detail, the motifs and devices by which his colleagues earlier in the decade had sought to pin down the elusive phenomenon of gangsterism. He compiles an anthology more evocative of movies in the early thirties than of the earlier period in which his subject is for the most part set.

This struggle to give form to experiences previously inaccessible to American film-makers, and the consequences of this struggle, is one of the two principal characteristics of many films made in the early thirties. The other characteristic was the urgency with which the past was explored, the insistence of its underlying question: 'What went wrong?'

By the spring of 1930 at least four million Americans were unemployed: by 1931 this figure had risen to eight million, and by 1932 to at least twelve million. Though Hollywood did not begin to approach the question of what went wrong with an answer that would satisfy the historian, it was able, through sound, to provide a wide spectrum of response to the Depression. It began to convey a sense of community. Rueful and brash, its ruefulness and brashness were anchored in the practicalities of making a living; and though it tantalized itself with the dream of a quick fortune obtained without effort, it did try to dramatize the theme of work. The collapse of trust in authority had been severe, and the individual could no longer pursue his interests without some awareness of how the society about him functioned. Hollywood found itself compelled to reflect, often in a confused way, both the anxieties of the Depression and the subsequent defence against these anxieties, the recrudescence of nationalism.

Certain countries in Europe had already experienced the effects of a breakdown in industrialism and a loss of national purpose, and some of them had invited a solution of the most extreme kind to these problems. The placatory peace treaty making of the twenties had been replaced in these countries by an undisguised belligerence. By 1930 Mussolini had already signed a concordat with the Papacy. Authoritarian governments were in power in Spain, Portugal, Hungary, Austria, Yugoslavia, Poland and Lithuania. Stalin had consolidated his position in the Kremlin. The Nazis won 107 seats in the Reichstag during that year, and the French began to build the Maginot line. The influence of the Depression, and of this increasingly aggressive nationalism, affected the tone of film-making everywhere.

A familiar theme was to be man's relation to the land, whether to the good earth or to the dust-bowl. William Empson's *Some Versions of Pastoral*, first published in 1935, obligingly catches an association of ideas in the air at this time. Empson demonstrates how pastoral can level political complexity to the simplicity of rustic wisdom—a levelling that can also seed its own kinds of complexity:

> The feeling that life is essentially inadequate to the human spirit, and yet that a good life must avoid saying so, is naturally at home with most versions of pastoral; in pastoral you take a limited life and pretend it is the full and normal one, and a suggestion that one must do this with all life, because the normal is itself limited, is easily put into the trick though not necessarily to its power. [1]

In the movies, Empson's kind of pastoral—it is often citified—emerges in the musical, in the cult of the proletariat, in the self as child and the child star, in the agrarian myth Leni Riefenstahl hoisted around the Führer and in the Socialist Realist demand that heroes should be positive. It is not surprising that a decade in which *Blut und Boden* and *Lebensraum* were impatient slogans should have begun in Pagnolism and ended with Scarlett O'Hara's affirmation that courage lay in a handful of soil.

This down-to-earth attitude was bound up with the swift changeover to talkies. It came into being before the Depression. Sound opened the floodgates to experiences that, in former years, had been accessible only in part, when filtered through the conventions of the silent screen. There was no longer any need for this refinement and transposition—the source of art, its admirers claimed. New conventions were required, but these were to be slow-yielding and even slower to be acknowledged. Moreover, until the Hollywood studios discovered the value of pre-recording and dubbing (which took time: they had to invent the moviola first), they were forced to register sound on a Vitaphone record during shooting and so found it impossible to control the quality of recording: fluffs, mistimings and the accidental cough could not be edited out, and the microphones picked up unintended effects, like footsteps, which emerged thunderously. Microphones had to remain immobile until the boom was devised: actors learned that they had to pussyfoot through this maze of sensitive ears; and the pre-sound cameras made a loud whirring that resembled, when recorded, the noise of a car after its silencer has fallen off. Cameramen had to enclose the camera and themselves in a stiflingly hot booth that could hardly be moved. Faced by these hazards, and the demand for talkies, Hollywood retreated. It was reduced, at first, to filming straight plays straight and to putting a premium on English stage actors with their clear diction.

The vogue for 'tea-cup dramas' soon palled—technicians, anyway, soon found means to bring back expressiveness to the image. (William Cameron Menzies, most extremely, designed mobile sets.) The aesthetes were probably less offended by this period of stilted filming than by the loss in stylistic decorum. There was no longer a need, as Seymour Stern wrote deploringly in 1936, to 'wrestle with the stringent dramatic exigencies of the silent black-and-white film'. [2] What the aesthetes did not admit, however, is that conventions must break down when new areas of subject-matter come into being. The new subject-matter needed to be wrought into some semblance of cohesion; and one way in which this could be brought about was by a technique that owed something to magic. 'The one value of film', d'Annunzio had said twenty years before, 'is its power of metamorphosis.' [3] Editing, lighting, camera movement and the leger-demain of the comedians entailed covert metamorphoses; but it needed the coming of sound, and the forced immobility of the camera, to revive the Méliès techniques of making a transformation within the image. It was no coincidence that this rediscovery took place at the same period in the animated cartoon, in the filmed revue and in the screen muscial, or that sound and image were first played against each other, with skill, in these forms. For the loosely-connected episodes out of which the animated cartoon, the revue and the musical were created depended for their impact not on motivated action but on the Circean powers of music and spectacular transformation.

Walt Disney discovered the most intriguing spell for these ingredients. Mortimer, alias Mickey Mouse, had been on the drawing-boards at the time when The Jazz Singer was released, and the addition of sound for his third public appearance in Steamboat Willie, which opened in New York in September 1928, was a key factor in the growth of his world-wide reputation. Disney was shrewd in recognizing the value of sound and, later, of three-colour process Technicolor. He was also fortunate. He had few assets or overheads and little to lose by experiment; and whirring cameras and immovable micro-phones raised no problem in bench work.

Walt Disney: *Steamboat Willie.*

His flair for playing sight against sound gave his animated cartoons a conviction that the silent cartoon or puppet play could never have had and frankly exposed the dehumanization inherent in the idea of metamorphosis. Animals do not deteriorate or die in his cartoons; under duress, they are merely transmogrified into different shapes. They are available for an unlimited amount of torture.

This technique and inhumanity are aspects of the assault on 'good taste' that appears to have been an unconscious driving force in Disney's life. The most gruesome of his early cartoons, *The Skeleton Dance* (1929), is the most dexterous in its handling of aural effects. His most ambitious use of sound, *Fantasia* (1941), also happens to be unintentionally his most grotesque caricature of culture. Admitting to having no ear for classical music, Disney adorned Beethoven's Pastoral Symphony with drawings of a coyness that seems to mock the feeling in the music. The indelibility of this caricature may, for some people, point to a falsity in the music itself. But certainly, the omnipresence of Disney's slickly-designed cupids and deer undermines the sublimity of pastoral, as Beethoven conceived of it. It presses the mind back to a nursery view of things, bounded on every side by mass-produced Disney toys.

Universal's *The King of Jazz*. Paul Whiteman.

Sennett's comedians had played out their gags in actual surroundings. In Disney's cartoons the image itself becomes the gag.
It was principally to compensate for the immobile camera and to bring
variety to songs that the filmed musical and revue also made such a
feature of transforming the image. Oil paintings begin to move, an
orchestra to rise out of a grand piano. It seems appropriate that
Universal's revue, *The King of Jazz* (1930), built around Paul
Whiteman's talents, should have had as its second item a cartoon
imitative of Disney, in which Whiteman was stretched and twisted like
a piece of indiarubber. Its finale—a melting-pot fantasy in which

folk singers from many nations step out of a huge chalice, and Whiteman blends their pastoral tunes into what a contemporary reviewer in *The Bioscope* described as 'a cacophonous blast' intended to represent the spirit of modernity—is typical, in microcosm, of the film's manufacture, its throwing together of every possible kind of appeal without any attempt at consistency: two-process Technicolor, a motley of elaborate stagings, every sort of orchestration and vaudeville act and, of course, a cast of thousands. And yet, like Whiteman's cacophonous blast, this charivari, as angular and generous, as conflicting in its energies and seemingly improvised as good jazz, is exhilarating.

Success depended on the melting-pot belief that anything will relate to anything else, so long as its parts are viewed as equal to each other: a view given added conviction by the failure of MGM's

MGM's *Hollywood Revue of 1929*. Laurel and Hardy.

Hollywood Revue of 1929, a medley which collapses beneath the weight of its unequal pretensions. Its cast included nearly every star in the Mayer stable, but the crippling restrictions of its recording system were evident from the start as the MGM lion opened its mouth and emitted the feeblest of roars. Only comedians who had practised their craft during the silent era, like Buster Keaton, Marie Dressler and Laurel and Hardy, manage fitfully to generate an atmosphere which sustains humour. The filming is least awkward when it is least portentous, as in the insouciant staging of Arthur Freed's stop-gap number, hastily composed, *Singin' in the Rain*.

Song and dance numbers tax the image-maker's ingenuity, and the musical stimulated technicians to discover means to re-mobilize the camera. But how far did their efforts serve new purposes? Ernst Lubitsch's *The Love Parade* (1929) opens promisingly in Paris with the snappy portrayal of a philanderer, then moves to the never-never land of Sylvana. The counterpoint of sound and image in the opening sequences enriches the action and discloses a new type of film comedy. A busload of American tourists read newspapers as their guide recites the history of the royal palace beside them; when the guide begins to talk about the royal finances the tourists, to a man, eagerly lower their newspapers. But as the story moves into fairy-tale romance, Lubitsch resorts to the distancing of the silent screen and appears unable to use sound to give verve to this romance. We notice how voice and lip movements are badly syn-chronized and perhaps find unconvincing the marriage of Maurice Chevalier as the ingratiating philanderer and Jeanette MacDonald

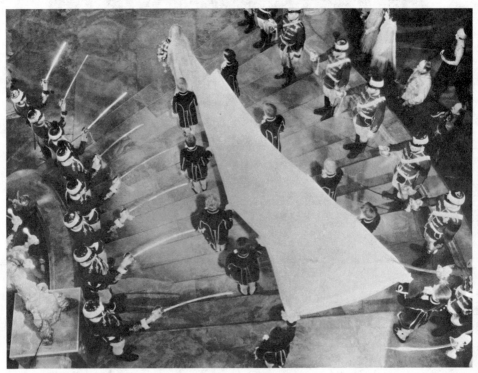

Ernst Lubitsch: *The Love Parade*.

as the genteel queen. (Yet the public welcomed this relationship, and the two actors were to be teamed together in *One Hour with You, Love Me Tonight*—both of 1932—and a version of *The Merry Widow* made in 1934.)

On the other hand, Rouben Mamoulian, with his first movie *Applause* (1929), does recognize how a bold use of sound can release film-makers from outdated conventions. His restless camera brings together the emphasis of German expressionism (menacing shadows and close-ups on bloated chorus girls), the delirious abandonment of a Vertov (as it spirals around Penn station) and a casualness of regard (in the subway sequence) that anticipates neo-realism. Mamoulian came to Paramount's Astoria studios in New York with a brilliant reputation as a Broadway stage producer. Yet film direction requires more than a theatrical flair, and Mamoulian appears to see his story, of a vaudeville star (Helen Morgan) who sacrifices herself to support her convent-trained daughter, as no more than an excuse for pyrotechnics. His style, more flashy than exploratory, evinces no personal timbre. Even his cynicism is perfunctory; his tracking shots along a chorus line of ageing, raddled actresses lack the ferocity that Sternberg was to bring in this year to his direction of *The Blue Angel*.

Applause is the skeleton for a realism typical of the thirties, which King Vidor began to flesh out in *Hallelujah* (1929). Al Jolson had given voice to a distress and, indeed, to a dimension of the American self denied by Puritanism, as Vidor appears to have recognized. In his autobiography *A Tree is a Tree*, he wrote of the Negro: 'The sincerity and fervour of their religious expression intrigued me as did the honest simplicity of their sexual drives. In many cases the inter-mingling of these two activities seemed to offer a strikingly dramatic content.'⁴ In *The Crowd* he had described the dehumanization of city life, in *Hallelujah* he turns in contrast to the shared warmth and suffering of a Negro community. But the manner in which he slipped round the taboos of his pink audience entails a sly pastoral strategy. He gambles on the assumption that audiences will accept Negro sexuality because they believe blacks to be children of nature and so less than human—a posture some of his actors comply with too willingly. At the same time he implies that his preacher, Zeke (Daniel Haynes), torn between metaphysical aspiration and desire for a good-time girl, can be a more complete human being than most filmgoers for the reason that he lives in a community which allows him to work out his interests openly. Vidor's sensitivity to shifts in feeling allows him to move back and forth between the detached location shooting that recalls newsreel, the stylized expressions of corporate life that owe something to the miracle play, and the presentation of some wonderful spirituals, that depends on the skills of the stage musical. These various genres fuse in the melting-pot of realism; a fusion that would have been impossible if Vidor had not extended the scope of sound equipment. He filmed much of his story without sound and then married it to wildtrack recordings:

a feat—he had no moviola—that drove one of his editors into a breakdown.

Some important pre-Depression experiments with sound took place in France, though the industry there, forever precarious, was shaken by the cost of installing new equipment. It was already financed largely from abroad. German studios, under threat from Hollywood, had expanded their markets by setting up international productions in Paris. Pathé had been taken over by Bernard Natan, pornographer and businessman, only interested in profits. Without sound facilities of their own, the French companies had to buy or hire equipment at stiff prices from General Electric and the German firm of Tobis. Foreign investors increased their hold. Banking interests and a Swiss electrical firm controlled Gaumont. Delluc's dream of a truly French cinema seems to have been lost.

But if Delluc's dream had faded, the French public, like the public elsewhere, appears to have been enchanted, at least for a short while, by the pleasure of going to films in their own tongue. The output of films in France rose steadily and the industry did not seriously feel the effects of the Depression before the end of 1932. Paramount and Tobis opened factory-cities near Paris, at Joinville and Epinay respectively, with the intention of mass-producing multilingual entertainments. A scene would be shot in one language; then another; and then another. It was not a productive method of working. Yet two valuable contributions came from it.

The first was valuable almost in spite of itself. Marcel Pagnol, aged thirty-seven and a successful playwright, thought that films had merit only as records of a theatrical experience. He had no feeling for the camera's capacity to reveal unexpected meanings in the visual world, or in the rhythm and syntax peculiar to film, and believed that when a talkie made sense with the sound switched off it was worthless. Paramount bought the rights on his popular play *Marius* and, typically, assigned the direction of this study in Marseilles dock life, rich in local detail, to a Hungarian fluent in several languages. This director, Alexander Korda, had built up a reputation as a producer in his home country. Graduating to Hollywood, he had laboured under a Fox contract. When Fox had fallen, he had lost his job and had wandered around Europe in search of work until eventually Paramount had signed him on. He directed three films for them, of which *Marius* (1931) is the only one to have become renowned.

It demonstrates triumphantly that a play can be transferred to the screen with a few minor modifications and yet be a satisfying experience in its own right. Korda took his two leading players, Raimu and Pierre Fresnay, from the original stage production, and both of them, with his assistance, realized themselves at once as screen presences. Raimu, with a physique as commanding as the bar behind which he stands and, in contrast, a voice that falls naturally into a hoarse patter, plays César, a café owner. Pierre Fresnay, appearing as his twenty-three-year-old son Marius, who yearns to escape from the café and sail the high seas, looks too old for the part and too sophisticated to convey the awkwardness of retarded adolescence but,

The Marcel Pagnol trilogy: *above, Marius: below left, Fanny: below right, César.* Pierre Fresnay, Orane Demazis.

like Robert Donat, he has a grace and a reticence unusual in actors that smooths over any disparity in casting. His coolness is deceptive; it holds in check intense feeling; as in the speech in which he tells his sweetheart Fanny (Orane Demazis) of his wish to go to sea. Technically, the film works against itself. The camera might be a lump of lead. It moves haltingly and more than once ends up in a position that tantalizingly half-blocks the view. The editing is too abrupt. Yet almost imperceptibly Korda draws our sympathy to Marius's imagination, to the Baudelaireian dream of the infinite, and in this way fulfils one part of Delluc's ambition. Above all, he resists Paramount's cosmopolitanism, and lavishes care on the idiosyncrasies of Midi behaviour and settings. He and Pagnol had realized that the texture and idiom of long-established communities give films their vitality and much of their worth.

Paramount sent Korda to London to work out his contract, where he soon established himself as an outstanding independent producer. He became a latter-day Disraeli and, more English than the English, lived within the maze of the imperial imagination. Meanwhile Pagnol remained faithful to Provence. *Fanny* (1932), directed by Marc Allégret, and *César* (1933), directed by Pagnol himself, continued the trilogy. They were as sane in feeling as *Marius*, and at moments Pagnol himself showed a flair for direction that belied his pronouncements. The trilogy and such later work as *La Femme du boulanger* (1939) were financially successful and often deeply moving, although purists may feel that Pagnol's principal contribution to the art of film was to finance *Toni* at a time when Jean Renoir's name was anathema to the bankers.

The other important pre-Depression use of sound came from René Clair at Tobis. Clair idealized the genius of working-class entertainers, Chaplin especially, and tried to identify himself with it. Yet he remained the bourgeois intellectual, sophisticated, critical, seeking for sources of energy outside his own culture. Detachment and a hint of dryness adhere to his most exuberant flights of invention. Sound so released his imagination that sequences in *Sous les toits de Paris* (1930), *Le Million* (1931) and *Le Quatorze Juillet* (1932) escape this charge. The climax to *Le Million* takes place at the opéra-lyrique. Downstage Sopranelli and Ravellini, two mountainous singers who loathe each other, sing a love duet, while upstage Michel and the girl he wants to marry sit in silent embrace on a park bench. An electric moon shines down on them; a stage hand, far above, scatters autumn leaves. Precise about the absurdity of opera, Clair clearly admires it also and portrays the singers and Sopranelli's claque—two august ladies who hurtle a bunch of roses at him—with an affectionate accuracy that places them among the sharpest of minor comic characters on film.

René Clair: *Le Million*. At the opéra-lyrique.

Like any evocation of nineteenth-century opera styles, this pastiche, to be persuasive, needs to exist within a mood strong enough to withstand the eclectic pressures of the present. In *Sous les toits de Paris* and *Le Million* Clair maintains such a mood precariously. Paris has to be a studio construction (and not only because of the difficulties of sound recording): it has to be controlled, distanced, often seen from the rooftops. In *Le Quatorze Juillet* he sought warmth in an identification with his working-class lovers, but could not escape memories of Pickford, Chaplin and Langdon. Even his best ideas, such as the mysterious, drunken millionaire who hands out money liberally, are cerebral. In a sense, Clair was unable to open himself to the tensions of the thirties and to its melting-pot of styles. In spite of his agile use of sound, his talent continued to float in the rarefied atmosphere of the silent age, most noticeably so in any comparison between the opera scenes in *Le Million* and the Marx Brothers' *A Night at the Opera* (1935).

The Marx Brothers, it seems at first sight, find the opera house so alien a place to them that they are aware of it only as a machine to be destroyed. Harpo fences with the conductor and misleads the orchestra into swinging from the overture of *Il Trovatore* to 'Take Me Out to the Ball Game', and Groucho appears in the stalls, selling peanuts. Philistinism has its advantages, for the breaking of social taboos opens up new areas for exploration – and the iconoclasm of the dadaists and surrealists seems mild when compared to the brothers' assaults. The twenties fade into gentility as Groucho verbally attacks Margaret Dumont, or, as the brothers leap onto the same blonde in *Horse Feathers* (1932) or as Harpo, more ominously, sweeps a stack of books into a fire.

In movie upon movie, Chico fingers out tunes on the piano with an endearing crassness, while Harpo seems to imbibe nostalgia at his harp. This sentimentality is as much part of the act as its humour and reflects on their determination to preserve a certain image of themselves. Arguably, their work deteriorated after they moved from Paramount to MGM in 1934, but they continued to draw strength from their formative experiences: their Jewish upbringing, the years in vaudeville, the structure of family life. In fact, they shuffled the ages of their actual kinship—Chico was the oldest and Groucho the youngest—yet in their screen characters Groucho forever resembled a five-year-old delinquent, fast in speech and with a charm that outwits (he believes) the maternal Margaret Dumont, Chico resembled a two-year-old, stumbling over words and never quite able to match his brother, while Harpo is like an infant immersed in destructive fantasies, wordless, in touch with a primitive kind of poetry. In their first film, *The Cocoanuts* (1929), a satire based on the Florida land boom of the twenties and transposed, almost unchanged, from their Broadway stage hit, they appear fully fledged, their personalities and relationships worked out, though Groucho, in his repeated threats to commit suicide, suggests a pessimism later to be sunk beneath a general grouchiness. With slight variations, they play the same gags again and again: the locked door routine, the bedroom confusion with three Grouchos in white nightcaps and gowns, the way Harpo hangs his knee like an umbrella on the helpless hand of anyone he does not like (they always have an instinctive knowledge of who will turn out to be an enemy or a friend).

Typically, when Chico and Harpo make music in *A Night at the Opera* they play for immigrants and children and not for the first-class passengers, and when Harpo swings on ropes or splits a backdrop during the performance of *Il Trovatore*, he does so in perfect timing to Verdi's rhythms: a humour that, far from destroying pleasure in opera, releases this pleasure from snobbery. Their breaking of conventions and proprieties, a postulate of realism, puts them in touch with a spontaneous creativity that Clair can only strive for. Harpo climbs through a porthole into a cabin where three bearded aviators sleep in one bed, and his eyes gleam wildly as he picks up a pair of scissors. He lifts one of the beards; a butterfly flutters out. . .

Horse Feathers. Harpo, Chico, Groucho and Zeppo Marx.

March of Time:
above left, King Cotton's Slaves: interior of a sharecropper's shack;
above right, King Cotton's Slaves: planters take the Rev. Claude Williams
from his car to flog him;
below left, Haile Selassie at the time of his League of Nations speech;
below right, Inside Nazi Germany.

9. The Depression:
The Media and Social Conscience

Radio had conditioned the public to sound as a vehicle for facts. In 1930 Darryl F. Zanuck, recently appointed Warner's production chief, announced that themes, in future, would be culled from the headlines. Without sound, this policy would have been impracticable, without the radio try-outs of the twenties, hardly conceivable at so early a stage. 'The talkies became an art,' wrote André Malraux, 'when directors realised that their model should be not the gramophone record but the radio feature.' [1]

The rapid discoveries of technology had opened up each of the mass media within an amazingly brief time-span; even so, the parallel in development between the radio and film industry in the United States was so close as to be uncanny. Before 1914 amateurs and small firms had operated radio without restriction. By 1919, after a savage war over patents, large combines such as the Radio Corporation of America, General Electric, the American Telephone and Telegraph company and its subsidiary, Western Electric, had taken over the field. During the twenties, radio, like the film industry, boomed and indeed outpaced the movies in growth (in 1924, for instance, Americans had invested over 358 million dollars in radio sets and spare parts). Listeners appointed their own stars; as with 'the Biograph girl', anonymity was no shield to fame. Gosden and Correll's comedy show, *Amos 'n Andy* — it began in 1928 and concerned two happy-go-lucky and lazy Negroes, played by whites — reached the top of the ratings. Like *The Birth of a Nation*, most popular of films, it was accused of racialism.

But radio had an edge over the cinema (and the press) in the immediacy of its news coverage. Its producers discovered an outstanding reporter in H. V. Kaltenhorn, and its surveys of the 1924 election, the Dempsey-Tunney fight of 1926 and the Lindbergh flight of 1927 established it as the most pulse-raising of the media. Throughout the thirties (and early forties) it dominated politics in nearly every country. Roosevelt and Hitler, and later Churchill and de Gaulle, depended on it to bolster national confidence; and only Stalin, among the leading politicians, muffed his chances when he spoke flounderingly to the nation after the Nazi invasion of Russia. In the United States radio was held responsible for the decline in newspaper readership. Film companies saw it as contributing to the Depression slump in box-office returns and were forced to take it into account; even Will H. Hays, who had fought to keep politics out of the movies, had to admit, tardily, in his report of 1939, the merit of 'pictures which dramatize present-day social conditions'.

But through a third agency, the advertising business, the two industries combined to lend weight to trivialization. Albert D. Lasker, of Lord and Thomas, one of the first and most adept of advertising agencies, quickly recognized how to exploit radio. Among his accounts were Lucky Strike and Pepsodent, which sponsored Amos 'n Andy — presumably one sponsor darkened teeth while the other whitened them. Lasker was one of the few people to make a fortune during the Depression and in 1932 alone acquired three million dollars. He had been a friend of Will H. Hays since his time in the Harding administration, and his company master-minded MGM's smear campaign against Upton Sinclair, when Sinclair entered the 1934 Democratic primary as candidate for governor: one of the first uses of modern advertising techniques in politics. In 1934, Photoplay, the fan magazine, broadcast the first programme devoted to film promotion, Forty-five Minutes in Hollywood, and at the same time Cecil B. DeMille began to preside over Lux Radio Theater. Hollywood stars appeared in this and other drama series. Meanwhile, Hollywood appropriated radio themes and gave star billing to such popular radio entertainers as Bing Crosby, Jack Benny, Bob Hope, Eddie Cantor, Rudy Vallee and Orson Welles. By 1937, ninety per cent of the sponsored national programmes were being transmitted from Hollywood. But by 1938 radio had been recognized as a threat to the movies, and Darryl F. Zanuck (who had moved to Twentieth Century-Fox) ordered Tyrone Power out of the Woodbury Soap programme; other studios issued similar orders.

The most striking and traceable interaction of the media occurred in the evolution of the March of Time newsreels. Roy Larsen, one of Henry Luce's aides on Time, had arranged to have items broadcast from the magazine, and these newscasts so attracted listeners that he developed them into a network programme, The March of Time. One of its appeals was that it dramatized the news — actors played 'memorable scenes from the news of the week'. Members of the Mercury Theatre company, including Orson Welles, Agnes Moorehead and Ray Collins, were among the regular performers. It is probable that Welles's parody of the March of Time style in the newsreel sequence of Citizen Kane is the most many filmgoers will know of the original series.

In 1934, Louis de Rochement, under Larsen's supervision, adapted the radio format to film. Some of his dramatic mock-ups in the earlier items, using amateur actors, look inept; but by taking up a firm opinion on the news and giving it a story line, he and his team made their rivals—Pathé, International Newsreel, Fox Movietone—seem out of touch with the political urgencies of the decade. Sometimes their commentaries sounded portentous, or spilled over into demagogy. On the whole, though, they handled information with the grace and economy of the parent magazine, and their profiles of public figures, such as the one on the union leader John L. Lewis, were models of elucidation. Most memorable of all, perhaps, was their voice-of-doom announcer, seconded from radio, Westbrook van Voorhis, who sounded as though he were about to explode as he forced out the closing words: 'Time . . . marches on!'

Primarily valuable in alerting the public to the dangers of Fascism, the recurring theme in these monthly panoramas was the threat to democracy—and 'democracy' became an overworked word in their commentaries. They reported on Huey Long's corrupt regime in Louisiana and the Nazi rallies of the American-German Bund managed by Gerald L. K. Smith. They carried an Academy award winning report on life inside Nazi Germany (1938) and an even more powerful one on refugees, which gave evidence of how German Jews were being persecuted. At home, among other socially important issues, they investigated the wheeling-and-dealing at Tammany Hall and supported La Guardia and Dewey in their campaign against the racketeers. The public quickly responded to this intelligence. In 1935, 432 American cinemas were showing the series regularly; by 1939 this number had nearly trebled. 'It has carried over from journalism into the cinema', said John Grierson, 'something of the bright and easy tradition of free-born comment which the newspaper has won and the cinema has been too abject even to ask for.' [2] Louis de Rochement left the programme in 1943 to set up as a feature producer, and in 1953, supplanted in function if not in value by television news services, *March of Time* came to an end.

John Grierson's appreciation of it reflects a viewpoint typical of the thirties, and one that he had helped to shape. Born in Scotland in 1898, he graduated from Glasgow University and visited the United States on a bursary to study communications. Walter Lippmann advised him to direct his attention to the most popular form of mass communication, the movies; and a period in Hollywood intensified his concern about the uses and misuses of cinema. On his return to England he became acquainted with S. G. (later Sir Stephen) Tallents of the Empire Marketing Board. In 1926 Tallents had called on Rudyard Kipling to discuss the work of the Board with him, and Kipling had suggested they should make a propaganda film to advertise Empire produce. He had recommended Walter Creighton for the job and indeed gone so far as to sketch out a scenario before withdrawing from the project altogether. In the event, Creighton assisted Grierson on the first EMB documentary, *Drifters* (1929).

Grierson had studied the Russian cinema intently. He admired its social concern and recognized in its techniques ways in which information about the complexities of modern society might be disseminated to a wide public. He believed this public to be bedazzled by the dreams promoted by advertising and the media, and his guiding passion was to educate it in the dynamic structures that underlay these distractions. As in *Turksib*, his programme was to show how nature created raw material and the stuff of food and then how industry and trade converted these products into the necessities of daily life. Quite frank about his ambitions—'I look at the cinema as a pulpit,' he wrote, 'and use it as a propagandist'[3]—he promoted his views throughout his career as an energetic producer and administrator, at first with the rapidly expanding EMB film unit; then in 1933, when he transferred his unit to the Post Office (the Empire Marketing Board having been closed down), he and such colleagues as Len Lye extended the uses of sound remarkably. From 1939 to 1945 he was to be Commissioner of a newly-formed National Film Board of Canada. Yet by 1935, as Alistair Cooke observed in the autumn issue of *Sight and Sound*, his programme had been largely superseded by the *March of Time* series.

It is odd that the most realistic documentary group in England, the GPO unit, our only sentient turners of history into news, should suddenly, by the production of a handful of fine American journalists, be left stranded; should suddenly appear as conscientious dramatisers of platitudes, should turn into a group of gentle academes roaming England with a camera and finding only what the already completed scenario had arranged for them to find.

The trouble was that the GPO film unit worked for a government agency—which curtailed its role as a critic of government policy. Compared to the freelance documentaries of Storck, Lods and Vigo, the tone of much of its work tended to be complacent. In an age of mass unemployment, when the economic bases of society were being called into question, its emphasis on craftsmanship and the processes of manufacture, though instructive, could be construed as a form of evasion. And when, in April 1940, the Ministry of Information took it over and named it the Crown Film Unit, its heroic involvement in battle still reflected an official view. The problem it had to face was perhaps insoluble. A documentary movement, to continue as a movement, needs to be subsidized, and government agencies, or millionaires, seldom tend to be disinterested: however reasonable bureaucrats may wish to be, in general their unconscious bias is to maintain the *status quo*.

Treasury support also gave Grierson the wrong sort of power. He distrusted the Hollywood monopoly and thought it had damaged the possibilities of film-making, especially in the United Kingdom, where it controlled many of the distribution outlets. Yet he seems to have been touched by its ambitions. He could be crushing to associates who strayed from the chosen path; in *Documentary Film*, for instance, Paul Rotha quotes Grierson's unforgivably cruel report on one of Arthur Elton's projects. In his articles, he frequently adopted a hectoring tone. Perhaps he felt that he needed this manner to sharpen lax minds; yet it also allowed him to cut corners too freely and encouraged him to dismiss any insight or formal intensity alien to his programme. Of Eisenstein's uncompleted *Que Viva Mexico*, he wrote: 'The clouds and cactus will pass for great photography among the hicks, but they are, of course, easy meat for anyone with a decent set of filters.'[4] Delluc's concern with the niceties of photogenics may have led him into the occasional silliness, but Grierson's brusqueness about the role of imagination and intuition in film-making perhaps explains why he failed to establish a tradition, as Delluc did, that nourishes talent.

A teacher who aspired to be an artist working in the Russian tradition, Grierson did not realize that the Russian techniques of montage were too cumbersome for his didactic intention. He was unable to transplant the Russian temperament to British soil. *Drifters*, his one attempt at direction, has repeated shots of fishermen pulling in nets with a few herrings caught in them, but apart from miming the monotony of labour, these shots tell us nothing about the condition of herring fishing or of the men who devote their lives to it. Fussy cross-cutting sets up no resonance in the contrast of images, and an extended observance of the seabed and of dogfish eating up the catch destroys the camera's identification with the men to no useful purpose. Compare it to Mikhail Kaufman's *Spring*, released in the same year, with its feeling for space, light and unusual detail—a snowman melting before some factory chimneys; Muscovite housewives, one of them wearing a pair of worn slippers, removing the second pane of glass on windows as the days grow warmer—and you become aware of an openness to the senses and a deftness unknown to Grierson.

More sensitive to words than to visual images, he might have made more of his information if he had been able to shape it as a radio feature. He could be perceptive about sound: 'Once you start detaching sounds from their origins . . . Your aeroplane whistle may become not the image of an aeroplane but the image of distance and height. Your steamer whistle may become not the image of a steamer but of isolation and darkness.'[5] Edgar Anstey's *Granton Trawler* (1934), which Grierson produced, succeeds in all that *Drifters* failed to do. It discovers beauty in windlasses, spars and a sail taut before a funnel pouring out black smoke, and it discovers beauty through its disciplined use of sound effects: the mutter of voices, the rattle of chains, the slap of the sea, the cry of gulls. The acute timing of these noises (and the absence of commentary) heightens the starkness of the images and strengthens their coherence, so that within twelve minutes it conveys the vision of a bleak and barely human world.

'England is the most fertile country imaginable for purely filmic material,'[6] wrote Paul Rotha in *The Film Till Now*. 'When recently visiting this country, Mr Eisenstein expressed his astonishment at the almost complete neglect by British film directors of the wonderful material that lay untouched.' Freed from the discipline of story-telling, the GPO film unit was able to explore the physicality of things. Grierson had looked to the Russians; Basil Wright, in *The Song of Ceylon* (1935), looks more to Flaherty, using the dissolves and soft-toned photography of *Moana* not as another tourist's guide to the colonies but as an evocation of Singhalese feeling: its reverence, above all, for the Buddha. Apart from one section, 'The Voices of Commerce', where Wright appears to have been more in awe of Grierson than the Buddha and imposes a hubbub of actors' voices reading business letters over a scrappy montage of telegraph wires and radio transmitters, he sustains this effect. Seldom has the agrarian utopia dreamed of by many film-makers of the thirties been so beguilingly described. Two years later Wright commended, in the *Spectator*, Ernest Hemingway's tactful commentary for *The Spanish Earth*. Wright recognized that finding the right tone for a commentary provides its director with his most awkward problem: a problem, however, that he himself solved in *The Song of Ceylon*.

Yet in creating a work of art, Wright, like Anstey, achieves a completeness that dissociates his film from its age. For a while, in Russia, the avant-garde and revolutionary politics had seemingly shared intentions: an awareness of kinship and a feeling for the dispossessed. But this connection was now ended, and any artist working within its tradition of experiment was liable either to arrive at a self-sufficient integrity that resembled a kind of death or a reliance on technique for its own sake that looked contrived. Wright's *Night Mail* (1936), co-directed with Harry Watt, for instance, shows how the post is carried from London to Edinburgh. It has music by Benjamin Britten and a verse commentary by W. H. Auden. And yet however ingenious and cheery it may be, its experiments in sound blur the underlying idea, conveying little about the lives of the letter-sorters in the train and seeing their work as merely an excuse for embellishment.

Cavalcanti's *Coalface* (1935) elegantly slums in the same manner, and all the more shamefully so in the light of the danger in coal-mining. It exhibits a numbness of imagination that was widespread at this time. Indeed a good deal of the political concern of the thirties, in England especially, seems more derived from an attempt to escape from despair than a desire to change social conditions. The non-Fascist nations appear to have been wholly incapable of dealing with the problems of totalitarianism, either in achieving social planning that did not resort to totalitarian solutions or in dealing with the aggression of countries given over to dehumanizing social structures. From the Japanese invasion of Manchuria onwards, this failure of nerve was to be omnipresent, perhaps because these nations themselves were, through industrialism, already committed to totalitarian modes of organization. It is typical of this decade that the Nazis and Russians should have modelled their film industries on the Hollywood assembly-line system of production, and that the Nazi documentary film-makers should have drawn their techniques from the Soviet cinema of the twenties. Every society seems to have been driven into some sort of denial of individuality, and the pressure of totalitarianism brought a uniformity to film styles in every country. With hindsight it is possible to see, for example, how far Paul Rotha's *The Face of Britain* (1935) is similar in sentiment and treatment to many Nazi documentaries in its presentation of the English countryside, attack on smoke pollution and concluding vision of a clean new age controlled by scientific planning.

Acknowledging the plight of the miner became a way of relieving this numbness of the imagination. 'Our civilisation', wrote George Orwell in *The Road to Wigan Pier*, 'is founded on coal, more completely than one realizes until one stops to think about it.'[7] While *Coalface* affirms the miner to be a good fellow doing his bit for the national effort, Orwell reports on his descent into the mine with a cold anger at the alienation of those who burn coal without thought for the risk and physical damage entailed by the men who hack it out of the ground. The miner at work, he tries to show, is the reality at the core of our shadowy and confused civilization.

In 1937, also, *March of Time* made a similar connection between mining and society in the United States, when it compared the universities and country houses, whose maintenance depended on coal, with the harsh conditions of the miners—in some areas two-thirds of the men had been unemployed for over thirteen years. But it is necessary to look outside England and the United States to find this sort of consciousness in documentary. Henri Storck, in Belgium, disturbs any complacency his audiences might have about industrial inequality by pointing out one of its consequences. In *The Borinage*, which he directed in association with the Dutch film-maker Joris Ivens in 1933, and in *Les Maisons de la misère* (1937), he conveys distressingly the relationship between factories and slums. Meanwhile, Ivens challenged

Henri Storck and Joris Ivens: *The Borinage.*

the Nazi cry of 'living-space' in *New Earth* (1934) by charting the methods in which rich soil was claimed from the drained Zuyder Zee. Ivens emphasized the toll in labour needed to bring about this man-made harvest. The tone of his commentary is sober – suitably so, in the light of later events. Though he was not to know it when he shot the film, the first crops taken from the Zuyder Zee fields were to be destroyed, because it was feared they would lower prices on the world market.

In 1931 Cecil B. DeMille, who had lost a small fortune on the stock exchange crash, went on tour of the Soviet Union and declared, as a parting shot, that 'There is something rotten at the core of our system.' In 1935, Clifford Odets of the Workers Laboratory Theatre went to Hollywood to work on *The General Died at Dawn*, and by the next year some of his left-wing colleagues, such as John Howard Lawson, Albert Maltz, John Wexley and the actor John Garfield, had moved West. By 1937, claims Murray Kempton in *Part of Our Time*, 'The Workers Laboratory Theatre appeared to have moved spiritually, if not physically, over to the Warner Brothers' lot' – by which time, in fact, Warners, under pressure from the Hays Office, was veiling topicality in wishful thinking. Murray Kempton believes that 'For Hollywood, and its Communists too, life was a piece of stage business. The Comintern was a musical and Spain the Rose Bowl. We are told this was a time when the Communists influenced Hollywood's most passionate creative minds; if that is true, we may wonder why so few of them felt any impulse to take time off and form independent companies.'[8]

The role of the writer in active Hollywood politics was less open to this sort of criticism. In 1933 Roosevelt's National Recovery Act gave workers the right to bargain collectively through unions of their own choosing, a right that re-mobilized the labour movement. (Since the Red Scare of 1919, its membership had dramatically fallen away.) Strikes rent the country, and clashes with the police occurred in Minneapolis, San Francisco and elsewhere. In 1934 Mayer and Thalberg decided to deduct a day's pay from the salary of their employees to help pay for their campaign against Upton Sinclair. Angered by this toll, MGM artists joined forces with their colleagues at other studios to assert their union rights. They founded the Screen Actors' Guild and the Screen Writers' Guild: there ensued a turbulent period of negotiation and conflict that culminated in the studio strikes of 1940. And they took action in other ways.

In 1936 the Motion Picture Artists Committee, led by Dashiell Hammett, sent aid to Republican Spain and to China in its struggle against Japan. In the same year Donald Ogden Stewart and Dudley Nichols formed the Anti-Nazi League, which soon raised assets valued at ninety thousand dollars and, among other gestures, had Leni Riefenstahl and Vittorio Mussolini dissuaded from staying in Los Angeles. By the end of the decade Leo C. Rosten could write: 'In the realm of international politics, Hollywood is more sensitive and responsive than most communities in the land.'[9] A number of the studios put pressure on their employees to renounce these activities. Martin Dies, a congressman, and Burton Fitts, a Los Angeles county district attorney, claimed that Communists had infiltrated these organizations and they opened a public inquiry. A few of these charges stuck; most did not. But some of these discredited allegations were to be revived in 1947 by the HUAC committee.

Political consciousness took different forms elsewhere. Recognizing the propaganda value of film, Mussolini delegated the industry to his son Vittorio, imposed a heavy tax on the dubbing of foreign films and in 1932 tried to mobilize Italian production by pouring money into Cinecittà, a large complex of studios near Rome. Antonio Maraini, secretary-general of the biennial Venice Fine Arts Festival, thought that the time had come to take the cinema as seriously as painting or sculpture and in 1932 organized the first Venice Film Festival to run concurrently with the art exhibition. Mussolini recognized the propaganda value of the festival and his minister of finance, Count Volpi, was appointed president. A grandiose picture-palace, in the Fascist style of architecture, rose on the shores of the Lido. The festival fulfilled a demand, and not only as some easily acquired publicity for the regime. It gave film directors a chance to publicize their work and to meet each other, and scholars, then as later, were to profit from its carefully-mounted film retrospectives. But although the idea of the festival was a good one, it did institutionalize the movies and, by putting them on the same level as 'art', threatened to raise them above the commonalty. Whether in fact festivals of the Venice kind could ever escape from a tendency to control culture was to be a point much debated in the late sixties.

Maraini was encouraged to set up the festival as an annual event in 1935, the year in which Mussolini's army invaded Abyssinia and in which politics overtly began to affect the competition. Italy won four of the eleven cups, sharing the two top awards with Germany; and Goebbels made an impromptu visit to boost this triumph. The competition, in effect, had become as bogus as the Mussolini Gold Cup, which was actually made of some inferior metal. In 1938 the scandal came to a head, as *The Times* cautiously reported on 2 September.

The American and British members of the jury resigned immediately after the last of the awards was published. It is understood that they have both taken exception to the award of the Mussolini Cup, the chief prize of the festival, to the German film *Olympiad* on the grounds that it is a documentary and not a feature film, and therefore ineligible. The action seems to have met with a wide measure of approval, for in certain quarters the opinion was expressed that in making their decisions some of the jury had allowed themselves to be swayed by political motives. Reuter's Venice correspondent states that the Mussolini Cup was shared between the film to which the objection was taken and *Luciano Serra, Airman*, the first film directed by Signor Vittorio Mussolini, the Duce's eldest son.

In fact, Roberto Rossellini wrote the scenario for this epic, and Goffredi Alessandrini directed it.

The French, angered by this rigging, organized the Cannes film festival with Louis Lumière as its honorary president. Ominously scheduled to open in September 1939, it had for obvious reasons to be postponed for the duration of the war. Venice had been compromised, admittedly, but it had been a milestone in the history of film and of ideas. It had recognized film-making as an art and had dramatized ways in which the notion of art, as of sport, could become tainted by nationalism and feelings of superiority: a hysteria about achievement, fostered by the media, which the defeat of the Axis did nothing to decrease. The controversy surrounding the showing in 1937 of Renoir's *La Grande Illusion*—the jury, stopped by festival officials from awarding it the Mussolini Cup, created a special prize for it—brought a new edge both to critical invective and to the serious analysis of film.

The widespread influence of the cinema and a new consciousness of its power brought out into the open once more the somewhat faded debate on whether the media could corrupt. Though no one understood the effect of films on the mind, the response to this mystery was largely to be of a negative kind. The New York police had first raided a movie show in 1904, and the American National Board of Censorship, run on an amateur basis, had been founded shortly afterwards. During the twenties the debate had seldom risen above the level of tabloid polemic. But developments in the fields of anthropology and child psychology allowed students of this subject to bring scientific or semi-scientific methods to bear on it, and their interest was to be positive in other ways. It became apparent that old films needed to be preserved as part of the national heritage, that film institutes and archives, in short, should be established. In 1935 the Italian government set up the Centro Sperimentale di Cinematografia, an organization with enough men of liberal temperament on its staff to prepare the ground for the post-war neo-realist movement; and a notable magazine associated with the Centro, *Bianco e Nero*, first appeared in 1937. In France Henri Langlois founded the Cercle du Cinéma (1935), which in the following year was re-formed as the Cinémathèque Française. A friend of the surrealists, M. Langlois's taste was less élitist or moralistic than that of some of his foreign contemporaries, and his later influence as a programme-planner on the New Wave generation of critics and directors was to be considerable.

In the United Kingdom *Sight and Sound*, 'a Review of Modern Aids to Learning', was first published in 1932. It carried articles on education, broadcasting and television, a trenchant film column by C. A. Lejeune – the equally trenchant Alistair Cooke took it over later – and an unsigned leader marshalling arguments in favour of a British Film Institute. In 1929, 300 education and scientific groups had set up a Commission to investigate the part film might play in education. 'How', the Commission asked in its report, *The Film in National Life* (1932), 'can we use a modern medium to develop the intelligence of a generation which has become cinema-minded?'[10] The Lampe Institute in Berlin had categorized films for school usage, but the British Commission wished to minimize censorship as far as possible and to make constructive proposals. It needed a permanent body to help it in its findings, and the British Film Institute, an active concern by 1933, took on this role. As the complexity of the educational problem was realized, the Institute branched out into areas only marginally connected with education.

And not without reason. For the question of how films might influence the young soon led investigators into other areas of inquiry: into psychology, aesthetics, sociology and the relativity of morals and taste. From 1929 to 1933 the Motion Picture Research Council of America, working with a grant from the Payne Fund, 'a foundation devoted to the welfare of youth', carried out a series of experiments intended to assess this influence. It published its discoveries in twelve monographs packed with graphs, statistics and disclosures, the contents of which Henry James Forman summarized in his book *Our Movie-Made Children* (1935). But while the Payne Fund researchers had been careful in drawing any conclusions from their facts, Forman not only paraphrased their views inaccurately but appears to have set himself up as a guardian of public morals. 'The road to delinquency', he wrote, 'is heavily dotted with movie addicts.'[11] His book stirred up a good

'The road to delinquency is heavily dotted with movie addicts':
Mae West in *She Done Him Wrong*.

deal of public anxiety, and grass-root reformers were able to use it as a weapon to force changes in studio policy.

Forman's alarmist slogans apart, the researchers had uncovered worrying evidence. They estimated that over seventy-seven million people in the United States went to the movies every week and that one third of this audience was made up of children and adolescents. In tests carried out over a three-year period, they discovered that children remembered about seventy per cent of what they had seen, and for a long time afterwards. They learnt, for instance, that many children had first become aware of anti-black feeling in themselves while watching *The Birth of a Nation*, though one girl said that its final racialist scenes had moved her to pity for the Negroes' condition: a reflection that led the Research Council to conclude, rather obviously, that films could stimulate differing responses.

For the most part made up of male researchers, the panel had little insight into its own motives and spent far too much time investigating ways in which films might stimulate sexual aggression in women. (It disapproved of this aggression.) While recognizing that the strongest film stories tend to give shape to impulses hostile to conventional morality, it acknowledged that it could not determine the extent to which a director might break taboos without alienating his audience. 'There is not a single vice in our code of society', writes one of the researchers, 'that some other group has not considered a virtue.' And yet, in admitting this point, the Council did not see how this relativity in morals imposed on it the obligation to study the irrationalities of its own community – of the protestant ethic in particular. Too eager to defend the *status quo*, it refused to accept the possibility that 'anti-social' tendencies might sometimes be therapeutic. It argued, for example, that the gangster movie frequently showed the criminal as attractive without asking why the audience might feel sympathy for him. It did not point out the double standard in a society which could preach the need for honesty and diligence and yet hold up for esteem, as eminent citizens, buccaneers involved in shady business dealings. It did not see how the figure of the gangster, that small-time capitalist who usually fails, might reflect on screen both the despair of the Depression and the morals of Hoover's America. It did not admit that a society usually gets the movies it wants, or that adults engaged in the monotony of factory work and children forced to play on the streets should naturally crave for fantasies in which sex, riches and the death of enemies are easily obtained. The Research Council avoided these issues and left it to Henry James Forman to blunder into a denunciation of public taste that by implication raised a terrible criticism of the standards he tried to defend.

So many of the characters lack occupation that in a real world they might be a concern to the police as having no means of support. They nearly all smoke to the number of eighty-seven and a half per cent. As to drinking, of the 115 pictures sixty-six per cent show it and forty-three per cent exhibit intoxication. Seventy-eight per cent of all pictures contain liquor situations.

As one sums up the people of the screen, always remembering that fine pictures have included many splendid characters, exhibiting fine manners and beautiful clothes, the total impression that survives is of a tawdry population, often absurdly over-dressed, often shady in character, much given to crime and sex, with little desire or need, apparently, of supporting themselves on this difficult planet. A people whom, for the most part, we should not want to know or live amongst.[12]

Forman is so concerned to deplore this bad taste that he fails to see its implicit hostility to conventional society. In *The Road to Wigan Pier* George Orwell was to present the matter in a different way.

In a decade of unparalleled depression, the consumption of all cheap luxuries has increased. The two things that have probably made the greatest difference of all are the movies and the mass-production of cheap smart clothes since the war . . . You may have three halfpence in your pocket and not a prospect in the world; but in your new clothes you can stand on the street corner, indulging in a private daydream of yourself as Clark Gable or Greta Garbo, which compensates you a lot for a great deal . . . It is quite likely that fish and chips, art-silk stockings, tinned salmon, cut-price chocolate (five two-ounce bars for sixpence), the movies, the radio, strong tea and the football pools have between them averted revolution.[13]

The Research Council suggested that the gangster film had weakened public morality by its manner of projecting subversive fantasies under the guise of fact. In many ways unusual, the gangster genre was most unusual, perhaps, in the speed with which it had acquired the trappings of actuality: gangsterism related to so many civic functions known to the public, such as the press, the law, the police, politics and commerce, that it needed to be described accurately to be credible. It was unusual, too, in its origins. Some critics have traced its pedigree to the French and German serials and to D. W. Griffith's *The Musketeers of Pig Alley*, but organized crime was so much a twenties phenomenon that such a derivation seems unlikely. Other critics have argued that it was the brain-child of a Chicago newspaperman, Ben Hecht, who wrote the screenplay for Sternberg's *Underworld* (1927).

Hecht claimed to have been dismayed by Sternberg's interpretation of his screenplay—and with some reason, for Sternberg showed little or no interest in the details of racketeering and used Hecht's subject as a pretext to return to his samurai view of human behaviour. He places his two men and a girl—George Bancroft as Bull Weed, a stupid and generous gang leader, Clive Brook as Rolls Royce, a destitute gentleman scholar, and Evelyn Brent as the poised Feathers McCoy—in an atmosphere of such spiritual refinement that most gangsters would find it incomprehensible. In the final scene Bull Weed comes to see that Rolls Royce is in every way his superior, gives up Feathers to him and voluntarily faces a police siege alone: arcane behaviour that Sternberg gives a certain plausibility by his intensely projected sense of stoicism; nearly every shot reflects his belief in the need to keep up appearances. 'To light a cigarette,' writes Andrew Sarris, in a monograph on this director, 'to grasp a coffee cup, to fondle one's furs is, for Sternberg, the equivalent to baring one's soul.'[14]

Kuleshov had discovered, through montage, what he was later to describe as an 'unreal geography'; Sternberg, through his use of lighting, creates a Cathay of the mind. His plots and characters defer to a sumptuous flow of images and his slender, tottering stories bear a rich swag. Everything depends on surfaces, on figures swathed in thickening and dissolving filigrees of light: a twenties conception of film-making that Sternberg persisted in throughout the thirties, carrying the silent screen aesthetic to its limits. Tolerated but little understood, he recognized that Marlene Dietrich was responsible for any appeal his films might have at the box-office, and he did not begin to win a more generous appreciation until the sixties, when a public sharing his selfconsciousness about technique and his ironic stoical view of life began to admire his series of Dietrich romances, from *Morocco* (1930) to *The Devil is a Woman* (1935), each of them more elaborate than the last.

Yet his taste for extravagance was not uncontrolled. Paramount had commissioned Eisenstein to prepare a screenplay based on Theodore Dreiser's novel, *An American Tragedy*, and when it was found unsuitable Zukor had urged Sternberg to take on the now expensive project—which he did, although the naturalism of the novel and its views on history were repugnant to him. In the event, he had difficulty in paraphrasing its complicated plot and used titles to summarize episodes he could not include. Dreiser was to disclaim any connection with the film released in 1931, and Eisenstein sympathizers were to see it as a betrayal—the main reason, perhaps, for its neglect.

Sternberg takes pains to convey the seediness of the Depression. He declines to follow the more naïve canons of naturalism when describing the monotonous effect of work in a shirt factory, and distils the experience, through a repeated machine movement, into an essence of dehumanization. Images of a lake, the clear rippling water where the drowning takes place, link the action and set the tone for Lee Garmes's photography, which discloses a cold beauty in drabness.

It has been said, wrongly, that Sternberg, by abandoning Dreiser's determinism, leaves his characters unmotivated and isolated from social pressure; yet the opening scene alone, in which Clyde (Phillips Holmes), as a bellhop in a grand hotel, accepts too large a tip from a woman who finds him attractive, establishes both a motive and pressure. Sternberg concerns himself with the individual and the particular and disdains to blame society for Clyde's cowardice. At his

Josef von Sternberg: *An American Tragedy*. Sylvia Sidney.

trial for murder, Clyde begins to lose his nerve during a gruelling cross-examination. His attorneys observe, coldly, that since he lacks courage he probably committed the crime: a deduction so harshly Sternbergian that it might seem like a lapse in Sternberg's sense of humour. Yet if we give it thought, we shall see it contains some truth, for in fact Clyde allowed the drowning to occur through cowardice. Unlike George Stevens's equally compelling and often beautiful version of the same story, *A Place in the Sun* (1951), which equates love with wish-fulfilment and attracts sympathy to the rich glamorous girl Clyde desires at the expense of the woman he has been living with, Sternberg gives us a Clyde virtually incapable of loving anyone and shows the woman he rejects in a favourable light. He only yields up his distrust of Clyde at the moment when, as the judge sentences him to death, Clyde turns to his mother and coolly smiles at her.

Hollywood had been slow to reflect post-war criticism of moral conventions, the belief that the sanctions and ideas of society were a hypocritical veneer on lawless impulse. If it reflected this impulse, it did so by implication: by showing family life as the last bastion of conventional virtue. An ambitious and unscrupulous hero will find himself burdened by a pious mother who represents not so much his conscience as a persecutor, someone who can be blamed for his failure in emotional development. He tends to respond to women as though they were either prostitutes or mothers. By the thirties the reliance of scriptwriters on this division had begun to appear fatigued, and though some of them continued to build their plots around it, the process had become a caricature of itself. Michael Curtiz's *Mammy* (1930), an extreme example, has Al Jolson in his black minstrel routine, worshipping his Mammy but also permanently on the run from her. He retreats into show business, where all questions of social and sexual identity are helpfully muddled, where his greed for praise can be satisfied by pleasing audiences, and where his engagement to a desirable girl, the ultimate betrayal of Mammy, can be excused—he falls victim to a backstage trick—as a form of theatrical dissimulation.

The Depression aroused a sense of betrayal and a distrust of authority that strained the bonds of family life as well as the allegiances of society. But other forces were at work to strengthen these bonds. The Payne Fund researchers, though perplexed, did hold on to the understanding that the young were likely to be the most hurt by the Depression and that Hollywood should, more than ever before, take on parental responsibilities. The studios reacted to this proposal by putting forward a variety of models for adult behaviour, many of them engaging. Yet their selection depended on intuition and box-office returns; they were as hesitant as their public in making moral judgements. John Ford's work at this time typifies this hesitation. Although he had often been tempted to retreat into an idealized past where a matriarchal or patriarchal rule can withstand any form of criticism, he was more concerned during this period to enact the ways in which the modern world could disrupt family life to the point where all certainties are destroyed. In the silent *Four Sons* (1928) a German widow experiences the death of three sons in the First World War and then joins her fourth son in New York. No one meets her on her arrival and she is soon lost in the big city. She sits on a pavement, bewildered by the crowds and a language that she cannot speak. The interest of this scene is that her dignity as a mother is broken not by war but by the city, and that Ford's style should gain in assurance at the moment of her collapse. It is as though he had acquired her former vitality.

Pilgrimage (1933) is sharper, more disillusioned, more convincing. Hannah Jessop (Henrietta Crosland), an Arkansas widow, breaks off her son's relationship with a neighbouring farm-girl by sending him to the front line. After his death, Hannah declines to acknowledge the existence of either the farm-girl or her illegitimate grandson. Ten years later a military commission persuades her to join a party of mothers on an official visit to the war graves in France. She feels a charlatan among the mourning mothers, but she mourns also, and the bitter irony of her condition stirs the poet in Ford: as in the wordless moment when the farm-girl and the grandson bring flowers for the grave to her departing train and her hand stretches out from the carriage window to receive them; as in the contrast between her and the jovial, pipe-smoking mother, who has nevertheless been afflicted by the death of three sons, or the mother who comes from Milwaukee and speaks only German. Irony for once tempers Ford's feeling for the elegiac and provides it with a depth seldom to be regained. The tough and indomitable Hannah gradually turns into an admirable character, though hardly a likeable one. As she stretches out her arms to her grandson, he cringes, and we recognize that her affections will always be controlling.

Pilgrimage is a product of depression, in every sense of that word, and no story conveying distrust of authority was to be more bitter than this one of a mother who kills her son and then must mourn his death as a sacrifice to the nation. Yet Ford discovers in this story a wholeness and strains of feeling that Sternberg, for instance, never reaches. A child may find models for adult life in Sternberg's films but he will never see how the child may become an adult. Clyde, like all Sternberg characters, seems to have sprung fully developed from the womb. He remains aloof. His smile in the con-cluding moments of the film comes as a shock because it has no connection with his past. On the other hand, Ford usually records the processes of growing up carefully.

The astringency of Sternberg's attitudes makes a welcome contrast to the sentimentality of *Mammy*, but it leaves too much out; and it is necessary to look elsewhere, to the first cycle of gangster movies, for intuitions about the structure of society and the family that deeply stirred the public.

Many gangster heroes reflect the self-sufficiency of Clyde and at the same time appear to be bound, in a Fordian way, by family ties and childhood pieties: a combination of estrangement and guilt that may seem to have been arranged to catch the teenage mind. But it is unlikely that Warner studios, who produced most of the gangster films, had been able to anticipate this result. A careful look at the most influential films in this first cycle, in fact, conveys the impression that the studio had unexpectedly tapped explosive energies (which are still barrelled in forewords and prohibitions warning the public of the gangsters' badness), that it was startled by these energies, and that it had the greatest difficulty in giving these energies a form.

For these first gangster films fit into no established category. They were neither satires on business ethics nor protests at slum conditions. Nor were they intended as nightmares, nor as definitions of some new, brutish kind of tragic hero. Yet all these possibilities were contained within them. As in many other cases where familiar conventions break down beneath the pressure of material as yet undiscriminated, we have no choice but to fall back onto a term that covers the failure of style to deal adequately with a sudden flood of actuality: that of realism.

Through his discovery of the West and his friendship with Old Timers and Redskins, Thomas H. Ince had created Westerns that were close to being documentaries. The producers and directors at Warner Brothers had much the same relationship to bootlegging, gang warfare and the skulduggery of politics. They tended to enjoy the same pleasures as the racketeer, especially gambling, and their business practices were often just as colourful. The gangster, on the other hand, was often fascinated by show business and its personalities. He dressed as flamboyantly as an actor. In his screen appearances, at least, he exhibited a theatrical flair in the way he stage-managed a city and, by treating ordinary things as though they were conjurors' props, could give them an unexpected function; it comes as a perennial surprise to learn that machine-guns may be hidden in a crate labelled

William Wellman: *The Public Enemy.*

'pineapples', or that a gasoline truck may contain hooch. At moments, the kinship between the mobster and the entertainment world was to tighten into irony, as when, in July 1934, Dillinger was shot down as he left the Biograph cinema in Chicago after seeing the crime drama *Manhattan Melodrama.*

The first cycle of gangster films, like Ince's Westerns, referred to the immediate past. It came into being as the age of gang terror was coming to an end, and it was no different from many other Depression movies in acknowledging that the 1920s had in some way failed and in wanting to know why. But it tended to be self-contradictory in this aim. For while it presented venality and greed rather censoriously, it remained uncritical of Jazz Age views on the good life. It frequently showed the gangster as a good dancer and had him dressed in black tie or tails. It gave his movements physical grace. It allowed him to expire as though he were Pavlova's swan. (Victims, however, usually died abruptly.) James Cagney's promotion from vaudeville hoofer to America's favourite tough guy excited no comment.

Hollywood also idealized memories of the Jazz Age by giving them a chromium-plated, art deco streamlining. Raffish glamour was no longer the prerogative of the aristocratic, the talented or the rich: the screen made it available, as a dream, to everyone. The immense popularity of Fred Astaire — from *Flying Down to Rio* (1933) to the end of the decade — marks this change. Astaire's superiority lay both in his dancing and in his ability not to appear superior; no one could feel resentment at his gifts. In a sense, the movies were still trying to work through ways of feeling and thinking that the novel had exhausted. In *Scarface* (1932), Tony Camonte's collection of shirts, one for every day of the year, and his death beneath the lights of a travel advertisement stating 'The World is Yours' approach the symbolism and texture of *The Great Gatsby* more closely than anything that had come out of Hollywood during the previous decade.

In *The Liveliest Art* Arthur Knight states that *Little Caesar* was so popular that over fifty gangster films and a great number of exposé movies had imitated it within a year. But *Little Caesar* presents all the elements of the gangster myth in an as yet unintegrated form. Its central character, Rico, is neither estranged from his family nor linked to them by feelings of guilt; he simply has no family. This part of the myth is directed onto Rico's henchman, Antonio, so guilt-ridden at the thought of his pious rebuking mother that Rico thinks him 'yella' and has him shot down, appropriately, on some cathedral steps. Another important aspect of the gangster myth also fails to cover Rico. Quite unlike his prototype in W. R. Burnett's novel, he has no overt sex life. This part of the myth — the expectation that gangsters should be sexually potent — is projected onto Rico's buddy, Joe Masara, a professional dancer who gives up crime to become a success in cabaret. Show business and crime may be linked, but show business offers the best opportunities to an élite of the talented and beautiful.

Rico is neither of these. An Italian immigrant played by Edward G. Robinson, an actor of Romanian Jewish origins, Rico is the perennial loser and outsider, a nobody who has sprung out of nowhere, who first comes to view in that most anonymous of places, an all-night diner. Ruthless enough to rise swiftly to the top of the underworld, he lacks the skill to hold onto power and soon slips back into the abyss. For years he moves from flophouse to flophouse, a tramp who drinks too much. A newspaper article describing him as a coward, and planted by the police, draws him out of hiding; and he is gunned down beneath a poster of Joe Masara and his radiant wife, advertising their latest show.

Rico has pathos. He makes the immigrant's mistake of taking the protestant ethic literally. He misreads the signs. His struggle for power is a struggle for a certain type of identity and he never obtains the social connections needed to secure this identity. Mervyn LeRoy and his scriptwriter, Francis Faragoh, are clearly baffled by him. Although they recognize his statistical significance—many immigrants, wishing to be accepted, suffered his kind of rejection—they seem unable to dramatize his fate within any of the accepted modes of fiction. They give his story the overtones of a Jacobean tragedy; yet this tentative bid for tragic status is qualified by the ironic 'little' of the title, and rightly so, for Rico remains small, even when compared to the mock-heroic Mussolini. His idiom becomes ornate when he snarls: 'If anyone turns yella and squeals, my gun'll speak its piece.' But the void about him shrivels this grandiloquence.

In his intelligent and deliberate way, Edward G. Robinson suggests the waste of a gifted man without appearing to play for audience sympathy. He attacks the part with a sardonic relish: an attack, however, that does not diminish Rico's failure to stake a claim on either the natural or supernatural world. He has no place in society. He can only define himself within the short-lived alliances of the underworld. Dying, he thinks of himself in the third person, like Othello. 'Mother of Mercy,' he groans, 'is this the end of Rico?' But he has touched depths of ignominy that Othello never knew of and his last words are no more than a placatory gesture towards some memory of faith. He has no faith. He has little feeling. Although he sends a lavish wreath to Antonio's funeral and joins the cortège in an expensive limousine, he can only feel restless. 'Gee,' he complains, 'we're moving slow.' Reformers missed the point when they argued that Rico embodied a wish fulfilment of the most subversive kind because his creators had given him no context in society or family life. The ferocity of their complaint, however, suggests how troubling was this image of alienated man, and how eagerly the public saw itself reflected in it.

In part to placate these reformers, William Wellman concentrates the opening scenes of *The Public Enemy* (1931) on the childhood of his central character, Tom Powers (James Cagney). Wellman does not reveal whether he thinks Tom's delinquency to be innate or implanted by his brutal policeman father. But in these opening scenes he does show how gang violence, far from being bound up with Prohibition, had been a social infection in the United States since before the First World War. He shows how crime and its environment are connected. For Wellman understood far better than LeRoy how he needed to describe the environment of criminals if he were to make their actions plausible.

His concern with the ways in which this culture is embodied in its buildings and streets opened up a manner of filming that reached its most complete expression in Wyler's *Dead End* (1937) and Curtiz's *Angels with Dirty Faces* (1938), where studio constructions of slum streets were so intricate that they tended to dominate the people who walked in them. But this emphasis on detail was not needlessly mannered. Anyone who has played as a child in city streets will have come to know every crack in the pavement and every irregularity in a brick wall: a prison-like experience recalled by these sets. In 1937 Congress passed a bill allocating half a billion dollars for slum clearance, and Sam Goldwyn invited Senator Wagner of New York, who had steered through this bill, as guest of honour to the opening night of *Dead End*. It was no accident that it and other films like it should have centred, however superficially, on the condition of slum children.

Wellman's insights are so central to urban life, and so unstudied, that they may pass unnoticed. One such moment in *The Public Enemy* consists of a bar-room seen full face from across the street in pouring rain; an image held until the sound of gunfire breaks in. On one level, the gunfire may be essential in furthering the plot. On another more valuable level, many people who have been brought up in cities will feel this violence to be related in some inherent way to the drabness of the bar-room: an awareness so bred in the bone that the spectator may register no surprise at seeing it portrayed on the screen. Yet this perception, and Wellman's use of sound and image, are far more imaginative than, say, Hitchcock's virtuosity with sound in *Blackmail* (1929).

But the inclusion of scenes from Tom's childhood is primarily useful in integrating the gangster myth. Because of them, Tom's close relationship as an adult with his God-fearing mother does not seem unexpected, while his long-standing antagonisms with the male members of his family help to widen the social implications of his actions. After his father's death, Tom directs his hostility to authority at his brother who had fought in the war and who struggles to make an honest living. Verbal battles ensue that allow Tom to score easy points in his own favour while pointing up his own exclusion from society. Why should his brother preach at him, Tom argues, when he killed in the war, and with apparent enjoyment, and when he now is so full of resentment at his low pay? These family quarrels and meetings have a sadness about them (very Irish in feeling and, like certain of John Ford's films, close in atmosphere to the plays of Sean O'Casey) that suggest some yearning for a primal harmony that has now been lost; a sadness underlined by a recurring motif, the playing of 'I'm Forever Blowing Bubbles' on a gramophone record.

It comes as no surprise, then, that Tom, who resists the idea of the family, should be seen as permanently regressed to states of infancy. His mother visits him in hospital after the shoot-up and calls him her baby—and indeed he resembles a baby, so wrapped up in bandages that he appears to be swaddled. In the final scene his mother and sister, hearing that he is about to come home, prepare his room as though expecting an accouchement, while 'I'm Forever Blowing Bubbles' plays on the gramophone. The doorbell rings; his brother opens the door; and Tom, murdered and still wrapped in bandages, falls into the hallway.

Tom deludes himself, then, in thinking that he has escaped from domesticity. But he does have one moment of protest so striking that it has been referred to as a turning-point in the cinema's history: a moment that occurs not during a gunfight but at a nervous moment in most households, at breakfast, when Tom with little justification thrusts half a grapefruit into his girl friend's face. In the next scene he picks up a high-class prostitute played by Jean Harlow, and in doing so replaces a solicitous, compliant and maternal woman with one as aggressive as himself. 'Give me your phone number,' she says, 'and I'll call you.' Wellman appears to be as dazzled by this relationship as Tom is; even so, Cagney's love scene with Harlow in a silky white

William Wellman: *The Public Enemy*. James Cagney, Jean Harlow.

boudoir has none of the dreamy remoteness of a silent screen romance. Harlow is as much the tough new kind of star as Cagney, and her candour speaks as directly to the audience as does his bluntness. But Tom is killed before this affair has had time to get going, perhaps fortunately; it would hardly have stood much investigation. Only the self-mocking Mae West could now make the figure of the vamp look plausible.

The style of *The Public Enemy* marks a considerable development on *Little Caesar*. Although its art direction reflects the influence of German design, Wellman knows how to give his sets the dimension and physicality that Le Roy had failed to achieve and he knows how to enact the spirit that underlies both Jacobean melodrama and the gangster thriller without falling into pastiche: the spirit in which people who live outside the laws of man and nature try to eliminate each other with devices of an ever more elaborate artifice—one such example being the truck that thunders coal down a chute at the moment when Tom's enemies wish to drown out the noise of a machine-gun. Even so, compared to Howard Hawks's *Scarface* (1932), the style of *The Public Enemy* looks transitional.

In a technical sense, *Scarface* is the purest of the early gangster movies. In content, though, it is packed with unnatural designs and intentions; even family relationships, however sacrosanct, are rooted in perversity, the question of incest hovering over Tony Camonte's closeness to his sister. Tony, alias Scarface, alias Paul Muni, is modelled on Al Capone (arrested and jailed for tax evasion in 1931), while the plot, devoted

Howard Hawks: *Scarface.*

to an underworld battle that occurs after the death of a gang leader, recalls the events that followed the murder of Arnold Rothstein in 1928. 'They'll be shooting each other like rabbits for the control of the booze business,' crows a newspaper editor, and Hawks does not cheat this expectation. He invites his audience into a pre-literate world where action has such a superiority over words that motives are often never given, and captures attention with a series of bloody crimes, each as brief and inconsequential as a nightmare. His sense of humour puts the nightmare into some sort of perspective and incidentally reveals that Tony is in the direct line of succession to Père Ubu, Alfred Jarry's stage buffoon who had stepped out of the avant-garde theatre, as it were, into the Sennett comedies. But in *Scarface* Père Ubu has become monstrously real and threatens to take over the cities. Humour saves Hawks from falling into the condescension that literate men often feel in their revulsion at the brutish. He passes no judgement on Tony and allows his audience for a while to consider the behaviour of this twilight mind.

Tony claims to enjoy serious plays and boasts that he will write his name over the town in big letters. But because he thinks words stand for literary achievements and executive status, they loom up as a target for his envy. He likes to put his fist through glass door-panels on which the names of rivals are painted and at one point directs his machine-gun at a hotel letter rack. He parodies verbal transactions by communicating with his gun. Angelo, his minute henchman, always failing to make connections, especially on the phone, takes this parody into burlesque. On one occasion when Tony and Angelo are at a restaurant, a rival gang rakes the place with bullets; and Angelo, at the phone, loses his temper because he cannot hear a word over the noise. On another occasion, provoked by some caller, he threatens to put a bullet into the receiver and later, as he dies, Hawks has him, somewhat obviously, crawl across the room to take a call.

Locked out of the world of words, Tony is all physical appetite and cunning. He seems incapable of remorse, as though a capacity for remorse depended on being articulate. He swells on violence, and he seems impossible. 'Do you like this?' he asks a girl, showing her his expensive new clothes. 'Kinda gaudy,' she mutters. 'Glad you like it.' Paul Muni's flamboyance fits this role like a glove. When this relished monster dies, he does so beneath arc lights, as though on a film set, as though his fictional nature had to be demonstrated before it could be extinguished. Even so, the reformers were incensed by him, and Howard Hughes had to interpolate a sequence in which a police chief states that gangsters, unlike the noble heroes of the Western, shoot their enemies in the back. This sequence, like most hasty interpolations, misfires: it adds to the gangster mystique.

Box-office returns had diminished in 1930, but the novelty of sound at first staved off the effects of the Depression. It was a different story in the theatre. 'Vaudeville in 1930', claimed *Variety* somewhat incoherently, 'stood motionless as a treadmill that moves backwards.'[15] Cinema owners, offering cut-price tickets and free marcel waves, worked hard to attract the public; but during 1931 attendances dropped by forty per cent, and when the studios reopened after the Christmas break, at the beginning of 1932, their managers had cut back on jobs and slashed salaries.

Take-overs and receiverships bedevilled the industry: Paramount, RKO and Fox went bankrupt, though part of the Fox organization escaped collapse and in 1935 was merged with Joseph Schenck's Twentieth Century Corporation. Altogether Hollywood cut back on expenditure by eighteen million dollars. (According to F. L. Allen, 'business as a whole lost between five and six billion dollars in 1932.')[16] Apart from the Loew Inc. cinema and theatre empire, only Warner Brothers was able, by cheeseparing, to ride the Depression unthreatened by closure. In 1932 one of its productions, *The Singing Fool* (1928), starring Al Jolson and directed by Lloyd Bacon, was still the best sound film at the box-office and had earned five million dollars. It was the only major company in that year not under the control of the Rockefeller, Morgan or Mellon groups.

By now all the major studios had taken up the assembly-line system of production which Irving Thalberg had initiated in the mid-twenties. Supervisors patrolled every department. Roland V. Brown, a minor talent who wrote and directed *Quick Millions* (1931), a desultory crime tale that launched Spencer Tracy as a star, and the droll, uneven *Blood Money* (1933), became a legendary figure in Hollywood—and ended his directorial career—when he knocked out one of these supervisors. But opportunities were just as limited in other countries. By 1935 the French film industry had utterly collapsed. A cottage industry came into being. Independent producers would join up with directors and actors to form small, transient companies. Unlike Hollywood, they did not need to capture world markets and they could gamble on adventurous themes. However, this apparent freedom did not lead to a director's cinema. Producers insisted on the guarantee of a good script before they would back a project. They looked for their model to the theatrical craftsmanship of Marcel Pagnol and Sacha Guitry, and they thought their policy vindicated when Renoir, improvising on the perfunctory script of *La Marseillaise*, brought in a box-office disaster. In the spring 1941 number of *Sight and Sound* André Bernheim was to support this policy by arguing—strangely, it may now seem—that the force of Duvivier's *Carnet de bal* and *Pepé le Moko* largely depended on Henri Jeanson's screenplays and that the writer Charles Spaak was mostly responsible for the brilliance of Renoir's *La*

Grande Illusion. In effect, most French directors tended to be as restricted as their contemporaries in Hollywood.

Hollywood studios devoted a great deal of time to improving the assembly-line method of production. When Preston Sturges in his screenplay for *Power and Glory* (1933) evolved a new form of film biography told in non-chronological order, his producer, Jesse L. Lasky, gave this innovation the name of 'narratage' and built his sales talks around it. But *Power and Glory* uses 'narratage' purely as a mechanical gimmick, and some years had to pass before Welles and Mankiewicz were to uncover a significant use for this technique in *Citizen Kane*. Hollywood tended to assess directors by their ability to modify a well-tried formula with the right amount (and no more) of novelty: precision engineering of a kind that as often as not gave an impression of slickness. The inventive Rouben Mamoulian conjured up an ingenious way of transforming Dr Jekyll into Mr Hyde (1931) and achieved some clever colour effects in *Becky Sharp* (1935), but he was seldom more than an exceptional technician. The same is true of Howard Hawks, who directed such well-paced comedies as *Twentieth Century* (1934) and *Bringing Up Baby* (1938), as well as the impeccable adventure story *Only Angels Have Wings* (1939): beautifully honed machines that gear an audience to laughter or suspense. But Hawks's toughness is too diplomatically couched, his urbanity too suave.

Fortunately no studio could iron out all idiosyncrasies. An output based on successful blueprints remained a producer's cigar-dream. It is possible that the Hollywood chiefs would have liked their audiences to have been robots; but audiences were always to be unpredictable and the Depression had increased their distrust of the hard sell. The collapse of the economic system had released strange forces. As Peter F. Drucker has written, it had shown 'man as a senseless cog in a senselessly-whirling machine which is beyond human understanding and has ceased to serve any purpose but its own'.[17] A situation reminiscent of Germany in the mid-twenties encouraged a trend in the German type of horror film. The public flocked to James Whale's rather chi-chi *Frankenstein* (1931). However, a number of films drawing a comparison between man and the beasts came closer to poetry. Walking through New York, the explorer Merian C. Cooper had a sudden vision of a huge gorilla towering over the Empire State Building: an image so powerful that it could be interpreted in a number of ways, though by the time Cooper and his director Ernest B. Schoedsack, with some help from Edgar Wallace, had worked through various drafts of their screenplay, the monster primarily represented the pathos of passion chained and the fury of passion released. Few films have contributed so many images to the folklore of the century as *King Kong* (1933). As the gorilla crushes a carriage on the El, peers

through a window into Fay Wray's bedroom, twiddles her between his
fingers or swipes at planes as though they were flies, he gradually
begins to take on the power of some primitive god in a Goya painting.
Willis O'Brien's special effects may be responsible for the conviction of
the images, but the source of their power lies in Cooper's flair for
sensing the widespread apocalyptic fear/wish that some godlike figure,
be it Scarface or King Kong, should take over the 'senselessly whirling
machine', and in his ability to conceive of this vision purely in
terms of film. *King Kong* brings together the fantastic type of imagination which Disney had liberated onto the screen and the naturalistic
care for detail of Cooper's adventure travelogues. During the worst
year of the Depression crowds packed the cinemas to be frightened
and consoled by its giant hero.

It caught the spirit of the moment; yet it represented only one
way among many in which the fragments of a communal fantasy could
be welded together. The first half of its story, for instance, concerns
the capture of King Kong on an island which the explorers feel to be a
prison; an idea which had been realized the year before, and far more
disturbingly, in an adaptation of H. G. Wells's *The Island of Dr Moreau*,
starring Charles Laughton. Dr Moreau experiments on animals and
virtually succeeds in transforming them into humans. His cruel
surgery and his bizarre theories about evolution anticipate the practice
of Nazi doctrines in the concentration camp experiments. Laughton
may be too pliant for the role, but in other ways *Island of Lost Souls/The
Island of Dr Moreau* (1932) has some claim to be among the most
disturbing films ever made. Its House of Pain and its dog servant and

Erle C. Kenton: *Island of Lost Souls*. Charles Laughton.

panther woman are horrifying, all the more so because the doctor's prison island, which visually resembles Boecklin's Isle of the Dead, is also the island of dreams where the self, godlike, imagines itself free to enact its most extreme wishes.

Sternberg's *The Blue Angel* had given a novel twist to the legend of beauty and the beast. The theory that some races are superior to others was very much in the air at this time, and the contrast between beauty and the beast could not help being infected by it. In Tod Browning's *Freaks* (1932), a group of circus freaks conspire to destroy a handsome pair of acrobat lovers who have mocked them for their inadequacies and cheated one of them, a dwarf. The woman acrobat ends up on display as a mutant, half-fowl and half-woman. A risible ending, yet the movie gave offence – Browning used actual freaks – and it was banned, though Browning's treatment was sensitive and in certain scenes, as in the gambolling of his monsters in a sunny glade, it touched the grotesque with gentleness.

The most elaborate working-out of the comparison between men and beasts occurred in *Zoo in Budapest* (1933). A zoo-keeper, a girl from an orphanage (Loretta Young) and a small boy, each of them in flight from the outside world, find themselves locked overnight in a zoo, and the small boy accidentally releases the animals from their cages. Quite what the director, Roland V. Lee, and his associates intended by their multiple metaphors for confinement and liberation is never given, and yet, like the makers of *King Kong*, they created a haunting concatenation of images – haunting, perhaps, because they recapture the complex sensations of childhood visits to the zoo. The thought that zoos may degrade the animals is qualified by memories of childhood pleasure in the proud independence of the beasts and the reassurance that their (and our) violence can be contained. Lee Garmes's camera covers the zoo from so many angles that he conveys the impression that he has enclosed both it and us within the dome of its lenses. He makes it plain that we and the three night visitors and the animals have some point of identification. What is less sure in this parable is the semi-divine status given to the zoo director, or the meaning of the spectacular sequence in which the animals break out of their cages. When guards appear in file carrying flares, like storm-troopers, and quell the animals with jets of water, as though the animals were Eisenstein's strikers, the action comes close to touching on Depression feelings about the socially intolerable, but never goes so far as to relate the animals to some human spirit of insurgency. In effect, the break-out of the animals is treated as no more than a flourish of cinematic energy, one of those meaningless spectacles by which Hollywood in the thirties often got round the problems it set itself.

What is remarkable, though, is the recurrence of the same motifs in every kind of Hollywood genre – evidence, maybe, of how the impact of the Depression had given a common preoccupation to most people. The emphasis on the same themes again and again is more like the repetitions of a newspaper item than the conscious patterning of novelists. Most of these themes stem from a distrust of the professions and the civic authorities and reveal a half-veiled sympathy for the criminal, an ironic involvement with the American need to get rich quick and a wish to acknowledge the damage the First World War had done to the spirit of the nation. (Many of the members of the breadline, it was noted, were veterans of the battlefront.) It is not surprising to learn, then, that some of the directors and actors concerned in evolving the most lively vehicle for these themes, the gangster movie, should have been among the more committed to social reform and to the promotion of social problem pictures.

Among these directors the one most committed to a left-wing view of social issues was probably Lewis Milestone, who had directed *The Racket* (1928), one of the earliest gangster films, and who during the thirties was to make his political sympathies more and more plain. Many critics have considered his film version of Erich Maria Remarque's novel *All Quiet on the Western Front* (1930) to be one of the finest of anti-war statements. But Milestone is one of those directors whose good intentions are often taken as a guarantee for talent; and almost every sequence in *All Quiet on the Western Front*, apart from its concluding moments, shows how limited his gifts were.

He was to find a more satisfactory outlet in *The Front Page* (1931), a close adaptation of the Ben Hecht–Charles MacArthur play, in which he emphasizes, as they do, both the heroism of its anarchist prisoner condemned to the electric chair and the social background of each of the characters who erupts into the reporter's room at the condemned man's prison. Howard Hawks, who remade *The Front Page* in 1939 as *His Girl Friday*, was to play down the political aspect of the play, to change its principal reporter into a woman (Rosalind Russell) and to concentrate on the tangled and amusing relationship she has with her editor (Cary Grant). But the difference between these two versions of *The Front Page* is more than one of temperament. Milestone's style is dominated by the influence of Pudovkin: camera angles and editing are less devoted to keeping the narrative on the move than to insisting on the physical relationship of the characters to their surroundings and on the sculptured presence of heads in close-up. Hawks, on the other hand, tries to heighten the vividness of each moment by sharp timing and by playing up the personalities of his two stars.

On the evidence of the Depression musical *Hallelujah I'm a Bum* (1933) Milestone was incapable of this skill, or perhaps thought it irrelevant. He had decided to take the world's conscience on his shoulders and was to work with the Group Theatre playwright Clifford Odets on *The General Died at Dawn* (1936) and with the Marxist documentarist Joris Ivens on *Our Russian Front* (1941). But it would be wrong to suggest that either Milestone or Hawks responded more effectively to the potential in the Hecht–MacArthur play. The point of the comparison is to show how, in relation to the main trends in Hollywood film-making in the 1930s, directors working at the time of a Depression that had hit their studios as well as the rest of society found it virtually impossible to exclude some form of reference to social anxieties, while directors at the end of the decade found it expedient to resist this pressure: after all, it took some time for Hollywood to realize how the threat of war and the loss of foreign markets had affected its box-office returns.

But in a sense Milestone had been an exception even in the early thirties: most of his Hollywood contemporaries did not feel the need to respond to social anxieties from some committed political position. In two topical films made at this time William Wellman and his screenwriters appear to have felt the Depression as in some way analogous in its shock to the death of a parent. In *Wild Boys of the Road* (1933), two boys leave home in order to relieve their parents who have been ruined by the slump. They join up with a gang of adolescents, found a boys' town and eventually end up in court. In *The President Vanishes* (1934) an American president pretends to have been kidnapped so as to bring a private Fascist army into the open and to remind the electorate of how valuable he is to them.

In neither film is Wellman a paternalist. He clearly welcomes hostile situations which force the individual into taking an initiative, to such an extent that his boys of the road are similar to gangsters like Tom Powers. Indeed, Frankie Darro, who plays their leader, is as agile, bouncy and good-humoured as Cagney; according to Wellman, Darro's minute stature alone prevented him from having an outstanding career in motion pictures.

The power of the reformers was such, however, that by the end of the decade Norman Taurog, dealing with a comparable theme in *Boys' Town* (1938), felt obliged to show his wild boys from the standpoint of a kindly Roman Catholic priest (Spencer Tracy). 'There's no such thing as a bad boy,' claims Father Flanagan, but in fact boys can be far worse than any to be seen in his town; even the most hardened delinquent that he has ever tried to reform (Mickey Rooney) is good-hearted. *Boys' Town* provides all the answers and would be odious in its sanctimony if it were not for the shrewd yet heartfelt acting of Tracy and Rooney.

Wellman, on the other hand, resents all presuppositions; the title of his most celebrated comedy *Nothing Sacred* (1937) catches his tone exactly. Siding with the maverick and even seeing the President as an accomplice to his own kidnapping, he engages most strongly with the sensations, even physical shock, that his individualists feel when stripped bare of all social protection; as when Tommy, one of the wild boys, accidentally walks into a telegraph pole, falls onto a railway track and has his leg severed by a train. He comes close in spirit to Jean Vigo's *Zéro de conduite* and Nicolai Ekk's *The Road to Life*, although his liking for enterprise never included a wish for revolution, as it did with Vigo and Ekk. In 1948 he was to be responsible for the anti-Red movie *The Iron Curtain*.

The effect of the Depression was such that while Warner Brothers put Wellman onto nearly every kind of picture, the same attitudes and plot patterns would emerge in nearly every one: a consistency even more noticeable in the case of Mervyn LeRoy, who in a matter of two years was to take on genres as unlike each other as the topical movie, the hard-boiled comedy and the musical. In *I am a Fugitive from a Chain Gang* (1932), based on the autobiography of Robert Elliott Burns, who twice escaped from a Georgia chain-gang and eventually was granted a parole by the New Jersey legislature (a happy ending which, perhaps uniquely in the history of Hollywood, was transformed into a pessimistic one on film), LeRoy turns the story's dispersal over space and time to his advantage by establishing a strong contrast between the Georgia

Mervyn LeRoy: *I am a Fugitive from a Chain Gang*

prison, where chains cripple mobility and men die from over-employment, and the world outside, where the unemployed are always on the move.

James Allen, his fugitive, is the antithesis of Rico in *Little Caesar*; yet both men are victims of the protestant ethic. Returning from the First World War, Allen angers his clergyman brother by refusing to settle down to office work. He wishes to build bridges, but he is unable to find employment and by mischance becomes involved in a hold-up and is sentenced to ten years' hard labour. After his first escape, he takes on a job in Chicago and works hard enough to win such social approval that the Chicago courts are willing to give him sanctuary. His brother describes him without irony as 'a man who showed his character by rising from nothing to be a prominent citizen'. But Allen also sets too much store on prominence and accepts the Governor of Georgia's promise that he will soon be pardoned if he serves a nominal sentence: a pledge that is broken. He escapes once more, but he is now a broken man, harassed by the fear of arrest; and the last image of the film is of a haunted face, fading into darkness. The critic Harry Alan Potamkin has pointed out how unusual this final image is, in the sense that it induces the spectator to revise his response to what has gone before.

Allen's well-intentioned struggle to escape from despair is among the most unequivocal examples on film of how the Depression could blight all hope. LeRoy at first presents the Georgia prison as a social evil that could be reformed; he then allows its atmosphere to inform the whole film and begins to see the prison as typical of a society in which officials are corrupt hypocrites and the promise of fulfilment through work or marriage revealed to be a thinly disguised invitation to slavery. Less concerned with describing the actual state of America in the twenties than its mood at the beginning of the next decade, LeRoy's skill resides in his evoking a grotesque situation without falling into the selfconscious devices employed by such novelists as Nathanael West. He is finely supported by Paul Muni's portrayal of Allen, the reticence of whose playing is so unlike the ebullience of his first leading screen performance in *Scarface* that he was to be acknowledged as Hollywood's most distinguished character actor.

As the Depression deepened, Warner Brothers moved LeRoy, as it did other directors, into the field of hard-boiled comedy. The main character in *Hard to Handle* (1933) is Chaplinesque without being sentimental or fanciful: a 'ballyhoo' promoter (James Cagney), whose only interest is to scalp the public. Organizing a dance marathon, he is chased down the street by irate competitors when the prize money is stolen; organizing a treasure-hunt on a pier, he is defeated when desperately poor crowds tear the pier apart. As a tribute to *Hard to*

Mervyn LeRoy: *Hard to Handle*. The dance marathon.

Handle, LeRoy was invited to appear as a member of the audience during the dance marathon sequences in *They Shoot Horses, Don't They?* (1969); yet it is probable that this hindsight wistful view of the Depression would have seemed foolish to LeRoy's public in 1933. Encouraging initiative and quelling self-pity, *Hard to Handle* makes no excuses for those who desire easy money, however poor they may be. In the words of Cagney's promoter, anyone who succumbs to this desire is 'like a cow bellowing to be milked', and the fat girl who attends the marathon in the hopes of seeing someone die sets the tone for this hard-eyed movie. LeRoy angles its bankruptcies, robberies and contricks so as to arouse laughter at the expense of the victim and although he allows Cagney a touch of Robin Hood – a favourite character on the Warner lot – he presents him as being at his most commendable in his manic enthusiasms.

LeRoy turned his hand to the musical in the same year, dealing in *Gold Diggers of 1933* with a subject that Lloyd Bacon's *Forty-Second Street* (1933) and a host of other musicals were to imitate: that of some gallant troupers trying to put on a musical good enough to melt the flinty hearts of metropolitan first-nighters. One reason why film-makers considered the souped-up imperatives of this subject desirable was that it allowed actors to move plausibly into musical routines; another more compelling reason was that it cashed in on the un-shakeable myth that all stage producers are sadists and all actresses prostitutes. But while *Forty-Second Street* dealt with these propositions in a straightforward manner, *Gold Diggers of 1933* enmeshes them with the theme of the Depression. In its main plot a producer sets up a musical about the Depression. In its subplot the sanctimonious brother of its central character and his lawyer are so tiresome in reiterating their belief that all actresses are prostitutes that they provoke two girls in the company to act this part and inevitably are infatuated by them.

In *We're in the Money*, a study of the Depression movie, Andrew Bergman quotes from 'Poverty Breeds Vice', an article in the *Literary Digest* of 1932 claiming that the 'inability to get work is forcing many young women either directly or indirectly into prostitution or at least into borderline occupations':[18] an argument that leaves unquestioned the assumption whether anyone has ever at any time been 'forced' into prostitution. Yet clearly the public's curiosity about this way of life and its confusions about the value of money were heightened by the Depression, and Hollywood did not hesitate to encourage this curiosity by suggesting that prostitution was one way in which the housewife or secretary could emancipate herself. Marlene Dietrich, Constance Bennett and Mae West, among others, were to put this idea assiduously into practice in a great number of movies; and in her autobiography, *Goodness has Nothing to Do with It*, Mae West states that not only did two of her vehicles, *She Done Him Wrong* (1933) and *I'm No Angel* (1933), break box-office records but that *She Done Him Wrong* saved Paramount financially at a time when its executives were thinking of selling out to MGM.

While Miss West makes prostitution seem innocuous by parodying the figure of the vamp, LeRoy in *Gold Diggers of 1933* damps down fears about the Depression by a form of play-acting. He dissolves everything into the values of show biz, putting unemployment on the same level as theatrical 'resting', gold digging on the level of pretence and Depression distress on the level of The Big Parade of Tears. In the same way that his stage producer is crucial to this transformation, comforting as well as cruel when he says 'I could make 'em laugh at seeing you starve, dear', since at least someone appears to be in control of the uncontrollable, so LeRoy's verve in taking over this Prospero role with his audience precludes indignation.

But within LeRoy's transformation of actuality into fairy-tale occurs another transformation even more outlandish in its audacity: the musical numbers in both *Gold Diggers of 1933* and *Forty-Second Street* choreographed and directed by Busby Berkeley. Berkeley's camera arabesques open up space in every direction and soon dispel the notion that the spectator may be watching a stage routine, taking him into a garish wonderland where visual expectations are confounded and substance becomes indistinguishable from its reflection. He transforms the idea of actress as prostitute into the idea of chorus-

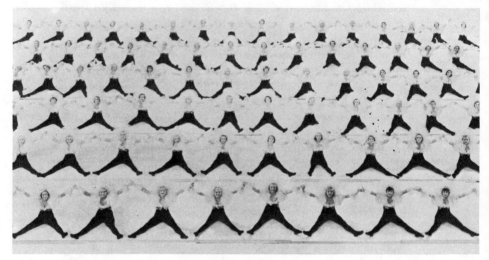

Busby Berkeley dance number: *Dames* (1934).

girl as sex machine, or even part of the human body, as he reduces a hundred girls to the shape of a violin, to the suspirious form of a sea anemone or to any other suggestion of the male or female genitals. Abstraction and the imperialism of technology here rival the ingenuity of Walt Disney and Leni Riefenstahl. An egregious tot (played by a midget), who peeps at girls, pulls up blinds on nudes in silhouette or hides under beds in the Honeymoon Hotel sequence of *Footlight Parade* (1933), is often the guiding intelligence to these events.

For all their tough practicality, American movies of the thirties gave light to some of the strangest fantasies of the cinema. Yet those who created these fantasies—and they include Busby Berkeley, Walt Disney and the Marx Brothers—were welcomed by the public and in no way thought of as recondite. They touched on a wish for the improbable in a materialist and mechanized society and they were talented enough to make the improbable look credible. In comparison, the Peeping Tom fantasies in *Le Sang d'un poète* and much other avant-garde eroticism of this time look forced. Berkeley raises cathedrals for the admirer of pin-ups; he brings the Méliès cinema to one kind of completion. He concludes *Gold Diggers of 1933* with a medley of Depression themes: men marching back from the war, joining the breadline, and being framed in a triple crescent while Joan Blondell sings 'Remember My Forgotten Man'. And not even he could quite cap that.

Hollywood's frivolity in this regard was enough to take King Vidor out of the studios to direct on private money *Our Daily Bread* (1934), the study of an agrarian commune that only rises to the promise of its subject in its concluding moments, as water is brought to the fields; for the rest, Vidor relies too much on a melodramatically conceived love affair with The Other Woman that recalls some of the weaker sequences in *Sunrise*. At this time, also, Pabst came to the United States and directed *A Modern Hero* (1934): a reputedly serious account of the Depression that failed at the box-office, however, and led to Pabst's return to Europe. Perhaps both he and Vidor had been overtaken by New Deal optimism, a confidence that Frank Capra had already anticipated in *American Madness* (1932) and *Lady for a Day* (1933).

Capra's power to set up meaningful connections between wishful predicaments and drab locations had been apparent in *The Strong Man* and *Long Pants*, the Harry Langdon comedies he had directed in 1926 and 1927. In much the same way as Langdon was to be a precursor of those innocent New Deal heroes Mr Deeds and Mr Smith, so Capra's fusion of the idealized and impoverished was to be more than an exploitation of the public desire for pie in the sky: the coherent way in which he developed his views on the human situation in the twenties and thirties would seem to confirm the seriousness of his involvement in them. The seventh child of Sicilian immigrant parents, he had been brought up as a Roman Catholic and in poverty. He must have found little that was unusual in the idea of a miracle in the tenement or in the juxtaposition of the Blessed Mother, with arms upraised, presiding over domestic squabbles and passions. Indebted though he was to at least one screenwriter, he was to signal the quality of his talent well before his long professional association with Robert Riskin; the Capra tone and the Capra gift for working out gags, for instance, had already matured by the time of his silent comedy *That Certain Thing* (1928). He appears to have recognized early on in his career that the gag consists of a series of physical events linked together by an improbable idea, a little like certain theological arguments.

Lady for a Day is taken from a Damon Runyon story in which a tough racketeer and his gang arrange that a street vendor, nicknamed Apple Annie, should spend some time in a grand hotel so that her daughter, engaged to some European aristocrat, should not learn of her penury. Apart from the improbability of racketeers taking part in such a benign conspiracy, the most salient feature of this story is its similarity to the Elinor Glyn type of romance that Hollywood had been so attached to in the twenties. In a sense Capra criticizes the appeal of this kind of romance, if only by contrasting the vitality of demotic America with the embalmed graciousness of upper-class living; but he then disarms this criticism by having Apple Annie and the racketeers discover that this kind of living fulfils their highest expectations. Where he comes closest to the prevailing mood of the early thirties is in the thought that the simulation of confidence, even in the form of a confidence trick, can spread confidence. Apple Annie actually becomes the lady she aspires to be.

He had enacted this idea more fully in his earlier film *American Madness*, which uncannily predicts the Keynesian tinge in the economic thinking of the Roosevelt administration. A switchboard operator at a bank misunderstands a remark overheard on the phone and spreads the rumour that the bank is on the point of financial collapse. A wave of panic spreads through its customers, who besiege it to withdraw their savings. But Dixon (Walter Huston), its president, not only thinks that investment is the answer to all economic problems, but also believes that firmness of character in itself has the power to counter-balance the unpredictability of the monetary system. He risks his own savings and the savings of his fellow directors to pay off the customers, and in doing so wins back confidence, diminishes panic and vindicates his policy that the running of banks should be based on an act of faith.

No one behaves rationally in this story. The customers may be hysterical, but their president is just as unreasonable in his hope to avert the crisis by personal authority alone, using the language of religion—hardly the most effective instrument of economic analysis—to describe the workings of the market, and persuading his fellow directors to part with their personal fortunes in a way that would leave unconvinced any banker worth his salt. Yet Capra clearly warms to this irrationality and has a splendid time with the scenes of mass hysteria. On reflection, though, his parable should arouse despondency in the spectator, especially as the course of events it describes was more or less to be enacted in real life. Unhappy the land that needs such heroes, maybe; yet such was the leader the United States wanted and got in Franklin D. Roosevelt.

While Capra's interests, so closely derived from his first-generation Sicilian and Roman Catholic upbringing, had a great appeal in the thirties and none in the late forties, the interests of another director of recent émigré origin, the Hungarian Michael Curtiz, were only to connect in any immediate way with the American public after the outbreak of the Second World War. During the thirties Curtiz was most at his ease with non-realistic themes: the crisply edited horrors of *The Mystery at the Wax Museum* (1933), the detective pleasantries of *The Kennel Murder Case* (1933) and the romances of *Captain Blood* (1935), *The Charge of the Light Brigade* (1936), *The Adventures of Robin Hood* (1938) and *The Private Lives of Elizabeth and Essex* (1939). Yet Curtiz did turn his hand to Depression themes, though rather dutifully. In *The Cabin in the Cotton* (1932) Richard Barthelmess, attempting his Tol'able David role once more but looking too old and plump for it, appears as Marvin Blake, the son of a cotton-picker, educated and then hired as an accountant after his father's death by his father's former employer. He becomes engaged to this planter's daughter (Bette Davis), discovers from the account books that the planter had cheated his father and uses this evidence to blackmail him into improving the condition of the cotton-pickers. Curtiz's treatment makes this story less a drama of divided loyalties than one of uncertain intentions. He reveals the pillaging cotton-pickers and Marvin Blake to be as dishonest as the planter, but to no other apparent purpose than to propitiate Southern audiences. His theme had little bearing on the actual situation, if a *March of Time* item of 1936 is to be believed: *Land of Cotton* reported that the one-crop system and not corruption was the primary cause of the decline of the cotton industry. Curtiz's Negroes fall into a Stepin Fetchit kind of servility and his whites are also degraded into stereotype; only Bette Davis as a Southern belle, both steely and soft ('I'd like to kiss you but I've just washed my hair'), escapes this fuzz of received ideas.

In the thirties Curtiz appeared to have felt at a loss when faced by the intrinsic perplexities of Depression themes. Untypical of Warner Brothers at this time, he directed *20,000 Years in Sing Sing* (1933) in such a way as to affirm the importance of authority. The Warden of Sing Sing grants compassionate leave to one of his convicts (Spencer Tracy) in the expectation that the convict will return to the prison at whatever cost: which he does, though the price of this gesture is that he has to die. Curtiz fudges any significance this idea might have had and undermines Arthur Byron's forthright performance as the Warden by having him act as a mute witness, though he knows it to be unjust, to the convict's execution.

He subscribed even more openly to equivocation in *Angels with Dirty Faces* (1938), in which James Cagney once more goes through the life-cycle of *The Public Enemy*. But in order to placate the Legion of Decency, his career is contrasted with that of a boys' club priest (Pat O'Brien) far less admired by the boys than he. The priest asks the gangster to feign cowardice when brought to the electric chair so as to destroy this admiration. From his concluding saintly close-up of the priest as he lies to the boys about the nature of the gangster's death and wins back their allegiance, it seems unlikely that Curtiz intended a satire on ecclesiastical hypocrisy, even though one of his screenwriters was the Marxist John Wexley.

In a despairing section of *L'Age ingrat du cinéma*, Léon Moussinac proposes that the cost of producing sound films and the shock of the Depression, though relatively muffled in France, were responsible for undermining the French avant-garde. Cautious businessmen had taken over the cinemas and grouped them into circuits. And the Commission of Censors, its power increased, now had the right to refuse a distribution certificate to any film made outside this system, so that for years Buñuel's *L'Age d'or* and Vigo's *Zéro de conduite* were banned. Yet the decline of the avant-garde—'that anarchic movement without a programme, only interested in anything that might be new'[19]—could be attributed to at least one other cause: the impact of *The Battleship Potemkin* on the ciné-club circuits.

For the subject of his third film, the documentary *Land without Bread* (1932), Luis Buñuel left cosmopolitan Paris for one of the poorest districts in his native Spain. His study of Las Hurdes, a village near Salamanca, shows starving goitered children with flies crawling over their faces, a thirty-two-year-old woman who looks as though she were eighty, an infant's death by malnutrition. But as so often in his films, Buñuel's impassivity before his subject is even more disconcerting than the subject itself.

In *What is Literature?* Jean-Paul Sartre has argued that the surrealist wish to destroy commonsense assumptions about the world is close in sympathy to the political desire for revolution. Yet the detachment entailed by surrealist contemplation of the strange was at war with the political notion of commitment. In *Les Maisons de la misère*, the Belgian documentarist Henri Storck, though clearly appalled by the nature of poverty, cannot resist dissipating indignation through his curiosity about cemetery ex-votos and a maggot-riddled horse's head lying beneath a bed. The appeal of committed filming and the older avant-garde impulse were hard to reconcile, but for those who kept out of politics, the results were to be even less satisfactory. Cocteau's *Le Sang d'un poète* (1932) looks like a wholesale conversion of Buñuel's passionate conceits into a cold chic, the refined cruelty of its tableaux lacking either the disturbance of confession or the force of disclosure. It seems merely an attempt to snub those members of the public who do not share its director's tastes, as snobbish in form as his conception of society and of poetry. The Prévert brothers' *L'Affaire est dans le sac*, released in the same year, is cliquey also but in a different way, an in-group romp whose humour probably gave more pleasure to its actors than it does to the spectator. On the evidence of *Adieu Léonard* (1943) and *Voyage surprise* (1947), its director Pierre Prévert was to reveal himself as distinctly less talented than his brother Jacques, the screenwriter and poet. Jacques's imagination was inclined to the fatalistic, the fantastic and the parabolic and drew its spirit from Paris street-songs, circus clowns, the popular theatre and the gangster movie. *L'Affaire est dans le sac* provided little opportunity for his gifts.

He was to have more of an opportunity when Jean Renoir invited him to revise the script for *Le Crime du Monsieur Lange* (1935). Perhaps because he had so little in common with Renoir insofar as the nature of his talent was concerned, his contribution to this film was to be of immense benefit to both men. Indeed, *Le Crime du Monsieur Lange* can be seen as a turning point in the career of both of them. With the coming of sound, but even more with the coming of the thirties, Renoir's style had begun to take on an inner coherence. His waywardness in storytelling, his apparent neglect of motivation or concern with the accidental and his at times abrupt editing began to appear like a criticism of manufacturing processes, as though he were using the technology of film to rebut technology itself. But while his style was to reveal itself as defined by the time he made the bitter tragi-comedy *La Chienne* (1931), it was only to achieve completeness in *Toni* (1934), where his deep-focus shots, tracking camera and multiple action within the image has the effect of socializing space.

He sees no point in underlining the fact that Toni and the other Spanish emigrants who come to work in Provence are working-class, and concentrates his attention on their feelings, their loneliness, their response to betrayal—and on finding a *mise en scène* for their relationships within the sun-drenched landscapes of Les Martigues near Marseilles. At the time of the left-wing Popular Front he directed *La Marseillaise* (1937) on money subscribed by the French trade unions; and yet, although he supported the Popular Front, he was unable to conceal his sympathy for the doomed king, Louis XVI (played by his brother Pierre).

He was conscious of the anti-technological tradition: Zola, Flaubert and his own father, Auguste Renoir. In his concern for the sensuous and the particular, he imitates these masters, but not uncritically. At this stage in his career he seldom relaxes into the derivative impressionism of *Le Déjeuner sur l'herbe* (1959). He may have felt competitive towards his father's genius, and he may have dealt with this problem by inhibiting his aggression—his fair-mindedness to his characters would have more impact, indeed, if he had been more trenchant in his assessment of them—yet he has his own eye for the behaviour, settings and faces characteristic of the 1930s. He seldom lapses into painterly or literary pastiche.

In *Le Crime du Monsieur Lange* Jacques Prévert was primarily to bring to Renoir's ruminatory talent a Commedia dell'Arte kind of brilliance, most evident in his characterization of Batala, the crooked publisher of pulp fiction and arch seducer—all rapid smiles and nervous gesticulation in Jules Berry's performance—whose intrigues cast a shadow over the tenement courtyard beneath his office window and who returns from the dead, seemingly, dressed as a priest. Prévert encouraged Renoir to abandon naturalism for a Balzacian realism in which individuals can be seen as typical of their class and society without forfeiting any of their individuality. Incompletely absorbed, however, this influence leads at times to pasteboard en-counters and to an insubstantial theatricality that Renoir was only able to resolve after a number of experiments culminating in *La Règle du jeu*.

But in one way Renoir goes beyond nineteenth-century narrative techniques. In order to match Prévert's wit, he evolved a bravura kind of camerawork as intricate in its virtuosity as anything Murnau had devised for *The Last Laugh*. As the camera glides back and forth between the various apartments surrounding the courtyard, it relates disparate actions and heightens the idea of community implied by the prospect of this courtyard: sensations very far from those Hitchcock raises from the courtyard in *Rear Window*. Its restlessness reinforces the theme of uncertainty inherent in Prévert's play with the ideas of illusion and disguise, and its celebrated pivot through almost 360 degrees after the Batala murder gives, as André Bazin has claimed, 'an impression of vertigo and madness as well as creating suspense'.[20] It reminds the spectator that *Le Crime du Monsieur Lange* was made during a year when the monetary system cracked up, when the French press was in an uproar over the suicide of Serge Stavisky, a swindler under protection from the Department of Justice, and when the possibility of a Fascist dictatorship was imminent.

Although Renoir echoes these crises and has Lange and Batala's employees form a publishing cooperative of a kind desired by many socialists in the thirties, he neither takes up some fixed political position nor conceptualizes his pleasure in the physical, indeed architectural presence of the community. But he does imply his position in the way he defines three of his male characters and their relationships to the women in the courtyard laundry: while the acrobat Charles loves one of these girls faithfully, and Batala seduces any one of them who comes into sight, Lange (who writes Westerns about Arizona Jim and sleeps with a prostitute) marries the woman who manages the laundry. Lange's prevarication and general passivity would seem to be bound up with the unreality of his novels, whose insubstantiality, in turn, stands in contrast to the rich inferences that Renoir, like his father, can draw from such mundane events as the sight of women toiling in the steam and fresh linen of a laundry shop.

On the whole, French film-makers appear to have been vague about the sort of society they would have preferred to the existing one. The best they could think of—at least insofar as their films were concerned—was a kind of opting out from responsibility in the manner of Chaplin's tramp. Jean Vigo, for one, had been greatly impressed by René Schwob's *Une Mélodie silencieuse* (1929), a collection of film essays, many of them concerned with the role Chaplin plays: and Schwob's theories about the relationship of the individual to society do capture attitudes prevalent in French films at this time. The cinema, Schwob believes, should concern itself with conveying both the power of love and the absurdity of those who isolate themselves from the community, especially of those whose satisfaction with the world and the self runs counter to the lover's desire to develop beyond his limitations. Chaplin's tramp represents this ridiculous self-centred figure at its most extreme; yet with one important qualification. Unlike the robot slaves in *Metropolis*, Chaplin's tramp can adapt himself to changing circumstances with a remarkable agility. His spontaneous powers of invention allow him to realize concretely the most varied qualities of the mind, and he is able to body in the course of daily life qualities that the surrealists had looked for in dreams, though often in vain. He is, thinks Schwob, superior to Keaton and all other comedians in the sense that he refuses to respect the logic of actual situations; he asserts the primacy of imagination over the tyranny of fact. In contrast to his brilliant display, the world appears a threadbare background and other people mere brutes.

A deep pessimism underlies Schwob's views. In attributing a role to the tramp very similar to Hollywood's interpretation of the gangster as a rebel whose actions cast into relief the inadequacies of society, he illuminates a crucial difference between the cultures of France and the United States of this time: that many French directors who used tramps as central figures in their films at this time preferred a passive rebel to an active one. Yet the kinship between these two kinds of rebel is greater than their dissimilarity. In less than the last resort, both of them are incapable of maintaining their individuality against social pressures, since one of them tends to disintegrate while the other is generally slain: and neither of them implies by his behaviour a reasonable argument for reforming society. Schwob tries to justify Chaplin's tramp on the grounds that like Picasso and the surrealists he resembles a *bricoleur* in his power to convert random pieces of stuff and junk into imaginative new forms; yet his view of the tramp as artist would appear to be as portentous as the view of the gangster as stoic hero.

It certainly fails to stand up to much reflection. In *A nous la liberté* (1931) René Clair contrasts the figure of the tramp as artist with the worker as robot — and allegedly modelled the career of his central character, Jules (Raymond Cordy), on that of Charles Pathé. Escaping from prison, Jules builds up a business empire as a manufacturer of gramophones, the key to his success being his organizing of factories on the same principles as a prison. Emile, a former prison friend, comes to seek his help, and when Jules recognizes that all Emile wants in the way of help is to know one of the girls who works in the gramophone factories, he begins to realize how unhappy he has become as a business tycoon. Abandoning his empire, he joins Emile as a tramp on the road, while his workers, liberated from the factories, take to fishing and dancing: a final sequence so limited in its expression of the good life that it may seem to be contemptuous of working-class pleasures.

The application of this story to Clair himself and to the condition of the French film industry is obvious: the director, like any artist, cannot function as a robot; he must be allowed spontaneity and enjoyment in his work. But in this sense, everyone is potentially an artist. Emile looks up from the street at the girl he loves as she sings at her window; then her voice drops an octave and he realizes that she is pretending to sing to the sound of one of Jules's gramophone records. In his treatise on laughter, Henri Bergson had proposed that the essence of the comic lay in reducing man to a machine; humour, on the other hand, presupposes that machine-like people can be restored to humanity. In spite of his wit, Clair gives little evidence of such a restorative poetry. He brings too great a geometric satisfaction to the scenes at the conveyor-belt and posits a misleading choice between his persecutory Sisyphean understanding of work and the nursery play of the liberated factory-hands; as Ermanno Olmi implies in *Il posto*, the choice is not between this type of work or this type of play but rather between kinds and qualities of involvement. In common with the surrealists and Chaplin's tramp, Clair seems incapable of imagining a society in which the wish for sustained work might be central to any notion of the good life, and because he is unwilling to imagine such a society, he falls into the kind of sentimental assumptions that Marcel Pagnol was also to exhibit in his portrait of Topaze: the assumption, in particular, that dictators might be kind-hearted. Yet would someone as ruthless as Jules be so willing to give up executive power in order to regain freedom?

Clair is unable to square his admiration for the criminal and anarchistic tendencies which he believes to be essential to the artist with his disapproval of tyrants who in fact enjoy the most complete autonomy of self-expression. Chaplin, who was to acknowledge a similarity between Clair and himself, and in *Modern Times* (1936) to appropriate the main idea of *A nous la liberté*, was to resolve this contradiction by seeing how the great dictator and the tramp could be aspects of the same self and how one actor could play both roles. Indeed, an important ingredient in Chaplin's talent has been his ability to find screen characters that allowed him to extend his analysis of the delinquency in the tramp: the progress from tramp-dandy through to tramp-murdering tyrant in *The Great Dictator* being completed in the figure of the dandy—mass murderer, Monsieur Verdoux. Yet another way in which Clair's contradictory views on the artist and tyrant can be resolved is to praise the tyrant as a kind of artist, as Wyndham Lewis and Ezra Pound did in their commendations of Mussolini.

For the French, the actor who most fulfilled the role of the tramp was Michel Simon. In *La Chienne* Renoir cast him as Legrand, the *petit-*

bourgeois Sunday artist who murders a prostitute, and in the final scene of the film presents him as a vagrant looking at one of his own pictures in the window of a gallery. In *Boudu sauvé des eaux* (1932) Renoir and Simon created a tramp without any interest in the arts, just someone who likes to stand and stare. But in a way Boudu is even more destructive than the Chaplin tramp. Saved from drowning by a bookseller named Lestingois, he responds to this gesture by spitting into Lestingois's most precious books, messing up his house and sleeping with both his wife and girl friend. After which he returns to the water in a sequence which appears to cross the threshold of the present into the past—a regression in feeling complemented by Boudu's amniotic immersion.

The filming moves back in memory, as it were, to a scene that recalls Auguste Renoir's pastoral impressionism. The camera looks up from a river to a café at the top of a steep bank. A band plays, a woman sings: an image that conveys both the gravity of a summer's day and the yearning implied by such a remoteness in space and time. The camera eye lazily contemplates an overloaded rowing-boat that contains among others Boudu and Lestingois's girl friend dressed in formal wedding clothes: grotesque bacchants in a paradisal glitter of water and trees. Boudu overturns the boat and bobs away like a walrus.

In later years Renoir tended to agree with those who saw this film as a satire on middle-class gentility; yet such an interpretation supposes a bond between the characters that Renoir's treatment avoids. Neither Boudu nor the bookseller and his friends come within distance of understanding each other. The comedy, indeed, depends on the contrast between Boudu's refusal to see them as other than exploitable things and their fascination with this unfathomable being, as self-absorbed as a baby.

In *L'Atalante* (1934) Jean Vigo gave Michel Simon and the figure of the tramp a different function. A friendly independent producer, J.-L. Nounez, had continued to back Vigo after the banning of *Zéro de conduite* and suggested that he should take some censor-proof subject for his next film and infiltrate any subversive comment he might wish to make through his treatment. In the event, Vigo and his screenwriter Alberto Riera modified Jean Guinée's innocuous story by interpolating the character of Père Jules (Michel Simon), the captain's assistant on the barge L'Atalante.

In common with Renoir, Vigo was haunted by memories of his father, who far from being a genius had been an unpopular anarchist and possibly a secret agent for the Germans during the First World War. At boarding-school the boy lived in dread of being exposed as his father's son; and yet Michel Simon has said that in later life Vigo resembled Hamlet in his eagerness to clear his father's reputation. In *L'Atalante* Vigo relates Père Jules, through his liking for cats and his anarchist past, to his father and also to Chaplin's tramp, of whom René Schwob had written: 'The superiority of this absolute solitary in a wicked world consists in his delivering a message of love to children. Everything else stirs in him a terrible contempt.'[21] But while Vigo had gained from Chaplin his confidence in elaborating on the most ordinary events by such means that they took on the metamorphic qualities of the imagination, he was only to respond to experience in this way in his two earlier films, *A Propos de Nice* (1930) and *Zéro de conduite* (1933). By the time he came to make *L'Atalante* he had relegated the Chaplin tramp to a secondary position, and in role Père Jules is undifferentiated from a pedlar and cabin-boy as attendants and witnesses to the main action. Although all three are fascinated by junk, and sometimes magically so—as when Père Jules runs a finger along the grooves of a gramophone record and seems to produce the sound of music—they are *bricoleurs* without power. Juliette (Dita Parlo), the captain's wife, becomes attracted by Père Jules and the pedlar at moments when she is depressed by the state of her marriage, but her interest in them is distanced. In a similar fashion, Vigo also appears to have moved beyond his fascination with Chaplin.

For two reasons. When Père Jules discovers that it is not he but the cabin-boy playing an accordion who has produced the sound of music, he exclaims: 'There are stranger things than playing a record with your fingernail. Electricity for instance.' Although restricted by his story to the relationship between the barge captain (Jean Dasté) and his wife, Vigo had now begun to address himself to such themes as the disquieting yet remarkable qualities of science, and when Juliette leaves her husband and wanders unhappily around Paris, he relates her depression to the more public Depression implied by the unemployed queuing outside a factory, the arrest of a pickpocket and by some desolate yet beautiful dock installations. His conception of the lovers and their relationship concentrates on the physicality of existence. At many points echoing Borzage's *Seventh Heaven*, he avoids Borzage's transcendentalism. As with Renoir, an awareness of materiality releases the imagination.

Unlike Renoir, he drew on few cultural resources. Not that it matters. He and his wife Lydou had for a while run a film club in Nice, yet his own work conveys the impression of a lyric spirit so intense that it can transmute every influence into its own idiom and derive its main inspiration from immediate experience. No other filmmaker has used the medium so testingly as a mode of self-development, taxing himself to such a point that the making of *L'Atalante* contributed to the illness that brought about his death at the age of twenty-nine. It was to be as serious a blow to the French cinema as had been the death of Louis Delluc.

Yet an element of good fortune lay behind the fact that he had achieved so much in so short a time. He had been fortunate in his marriage, in his partnership with J-L. Nounez and in an extraordinary visit to Paris which by chance had brought him into contact with Henri Storck, Jean Lods and Jean Painlevé. He was also to meet Boris Kaufman, whose parents had fled from Russia after the Revolution. A student at the Sorbonne, Kaufman talked animatedly about his legendary elder brothers, Denis and Michail, and fired Vigo's imagination with stories about their exploits as film-makers. Then Denis, alias Dziga Vertov, became a real presence when he sent Boris his Debré camera. It was with this camera that Boris and Jean began to shoot *A Propos de Nice*.

Beginning in a casual, almost doodling fashion, Vigo picks up the underlying pattern in various shots of road-sweepers, tennis-players and other activities: a non-figurative interest in tempo, similarities in shape and editing that bring him closer to Ruttmann than to Vertov. But his filming tightens in the scenes on the Promenade des Anglais, revealing his increased involvement in his subject as he observes faces marked by age, greed, deformity and suffering; and by the concluding sequences he is able to intensify the most wide-reaching relationships between images with the accent of personal conflict. *A Propos de Nice* was admired on the ciné-club circuits and led to Vigo's meeting with J-L. Nounez, who invited him to make a film about the Camargue horses. But Vigo preferred to work on either a story about his boarding-school experiences or one about the anarchist Eugène Dieudonné's sufferings in prison. He finally chose the idea of *Zéro de conduite*, which allowed him to relate his interest in anarchism and the effects of prison with his memories of school, while avoiding the explicit parallelism that Clair had drawn from his equation of prisons and factories.

He did this by converting his implied parallels into a series of metaphors: metaphors that were unlimited and even volatile in their relation to each other. Schwob had described Chaplin as a monkey among grotesques, capable of discovering in daily life what the surrealists had looked for in dreams. Vigo's schoolboys are like Chaplin in this sense, and so is his use of film. The richness of his images, the freedom of his editing, the use of slow motion, or fantastic ideas (the headmaster at the school is not only small-minded but a dwarf, and the guests at Speech Day are represented by wooden dummies) is never experimental for its own sake. He instinctively recognized in his power of transformation something that scientists have since confirmed: that human perceptions are not fixed, like those of a camera, but dynamic. He helps to show how perception may be linked to those mental processes that generate dreams. In comparison to him, many surrealists appear to be literalist interpreters of dream iconography.

In its opening sequence two boys are travelling back to school in a nondescript railway carriage. A shot of one of the boys, his hands pressed against the carriage window, projects a feeling of confinement. But as the boys make rabbit-shadows, pretend to be birds, stroke two blown-up balloons as though they were breasts and smoke cigars, Vigo transforms the carriage into a mysterious and magical cavern (like a cinema?) where anything could be possible. The smoke streaming past the window and Maurice Jaubert's eerie, strident music relate this grimy place to dream memories, an association carried through into subsequent scenes: at the railway station, with its looming grotesques, and in the dormitory, where a master, seen through a diaphanous sheet undressing for bed, could be taken for a shadow-puppet.

In the corner of the railway carriage slumps Huguet, the usher, who likes to imitate Chaplin's walk. Huguet, as Chaplin's surrogate, mediates between the boys and the caricatured adult world and also may remind the spectator of how intelligently Vigo understood Chaplin's art. Vigo never schematizes, never attempts a direct political allegory; it would be futile to ask whether the school staff represent adult authority as Vigo sees it, or purely as the boys see it. If he is involved in politics, he is so primarily in his struggle to free his audience from perceptual laziness.

Jean Vigo: *Zéro de conduite.*

10. Utopianism and Despair

An increased respect for authority and a decline in both social criticism and intellectual freedom were noticeable in Hollywood productions during 1933. In March of that year Franklin D. Roosevelt took office, and *Variety* was so impressed by his tonic appearances on the newsreels that it named this 'Barrymore of the White House'—a description that angered Republican John Barrymore—the star of the year. The New Deal did not sweep away the Depression, but it did raise hope once more, and the Hollywood studios quickly registered this optimism, if only at first in the form of a musical, *Stand Up and Cheer*, and a Disney cartoon, *Three Little Pigs*, with a song intended to whistle away all fears of the Big Bad Wolf.

As they became more confident, people began to reassert their trust in the country and its institutions. The influx of immigrants had decreased. The population was stabilizing itself and assuming a cohesive identity. There was a growth of public interest in American history. At the same time, the consolidation of dictatorships in Germany, Italy and the Soviet Union strengthened the instinct for caution. Hollywood turned to domestic themes. It began to preach isolationism. It became utopian—more interested in how things should be or might be than in how they were. In *Footlight Parade* (1933) Busby Berkeley had his girls form into the shape of the Republic's Eagle and then re-form as Roosevelt's head.

Increased pressures in censorship were among the reasons for this change. In 1930 Martin Quigley, a Chicago publisher of film trade magazines, and Father Lord, s. J., reframed the 1927 Hays Office studio recommendations into a Production Code intended to deal with the dangers raised by the spoken word. Quigley realized that the Code could only be enforced with public support. During the slump he had observed the industry move into a new permissiveness; and in 1934 he received support for his policies from the Roman Catholic bishops and certain pastors in other denominations. They formed the National Legion of Decency. Previous attempts at censorship had been vitiated by the conflicting opinions of those who wished to be censors. The Legion was dogmatically single-minded in its views. And with twenty million American Roman Catholics to support it, it could exercise great strength on the box-office-conscious studios. It arranged that the

Frank Capra (back to camera) directing
Claudette Colbert and Clark Gable in *It Happened One Night*.

MPPDA (the Motion Picture Producers and Distributors of America Inc.) should set up a Production Code Administration under the direction of the Roman Catholic Joseph I. Breen. Between 1934 and the anti-trust decree of 1948, this Administration was to supervise the content of about ninety-five per cent of the films made in the United States. Any film released without Breen's approval was liable to a $25,000 fine and, more seriously, to a condemnation by the National Legion of Decency.

It has often been assumed that the Legion primarily objected to obscenity; but in fact its aims were political. In August 1938 it stated:

The Legion views with grave apprehension those efforts now being made to utilize the cinema for the spread of ideas antagonistic, not only to traditional Christian morality but to all religion. It must oppose the efforts of those who would make motion pictures an agency for the dissemination of the false, atheistic and immoral doctrines repeatedly condemned by all accepted moral teachers. Films which portray, approvingly, concepts rooted in philosophies attacking the Christian moral order and the supernatural destiny of man serve not to ennoble but rather, to debase humanity, and as such, these films are an affront to right-thinking men and women. [1]

Supporting the Fascists in the Spanish Civil War, the Legion tried to stop cinema managers from showing Walter Wanger's production, *Blockade*; it became an ally to Martin Dies in his campaign against Hollywood's left-wing associations; and it was not to be immune from charges of corruption. 'The Legion's actions lend credence to rumours that it will sometimes compromise where sufficient contributions are made to the Church,' [2] claimed Ephraim London, the distinguished attorney, at the time the Legion withdrew its condemnation of *The Pawnbroker* (1963). Yet the Roman Catholic clergy was far from being wholly responsible for the new censorship. Box-office figures imply that the majority of the public welcomed this retreat from disturbing issues.

By 1935 Hollywood was the second most powerful industry in California. Its thirty-nine studios employed over 9,000 people and its assets were valued at ninety-seven million dollars. By 1936 all the major studios were financially viable once more, though none of them was to find film promotion as easy as it had been in the early twenties.

André Malraux, shooting *L'Espoir* on location in Spain, described the dangerous adventures of some Republican pilots with a Hawksian verve and later re-conceived the events of the film as a novel, a reversal of the usual procedure. (The novel was published in 1938, the film remaining undistributed until after the Second World War). But Malraux was too immersed in the war to have a coherent view of it. He thought in terms of splendid incidents: the German pilot who crashes a Republican plane and then admits he has

lived too long in the mines; the Spanish farmer, airborne for the
first time, trying desperately to locate familiar terrain; most impressive
of all, the unending procession of wounded and dispossessed refugees
stumbling up the mountain paths of the Pyrenees to the reiterated
rhythms of Darius Milhaud's score. Yet Malraux's enthusiasm for
military discipline or the peculiarities of heroism and destiny consorted
oddly with his left-wing sympathies, and his highly-wrought imaginings
were often achieved at the expense of actual complexities. Historians
may wish that he had analysed the ebb and flow of the war more
closely.

Joris Ivens was to do just that in *The Spanish Earth* (1937). A
group of New York writers, including Archibald MacLeish, Dorothy

Joris Ivens: *The Spanish Earth.*
Ivens and Hemingway in Spain;
the blitzed university, Madrid

Parker and Lillian Hellman, formed a company known as Contemporary Historians in order to raise funds for Ivens. They wrote a script for him. He went off to Spain, taking Dos Passos with him as a translator. In his memoirs *The Camera and I*, Ivens says that he was so bewildered by his impressions of the war that he discarded the script and went to Paris to rethink his project. He met Hemingway, who told him that he 'saw no particularly deep implications in this war and was pretty sceptical when I described it as the first test of fascism in Europe'. [3] But Hemingway was open to persuasion. He came to Spain, joined the film unit as an assistant and self-effacingly made himself useful. He later wrote an admirable commentary for the film, which Orson Welles was invited to read. But Welles's manner proved to be too declamatory, and the unsuspecting Hemingway was asked to make a trial recording — or so he was told — to help out the film editors; and this was the recording used on the final version of the film.

It contrasts two subjects: the terror of Madrid under fire and the setting up of an irrigation scheme in a commune village just south of Madrid. (In the hopes of encouraging American intervention in Spain, some of Ivens's friends arranged a preview of *The Spanish Earth* at the White House; and President Roosevelt, wishing to offer token support, suggested they should re-edit the film to give more importance to this irrigation scheme.) As it stands, the contrast between the two subjects is ill-adjusted; but then *The Spanish Earth*, like *L'Espoir*, was made under far from ideal conditions, during periods of street fighting and aerial bombardments. It is an outstanding documentary, and not only in its immediacy. In certain scenes, as when it captures the chill of a besieged, seemingly empty Madrid or observes the abrupt death of a bookseller during an air-raid, it becomes a work of art, balancing moments of extreme tension with John Ferno's photography of the Spanish landscape, mellow in sunshine and shadow, and with the Courbet-like pleasure in stability that Ivens discovers in women washing laundry by a river or sweeping a deserted village street.

The New Deal had blurred any notion of a Manichean conflict between left and right; it tended to defuse extremists. Pare Lorentz's documentaries, *The Plow that Broke the Plains* (1936) and *The River* (1937), reflect this moderation. Like Grierson's GPO Film Unit productions, they were government sponsored: the first to be so by an American government agency in peacetime. A supporter of the New Deal, Lorentz had written a eulogistic book called *The Roosevelt Year: 1933*, which had encouraged Rexford Tugwell of the Resettlement Administration to commission him to produce a film on the history of the dust-bowl tragedy. From the start things went wrong: Lorentz had trouble with his cameramen—Ralph Steiner, Paul Strand and Leo Hurwitz—who found his amateurism unforgivable and who wished to take up a more critical stance than he did to a society whose greed had eroded the land; it was overgrazing and over-ploughing that had allowed the drought and high winds of the early thirties to lay waste the plains from Texas to South Dakota. Lorentz had also aroused resentment in Hollywood and had difficulties in getting hold of the stock footage necessary for his treatment. In spite of these difficulties, he alone must be held responsible for the pseudo-poetical blare of the commentary, the dullness of the imagery and the clumsiness with which he relates these images to Virgil Thomson's music. *The River* is just as bland (apart from a compelling sequence of the Mississippi in flood shot by Floyd Crosby) and conveys as little information about the river as *The Plow* had done about the land. Lorentz appears to have had little interest in people and takes the New Deal enthusiasm for seeing everything in terms of national emblems to an extreme.

Frank Capra was to use national emblems far more effectively and during the mid and late thirties to touch the public nerve again and again. But the film with which he made a fortune for Columbia, won Academy Awards for both his stars and himself and opened up a new trend in Hollywood filming was to be deliberately apolitical. For though *It Happened One Night*, the sleeper of 1934 and possibly the most renowned sleeper of all time, includes scenes that show Depression poverty, its appeal to the public lay mainly in its sophisticated whimsy: its recognition that lovers, however bad the times, create a private world of their own. The bantering wit of *It Happened One Night*, and its mood—tough yet compromising, sophisticated yet feeling—were to permeate a cycle of thirties films about adult lovers, including the elegant Thin Man series with William Powell and Myrna Loy, the Fred Astaire and Ginger Rogers partnership and the unlikely conjunction of Marlene Dietrich and Gary Cooper in Borzage's *Desire* (1936). It culminated in perhaps the finest of Hollywood comedies, George Cukor's version of Philip Barry's stage play *The Philadelphia Story* (1940).

While Depression reporters had been thought of as muck-rakers, their profession now seemed to have become the fastest elevator to the social heights. In *It Happened One Night* Capra and his screenwriter Robert Riskin have their reporter (Clark Gable) marry a runaway heiress (Claudette Colbert). In *Mr Deeds Goes to Town* (1936) Capra has Jean Arthur's sacked reporter win a scatty heir. His Mr Deeds is a pastoral clown or rube like Harry Langdon, noble as well as innocent, with a forename as emphatic in its significance as the forename of his successor, Jefferson Smith, in *Mr Smith Goes to*

Washington (1939). Capra and Robert Riskin aim for this political reference in the widest way possible. They have Mr Deeds played by Gary Cooper, who had established his reputation with *The Virginian*. They have him in his tall, gauche way resemble Abraham Lincoln. They have him stand before Grant's tomb and acknowledge that the great general had once been an Iowa farmboy.

Does this lineage embody some important American virtue? It would seem not. Mr Deeds plays the tuba ineptly, writes bad poetry and enjoys home-made apple pie. Smart people think him a screwball, but nice ones—like us, Capra would nudge us into thinking—see him as an individualist who resists the worst trends in civilization. He seems incorruptible. Inheriting two million dollars, he claims he has no need for money: an indifference to wealth that has the contradictory effect of rendering meaningless his later generosity, as when he is moved by the sight of starving farmers and offers them handouts, good deeds that entail no sacrifice. It is unlikely that Capra or Riskin intended a satire on the New Deal itself, or a satire in particular on the inherited wealth of such figures as the patrician President Roosevelt. Capra and Riskin never examine the possibly corrupt origins of Mr Deeds's wealth. They see money as in some way magical; it need not be earned and, when obtained without labour, need not arouse feelings of guilt. The farmer who threatens to shoot Mr Deeds, and who presumably represents the revolutionary impulse, is dismissed as crazed through starvation.

Mr Deeds has his enemies. His aunts denounce him in court as mad. Established poets mock his verse. A newspaper editor wishes to expose him as a dangerous fool. But opposition crumbles at the sight of his radiant integrity—and at the first sign of his ability to

Frank Capra: *Mr Deeds Goes to Town*. Gary Cooper (first left)

use his fists. 'Gee Mr Deeds, you're swell,' gurgles Jean Arthur throatily as she capitulates. But is he? He misuses his power, wanting to cut his subscription to an opera company on the grounds that if opera were any good it would pay its own way. No vote-catching politician could put the populist case better.

During the thirties many suburban houses bore the words 'Shangri-la' on their gates, Shangri-la being the paradisial kingdom in James Hilton's novel *Lost Horizon*. Dickens had described a similar kind of alienation between life at home and at work in his portrait of Mr Wemmick in *Great Expectations*, but this kind of alienation was to be far more extreme in the late thirties. It was appropriate that Capra should have been chosen to direct *Lost Horizon* (1937) and appropriate that he should have been unable to relate its legendary kingdom in any meaningful way to contemporary anxieties. For Capra's utopianism could only be realized as a neo-classical kind of frigidity. However hard he and Riskin strain their plots, they are unable to set up a living connection between their heroes and the ideals of the Founding Fathers as suggested by Washington statuary.

While Mr Deeds inherits money, Mr Smith inherits the spirit of the constitution. His father, a newspaper editor on the frontier, had been murdered for honest muck-raking, and Mr Smith, a teacher who wins the admiration of his pupils, tries to uphold his father's beliefs. A senator dies, and the Governor of the state, on the advice of his children, and after he has convinced himself that the diffident young man will support the party machine, has Mr Smith nominated. But Mr Smith stands up against the power of the party boss (Edward Arnold) and his compliant associate, Senator Payne, by filibustering one of their

Frank Capra: *Mr Smith Goes to Washington*. James Stewart.

bills—intended to sanction the industrial take-over of some land that Mr Smith has earmarked as a recreation centre for children. Senator Payne, a former friend of Smith's father, is so disturbed by Smith's integrity that he breaks down before Congress and admits the corruption of the party machine.

At least two implausibilities undermine this story: one of them being that seasoned politicians should fail to recognize Mr Smith's strength of character, the other that a tough operator like Senator Payne should so easily collapse. Both arise from the assumption that while Mr Smith has been strengthened by ancestral grace, the metropolitan senators have been distracted from this grace by their pursuit of self-interest: an idea that may be comforting to those who find the intricacies of wheeling-and-dealing too hard to understand, but one that does not stand the test of actuality. And in fact, *Mr Smith Goes to Washington* outraged many senators, and the American ambassador in London, Joseph P. Kennedy, tried to have it banned.

Capra makes excessive demands on the two actors who have to bear the burden of implausibility. In later years James Stewart, who plays Mr Smith, was to fall into mannerism with this sort of role, yet on this occasion he manages the naïvety, spiritual authority and dogged-ness that make up the character of this fool who becomes a judge: a transformation that William Empson has pointed out to be typical of certain kinds of pastoral heroes, the most eminent example being Christ. Whether Capra was conscious of this sacramental aspect to his hero or not, he does not allow it to override his secular concern with Mr Smith as a schoolmaster. The collapse of Senator Payne is another matter and it overtaxes Claude Rains, in spite of his flair for playing ruthless men vulnerable to feeling.

Yet what distinguishes *Mr Smith Goes to Washington* most of all is its spaciousness of vision. Capra appears to have been sufficiently stirred by the prospect of world war to have found a means by which to give life to his corporate symbolism. He had filmed Mr Deeds's visit to the Washington monuments as though it were a perfunctory travelogue, but he was to film Mr Smith's comparable visit with an expressiveness that suggests he may have really felt some connection between these paternal emblems and the damage war might inflict on American life, especially its children. The rhetoric of his filming is all the more convincing for being subdued, softening the marmoreal and very unlike Leni Riefenstahl's ambition to give camera movements the portentousness of nationalistic architecture.

Mr Smith is a type of hero remote from the Depression world of gangsters and tramps—a type evolved out of many factors, among which Thomas Dewey's success at City Hall in bringing so many gangsters to book played some part. But the world-wide resurgence in nationalism was to be more pressing than any other factor, and the American need for Sir Galahads was complemented by the Socialist Realist heroes of the Soviet Union and the positive heroes of Nazi fiction. In this process children were as much idealized as adults. From 1935 to 1938 Shirley Temple was to be the top box-office star in both the United States and Great Britain, and in 1937 the presence of the fifteen-year-old Deanna Durbin in *Three Smart Girls* made $2m gross for Universal.

Possibly the most illuminating example of this change in mood was a B feature which enjoyed such popularity that MGM returned to its subject thirteen times altogether, and Louis B. Mayer declared it to be his most cherished property. The Andy Hardy series consisted of small-town family stories of an almost defiant provinciality. *Love Finds Andy Hardy* (1938), the second in the series, is based on the relationship between the mildly delinquent Andy (Mickey Rooney) and his stern kind father, Judge Hardy (Lewis Stone). Andy's naughtiness and candour with his father and the Judge's amazement at his son's authority in handling newfangled inventions like radio transmitters and automobiles take on such a dramatic resonance that the women in their lives seem to be little more than background figures. Mrs Hardy has cooked for the family for thirty years but has difficulty in keeping her position, and the Judge has to exercise the utmost tact in introducing a new cook to the house. Betsy (Judy Garland), the girl next door, pines for Andy though she knows he has eyes only for glamorous girls. 'I'm too old for toys,' she sings, 'too young for boys.' And Andy is grudging in praise of even her prodigious gift as a singer.

The public welcomed Mickey Rooney and Judy Garland enthusiastically but not so enthusiastically, perhaps, as they had welcomed another Mickey. 'In Africa,' writes Richard Schickel, 'it was discovered that some native tribes would not accept gifts of soap unless the bars were stamped with the Mouse's outline. A traveller in China reported seeing his likeness peering from a window in Manchouli. It was reported that in Japan he was the most popular figure next to the Emperor.'[4] Totalitarian governments elsewhere were not so easily impressed. The Nazis denounced Mickey as a lie; they knew, they said, that mice were dirty. The Soviets had more trouble in defining him and after a certain amount of terminological wavering pinned him down as 'a warmonger'. They created a competitor known as Yozh, or porcupine, who had, claims Mr Schickel, 'a suitably prickly—and correct—Marxist-Leninist attitude to world conditions'.[5]

In France, and to a lesser extent in Hollywood, heroes could only be tolerated if they were in some way doomed. Under the shadow of war Julien Duvivier and Marcel Carné were to take to an extreme the romantic pessimism that Feyder had tapped in *Carmen* and *Thérèse*

Raquin, a pessimism resulting from the belief that the circumstances of the world will necessarily crush youth, or the spirit of youth. With Duvivier, the pessimism was unexpected—*Poil de carotte* (1925; remade 1932) and *Allo Berlin, ici Paris* (1932) had given little intimation of it. But then in the mid-thirties he began to pin down a mood of despair so prevalent at that time with *Un Carnet de bal* and *Pépé le Moko*.

Un Carnet de bal (1937) consists of a series of sketches linked by the idea of a widow who restlessly seeks out the various men she had danced with on one memorable night in her youth; she learns that one of them is dead and that all the others have changed, most of them for the worse. Duvivier's treatment of this slight script is unjustifiably complicated—as in the episode he shoots to no useful end with tilted camera angles—and he over-emphasizes the mood of regret to the point of losing the spectator's sympathy. *Pépé le Moko* (1936), however, continues to have all the self-sufficient vitality of a well-constructed thriller; Duvivier cross-breeds the format of the gangster movie with the exoticism of Sternberg's *Morocco*, one of the most successful attempts by a French director to appropriate American styles. He presents his doomed hero Pépé (Jean Gabin) as an exceptional man, intimating that three thousand women will mourn his death. Trapped in the Casbah quarter of Algiers, a labyrinth of tenements propped on a hillside that descends to the sea, Pépé, a professional killer, knows that he will be protected by the underworld if he stays within its walls. But inevitably the woman he most loves becomes an unsuspecting party to his betrayal. He falls into a police trap in the outside world and kills himself before barred dock gates as he watches the liner with his loved one put out to sea.

Duvivier not only plays up the tourist exoticism of the Casbah but has its criminals sick with nostalgia for Paris. He insists on the inevitability of fate and misses few romantic opportunities: an elderly whore, mascara-stained tears running down her plump cheeks, listens to a cracked gramophone recording of a Paris *chanson*, an informer accidentally knocks a mechanical piano into tune at the moment he is shot. Yet Duvivier hardens these effects with an American terseness of pace and economy of camera movement, swiftly presenting the intricate communities in downtown Algiers and the Casbah, while keeping up an omnipresent atmosphere of rumour and marshalling one of the finest galleries of corrupt faces on film. He elicits from Lucas Gridoux a remarkable performance as Slimane, the sly detective, and an even more remarkable one from the tight-lipped and impassive Jean Gabin.

The imminence of war cannot account for the despairing mood of *Pépé le Moko* and the other *films noirs* of the time; at best an outward threat could only have mobilized a pessimism of such conviction, not initiated it. More probably, its origins are to be found in the conflict between a Baudelairian distaste for popular culture and the sense of exclusion from any communal vitality that many artists felt during the inter-war years, a conflict which the makers of the *films noirs* exemplify so well in their wish to maintain an aristocratic symbolist ideology while embarking on popular themes in a populist manner. Wishing to have the best of two bad worlds, they worked themselves into a wholly untenable position, the falsity of which would have been immediately apparent without the convincing presence of Jean Gabin: for Gabin was able to create working-class characters who could project an aristocratic stoicism and disdain in the face of defeat.

He was to star in the two Carné-Prévert films which gave the *film noir* its most complete expression. Carné was only twenty-nine when he directed *Quai des brumes* (1938). He had been Feyder's assistant on a number of films and had established a reputation in the ciné-clubs with his documentary *Nogent, Eldorado du dimanche* (1930) and, in the commercial cinema, with *Jenny* (1936) and *Drôle de drame* (1937). But his interests were to darken abruptly with *Quai des brumes*. A variety of disillusioned people, including a murderer (Gabin), the woman he loves and a depressed artist, gather at a café by the harbour of Le Havre. There is talk of a boat to Venezuela; the artist commits suicide; and the murderer, who has been explicitly associated with a stray dog, is shot down in the streets. All the hallmarks of the Carné-Prévert partnership are here: heavy atmospherics, sharply defined minor characters (bait for major actors), the inescapable hint of some allegorical scheme being

Marcel Carné: *Hôtel du Nord.* Louis Jouvet.

worked out beneath the apparent lack of purpose. In *Hôtel du Nord* (1938) Carné replaced Prévert with Henri Jeanson as his scriptwriter and Gabin with Louis Jouvet as his leading actor. A pair of young lovers come to the seedy hotel with the intention of killing themselves, their plan misfiring when the young man only wounds the girl and then lacks the nerve to shoot himself. The other more colourful residents in the hotel also seem locked in self-pity, bitterness or reveries of flight to Port Said. Less coherent in structure than its predecessor, *Hôtel du Nord* is at its most memorable in Louis Jouvet's performance as a petty swindler.

The Carné-Prévert *Le Jour se lève* (1939) has Gabin as François, a workman wanted by the police for murder, barring himself in his attic bedroom at the top of a high apartment-block. Armed police beleaguer the otherwise empty building. Gunfire rakes the attic door; François pushes a wardrobe in front of it. But he resists the police in a token fashion and for most of the time lies on his bed and reviews the events that brought about his crisis: flashbacks dovetailed with a skill that was to be much imitated. Carné presents François's last hours with such an economy of effect that certain critics have seen the whole film as a metaphor for all men at the moment when they approach death. André Bazin was so impressed by Carné's spare use of furnishings in the attic that he was tempted to describe his style as 'metaphysical'. Yet Carné and Prévert cannot resist a boulevard kind of theatricality that excludes the spiritual intensity ascribed to them.

It seems wilful to read metaphysical meanings into their passionately secular concerns: meanings, moreover, that do not square with the circumstances responsible for François's situation—his murder of Valentin (Jules Berry), a sadistic dog-trainer, and his involvement with two of Valentin's women: Clara (Arletty), who is Valentin's music-hall partner, and Françoise (Jacqueline Laurent), a girl infatuated by him. Prévert conjures up a dazzling range of correspondences and contrasts between these characters. But his evolved description of the conflict between François and Valentin distracts attention from the main theme—the alienation of François from any condition of being or labour—and he fails to account for François's wish to risk death for the sake of a *crime passionel*. Like Ingmar Bergman, Prévert has an impatient talent. Social problems often yield up their meanings slowly; but Prévert would seem unable to tolerate this process and avoids it by evolving brilliantly theatrical yet facile solutions to all difficulties. The film ends with a stroke that to some extent cancels out its previous glibness. François shoots himself at dawn and, as he lies on the floor dying, his alarm-clock begins to ring. With this one imaginative stroke, his suicide and the principal reason for his suicide—his intolerable life as a worker—are brought together.

'Francois shoots himself at dawn . . .' Marcel Carné: *Le Jour se lève*.

The kind of hero played by Jean Gabin is a curious amalgam: a Marius whose wish to run away to sea is in some way or another blocked, a murderer who denies his guilt, a stoic whose courage is presumed to reside in his impassive acceptance of death. To make a character of this kind plausible it was necessary to postulate a malign fate that somehow robs the individual of responsibility for his actions; or at least such a thought appears to have been uppermost in the mind of Fritz Lang when he directed his first two American films, *Fury* (1936) and *You Only Live Once* (1937). In *Fury*, Joe Wheeler (Spencer Tracy) is jailed for a crime he did not commit and only narrowly escapes death at the hands of a lynch-mob. In *You Only Live Once*, Eddie

Fritz Lang: *Fury*. Spencer Tracy, Sylvia Sidney.

Taylor (Henry Fonda) is put to death for a murder that the audience will feel to have been an act of manslaughter. Yet what is so noticeable about these two stories is the extent to which Lang and his screenwriters have been forced to contrive their plots in order to reach their conclusions and how, for all their contrivance, they manage to incorporate so little actual experience. Lang brings a great theatrical flair to the lynch-mob scenes in *Fury*. Perhaps in a wish to compensate for Hollywood idealization, he ascribes bad motives to nearly everyone. Louis B. Mayer, who could not bear seeing the worst in people, at least on the screen, was furious at Lang's disenchanted view of human nature—in *Fury* Lang has a right-wing strike-breaker leading the lynch-mob and a cinema audience relishing a newsreel of a man burning to death—and ordered Lang to be kept off the MGM lot. In fact, Lang is more effective at dramatizing states of mind than actual situations, an instance being the anxious and precarious sense of happiness shared by the lovers as they flee across the countryside in *You Only Live Once*.

The idea of the doomed hero usually needed some sort of contrivance or distortion of fact to be given substance—as in Henry King's *Jesse James* (1939), where the delinquent James brothers are presented as righteous avengers putting down the wicked men in authority, a distortion of the legend that however never quite achieved the falsity of its successor, Nicholas Ray's *The True Story of Jesse James* (1957). But the idea of the doomed hero could be given substance in another rather odd way: he could be thought of as English. According to Hollywood, the English gentleman was honourable, stylish and futile: a belief reinforced by the abdication of Edward VIII in 1937, which H. L. Mencken had thought 'the greatest news story since the Resurrection'. The ethics of Empire could be admired because the British Empire was so evidently on the verge of disintegration.

In *The Petrified Forest* (1936), Archie Mayo's version of the Robert E. Sherwood play, Leslie Howard as Alan Squire, an English writer who believes himself to be among the last of the intellectuals and looks forward to the imminent prospect of mankind's extinction, finds himself faced by Duke Mantee (Humphrey Bogart), one of the apelike gangsters that Squire predicts will shortly take over the world. Sherwood appears to have derived this conflict from the poetry of T. S. Eliot—the hollow man versus Sweeney. His received ideas are hardly helped by the location for this meeting, a BAR-B-Q on the edge of a desert made up of studio backdrops. Whatever energy the film may have comes from Bogart, who uncovers a pathos and ferocity in his role that exist nowhere in the text—yet Warner Brothers had wanted either James Cagney or Edward G. Robinson for the part and had only cast Bogart on the insistence of Leslie Howard.

At the end of the film, Squire incites the Duke to kill him in the knowledge that his life insurance will help a Sunday painter (Bette Davis) to escape to a more civilized country; yet this act of altruism, far from seeming heroic, will strike most people as absurd. For though Howard is presented here and elsewhere (as in *Gone with the Wind*) as an ideal to be looked up to, the English gentleman who renounces pleasure for the sake of virtue, he merely comes over as being as self-abnegating as any Hollywood priest. Audiences found themselves guiltily, yet rightly, preferring the virility of Bogart's Duke or Clark Gable's self-seeking Rhett.

Hollywood derived its myth of the English gentleman less from the British cinema than from its literature and theatre. During the twenties Paramount had relied heavily on the novels and plays of James Barrie, Elinor Glyn, P. C. Wren and Rudyard Kipling. Clive Brook and Ronald Colman had imported the Du Maurier style of acting and as time went by they were to be joined by, among others, Cary Grant, Claude Rains, Robert Donat, Basil Rathbone, Sir Cedric Hardwicke and Sir C. Aubrey Smith. In effect, Hollywood became one of the last bastions of the British Empire. The Bel-Air cricket match described in the opening pages of Evelyn Waugh's novel *The Loved One* is hardly far-fetched.

Yet one British film did have a lasting effect on Hollywood: *The Private Life of Henry VIII* (1933), in which Alexander Korda, aided by a French cameraman, Georges Périnal, and a Hungarian designer, Vincent Korda, tried to sell the Englishness of the English to a world public. In the manner of Lubitsch, Korda reduces the status of the tyrannical king (Charles Laughton) to that of an endearing Bluebeard and then levels him down further by deliberately confusing his sexuality with over-eating. A bantering kind of humour derived from the Cochran revues and from *1066 and All That*—a spectator at Anne Boleyn's execution asks the woman sitting in front of him to remove her hat—identifies the heartlessness of the king with the mood of the film itself. This sleight of hand is managed with a neatness of plot and repartee that (as Pauline Kael has observed) British film-makers have often bought at too heavy a price.

Korda's affection for English palaces, snobbery, humour, professional actors and beautiful women projects an image of the country as highly coloured as the Marseilles of *Marius* and one that was to be just as successful at the box-office. But when Korda went on to film other private lives—those of Rembrandt and Don Juan among others—he was unable to repeat his success and the City of London investors who had been encouraged to support him were soon shaken to discover that they had lost a fortune on his extravagant productions. By 1937 his company, London Films, and his studio at

Denham were insolvent. Yet in all fairness to him it should be said that he did try to escape from English neatness in the 1936 film that brought him to ruin, *The Shape of Things to Come* (later titled *Things to Come*).

In his script for it, H. G. Wells attempts to refute Fritz Lang's conclusion to *Metropolis* by describing a world of the future in which scientists have become the trustees of civilization and refuse to ally themselves with the war-lords: a scenario that allows Wells to make some predictions about the future that continue to be fascinating, however inaccurate passing time may have proved them to be. He posits a world war lasting from 1940 to 1960; a wandering sickness, similar in effect to radioactivity, that covers England in 1966; a hippie community that takes over the country from the machine-age technocrats in 1970 and a missile attempt to reach the moon in 2036. But his script is too much a stagy debate, and William Cameron Menzies, the eminent United Artists designer whom Korda brought into the project as a director, was unable to give it emotional reality. Menzies created some magnificent settings, the best of them being his space-age London, in which buildings take on such personality that they almost seem to come to life. Yet this display remains uncoordinated with the rest of the action. If Menzies had been more assured as a director he would have scotched many of the ideas of Menzies the designer. Yet *Things to Come* remains one of the most interesting contributions to the utopian spirit of the thirties and was to lead to a curious tradition of English after-life movies, of which Michael Powell's *A Matter of Life and Death* (1946) is perhaps the most memorable.

A different sort of heartlessness and different kind of Englishman appears in Alfred Hitchcock's *The Man Who Knew Too Much* (1934). Hitchcock had been directing since 1922 but a number of miscalculations had brought his career to a low ebb in the early thirties; at which time Michael Balcon, who had been his first employer, invited him to direct *The Man Who Knew Too Much* at Gaumont British, arranging for Ivor Montagu to be the assistant producer. The association of these three men was to be productive. Hitchcock brought to it his expertise and awareness of the latest American techniques, Balcon a flair that owed something to the production methods of the German studios (in the twenties he had sent Hitchcock to work for a while in Germany and, like him, admired the films of F. W. Murnau) and Ivor Montagu an intimate knowledge of the Soviet cinema. These eclectic influences were fused in such a way that Balcon's wish to realize a national style of film-making (of a genuine kind, as opposed to Korda's ersatz) was to be fulfilled in the four films he produced with Hitchcock as his director.

Bob Lawrence (Leslie Banks), the man who knows too much, is an upper-middle-class Englishman who responds to a painful crisis in a characteristically English manner: with a tentative and rather fantastic capacity for improvisation. He muddles his way through, never losing his sense of humour, however difficult the going might be. Although he may seem ill-equipped to cope with the dangerous international intrigue he finds himself involved in, he demonstrates that flexibility of his kind is one possible way of dealing with the lunacies of an Alice-in-Wonderland situation. He defeats his enemies because he is without their intensity of purpose and rigidity of mind. In this sense, he is a model for nearly all the leading characters in the films Hitchcock directed in the 1930s and in Michael Balcon's post-war Ealing comedies.

Bob Lawrence's lack of preparation yet effortless superiority may have comforted those of his fellow countrymen who had recognized how unprepared they were for the Nazis. Secret agents hold his daughter hostage so that he will not disclose a cryptic message, key to the possible assassination of a foreign statesman. At first Lawrence falls in with this piece of blackmail, arguing (rightly, it may seem) that he sees no reason why he should risk the life of his daughter to save the life of a foreign statesman whom he has never heard of: yet subsequent events prove him to have been wrong. Hitchcock was later to show the political consequences of Lawrence's argument, which anticipates almost to the word Neville Chamberlain's statement on the invasion of Czechoslovakia. In *The Lady Vanishes* (1938), various English characters on a foreign train react to a dangerous situation at first by denying its existence and then by wishing to surrender to the enemy. Mr Todhunter (Cecil Parker)—saying that he would rather be called a rat than die like one—waves his white handkerchief. But enemies of this kind cannot be placated and Mr Todhunter is shot down. *The Lady Vanishes* could be seen as a satire on the attitudes that led to the signing of the Munich Pact.

Hitchcock may admire Bob Lawrence's decency, kindness and coolness in the face of danger, but he does not invite the spectator to identify with him uncritically. In his class origins and working methods, moreover, Hitchcock himself is wholly unlike this kind of Englishman. He never muddles through. He is always in control, fearfully. Interested in what is ordinary about ordinary life (like many of his contemporaries in the 1930s, the age of the common man), he recognizes in a way few others did that this sense of the commonplace lies in the far from complacent chanciness of urban life. The opening sequence of *The Man Who Knew Too Much* brings together a woman taking part in a shooting match at St Moritz, her suave competitor and a far too affable stranger (Peter Lorre) who takes too great an interest in her daughter's chiming watch. These relationships

Alfred Hitchcock filming the opening scenes of *The Man Who Knew Too Much*.
Peter Lorre (in fur coat).

seem to be random; yet Hitchcock's camera movements bind them
together with an insistence whose motive remains undisclosed. He has
his camera glide here and there, setting up emphases and framing
shots with the confidence of a Murnau: a confidence, though, that has
nothing in common with Murnau's use of this technique to enact the
sensations of his characters. If Bob Lawrence stumbles onto a cryptic
message which overturns all his presuppositions, Hitchcock, it could be
argued, imposes a cryptic message on everyday events. He has his
camera observe a mountain range through a window, then pulls it
back to reveal the hotel dining-room of which this window is a part.
Quite why this backward-moving shot should be so chilling is never
clear, though the end of the sequence provides a partial answer when
the camera returns to the window once more and focuses its attention

not on the mountain range but on a bullet-hole in the glass. Yet the initial anxiety remains unaccounted for.

Hitchcock was more or less to admit to the cynicism inherent in his need to mystify when he claimed that the cryptic message and other devices like it are no more than 'MacGuffins'—a term derived from Kipling to cover the purpose of an intrigue, whether it be to discover secret plans, or whatever—the point about 'MacGuffins' being that they consist of nothing. Intrigues and chases should be intrinsically meaningless, he believes, as when in *The Lady Vanishes* men die for the sake of a tune, the value of whose coded message they have no way of knowing. Yet it would be as foolish to take Hitchcock's cynicism on its face value as it would be to accept François Truffaut's view that Hitchcock elaborates a philosophy of the absurd out of it. Genuine anxieties and genuine intuitions do emerge in his filming. Working in a country where no serious tradition of film-making existed—his films were considered 'difficult' in the mid-thirties—he was yet able to relate himself to the culture in which he had been brought up, as in the music-hall sequences of *The Thirty-Nine Steps* (1935), and to the work of the more talented film-makers abroad. The concluding sequences of *The Man Who Knew Too Much*, though based on the Sidney Street siege, owe something in style both to Sternberg's *Underworld* and to the mysterious, abrupt executions in Dovzhenko's *Arsenal*. And in his quickly enacted killing of a decent policeman, Hitchcock touched on a poignancy that he was never again to achieve in his later career.

Although John Ford was to venture into the field of Anglo-Indian imperialism with *Wee Willie Winkie* (1937) and *Four Men and a Prayer* (1938), his most notable film in mid-decade, *The Informer* (1935), was to be set in Ireland during the troubles and given a *Kammerspiel* treatment—high-pitched lighting on faces, dark backgrounds—to keep down costs. At the end of the decade his talent was to reach full maturity while directing *Young Mr Lincoln* and *Stagecoach*, both of which were released in 1939.

In an article on *Young Mr Lincoln*, Eisenstein wrote that it had brought the daguerreotype to life once more and praised the way in which Ford had stylized the personality of Lincoln through his use of silhouette. Eisenstein appears to have seen this figure—'reminding one simultaneously of an old-fashioned semaphore telegraph, a well-worn windmill and a scarecrow'[6]—as a precursor of his own Ivan the Terrible; yet Ford was temperamentally very different from Eisenstein and in *Young Mr Lincoln* managed to create something more than an abstraction of Griffith's vision. The achievement, rather, was to adapt Griffith's pastoralism and the facts obtained from Carl Sandburg's

John Ford: *Young Mr Lincoln*. Henry Fonda.

biography of Lincoln to the political complexities of the 1930s without distorting the spirit of either.

Ford's admiration for Lincoln had always contained an undertow of scepticism and fear. In the *Prisoner of Shark Island* (1936) he had described the appalling mis-trial and punishment of the doctor who had unsuspectingly tended Lincoln's assassin and implied that the mass hysteria aroused by Lincoln's death had been mainly responsible for this act of injustice. He and his scriptwriters have nearly always shown Lincoln as a demagogue, his gift for swaying the public mind as a kind of black magic. At the same time they have acknowledged that the sinister element in Lincoln resides less in his power than in his awareness of power: in the knowing way in which he freezes litigants with his penetrating stare or towers over other men by wearing a tall, black, stovepipe hat.

In *Young Mr Lincoln* Ford distinguishes Lincoln from the demagogues of the thirties by showing him use his power beneficently and risk his life in facing a lynch-mob. He recognizes that Lincoln most differs from other demagogues in his grief; his ambition as a lawyer being broken by Ann Rutledge's death. When Lincoln tells the mother of the accused man that she reminds him of his own mother, he lays claim to identifying with her suffering, as well as admitting, perhaps, that there exists a potential murderer in himself. He is a man of his time in admiring this mother as the self-abnegating servant of men, 'giving everything and expecting nothing', but he rises above such considerations when he puts aside self-interest to serve justice.

Ford's skill is nowhere so evident as in the way he manages the transition from the rural Salem of the opening scenes—probably the finest example of thirties pastoralism—to the modern-sounding paradoxes of the courtroom, where the eliciting of truth must depend on cunning and the dubious exercise of rhetorical power. He manages this transition in part through a fairground sequence, in which Lincoln's guile and sociability are established by his response to a pie-eating contest and a tug-of-war, and his relationship to the past brought into relief by a parade of veterans who had taken part in the American Revolution. Ford had used a similar device in *Steamboat Round the Bend* (1935), where some comic rustics convert a waxwork museum of American statesmen and frontier heroes into a show of fantastic monsters and then feed these dummies into the steamboat furnace in order to win a race. He was later to contrast frontier showmen and legendary frontier heroes in both *My Darling Clementine* (1946) and *Wagonmaster* (1950), but never with such emblematic sharpness as in *Young Mr Lincoln*.

Ford has said that *Stagecoach* was based on Maupassant's story *Boule-de-suif*; yet the resemblance between the two is slight. In Maupassant's story a group of French travellers, in flight from the Germans during the Franco-Prussian war, curry favour with a prostitute so as to have her save their lives by sleeping with an enemy officer, and then treat her with contempt. The travellers are merely targets for Maupassant's hatred of the bourgeoisie; but in *Stagecoach*, Ford and his screenwriter Dudley Nichols demonstrate that the typicality of their various travellers is of a different kind. If their priggish salesman, self-righteous banker and haughty lady, on the one hand, and their drunken doctor, prostitute and hick criminal, on the other, behave as members of their various social classes are supposed to, they do so as a defence against the uncertainties of a mobile society. In *The Americans* Daniel J. Boorstin points out how in the nineteenth century the cramped condition of most forms of travel was a great social leveller; and Ford's travellers do change as they face the terror of the Apaches. Yet in changing, they continue to be types: the salesman turns out to be a coward, the banker an embezzler and the drunken doctor a hero, while the hick criminal and the prostitute become a less plausible archetype, the eternal lovers—the doctor hoping, rather wistfully, that their love will allow them to escape the pressures of civilization.

John Ford: *Stagecoach*.

If this typicality helps to increase the crisp pace of Ford's narration, which moves at the speed of his runaway stagecoach, it also gives him a certain latitude with his cast, its formality providing a structure for a kind of acting so relaxed that it suggests that Ford's cast might have been putting on a party charade for his benefit. From *Straight Shooting* on, Ford has encouraged this dynamic sort of casualness, and with John Wayne as Ringo Kid, the hick criminal, he was to bring this manner to perfection. *Stagecoach* finely balances precision with a feeling for the extemporized. It has been praised for its historical accuracy (and Margaret Thorp has claimed it to be the first movie ever to use folk music of the right period), yet in its vivid sense of the present moment it avoids the deadness of historical reconstruction.

Ford's optimism appears unusual in an age given over to the elegiac. Melancholy and doom had become the stuff of bestsellers, and Ford was to film two of them, *The Grapes of Wrath* and *How Green was My Valley*, as the old decade gave way to the new. With Europe on the verge of totalitarianism, Hollywood turned to the south as a repository for guilt-laden fantasies. Titles can be revealing, and the

Victor Fleming: *Gone with the Wind*. Clark Gable.

great epic on the Civil War was no longer to be called *The Birth of a Nation* but one based on Margaret Mitchell's novel *Gone with the Wind*.

It has been said that William Wyler filmed *Jezebel* (1938) to pre-empt this epic and to ease Bette Davis's disappointment at not being cast as Scarlett O'Hara. His packaging matches her elegance in a way that anticipates the style of *The Magnificent Ambersons*, though his screenplay (John Huston has one of the credits) is without the Wellesian wit or sense of passing time. His sharpness is of a different and more morbid kind, analysing Jezebel's cruelty to her lover Preston Dillard (Henry Fonda—white face, tufted hair, like some angel of righteousness) as partly a release from frustration at being a woman of character in a society where women are treated as chattels, and partly a wish to elicit violence from him. Wyler places such an emphasis on masochistic motive that it is possible to see both the death of Buck Cantrell, one of Jezebel's admirers, and the defeat of the South as voluptuous forms of suicide. At the end of the film, Jezebel accompanies the dying Preston Dillard to a yellow fever colony and moves through a burning town to her certain death, welcoming apocalypse with a consummate pleasure.

Gone with the Wind (1939) is even more extreme. At various stages in its shooting George Cukor, Victor Fleming and Sam Wood took over as director, but most credit for its appearance on screen must lie with its producer. *Memo from David O. Selznick*, a selection of correspondence, reveals the extent to which Selznick took control over every department of his studio. Obsessed, risking everything, he was as persistent as an Al Jolson in his wish to move audiences to tears. In this he succeeded. Making no concession to contemporary opinion—his Negroes are either effete or quaint, his Scarlett idealized in her emotional difficulties—he created a type of kitsch that weathers all fashion. He is so involved in a showman's vision of tragedy that he carries his audience along with him, showing a Scarlett (Vivien Leigh) who has been given everything—wealth, beauty, loving parents, admiring beaux, a fine country home—and must lose everything but her beauty. And as the hours pass, he has his audiences move with her through death and destruction, with only the slightest lightening of mood. She marries Rhett, a Southern buck, who builds her a house so garish that it would seem to parody the production values of the film itself. But even here she cannot find happiness and recognizes that she must return to the charred soil of Tara, the family estate.

Gone with the Wind complemented the flamboyant picture temples of the inter-war years and satisfied a public need for mass-consumer baroque. It made over seventy million dollars for MGM in the United States and Canada alone. But historical romance also had other shrines. If *Gone with the Wind* was mass-consumer baroque, then the conversion of Garbo and Dietrich into screen goddesses could be seen as mass-consumer classicism on the one hand and mass-consumer rococo on the other. Sternberg had fabricated Dietrich, gauzing, wrapping, mummifying her as an act of will that had no relation to history, geography or what the public might have wanted. He snared the spectator in a web of light and shade, in which all Dietrich had to do was to repose like some carved Aztec stone.

The processes by which Garbo had been transformed were more complicated. Louis B. Mayer had invited her and Mauritz Stiller to come to Hollywood in the mid-twenties, and it seems likely that her screen personality at this time was quite different from her later one. Alexander Walker has claimed in his book *Stardom* that in at least two of the films directed by Clarence Brown, *Flesh and the Devil* (1927) and *A Woman of Affairs* (1928), she 'embodied eroticism more intensely than any other star of the period'.[7] But the Garbo of the thirties— the Garbo of *Grand Hotel* (1933), *Anna Karenina* (1935), *Camille* (1936) and *Conquest/Marie Walewska* (1937) was to be remote, a dreamy Nordic Madonna. Rouben Mamoulian's choreographic direction of *Queen Christina* (1933) allowed Garbo to realize this kind of presence through a series of almost balletic gestures: the drifting, caressing sway around the inn room where she has stayed with her lover ('I was memorizing this room. In future I shall live long in memory of this room'), a sway timed to a metronome; the decisive, broken movement of her arms as she removes her crown at the abdication; or the sustained final shot of her, blank-faced, as her ship pulls out to sea, as meaningful, or meaningless, as the spectator may wish it to be.

The impulse that transformed Dietrich and Garbo into screen goddesses may have been no more than a sophisticated variation on the male wish to transform women into objects. But if Hollywood could be casual with women, it could be just as casual with history. It had no tenure on the past, seeing it as either a pretext for exoticism or a means for commenting on the present. When Warner Brothers assigned William Dieterle to a series of historical biographies, *The Story of Louis Pasteur* (1935), *The Life of Emile Zola* (1937) and *Juarez* (1939), the studio was so eager to point out the similarity between past and present that it made little sense of either.

Dieterle's Zola might be a man of the early 1930s, fit subject for a Warner Brothers' topical film. During a slump, he writes newspaper reports on the maltreatment of prostitutes and exposes the corruption of those in authority. He becomes involved in the Dreyfus affair— injustices of an *I am a Fugitive from a Chain Gang* kind—and has his books burnt. But in suggesting a likeness between the Dreyfus persecution and the behaviour of the Nazis, Dieterle manages to avoid any reference to the most salient issue in this affair: the anti-semitism of Dreyfus's opponents. He never once mentions that Dreyfus was a Jew, and presents the Dreyfus household as a representative American WASP family, with a daughter resembling Shirley Temple.

Dieterle based *Juarez* on a play by Franz Werfel and filmed it with far more panache than *The Life of Emile Zola*, eliciting a clean-edged photography from Tony Gaudio, pacing his narrative tightly and providing Juarez with a silhouette as vivid as Ford's Mr Lincoln— appropriately, since Juarez modelled himself on Lincoln, rather like that other hero of 1939, Capra's Mr Smith. (Paul Muni, who had also played Zola, presents Juarez as a monolithic figure with sly, restless eyes: one of his best performances.) Dieterle balances sympathy in the conflict between the murderous yet honest Juarez and the futile yet graceful Emperor Maximilian (Brian Aherne—who was usually cast at this time as various kinds of ineffectual Englishman). He brings out the pathos both in the Emperor's execution and in his wife's madness. But on the debit side, his treatment appears directed to one end: to preach isolationism. He had no personal reason, it would seem, for being anti-European. For all that, he took care to build his film around Juarez's denunciation of 'the butchering, destroying powers of Europe' and his wish to remain at a remove from them.

No other film-maker was to achieve so much in the 1930s as Jean Renoir in the fifteen films he was to direct during this period. No one understood better than he the underlying themes of this decade, or explored more widely the range of conventions available to it, or withstood more boldly its tendency to streamline.

In *La Grande Illusion* (1937) he appears at first sight to be practising the same technique as in *Le Crime du Monsieur Lange*: that is, of describing a complicated and unusual social structure – the relationship of Frenchmen to each other and to their German captors in a prisoner-of-war camp – by means of a theory of types, and by this theory communicating something of the conflicting interests that made up the climate of Europe in 1914. He brings to the practice of this theory a certain complexity, by showing how two officer gentlemen on opposing sides, Boïeldieu (Pierre Fresnay) and Rauffenstein (Erich von Stroheim), can have a greater kinship with each other than with the men in their command and how Maréchal (Jean Gabin), a soldier of peasant origins, and Rosenthal (Marcel Dalio), a soldier from a wealthy Jewish family, have more in common through their wish to survive than ethnic and class tensions might imply.

Renoir realizes the significance of these kinships in a way that places the theory of types within a context. He demonstrates how thinking in terms of types is liable to exacerbate the conditions that lead to war. In Feyder's *La Kermesse heroïque* (1935), the women in a beleaguered Flemish town think that they can emasculate their Spanish overlords by kindness; and the passivity intrinsic to this kind of resistance is reflected in Feyder's style. He constructs the film out of a series of elegant set pieces, holding up the past to intricate inspection, as though with a pair of tweezers. Everything is static and fixed. But Renoir, whose understanding of resistance is never passive – none of the prisoners of war denies the need to escape – and whose concern is to distinguish not so much between courage and cowardice as between the heroic, suicidal kind of courage represented by Boïeldieu and the cunning yet more effective kind of courage represented by Maréchal, takes up a dynamic relationship to the experiences he describes. If Feyder's treatment resembles a sequence of minor Dutch paintings, Renoir's treatment is more like a symphony in which themes may interact and modify each other. His film consists of a prelude and three movements, each linked to the other by a travelling shot of a landscape filmed from a train window; and these travelling shots, which appear to dissolve and renew the landscape before our eyes, like images that pass through the mind at the moment when it enters sleep, indicate the technique that Renoir was to bring to perfection in *La Grande Illusion* and *La Règle du jeu*.

Although Renoir had intimated this process of regression in the final sequence of *Boudu sauvé des eaux*, he was to work it out with a far greater understanding of its meaning in *La Grande Illusion*. Boïeldieu and his men make ceaseless attempts to escape. After each failure they are transported from prison camp to prison camp until they end up in a medieval castle commanded by Rauffenstein. Each of these camps takes them a step further into Germany, into closer security, into an increasing physical coldness, into deeper states of despair. And each of these stages in their journey marks a stage backwards in time, as it were, until they reach the feudal conditions out of which, Renoir implies, the tensions that led to the Great War emerged. Similarly, Renoir's filming shifts from a heightened kind of naturalism into an oceanic realism that can freely carry an overt kind of symbolism. In the snowbound castle Boïeldieu and Rauffenstein most completely live out their strange code of behaviour, the archaic nature of which is symbolized by the manner of Boïeldieu's death. In white gloves and playing a penny whistle, Boïeldieu leaps across the fortress parapets in order to distract the German troops while his men escape. Rauffenstein has to shoot him down: the ostentatious futility of his death appearing to be an epitaph to the Greek ideal that a life may be fulfilled by death in action, an ethos inherited by the officers who died in Flanders.

In the final episode of the story Maréchal and Rosenthal escape into the snow. Almost dead from exposure, they reach a farm-house, where a young German widow takes them into her protection. They wait for spring; and Maréchal becomes the widow's lover while Rosenthal works on the farm. As the two men recover from their ordeal, Renoir's style appears to abandon its fantastic element, so that when the widow washes Rosenthal's feet, a Christian reference already signalled earlier when a soldier washed Maréchal's feet, or when Rosenthal carves a Jesus crib out of potatoes, the symbolism seems at odds with Renoir's return to naturalism, however well-meaning his intention in describing a community that transcends religious or racial considerations.

In *La Grande Illusion* Renoir handles narrative with a freedom usually associated with the novel, although his fluent camera movements and deep-focus photography allow him to render vivid qualities that a novelist can only imply, such as the subtle variety of the relationships or the haunting presence of the castle in the snow. And it is unlikely that a novelist could have presented so tersely a character as strange as Stroheim's Rauffenstein.

In a sense *La Règle du jeu* (1939) is even more novelistic since its structure takes the form of a confession, a form that is unusual in films, if not in novels. In one of the earlier scenario drafts for this film, Renoir had his central character, Octave, study music with a distinguished Austrian conductor and fall in love with the conductor's daughter. Later the penniless Octave lodges with the daughter and arouses resentment in her husband, a French lawyer. In the completed film this situation has been modified: Octave's relationship with Christine and her husband, the wealthy Marquis Robert de la Chesnaye, is far more complicated, its tension veiled by good humour, while Octave's dependence on the couple is to some extent compensated for by their need to use him as a confidant. In the completed film, too, Christine's conductor father has died long before the beginning of the action, his cherished memory playing an important part in her friendship with Octave.

The significance of this dead father is increased by the fact that Renoir himself plays Octave. In one poignant scene Octave pretends to mime the role of a conductor for Christine, raises an invisible baton and then drops his arms despairingly. Renoir, of course, is playing a character in fiction, and yet Octave's modesty in this scene is so like Renoir's modesty in interview about his own father that it would be hard not to see the character and the actor at this point as identical. One of the attractions of *La Règle du jeu* is that Renoir should feel the

Jean Renoir: *La Règle du jeu*. Renoir as Octave (right),
Roland Toutain as the aviator.

need to apologize for himself and to acknowledge his inferiority to his father. Touched by such candour, the film itself takes on the attributes of an engaging human being.

If a confession draws back the curtains on the mind of the person who confesses, then *La Règle du jeu* in its totality can be seen to disclose something of Octave's mental landscape. But Octave in his role of confidant is a father confessor as well as the one who confesses, someone who sets the action in motion and who discloses the interiority of the various other characters. In *La Grande Illusion* Renoir had worked out a means by which his film could embody regressed and fantastic states of mind without resorting to expressionistic techniques. In *La Règle du jeu*, where nearly every one of his principal characters has a confession to make, he has to open up this perspective of regressed mental states in many directions. And yet in the same way as the spectator may feel an intruder into the privacy of these characters, so the characters can be seen as intruders into each others' lives. The structure of the film is based on this parasitic kind of dependence, and it is this parasitism that brings about the retreat into disorder.

At the opening of the film a Mozart overture implies by its presence an emotional stability that none of the characters is ever to reach; in this sense, its effect is like the cherished memory of Christine's conductor father. André Jurieux (Roland Toutain), an outstanding aviator, lands at Le Bourget after having flown the Atlantic alone. Greeted as a hero by the crowd, the equivocal nature of his heroism becomes evident when he complains over the radio that his flight has been worthless because the woman he loves—Christine— has not come to welcome him at the airport. By shaming Christine in this way, André has not only broken the rules of the game by publicizing his love for her, but also has intruded into her privacy. Later, by threatening suicide, he forces Octave to bring him as a guest to Christine's house-party in the country: an embarrassing intrusion that Christine's husband, the Marquis, tries to compete with by bringing a poacher into the house as a servant. In the same way as this poacher disrupts the servants' quarters by his intrusion into a game-keeper's marriage, so André and Octave by their actions precipitate a succession of disasters in the rooms upstairs; and the house-party, which had hardly begun calmly, with its pillow fights and unconcealed malice among the guests, turns into a bear-garden with Octave dressed up as the bear. Chases, fisticuffs, pistol shots: the regression into infancy begins to be strident as the guests squabble like unattended children and Renoir resorts to the techniques of farce.

He describes a formalized society which has fallen into disorder because almost everyone in it refuses to play the role allotted to him. Typical of this disorder is the fact that the host at the party, the *grand seigneur*, should be a Jew: someone the aristocrats of the Boulevard Saint-Germain would think of as the perennial intruder, who is yet described by his chef, one of the few characters in the film to observe the rules of the game, as 'un homme du monde'. It is typical of Renoir's irony that this Jew should not only have the character of an admirable aristocrat but yet by his confession bring about disorder. At a concert party, in which some of his guests dressed up as skeletons leap about to the music of Saint-Saëns's *Danse macabre*, the Marquis displays a fairground organ, the latest acquisition in his collection of clockwork toys. As he stands beaming with gratification before this thundering animated piece of machinery, it becomes clear that the Marquis would like to control his guests in much the same way as he controls his toys: a wish that by its nature renders him ineffectual, so that he is unable to avert the impending catastrophe.

Renoir has frequently allowed his characters to reveal their motives through play-acting, as when in *Une Partie de campagne* (1938) he has Jacques Brunius as a lecherous salesman burlesque the love-rites of a faun. And play-acting, too, allows him to change conventions unobtrusively, moving from one style to another, as in *The Golden Coach* (1952). He had already mastered this technique by the time he came to direct *La Règle du jeu* and moves without strain from the newsreel naturalism of his opening scene, through the Dance of Death stylization of the middle sequences, to the Commedia dell'Arte treatment of his concluding chase. But even in his most naturalistic sequences he uses locations as though they were a stage on which his characters can act out their most private feelings, corralling great areas of space for them through his deep-focus photography and sweeping camera movements.

It is psychologically appropriate that these intrusions, and the deaths that result from them, should be bound up with confused states of mind: that André should be killed while 'accidentally' wearing Octave's overcoat and that by the end of the film, and without explanation, Octave should be seen wearing this overcoat once more; or that Octave's apparently generous renunciation of Christine should help to bring about the death of his rival for Christine's love. But how far do the final scenes of the film act out Renoir/Octave's imaginings or actual events? Throughout the story a deliberate use of ambiguity bedevils any literalist interpretation of events, as in the double-time system—the house-party, which appears to last only a weekend, is in fact spaced out over the period of a week—or in doubts raised about the number of guests at the party, or about the geographical placing of the country house, La Collinière, in relation to Paris.

At the same time, Renoir's intuitions about the nature of jealousy give substance to his comparison between France on the eve of the 1789 revolution and its condition before its collapse of 1940, to his comparison between the fate of the characters in Beaumarchais's *The Marriage of Figaro* and Christine's guests. For in *La Règle du jeu* Renoir assumes that the social order has already changed and the game no

'Corralling great areas of space.' Jean Renoir: *La Regle du jeu*.

longer has meaning, and so is able to show, if only by implication, how naïve Hollywood's view of the upper-class European as the last curator of civilization had become. If certain privileged people still do uphold the rules of the game, most of them do so cynically, as Renoir reveals when he has the Marquis hypocritically tell his guests how deeply he regrets the death of André—the man who had almost destroyed his marriage. Renoir concludes the film with a shot of shrubs in pots laid out in a neat row: a sardonic comment, if anything, on a symmetry that no longer has any social meaning. The only character in the film who observes the rules of the game as though they were unchangeable law is the gamekeeper, and he is shown to be broken by his rigidity.

La Règle du jeu registers a breakdown in conventional ideas about morality as well as about social order, and its style is sensitive to these changes; indeed, Renoir's reticence about motives, his spatial configurations and his use of camera movement anticipate by about twenty years the interests of the French and Italian New Wave. In *La Règle du jeu* he not only summarizes many of the main preoccupations of film-makers in nearly every country but points out one possible way in which they could move in the future. It is not surprising, then, that its first audiences should have responded to it with bafflement, if not with hostility, and that it should have been swiftly withdrawn from circulation.

Part Four: 1940–1956

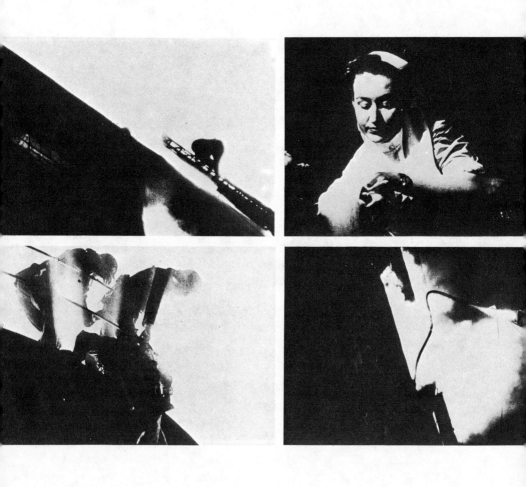

Humphrey Jennings: *Fires were Started*.

11. The Second World War

Women bolstering their confidence by wearing huge, elaborate hats; ashtrays full of stubs and smoke-filled rooms; brief, casual encounters; jealousy often figuring as poisoning; terror and consolation at evidence of the supernatural—the war's signature on the movies was unmistakable. And they, in turn, recorded the unsettling effects of war: how it took people away from home, separated the sexes and increased anxieties about death. The war drove the two principal trends in 1930s filming—towards realism and towards romance—to extremes. It was like the separation of the sexes, or the separation of the masculine and feminine components in everyone. Realism came to mean the inconvenient subject, the awkward fact, the discomforts of restriction; while romance came to mean the engulfing release of desire.

The Axis may have been the enemy, but its infection was hard to contain. As victory began to look certain for the Allies, newsreels grew more aggressive and cruelty more strident, even in such programme-fillers as the Tom and Jerry cartoons or the Three Stooges. Often the belligerence was reassuring: the musical was never to be so vigorous, or yearning, as now. Florenz Ziegfeld, a legend, was frequently referred to as though he were a god (and, godlike, did not appear in the post-war *Ziegfeld Follies*): an apotheosis owing something, perhaps, in this era of rationing, to the famous Ziegfeld parade in which girls were presented like platters of food. Pin-ups were called cheesecake. Eroticism and exoticism took the form of Rita Hayworth and Carmen Miranda, known on one celebrated occasion as 'The Lady in the Tutti Frutti Hat'. Howard Hughes, as a kind of Pygmalion, spent years of effort trying to breathe life into his Galatea, cheesecake to end all cheesecake, Jane Russell in *The Outlaw* (1944).

This was the outward show. In films for women the world was experienced as dark and treacherous. However much they might be veiled, jealousy, loneliness and loss could not be avoided. The sufferings of Scarlett O'Hara gave comfort. In London *Gone with the Wind* dominated Leicester Square from April 1940 to the spring of D-Day. 'During the long blitz you went into Leicester Square early in the morning, after a long night of bombing, and found the queues already circling the theatre,' wrote an anonymous diarist, quoted by Guy Morgan in *Red Roses Every Night*.

'It was the general experience of managers in the bad years,' confides the diarist, 'that the public would not sit through the ordinary talkie-talkie tea-table picture. We wanted action, movement, colour, music, comedy—some sort of proxy release. We would tolerate heavy drama (i.e. Bette Davis) but not a whimsical fantastic love affair. The enjoyment or non-enjoyment of programmes was always profoundly affected by the newsreels.' The documentary was never really popular, 'except *Target for Tonight* and *Desert Victory*, both showing power to strike back'. The public avoided war films and had no taste for resistance themes, although '*One of Our Aircraft is Missing* did well, *Casablanca* did marvellously, as a lush romance'.[1] In 1942 British audiences were divided in their opinion about *Mrs Miniver*, but they liked *In Which We Serve*, *Yankee Doodle Dandy*, *Holiday Inn*, *The First of the Few*, *The Little Foxes* and *Dangerous Moonlight*. In 1943 *Random Harvest* swept the country, and the Rank release *The Man in Grey* was a surprising hit. On the whole, young audiences were sceptical about attempts at realism and were quick to spot the bogus. The forces had little time for war pictures. Unexpectedly, perhaps, they approved of Carol Reed's *The Way Ahead* (1944).

Although unpopular, documentary was endured. Mobile projectors, sent out by the Ministry of Information, travelled the country and between August 1943 and August 1944 over eleven million people

Ministry of Information van carrying mobile projector and documentary films.

went to these programmes. In 1941 Dilys Powell visited a munitions factory in South Wales where, during a midday screening of some documentaries, the sound of voices was 'incessant and savage'. Yet people insisted on more of these programmes, and on the evening of the same day she observed some miners and their wives as they 'sat rapt and silent through a documentary record of the making of an airscrew'. [2]

Documentary, moreover, was to be a stimulus to the film industry in general. At the time when Chamberlain declared war on Hitler's regime in September 1939, the collapse of the industry, already unnerved by the financial difficulties of 1937, seemed imminent. The public did not go out in the blackout, studios had been requisitioned, actors called up and film stock curtailed. In the Sunday papers and *Picturegoer*, Michael Balcon commented on the flight of film personalities to Hollywood. 'Between the Munich agreement and the beginning of the war—and even since then—streams of British subjects have been hurrying across the Atlantic.' [3] Then the situation changed. The public grew used to the tense boredom of the phoney war. It started going to the movies once more, and with increased enthusiasm: by 1943–4 twenty-five million tickets were being sold each week, equivalent to everyone in the British Isles visiting the cinema twice a month. From the summer of 1940 to the defeat of the Germans in North Africa, the country was besieged by the enemy; and yet, however appalling the threat, it did at last free the film-makers from a dependence on American finance and gave them a communal theme.

At the outbreak of the war, the government had set up the Ministry of Information to deal with the problems of propaganda and censorship. It included a film division, at first directed by Kenneth Clark and then by Jack Beddington. In April 1940 the division took over the GPO Film Unit and in November of that year renamed it the Crown Film Unit. Grierson had left for Canada. Alberto Cavalcanti was in charge (at least for a while, but his Brazilian passport rendered him *persona non grata* and Ian Dalrymple took over at the time of the renaming), and Cavalcanti had promoted the talents of two men who were to be key figures in the documentary movement: Harry Watt and Humphrey Jennings.

In the spring issue of the 1941 *Sight and Sound*, already slim from the paper shortage, Basil Wright suggested how war had influenced the techniques of documentary: non-professional actors were being handled with greater flexibility, narrative structures simplified and the cult of Russian montage quietly forgotten. Jennings was to be an exception, perhaps; his delicate, complex films were to profit from many of the GPO Film Unit's researches into the fields of editing and sound recording, but this streamlining certainly applied to Watt and to others. Under Cavalcanti, Watt had been responsible for a number

Harry Watt: *Target for Tonight.*

of shorts, including *Squadron 992* and the admirable *North Sea*; then in 1941 he directed the documentary feature *Target for Tonight.*

It now seems as evocative of its period as an ugly narrow-armed utility chair. The bleakness of its aerodrome setting and the awkwardness of its editing and camera placements capture the austerity of the period with a zeal so puritanical that it begins to assume the conviction of a style. It covers an aerial reconnaissance of Germany, the pinpointing of targets by photography and the ensuing successful raid. Watt's actors were people actually involved in this work, and he in no way explores their personalities; so far as he is concerned, they might be parts of a machine. If he does relax into appreciation, it is in fact into an appreciation of machines: clear-edged images of planes taking off from a desolate runway or flying low against a cold northern sky. He resists any drift towards the ferment of drama, as though he believed fiction to be dishonest; and it was suitable to this literalist intention, as it was to Rossellini's *Rome, Open City,* that the uses of photography, in this case of aerial photography, should have been crucial to his subject. His scruples were justified. We see here for the first time the nervous, rather wooden decency of the British under stress, a response which professional actors were to work up into a mannerism, the stiff-upper-lip routine.

One sequence, which offers the satisfaction of looking down at bombs falling on Germany, was to become a cliché in war films: to be exorcised in part by Stanley Kubrick's parody of it in *Dr Strangelove*, when Slim Pickens's Major 'King Kong' descends with a whoopee on the back of a nuclear bomb. But on the whole *Target for Tonight* avoids overt propaganda, describing the action of people at work without raising the question of the work's value. It makes no chauvinistic claims and its aggression is usually veiled. It can be usefully compared to the Nazi *Baptism of Fire* (1940), where self-justification – the commentator announces that God will judge Chamberlain harshly for having unleashed the war – and an increasingly violent rhythm of attack dominate a picture of the Polish blitzkrieg intended to terrorize neutral nations. The independent feature *In Which We Serve* has Noel Coward tautly sneering at the cowardice of the 'macaronis' (although the man who put together this production was an Italian, Filippo Del Giudice), and at least one Pathé Gazette at the time of the Rhine crossing has its commentator gloating over the 'obsequious smiles' of the defeated Germans, 'a backward race', and takes pleasure in the fact that American troops have wiped out a town because of a persistent enemy sniper. But most war documentaries avoided such a tone. They purveyed information; they were diagrammatic; and the conflicts they faced centred less on nationalism than on man's difficulties with nature and the bureaucrats.

The war was seen at this stage as a necessary evil. Yet even when the siege had ended, in 1943, the Crown Film Unit production *Western Approaches*, scripted and directed by Pat Jackson, concentrated more on

Pat Jackson: *Western Approaches.*

the endurance of some shipwrecked merchant seamen than on the meaning of the war, and a foxy U-boat commander who uses the lifeboat as a decoy comes poor second, as a raiser of suspense, to man's struggle with the elements. It was implicit in this project that Jack Cardiff should photograph it on location, although colour equipment was cumbersome at this time, especially in a crowded lifeboat on heavy seas. (The twenty-eight-foot lifeboat contained twenty-two merchant seamen, a production team of five, plus all the equipment. Shooting took place twenty miles out of Holyhead, Wales, every day for six months.) We need only contrast the result with Hitchcock's studiobound *Lifeboat* (1944) to see how far the risks had been worth-while. Jackson catches the quality of the Anglo-American convoys precisely and he is informative about the precautions taken by their phlegmatic commanders, but it is Cardiff's skill with Technicolor—his ability, for instance, to conjure up the sensation of towering blue-grey waves—and the accompanying elegiac music by Clifton Parker which stays in the memory. Maps, the lore of seamanship, a plot reliance on such means of communication as radio, voice amplifiers and flickering lights connect dry practicalities with sublime nature and check the English taste for a sweetened kind of romanticism. Jackson is never explicit about this being a people's war, as Humphrey Jennings was to be, yet his casting of the men in the lifeboat—the faces marked by character, the absence of class caricature, the carefully natural dialogue—implies such an assumption and reminds us that the movement towards neo-realism occurred not only in Italy. Historians will find valuable this record of the permanently depressed and slightly deferential behaviour of working-class men, a manner which had been reinforced by the Depression yet was soon to disappear.

David MacDonald and Roy Boulting, who co-directed *Desert Victory* (1943) for the Army Film Unit, also concentrated on reportage. But they were too close to the subject and they underplayed the importance of the October 1942 victory at El Alamein and the subsequent breakthrough to Tripoli. On its first release, audiences came to the film with some knowledge of the battle; a present-day spectator may feel at a loss with the events. Its evidence, in the form of maps and a commentary, is inadequate. Its makers give the perhaps false impression that they are more fascinated by American Sherman tanks than by people. They know nothing of what went on behind the enemy lines: how General Stumme, for instance, had a heart attack on the first day of battle and Rommel was rushed out of hospital to reassume command. The filming seldom rises above newsreel level—soldiers silhouetted against the dawn sky, guns flashing in darkness. The restrained commentary gives British casualties as twenty thousand dead in twelve days and nights of battle, and the general honesty of the treatment almost redeems the film from its inadequacies.

Roy Boulting was to be involved in both the later Victory documentaries, and he and his brother John were to be responsible for some of the more imaginative productions of the 1940s. But *Seven Days to Noon* (1950), which touched on the fear of nuclear destruction, a fear that overshadowed life at that time yet was seldom referred to on the screen, seems to have drained their powers of invention. During the fifties they aimed for easier targets: satires on the Trade Union movement and the army. They had lost the sense of adventure and the hope that had characterized the earlier stages of their career. For when they were twenty-five, Roy had directed and John produced *Pastor Hall* (1939), based on Ernst Toller's play about Pastor Niemöller. Like Cavalcanti, Jennings and Kevin Brownlow later, they seem to have been haunted by the thought of how they would have responded to Nazism if it had taken root in England. *Pastor Hall* has a studio-bound German village setting, but its acting—especially Wilfred Lawson's incandescent portrait of the Pastor—and its mood establish it as English in feeling. Stormtroopers take control of the Pastor's village; they send him to a concentration camp when he refuses to pay lip-service to their doctrines, and eventually, it is implied, put him to death. The Boultings present the horrors of the concentration camp soberly and without equivocation, which must have required courage at a time when the British, both on the left and the right, tended to be placatory towards Nazi Germany.

Many of the Boulting plots of the forties invoke extreme anxiety (*Thunder Rock*, *The Guinea Pig*, *Brighton Rock* and even their 1968 thriller *Twisted Nerve*). The Victory films did not allow Roy Boulting this kind of investigation, and he was further cramped by the unusual production set-up of *Tunisian Victory* (1944). Although the events of this feature follow on from its predecessor like a sequel—the sudden 1,500-mile retreat of Rommel's army to Tunis to deal with the Allied offensive there allowed the British to make their swift breakthrough to Tripoli—the Tunisian campaign differed from the battle of El Alamein in one noticeable way: it was the first in which American and British armed forces worked together, a trial run for the more complex organization of the June 1944 'Overlord' landing in Normandy. Suitably, therefore, the film was an Anglo-American production, and John Huston, Frank Capra and Anthony Veiller joined with Roy Boulting in various directorial capacities. But the association was unfruitful. A Hollywood exultation in glossy images of power—a way of looking at the take-off of Flying Fortresses, the laying down of roads, even the conspicuous waste of hardware—and a Hollywood expertise in editing and use of a more sensitive type of black and white film stock (some of the images have the quality of a Robert Capa photograph) give it an intermittent glamour. But overall, this style undermines confidence. The commentary slips into a hectoring and sentimental manner, which a later Anglo-American production, *The True Glory*, was to avoid. It reminds us that 'Arab kids are no different from the kids at home' and that the troops are bringing back smiles to their faces. It smooths over difficulties in the Atlantic partnership by dealing with it on a Huckleberry Finn level and refers to the French forces who occupied Tunis with affectionate contempt as 'old Alphonse'—the relationship with the French was, needless to say, edgy.

Burma Victory (1945), last in the Victory series and the most interesting, covers the campaign to open the route to China, the founding of the South East Command under Mountbatten, Slim's astonishing tactics and the terrible battle for Mandalay, with shots of planes zooming over the pagodas. It, too, plays down Anglo-American tensions; but apart from the death of Wingate, an event of epic stature, the importance of human activity recedes before the presence of nature. The jungle undermines everything; yet the jungle can take on a baleful splendour, as when at dawn birdsong brings it to sudden life. Roy Boulting, who directed the film, communicates the prickly heat and other sensations of a sweltering summer, as well as the fatigue of plunging through the rain and mud of an interminable monsoon. Men climbing a hill look like ants on a wall. British film-makers were never again to come so close to the extremism of the Russian war documentaries. Shots of the British dead were for once left uncensored: the tangle of crashed gliders, the graveyard in the clearing, the garden heavy with corpses.

Most Ministry of Information productions idealized the role of the fighting man. They were impersonal, non-evaluatory, officially acceptable. The tensions of war gave them a heightened gravity: yet some of them—the documentaries of Humphrey Jennings, for example—had more than that.

It could be argued that Jennings's interests should have ruled him out as a government chronicler of the blitz. A surrealist painter during the inter-war years, and a follower of Magritte, he had developed an eye for the incongruous—and he had developed this eye for irreverent perception in other ways. He and his friends had studied the anthropological writings of Malinowski and Freud. They had founded the Mass Observation movement and collected information on the unconscious customs of the British, in much the same way as Malinowski had documented the behaviour of South Sea Islanders. Fascinated by science, Jennings had filled a trunk with notes for an uncompleted book on the Industrial Revolution. He admired the

'An eye for the incongruous.' Humphrey Jennings: *London Can Take It*.

genius of its inventors, yet at the same time recognized how the misuse of this technology had reinforced class distinctions as well as despoiling large areas of Britain. He was a socialist who revered the poetry of Blake. But like many Romantics of his generation, he had been impressed by the neo-classical ideas of T. E. Hulme and T. S. Eliot and had been especially impressed by their doctrine of creative impersonality, a doctrine that was deeply Romantic in inspiration. As a surrealist he had been drawn to the notion of the collective unconscious, the shared dream of a whole people, and this cult of impersonality had been buttressed by his work as a member of the Mass Observation movement. All these interests fitted him for the role of documentary maker for the Crown Film Unit.

He was fitted for it, too, in other, less appealing ways. His socialism was paternalist; it assumed that it knew what was best for others; it was close to the spirit that had brought about the Education Act of 1944. He believed dogmatically that the kind of humanism represented by the music of Beethoven and Sibelius was both central to human experience and beneficial. For instance, E. M. Forster's commentary to *Diary for Timothy* (1945) worries over the fact that Beethoven was a German but in every other way proposes a universal value in its middle-class interpretation of culture. Admittedly, the war had allowed all classes the chance to enjoy some of the benefits of this culture, if only through the concerts and plays broadcast by the BBC.

Yet it was an idea of culture both imposed and slightly unreal, as Jennings unintentionally demonstrated in *Listen to Britain* (1941) when he cut together a scene of Flanagan and Allen, the comedians, appearing at a midday factory concert with shots of Myra Hess playing Beethoven to rows of sensitive faces. This idealized view of an integrated culture patronized the public by making the false inference that it knew what was good for it.

'Our inheritance was left to us by no testament,'[4] wrote the French Resistance poet René Char. Jennings's distinction was to have recognized this inheritance at the moment when it seemed that it would be destroyed. He films the immeasurably precious qualities of ordinary life with the intensity of a desert island castaway sending off his last message in a bottle: the modesty and friendliness of the Londoner in the blitz, the angular grace of its women, the loveliness of the countryside, the pleasure of its communities. But he also felt that this culture had to be seen as respectable. He not only recorded the atmosphere of English life but set himself up as its publicist. He took on a heroic tone in promoting the view of the war as a people's war, a tone more appropriate to Beethoven than to the temperament of the people who were his subject. His thinking is of a kind that can easily lapse into disillusion, and his post-war films were intended to be sour. He died in 1951. It is unlikely that he would have admired the working-class culture that took over the British media in the mid-sixties or felt any sympathy for the critical attention now paid to the Hollywood film.

However, he had been chronically irritable before the war as well as after it. Joining the GPO Film Unit in 1934, he began to reveal the extent of his talent three years later in his short documentary *Spare Time* (1937), a downcast study of working-class hobbies filmed in Bolton, where one of the Mass Observation surveys had taken place. Its best moments—such as the street scene of a band playing the National Anthem, escorted by a gauche Miss Britannia and some old men in Union Jack waistcoats—are filled with revulsion. But his hostility had diminished by the time he came to direct *The First Days* (1939). He had begun to identify with his subject and, apart from a shot of a Christmas Island statue lodged beneath the neo-classical portico of the British museum, he had abandoned his knowing use of surrealism. His images carry a wealth of meaning. As on *Spare Time*, he worked in association with his Mass Observation colleagues; and *The First Days* covers the phoney war in much the same way as does one of their best surveys, *War Begins at Home*. But his technique looks back to an earlier survey, one made at the time of the Coronation in 1937, which added support to Freud's view that at key moments in a nation's history 'psychic processes' of a communal nature are liable to emerge: an idea somewhat cast in doubt by the existence of Riefenstahl's *Triumph of the Will*, where such psychic processes might be more fairly described as hysterical suggestion. If Jennings avoids patriotic sentimentality, he does so through the closely-meshed musicality of his editing and a sympathy for the oppressed that could extend beyond his own country-men; as in *A Defeated People* (1945), where he invited the spectator to identify with the hardship of the Germans in the first post-war winter.

His orchestration of images was to be most effective in *Listen to Britain* (1941): its contrasts between night and day, city and country-side, colliery and street needed no commentary to communicate the tensions of impending invasion. In subsequent films he tended to be ambitious in a literary manner, including a long quotation from Sir Walter Raleigh in *Fires Were Started* (1943) and modelling *Diary for Timothy* on the essay form. He risked turning his films into illustrated lectures. Even so, he was usually able to realize his ideas in visual terms; a good instance being the moment in *Diary for Timothy* when the miner Gyronwy, hospitalized in a stately country mansion, looks up at a ceiling painted in the manner of Tiepolo and asks himself whether the unemployment and starvation of the thirties will recur after the war is over.

Perhaps other Ministry of Information documentaries, such as Jack Chambers's *Night Shift* or the Army Film Unit's *A Date with a Tank,* convey the war atmosphere more directly. Jennings's sensitive medi-tations compel attention in another way. They are the most complete embodiment of the social and political interests of the British docu-mentary movement and develop the genre as far as it was possible to develop it within the limitations of a government agency.

Early in 1939 Michael Balcon had written to the government sug-gesting ways in which his studio might be put to the service of the country. He received no answer. But then he got in touch with Kenneth Clark at the Ministry of Information, and soon Ealing was producing war documentaries as well as its usual Will Hay and George Formby comedies. Cavalcanti had now joined Balcon's team as a producer and both men wished to bring the techniques of documentary into the feature film, although they were to experience a number of setbacks with this project, the saddest being the death of the promising young director Pen Tennyson in an aircrash.

By 1941 Ealing was producing six features a year as well as its quota of Ministry of Information documentaries: output was stimulated by the fact that the studios were within range of the enemy bombers. *Next of Kin* (1942), sponsored by the War Office, began as a short documentary on the theme that careless talk costs lives, but then its director, Thorold Dickinson, found that he had enough to go on with to develop the subject into a low-budget feature. *The Big Blockade* (1941), made in association with the Ministry of Economic Warfare, gave a semi-fictionalized account of the British attempt to stop supplies getting through to Germany. William Whitebait, writing in the *New Statesman*, described it as a collage in the manner of the *March of Time* newsreels. He thought it only fitfully effective.

In the next year Charles Frend, the director of *The Big Blockade*, was to achieve a more coordinated effort with *The Foreman Went to France* (1942). Based on an incident mentioned in the newspapers and worked up into a story by J. B. Priestley, this unusual film can be seen as a prototype of the Ealing comedies, though it was to be far more caustic in its criticisms than any of its successors. By the end of the war many film-makers were to romanticize 1940 as the *annus mirabilis* of the British people: an idealization that *The Foreman Went to France* rejects. It begins with two firewatchers in the blitz recalling the part played by the foreman in saving the country from defeat, then moves back in time to 1940 and to some workmen in a pub grousing about the universal incompetence of their managers. The foreman wishes to go to France to bring back some highly secret machinery crucial to the war effort, but his superiors dismiss the possibility that France might be defeated. In fact, the foreman's eventual search for this machinery is no more than a MacGuffin, as Hitchcock would call it, an excuse for Priestley and the screen-writers to suggest that the corrupt social structure in France, which had helped to bring about the country's downfall, was similar to the one in Britain. Frend's direction sharpens this point by showing his France to be no more than a looking-glass reflection of England, with markedly English actors like Robert Morley and Ernest Milton playing French collaborators who try to foil the foreman's rescue operation. At the climax of this story, the foreman fights someone who seems to be a senior British officer in an English country house; yet the officer is a German spy and the house is in France.

The main point of this comparison, it would appear, was to awaken a sense of guilt in British audiences. 'It's our fault it happened,' says the foreman to an American woman whose sister has been killed in a bombing raid. 'We've been half asleep. But we're waking up at last.' It is possible to draw at least two inferences from this comparison: that the makers of *The Foreman Went to France* not only wished to hold the ruling classes in Britain responsible for the war but also wished to exacerbate a public already irritated by the bureaucratic way the war was being conducted at home—a hostility that was very real and could appear in the most unlikely contexts, as in Leslie Howard's *The First of the Few* (1942), a selfconsciously noble study of Mitchell, the inventor of the Spitfire. Howard reveals that the greatest threat to Mitchell's invention and to Mitchell's fatally undermined health was the pro-crastination of slow-witted civil servants. In *The Foreman Went to France* two soldiers, very conscious of the regulations, try to stop the foreman from appropriating the machinery, then decide to help him steal it with all the schoolboyish bravado of some delinquents joining, say, the Lavender Hill mob. Even so, the scene in which one of these soldiers is shot, as enemy planes strafe the refugee-jammed roads of France, shocked the British public. As the foreman says, the war means little until you have seen something of its effect with your own eyes.

Charles Frend: *The Foreman Went to France.*

Alberto Cavalcanti, who produced *The Foreman Went to France*, was to hammer home this idea when he directed *Went the Day Well?* (1942), a film version of a Graham Greene story about the invasion of an idyllic English village by some German parachutists disguised as a Mass Observation team. The astringent tone of his comedy only just saves it from lapsing into despair. But as the war continued, the public began to lose interest in anything that might be thought of as bracing, and Ealing reflected this change in taste. Horror tales and melodramas were to ventilate feelings of persecution while luxuriously-designed period films compensated a little for the austerities of rationing. This change in taste was not to be entirely negative in effect: Cavalcanti's ingeniously constructed anthology of horror stories, *Dead of Night* (1945), and Robert Hamer's stylish *Pink String and Sealing Wax* (1945) demonstrate how it brought about a remarkable improvement in technique.

The Rank Organization, controlled by J. Arthur Rank, a Methodist millionaire whose family had made a fortune in flour, was to play an important part in this change of taste. Rank has often been held responsible for the decline in quality and output of the post-war British film industry on the grounds that, badly advised, he followed Korda's path to ruin by attempting to win a place in the American market with spectacular productions. Certainly the Rank Organization's main emphasis on showbiz values was remote from the commitment to actual situations of the Crown Film Unit; and it could be argued that Rank had a depleting effect on every aspect of British film-making. But such an argument depends on our wrongly assuming that Rank had a stranglehold over the industry. In 1943 a Monopoly Commission set up by Parliament had looked into the question of the Rank Organization's power—its ownership or control over fifty-six per cent of the studios and about ten per cent of the cinemas in the United Kingdom—and found it acceptable. (The Palache report of 1943 states that the Gaumont British and Odeon circuits controlled 549 of the 4,750 cinemas still open in the United Kingdom during the war. The power of the Rank Organization came closer to a monopoly in the London area, where it controlled 204 of the 360 cinemas in use.)

A bitter experience lay behind Rank's desire for power. In 1934 he had founded a film company, British National, with the intention of producing documentaries to promote Methodism. His partner in this venture had been the rich and eccentric Lady Yule, who had once trained forty horses to dance the quadrille ('to show that English horses can be trained to do anything'). But when Rank learned that no one would distribute his documentaries, he had decided quite logically to become a distributor himself. In 1939 he joined the board, and then became chairman of the Odeon circuit. In 1941 he was instrumental in the Odeon take-over of Gaumont British. He became a member of the board of the Crown Film Unit, which (like the Army and Royal Air Force Film Units) worked at the Rank-owned Pinewood studios. Even Balcon at Ealing had to make a deal with him to gain distribution outlets.

Although the Rank Organization became over-ambitious in its wish to compete with Hollywood, some of its Gainsborough studio romances were to weather the years better. Leslie Arliss, who directed *The Man in Grey* (1943), was to anatomize the calculation that underlay so much of the snobbery and social climbing of the Regency period. In at least one scene, he comes close to the atmosphere of Marcel Carné's *Les Enfants du paradis*: the scene in which virtuous Clarissa (Phyllis Calvert) watches Stewart Granger, as an actor impersonating Othello, almost strangle his Desdemona, played by the wicked Miss Shaw (Margaret Lockwood). As the plot almost ingenuously reveals, the motives of these characters seldom escape some tinge of sadism. Miss Shaw eventually murders Clarissa and receives her presumably desired reward when Lord Rowan (James Mason) beats her with his riding crop as she crawls across a Persian carpet.

The Rank Organization also produced films with a more direct bearing on the war. Frank Launder and Sidney Gilliatt were to make *Millions Like Us* (1944) for it, with some financial support from the Ministry of Information, while Michael Powell and Emeric Pressburger, working for their own company, Archers, were to depend on its distribution system. Powell, whose pre-war career had included *The Spy in Black* (1939), was to direct *One of Our Aircraft is Missing* (1942) and *The Life and Death of Colonel Blimp* (1943) with Pressburger as his producer—creating in all of these films a considerable dramatic *éclat*. The opening sequence of *One of Our Aircraft is Missing*, in which an apparently empty plane crashes into a telegraph pole, is typical of Powell's feeling for the uncanny, a feeling that often softens the professionalism of his technique.

Rank also distributed Anthony Asquith's *We Dive at Dawn* (1943) and *The Way to the Stars* (1945), both of them Two Cities productions elaborating on the homo-erotic romanticism of Noel Coward's *In Which We Serve* (1942). If *The Way to the Stars* captures something of the atmosphere of the 1940s, it does so less through its content, which refines the experience of the forties to the point of depleting it, than through its choice of stagy conventions and mannerisms in dialogue—the precious theatricality of Terence Rattigan's screenplay being underlined by Asquith's placing of his credit titles against ruffled satin, and his preference for a kind of lighting that imitates the glossy stiltedness of society photographers' portraits of that time.

Film-makers in the concluding years of the war did not invariably romanticize its supposedly finest hour. In Carol Reed's *The Way Ahead* (1944) two Chelsea pensioners, who recall the glorious days of spear warfare and hold their juniors in contempt, act as a chorus to an episodic story that shifts from 1939 to 1941 and then to 1943. Eric Ambler and Peter Ustinov were commissioned to write a script that would encourage enlistment in the infantry and were obliged to show their pensioners' scepticism give way to admiration. But it is hard to escape the thought that they might have been more in sympathy with the pensioners' scepticism than the project allowed. They present a people's war as seen by the people and without heroics, centring their restless story on no one character or group in particular and depending, at least in the 1939 sequences, on the humour of disillusionment. Carol Reed's skill in weaving together the various strands in this episodic plot, his sense of comic timing and his ability to bring out the best in his actors are largely self-effacing, and so, too, is his evolution of a technique to deal with the subject of group behaviour, a technique that was to reach its most complete form in *The True Glory* (1945), which he was to co-direct with Garson Kanin.

It reports on the Normandy landings, the big push through France (with troops moving much faster than the anticipated supply of detailed maps), the hold-up in the Ardennes, the capture of Berlin and the peace celebrations of May 1945. The arrival at Belsen punctures this euphoria. At the beginning of this feature documentary, a pseudo-Shakespearean commentary gives way to a medley of voices, including Eisenhower's, recalling the great invasion. These memories are played against a compilation of newsreel shots or photographs, so tightly edited that they hardly ever last more than three seconds on the screen. The camera seldom appears to move. The sweet casualness of the voices blends with the doom-like sense of mechanized armies converging on victory.

During the harshest years of the war the British public flocked to the cinema for comradeship, warmth and the promise of a less austere life, and, for a while at least, the film-makers were able to satisfy this need: the tragedy (or comedy) of this situation was that so many of these talented directors were to continue playing the same increasingly flat tunes for the next thirty years. During the period 7 September to 5 October 1940, when Londoners had to live through thirty-eight major air-raids, the cinemas were always packed, and cinema managers responded generously to this enthusiasm. On the Granada circuit they would warn the staff that enemy aircraft were in flight over the North Sea by passing on the code message 'Red Roses'. Business continued as usual, even on the nights when the whole of London seemed to be ablaze. 'When the last performance finished,' writes Guy Morgan in *Red Roses Every Night*, 'the audience stayed on, and with bombs dropping outside, cinema staffs gave them not only sanctuary but a show: the full advertised programme again, three stand-by features, two half-hour shows by the house organist and the feature organist (the favourite tune being *The White Cliffs of Dover*), followed by an impromptu sing-song and dancing on the stage.'[5] The Granada, Clapham Junction, once showed five feature films in one night.

Early in 1940, a few weeks before the fall of France and almost two years before the bombing of Pearl Harbor, an exhibitor from Atlanta and an exhibitor from New Orleans arranged with the US government to set up an organization known the Committee Co-operating for National Defence. This committee arranged that ten thousand exhibitors should collect funds for the war effort and give more screen time to the newsreel. (The artisan working in armoury, arsenal and plane factory became, it was said, number one American film hero of 1940.) It distributed films to the forces and scotched a Japanese plan to buy up all existing laboratory stock shots of the US Navy. With

John Ford: *They were Expendable.*

America's entry into the war in December 1941, it was renamed the War Activities Committee–Motion Picture Industry, and one of the vice-presidents at Twentieth-Century Fox, Colonel Darryl F. Zanuck, was put in charge. By April 1943 Zanuck could report that his team, as well as organizing War Bond and Service Fund campaigns, had completed sixty-three training films.

In 1941 the Hollywood studios raised over two million dollars in relief-fund drives. But they were to be much slower in adjusting their production schedules to the war in Europe—a production could easily take two years in passing from its initial planning stage to its release date—and as the new decade began, they were still mining subjects and treatments more typical of the pre-war years.

The romanticism of *Gone with the Wind* was to be reflected in Wyler's *Wuthering Heights* (1939) and Hitchcock's *Rebecca* (1940). Hollywood seized on a mood of sepulchral mystification with the wholeheartedness that it had once brought to the topical film. Herman J. Mankiewicz and Orson Welles constructed parts of *Citizen Kane* on the model of those revue sketches that end with a pay-off line; but they were to be inimitably of the 1940s in their opening sequence, in which the camera glides forward, through dissolving images of the Xanadu estate, to Kane's deathbed and his flurried crystal snowball.

Rebecca opens in a similar fashion, with its camera edging forward through a dank, leafy garden to a shrouded country house called Manderley. In the past, such evocations of the eerie—of entombed emotions brought to light—had been the preserve of the horror movie. Hollywood studios now applied it to nearly every genre.

In perhaps his most valuable essay on films, 'L'Evolution du langage cinématographique',[6] the French critic André Bazin proposed that Gregg Toland's fluent camerawork and deep-focus photography in *Citizen Kane* and Wyler's *The Little Foxes* (1941) allowed audiences a new freedom in interpreting the image, since these techniques no longer conditioned the spectator—as did suspense editing or other types of narrative control. The screen could be as open as the stage, its actors allowed to be ambiguous in motive. Through this argument Bazin was able to relate *Citizen Kane* and *The Little Foxes* to films that appeared at first sight stylistically remote from them, such as Rouquier's *Farrebique* (1946) and the first examples of Italian neo-realism. In *Farrebique* Rouquier shows his peasants baking their bread with as little editorial interference as possible; he allows the scene to unfold at its own pace and invites the spectator to exercise the same freedom of perception as he would on events taking place outside the cinema. In *The Magnificent Ambersons* (1941), Orson Welles practises the same technique when he has Agnes Moorehead and Tim Holt engage in a lengthy, semi-improvised dialogue before a

Orson Welles: *The Magnificent Ambersons*. Agnes Moorhead, Tim Holt.

camera that neither moves nor stops watching them, however much they may pause or change the focus of attention. In this sequence Welles begins to approach an idea proposed many years before by the painter Fernand Léger, who had said that a film showing in detail twenty-four hours in the life of an ordinary married couple would cause a world-wide scandal. Welles also anticipates the views of Cesare Zavattini, the leading neo-realist screenwriter and theoretician, whose most cherished wish was to record on film ninety consecutive minutes in a man's life.

In a sense, Bazin's discovery of a likeness between Welles/Wyler and the neo-realists was perverse; many critics, indeed, would prefer to think of them as polar opposites. They would argue that Welles and Wyler think in terms of style, while the neo-realists try to conceal evidence of style in order to heighten the impression of substantiality in the world. 'What De Sica can do, I can't do,' said Welles. 'I ran over *Shoeshine* recently and the camera disappeared, the screen disappeared, it was just life . . .'[7] *Citizen Kane* and *The Magnificent Ambersons* are packed with an over-abundance of stylistic devices, and although some of them were techniques that the neo-realists were to use, neither film creates an effect of naturalism.

Both *Citizen Kane* and its central character are like the proverbial onion: to peel away their pretensions is to peel them away to nothing. Kane's friends believe that if he had been less corrupted by wealth he might have been a sincere socialist, a citizen or *citoyen* like Danton. Some of them turn against him because they believe that he has betrayed his principles. Yet in fact Kane has no principles, and by extension the self-pity in which he shrouds his defeat contains no dramatic meaning. For all his worldly power, his role in the plot is insubstantial, being no more than a foil to the other characters. 'What would you have liked to have been?' asks Thatcher, his former guardian, and the young tycoon answers: 'Everything you hate.' Kane believes that he controls the media. Yet he is very much their creature, supporting the fashionably most sensational performers of his age, Mussolini and Hitler. Even the pun in his name is deceptive. He may be shunned or loathed by many, but he is no Cain. He can hardly be thought of as a wicked or tragic figure. At certain moments Welles plays him as though he were a naughty boy, endearing in his wit—as when he answers reporters who tell him there is no war in Cuba. 'You provide the prose poems. I'll provide the war.' At other moments Welles places Kane's more serious affirmations in an ironic context—as when on a newsreel Kane enunciates: 'I am, and have been, and always will be, an American.'

The trouble is that Kane is no more than the sum of his theatrical gestures. And to see him purely as a victim of the media, or as a satirical portrayal of William Randolph Hearst, in no way adds to his substance, since the film itself offers no alternative to its legerdemain. In its miscellany of styles it resembles not only Kane's personality but also Kane's castle, Xanadu, with its jumble of artworks; in much the same way that Xanadu, as it awaits the auctioneer after Kane's death, resembles the disarray of a film studio. *Citizen Kane* is a film that Kane himself might have made, and indeed did make, for the actor playing him and the director responsible for the film are both aspects of one of the most astonishing fictions in the cinema: the public mask of the professional entertainer and amateur conjuror known as Orson Welles.

Even so, the film is only partly convincing as an egotist's vision of himself. It is beautifully effective when Welles presents himself as a master of cinematic devices and atmospheres, far less effective when he

Orson Welles: *Citizen Kane.*

presents himself as an object of pathos—Kane lost in the corridor of mirrors. Welles's touch falters whenever he has to enter the realms of feeling. Like many egotists, he fails to recognize the egotist's tragedy: his inability to respond to people as other than things to be used. And this failure diminishes any meaning the plot might have. The reporter who tries to discover the mainspring to Kane's life is forced to learn that his search is futile; and even if it is assumed that Kane's famous final word, 'rosebud'—which, as the reporter never learns, was inscribed on the base of a child's sled—represents some primal love that has been denied, it is still hard to believe that the loss of such a love will mean much to so carapaced a prince. Yearning of this kind is just one of the bogus ways in which Welles/Kane dramatizes himself. In the same way, the plot structure of the film— its dependence on an intricate time scheme and on the conflicting memories of Kane's associates—does no more than contribute to the subtle self-flattery of Welles/Kane. For all its complexity, it cannot conceal the fact that the egotist is cut off from experience. *Citizen Kane* is full of yearnings for a childhood that actually was despised (hence Kane's self-pity) and forebodings and grandiose schemings about a future that of its nature cannot be predicted. But where it does touch on a certain truth is in its recognition that Kane's wish to achieve a godlike status must always lead to embitterment.

The Magnificent Ambersons elaborates further on this feeling of having missed out. Its plot is bound by three love affairs, all of them unrequited. Like many of its characters—the local gossips who whisper to each other about changes in the Amberson household, or the unmarried relatives in the household who feel excluded and yet are fascinated by the events they are excluded from—the spectator feels himself to be peripheral to the action; he is seldom allowed to witness the crises on which the plot turns. The principal event of the film, the impact of mechanized transport on all the characters, an impact which changes them all, takes place off-screen and catches nearly everyone by surprise. 'The town heaved up in the middle, incredibly,' says Welles in the role of the narrator, as though this catastrophe were some burrowing by gigantic moles or nightmare about the primal scene. It would be misleading to say that Welles modelled *The Magnificent Ambersons* on Greek tragedy and its exclusion of violent action from the stage. His avoidance of the immediate seems preconditioned by a rigid need to protect an egotist's viewpoint. He in no way faces the choice of whether he should remain in the kingdom of reverie or not, and even presents the actuality of the last great ball in the Amberson home, an event which accretes in family memory as evidence of its former greatness, as though it were no more than a funeral dream. Both *Citizen Kane* and *The Magnificent Ambersons* mark a retreat from experience into the untested ruminations of adolescence. In their type of humour and interest in the practicalities of money and work, they clearly emerge from the conventions of 1930s film comedy, but without the feeling for community on which these conventions depend. Indeed they signal the dissolution of one kind of approach to film and the emergence of another more essayistic and personal kind.

The same might be said of the comedies directed by Preston Sturges in the early 1940s. In *The Great McGinty* and *Christmas in July* (both 1940), *Sullivan's Travels* and *The Lady Eve* (both 1941), *The Palm Beach Story* (1942), *The Miracle of Morgan's Creek* (1943), and *Hail the Conquering Hero* (1944), Sturges takes many of the comedy techniques developed in the thirties and many of its attitudes—such as its snobberies about class and wealth—and perhaps unintentionally pushes them into caricature. In his way as self-reflexive and self-centred as Welles, he packs in allusions to Paramount (for whom he worked) and its chief of production Ernst Lubitsch, parodies all sorts of Hollywood styles, mocks the topical film and flaunts all the showbiz values that the more serious people in Hollywood had affected to despise during the years of the Depression. His films seem to have been manufactured by some studio team that has lost all pretence at polite restraint and probably has gone berserk. Their disembodied vitality, like the fevered brilliance that can precede total collapse, encourages the belief that Hollywood had entered its death throes in the early 1940s.

In a remarkable essay written with W. S. Poster, and as extravagant as its subject, Manny Farber has suggested that Sturges was able to release these primitive energies by bringing together the *Mr Deeds Goes to Town* type of plot with the impetus of early Sennett. But he was not alone at this time in his passion for brashness and speed. The pace of life had changed. Many films of the forties look as though they were 1930s films being rushed through the projector: a change in pace that was not only bound up with a liking for ornate dialogue – dialogue which seemed to sprout in every direction, to fill every crevice of silence and to become more and more mannered as its speed was increased – but most obtruded in stories that pivoted on life and death issues, such as Hawks's *His Girl Friday* (1939), Huston's *The Maltese Falcon* (1941) and Wilder's *Double Indemnity* (1944).

Sturges's father had been a wealthy businessman, his mother a lady devoted to high culture. His films reflect the quirky, often contradictory thoughts of an eccentric almost as rich as Kane, who is unworried by the fact that he is dissociated from the pressures that most people live under. In *The Palm Beach Story* he shows his fellow-rich, in the guise of the Ale and Quail Club and the Hackensecker family, as mildly crazed by their freedom to exercise any whim. Enjoying this amiable madness, he assumes approvingly that all the poor wish to do is to achieve the same condition, like the young couple in *Christmas in July*, who submit themselves to all sorts of idiocies to gain a fortune. He has trouble, though, in squaring his complicity in this wish to make a fast buck with his disquiet at those who wish to make a fast buck by fleecing the rich: a contradiction that he gets around by bringing out an unfailing recipe – the balm of love. In *The Lady Eve*, a brewer's heir (Henry Fonda) believes that most of his fellow passengers on a liner are gold-diggers and politely avoids everybody's company; he is so sequestered, in fact, that professional confidence tricksters find him easy bait. His adventures would end in disillusionment if Sturges did not believe that he and the cardsharper's daughter (Barbara Stanwyck) were not ideally suited to each other, both of them being

Preston Sturges: *The Lady Eve*. Henry Fonda, Barbara Stanwyck.

the children of individualists who have clambered to the top of their not too unlike professions. But Sturges is less intent on showing how the cardsharper's daughter becomes a loyal and loving wife than on showing how a priggish heir can be transformed into someone who delights in the moral imperfections of the world.

In his way, Sturges is as unworldly as his brewer's heir. He seems to have got most of his views on life from the movies and somehow (effectively) jumbled all their insights up. But one kind of movie clearly perplexes him: the topical films produced by Warner Brothers in the early thirties. In *Sullivan's Travels*, a good-humoured, rich film director (Joel McCrea) decides to turn from his profitable career as the maker of musicals with titles like *Ants in Your Pants of 1941* to an indictment of poverty called *Brother, What Art Thou?* He decides that he needs to do some research, but, in his unworldly fashion, he finds it almost impossible to join the *lumpenproletariat* dressed as a tramp. He is cosseted by servants and studio agents, and when he decides to steal a ride on a freight train, his butler as a matter of course phones the railway station to find out the times when freight trains pass. All that he brings back from his first trip into poverty is an independent woman (Veronica Lake), who pities his helplessness. 'The nice thing about buying a man food,' she says, 'is that you don't have to laugh at his jokes.'

But eventually Sullivan does enter the world of the dispossessed. Knocked on the head and robbed, he is arrested and sent to a chain-gang penitentiary; and thus Mr Deeds begins to wish that he were a fugitive from the chain gang. Attending a film show at a Negro revivalist church with other convicts, he observes the audience laughing at a Mickey Mouse cartoon. He decides that his butler and studio advisers have been right all along in believing that the public is only interested in subjects it knows nothing about, and that only the morbid rich are concerned about the poor. It is doubtful whether Sturges intended this conclusion to be cynical, or intended a satire on the topical film. He operated in a dream world, and his ideas would probably be incomprehensible if he did not communicate them through the idiom of past movies. He joins with Welles in being among the first of the Hollywood directors to play on their audiences' knowledge of Hollywood and its films.

Manny Farber believes that Sturges's interests were primarily aesthetic, his plots being 'developed chiefly to provide him with the kinds of movements and appearances he wants, with crowds of queer, animated individuals, with juxtapositions of unusual actions and faces. These are then organised . . . to evoke *feelings* about society and life which cannot be reduced to doctrine.'[8] But organization is perhaps too strong a word for this modulation of surface effects. Often, as in *Sullivan's Travels*, the highly textured presence of supporting actors like William Demarest, Franklin Pangborne and Eric Blore threatens to dominate a composition in which the central characters are less interesting in their eccentricity. At such times, Sturges is barely able to control his scattiness.

The same danger arises with John Huston's *The Maltese Falcon* (1941). Huston had gained a reputation as one of the screenwriters working on the various social biographies directed by William Dieterle in the late thirties; yet in his first feature as a director he was to turn to a Dashiell Hammett thriller—previously filmed by Roy del Ruth in 1931 —which implicitly derides any notion of social purpose. Huston presents its location (San Francisco) as more an atmospheric backdrop than an actual place. And each of the liars or dissimulators who invade the office of the private detective Sam Spade, or summon him to their hotel bedrooms—they include Peter Lorre as Joel Cairo, a man of many passports and uncertain sexual identity, Sidney Greenstreet making his Hollywood debut as the stout yet elusive Mr Gutman, Mary Astor as Brigid O'Shaughnessy, the most inventive of these fabulists, and Gladys George as the hypocritical and predatory widow, Iva Archer—each of them might have been whistled up out of nowhere. Although they are ruthless self-seekers, the object most of them seek, the jewel-encrusted golden statue of a falcon that had once belonged to the Knights of Malta, is as much a MacGuffin as Kane's 'rosebud' and provides just as much of a disillusionment. Most of these villains join in the search for the falcon less for financial reward, it would seem, than for the

John Huston: *The Maltese Falcon*. Humphrey Bogart, Peter Lorre, Mary Astor.

pleasure of testing out their powers; they might be participants in the 'great game' of imperialism. They spring up before Spade (and the spectator) as a succession of spectacular appearances, and, their greed apart, seldom reveal their motives. Like Spade himself, none of them has a home; they are transients who live in hotel bedrooms and rented apartments.

The effect, appropriately, is of a world ceaselessly on the move, in which everyone is a refugee; an unsettled wartime condition which also typifies John Huston's gifts as a director. He is as elusive as his characters, revealing qualities rather than a fixed viewpoint in his style. He clearly enjoys the company of seedily raffish characters, people who are slightly askew: gamblers, unprincipled tacticians, outsiders deplored by conventional society. He is amused by these characters in the same way as William Powell, in the Dashiell Hammett Thin Man series, had been amused by certain members of the underworld. But he is also detached, sardonic and in taste slightly 'camp', rather as Welles and Sturges are. It is notable that *The Maltese Falcon* is among the first Hollywood films to make explicit the theme of male homosexuality (among its crooks)—a theme which may in part account for its pervading *nostalgie de la boue* and for the cruel final-reel reprisals taken against Brigid O'Shaughnessy, but not against the other criminals, when the men gang up against her. James Agee, writing some of his best film criticism at this time for *The Nation*, tended to overrate Huston's talents, but it is possible to see why this graceful Irish writer should have warmed to Huston's Irish wit.

Huston's response to his characters appears to waver between the murderous and the sympathetic; and Humphrey Bogart, who plays Sam Spade, is ambivalent in a similar way, as though he had modelled his performance on Huston. But Bogart's appeal in this role lies in more than in his amused stoical manner or impassive yet wry face. In general, his appeal is complex. He had played second string to James Cagney throughout the thirties, and the Warner Brothers' casting agency had seen them as members of the same type, but he and Cagney had little in common. If the generous and ebullient Cagney often seemed cast against type as a gangster, Bogart on screen always seemed to be permanently locked in a struggle against an innate irritability and meanness. His moments of kindness are usually surprising. It is part of the complicated impression created by this actor that though he should have played tough guys, he should have been exempted from military service on the grounds of ill-health. The same was true of Alan Ladd, though Ladd never had the interest of Bogart, who could wreathe cruelty in charm and counterbalance his slurred speech and frail physique with an ironic manner that suggested strength.

For generations of adolescents he came to represent an ideal of integrity under pressure, as well as being a one-man advertising agency for the cigarette. Yet most of the characters he played were neurotics, and many adolescents must have felt him to be less an adult to admire than someone like themselves, masking all sorts of disturbances under an assured manner. It is interesting that in *The Maltese Falcon* the camera should identify with Sam Spade at the moment when drugs render him unconscious, so that the spectator sees Mr Gutman as Sam sees him, both towering and out of focus: an expressionistic trick appropriate to the psychiatry-haunted movies of the forties, but apt, too, for the kind of characters played by Bogart, men on the verge of a breakdown. However, when Huston pushed Bogart's talent to its limits in *The Treasure of Sierra Madre* (1947) and in doing so revealed that it was less restricted than might have been supposed, he and Bogart were unable to make convincing the final scenes of madness. Perhaps the real thing was too encroaching to be turned into a statement.

Hollywood directors were to rifle Chandler, Spillane and other thriller writers apart from Hammett for ideas, but few of them were able to extend the field that Huston had opened up in *The Maltese Falcon*. The beating up of the tough guy was to become a set-piece of voluptuous monotony. In *The Glass Key* (1942), Jeff (William Bendix) spends a leisurely twenty-four hours knocking out young Ed (Alan Ladd, as inscrutable as Fu Manchu) and then reviving him with cold water: losses of consciousness described with the kind of image distortion that Pabst had practised in *Secrets of a Soul* and sometimes, as in Edward Dmytryk's *Murder My Sweet/Farewell My Lovely* (1944), carried out with considerable skill. Dmytryk appears to have recognized how the blackouts of his punch-drunk heroes epitomized the random shocks of light and movement in a city at night. And he appears to have had no illusion about the supposed toughness of Phillip Marlowe when he cast baby-faced Dick Powell in this role.

To many people in the audience, daily in touch with death in the blitz or at the front, the suffering of these tough guys must have looked pleasantly unreal, an exhibition of passivity a little like the swooning of heroines in Victorian novels. With hindsight it is possible to imagine that this lack of credibility was intentional and that the thriller burlesqued the experience of war so as to make it less intolerable, reducing death to a simulation without grief and persecutors to cosy figures like Sidney Greenstreet and Peter Lorre. But the insubstantiality of these charades has become all too evident with the passing of time. Greenstreet and Lorre were to be given top billing in *The Mask of Demetrios* (1944), yet for all their skill and for all the relished exoticism and amorality of their subject, they were unable to conceal its poverty of invention.

But this over-fabricated sense of illusion satisfied a usefuı purpose. It asserted escapism defiantly, rather in the manner in which women applied make-up at this time, as though it were Sioux war-paint. It also had an economic motive. Having lost most of its markets in Europe and Asia, Hollywood had mounted a campaign to win moviegoers in South America. Disney went on a goodwill tour there and produced *The Three Caballeros* (1944), while the other studios usually managed to work flattering references to Latin America into their movies. Well-to-do honeymooners no longer went to Monaco in these movies but to Rio, and everyone claimed to enjoy coffee. But somehow this promotion had little heart in it, and though South America was geographically close, it seldom gained more credibility on the screen than as a wobbling back-projection. Exotic locations set in other countries hardly fared better. Nobody, it seemed, believed that happiness could be more than fleeting. The tents, deserts and heavily draped bedrooms where Maria Montez, Carmen Miranda and Dorothy Lamour conducted their sultry affairs always managed, perhaps deliberately, to seem provisional.

The relationship between stars and their audience had also changed. Formerly, when Ronald Colman or Gary Cooper had joined the Foreign Legion, they had acted with enough authority to distract the spectator from observing too closely the studio-contructed desert with cycloramas rising above sand-dunes. But the stars no longer had this sort of ivory-tower authority. Many of the men worked at the studios only occasionally, between periods of war service, while

many of the women raised money for war bonds by dancing with GIs
or by touring the country. And the relaxed informality of shows in the
jungle, in which the stars would joke about mosquitos and the heat,
was to modify the conventions of screen comedy. A new kind of self-
deprecating sophistication came into being, as when in one of the
Paramou.it Hope-Crosby-Lamour 'Road' series, travellers pass a
mountain (or paramountain) ringed by cardboard stars.

By a strange contradiction, the further Hollywood moved away from
naturalism, the closer it came to making documentaries about itself.
Its studio sets began to resemble the bizarre architecture of Grauman's
Chinese Theatre and of the older Los Angeles villas. It was as though
Hollywood wished to point up the difference between fiction and the
all-important and often tragic newsreel. It withdrew into itself, it
mocked its own power to create illusions with a loss of confidence that
had nothing to do with the wartime restriction on film budgets. It was
typical of this period that the slapstick in Olsen and Johnson's
Hellzapoppin (1942) should have relied on some fairly crude gags about
studio mismanagement and confusions in the projection box. The age
of camp had begun, or at least that was the way certain critics of the
sixties were to see it.

This division between daily experience and illusion was quite different
from the utopianism of the thirties. During the Depression Sternberg
had been able to summon up extraordinary Moroccos and Cathays
of the mind, but by the forties this sense of inspiration had become
strained: exotic places, after all, were places where the young were
dying, and nearly everyone wanted to return home, however serious
conditions might be there. In *The Shanghai Gesture* (1942) Sternberg
had every opportunity to excel himself once more: the settings
designed by Boris Leven and Howard Baker for Madam Gin-Sling's
casino and private banqueting-room are of great atmospheric power;
yet he seems to have been uninspired by them. His actors merely
go through their paces or fall into mannerism. His talent had not
so much dried up as become disengaged. In 1943 he directed a
March of Time kind of study of Madison, Indiana, called *The Town* for the
US Office of War Information. Reversing his usual strategy, he did not
heighten the exoticism of the exotic, but showed how the exotic could
be discovered in the most homely of places. He begins the documentary with a series of shots of exotic architectural features (an
Italian campanile, etc.) and then reveals how these features are all part
of Madison, a town as American as apple-pie. Sternberg's affection
for the Mid West is clear, and his filming reinforces the thought that
any attempt to define American identity would entail the analysis of
many kinds of exoticism. If you live in such a country, you do not
need to travel to Cathay.

Such an awareness of the strangeness intrinsic to the familiar, often occurring when the self feels estranged from custom or habit, recalls the uncanny sensations that André Breton and his friends had felt when contemplating the streets of Paris on the eve of the First World War. A number of the leading surrealists had emigrated to the United States at the beginning of the Second World War; some of them were to influence the New York school of action painters, and some of them were to take part in Hans Richter's surrealist feature *Dreams That Money Can Buy* (1944). There had been American avant-garde filming of a desultory kind in the thirties, but it needed the war and the surrealist influx to give this activity any force. American avant-garde directors of the forties were to be quite different from their successors in the early fifties and sixties, whose experiments appear to have been largely determined by an ambivalence to the myths and values of Hollywood. The 1940s generation looked to French art for its model and in particular to surrealism.

Maya Deren was one of the more talented figures in this generation. Audiences conditioned to Hollywood blandness must have been startled by the confessional nature of *Meshes in the Afternoon* (1943), which she co-directed with Alexander Hammid. Its jump cuts and un-explained recurrences (a falling knife, a falling key) relate it to the contents of dreams. Although its symbolism seems at times over-calculated in a surrealist manner, she projects her anxieties about a love affair—especially her anxiety that passion and violence may be inextricably confused—with considerable power. Her later career was to be disappointing, with its tame reports on dancers and dancing and, habitual to the avant-garde, excursions into a Jungian kind of mysticism. But in *Meshes in the Afternoon* she composed her images with an authority that rescues even some of her less convincing ideas from sensationalism. She added to this authority by herself appearing in the role of dreamer protagonist. Arising out of French techniques of the 1920s, *Meshes in the Afternoon* at moments anticipates Cocteau's *Orphée*. Yet the liquid blacks of its photography and its deployment of space and large close-ups affiliate it just as securely to the techniques of Hollywood romance.

In at least two important respects, though, Hollywood surrealism was to differ from avant-garde surrealism. The studios' awakening to the charm of the incongruous was to be for the most part instinctive and to owe little or nothing to French theory. It was largely stimulated by the wartime rediscovery of mankind's craving for violence and—to use a phrase popular in the journalism of the time—by 'the crisis of identity' that was apparently endemic in the 1940s: a crisis outwardly more staid on screen than certain critical writings associated with the avant-garde film-makers might lead us to suppose.

In *Magic and Myth of the Movies*, a book published in 1947 about the unconscious themes in certain Hollywood movies (which anticipates remarkably some of the ways in which Hollywood was to develop), Parker Tyler describes this identity crisis in terms that give the Hollywood romances the polymorphous-perverse enchantment of a Jean Genet novel. Mr Tyler usefully points out how moviegoers were made aware of the importance of psychiatry by press and film publicity on the treatment of shell-shocked soldiers, but in his elaborate description of the myths underlying these romances he sometimes makes them sound more like the product of the snake-pit than any viewing of them might suggest. Gore Vidal took Mr Tyler's fascination with the theme of transvestism and ambisexuality to an extreme (which Mr Tyler believes parodied his views) in his novel *Myra Breckinridge*, a mock-tragic account, filmed lamentably in 1970, of a multiple sex change which belongs firmly to the knowing culture of the sixties: a culture in which someone like Andy Warhol could take on an international stature and which Hollywood directors of the 1940s, if they could have foreseen it, would have found at best perplexing.

For though the forties' crisis in identity forced a shift in interest from allegories about society to allegories about the mind, Hollywood resisted the implications of this change. It was not until the late forties, and in France, that Alain Resnais and others were to explore the similarity between screen and mental images: the speed with which the mind can move back and forth over time, or back and forth between sequences derived from observation and sequences based upon a conflation of memories. When Hollywood used flashbacks in the 1940s, it tended to use them ponderously.

But Hollywood had increased spectator identification in other ways. New black and white panchromatic film stock of high definition and colour processes of greater speed and sensitivity (a breakthrough by Technicolor at the time of *Gone with the Wind*) allowed directors to invoke atmospheres of an enveloping intensity with black and white film—streets and piers glittering in the rain, fogbound runways, rooms shrouded in shadow—and to achieve jewel-like mesmerizing hues, as in the Twentieth Century-Fox musicals, with colour. Credit sequences often signalled this wish to hypnotize—wind riffling the pages of a book, the sea washing over letters written on sand—though the incidents that followed seldom lived up to the expectation aroused by these credits. For Hollywood wanted to enact moods of a Maya Deren kind without giving up the conventions of the naturalistic screenplay; and though certain directors with experience of the German cinema of the 1920s (Billy Wilder, Robert Siodmak, Fritz Lang) were to be among the more adept at practising this awkward carpentry, even they could not conceal most of the ill-fitting joints.

Fritz Lang: *The Woman in the Window*. Edward G. Robinson on the platform.

Lang's *The Woman in the Window* (1944), for instance, tries to draw audiences into the vortex of a nightmare. A professor of criminology (Edward G. Robinson) meets up casually with a *femme fatale* (Joan Bennett), murders a private eye who is blackmailing her and then, under pressure from the police, takes an overdose of sleeping pills— only to awake comfortably from this death/sleep/dream at his club. The trouble with this fantasy is that its motive—the desire of a middle-aged man to have an affair with an attractive young woman— remains untested by actuality; for the plot avoids the physical pro- babilities of such a relationship and in place of them provides a murder, which the professor justifies with the familiar wartime plea that 'if I hadn't killed him, he'd have killed me'.

Lang obviously enjoys reconstructing his favourite legend of *Der Müde Tod*, in which Death tracks down its victims in a human guise, here of a *femme fatale*; and indeed his use of a dream convention would be pleasantly innocuous if he did not use it to lend conviction to a dispiriting theory. In personal terms, his story shows how even the most secure individual can be undermined by unconscious impulse; in more general terms, how the self-protecting mechanisms of society can collapse under the least pressure from its enemies. In *M* he had invited the spectator to sympathize with a child murderer and to recognize the psychotic element in everyone (and in this sense to counteract the Nazi wish to liquidate refractory minorities). In *The Woman in the Window* he less boldly follows the fashionable mid-1940s' belief that the core of sanity in everyone, like the institutions that uphold society, resembles a small light that can easily capsize as it sways across dark turbulent seas.

Michael Curtiz: *Yankee Doodle Dandy*. James Cagney.

However much Hollywood tried to trivialize anxieties about the self, or to reassure, it could not escape from these anxieties; and often they were most present when most denied, as in the musical. The Depression musical had viewed a national emergency through the rose-tinted spectacles of show business; the war musical differed from it only in sometimes retreating into the immediate past. Michael Curtiz's *Yankee Doodle Dandy* (1942) embodied American virtue in the person of the master showman and writer of patriotic songs, George M. Cohan — 'the whole darned country squeezed into a pair of pants'; and Curtiz's tight editing and James Cagney's performance in the leading role, which won him an Academy award, generated a vitality which less chauvinistic times have failed to dissipate. Just as vigorously, the Arthur Freed and Busby Berkeley musical *For Me and My Gal* (1942) cocooned the spectator from the war and at the same time placated the conscience by taking a stern line on cowardice ('You'll never make the big time because you're small time in your heart') and eventually having Judy Garland go and entertain the troops. But basically the screen musical was much the same as it had been fifteen years before. Even Busby Berkeley's *The Gang's All Here* (1943),

Arthur Freed and Busby Berkeley:
For Me and My Gal. Gene Kelly, Judy Garland.

Busby Berkeley: *The Gang's All Here*.

with its topical jokes about B1 vitamins, war bonds, good neighbour policies, wolf talk, doughnuts, coffee and Carmen Miranda's hats, and generally its feeling for the 1940s (captured in the suave background murmur of Benny Goodman's band, a hero who goes off for service in the Pacific and Alice Faye as a superstar who dances with GIs) keeps to a familiar story line. Indeed its main idea—of a touchy businessman (Edward Everett Horton) cajoled into putting on a show at his private estate—looks back not only to *Flying Down to Rio* but to the Broadway musicals of the 1920s; while its Busby Berkeley choreography is most novel in the fluorescent brilliance of its colour.

All these musicals made some token reference to the war. But by 1944 one musical at least was to be without such references, MGM's *Meet Me in St Louis*. Although it has been claimed that the MGM Andy Hardy series asserted the wholesome nature of provincial family life at the expense of neglecting more urgent themes, it did dramatize community values. *Meet Me in St Louis* isolates itself from even these concerns. Its principal location—the Smith home and the grass-verged street beside it—is ostentatiously studio-built. George Folsey's bright colour photography heightens this sense of a warmly-quilted theatricality. It offers a view of St Louis restricted to the emotional problems and domestic interests of one group of middle-class women, a view quite unlike St Louis as it actually was at the turn of the century. (With its brothels and ragtime, St Louis was considered the most infamous city in the United States.) Its women mostly concern themselves with the cooking and eating of high-caloried foods; its men tend to be passive, or noticeable by their absence. The Smith girls easily subdue fractious Papa, and although Judy Garland, as one of them, manages to wring pathos out of her torch song for the boy next door, love conflicts are more wished-for than experienced and lovers more dream-like than realized. Of all the small lights swaying in turbulent waters, *Meet Me in St Louis* is the most protected in its denial of the surrounding darkness.

For its director, Vincente Minnelli, it represented a *tour de force* and consolidation of talent, in the sense that he was able to elicit so much wistfulness, humour and happiness from so limited a fantasy. Part of its continuing appeal is that his turn-of-the-century St Louis now seems so flamboyantly a 1940s idealization of the unobtainable: in its elaborate hairstyles, dresses made up of yards of unrationed material and visions of cream cake. Like Sternberg's *The Town*, though less overtly, it dramatizes the exoticism implicit in an American homeliness.

The extent to which this account of calf-love is remote from the wartime anxieties of women separated from men becomes clear in any comparison with David O. Selznick's *Since You Went Away*, released in the same year: a curious production that shows all the usual signs of Selznick's tendency to over-inflate. Selznick, who wrote the screenplay as well as producing the film, was presumably trying to recapture his *Gone with the Wind* kind of audience; but his story was too slight and the present-day period in which it was set too austere to bear his passion for excessive production values. Indeed, a superfluity of actors and lavish dresses hinder any dynamic his story might have had, as do John Cromwell's subdued direction and Claudette Colbert's listless performance as the wife pining for her husband to return from the war. Yet Selznick's taste for the exhaustive and his ability to divine mental pain in the most unlikely circumstances do yield up a good deal of 1940s atmosphere, as when Jennifer Jones, still living out the dying chords of *The Song of Bernadette*, becomes a hospital nurse, or Claudette Colbert, as her mother Mrs Hilton, takes on a job in a steel factory and meets a female Russian welder, who praises her as typical of America at its best. (Few actors playing leading roles in these years managed to escape being described by some minor character as typical, in one way or another, of their nation.) But the enterprise as a whole is so low in voltage that a bulldog steals scene upon scene.

It was left to Bette Davis, her screenwriters and directors to dramatize the idea of loneliness to the point that it took on the power of a national myth. Her Charlotte Vale in *Now Voyager* (1942) consolidated

Irving Rapper: *Now Voyager*. Bette Davis.

her reputation as a great star, giving her the opportunity to go through her paces, from crushed spinster (like the second wife in *Rebecca*), to attractive socialite bemused by the success of her appeal, to the mature Other Woman, unable to marry her lover Jerry (Paul Henreid) and resigned to the vicarious satisfaction of helping her lover's disturbed daughter ('Oh Jerry, let's not ask for the moon. We have the stars'). She and Irving Rapper, her director, play on the spectator's sympathy in two quite opposing ways: they submerge him in one of the most oceanic of Hollywood romances, while at the same time they lay bare the mechanism of the star system. It is as though they were making a clandestine documentary about Hollywood. In the same fashion, Bette Davis manages to give the impression of being both the craven Charlotte and an imperious actress working for her public. If the film projects Charlotte's sense of fragmentation through its metaphors of voyaging, seas and cosmic space, Bette Davis brings reassurance to this identity crisis by playing it out with the tenacity of a welder beating targets in the war effort.

A key figure in Charlotte's recovery, acted by Claude Rains in a gravelly, sleepy manner, is the psychiatrist, Doctor Jaquith. Little is seen of the techniques he uses at Cascade, his country sanatorium; but it is possible to infer that he frees Charlotte from her inhibitions mainly by encouragement. His authority, then, is unlike the coercive style of the film itself, which presumes that its audience consists of Charlottes in search of a father-figure less benign than he. But while it might be argued that this coercion reflects the increased authoritarianism of wartime government, it might also be argued that the film makes evident one of the war's few positive contributions: the change it brought about in public attitudes to neurosis. Mental breakdown, a subject previously thought of as a guilty family secret, was now discussed everywhere with a theological fervour. *Now Voyager* has this openness—indeed, it presents Charlotte's illness with the emphasis appropriate to a saint's dark night of the soul. Its whole-hearted belief in its own value tends to disarm any ironic response in the spectator.

Yet a sense of irony is useful in considering Hollywood's unrelentingly solemn view of psychiatry. *Random Harvest* (1942) offered a male variation on Charlotte's journey through breakdown to redemption; better than most films in this genre, it allowed Ronald Colman far too long to rediscover the door, both symbolic and real, which his key could open. In this it differed from others of its kind. Hollywood all too easily glamorized the suffering of the mentally ill or over-simplified their problems, a case in point being the Paramount screen version of a Broadway musical, *Lady in the Dark* (1944). Its subject—the breakdown and cure of Liza Elliott (Ginger Rogers), the editor of a fashion magazine—allowed the studio to bring together psychiatry and the glossy world of fashion in a manner that quelled reproach, and also to take a side-swipe at the mannish arrogance of women who had taken over posts that in peacetime were reserved for men.

Liza has lost touch with her femininity. Imitating men to the point of caricature, she feels insecure in her work: a condition that Mitchell Leisen, the director, presents in a manner needling enough to unsettle most career women. He has Liza wear dresses in her dreams that over-compensate for her repressed femininity: lavish dresses in tulle and satin that in wartime must have gratified audiences de-

Mitchell Leisen: *Lady in the Dark*. Mischa Auer, Ginger Rogers.

prived of such luxuries. Leisen's unkindness is such that in Liza's wedding dream he goes far beyond the decorative extravagance of *Meet Me in St Louis* to the point where he enters burlesque. It is possible Leisen did not recognize his contempt for Liza. Yet it becomes more and more apparent as the story develops. If motives at the beginning of the story seem to ask for a Freudian reading, they invite a Pavlovian interpretation by its end. Liza becomes machine-like as she moves into love and marriage with an associate she had formerly despised: the key to this reflex being the explicitly stated theory that all Liza need do to recover from her breakdown is to find a man who will dominate her.

Hollywood had begun to realize that its pre-war view of human character as either good or bad no longer had relevance in a time of war, when the most obedient of citizens might turn out to be the most honoured of combatants. The eponymous housewife in Michael Curtiz's *Mildred Pierce* (1945) achieves social status as a 'self-made' woman by building up a chain of successful restaurants. In order to keep Mildred's reputation untarnished, the violence of her ambition is displaced onto her daughter Vida, so that Mildred may seem to be motivated purely by a well-meaning desire to serve this adolescent child. The interest of both the film and the James M. Cain novel on which it is based is that neither of them denies this displacement. Both of them assume that Mildred's guilt over her greedy career can be implied by grafting onto it a murder story, in which doubts are raised as to whether Mildred was responsible for the murder.

Curtiz sees Mildred as typifying the protestant ideal of the hard selfless worker, incapable of enjoying the rewards of labour. But this interpretation of Mildred as a puritan fails to tally with her snobberies about wealth and class. It is central to the fantasy embodied by Mildred (Joan Crawford) that she should fall in love with a leisured Southern gentleman, Monty Berargon (Zachary Scott), the snobbery in her desire being veiled in part by the revelation that Berargon is a cad, and in part by its being projected onto Vida, who also desires Berargon and who eventually shoots him. In dying, Berargon murmurs Mildred's name; and though the inference that she might be his killer is factually wrong, it seems right emotionally. Curtiz works hard to win audience sympathy for Mildred: he shows her to be lonely, helpless and afflicted by the death of her second daughter, but he cannot conceal her similarity to Vida, at least not entirely; for only an ambitious snob would flinch so readily when taunted for being a waitress. In a more candid film, the right man for Mildred would have been Wally Faye (Jack Carson), a tough businessman who protects her interests but who lacks class and can be crude. Mildred's first husband, on the other hand, has class but lacks ambition and money and is soon whisked out of sight. Propriety requires a reconciliation with him in the final reel, but by then Mildred has earned a mink coat, and much else besides, by her own efforts.

Curtiz's treatment of this story is broken-backed, the labyrinthine mystification of the opening sequence, with its murder by a shattered mirror in a room filled with pools of shadow, giving way to soap opera uneventfulness, as Mildred bakes cakes to pay for Vida's dresses. Mildred's gentility is even more dispiriting than her masochism, although it is her pleasure in self-degradation that appears most in keeping with the seedy Los Angeles night-clubs, beach houses and restaurants: an identification of character and ambience that sets her apart from the more lively opportunists of the thirties.

Hollywood's equivocation about the bad motives of its more respectable screen characters appears to have been heightened whenever its stories brought these characters geographically close to the film colony. James M. Cain, who wrote the novel of *Mildred Pierce*, also wrote *Double Indemnity*, which Billy Wilder was to film (1944), with a screenplay by Raymond Chandler. Wilder was something of an exception in Hollywood, being as irreverent about certain of its sentimentalities as Stroheim had been twenty years before. He in no way

Billy Wilder: *Double Indemnity*. Fred MacMurray, Barbara Stanwyck.

conceals the cupidity of his two adulterers (Barbara Stanwyck and Fred MacMurray), matching the meanness of their affair so perfectly with the mock-Spanish Los Angeles house where it begins and ends that one seems to be inseparable from the other. But he could be as much caught up in Hollywood uncertainties over public taste as anyone else. In *The Lost Weekend* (1945) he tried to justify interest in the unpleasant alcoholic Don Birnan (Ray Milland) by suggesting that someone who aspired to be a serious writer should be forgiven a great deal. Fortunately Ray Milland's irritability dents this attempted idealization in much the same way as Joan Crawford's wish, in playing Mildred Pierce, to be thought pliant and forever close to tears seems incompatible with the formidable impression usually made by the future president of Pepsi-Cola. In fact, Curtiz uses Miss Crawford's totemic features and limited range of expression to give an incongruous distinction to a nondescript role. Mildred walks through the action as though she had inexcusably blundered into someone else's dream: a performance that won Joan Crawford a large following and an Academy Award.

During the thirties Michael Curtiz had been ill at ease with the social idiom of the United States. But the disadvantages of being an emigré were to work in his favour during the war years. Two of the films Curtiz directed in 1943 were to be splendidly typical of the period: the excesses of one of them being later regretted, the mood of the other, far from dating it as the mood passed, giving it an almost timeless permanence. Both of them were to be scripted by Howard Koch.

Mission to Moscow, one of the strangest products of the Soviet-American alliance, swallows hook, line and sinker Ambassador Davies's pro-Stalinist account of the Moscow purges of the late 1930s. Roosevelt

Michael Curtiz: *Mission to Moscow*.

had sent the ambassador – 'a hardboiled businessman who will get me the facts' – to Moscow via Berlin. In the film the ambassador, played by Walter Huston, watches a platoon of Hitlerjugend cross the station. Without leaving the platform he is able to sum up the nature of Nazism. In Moscow he is less prescient. Charmed by the friendliness of Russian soldiers at the border, he is even more charmed by the old world quaintness of Kamenev and Viroshilov – who in this view might be brothers to the comic Russian agents in Lubitsch's *Ninotchka*. The ambassador is so ingenuous that he refuses to have his rooms checked for hidden microphones. A reception at the Kremlin has its guests in dinner jackets, a Max Steiner waltz and the kind of conversation which can include remarks like: 'And have you read Karl Marx?'

In a lengthy introduction the ambassador himself appears and sanctions the pro-Communist attitudes of this two-hour film. *Mission to Moscow* skirts the implications of the Nazi-Soviet pact, divides

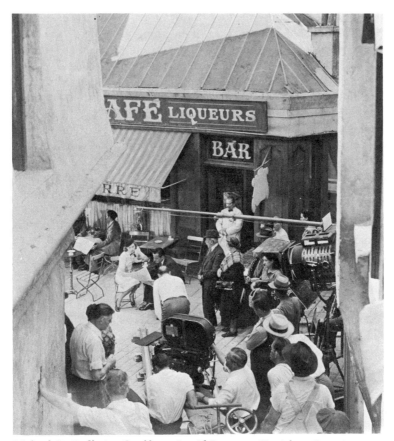

Michael Curtiz filming *Casablanca*. Ingrid Bergman, Humphrey Bogart.

American businessmen into either pro-Communists or pro-Nazis, puts over a sanctimonious view of politics and seems unable to distinguish differences in quality between Roosevelt, Churchill and Stalin (all three being shown as great men with the common touch). It supports whole-heartedly the official Soviet view of the 1937 Moscow show trials. 'After twenty years' trial practice I'm inclined to believe these confessions,' states Davies; and Curtiz's filming in no way qualifies the belief that Radek, Yagoda and the rest were saboteurs working for the Germans.

Curtiz and Koch minimize political motive in *Casablanca*. Rick, their main character (played by Humphrey Bogart), had fought in the Spanish Civil War on the republican side. But by the time the film begins, he has moved to Casablanca where he runs the Café Americain with a studied neutrality. Rick's former involvement in politics is mentioned very casually. By implication, he has been embittered less by the outcome of the Civil War than by the supposed defection of a girl-friend, Ilsa. Conveniently, Ilsa (Ingrid Bergman) comes to Casablanca with her lover, a resistance movement hero, and conveniently her lover is murdered, so that she and Rick can be reunited and (in one version of the film) leave Casablanca together.

But the film is at least political in the mood it conveys: its sense that all happiness is transient, its sense that we are all in the same predicament—established by the opening shot of a spinning globe. Nightly a group of foreigners comes to the Café Americain. At first sight the Café appears to be a luxurious night-club and gaming-room insulated from the world at large; it might be Hollywood at any period of its history. But most of its visitors want to escape from Morocco and all of them are prey to the ideological and ethnic tensions of war. Curtiz and Koch play the wish for international solidarity against isolationist fears. They marshal some of Europe's finest actors— including Peter Lorre, Sidney Greenstreet, Marcel Dalio, Conrad Veidt and Claude Rains—and have them appear as devious foreigners. Yet they show these foreigners to be most fine when most true to their foreign natures (as when Frenchmen in the Café sing the Marseillaise in defiance of some German officers). Most strikingly of all, they imply that none of these foreigners would have survived in wartime if they had not been corruptible.

No Hollywood film in the previous decade would have dared assume that to survive in war you need to be touched by its corruption. But the change in morality covers a wider ground. In the thirties, screen gangsters had run gambling-rooms as a side line. In the forties, movies did not limit gambling to the underworld. In Rick's café everyone joins in. War, it seemed, had shown life to be a gambling situation and all moral values as relative. If the American Rick can involve himself honourably in underhand deals, so non-Americans, too, can be both less than perfect and admirable. For all its romanticism, *Casablanca* refers to issues familiar to most people. By 1943, the public no longer thought of Morocco as some make-believe country. Casablanca as an actual place was mentioned most days in the newspapers. The film's popularity at the time of its release was to be boosted by the Anglo-American capture of the city and by the conference subsequently held there.

The romantic yearnings of *Casablanca* were by chance to be modified by the matter-of-fact. In the case of other films, the matter-of-fact was to be incorporated into romantic subjects in such a way that critics were inclined to describe the result as a new form of realism. David Lean's *Brief Encounter* (1946) is as good an illustration as any of how this response came about. Based on a one-act play by Noel Coward, *Brief Encounter* enacts the reveries of a housewife (Celia Johnson) as she sits at home with her husband listening to a recording of Rachmaninov's Second Piano Concerto. Lean never raises the question as to whether Laura's reveries are based on memories or wishful thinking; he expects his audience to assume that they evoke events that actually happened to her, even though the structure of his film could allow for this ambiguity. But, if only by implication, he does try to differentiate between types of fantasy: on the one hand, a type of fantasy inherited from the Marcel Carné *films noirs* of the thirties, and characterized by its dispiriting and soiling qualities, in this case of a suburban town with its cinema, tea-room and grimy railway station; on the other hand, Laura's faintly-caricatured imaginings signalled by huge close-ups on her face and dissolving images. The 'realism' of this style presupposes that the romantic conception of the town as a prison in some way destroys the less substantial romanticism of Laura's imaginings.

Laura dreams of her few brief encounters with a doctor, Alec Harvey (to which role Trevor Howard brings a sense of circumstance only hinted at by the script). But her dreams are so unphysical that she might be thinking not so much of a lover as a son: a possibility that seems to have occurred to those involved on the film, for Laura's meetings with Alec at the railway station and in the town are like nothing so much as a mother's mid-term visits to a boarding-school, while the one occasion when Laura comes close to sleeping with Alec is associated with an accident to her actual son. But if in suggesting that the beloved stranger may be a member of the family circle, Lean works in the same vein as certain American directors, he differs from them in leaving

David Lean: *Brief Encounter*. Celia Johnson.

Laura's gentility undefined. Laura may be as genteel as Mildred Pierce, yet no one would think of accusing her of murder. Lean increases the sense of restriction in her life by providing no genuine alternative to it, and he blocks many of the implications of his story by leaving unexamined the question of whether Laura has been limited in some way by her class-conscious milieu. Indeed, he heightens this snobbery by having Celia Johnson give the middle-class Laura the accents and manners of an upper-class woman and by reducing his working-class characters—the porter and buffet waitress at the railway station—to comic grotesques. As an alternative to her impoverished life, he provides the exoticism of a Rachmaninov piano concerto and some expressionistic reflections on a railway carriage window. His pessimism (and perhaps contempt) throws some light on the direction he was to take as a film director; for Laura, surely, is a precursor of those millions who have been thought satisfied by the romanticism of his *Lawrence of Arabia* (1962), *Dr Zhivago* (1965) and *Ryan's Daughter* (1970).

Most of the actual war films produced by Hollywood during the war were intended to reassure wives and girl friends, like letters home from the front. James Agee found *Guadalcanal Diary* (1943) 'serious, simple and honest', but pointed out that it did not give a 'remotely adequate image of the first months of that island'.[9] Softening one of the more ferocious of the Pacific campaigns into a Huckleberry Finn adventure story, Lewis Seiler, its director, emphasizes the racial ease that existed among the troops and the bravery of priests. Faces remain unstrained, officers paternal. As Lionel Stander's goofy GI remarks: 'It's nothing compared to the war in *Gone with the Wind*.' Too often Hollywood presumed the GI to be as celibate and dedicated as Roman Catholic priests are supposed to be; and the sentimental cheeriness of *Going My Way* (1944), with Bing Crosby as a singing priest, seems to have spread everywhere. It certainly rings through *A Bell for Adano* (1945), an idealization of the GI in occupied Italy very unlike Rossellini's rueful study of him in *Paisà*.

Some sort of positive response to the Nazi threat had to be discovered, but values could not be tested, as in Europe, by the need to resist an enemy occupation or blitz; and Hollywood continued to rely on the populist values of the thirties, values that now lacked conviction. Traditionalists looked to religion and the sanctity of family life, progressives to a watered-down Marxism. At this time studios willingly employed the men later to be stigmatized as the Hollywood Ten. One of them, John Howard Lawson, wrote the screenplay for Warner Brothers' *Action in the North Atlantic* (1943), in which a convoy of liberty ships eventually manages to sail into a Russian harbour to the encouraging cheers of Soviet citizens. 'What's that mean,' asks one American sailor anxiously of another, '*tovarich?*' Populism of this kind tended to exclude insight into character, but it could include some splendid action at sea.

But why were the men fighting? General George C. Marshall seems to have been fully aware of this problem when he asked Frank Capra—who had joined the Signals Corps—to indoctrinate 'the pleasure-loving soft citizens' army, fifty to every one professional soldier'.[10] With his instinctive grasp on populist rhetoric, Capra was well-chosen for this job. But he was intolerant of individual differences and often undiscriminating. Occasionally his reductionism could be trenchant; sometimes it was merely simplistic. In *Prelude to War*, the first of the six *Why We Fight* compilations which he supervised and in part directed, he harkens back continually to his Italian origins, seeing the prelude to war in terms of gangsters and rosaries (crudely epitomized by the shot of a shattered cathedral window with a poster of Hitler beyond it). He acknowledges the plurality of American culture by tracing the most worth-while of American values to Moses, Mohammed, Confucius, Christ, Jefferson, Garibaldi and—with some shots from *Mr Smith Goes to Washington*—George Washington. As if this summary were not confusing enough, he then describes each of the three members of the Axis separately, cutting between Berlin, Tokyo and Rome, and between them and each of the Allies, in such a way as to recall the formalist equations of Ruttmann's *Melody of the World*. He concludes *Prelude to War* with some horrific newsreel material of the Japanese attack on Shanghai; and he was to use a similar kind of punch ending on the other compilations.

Working at first in Washington and then in Hollywood, Capra assembled his compilations with the greatest difficulty. He had obtained a valuable hoard of newsreel stock from army archives, but he was never given a studio and his equipment was inadequate. By expertise alone, he and his colleagues created a dynamism and satanic glamour based in part on the techniques of *Triumph of the Will*, which had impressed them. He was later to say that his compilations had defined government policy between the wars; in fact they are, at best, primitive moralities. The commentary to *The Nazi Strike* hails Hitler's rise to power as 'the most fantastic play in history'. Seldom has the black octopus spread with such panache across the maps of Europe. Capra appears to have admired energy in almost any form. Yet it is not surprising that someone willing to work for so many years for Harry Cohn should have been tantalized by despotism: a fascination that emerges as far back in his career as *The Bitter Tea of General Yen* (1932), where he had deified the murderous war-lord, General Yen, by posthumously transforming him into a force of nature, the wind that blows through Barbara Stanwyck's hair. His rhetoric is nowhere so apparent as in his conclusion to *The Nazi Strike*, which he builds up into a crescendo of terror over the blitzing of Warsaw and the betrayals and executions that follow the Nazi take-over of the country, a crescendo which modulates into the voice of Churchill commending courage, with a choir singing *Onward Christian Soldiers* in the background. It is a little like Christmas goodwill transmitted over street amplifiers.

Among these compilations *The Battle of Russia*, in the main put together by Anatole Litvak, was exceptional. Yet it was characteristic of this period – when Soviet film-makers and the more reactionary administrators in Hollywood could unite to send greetings to the VOKS conference of 1942, and when the right-wing Capra could be revered in Russia to the extent that Pudovkin praised *Prelude to War* as the prototype of the future international film because it 'can be fully under-stood everywhere', [11] and *It Happened One Night*, retitled as *New York–Miami Bus*, could become the most popular stage play on in Leningrad during its siege – that *The Battle of Russia*, while confirming General MacArthur's belief that the Soviet struggle was 'the greatest military achievement in history', could yet survey the Russian past without once mentioning the ideals of the October revolution.

The Russians produced a number of feature documentaries on the war within their frontiers. Some of them were to be shown in the West, and one of them, *Moscow Strikes Back* (1942), with a commentary by

Leonid Varlamov: *Stalingrad.*

Albert Maltz (later to be one of the Hollywood Ten) and spoken by Edward G. Robinson, was to win an Academy award. Litvak took much of his material from these documentaries and did manage to recapture something of the unbelievable experiences undergone by the Russians. But of necessity he had to edit down the available footage, and in doing so lost the sense of endurance that gives so much power to the Russian originals. It may be that Leonid Varlamov weakens his *Stalingrad* (1943) with a raucous commentary praising Stalin and Voroshilov, and yet he conveys an impact that Litvak, for all his reliance on Tchaikovsky, cannot communicate. Varlamov had a distinguished team of cameramen at his disposal, and it was usually at the right place at the right time and able to seize on such memorable moments as the only surrender of a field-marshal (Paulus) in the war, the bustling appearance of Khrushchev as mayor of the city and the sight of long lines of defeated German soldiers, many of them very young, trudging in makeshift sandals through snow. But as so often in Russian films, heroism seems to be defined through an identification with an epic landscape, the ruined city rising out of the plains, the steely melancholy of the Volga.

Working for the forces encouraged a number of Hollywood directors to break away from the major studios at the end of the war. Capra was one of these directors, setting up his own company, Liberty Films, with George Stevens, who had been an associate on the *Why We Fight* series. Liberty Films had to be disbanded in 1947. Capra, the populist, had lost touch with public taste; and apart from *State of the Union* (1948), a vehicle for Spencer Tracy and Katharine Hepburn, none of his post-war films were to have the impact of his earlier work.

Walt Disney, on the other hand, had been a successful independent from the beginning of his career. He was to load his already heavy wartime schedule with two war projects, cooperating with the Signals Corps to produce an instructional film, *Two Down and One to Go*, and to turn over all his facilities to the making of a full-length animation feature, *Victory through Air Power* (1943), in order to illustrate the theory of a friend of his, Major Alexander de Seversky, who believed that long-distance bombers might be the key to victory. Richard Schickel claims in his biography of Disney that 'the curious appeal of strategic air power to people of rightist political leanings has never been analysed'[12]; and events were certainly to disprove the Major's theory before the end of 1943, so that the film never gained more than a limited circulation. Yet the techniques devised for it by the Disney studio make it a model of exposition, and certain sequences concerned with the history of the aeroplane—they contain some dazzlingly inventive ideas—alone give it value. Many of its deductions are

Walt Disney: *Victory through Air Power.*

pessimistic, and in a way that is less revealing of wartime anxieties than of Disney himself. He argues, by false analogy, that the Germans and Japanese have a geographical advantage over the Allies and suggests that the war will continue until 1948.

In 1943 John Huston, who had been appointed a captain in the Air Force, directed *Report on the Aleutians* for the Signals Corps. The presence of a fuelling station, seemingly at the end of the world, appears to fascinate him in much the same way as later he was to be drawn to the image of the isolated ranch in *The Unforgiven* (1959) and *The Misfits* (1960), while his imaginative combination of tawny brown, rust red and ochre anticipates his colour experiments in *Moulin Rouge* (1953) and *Moby Dick* (1956). But his aestheticism is uninvolved with the subject; his attitude is ironic; and it was fitting that the Aleutian campaign should never have taken place, and that the documentary should fade out without conflict or affirmation. *The Battle of San Pietro* (1944) is very different. Its emphasis on the cost of battle, on death both among American troops and Italian civilians, marks it out as a pre-cursor of Huston's remarkable *The Red Badge of Courage* (1951), in spite of its drab middle-distance filming. An impassioned, quietly spoken commentary in no way tries to conceal the futility of war. In 1945 Huston directed *Let There Be Light*, a documentary on the psychiatric treatment of shell-shocked soldiers. He has claimed that working on this subsequently banned film was one of the most important experiences in his life.

John Ford was to be appointed lieutenant-commander in the Navy and to work mainly for Intelligence as Chief of the Field Photographic Branch. He was to be at his finest at the beginning of the decade with *The Grapes of Wrath* (1940). Although he was later to say that he had no sympathy for John Steinbeck's left-wing politics and

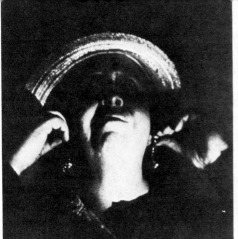

John Ford: *The Grapes of Wrath.*
Jane Darwell.

Mark Donskoi: *My Childhood.*
Massalitinova.

had responded to Nunnally Johnson's screenplay of Steinbeck's novel as disinterestedly as he did to any project, his identification with his principal characters, the dispossessed Oakies, emerges strongly. The story of *The Grapes of Wrath* describes a journey, rather like *Stagecoach*, but of a greater complexity in meaning and quite different in spirit: being a sort of anti-Western, in which the Joad family's arduous lorry trek from the dust-bowl desolation of Oklahoma to the orange groves of California does not lead to a Fordian statement about the promise of the Republic but to disillusionment and to a tentative demand for organized labour.

In its intensity it transcends the pastoral themes of the previous decade, in much the same way as a Russian film trilogy, Mark Donskoi's adaptation of Maxim Gorky's autobiography, was to do. The imagery of *My Childhood* (1938), the first part of the Donskoi trilogy, manages both to convey the boy Maxim's relationship to the adult world and its problems and to have the timeless quality of a child's imagination, bringing together impressions of epic figures from legend with figures from the family circle. In both *My Childhood* and *The Grapes of Wrath*, an elderly woman—to the child as old as the history of the race—is the main object of attention. As Massalitinova dances in a slowly cumbersome yet graceful way by her stove or Jane Darwell's Ma Joad looks through some old postcards and then at herself in a mirror, they evoke a youth all the more awesome because it occurred in some uncharted time before the child came into being.

Both Donskoi and Ford raise pastoralism into myth, Donskoi counteracting the abstraction of myth by his sense of humour and feeling for the hard and arbitrary nature of existence, Ford by the documentary care that he and his cameraman, Gregg Toland, bring to nearly every scene. An almost pitiless concern with the textures of wood, sand, taut lined faces and of such familiar objects as dented buckets has the effect of making credible events of a nightmarish dimension, such as the destruction of the Joad homestead by a caterpillar tractor or the exploitation of the workers at a Californian labour camp. Toland's photography, which has the airless beauty of certain botanists' engravings, appears to imitate the style of some remarkable photographs taken by Dorothea Lange on a visit to the migrant camps in 1936, a style to be subscribed to by Walker Evans in his photographs for James Agee's *Let Us Now Praise Famous Men* and by Flaherty in his documentary *The Land* (1940). The sharp focus of this style relieves Steinbeck's symbolism of much of its pretension.

War service brought about a change in Ford. In the post-war years he was inclined to see his characters from an officer's viewpoint, the relationship between the captain and his batman in *She Wore a Yellow Ribbon* (1949) being typical. Officers tended to be quixotic, their men to be Sancho Panzas. Yet if Ford grew more paternalist in his conscious attitudes, the quality of his filming continued to be tender: a quality evident in the few scenes he shot for Gregg Toland's reconstruction of the Pearl Harbor disaster, *December 7th* (1943).

In the previous year he had compiled *The Battle of Midway* (1942), and a comparison of the two versions of this documentary is as good a record as any of how he could transform indifferent material. He himself had shot part of the first version with a 16mm. camera during a Japanese air-strike on the mid-Pacific island of Midway, but while filming he had been wounded in the arm. Various other members of the Field Photographic Branch had edited the rushes into a propaganda film of so stilted and aggressive a kind that it had an effect contrary to the one intended. On coming out of hospital, Ford re-edited these rushes into a longer compilation, one that was distinguished enough to win him an Academy award.

He begins it, characteristically, by concentrating on seemingly marginal events: shots of birds on the island, American folk at home talking about their boys in the forces, an accordion playing *Red River Valley* as the sun sets. He establishes a mood that the battle will be shown to destroy. During the air-strike sequences he not only paces the action with a mastery unavailable to his colleagues but gives the monotony of the bombing some significance by relating it to the humanity of its victims. The first version of *The Battle of Midway* reports on the destruction of an American hospital and the burial of its dead with an editing so insensitive that it kills the images. Its commentary is over-compensatingly belligerent, snarling that '20 of them will die for every one of us.' Ford edits this material in such a way that the funeral becomes one of his typically statuesque ceremonies. His commentary restricts itself to listing the names of the officers present.

A similar transformation of subject-matter occurs in *They Were Expendable* (1945). Ford appears to be at his most authoritarian. He responds to the despotic figure of General MacArthur with reverence, accepts the way the war is being conducted without criticism and idealizes the crews of two torpedo-boats as unwavering patriots. But by the very fact that he deals with an American defeat, the withdrawal from the Philippines in 1941, he turns all these attitudes on their head; so that his idealization seems less a trick of propaganda than a way of achieving a style both epic and elegiac. If his torpedo-boat crews appear to welcome regimentation, they do so as a necessary comradeship in the face of loneliness and fear. If Ford's respect for naval ritual may seem disquieting, it seems less so in the context of such a sadness, a mood most strong in the finest scenes, as when officers hear of the Pearl Harbor bombardment in a Filippino night-club or when some of the men listen to a broadcast from San Francisco while sitting in a remote Pacific island bar.

William Wyler had as much reason as anyone in America for being anguished about the war in Europe. He had been born in Alsace in 1902 of a Swiss mother and a German father and brought to the United States in 1920 by Carl Laemmle, who was one of his relatives. In *The Little Foxes* (1941) he was to elaborate on many of his interests: his feeling for the past and the Southern states, his taste for spacious camerawork and theatrical settings—the roses Regina (Bette Davis) cuts in her garden are ostentatiously artificial. And its theme did not exclude his habitual fascination with cruelty. But the primary value of *The Little Foxes* is that Lillian Hellman's screen adaptation of her stage play allows him specifically to relate these interests to the theme of Nazi evil.

He has always been divided in his feelings about predatory people. Much of the tension in *The Desperate Hours* (1955), for instance, in which three escaped convicts beleaguer and torment a middle-class family, derives from his ambivalent response to their cruelty, although

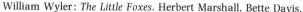

William Wyler: *The Little Foxes*. Herbert Marshall, Bette Davis.

consciously his sympathy may have been with the family. In *The Little Foxes* his description of cruelty in some of its more subtle guises is painful, and yet without it the allusion to the Nazis could have been brushed aside. As Wyler presents them, Regina and her two brothers have the presence of evil. The sequence in which Birdie, a gentle defeated Southern lady, talks too much at table and then approaches her husband, one of the two brothers, anxiously asking 'Was I all right?' and has her face slapped, or the suspense generated by the heart condition of Regina's husband (Herbert Marshall), who carries within him, as it were, an unexploded bomb that Regina will clearly trigger off, dramatizes the impact of evil most vividly: in the context of which the balletic grace of Wyler's camera movements and his use of deep-focus shots do not open up space nor, as André Bazin claimed, bring ambiguity into the image so much as increase narrative impetus and heighten an ugliness in motive by a contrasted elegance in manner.

Wyler directed *The Little Foxes* for Goldwyn; but he was to direct *Mrs Miniver*, appropriately, for MGM, since the Miniver family is supposed to be as cosily representative of England in the blitz as the Hardy family had been of the United States during the New Deal. But it would be pointless to fault *Mrs Miniver* for its lack of verisimilitude. It is not that sort of film. Like Mervyn LeRoy's *Waterloo Bridge* (1940) it is closer in kind to the romances of Mizoguchi; and on these terms, Wyler's skill is admirable in drawing out the radiance and pathos of his actresses, in evoking the departure of the small ships to Dunkirk or in playing on the expectations of his audience.

William Wyler: *The Best Years of Our Lives.*

(Everything would suggest that Mrs Miniver's son will be killed in battle, yet it is his fiancée and not he who dies, and in an unusual way.) Typically, Wyler's most effective scene concerns an intrusive predator, the Nazi pilot who breaks into Mrs Miniver's kitchen and demands to be fed. Wyler has said that he intended the pilot to be a surrogate of Mrs Miniver's son, and the effect of this scene, indeed, is to act out tensions denied by the bland reassurance of the rest of the film. *Mrs Miniver* may project the responsibility for destruction onto the enemy, as most war propaganda does, but this scene intimates that war symbolizes the destructive impulse in everyone; and that nearly everyone at one time or another wishes to blitz a home of Mrs Miniver's kind.

Wyler was to direct two war documentaries, *Memphis Belle* and *The Fighting Lady* (both 1944). He was to say that the film-making of his friend, George Stevens, had been profoundly changed by a visit to Dachau; but few directors have been quite so transformed by active service as he, a transformation that marks *The Best Years of Our Lives* (1946). Although its technique is as elaborate as any he was to use, its aim is self-effacement. Complicated camera movements are so arranged as to eliminate any experience of the camera as a mediating presence, so that the spectator may believe himself to be the constant companion of the soldier, sailor and airman who are trying to rehabilitate themselves to the nondescript strangeness of their home town.

The opening of the film is startling in its muted talk and throwaway tragic revelations, such as that of the sailor, who reveals that he has

William Wyler: *The Best Years of Our Lives*. Dana Andrews.

lost both his hands in the war. (Harold Russell, who plays the part, had himself been so mutilated, and the nature of his condition would appear to have sobered the other performers.) But even more startling is a scene in the cockpit of an aeroplane, in which the returning combatants look down on their native town in a sustained gliding shot that anticipates CinemaScope in its breadth of visual information. It is soon clear that Wyler has adapted his technique to record nuances in feeling, not to heighten behaviour. Avoiding the spatial disruptions entailed by any use of the close-up, he relies on flowing camerawork and set-ups of a kind that focus attention on the eye movements of his actors. As André Bazin has noted, he makes the direction in which his actors glance essential to the structure of his compositions, as though these looks were lines cutting across a picture plane. If Murnau had moved the camera to evoke lyric sensations, Wyler moves it 'to analyse sentiments', as Michelangelo Antonioni, one of his successors, has put it; even the panoramic cockpit view of the town conveys the impression of looking introspectively into the self.

The atrocities disclosed by the war could have encouraged a blank refusal to know the truth; in fact, many people were ready to learn the worst. *The Best Years of Our Lives* contributes to this process of paring away illusion and lies. Its screenplay is by Robert E. Sherwood, and on this occasion at least Sherwood resisted his inclination to search out transcendental meanings: there is a wish to show things as they are, however ordinary they may be. Indeed, Sherwood's subject, the nature of post-war readjustment, contains within it the idea of legends being stripped down and idealizations diminished: a process that Wyler is often tempted to take to the verge of degradation, as in the scenes where Dana Andrews's fighter pilot has to face the contempt of customers as a drugstore assistant, or Fredric March, as a tippling ex-sergeant reinstated as a bank official, has to decide on whether another veteran should be granted a loan. A mood of dismay permeates the whole film and even touches its ironic title; for the wife who claims to have wasted the best years of her life awaiting her husband's return has in actuality been kept busy by a succession of lovers.

The theme of rehabilitation was to be taken up by other directors. Fred Zinnemann, for instance, was to make a star of Brando by casting him in his first leading role as a paraplegic in *The Men* (1950). But *The Best Years of Our Lives* towers over these other films: in part through its exhaustiveness (it lasts for more than two and a half hours), in part through the assiduity with which it works towards some hope for its leading characters. It was a solitary achievement. As Wyler himself was to say, its sympathies would have been impossible two years later. And indeed the House Un-American Activities Committee was shortly to attack him for his remarkable *Carrie* (1952). The Cold War had already set in.

Jean Grémillon: *Lumière d'été.*

The Vichy Cinema

By June 1940 the French film industry was paralysed. Mobilization had emptied the studios and disrupted shooting on – among other projects – Clair's *Air pur* and Grémillon's *Remorques* (completed in 1941). In the meanwhile – Tobis and ACE being already German-owned – the German authorities had no trouble in taking control of the distribution networks. Setting up their own production company (Continental) at the Hôtel Crillon, they appointed a certain Dr Dietrich as supervisor and ordered that the principal item on all film programmes should be their newsreel *Deutsche Wochenschau.* During showings of this newsreel, doors had to be locked and auditorium lights kept on, while two armed policemen stood guard by the screen, looking down at the audience. By the end of 1940 American movies were no longer being imported. The French public saw this as no reason for going to see Continental films, even though many of them were quite successful imitations of Hollywood comedies and musicals. Recognizing the nature of this hostility, Dr Dietrich determined to combine forces with the Comité d'Organisation de l'Industrie Cinématographique (COIC), which the collaborationist Vichy government had set up in December 1940.

Dietrich's ambition in financing the Comité was to be turned awry. For although COIC had expelled all Jews from the industry, forbidden trade-union activity and was strictly to control the activities of its personnel, some of its employees did manage—in the twenty-nine films produced in 1940, the seventy-eight in 1942 and the twenty in 1944—to insert clandestine and at times cryptic messages of support for the Free French. The first of these films (and it raised morale throughout France) was Daquin's *Nous les gosses* (1941). Others included Carné's *Les Visiteurs du soir* (1942), Grémillon's *La Vie est à vous* (1944) and Carné's *Les Enfants du paradis* (1945). Audiences became sensitive to political nuance, too much so perhaps; and both Clouzot's *Le Corbeau* (1943) and Delannoy's *L'Eternel Retour* (1943) were condemned, somewhat unfairly, as Nazi propaganda. Yet sometimes audiences were justified in assuming they were being subjected to Nazi propaganda, as when they had to sit through Marshal Pétain's anti-semitic peroration at the end of *Les Inconnus dans la maison* (1942).

In two articles on *The French Cinema during the Occupation*, published in the 1946 spring and summer editions of *Sight and Sound*, Hazel Hackett noted that by 1942 audiences had begun to resemble authors rather than spectators, spinning their own films out of webs of allusion. She states that the Vichy censorship had largely kept the industry to historical subjects, myths and symbolist treatments, its only freedom being to 'ignore reality'. It is possible, though, that the restriction was less severe than she claims. Myths and overt symbolism had always been important to the French avant-garde, and its notion of 'reality' had seldom been more than token; as in its choice of seedy urban locations or moods of Baudelairean despair. But the most typical attribute of the Vichy films (taking a tendency in avant-garde thought to an extreme) was their sealed-off, rarefied settings, in which isolated groups of characters lacked almost any restraint on their behaviour. It is worth observing that Jacques Prévert, who had been at home with subjects of this kind since the mid-thirties, was not only free to continue developing these interests during the war years but was also able to bring his talents as a screenplay writer to their full maturity at this time.

In Grémillon's *Lumière d'été* (1943)—Prévert wrote the script, as he had for *Remorques*—one such isolated group finds itself stranded in a hotel in the Massif Central. It is typical of his enterprise that an alcoholic painter, played by Pierre Brasseur, should see himself as a modern Hamlet and relate France to the rotten state of Denmark: an allusion that the Vichy censors, who banned the film, did not miss. Prévert underlined the allusion by contrasting the decadents in the hotel with a gang of workers blasting a rock face in the valley below—a contrast that, for all its bravura, tends to be too schematic and to

Claude Autant-Lara: *Douce.*

insulate Prévert's theme from some of the more pressing issues facing his wartime audiences. It all seems very remote from the forties. And Grémillon's concern with sensibility appears disproportionate to his subject (in a way that Jean Renoir's treatment of the thematically similar *La Règle du jeu* does not). Yet his pleasure in atmosphere—sun-parched rocks, a golden eagle wheeling overhead, the quality of light seen through hotel windows—sets up its own kind of credibility. The same argument could be raised against Claude Autant-Lara's *Douce* (1943), in which Autant-Lara uses a self-destructive love affair as a point of departure to explore the reactions of an aristocratic family to the changing social attitudes of the late 1880s. A deracinated theme—and Henry James had argued that deracination of this kind was intrinsic to romance—yet a theme that brings its own benefits: it frees Autant-Lara's powers of sensibility and allows him leisurely to delineate velleities of feeling in a manner that few of his later, more urgent subjects were to afford.

With hindsight, its is possible to enjoy many Vichy films as autonomous and imaginative artifices that never quite avoid a sense of precarious studio carpentry. Jean Delannoy's *L'Eternel Retour*—with a screenplay by Jean Cocteau and very much a Cocteau film—is of this type. Its Tristan and Iseult, idealized to the point of implausibility, are surrounded by envious grotesques. Yet Delannoy realizes the notion of transcendental passion effectively and puts over the mythic business of poisons and potions with enough conviction to make an improbable story acceptable as a sort of dream. Jean Epstein's influence is noticeable throughout, and was to be even more marked on Cocteau's own *La Belle et la bête* (1946), which managed to sustain the atmosphere of a fairy-tale on a minuscule budget.

Marcel Carné's *Les Visiteurs du soir* tries to work the same magic at greater expense. It tells of how, sometime in the late fifteenth century, two minstrels signed a pact with the Devil which allowed them to seduce whomever they wished. Prévert's script at moments has the unpredictable invention of a late Shakespeare play. But for all that, his technical skill and some spectacular effects cannot redeem a slight idea. Camera movements are over-complicated, and Georges Walkevitch's main setting—a gleaming white castle that might have been derived from the pages of *Les Très Riches Heures du Duc de Berry*—is far too dominating. Monumentality stifles this production. Whatever life it has resides in Jules Berry's performance as the Devil. When reminded of the many disasters he has brought about, Berry's Devil carelessly (and inimitably) replies: 'I must pass the time somehow.'

Prévert and Carné were to be closer to the spirit of Shakespeare in their next production. Indeed, *Les Enfants du paradis*, filmed for the most part in Nice during the war, but not released until 1945, could be seen as a commentary on the way in which such Romantics as Hugo, Berlioz and de Musset interpreted Shakespeare. It is, in the best sense of the word, a pastiche. Prévert's screenplay intimates that he was more interested in evoking the intellectual and aesthetic atmosphere of the 1840s than in reconstructing the material aspects of the period and, like Shakespeare, more concerned with relating himself to an idea of the past than to observing historical verisimilitude. As always, he thinks through a maze of analogies, cross-references and Wildean paradoxes. He manages to work out some of his parallels very closely, the most central of them being his noted similarity between two implicitly anti-bourgeois classes, criminals and actors: so that a mercenary killer, François, can think of himself as an artist in crime, while at the same time a great actor, Frédéric Lemaître (Pierre Brasseur), feels no compunction in living lawlessly. Both men take on being, and indeed accrete formidable personalities, through their megalomaniac identifications. The irony is that both of them do achieve a kind of art in their madness.

It might seem that Prévert is evaluating a Romantic idea about the way human beings can realize themselves. But in fact he so enters into the period's spirit of panache that his intentions can hardly be viewed as historical in this sense. His identification with Romanticism is complete and uncritical: a relationship that seems to be bound up with his coming to maturity as a film writer. At their most Romantic, his characters might be walking versions of any of his previous screenplays. They become selfconscious about the symbolic nature of their actions. They ceaselessly draw parallels between themselves and events in such Shakespeare plays as *Romeo and Juliet* and

Marcel Carné: *Les Enfants du paradis.*

Othello. They are enclosed within their own theatricality. Relishing this theatricality, Prévert misses no opportunity of exploring the repertoire of illusions and stage devices suggested by it. And through the figure of the mime Baptiste (played by Jean-Louis Barrault), he is able to work out a favourite theme: the difference between the Ideal and the Real in both love and art.

It would be misleading, though, to follow the logic of Prévert's Romanticism and to argue that he realized his talents at the sad expense of losing himself within some delusional and self-isolating system of thought. For he does reflect the genuine anxieties of a society under occupation, although these anxieties are somewhat concealed by their Romantic guise. Members of the Resistance movement, or even those who did no more than decline to admit defeat, were like his criminals and actors in their hostility to the ruling powers, or in their belief that when they came out onto the streets they had to play roles. Glints of such a reference occur when François, the mercenary killer, raises the question, 'Why ask people their names when they hide their real selves?', when Frédéric Lemaître refers to himself as acting all the time, or when Baptiste points up the contrast between silence and words. The scene in which Baptiste silently accuses a pickpocket by miming his act of stealing a watch is not only one of the most remarkable in any film, it can also be understood without strain as a comment on the way in which Frenchmen accused their oppressors.

The Carné-Prévert partnership was shortly to founder, but on this occasion Carné brought such excitement to Prévert's ideas that he really was able to incarnate a poet's dream. Seldom has the feeling of life backstage, or of miraculous stage performance, been so fully realized. Exceptional acting—but in different, even conflicting styles—by Arletty and Casarès, as well as by Brasseur and Barrault, are coordinated: the effect of the tender love scenes between Barrault and Arletty, for instance, very much depending on a director's tact. And for once Carné's nervously flamboyant style appears compatible with his subject.

While the war brought this partnership to fruition, it also ushered in a new generation of film-makers, two of whom were to be of unusual ability. One of them, Jacques Becker, a long-time assistant on many of Renoir's films, first attracted attention with his feature *Goupi Mains-Rouge* (1943). Although his short career was to be uneven in its output—he died in 1960 at the age of fifty-four—he did manage in that time to direct the ironical and pleasing comedy *Edouard et Caroline* (1951), *Casque d'or* (1952)—memorable for its pagan description of a love affair that ends in a violent death and for its sensuous response to landscape—and *Le Trou* (1960), one of the best film accounts of a prison escape. It has been claimed that Becker's manner in filming this escape was indebted to Robert Bresson. If so, this sympathy is understandable, for Bresson was not only Becker's contemporary, but also the most gifted French film-maker to emerge during the war: *Les Anges du péché*, with dialogue by Jean Giraudoux, being released in 1943, and *Les Dames du Bois de Boulogne*, with dialogue by Jean Cocteau, in 1945.

Based on an anecdote, almost an aside, in Diderot's *Jacques le fataliste*, *Les Dames du Bois de Boulogne* tells of how a society lady takes revenge on a lover who has rejected her by arranging that he should marry a *demi-mondaine*. But this scandal, which has the force of a broken taboo in Diderot, loses much of its significance when transposed into the twentieth century; and the casting of Maria Casarès, all cold will and intensity, as the society lady Hélène and the feminine, sunny Elina Labourdette as the dancer—Bresson shows nothing of her supposed activities as a prostitute—adds weight to the feeling that the gentleman was not so much tricked as lucky. But in spite of this disparity between intention and effect, *Les Dames du Bois de Boulogne* remains intriguing in many ways: above all, because it is both unlike Bresson's later approach to film-making while in many respects anticipating his development. He was never again to work with professional actors (and Casarès, as Hélène, employs the grandest of theatrical styles) or to depend on a plot so dramatic in its reversals. At the same time he was to concentrate more and more on two of the stylistic techniques tentatively raised here: that of refinement—paring down his images to the sparest kind of statement possible—and that of repetition, certain scenes or locations occurring again and again with little variation. (In this case, he emphasizes the motif of tears and tear-laden faces.) He relies on close-up far more than did most directors in the forties, making a slightly grotesque play with the convention by which ladies wear hats at the dinner table and declining to conceal the observation that Casarès's head appears enormous in relation to her shoulders.

The oddity is that he was to discard this type of histrionic presence in his subsequent work, although he seems to be more fascinated by Hélène than by any of the characters around her. Few, if any, of his later protagonists were to be as active as she, or so controlling: an idea succinctly conveyed by the way in which she manages the lift outside her apartment, blocking, if she so wants, the departure of her guests. It is typical of Bresson that the final scenes should show her control to have been delusive: the lovers, we are led to suppose, will be happy together in spite of her malice. Even so, these final redemption scenes—the religious overtones are overt—are too arbitrarily related to the rest of the story and indeed too crude. In future Bresson was to deal with the theme of fate, and its mysterious workings, far less explicitly, allowing it to creep through interstices, as it were, so as to permeate the whole plot.

Roberto Rossellini: *Germania, anno zero*.

12. Neo-realism and the Cold War

Aptly named, the Cold War (a term popularized, if not invented, by Walter Lippmann) was a time when the public imagination seemed to have frozen over. The spirit was numb, generosity appeared lost. The so-called war was more a deadlock in international relations than a series of actual events. Winston S. Churchill's Fulton speech in March 1946 and the Truman Doctrine of March 1947 marked important stages in the public awareness of a possible third world war. The Berlin Blockade and the Korean War were to intensify it. In this sense, such anti-Red movies as William Wellman's *The Iron Curtain* (1948), George Sidney's *The Red Danube* (1949) and Leo McCarey's *My Son John* (1952) were quintessentially Cold War statements. But the war was more than a conflict between Communist and non-Communist wishes. The revelations of the Second World War—the power of the atom bomb, in particular, and the obscenity of the concentration camps—had brought about a change in mankind that was, and still is, incalculable. The shock of this change had still to be assimilated; it was felt to be too overwhelming, perhaps, to be grieved; and the Cold War was one of its consequences. It was a little like the acrimony, or dullness, or sense of triumph that can occur when a family fails to mourn the death of someone in their midst.

But again, it would be misleading to limit the war's influence on the film industry to movies that directly or indirectly reflected fears of world annihilation or apocalyptic feelings, though clearly the projection of these fears and feelings did result from it. Even so serious an enterprise as Ingmar Bergman's *The Seventh Seal* (1957)—let alone Robert Aldrich's *Kiss Me Deadly* (1955) or Don Siegel's *Invasion of the Body Snatchers* (1956)—must seem insubstantial in the light of its incapacitating effect. A major stumbling-block in defining the Cold War is that we are still so much part of it.

Its immediate influence was that audiences looked for qualities of warmth, however simulated. Critics praised the Italian neo-realist films for their spontaneous humanity and discounted their often contrived sweetness, in much the same way as they had once underplayed Chaplin's self-pity. By force of custom, the little man's stand against the big battalions was allowed to be sentimental. Other members of the public sought warmth in such protracted commercials for domestic luxury as *Mr Blandings Builds His Dream House* (1948), while yet others sought it in the comfortable pessimism of the French art films of the 1930s and the Occupation. (Duvivier, Carné and Feyder were the most popular of the French directors.) The art film enjoyed great prestige during the Cold War, just as it had in Germany in the years after the Kaiser's defeat, on the grounds presumably that the prospect of high culture would sustain the self in a time of deprivation.

Hollywood felt the Cold War more sharply. It was to be one of the first victims of the Congressional witch-hunts. In the thirties and early forties it had managed to placate the House Un-American Activities Committee; but under the HUAC investigations of 1947, chaired by J. Parnell Thomas (who was later sent to prison for embezzling public funds), it lost its nerve. The Alger Hiss-Whittaker Chambers case of 1948 which, as Alistair Cooke wrote, put a whole generation on trial, might not have taken place if the Thomas Committee investigating Hollywood in Washington had not perceived how effective its bullying tactics could be. Recognizing how vulnerable entertainers were to public opinion, the Committee pressed its charges unscrupulously, while many of those investigated, including some who were Communists, declined to speak frankly for fear of losing employment.

The Washington investigations had an atmosphere of unreality, yet many of their consequences were to be all too real: ostracism, unemployment, exile, the break-up of families, heart failures and suicides. They brought into disrepute leaders in the film industry who had either informed on their colleagues or absurdly set themselves up as authorities on world Communism. They were to be responsible for the fines or gaol-sentences imposed on those writers, producers and directors, known as the Unfriendly Ten, who had refused to testify, pleading the First Amendment. They were to frighten the bankers, who put pressure on the studios and casting agencies to compile black lists of increasing length naming alleged subversives who were on no account to be employed. 'The black list was a time of evil,' wrote Dalton Trumbo, one of the Unfriendly Ten, 'and no one on either side who survived it came through untouched by evil.'[1]

But on the whole the meaning of the Cold War was too diffuse to be articulated on the screen, and Hollywood was to register it only as a disturbed person might: by settling more deeply into its fixation on jealousy. Hitchcock and Ben Hecht took a magazine story about an actress who sleeps with a Nazi spy and transformed it into *Notorious* (1944, released 1946), an intricate parable about jealousy. In *Suspicion* (1941) Hitchcock had cast Cary Grant as a possible murderer; he had taken advantage of Grant's ability to look both protective and at the same time detached in a glazed, slightly lunatic way, and he had elaborated on the similarity between jealousy as a poisoning of the mind and actual poisoning – as in the scene where he has the putative murderer approach his wife with a glass of milk that may contain poison. He was to play on audience memories when he cast Cary Grant in *Notorious* as the strange FBI agent who arranges that Alicia, whom he loves, should become the lover and then wife of a Nazi spy in Rio.

The beautiful Alicia (Ingrid Bergman) is seen very much through the eyes of Hitchcock/Devlin (Cary Grant): a slandered figure implicitly accused of being Nazi-tainted, promiscuous and an alcoholic. When the Nazis begin to poison her with arsenic, Devlin thinks that she

Alfred Hitchcock: *Notorious*. Cary Grant, Ingrid Bergman.

has taken to drink once more and excuses himself from further action. But if Alicia is perceived with all the confusions of a jealous mind, then the same is true of Devlin. He first meets her on the evening after her father, a Nazi spy, has died in gaol. She is drunk and spending the evening with some friends, and the filming tries to imitate her state of mind: figures swim in and out of the frame and camera angles are tilted. The spectator sees Devlin as no more than a shadowy silhouette, potentially either a persecutor or protector.

However distrustful this relationship may be, it looks relatively straightforward when compared to Alicia's marriage to the Nazi agent (Claude Rains). Alicia lives out her Electra complex by marrying this older man, one of her father's peers, and by displacing his possessive mother. At the same time, her husband and Devlin are jealous of each other; while Alicia's mother-in-law takes pleasure in slowly poisoning her. Hitchcock succeeds in persuading his audience to accept this far-fetched tangle of jealous intentions, in part because the mood he creates, of self-disgust and degradation, was so true to the moment. 'Life is dirty,' says the revue artist in *Rome, Open City* who betrays her lover to the Gestapo, and this sense of dirtiness is the implied theme of *Notorious*, however glossy its presentation. One incident illustrates Hitchcock's feeling for the moment. Over a year before the first atom bomb was dropped on Japan, he had decided that his MacGuffin, the mysterious substance contained in the wine bottles of the Nazi agent's cellar, should be something potentially far more destructive than any poison: uranium.

Father-figures and lovers who turned out to be Nazis had become staple characters in American films. Hitler might have risen from the dead. Hollywood had little to offer in the way of hope or belief at this time; no wonder the Thomas committee was able to have its own way so easily. In *Gilda* (1946), Mundsen, a Nazi with plans for world conquest, resembles Rick in *Casablanca* in the sense that he runs a casino in outlandish Buenos Aires. But the spirit of this film is far from the spirit of *Casablanca*. Mundsen employs Johnny, then discards him for Gilda (Rita Hayworth). Johnny drifts back into their lives and manages to torment them both: manoeuvres that recall the behaviour of the three principal characters in *Notorious*, though motives are now openly sado-masochistic. But while *Gilda* is compellingly unpleasant, the travesty of forties' themes and genres through repetition was more often to lead to absurdity. In *The Unsuspected* (1947) Michael Curtiz develops the extravagances of *Mildred Pierce* to the point where they lose all conviction, reaching an extreme of forties' expressionism in his use of velvety shadows and distorted images. And forties' romance was to come even closer to self-parody in Jean Negulesco's *Humoresque* (1947).

Its absurdities are such that it is hard to believe that its screen-writer Clifford Odets and its leading actor John Garfield had been members of the socially conscious New York Group Theatre of the 1930s, although the character played by Garfield has a fleeting resemblance to the hero of Odets's play *Golden Boy*. Paul is a violinist, a self-confessed genius, whose career is promoted by a society hostess in exchange for his sexual favours. If Odets intended his subject to be a satire on success, Negulesco certainly conceals any tendency to irony. He assumes that the spectator will have the thick-skinned sensibility of the audiences who applaud Paul's sickly playing of the *Liebestod* from *Tristan and Isolde* and declines to see the hostess as a comic figure. Joan Crawford, anyway, swamps the character in self-pity and presents her as a kind of intellectual. 'Martinis', says the hostess in a typical quip, 'are an acquired taste, like Ravel.' Everyone conspires to present her as a great lady and, in the final sequence, in which she walks out into the sea to the sound of a radio blaring out Paul's *Liebestod*, as a great lady of tragic dimension.

If Hollywood is to be believed, Malibu beach was strewn with the corpses of celebrities who had drowned themselves. George Cukor's

Malibu beach, in George Cukor's *A Star is Born*. James Mason.

version of the Dorothy Parker and Alan Campbell screenplay for *A Star is Born* (1954) is so hysterical that the spectator feels as confined as Judy Garland's Vicki, born in a trunk, or James Mason's Norman, who drowns himself. Judy Garland's evangelical singing is matched by Cukor's heightened expression, with its audience-enveloping camerawork and effulgent colour sense. It is interesting that William Wellman's 1937 version of this screenplay had distanced itself from the self-dramatizations of Hollywood, giving the impression of being an anthropological report on an alien culture. Wellman and Parker had provided a *New Yorker* view of Hollywood. Cukor communicates the film community's fascination with itself. Neither version is better than the other; both are complete in themselves.

Clearly the veer towards self-abandonment, towards drugged states of mind, towards inundation was irresistible in post-war Hollywood. Trying to repeat the success of *Gone with the Wind*, David O. Selznick re-used many of its ingredients in *Duel in the Sun* (1946). But somehow the recipe had got muddled and the result was hallucinatory. Character gave way to phantasmal caricature and emotionality to the rhetoric of lust. The endurance of Scarlett in the face of catastrophe was reduced to the degradations of Jennifer Jones's Pearl Chavez. *Gone with the Wind* had had sufficient pathos to be accepted by some as a tragedy. *Duel in the Sun* was not even *grand guignol*; it was *sui generis*, a Disneyland paean to tumescence.

Hollywood film-makers had great difficulty in accommodating themselves to the disturbing re-interpretation of personality induced by war. Hitchcock was to commission Salvador Dali to design the dream sequences in *Spellbound* (1945), but no one could take surrealism as more than a temporary amusement, while the expressionist techniques derived from the German cinema, though often used, tended to look either strident or mannered. The limitations of naturalism were also to be striking. In Edward Dmytryk's *Crossfire* (1947), a soldier (Robert Ryan), who is unable to tolerate the sadistic inclinations released in him by war, projects this badness wildly onto Jews. Instead of encouraging an understanding of the soldier's mind, Dmytryk merely imitates its content. In much the same way as the soldier uses Jews as scapegoats, so Dmytryk has the soldier become an object of hatred, 'the anti-semite'. (In Richard Brooks's novel *The Brick Foxhole*, the murder victim had been a different object of popular contempt, 'the homosexual'.) The view of society in *Crossfire* is wholly in the service of fantasy, in the sense that it invites the audience to identify with a police investigator who tracks down the soldier mercilessly.

Although Wyler had arrived at a way of filming a society that was both realistic and yet could incorporate the jealous fantasies of a betrayed husband (in *The Best Years of Our Lives*), he could only achieve this incorporation at the cost of suggesting rather than revealing the intrinsic meaning of these fantasies. In contrast, *The Blue Dahlia* (1946) was to present an identical situation as a vortex of terror dissociated from any sense of community. It seemed impossible to reconcile the need to report accurately on the condition of society with the need to describe the more mature post-war conception of human personality. Howard Hawks was to be far more explicit than Wyler about the fantastic basis of aggression in his treatment of Raymond Chandler's novel *The Big Sleep* (1946), but he was only able to be so by divorcing his story from any verifiable social context or coherent view of character. As in *Scarface*, his actors—Humphrey Bogart and Lauren Bacall especially—had to work with roles that were little more than bizarre impulses in the Chandler imagination. A new kind of film-making was coming into being in which, to paraphrase Hugo Münsterberg, the outer world would be woven into the mind and shaped by acts of attention. But Hollywood at this time was only capable of approximating to it. If *Laura* (1944) for instance, partly directed by Rouben Mamoulian, partly by Otto Preminger, was saved from vapidity, it was saved by the presence of Gene Tierney in the title role and by the half-recognition that its action reflects the thoughts of jealously possessive Waldo (Clifton

Webb), an idea brought out to brilliant effect by showing his apartment to be almost identical to Laura's.

On the whole, Hollywood preferred to describe jealousy behaviouris-tically and within naturalistic terms. Joseph L. Mankiewicz presents jealousy with evasive skill as a motiveless malignancy in *A Letter to Three Wives* (1949), where the jealous letter-writer is never shown, and also in *All About Eve* (1950), where Anne Baxter plays a jealously ambitious actress in an impassive fashion. But for all their wit, both these films remain on the level of sophisticated prattle and rather lamely justify their shallowness by claiming that all women are, of their nature, dangerously enigmatic. Mankiewicz was later to turn his hand to Cleopatra.

Hollywood may have been unnerved by the Cold War, but it was to be overwhelmed and eventually ruined by a number of more immediate difficulties. The most urgent of these problems was also one of the easiest to solve: the need to recapture European markets. Fortunately for the film industry, the US State Department, acknowledging the propaganda value of Hollywood movies, put pressure on the bankrupt nations of Europe to exhibit these movies as part of a package deal which included trade and cash concessions. Léon Blum weakly de-fended the Blum-Byrnes agreement of 1946, one section of which stipulated that seventy per cent of French screen-time should be devoted to American films, by arguing that the Italians had negotiated a far worse settlement. The French film industry once more seemed on the point of collapse, studios closed, and unemployment rose to seventy-five per cent, among the unemployed being Bresson, Becker, Grémillon, Autant-Lara and Carné.

The State Department also put pressure on the Rank empire in the United Kingdom. The Labour government, elected in 1945, had been unsure whether to nationalize the film industry, and in June 1949 the London correspondent of the *International Motion Picture Almanac*, writing for the American reader, blamed the President of the Board of Trade for the precarious state of British films. 'Industrious academic theoretician Harold Wilson has been subjected to a remarkable barrage of acid criticism throughout the year, with the accusation being made that it is he who was the sole architect of the industry's current des-pair.' But American resentment at Harold Wilson was in part directed at Wilson's success in managing to stave off the American incursion by three measures: he had imposed a forty per cent quota, he had founded the National Film Finance Corporation to subsidize British productions and he had implemented a scheme devised by Wilfred Eady, a civil servant, by which films made in the United Kingdom received a cut from box-office takings (levied by H.M. Customs and Excise) in direct proportion to their earnings in Great Britain: a scheme which, although it supported the commercially successful film, hardly encouraged the 'quality' film.

Hollywood was to find one of these measures an incentive. Since the days of MGM's administrative fiasco over *Ben Hur*, the studios had avoided sending film units abroad. The attractions of easy money, combined with the lower cost of living in Europe and the prospect of unfreezing blocked American currency, induced them to set up bases abroad, at first in the United Kingdom and Italy and then in Spain. The British film industry, however, was to receive only a short-term advantage from American investment, and the slump of the late sixties was to be aggravated when American companies left the country.

Apart from its tough post-war struggle for foreign markets, Hollywood had to face other difficulties. In 1947, after nine years of litigation, the US government found itself legally able to break the monopolistic position of the major studios and by 1950 had forced most of them to separate their means of production from their means of exhibition and to stop the practices of price-fixing and block-booking. It was to be a setback: but the studios were to be even more alarmed by another development. As early as 1928, men as dissimilar as Adolph Zukor and Léon Moussinac had predicted the catastrophic effect television would have on the other media; and although less prescient studio executives were to shrug off the threat in 1946, a boom year at the box-office, all of them were to be in a state of panic by 1949, which was known as 'the year of the television jitters'.

By 1949 forty per cent of the American population was able to watch television. The revenue of the TV companies was to increase dramatically: the earnings for 1951 being double those of 1950 and seven times as much as those for 1949. Cinema receipts, in the meanwhile, moved in the contrary direction: the $1,512m takings of 1946 giving way to $1,247m in 1950, then $1,134m in 1952—and the steep decline continued. Exhibitors used all sorts of means to win back audiences. One of them, the Drive-In theatre, was to be popular, but not popular enough to halt the decline. Then the studios had the bright idea of competing with television in areas where television could not compete: by enlarging the size of the screen, by introducing stereoscopic devices and by improving colour processes. Fortunately, the technical problems raised by these developments—primarily, different kinds of projector and camera lenses—had been for the most part solved, some of them as far back as in the 1920s. Cinerama opened on Broadway in 1952. It brought in huge crowds, but was too expensive to set up to be more than a big-city attraction. 3D enjoyed a temporary fashion—and Warner Brothers' *House of Wax* (1953), with its burning dummies seeming to liquefy onto the spectator's lap, was thought pleasurably disquieting—but the public found the need to wear 3D spectacles tiresome and the novelty soon faded.

Potentially the most promising of these developments was to be Twentieth Century-Fox's CinemaScope, which opened the way to many 'Scope imitations. Discovering a formula for commercial success with its carefully prepared CinemaScope epic, *The Robe* (1953), Fox began the age of blockbuster presentations. But the days of Hollywood as an industry were numbered. The market no longer needed a steady day-to-day factory output. The tempo of production had changed. Independent companies would sometimes take up to five years or more on their films. The major companies diversified into other commodities. It was as though the daily press had given up journalism for the occasional three-decker novel. Television now provided the journalism and the soap operas, and soon many of the Hollywood film lots had been turned over to the makers of TV series.

If Hollywood had responded to the shock of war by retreating into Cold War attitudes, film-makers elsewhere were to come closer to the processes of mourning. Hollywood had seen the war primarily in terms of the separation of men and women. European directors, and Italian directors in particular, were to see it primarily in terms of the damage it had done to children.

In an essay on Donskoi's *My Childhood*, the psychiatrist Erik H. Erikson has suggested some of the ways in which the film has the young Maxim discover his adult self, and the meaning of his Russian heritage, through his various identifications. Many of Erikson's arguments could be applied to 1930s films from other countries. The boys in *Zéro de conduite* try optimistically to free themselves from tyranny: and even in the morally severe Warner Brothers gangster films childhood was presented as a time of release. The Depression had forced people to take on responsibility for themselves: a situation dramatized in King Vidor's *The Champ* (1931), where the natural parent and child relationship is inverted as a small boy bolsters the courage of his alcoholic boxer father and brings him back to the ring. Child stars of the thirties, such as Temple, Bartholomew, Rooney and Garland, were admired for their precocity and often behaved, to the point of caricature, like adults. The brassiness of Shirley Temple, most popular of these stars, gave her the apparent autonomy of a Mae West or W. C. Fields.

But these attitudes to childhood had changed by the time Vittorio de Sica and the writer Cesare Zavattini came to work on their first film together, *The Children are Watching Us* (1942). De Sica and Zavattini saw the child as a focus for a kind of consciousness that epitomized the intentions of neo-realism. Through the child's sense of time—lingering, intense and consecutive—they came to realize how film needed narrative structures that did not rely on the model of stage drama. In the child's spontaneity and freshness they recognized modes of behaviour that showed up by contrast the contrivance

Vittorio de Sica: *The Children are Watching Us.*

of the professional actor, much as a child's candour can expose the vanities of adults. They believed that the theme of a child victimized by adults could stand as a criticism of adult society in general. The more passive and vulnerable a child was thought to be, the more likely was it to stir feelings of guilt in the spectator.

Such a strategy was soon subjected to diminishing returns. It was a form of moral blackmail. Like those public charities which justify themselves on the pretext that social injustice is part of an unchangeable human condition, it based its claims on a questionable ideology. In *Bicycle Thieves* (1948), for example, de Sica and Zavattini

Vittorio de Sica: *Bicycle Thieves.*

draw some unexpected deductions from a workman's failure to put a lock on his bicycle. The workman tries to steal someone else's bicycle after a prolonged search for his stolen one, and, when caught, has to suffer the ignominy of a rebuke delivered before his young son. De Sica allows for all sorts of inferences in his treatment of this theme: to see it as a commentary on the high level of unemployment in Italy at this time (twenty-two per cent of the work force) or as a parable on the innate corruption of mankind—in the final sequence the boy gives his hand to his father, as though they were Adam and Eve leaving the Garden of Eden. What de Sica avoids suggesting, though, is that the father was a fool to leave his bicycle unlocked at a time when thieving was a national occupation in Italy. He does his best to block this thought by showing the father to be as passive and unworldly as a child and therefore someone to be patronized.

Through his portrait of Peachum in *The Threepenny Opera*, Brecht had implied that all claims to charity are a form of licensed thievery. He had recognized how in an unjust society the exploited can exploit the exploiters in a way that traps everyone into some form of guile. De Sica and Zavattini are not willing to accept responsibility for this conception of society. They reduce everyone to a childlike state, as though everyone were a child in the sight of God. Their childlike perception of the minutiae of daily life tends to be passive, for all its delicate precision. They cling to the surface of things, and in their clinging assume a perpetual complaint. Brecht had understood that once adults slip back into childlike states of mind and displace responsibility for the community elsewhere, they prefer to complain rather than take action when the community fails to satisfy their needs; and since these needs are seldom satisfied, they tend to imagine that their lives are ordained by some malignant power.

For de Sica and Zavattini, this fantasy took the form of believing, as St Augustine had done, that mankind is innately wicked, though they did not follow St Augustine's inference that the only way this wickedness can be curbed is through the strict exercise of authority: an argument that might have led them back to the political position they most wanted to combat.

For although Mussolini's Fascism had been ostensibly destroyed, its influence persisted everywhere in post-war Italy. The better neo-realist films tended to include many of the confusions and hesitations of this new-born society: its superstitions, both pagan and Christian, its vaguely Marxist yearnings and its hunger for dependence (in part assuaged by the United States). The enthusiasm stirred by these films throughout the world also reveals how far they embodied an ideology of more than national interest. They embodied, in fact, a naturalism based on conservative assumptions that both placated and reassured the despairing public of the Cold War years. Audiences in nearly every country appear to have been moved by their evocation of childhood fragility, and to have taken comfort in their denial of the potential in every human being.

The burden of post-war guilt must have been overwhelming. In some countries the denial of this guilt took the form of a manic materialism, as in the 'economic miracles' of Germany, Japan and indeed Italy. In other countries it emerged as a weariness of mood in which Augustinian beliefs had some appeal. The Augustinian—and adroit— screenplays written by Graham Greene for *The Fallen Idol* (1948), which is concerned with the irreparable corruption of a child, or *The Third Man* (1949), which is concerned with the murder of children, illustrate vividly some of the ways in which compassion and self-pity could be confused. In *The Third Man*, Harry Lime's girl friend tries to justify his appalling crimes by saying, 'He never grew up. The world grew up around him, that's all—and buried him': an understanding of gangster behaviour that Wellman and Cagney would have found incomprehensible.

The idea that society had somehow conspired to destroy children was to be extended to take in the idea that it had conspired against all adolescents—as in Nicholas Ray's *They Live by Night* (1948)—and then to be extended to take in everyone, as though implying that the universe were geared to crush the child in every adult: the death of Maciek in *Ashes and Diamonds*, of Michel in *A Bout de souffle* and of Accattone in *Accattone*, the end of the carnival in *I vitelloni* or the final defeat of the clerk in Olmi's *Il posto* depend for their meaning on this postulate. Self-pity was the keynote to the late forties and 1950s and the main characteristic of the younger stars. If Marlon Brando, James Dean and Marilyn Monroe had anything in common, it was a wish to solicit pity from their audiences. They caressed objects, or themselves, in a manner that implied a loveless childhood; they were soft; and they enacted the idea, popular in the fifties, that parents were usually to blame for their children's problems, an idea that would have sounded strange to the young stars of the 1930s. Tracy, Cagney, Gable or Hepburn never behaved as though the world owed them a living.

The Children are Watching Us initiates this process of blame. Yet it is extremely moving as a description of how young Prico becomes a victim of his parents' passions. Shortly before committing suicide, Prico's father interrogates him with brutal desperation about his mother's affair with a cruel and negligent lover. By the end of the film the child has been confined to an ecclesiastical boarding-school; he is dwarfed by its austere surroundings, and he wears a uniform. As his cold mother leaves him after a short visit, he fails to respond to her embrace. It seems likely that he will continue to remain among priests.

Although mother-love can be a mawkish theme in the Italian cinema, especially when the mother-lover is middle-aged, de Sica avoids sentimentalizing this theme by his awareness that Prico is engaged in a far from pretty conflict. Accidentally on purpose, the boy knocks a flower-pot off a balcony onto a pair of lovers seated below; and going through a breakdown on a train journey, he imagines that he sees his disturbed thoughts reflected on the carriage window. His memory of a Punch and Judy show, before which other children had cried, reflects his desire to take revenge on his parents. He would seem to identify with his mother's cruel lover and in a sense, and in spite of his passivity, he lives out his wishes. What is uncertain, though, is the extent to which de Sica and Zavattini see the end of the film as a defeat, the extent to which they admire or distrust the priesthood.

But then they present an ambivalent response to authority in general, in much the same way as Fellini was later to do. Prico's response to authority often verges on the naughtily cruel, as in his view of an imperious grandmother carried about in a chair, or of a plump aunt struggling to get into her corset; a cinematic way of looking at others, part mischievous, part awed, that originates with Chaplin and Stroheim. De Sica and Zavattini—and indeed Fellini—are poets who both celebrate and criticize the gentility of the Italian lower middle-classes. They draw a good deal of fun out of their picture of the seedy, pretentious conjuror Professor Gabrieli, who is angered by Prico's sharp-eyed awareness of how he carries out his tricks, or the prim miss who dives with fastidious disgust into the sea when told that a boring acquaintance has arrived. Above all, they are poets who celebrate the quiet, forgotten lives of seamstresses and maids. They were among the first to recognize a theme that later film-makers were to find important: the loneliness of suburban domesticity. In *Umberto D* (1951) the camera idly watches, like a small boy, the unexplained routines of a maid, as though the whole world depended on her every movement. Indeed, the central feeling in their early cycle of films, extending from *The Children are Watching Us* through *Shoeshine* (1946), *Bicycle Thieves* (1948), *Miracolo a Milano* (1950) to *Umberto D.* is the pessimistic one of someone hungering for love in a loveless world.

But the rhetorical form which their pathos often takes threatens to stifle feeling. De Sica had been a *jeune premier* in the theatre and cinema of the 1930s; he had known how to ingratiate himself with audiences all too well, and his overcalculation of audience response in his first film as a director soon makes it clear that his 'realism', for all its location shooting and non-professional actors, is derived from the music-hall coquetry of Chaplin—as in the typical scene

Vittorio de Sica: *Umberto D.*

where Umberto D holds out the palm of his hand to beg and then, as a friend passes by, proudly turns his hand over and looks up at the sky as though expecting rain. Childlike, he is also clownlike: it is a strategy that Chaplin had often followed.

Yet in all fairness to him, Chaplin had acknowledged the war by bringing together the tramp and the mass murderer: with Hitler and then, in 1947, with Landru. *Monsieur Verdoux* reflects the spirit of the Cold War in its denial of grief—callous in its misogyny and in the casual way that Verdoux announces the death of his crippled wife and child. Chaplin plays Verdoux's preparation for death as though it were a last performance and appears to assume that bravado might be a token of integrity. Some of the war criminals hanged after the Nuremberg trials reportedly behaved in the same way, though it is more likely that Chaplin's model was the disdainful guillotine-bound aristocrats of Griffith's *Orphans of the Storm*. As Chaplin sees him, Verdoux is an aristocrat who dies in complicity with the revolutionary desires of the proletariat.

Chaplin remains a clown in the face of death. In the same way, de Sica—and Frank Capra also—continued to think of themselves as entertainers as they moved from themes of some social urgency to fairy-tales where magic resolves any difficulty and conflicts were schematized. In de Sica's *Miracolo a Milano* and Capra's *It's a Wonderful Life* (1946) Paolo Stoppa and Lionel Barrymore respectively play financiers as though they were ogres and as though the structure of capitalism had become fixed at the time of the robber barons. Both these films cheat the spectator by bringing in a *deus ex machina*. They present their fantasies omnipotently, yet it seems improbable that de Sica and Capra believed in their miracles. Their fairy-stories present the adult world as though seen by a child; and again, it seems improbable that they could have believed any child would view the adult world so blandly.

Yet it was through the agency of children that at least one film-maker, René Clément in *Jeux interdits* (1952), was to delineate movingly the dissociations that can halt the processes of mourning. Clément had already come close to its subject in his tribute to the French railway-men who took part in the Resistance movement, *La Bataille du rail* (1944–6), in particular the sequence where he enacts the execution of a group of hostages. As the railwaymen are lined up against a wall, one of them looks up at a plume of black smoke rising from a factory chimney, and his glance seems to mingle fear, resignation and a touch of amazement. The death of these hostages conveys such a sense of waste that it appears to demand some sort of interpretation—to see the men as martyrs for their cause, perhaps—yet the structure of the se-quence is such that it only allows for the kind of meaning that post-war writers of the temperament of Albert Camus, say, would have allowed it: that death signifies the obliteration of all meaning.

Its force depends on serious considerations of this kind and not on the excitement sometimes associated with the theme of death, as in those films about collaborators in which the experience of dying is con-fused with pleasurable anxieties about torture. Clément was to touch on these pleasurable anxieties in *Les Maudits* (1947), but on the whole left them to his contemporary Henri-Georges Clouzot—who was to pro-mote them with relish in *Manon* (1949), *Le Salaire de la peur* (1953) and most grotesquely in *Les Diaboliques* (1955). Yet it may be wondered why Clément treats so much of the action in *La Bataille du rail* as though it were a boy's adventure story, with train wreckings that at moments take on the tone of farce: a question to which *Jeux interdits* suggests an answer. For, whether consciously or not, it has the same theme as its predecessor and yet inverts its meaning. While the railwaymen in *La Bataille du rail* behave like children when threatened by death, the children in *Jeux interdits*, under a similar

René Clement: *Jeux interdits.*

pressure, imitate the burial rites of adults without understanding their significance.

A five-year-old girl flees with her parents from the German invasion; a plane strafes the parents; and the girl, numbly failing to comprehend her parents' death, grieves over her dead dog. She meets an eleven-year-old peasant boy who encourages her to bury the dog according to Christian ritual and then brings her into his family. Fascinated by the idea of funerals, the children construct their own pet cemetery in a barn beneath the impassive stare of an owl whom the boy thinks a hundred years old. They steal crosses from a local graveyard and a crucifix from the church: acts that burlesque Christian ceremonies as well as admitting their therapeutic value. But for all its comedy, *Jeux interdits* in no way defends itself against the painful and irreparable damage of war. At its conclusion the girl is dispatched to a transit hall for displaced persons. Labelled yet lost, she whimpers the boy's name; like Prico, she is overwhelmed by feelings beyond her comprehension.

The blitzed cities of Europe were to be the most suitable backdrop for the theme of the traumatized child. *Jeux interdits* shows, however, that landscape could have the same function. It could be argued, indeed, that the wish for 'realism' in the cinema contained within it the fantasy of a flinty earth which nothing could restore: Rouquier's *Farrebique*, which revitalized the French documentary movement, is a study in rural poverty, while many Italian neo-realist directors were to

Georges Rouquier: *Farrebique.*

be preoccupied by the problems of agrarian reform. And the Hiroshima fear that mankind had exploited the earth to a point of exhaustion was gradually to be acknowledged, as in Fellini's depressed response to windswept and inarticulate mountain communities.

Hollywood was to recognize this theme in a series of handsomely photographed films, though never with Fellini's melancholy. Jean Renoir's *The Southerner* (1945) is as much a wonderful tribute to the American cinema, to Ford's *The Grapes of Wrath* and to Griffith, as an account of a Texan farmer's struggle to render arid land fertile. *Johnny Belinda* (1948) also looked back to the mood of dust-bowl disaster movies, but played down tragic implications by having deaf-mute Belinda (Jane Wyman) learn how to speak and to protect her baby from a murderous father. On the whole, Hollywood preferred to forget about the dust-bowl, and it idealized nature to the point of over-ripeness. In *The Yearling* (1946) a veteran director, Clarence Brown, transformed a frontier community into a Garden of Eden as distanced and self-enclosed as the ararian idyll of *Tol'able David.* Archaic speech increased this sense of distancing. Brown involved the spectator whenever he touched on the relationship of the boy Jody (Claude Jarman Jnr) with a hunted bear and Flag, a

Robert Flaherty: *Louisiana Story*.

befriended fawn—the death of the fawn being the boy's first heartbreak. He was to employ the same actor and to apply the same sort of craft in *Intruder in the Dust* (1949), which also managed to look faintly unbelievable.

It was left to Robert J. Flaherty to take to an extreme this kind of silent film sensibility. Generously sponsored by the Standard Oil Company (NJ), *Louisiana Story* (1948) is constructed around an insignificant anecdote about a Cajun boy's meeting and friendship with a team of oil prospectors. Its interest lies mainly in its style. The camera glides across the Petit Ansse Bayou, catching the reflection of cypress-trees laden with trailing Spanish moss in such a way that they seem to float over the water. It attempts to identify with the boy's awe before a landscape that is exotic to the point of being unreal. Richard Leacock's camerawork, Virgil Thomson's sonorous music and Helen van Dongen's editing all contribute to this achievement, yet Flaherty was responsible for more than coordinating the talents of others. As in *Nanook*, he uses technology to vivify sensations that technology has dulled in most people; and no one has been able to convert the mechanical apparatus of the film-maker into a sensitive vehicle for intuition as well as he. His images take on sentience.

Sequences often consist of long-held shots, in which the eye can adjust itself to the need to look carefully and the mind remain undistracted by imposed explanations. Most of these sequences are like short films in themselves. In common with Clarence Brown, Flaherty

Robert Flaherty: *Louisiana Story.*

resorts to totemic relationships, though with the different purpose of connecting these short films. The boy attempts to steal some alligator eggs, and the roar of the disturbed alligator parent is exactly like the later sound of an uncontrolled fire at the oil-well. Flaherty films an oil-rig as though seen through the boy's animistic imagination so that it appears to be a kind of dragon. The absence of commentary helps to achieve this transformation and in other ways deepens mystery. For by never explaining why the boy should be canoeing through the Bayou, or what his motives might be, Flaherty is able to give his journey the incorporeity of dreams. At other moments, his reluctance to impart information leads to a certain blankness, as in the boy's friendship with the oilmen, all smiles and nods. Flaherty's technique was to be influential. Arne Sucksdorff was to work from it on *The Great Adventure* (1953) and *My Home is Copacabana* (1964), and Antonioni has been able to develop it to include areas of urban experience that Flaherty felt no sympathy for.

Flaherty seems to have escaped the mood of the Cold War — the Cajun boy is primarily a composite of Flaherty's own recollections of a childhood sense of wonder and adventure. At first sight, it may seem that Luis Buñuel, who had re-emerged on the international scene in 1950, also avoids the mood of the times. For although *Los Olvidados* deals with the subject of damaged children, it carefully avoids neo-realist pathos. Buñuel's career had suffered an eclipse after *Las Hurdes*. He had gone to the United States, worked as a sound-dubber in Hollywood, taken part in some anti-Nazi compilations and joined Warner Brothers as a producer. In 1947 Oscar Dancigers had invited him to Mexico on the understanding that if he made two commercially successful films he would be free to choose the subject·of his third one, which in the event turned out to be the award-winning *Los Olvidados* (1950).

Its form recalls certain dreams in which details appear clear to the point of over-significance and at the same time disconnected. It seems to be both purposeful and incoherent, without a theme, without a central character and without a central set of relationships. Gabriel Figueroa's sober photography imposes some consistency on the images; yet Buñuel's style, which moves from the naturalism of its opening sequences to a stress on incongruities and repetitions that occur without apparent reason, almost wilfully disrupts Figueroa's consistency (or so it seems). As with a dream, it is necessary to extra-polate an interpretation to uncover the underlying form of the film; once this key has been found, however, it is possible to relate the various details to each other.

Buñuel sets his opening scenes in a market-place on the outskirts of Mexico City and films them in a neo-realist manner, alluding specifically to *Shoeshine*. It is a deceptive opening. Buñuel has said: 'Neo-realist reality is incomplete, official and altogether reasonable; but the poetry, the mystery, everything which completes and enlarges tangible reality is completely missing.'[2] He soon begins to establish an image in the mind of the spectator that is far from the concerns of neo-realism. Seeming to see the market-place as resembling Langland's field of folk, a medieval representation of all life on earth, he mingles his characters and types without undue emphasis on any one of them and only gradually allows three boys to distinguish themselves from the rest of the crowd. He draws no moral contrast between these boys (though their intentions are very different) and he makes no judgements. Wide Eyes has been abandoned by his father—something that often happens, apparently, to children from poor Mexican families —and weeps as he waits for his father's return. Jaibo, an orphan and delinquent, plans to rob a blind beggar. Pedro exists in a moral zone between the two other boys. Kindly by nature, he befriends Wide Eyes; yet he is under Jaibo's sway and joins up with him to commit a murder.

All three boys have been abandoned by their fathers; and Buñuel's aim, it would seem, is to describe the conditions that obtain when

Luis Buñuel: *Los Olvidados.*

children are so abandoned. He shows them enter a state of disorder rather similar to the one described in *L'Age d'or*; but whereas in *L'Age d'or* his sympathies for anarchism, both as a form of politics and as a state of mind, had been explicit, his views had become far more complicated by the time he came to make *Los Olvidados*. Although attracted to disorder, irrationalities and assertions of personal freedom, his imagination also seems to yearn for an extreme authority – be it a stern father, a paternalist society or an Old Testament kind of God.

In this sense, he has the mind of a medieval heretic who presents himself under the contemporary guise of a surrealist. He is fascinated by medieval forms of hysteria: trances, fits and mystical therapies. He was to use the structure of a medieval *exemplum* in *Simon of the Desert* (1966) and of a medieval fable in *The Milky Way* (1969), which tells of two pilgrims who witness a succession of miracles. His distaste for naturalism and his almost clinical annotation of grotesqueries of every kind owe more to an important tradition in Spanish painting and literature than to surrealist doctrine.

Yet his interests are more than antiquarian; they carry a particular urgency in the post-war era, at a time when mankind has become as frightened at the prospect of nuclear war as once it had been of the plague, and when the promotion of apocalyptic and millenarian notions has once more become widespread. (He is not alone among film directors in drawing a parallel between our condition now and the decline of the Middle Ages.) He is a man living in the present-day world. His review of the archaic traces in the contemporary sensibility contains modern insights and a modern agnosticism. Many of the puzzles in his work evolve logically from a viewpoint which is both God-haunted and yet sceptical of God's existence, a religious metaphysic centring on a void.

In questioning the claims of authority, he questions his own right to make judgements. In collecting evidence of superstition, he reveals a collector's delight in the wide variety of the field for investigation. He is most reverent when exhibiting the socially profane. A Buñuel dream sequence, often hard to extricate from any other Buñuel sequence, cannot simply be interpreted in psychoanalytic terms, although his imagination often appears shaped by the pressures of jealousy. His style defies translation into the modern categories of knowledge. It describes the incongruous and unnatural with a matter-of-fact concreteness that a medieval scholar would find familiar. And it often raises dramatic effects by shifting ground unexpectedly, so that the spectator remains uncertain whether he is looking at medieval phenomena from within a modern framework or at modern phenomena from within a medieval framework.

If his films resist interpretation, they do so in part because he himself is sceptical about the claims made by his characters, especially those of them who lay claim to be authorities. His paternalists often turn out to be hypocrites or seducers or, like the priest in *Nazarin* (1959) and the uncle in *Viridiana* (1961), as much tormented by self-doubt and destructive feelings as anyone else. A number of them appear in *Los Olvidados*, the most prominent among them being the blind beggar, swathed in musical instruments, who adopts Wide Eyes. He seems at first a figure to be pitied. But he soon reveals himself to be a tyrant and eventually a monstrous commentator on the action when he screams from a rubbish heap that children should be killed before their birth. He may appear to represent Buñuel's outlook at this moment; yet it would be wrong to give him this kind of status, for the principal effect of Buñuel's narrative, as it moves swiftly from one viewpoint to another, is to minimize any notion of authority. There are many other pretenders to authority. Pedro meets two of them: an elderly pederast and the liberal director of a remand home, the liberal director doing more harm to him than the ineffectual pederast, in the sense that his policy of allowing delinquent boys freedom of choice leads indirectly to Pedro's death. Buñuel appears unable to involve himself in the director's liberalism, and the scenes at the remand home, which recall the ways Warner Brothers used to handle the theme of good citizenship in the thirties, are the weakest in the film.

Buñuel spends more time in considering Pedro than the other boys, entering his home and even his dreams, observing his mother and younger siblings, his death and the disposal of his corpse on a rubbish dump. But Pedro is too subservient to be the protagonist of the film, while Jaibo remains too distanced and unexplained to take on this role. For instance, Jaibo seduces Pedro's mother, but he never pretends to be a surrogate father. Perhaps Buñuel remains cryptic about him because to tell more would oblige him to make a judgement. Or perhaps he feels too identified with Jaibo's iconoclasm to see him clearly. He shows Jaibo frequently beating people with a stick, and these beatings take on the quality of a futile obsession.

From one point of view, the three boys would appear to be parts of the same person. They often seem to swap identity. Standing aside from the manifest content of the film for a moment, it is possible to infer that Pedro's dream about his mother is identical with Jaibo's intentions, in that both boys seem to share in the fantasy of wishing to rob mothers and mutilate fathers. But Buñuel himself resists this kind of summary and indeed to explicate the story in this sort of way is to risk damaging its texture of feeling.

Buñuel refers to the principal images of Pedro's dream throughout the story and in such a way that they would appear irreducible to rational explanation. The abrupt inconsequence he allows to certain acts, as when the blind beggar tries to cure a sick woman by rubbing a dove along her back or when Jaibo kicks a legless and armless man out of his cart, blocks any wish on the part of the spectator to relate them to some authoritative director's view of the plot. He teases his audience by stirring up its desire for coherence without satisfying this desire; he raises repetitions and contrasts that hint at some pattern, though this pattern never emerges. Yet his enterprise is not self-destructive. He allows the spectator to recognize that each event may have its own dignity while remaining independent of any context, that each event can be its own autonomous ceremony. In denying authority to himself, Buñuel undermines the authority of the critic in every member of his audience. He trades in mysteries; and the value of these mysteries is commensurate with the extent to which they stay in the spectator's memory.

The same is true of Robert Bresson. In common with Flaherty, Buñuel (and Dreyer), Bresson has returned to a silent film aesthetic that emphasizes both the self-sufficiency of the image and the implied doctrine that only through editing should the image be brought to life. It is interesting that this return to an abandoned aesthetic should have entailed a return to a view held by many critics at the end of the twenties: that the art of film is in some way analogous to theology. But while Buñuel proposes a metaphysical awareness in which the presence of God is most painfully felt through His absence, Bresson proposes a metaphysical awareness that asserts the existence of God, and yet qualifies this assertion by showing how His influence on the world is imponderable.

His belief that young people of a certain spiritual intensity can bear witness to the metaphysical perplexities of existence was first to be dramatized in *Le Journal d'un curé de campagne* (1950). He has since claimed that he lacked sympathy with the ideology of the Georges Bernanos novel on which the film was based and now feels distaste at its view that piety may be reinforced by a denial of the physical world, a rejection so extreme that it can include the loss of good health.

Yet in his stubborn behaviour, slyness and isolation, the curé is truly a Bressonian hero. He makes concessions to no one; and in this he is like Bresson himself, whose choice of unemphatic images that take on energy through their interaction, whose ellipses in thought and whose refusal to ingratiate himself with the spectator, are perhaps most fully realized in *Un Condamné à mort s'est échappé* (1956). Basing its action on André Devigny's actual escape from German internment in 1943, Bresson conceives of his subject on two levels, neither of which resembles reportage. On one level, he describes with an almost obsessive care for detail the routines of prison and the physical preparation for escape. His stylistic concern to achieve the maximum tension with the minimum of elaboration is echoed in the economy with which the condemned man effects his escape. On the other level, Bresson reads into the escape an allegory of chance and purpose, intimated in his epigraph 'The wind bloweth where it listeth', by showing how the success and failure of various attempts at escape largely depend on coincidence. The argument he proposes is of a kind intended to remind the spectator of the mystery inherent in human

'Predestined to escape . . .' Robert Bresson: *Un Condamné à mort s'est échappé.*

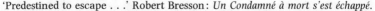

existence; at the same time it does imply the paradoxical conclusion that the workings of chance are so omnipresent that they may be fairly taken as evidence of some supernatural purpose or fate. Retrospectively, it may be concluded that the condemned man was as predestined to escape as his fellow prisoners were predestined to fail: a shocking line of thought that Bresson was to move away from after the making of *Pickpocket* (1959). In his later work, *Mouchette* (1967), *Une Femme douce* (1969) and *Quatre Nuits d'un rêveur* (1971), he has on the whole given up any allegorical reference. He has not only become less severe in his attitudes to his young central characters but also allowed them to be less severe in their relationships to others. He has even begun to forgive them their pleasure in youth and the senses.

No one could be further in taste from the exacting Bresson than Max Ophüls; indeed, these two directors might be temperamentally the opposite of each other, even though both of them related their work consciously to an age of austerity and international tension. After directing *Liebelei*, Ophüls had taken on various engagements in France and Switzerland—none of his films during this time being especially distinguished—and then in 1941 emigrated to the United States. Like Buñuel, he was to have a hard time in Hollywood. Yet *Letter from an Unknown Woman*, which was released in 1948 with little publicity, reveals the assurance of a practised master, remarkable in that Ophüls was able to summon up a convincing fin-de-siècle Vienna in a Hollywood studio and by style alone partially to conceal the flaws in his plot (drawn from a story by Stefan Zweig).

As a child, the unknown woman had become infatuated with a concert pianist—and to such an extent that she is willing in later years to leave her husband and child to join him at a moment's notice. But while she is fixated on this one man, whom she has seldom seen and scarcely spoken to, he by contrast happens to be so promiscuous in his affections that he finds it impossible to remember that he had once been the lover of the unknown woman. Ophüls not only converts this absurd situation into a bitter-sweet comedy about the random nature of desire but also manages to conceal the implicit snobbery of the whole enterprise. For the only difference in content between the unknown woman's passion and any bobbysoxer infatuation is that she falls in love with a concert pianist and therefore is a creature set apart in sensibility. Audiences were encouraged to infer that this idea of superiority, represented as much by the Vienna of Ophüls's imagination as by her choice of lover, had brought prestige to a trite theme.

Yet Ophüls was to keep to novelettish subjects for the rest of his career. Perhaps he wanted to, in much the same way as certain French directors of the twenties had wanted to work from *feuilleton* stories. He seems to have been aware in *Caught* (1949), *La Ronde* (1950), *Le Plaisir* (1952), *Madame de . . .* (1953) and *Lola Montès* (1955) that his talent lay in discovering the nuance that can transform banalities into insight, either by drawing out unexpected qualities in his actors, by identification with the sensitivity of his heroines or by the incantatory effect of his extended camera movements. Yet his displays of sensibility can be sometimes self-absorbed to the point of being precious and sometimes (in contrast to *Liebelei*) touched by vulgarity. He no longer seems quite to have believed in the romance of Old Vienna; it had become a trade mark by which he was known in Hollywood and the studios of Europe. By nature a ribald man (like Mizoguchi), his choice of themes might have become more true of him if he had lived on into a more permissive age.

While Ophüls elaborately tried to restore the past, Roberto Rossellini tried to awaken his audiences to the fragmented nature of the present — neither, in the process, discovering much in the way of a hopeful prospect. Rossellini, son of an architect responsible in some part for the planning and construction of modern Rome, had been attracted to film-making after his father's death and had entered the Fascist-controlled industry in the late thirties. Impressed by the ideas of Francesco de Robertis, a naval officer and writer who had promoted a documentary type of film using non-professional actors, he was to work with de Robertis on *La nave bianca* (1941), the first of three war films made in support of Mussolini's regime. (The other two were *Un pilota ritorna* and *L'uomo della croce*.)

La nave bianca takes place on a destroyer and hospital-ship (the white ship of the title), its theme being that the state protects its navy in any circumstances. With hindsight it is possible to describe this paternalism and its solemn and rather sad invocations to 'la patria' as Fascist; and yet with hindsight it would also have to be admitted that these concerns have continued to fascinate Rossellini in such avowedly anti-Fascist projects as his television documentaries, *La Prise du pouvoir de Louis XIV* (1966) and *Socrate* (1970). The destroyer scenes have some views of guns sweeping the horizon that recall *The Battleship Potemkin* and a visitor's enthusiasm for ships' machinery, yet Rossellini's sympathy for lower-deck sensitivities and elegiac mood (a mood which dampens aggression) recall the pre-Nazi submarine movie *Morgenrot*, which Hitler admired, and the Japanese war film *Five Scouts*. The hospital-ship scenes lower the temperature even further and include nurses, who do not so much act as a contrast to the destroyer scenes as add to the mood of passivity. Much of the story concerns itself with a young sailor's attempts to keep in touch with his girl friend, a little like the young welder in Olmi's *I fidanzati*. But while Italian directors of the sixties were to be exercised by the ways in which an industrial society could mutate feelings, Rossellini avoids this problem and allows his sailor to find comfort in convalescence. The final shot of the film is not of some gun or flag but of a Red Cross badge worn by a nurse. *La nave bianca* invites the spectator to accept the role of invalid and to abandon himself to benign authority; rather unusual as propaganda, it appeals for inertia.

To some extent, Rossellini also retreats from responsibility in *Rome, Open City* (1945), by idealizing the courage of a partisan leader and a priest and by over-dramatizing the hardships they have to face, as though he wished to show that ordinary people would find too great the need to resist the German forces of occupation and therefore would have every excuse to lie low. The hazardous manner in which Rossellini went about his filming—the Germans had only just retreated from the city—suggests that he himself was all too aware of the temptations of cowardice and was trying to evolve a form in which such a conflict could be enacted.

He intended his technique to be free enough to combine reportage with fiction. In fact the project began as two documentaries which Rossellini later dovetailed into a single plot: one is about Don Morosini, a priest and member of the Resistance who was shot by the Germans, the other about the Resistance activities of Roman children. Rossellini had trouble in finding a link for these documentaries, but it was to be the least of his worries. He had very little film stock. He could seldom afford to reshoot, and often his shots had to be kept brief in length. He could not avoid abrupt editing or photography of an uneven quality. By Hollywood standards, maybe, his technique is unprofessional. But he was not making a Hollywood film: and he was able to turn his limitations to an advantage. He does not try to lull his audience with narrative fluency, but uses rawness to simulate the immediacy of newsreel. At the same time, his style makes no claim to objectivity as the newsreel does. It has the tentative quality of certain thought. Like Vertov and Renoir before him, he came to discover that film-making, as it recorded events, could also record the mind's involvement in a subject—in this case, as it investigates the conditions of a city under occupation and tries to elucidate those factors in the past which determine the future. But above all, it could dramatize the state of mind of a timid man locked in the present with the things he most fears.

The intensity of experience that underlay this improvised search saves it from the charge of amateurism; for no amateur worth the name would submit himself to such risks. At its first showings, the immediacy of *Rome, Open City* was to have a great impact; later its idiosyncratic method was to count against Rossellini, and the public was to be as distrustful of him as it had been of Renoir in the thirties. Yet those aspects of his technique that most irritated the public were

to be those that most attracted young French directors and critics of
the late fifties. Truffaut, Godard and Rivette, among others, were to
subscribe to his belief in the feature film as an essay form, a highly
personal meditation in which fiction and reportage could be combined.
They were to imitate his abruptness of editing, although it was no
longer unavoidable, and they were to make a calculated use of the jump
cut. Jean Rouch and Louis Malle especially were to recognize how
some of his studies of alien cultures, such as *India* (1958), could
assist the anthropologist.

But *Rome, Open City* has none of the detachment of anthropology.
Rossellini's guilt, his terror, his involvement in immediacies blur

Roberto Rossellini: *Rome, Open City.*

his powers of observation. He confuses both the journalistic and
tragic possibilities of his theme. He fails to face up to the question of
Italian culpability in the German occupation, nor does he admit to his
own guilt. He denies self-disgust by displacing it onto the sexuality of
others and he denies self-hatred by displacing it onto the Germans.
For instance, he desexualizes the good characters, such as the housewife
Pina (Anna Magnani), the priest Don Pietro (Aldo Fabrizi) and the
Communist partisan leader (Marcello Pagliero) by seeing their motives
as purely religious or political, while he describes the motives of the
treacherous revue artist Marina, or of the Nazi major and Ingrid, his
accomplice, in terms of a perverse sexuality. It may be true that
collaborators and torturers are destructive in every area of life,
including the most personal, but Rossellini neither demonstrates this
theme nor gives it the attention it requires. By providing no effective
alternative to this implied omnipresence of sadism, he forces himself
into taking up an extremely pessimistic position.

The consequences of this pessimism are twofold. Throughout the film its good characters set their hopes on the future. 'We are fighting for something that must come,' says Francesco, a Communist printer, to his lover, the widow Pina, 'a better world for our children.' But the film fails to realize this idea. The Roman children caught up in the Resistance movement are only tenuously related to either the adults or the city, while Pina's feelings for her son, or Don Pietro's guardianship over the children in his parish, are not strong enough in themselves to counteract the prevailing mood of defeatism. Both Pina and Don Pietro are on their own; their goodness is desexualized and is based on a separation of men and women; and because Rossellini will not tolerate the idea of the family as the unit most capable of withstanding fear, he depletes his account of the ideas for which the partisans were fighting. Although the first reviewers of *Rome, Open City* were filled with admiration at its directness, many of them, even then, were conscious of how Rossellini had failed to discover positives of a kind that could offer an alternative to despair. James Agee doubted whether 'the basic and ultimate practising motives of institutional Christianity and leftism can be adequately represented by the most magnanimous individuals of each kind',[3] while the Italian critic, Franco Valorba, argued that 'both priest and communist use the same concept of liberty, patriotism and justice; each of them uses these concepts in a different way, yet each of them is unaware of the difference.'

A central impulse in neo-realist thought has been to find an ideology that would reconcile the conflict between Roman Catholicism and Marxism and thereby resolve the most serious ideological division in post-war Italy. It is interesting to observe, though, that the two most adventurous attempts by film-makers in the sixties to breach this gap, Olmi's *A Man Named John* and Pasolini's *The Gospel According to St Matthew*, depended for their effect on a separation of male and female. In the same way, Rossellini presents Don Pietro as a holy fool of God—a prototype for St Francis of Assisi in *St Francis, Fool of God*—a simplistic interpretation of the priest's character that solicits a passive, confiding response (rather as *La nave bianca* does). And even though Rossellini allows the partisan leader to be more virile than the priest, he would seem to find this virility intolerable and has to neutralize it. He has the partisan leader tortured in a sequence in which his mutilated body comes to resemble a baroque crucifix of Christ in His agony. The priest, who has to watch these acts of torture, is presented with a situation that would seem to mock his painful helplessness before the agony on the cross.

The second consequence of Rossellini's pessimism is that since he is unable to find an adequate challenge to the forces of sadism in himself, he finds himself more and more obliged to take up an identification with the torturers. Perhaps unintentionally, he modelled the structure of his torture sequences on an incident in Sardou's *Tosca*, in which the wicked Scarpia presses Tosca to tell him the hiding place of a wanted man by forcing her to listen to the screams of her lover as he is broken on the rack. For all his apparent sympathy with Tosca, Sardou invites the spectator to identify with Scarpia. The sadistic implications of this kind of plot device are even more plain in a Nazi movie, Veidt Harlan's anti-semitic *Jew Süss* (1940), in which the Jew tries to seduce an Aryan girl by having her listen to the screams of her tortured lover. The Jew is wicked because he behaves like a Nazi; but because he is a Jew, Nazi audiences were able to acknowledge this wickedness and so to assuage their guilt a little.

Although he was to try to bring together the motifs of traumatized child, the wish for patricide and the ruined city in *Germania, anno zero* (1947), Rossellini was unable to relate them to any central interest. His talent at this time was devoted to a lyrical, almost schizoid awareness of the fragmented nature of the momentary. Like most Italian directors, his work tends to veer between a certain grandeur of statement and a certain grandiosity. He nearly always achieves grandeur when dealing with abrupt crises, like the execution of Don Pietro in *Rome, Open City* and the shooting down of Pina in the streets (an event imitated and transposed into a mood of dry buffoonery by Jean-Luc Godard in the concluding sequence of *Les Carabiniers*), or, in *Paisà*, the brief shot of a child howling in the streets of a village where all the inhabitants have been hanged, and the scene in which the partisans are drowned one by one in the Po river. It is probable that Rossellini's fragmented awareness of immediate experience is bound up with icy thoughts of terror at the prospect of violent death.

Yet newsreels of the blitzed cities of Europe–of Warsaw, Coventry, Berlin–could melt the imagination. All attempts to achieve realism in the cinema had to be accommodated to this terrible evidence of mankind's capacity for aggression. Film-makers were only able to tolerate this realization in part, like everyone else, and a sense of humour was very much needed to combat a sense of despair. At the height of the London blitz Humphrey Jennings could note the amusing incongruity of a house severed by an explosion, one of its bedrooms hanging out over the street. It was observed that children thought ruins the playground of their dreams, although the dream could easily turn into nightmare if the child found itself lost in this never-ending landscape of rubble.

Such a thought underlies the Ealing comedy *Hue and Cry* (1946), directed by Charles Crichton with a screenplay by T. E. B. Clarke. Boys playing among the bomb-sites of Southwark, a London borough south

Charles Crichton: *Hue and Cry.*

of the Thames, find not only that their surroundings stimulate fantastic war games but that they also provide a setting in which anything might be possible. One of them thinks that he spots a connection between a serial in his favourite comic and various random events in the actual world and, in the manner of *Emil and the Detectives,* his hunch proves to be correct. But the fun of a chase soon sours when he discovers that he and his friends have become involved with a gang of black-marketeers.

The boys are Chaplinesque in their absurd willingness to take on a much stronger enemy. The Ealing comedies in general assumed the spirit of Chaplin, though with one important qualification: all of them diminished his sentimentality and ferocity by their sense of fair play. In a semi-imperial fashion, nearly all of them placed initiative in conflict with the deadening effects of a bureaucracy webbed in red tape. They appealed to a boyish *Gunga Din* sense of humour and adventure, and at the same time had the grace not to idealize the boyish. (A far from angelic choir of small boys with angelic faces singing 'Oh, for the Wings of a Dove' in *Hue and Cry* parodies one of the more unctuous moments in Jennings's *Diary for Timothy.*) But the pleasure taken by the

Ealing team in illegal enterprises did rest on the assumption that those involved in these enterprises were decent enough to know when to check the illegality of their actions, and it did also resort to a vagueness about which sorts of criminal behaviour it should approve of. The boys in *Hue and Cry* use the buildings and sewers of London with the insolence of a Harry Lime, yet when they come face to face with the black-marketeers they find themselves confronted by monsters. Ealing, it would seem, applied one rule of law to the sons, another to the fathers.

It was to remain fairly consistent in practising this ingenuous morality. But as the years passed, its techniques changed. Inventions became bolder, rivalling anything Hitchcock might have thought up in the thirties, as when in *The Lavender Hill Mob* (1951) the mob smuggle gold bullion out of the country in the form of souvenir Eiffel towers. Filming became more and more stylish, reaching perfection in Robert Hamer's *Kind Hearts and Coronets* (1949), a Wildean comedy with a Wildean wit in its editing. At the same time the satirical intention behind so much Ealing work (as in *The Foreman Went to France*) began to flag. It was not only a financial crisis that brought the Ealing comedies to an end in the mid-fifties; its belief in the capacity of gallant little amateurs to muddle through any difficulty was to seem painfully incompatible with the condition of England at this time.

The Ealing comedies were cosy; and *Hue and Cry*, for instance, no more than glimpses the spectres on the bomb-sites. But in *Germania, anno zero*, Rossellini not only has a scene in which a gramophone recording of a Hitler speech is played in the ruins of the Reichstag, but presses home this point by having a schoolmaster corrupt a boy with Nazi doctrines concerning the disposability of people. Young Edmund feels justified in taking the life of his sick father; he then commits suicide. It was as though Nosferatu were once more to stalk the streets of a shrouded Bremen. For obvious reasons, many films at this time included scenes set in the after-life, seances and the appearance of revenants, or dwelt on fantasies about labyrinthine cities controlled by some monster at their heart. David Lean was to use the idea of the revenant amusingly in *Blithe Spirit* (1945) and the idea of the haunted city in his fine Dickens adaptations *Great Expectations* (1946) and *Oliver Twist* (1948); while Carol Reed was to enter Dickensian territory in *Odd Man Out* (1946), where a wounded, hunted IRA gunman (James Mason) is involved in a series of encounters with various strangers, some of whom may be police informers. Reed captures the moods and atmospheres of these various meetings with economy, though his liking for tilted camera angles reaches a flurry of selfconsciousness in the concluding sequences, in which a mad artist preaches to the dying gunman.

He was to continue working with these expressionistic techniques in *The Third Man* (1949) and discovered a romantic enchantment in the ruins of a Vienna divided among the four major powers. His screenplay, by Graham Greene, has a writer of the Zane Grey type of novel enter into a situation more in keeping with a blitzed city; the writer finds himself caught up with a group of cultivated racketeers who trade in diluted penicillin and who seem to rise out of the ruins like phantoms. It is typical of Greene that the behaviour of his principal villain, Harry Lime (Orson Welles), should seem to parody Christ: Lime purportedly rises from the dead, is the third man seen walking beside his disciples and inverts Christ's intentions by being party to the death of children.

The flair and melancholy of this thriller owed almost as much to Alexander Korda and Orson Welles as to Carol Reed and Graham Greene. Yet its baroque elaboration must have appeared surprising to anyone who had lived in Vienna during the last months of the war. The theme of ghosts and guilts was too easily available; it denied emotional significance to devastation; indeed, it gained its energies from this denial. The nature of Welles's contribution is controversial. He and Joseph Cotten (as the writer) relive once more the self-pitying friendship of *Citizen Kane*, while at moments Carol Reed seems to be influenced by the detached bravura of the early Wellesian style. But then, rather like Hamlet, the Wellesian type of egotist is naturally drawn to ghosts.

The most distinctive exploitation of the ghosts lurking in the ruins was to be Jean Cocteau's *Orphée* (1949). Its central idea portrays the most flattering form of self-love: a poet who penetrates his own mirror reflection. Yet in spite of its chic metaphysics, Cocteau's retelling of the Orpheus and Eurydice legend—he had first cast it in the form of a play in 1925—has the ring of autobiographical truth. He conceives of the world of the living and the world of the dead as a contrast between a paranoid, existentialist-minded present and the recent wartime past. Death (Maria Casarès) rides by in a limousine flanked by outriders in black leather, who might be Wehrmacht bully-boys or predecessors of the Hell's Angels; her car radio emits surrealist bulletins that recall the seemingly nonsensical coded orders broadcast by the BBC to the French Resistance; the stern judges of the underworld are like members of the *Conseils d'Epuration* at the end of the war; while Cocteau's setting for the underworld, the awesome bombed military academy at St Cyr, has only been challenged as an imaginative choice of location by Orson Welles's use of the deserted Gare d'Orsay in *The Trial*. This conception would have been stillborn, however, without the performances of Maria Casarès as

Jean Cocteau: *Orphée*. Maria Casarès.

Death and François Périer as her chauffeur. Smartly dressed, a cigarette usually clenched between tight lips, sharply contemptuous of fools and, like certain members of the Resistance, willing to risk everything on her mission, Maria Casarès transforms a metaphysical stereotype into a passionate figure that might have emerged from a tragedy by Racine.

Enough of Cocteau's own experience enters into this treatment to give a certain urgency to his trick effects, which include reversed shots (so that a man seems to rise like a plank from the floor), back projections, in negative, of trees and blitzed houses, Méliès-like vanishings and the dissolving surface of a mirror created in a vat of mercury. But the presence of one traumatized child in this ruined landscape would have shattered Cocteau's *tour de force*: he imitates the tautness of neo-classical tragedy without ever achieving the tragic. In his yearning for classical order, he is completely Romantic.

The differences in intention between the Wellesian kind of cinema and the Italian neo-realists is not so great as it may appear to be at first sight. It could be argued, indeed, that many of the more complicated forms of narrative used in the sixties, which surely could be described as the age of Kane, evolved out of the seemingly passive impressionism of neo-realist doctrine. The anti-symbolist effects practised by Jancsó in his first features—rituals that have the effect of cancelling out the meaning of ritual—take the neo-realist wish to show things as they are to its logical conclusion. John Cassavetes' mannered improvisations owe as much to the neo-realist belief in spontaneity as to method acting, while the elaborate styles developed by Antonioni and Fellini began, as they have admitted, in neo-realism.

Cesare Zavattini, who wrote screenplays for Blasetti, de Santis, Emmer and Castellani as well as for de Sica, and never took on the role of director, was to be its most important theoretician. In his wartime diary *Sequences from a Cinematic Life*, Zavattini saw neo-realism as a reaction against propriety. During the Fascist period, he wrote: 'It was as if, by law, we had to wear a papier-mâché nose.' He wanted in contrast candour, spontaneity, directness. 'Set up a camera in the street, in a room, see with insatiable patience, train ourselves in the contemplation of our fellow man in his elementary actions . . . The wonder must be in us, expressing itself without wonder: the best dreams are those outside the mist, which can be seen like the veins of leaves.' [4]

Yet in suggesting directions that would lead away from the drama-derived conventions of the well-made film, Zavattini saddled the film director with problems of selfconsciousness already familiar to the novelist. For in trying to 'see with insatiable patience' things as they are, the neo-realists were obliged to become amateur epistemologists and to wonder how far the mind's capacity for interpreting the present was conditioned by its own past experiences. To understand the present it was necessary to recognize how observation depends on memory. To understand the past, as it exists outside memory, it was necessary to reconstruct the available evidence as history.

Although the part played by memory in observation had been more intimated than explored by the film-makers of the forties, Alain Resnais had already begun to experiment—in such documentaries as *Van Gogh* (1948) and *Guernica* (1950)—with the tensions that an editor can obtain when he places images of the past against images of the present, or photographs of paintings against photographs of the places and objects that the painter had used as his motifs. Resnais had worked as an editor for Nicole Védrès on her compilation *Paris 1900* (1947), and nearly all of his documentaries and a number of his feature films contain an implied auto-criticism of the art of compilation. Perhaps the most important question they raise concerns the reliability of the media—especially the value of newsreel as history—in analysing any problem of time and memory.

It is relevant to these interests that his subject in *Nuit et brouillard* (1955) and his first feature *Hiroshima mon amour* (1959) is neither the Nazi concentration camps nor the nuclear destruction of Hiroshima, though these traumas of the Cold War play a large part

Alain Resnais: *Nuit et brouillard.*

in their content; his subject is the mind's struggle to accommodate
itself to these intolerable events. He compiled *Nuit et brouillard* out of
meditative sequences in Eastmancolor shot at Auschwitz ten years after
the war had ended and cut still photographs and newsreel shots of the
camp at the time when it was still in operation into these sequences. He
tries to show how an interaction of the present and past can modify
their separate meanings. In the present-day sequences the camera seems
to transform rusty barbed wire and decaying huts into sculpture as it
glides past them. A nondescript place assumes beauty of a kind that at
one moment recalls one of Van Gogh's paintings, as crows rise from a
cornfield. And by relating the newsreel shots and photographs of the
camp as it actually was to this landscape, he purges these images of the
terror they have acquired in the minds of many who have seen them.
He brings together these records of the past with such clinical detachment that he begins to raise doubts about the accuracy of these
records: about whether these images can deepen an imaginative
understanding of the experiences lived through by the camp prisoners
or merely extend the ramifications of private fantasy. Jean Cayrol's
commentary recounts in a decorous and measured prose how the
camp was built according to a systematic philosophy based on an
inversion of the principles of reason, while Hanns Eisler's spare
atonal score augments the view that Resnais was trying to create
a work of art out of the mind's need to transform painful thoughts
into art. In the light of this method, which Resnais has continued to
practise, it is immaterial that the sequences in *Hiroshima mon amour*

Alain Resnais: *Toute la mémoire du monde.*

devoted to flashback memories of the nuclear destruction of the city should have included extracts from a Japanese feature film in which the catastrophe was reconstructed in the studio.

Resnais's documentaries mark a stage in a process of abstraction that was to become more and more evident during the late fifties and to assert itself fully in the sixties: a formalism that was international. Serge Bourguignon in France, Hiroshi Teshigahara in Japan and John Boorman in England—to take three names almost at random—were all to conceive of sequences and model the composition of their images on the styles of various American action painters. But Resnais has been less obtrusive in technique than some of those who took the process of abstraction further. He is much closer in spirit to the neo-realists and their recognition that the film-maker should bear witness to the uniqueness of his perceptions: a position arrived at by introspection and a winnowing away of the inessential.

Much that was important in the so-called New Wave movement, in fact, developed out of neo-realism. André Bazin's understanding of how important it had been in opening up new ways of thinking in terms of film was not only to diminish critical scepticism about the achievements of Jean Renoir, Buñuel and Vigo, who had previously been thought of as wayward in their reluctance to work from a screenplay, but also to influence at least two of his admirers, François Truffaut and Jean-Luc Godard—both of whom have ingeniously adapted his interpretation of neo-realism to suit their own needs and in doing so have often obscured their debt both to him and to neo-realism. It comes as a surprise to learn that Truffaut was continuously inspired by memories of *Germania, anno zero* while making *Les Quatre Cents Coups*.

But if Resnais was to think of the reconstruction of the past as a form of auto-criticism, both of the image as well as of fallible memory, others were to think of this reconstruction of the past in a more literal way. 'The reality buried under the myths slowly flowered,' states Zavattini. 'The cinema began its creation of the world.' Perhaps Zavattini's idea underplays the fact that perception is usually conditioned by the nature of one's own history, and it would seem to be dominated by the wish to obliterate the recent Fascist past by starting everything anew. But then the Italians have always had an uneasy relationship to their own past, even though modern historical studies may have begun in Italy. Until recently views on the origins of the Italian state in the nineteenth century have been clouded by legend. The two social forces that were most inclined to strengthen the Italian sense of national identity in the thirties had been among the most anti-historical, for both the Fascist state and the Church had promoted a trust in the immutability of certain élitist values. And the great heritage of Italian art also reinforced this distrust of history. It was easy, when interpreting the past through its paintings, sculpture and architecture, to confuse history with aesthetics and to convert the past into a timeless museum or to see it as a form of decoration. The first Italian epic-makers had done exactly this when they had reinforced the idea of an eternal past by decorating sets with authentic antique furnishings.

In a sense, Luchino Visconti was to follow in the footsteps of these Italian pioneers. Selfconsciously aware of his patrician descent, he has plundered past epochs for their cultural loot—the kind of loot prized in aristocratic circles—and rearranged it to suit his own decorative purpose. His interpretation of the Risorgimento in *Senso* (1953) was less derived from primary sources than from a haze of received opinions about the value of Stendhal, Verdi and the work of certain nineteenth-century Italian painters. In general, Visconti draws life from an appreciation of the creative insights of others, but even in his most sensitive of references to high culture, he tends towards a literalism that dehumanizes the experiences of his characters. He often gives the impression of having passed through a larger part of the twentieth century untouched by the concerns that have given shape to the modern movement in art, and appears most at home in his stage productions of nineteenth-century opera, where his antiquarian sensibility and liking for a heightened naturalism are most sanctioned by tradition.

Luchino Visconti: *Ossessione.*

Ossessione (1942) and *La terra trema* (1948) are both landmarks in the history of neo-realism: the first for being the first film of neo-realist intention, the second for its boldness. Visconti's boldness is such that he allowed the fishermen of Alcitrezza to speak in dialect and made no attempt to fit his leisurely pace to the snappy ninety-minute format. Even so, he did allow the filters of high culture to enter in between the spectator and the events described in both these films.

During the forties a number of Italian writers — Cesare Pavese being the most outstanding — had tried to escape from the claustrophobic snobberies of the Italian literary tradition by seeking fresh modes of expression in American fiction. Visconti may have been aware of this trend when, following Jean Renoir's advice, he decided to base his first feature on James M. Cain's novel *The Postman Always Rings Twice*. But his *Ossessione* is far from the conventions of the dime novel, or from the American idiom and tawdry metropolitan settings of *Double Indemnity* and *Mildred Pierce* (both of them based on Cain novels). He transposed its action to the Po valley, to those watery marshlands where Rossellini was to film *Paisà* — though in his treatment the land looks as sun-parched as Verga's *mezzogiorno*. And he infused Cain's low story with a grandeur that recalls Verga's attitudes to passion and death, bringing a sensuousness to its gestures that recalls Flaubert. His perception of nuance and his ability to sculpt figures against their surroundings were impressive, yet they were also in the main pictorial.

For all its display of Latin temperament, the strongest feeling communicated by *Ossessione* is Visconti's wish to be known as the creator of a masterpiece.

Yet if he just avoids making an embalmed art object out of *Ossessione*, he does so through a tension that has continued to be generative throughout his career: a tension that arises from a clash between his decorative ambitions and a disrupting energy that owes something to his aristocratic distaste for middle-class culture in all its forms and something to his mixed feelings about his own patrician upbringing. On one level, he has cast himself as the outsider, in sympathy with inclinations of an omnipotent and sado-masochistic kind; on another, more thoughtful level, he was for a while to see himself as a Marxist consciously working within a dialectical materialist theory about the ways in which society can change and in which the members of any society can be both individuals and representatives of their class. Yet the conflict he gives vent to in his films, of an iconoclast and snob forever at war with each other, is not unusual in Italian film-makers and writers; what is unusual about it, though, is the manner in which it has been tempered by the mellow influence of Jean Renoir.

Almost by chance, Visconti had met Renoir and been invited to join Cartier-Bresson and Jacques Becker as assistants on *Une Partie de campagne* (1938). He was to be impressed by the spirit of a family community that Renoir brought to the unit and by Renoir's insistence that film-making should be considered as closer to the individuality of the arts and crafts movement than to the impersonality of mass production. Even so, Italian Marxists have been suspicious of the socialism that Visconti in part acquired from Renoir. They believe that he finds an unjustified glamour in poverty. Orson Welles's complaint that Visconti filmed the young fishermen in *La terra trema* as though they were models in a fashion magazine has some truth to it, and even more truth in regard to its luxurious sequel, *Rocco and His Brothers* (1960).

These criticisms have not deflected Visconti in the least. He has been among the most consistent of film directors in pursuing his own interests and, like Stroheim, he has refused to be other than himself. Allied to his connoisseurship is a Teutonic will to push themes to a point that exhausts everyone, apart from himself. Audiences at the first showing of *La terra trema* at the Venice festival were not only baffled by its Sicilian dialect but also stunned by its three-hour-long revel in the sensuous pleasures of each moment. Its opening shot, in which fishing vessels (at first no more than small lights on the water) gradually ebb into port as dawn breaks and a church bell clangs, acquired such force by its length that the screen seemed to extend into Cinerama and the sound of the bell to take on a stereophonic dimension. At such moments, and Visconti was to create this sort of impression once more at the beginning of *Death in Venice* (1971), his talents as an opera producer and film director come together to achieve a magisterial strength. Perhaps more than any other exponent of neo-realism, he has been able to show how flexible its programme can be, how it can take in almost every type of genre, how it can relate location shooting to the most abandoned kinds of theatricality. In following its tenet to show things as they are, he has felt free to move from the actual to the ideal, from (to mention two of his more underrated films) the *verismo* filming of a Franco-Algerian community between the wars in his version of Camus's novel *The Outsider* (1971) to the deliberate artifice of his settings for his Dostoyevsky adaptation, *White Nights* (1957).

But the wish to reconstruct the past, whether as history or legend, whether in terms of realism or naturalism, was to be widespread in the post-war cinema. It is one of the supports underlying a new strength in the Western, a prime instance being John Ford's *My Darling Clementine* (1946)—which is historically more selfconscious and structurally more complex than his former work in this genre. Ford's clearest statement of the ironies implicit in the contrast between the past as legend and as actuality occurs in *The Man Who Shot Liberty Valance* (1961). The appeal of the past is evident not only in the revival of silent-screen narrative techniques—that is, a greater dependence on the image—by Flaherty, Buñuel and Bresson, but also in stories that evoke the making of silent films: among others, René Clair's *Le Silence est d'or* (1946), Billy Wilder's *Sunset Boulevard* (1950) and the Gene Kelly–Stanley Donen *Singin' in the Rain* (1951), a delightful MGM musical released in the year of Louis B. Mayer's departure from the studio—an event that more than any other, writes Penelope Houston in *The Contemporary Cinema*, marks the end of Hollywood confidence. All these films react to the silent period as though it had occurred at the beginning of time, so that it appears to be far more remote from their age than it does to us now; and Wilder, especially, uncovers a dread in his sentimentally affectionate response to the past—as when, in *Sunset Boulevard*, he shows up the repulsive absurdity that accompanies the pathos and talent of the once-great screen star Norma Desmond (Gloria Swanson)—that suggests a reluctance on his part to see the past as little more than a living death. The wish to reconstruct the past contained a measure of self-indulgence. Renoir's *The Golden Coach* (1952) and *French Can Can* (1955) were knowingly 'period' in a way that his *Madame Bovary* (1934), for instance, had never been: time-machine trips away from the bleakness of the fifties.

By 1949 the Italian film industry, like the film industries in France and Great Britain, had entered a period of slump, and for the same reasons. It petitioned the government to protect it against the American control of distribution rights; and the Social Democrat government responded by appointing Giulio Andreotti, one of its ministers, to take charge of the industry. Within a short time Andreotti had tripled the distribution of Italian films within the home market. But he also took action against the neo-realists, on the grounds that social criticism of any sort was probably Communist inspired and certainly a threat to the *status quo*. In 1955 one of the ministers in this government was to say: 'Film is escape, relaxation, forgetfulness for the poor. The people have need of bread and circuses.'[5] Andreotti had sweeping powers. He could ban the export of all Italian films (and the neo-realists depended on foreign earnings), he controlled all bank loans (producers were obliged to submit all screenplays to the government-owned Banco di Lavoro) and he had the right to impose censorship (many of the neo-realists were to feel censorship as directed in particular against them). In 1949, the year of these reforms, Italy signed the Atlantic pact. In 1950 de Sica went to Hollywood, and Luigi Chiarini, a leading spokesman for the neo-realists, was fired from the editorial board of *Bianco e nero* and from the directorship of the Centro Sperimentale.

The spirit of social criticism seemed broken. De Sica went so far as to provide, if not bread and circuses, at least *Bread, Love and Dreams* (1953). In 1959 Rossellini returned to memories of the war years with his bland *Il Generale della Rovere*, casting de Sica in the role of a confidence trickster. Yet during the fifties neo-realism continued to exercise great influence throughout the world, while in Italy its spirit was kept alive in a subterranean fashion. It moved away from public themes into private ones. Michelangelo Antonioni was to direct *Cronaca di un amore* in 1951, both neo-realist and intro-spective in intention. (Antonioni had previously written screenplays for Rossellini and de Santis and made a number of documentaries.) Two years later Federico Fellini was to direct *The White Sheik*. He too had received his grounding in film with the neo-realists, writing screenplays for Rossellini and assisting him on *Rome, Open City* and co-directing a feature with Alberto Lattuada. But in the main neo-realist ideas were to remain dormant during the fifties and only to quicken once more in the next decade, and in new forms, most notably in the work of Olmi, de Seta and Zurlini.

Neo-realism had been brought into being by events that had also given shape to post-war French existentialism, and it is not surprising that both movements should have qualities in common: a concern with immediacy, states of being and questions of bad faith, a hostility to dogma and institutional authority, and an openness to misrepresentation. In the United States as well as in Italy, neo-realist techniques were to be appropriated and used in ways that the neo-realists would have disclaimed.

Much of Elia Kazan's filming between 1944 and 1950 is close to neo-realism, especially his taste for location shooting, sympathy for the underdog and talent for merging professional and non-professional actors. But Kazan had begun his career with the Group Theatre and was to remain true to its tradition of assessing plot ideas in terms of their propaganda value. His first feature, *A Tree Grows in Brooklyn* (1945), was adapted from one of his stage productions and based on a novel by Betty Smith. It appears remarkable now for Kazan's ability to discover the dramatic possibilities inherent in commonplace events and in the least likely character traits of his actors. Yet James Agee, who found it deeply moving, was inclined to praise its neo-realist qualities in 1945. He liked its solid-looking city streets and its sharpness of observation—a shot of a girl 'hesitant on a curb which has the lovely authenticity of a wild animal startled by a flashbulb . . . a shot of Joan Blondell's bent hustling back, the thin dress propped and ridged through her underwear.'[6]

Louis de Rochemont, who had formerly supervised the *March of Time* series and who had now turned independent producer, came together with Kazan to evolve a type of movie that would do justice to de Rochemont's gifts as a journalist and Kazan's feeling for dramatic nuance. The result was the badly shot yet ingenious thriller *Boomerang!* (1947). Kazan continued to use its techniques in subsequent movies to describe a wide variety of American attitudes, linked to the subject of civic incompetence in *Boomerang!* and *Panic in the Streets* (1950) and to the subject of racialism in *Gentleman's Agreement* (1947) and *Pinky* (1949). But his desire to be both a social conscience and a provider of staple entertainment registered in the far-fetched and contrived nature of his plots. *Pinky,* for instance, depends on two hypotheses that the film fails to test sufficiently: that a mulatto nurse, who hates an elderly landowner whom she believes exploits coloured people and holds them in contempt, will yet be willing to look after this tough old reactionary; and that the landowner will soften sufficiently to bequeath her house and estate to the nurse. In *Gentleman's Agreement* Gregory Peck plays a journalist who decides to write a series of articles entitled *I was Jewish for Six Weeks.* 'Dynamite,' enthuses one of his colleagues (Celeste Holm, her habitual veneer of sophistication for once beginning to crack). It sounds like studio talk, and Kazan presents it without a trace of irony. In other ways, too, his sense of reporting was well enmeshed in the values of show business. To be sure, John Ford had cast the wholesome white actress Jeanne Crain as the coloured Pinky, but it was Kazan who had seen that his journalist should finally turn out to be a Gentile.

Perhaps he was too much a part of the volatile, publicity-conscious culture that he was trying to describe. His career reveals no settled conviction, apart from the understandable wish to be accepted. In promoting 'realism', he subscribed to a fashion which Hollywood executives, quivering on the edge of bankruptcy, and TV executives, on the look-out for inexpensive subjects, were both to commandeer: a reversal of policy most strikingly demonstrated by MGM, which had formerly been the most conservative of the major studios. (In 1951 Dore Schary, vice-president of the company, known for his relatively liberal views, succeeded to the title once held by Louis B. Mayer.) Most of the independent film-makers were to make deals with the major studios and to subscribe to policies they had once thought to despise. Kazan was no exception. And his appearance before the House Un-American Activities Committee on 10 April 1952, when he denounced some of his one-time Group Theatre associates as Communists and described each of his stage productions and films in turn as healthily American, dramatized the extent to which he had lost his nerve.

Fortunately his films are not the pap he made them out to be. They show that he had seen little to trust in American institutions, and his appearance before the House Committee could hardly have increased his sense of confidence. He was to enter into a period when his work would be characterized by frenzied camera movement, over-emphatic symbolism and self-abasing confessions. Yet it would be wrong-headed to believe that his ordeal before the House Committee was primarily responsible for this change, though it may have played some part. The moment when his style changed can be pinned down to a scene near the end of *Panic in the Streets*, where he brings out the implicit meaning of a parallel between criminals and plague-carrying rats stridently, by having one of the criminals clamber up a ship's mooring. He no longer appears to have believed that content could body forth its own meaning. In *A Streetcar Named Desire* (1951),

Elia Kazan: *A Streetcar Named Desire.* Vivien Leigh (left).

Elia Kazan: *A Streetcar Named Desire.* Marlon Brando.

based on Tennessee Williams's stage play, he no longer allows his style to emerge unselfconsciously from observation and feeling, but imposes it on his subject like a signature.

He began to write his name on the sky. Yet even at his most self-demonstrative and hysterical, he never quite lost his sense of dramatic strategy or power to elicit the talent of his actors. He has much in common with Arthur Penn. An uneasy mixture of percipience and idealization mark both his *East of Eden* (1955), cult film of the 1950s, and Penn's *Bonnie and Clyde* (1967), cult film of the sixties. But he has a creative nub to his personality, however fissured, that Penn so far has given little evidence of having. He can take off into excess and then consolidate his gifts with themes that allow for steady discovery. In the sixties he twice moved into the field of the semi-autobiographical film; and yet, while *The Arrangement* (1969) has a show-business keenness for strong scenes and glamorous performances and also loses direction in a kind of show-business panic, the privately financed *America, America* (1963) avoids this sensationalism. It tells of how a young Anatolian shepherd emigrates to the United States—but at a terrible cost to his being. Kazan keeps to the particular and in doing so, paradoxically, manages to illuminate the condition of all immigrants. The experience of *America, America* adds to the meaning of those well-known nineteenth-century photographs of cowed figures waiting on Ellis Island.

The Anatolian shepherd tries to obtain money for his journey across the Atlantic by marrying the daughter of a rich merchant. The remarkable way in which Kazan works out this incident does not distort character to suit some preconceived idea about the identity crises of adolescents, as was the case in *East of Eden*. He respects the unique nature of their relationship, perhaps because he was responding to a culture to which he was not habituated and could observe with a certain detachment. And for once his taste in making biblical comparisons is not forced. Few careers have been so variable in the

Elia Kazan: *Wild River*.

quality of their inspiration. In the light of both *Wild River* (1960), an elegiac recall of New Deal enterprise, as sensitive as Renoir's *The Southerner*, and the frenzied mannerisms of *Splendour in the Grass* (1961), it is possible to deduce that Kazan, perhaps more than any other director, needs frequently to recharge his metropolitan talent by returning to nature at its most meanly rural.

The uneasy compromise between muck-raking reportage and kitsch that Kazan had achieved in his first years in films was to be imitated by Enterprise Pictures, a group of independent film-makers that had infiltrated itself into the distribution system of MGM in the immediate post-war years. Lewis Milestone was a member of this group and so was Robert Rossen who wrote the screenplays of Milestone's *A Walk in the Sun* (1944) and *The Strange Love of Martha Ivers* (1946), and who was to make a striking impact with his second film as a director, *Body and Soul* (1947). Rossen edited the concluding boxing-match of *Body and Soul* with the same feeling for pace that he was later to bring to the pool sequences in *The Hustler*, but in every other way he appears to have been trying to work a vein that Odets had exhausted in the thirties. The conflict he sets up between spiritual values and the appeals of materialism never quite connect with the events in the life of his Jewish boxer (John Garfield). He was to be more incisive when filming, for Columbia, Robert Penn Warren's novel *All the King's Men*, which includes a barely disguised portrait of the Louisiana demagogue Huey Long. His manner of probing into political corruption was often to be imitated, but seldom with such honesty.

Enterprise Pictures was managed by Stanley Kramer, Carl Foreman (both of whom had been seconded to army film units in the war) and Richard Fleischer. Stanley Kramer was so adept at publicizing the company that many people thought he ran it alone. In 1947 he formed Screenplays Incorporated, which was managed by George Glass, Carl Foreman and himself, and evolved a profitable policy of shooting low budget films quickly on location. *Champion* (1949), one of a cycle of boxing films modelled on *Body and Soul*, made a star of Kirk Douglas. It was completed in twenty days at half a million dollars and earned back more than four times that amount in the American market alone. Kramer competed with television by using its cut-price techniques. But he also took the precaution of employing highly competent film-makers like Fred Zinnemann (who directed *High Noon*, *The Men* and *The Member of the Wedding*) and Laslo Benedek (*Death of a Salesman*, *The Wild One*). Carl Foreman wrote the screenplays for some of the more high-minded of these movies. 'During the making of *High Noon*,' wrote Foreman some years later in *Films and Filming*, 'I felt that I was ready to direct my next screenplay. However, in 1951 I was subpoenaed by the Un-American Activities

Robert Rossen: *Body and Soul.*

Committee, and my refusal to co-operate with it resulted in a quarrel with Kramer and Glass (who had already "named names"), my departure from the company and subsequent black-listing in the American film industry. For five years I made no films, the black-listing remaining effective in Europe.'[7] (Foreman made no films, but he did work as a co-scriptwriter on *The Sleeping Tiger*, 1954.) Meanwhile, Kramer's policy had proved so effective that he had begun to attract wealthy backers. In 1951 he came to a remarkable agreement with Columbia in which he was free to use their studio facilities while retaining complete independence.

Kramer promoted Art and Social Conscience as though they were commodities. Few of the films he produced at this time – he was only to turn to direction in 1955 with *Not as a Stranger* – were comparable in journalistic skill to Litvak's *The Snake Pit* (1948), Huston's *The Asphalt Jungle* (1950) or Wilder's *Ace in the Hole* (1951). But his entrepreneurial ability did mark him out as one of the few men in the film industry capable of competing with the appeal of television. He did not have a monopoly on false realism, though, and television was to outbid him handsomely with Paddy Chayevsky's TV play *Marty*, which Delbert Mann filmed in 1955. *Marty* puts forward the argument that unattractive people can still be lovable. Ernest Borgnine and Betsy Blair as its butcher hero and girl friend fail to demonstrate this argument; and Chayevsky's script reeks of self-pity, in spite of his understanding of Marty's character and his ear for the Bronx idiom. 'Realism' for Chayevsky is a kind of anti-commercial selling something repellent and yet relying on the glossy techniques of Madison Avenue.

The same wish to persuade underlies another more dramatically brilliant television play, Reginald Rose's *Twelve Angry Men*, which Sidney Lumet was to film in 1957. Davis (Henry Fonda), an architect in a white suit, convinces his fellow jurymen that a young Puerto Rican is probably innocent of the crime he has been accused of – by undermining each of their prejudices with the mastery of a Wyatt Earp cleaning up Tombstone. Rose packs the jury with bigots and turncoats. But if he is too gloomy in his view of representative democracy, he is probably too sanguine about the architect's powers of persuasion. Rose's aim, it would seem, was to reassure the embattled liberal. Yet while *Marty* was a success at the box-office and won Ernest Borgnine an Academy Award, *Twelve Angry Men* took a long time to earn back its production costs.

Bigotry, especially in relation to the issues of racism and delinquency, was to play a large part in Richard Brooks's film version of an Evan Hunter novel, *The Blackboard Jungle* (1955). Richard Brooks does all he can to distinguish the turbulence in a New York technical college from the innocuous personality of his central character, an idealistic schoolmaster. The schoolmaster comes over as a *tabula rasa*, on which the conflicts exercised in the college would seem to be written; it is as though the events in the college represented his most private fantasies. His edgy relationship with his wife and her frustrated wish to have a child are illuminated by his ineffectuality with the delinquent boys and, in particular, by his homoerotic friendship with a coloured youth (Sidney Poitier). Brooks reveals little regret at the way the college wastes the potential in its students; and for all his liberalism, he would seem to have committed his feelings to youthful violence. Perhaps in compensation for these feelings, he allows the Sidney Poitier character to correct white folk on their social attitudes: a role which Poitier was to play again and again, and with increasing missionary zeal, over the next decade. The main interest of *The Blackboard Jungle* is that, whether intentionally or not, Brooks enacts confusions that were typical of the fifties. Buñuel had been far more explicit about some of these confusions in *Robinson Crusoe* (1952), where an ageing and half-mad imperialist, Crusoe, is horrified when Man Friday tries to please him by putting on a woman's dress.

Part Five: 1956–1970

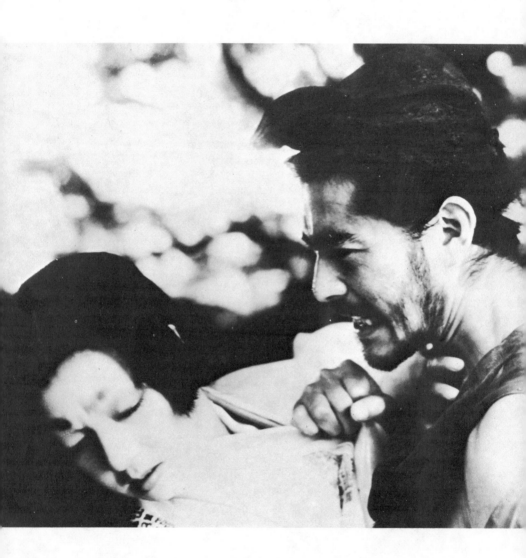

Akira Kurosawa: *Rashomon*. Machiko Kyo, Toshiro Mifune.

13. *Internationalism*

The Bandung conference of 1955 had publicized the existence of the underdeveloped countries, given substance to the idea of a Third World and begun to unsettle the Cold War balance of power. Jet travel and satellite television were seemingly to shrink the world further. The kind of isolationism Neville Chamberlain had once proposed about Czechoslovakia, although privately maintained by many, no longer appeared tenable in public. 'How horrible, fantastic, incredible it is that we should be digging trenches . . . because of a quarrel in a faraway country between people of whom we know nothing.'[1]

From the beginning of the fifties the major film festivals were to reflect the new internationalism, vying with each other to discover talent in faraway countries: among others, Torre Nilsson in Argentina, Bardem and Berlanga in Spain, Cacoyannis in Greece. Some of these directors failed to consolidate their achievement; yet a few of them, and one or two previously little-known film industries, were to prove more durable. The re-emergence of Luis Buñuel as an important figure on the international scene has already been mentioned, and the Polish film industry will be discussed later. In the meanwhile, three outstanding events in the world cinema of the fifties need to be enlarged on: a revitalized Swedish film industry, in the main due to the contribution of one man, Ingmar Bergman; the acknowledgement of a major Indian film director in Satyajit Ray; and the recognition of a Japanese tradition in film-making, about which the Western public had previously known next to nothing.

Ingmar Bergman

During the thirties the Swedish film industry had, relatively speaking, entered the doldrums: there was no one to match the brilliance of Stiller or the visionary intensity of Sjöström. And then, in 1944, Alf Sjöberg directed *Frenzy*. Well known at home as a stage producer and actor—his first film had been *The Stronger* (1929)—Sjöberg was an eclectic in his range of film styles and strove too hard to win international attention (an attention necessary to the Swedish film industry, though, which relies on the money made by foreign distribution). But on one occasion at least his theatricality was to marry harmoniously

Ingmar Bergman: *Cries and Whispers*. Liv Ullmann.

with his subject-matter, a screen adaptation (1951) of Strindberg's play *Miss Julie*. Sjöberg is at his best in *Frenzy* when his sense of style is least obtrusive, as during the moments when he builds up the atmosphere in his school location—an atmosphere more appropriate to a nineteenth-century Prussian academy, maybe, than to a Swedish school in the mid twentieth century—or choreographs scenes of bustle and conversation on the school stairs; at his worst when he resorts to a shorthand of swaying lamps and fearful shadows to suggest the terrorizing and death of a shop-girl (Mai Zetterling). In fact, the vitality of *Frenzy* arises from other sources: partly from Sjöberg's gift for eliciting exceptional performances from his actors—in this case from Stig Jarrel as the sadistic schoolmaster who drives the shop-girl to her death—and partly from the intensity of a screenplay dominated by the idea of an omnipresent evil. The writer of this screenplay, a young drama student, had only a marginal influence on the film; but in the light of Ingmar Bergman's later output, this influence now appears important. It is possible to surmise that Sjöberg provided the technique and much of the accomplishment of the final effect, Bergman the semi-autobiographical record of adolescent perplexity. The same kind of allocation of responsibility can be ascribed to *The Woman without a Face* (1947), scripted by Bergman and directed by the veteran Gustav Molander. Once again a fluent narrative style embodies a recollection of adolescent passion, naïve in statement, lacking in proportion, yet rawly, even hysterically felt. Both screenplays imply a struggle to differentiate feelings of affection from desires of a more cruel kind.

Of his first films as a director, beginning with *Crisis* (1945), Bergman has said that he prefers that they should be forgotten; and on the evidence of *Port of Call* (1948) and *Prison* (1949), his wish deserves to be respected. Picturesque views of docks and moored ships apart, they offer little more than an attempt to contain melo-dramatic happenings within a naturalistic, even drab framework. But in the same year as *Prison*, Bergman embarked on *Thirst*, and from almost its opening moments reveals the assurance that typifies his later work. At this stage in his development his dis-tinction lies less in the working out of content (a complicated story that never quite knits together either thematically or as a plot) than in his ability to use the camera both in close-up and in some in-ventively managed two-shots to hint at the unspoken thoughts of his characters. In effect, Bergman had already discovered the secret of sustaining such tension in a sequence that he could hold a shot long beyond the spectator's natural expectation. His accurate sense of camera placement and his sense of timing (both of action within the frame and in editing) had already begun to mark him out as a distinct talent.

During the fifties it became plain that Bergman had an unusual gift for finding fictions, of a widely varied kind, that could act as vehicles for his own conflicts. His freedom to pursue this semi-autobiographical direction speaks admirably for the policy at Svensk Filmindustri. Even so, the invention with which he converted his narrow, often monotonous interests into such richly dramatic plots and images is entirely his own. His mastery of tragic idyll (*Summer with Monica*, 1953), modern comedy (*A Lesson in Love*, 1954), period comedy in the lavish and witty manner of Stiller (*Smiles of a Summer Night*, 1955), medieval allegory (*The Seventh Seal*, 1957) or intro-spective realism (*Wild Strawberries*, 1957) demonstrates a scope that other directors may have equalled, perhaps, but none with the same emotional commitment to certain themes and symbols: a corpus of meaning (in the main accreting around the problems facing one devil-haunted artist in particular, i.e. Ingmar Bergman) steadily to be worked on through many genres. This sense of a governing intelligence involved in the process of self-discovery was heightened by Bergman's custom of employing the same group of actors—among the more notable being Naima Wifstrand, Eva Dahlbeck, Bibi Andersson, Harriet Andersson, Ingrid Thulin, Liv Ullmann, Gunnar Björnstrand, Max von Sydow and Anders Ek—and of restricting himself to the service of two great cameramen, Gunnar Fischer and Sven Nykvist.

Bergman was eventually to put aside this symphonic virtuosity for a more austere approach, in style not unlike certain kinds of chamber music—a musical analogy appropriate to so musical a talent. As it appeared in his so-called trilogy (*Through a Glass Darkly*, 1961, *Winter Light*, 1963, and *The Silence*, 1963), the new discipline tended at first to lead to an edgy stiffness. But as the decade went on, Bergman managed to modulate his new technique so that a story containing two or three relationships at most could subtly reflect issues of a general nature—such as the theme of war in *Shame* (1968). There was still a tendency to lose problems in over-emphasis, as in the otherwise fine *Persona* (1966), and *Hour of the Wolf* (1968), but on the whole Bergman moved into the quieter accent. He continued to refine on his mastery of the close-up—and he was to remain incomparable when filming the barely observable fleeting expression. His sense of time grew even more precise; not so much time as it passes as time felt on the pulse.

The limitations of his career would appear to be twofold. Unconsciously, perhaps, he subscribes to a notion of culture as something Olympian, cold and selfconscious in its symbolism: the kind of *Kultur* once represented by Thomas Mann, whom Bergman admires, and which no longer obtains in most countries in the West. Working within the assumptions of this kind of culture allows him easily to refer to art with a capital A (as in the lecture on Mozart's Tamino in *Hour of the Wolf*), to make metaphysical statements and to produce crossword-puzzle type allegories that most film-makers elsewhere would find unmanageable, thinking these references either pretentious or irrelevant to their experience. Not so Bergman. A culturally isolated society allows him this kind of symbolism; yet even he cannot avoid the impression, sometimes, of having built his plots out of a pack of intellectual cards.

The other limitation is that he appears not only to dislike the majority of his characters but to feel distaste for humanity itself. So often when he slips into over-elaboration or into morbid gloating he conveys the sense that in rejecting the bad he rejects the good also. So often he directs his most lacerating attacks on good yet defenceless people. In the very considerable *Cries and Whispers* (1973) he made these difficulties into his theme, contrasting two kinds of pain: the involuntary suffering of Agnes (Harriet Andersson), who is dying from some appalling illness, and the masochistic self-inflicted pain of her sister Karin (Ingrid Thulin). But although he wishes to distinguish these two kinds of pain, Bergman continues to confuse them, and he films Agnes's death in a manner more suitable to *grand guignol* than to tragedy. He has a flair for *grand guignol* and, at moments, an awareness of the tragic: but—and it is a big 'but' that echoes throughout his career—a fascination with the destructive has often tempted him to confuse the two.

Satyajit Ray

Bergman began to achieve an international reputation in the early fifties, Satyajit Ray a little later in the decade. Though Ray is not the first Indian film director to have been acclaimed outside his own country— K. A. Abbas and Bimal Roy had already shown work at the festivals— he is the only one so far to deserve mention in the same breath as the masters of the cinema. As a young man, he had met and been encouraged by Jean Renoir, during the time when Renoir was in India filming *The River* (1950). In London, as a trainee in advertising, he had been an assiduous filmgoer and had been especially impressed by de Sica's *Bicycle Thieves*. Then, despite many practical difficulties, he had filmed Bibhati Banerji's novel *Pather Panchali*; and it was with *Pather Panchali* (1955) and the other two films in his Apu trilogy— each is self-sufficient — *Aparajito* (1957) and *Apur Sansar* (1959) that he began to win the attention of an international audience.

Ray has such a feeling for the way in which a sequence can unfold naturally yet unexpectedly and has such an eye for the intimacies of a relationship, for the surroundings his characters inhabit or the objects they use, that it is possible (just) to think of him as an impressionist. For so long charged with ignoring the more serious problems of contemporary India—the corruption of its executive class, the failure to eradicate the caste system, the inertia, the appalling poverty and starvation, so striking in his birthplace Calcutta—he has been tempted to refute his critics in such later films as *The Adversary* (1970), *Company Limited* (1972) and *Distant Thunder* (1973), though often at the expense of forcing his talent. Yet even with the Apu trilogy it made no sense to argue that his talent was limited to his powers as an observer. Perception does not precede insight, and Ray's awareness of the historical processes that have affected India during the past century and of its social conflicts—such as the one between the religious view of experience and the pragmatic values of technology —has been at least implied from the beginning of his career. 'If you go to Benares,' he has said in a BBC television interview (*Release*, May 1968), 'you'll feel that India has never changed, while if you go to Calcutta you can see the old and new existing side by side; it's such an important element of the social life in India that you can't escape it.'

His output has been prolific. Apart from the Apu trilogy, key films have been *Jalsaghar* (1958), *Kachenjunga* (1962) and *Charulata* (1964). Something of his development over the years can be suggested by a consideration of two other key films, *Mahanaghar* (1963) and *Days and Nights in the Forest* (1970). The first of these, *Mahanaghar*, is one of the few convincing film studies of business relationships. It is so, in part, because India still undergoes changes of a kind that most of Europe underwent in the nineteenth century, and Ray feels free to analyse this society according to the prescriptions (or so it now seems) of the early nineteenth-century novelists. Arati, his heroine, might have stepped from the pages of Balzac. She is a compliant wife, in a household dominated by men, forced by circumstances to go out to work and to begin asserting herself. Ray draws a fine distinction between Arati's apparently benign employer and her querulous, demanding husband. The employer has an unacknowledged power over Arati and can afford to be benign; he only becomes tyrannical when she brings the scruples of private life into their association. Arati resigns, confident that she and her husband will find jobs elsewhere in the city. The commitments and strains of marriage, she learns, do not apply to the promiscuities of commerce.

Arati and the other characters fill the definition of nineteenth-century realism proposed by the Marxist critic, Georg Lukács. They are both individuals and social types. The city they inhabit—Calcutta—is more than a scenic background, and its economic and class structure play an important part in their motivation. (The collapse of the private bank at which Arati's husband works is crucial to the denouement.) Even the most trivial of objects, like a tube of lipstick, are made dynamically essential to the plot. Putting on lipstick is an outward sign of emancipation: Arati's sexuality will no longer be her husband's property. At the same time, wearing lipstick is a recognition that she will be using her sex, in a sense dishonestly, to help sell knitting machines.

Ray is supremely economical. *Mahanaghar* wastes nothing. Yet it is also predictable. Compare it to Antonioni's *The Eclipse*, similar in theme, made at much the same time, and it becomes evident that the sensibility of *The Eclipse* eludes definition. Antonioni explores areas of the present out of which the future is emerging; and we need that future to find a language adequate for this exploration. The main point of Lukács's attempt to define nineteenth-century realism was to establish a human centrality in modern literature. *The Eclipse* shows how this centrality is shifting, perhaps disappearing. If *Mahanaghar* has the vitality of immediate experience, it has so because Lukács's type of criticism delineates the creative process without touching on the ways in which the creative mind transforms prescriptions into insight. Ray has deft powers of intuition. He allows his material to take on an independent life; he neither forces nor imposes on it; yet he somehow manages to allow order to emerge from the flux. The strength of his art lies in its predictability. We have seen it all before, though perhaps never consciously and never on the screen: our perception is enlarged by his insight. Witness the complicated sequences in Arati's overcrowded home – an appearance of casual spontaneity, yet no gesture or movement is extraneous.

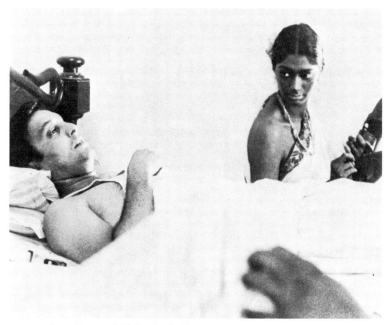

Satyajit Ray: *Days and Nights in the Forest.*

Days and Nights in the Forest marks an advance on *Mahanaghar* to the extent that it embodies areas of sensibility and uses a technique of an Antonioni kind. Four rather worldly men leave the city – one of them is hoping to recover from an embittered love affair – and travelling camera shots have the effect of evoking the mystery of the forest into which they enter. With some coercion they take over rooms in a private rest house, and in this peaceful setting their irritation, bouts of lassitude, venality, citified manners and bragging appear not only out of place but strange. Their behaviour deteriorates: one of them accuses a servant of stealing a wallet, another has a rather brutal relationship with a peasant girl in a near-by village. Belatedly they try to justify their behaviour: they feel so trapped in their jobs, on holiday they need to break regulations.

The camera watches them detachedly. It is often placed behind them as they move through the forest, so that the forest takes on as much presence in the story as they do. In the forest they come into touch with an India they would prefer to forget. Ray shows their meeting with two cultivated women, and it becomes apparent that all the women in the film, including the peasant girl and the sick, possibly dying caretaker's wife, are in touch with suffering in a way that the men wish to deny. One of these women, played by Sharmila Tagore, tells the most sensitive of the men: 'You've never faced any great sorrow in your life.' She herself has been inwardly changed by the death of her mother in a fire and the suicide of a brother. The mystery of the forest holds within it something of the perhaps intolerable beauty of nature: a beauty intolerable in the sense that a capacity to respond to it depends on a capacity to face such pain. In the Apu trilogy Ray had shown his young hero as welcoming the sight of a train and, later, trying to master the world though a knowledge of science and literature. He had also shown this sense of omniscience crumble: Apu must suffer the death of his parents and young wife. Yet Ray recognizes that the vanity of his hero is such that he will not tolerate much suffering. For a number of years the bereft Apu abandons his infant son, and then—as the disquieting conclusion to *Apur Sansar* implies—takes him away from his grandparents in such a way as to suggest that he will bring up the child badly.

The Japanese Cinema

There had been something of a scandal at the Cannes Film Festival when *Pather Panchali* was shown there in 1956. Some of the jury had missed its screening; no one, it seems, had anticipated a master-piece from Bengal. A different sort of embarrassment surrounded the showing of Akira Kurosawa's *Rashomon* (1950) at Venice in 1951. The studio chiefs at Toho had almost failed to send it to the festival. Like other Japanese producers, they did not expect to win a place in foreign markets and they feared to lose face. Their hesitation was not unexpected—the Japanese have always been uncertain about the film market beyond the Far East. During the thirties, at a time when Japan had been at its most chauvinistic, its intellectuals had usually despised local productions and preferred the few French films imported under a severe quota restriction. Its directors had tended to disparage their own work when speaking to foreigners. The industry had barely tried to export its films and it had been tentative in aiming for world-wide publicity.

In spite of this, something of its size and achievement had filtered through to the West. (In 1927, a representative year, the industry had produced 700 films.) The English magazine *Close-Up* had run a number of informed articles on some of its more gifted people, in one of them praising Sadao Yamanaka as a prodigious talent, in another describing the career of Teinsuke Kinugasa, an actor who had turned director. Indeed, Kinugasa's *Crossways* (1928), perhaps too derived from the German and the Soviet cinema, had been admired in the

Yasujiro Ozu: *Good Morning* (1959).

West and a copy of it was preserved in the British National Film Archive. (Recently Kinugasa discovered a print of his *Page of Madness* (1926) in a garden shed. An outstanding example of avant-garde experiment in the twenties, it demonstrates how skilfully Kinugasa had mastered the idiom of German expressionism and given it a fluency that few of the post-*Caligari* films ever had. None of this appears to have been known about in the West during the thirties.) In 1938 Tomotaka Tasaka's war film *Five Scouts* won a Popular Culture Award at Venice, but it probably gained few admirers outside the Fascist countries. Ozu and Mizoguchi were no more than names to ciné-club members.

The producers at Toho, then, had some reason to be unsure about *Rashomon*, fearing it to be too Japanese to be intelligible to Europeans, and too untraditional in its plot structure to be typical of the industry. But eventually they yielded to Italian persuasion. The film was shown, and it won the Grand Prix. In 1954 Kinugasa's *Gates of Hell*, with its rainbow colour harmonies, won an award at Cannes. The discovery of the Japanese cinema was under way.

Kurosawa based his screenplay for *Rashomon* on a well-known story by Ryunosuke Akutagawa, in which four witnesses, either involved in or present at a rape and a death in a forest, offer contradictory interpretations of these events. This story is enclosed within another story about three travellers taking shelter from a thunderstorm under the ruined Rasho gate at Kyoto, sometime in the eighteenth century. The director then summons up vivid polarities, evoking in the forest scenes a fairy-tale atmosphere, as the camera glimpses a mysterious veiled lady in white riding through a glade, and also a nightmare of flashing swords, running blood, and loquacious groaning ghosts. In the scenes beneath the gate he goes to another extreme, enacting remorse at his vision of glamour and violence with buckets of rain, an abandoned crying child and some lost, homeless travellers. He pitches from one absolute in feeling to another, almost incapacitating the action with excessive tension.

It seems too much. Background music—modelled on Ravel's *Bolero* —thrums to the point of monotony. Shots of the sun glinting through leafy branches and people trudging through the forest are repeated to the point of destroying the initial impression. Yet the qualities that Kurosawa over-emphasized were the qualities most admired by the audience at Venice, who did not know that Kurosawa's distributors had been so worried by the performances of his actors that they had put out a poster showing the actors caricaturing their roles. The Venice audience thought this grotesque behaviour typical of the Japanese and warmed to its exotic appeal. Yet *Rashomon* has proved to be more than a curiosity, and it has had an influence comparable to *Citizen Kane*, with whose plot structure it has some affinity. It is unlikely that a more subtle film would have made this impact on the West.

Rashomon touched on a basic perplexity of the post-war period. Its conflicting attitudes to the violence in the forest—the woodcutter's guilt, the monk's complacency, the bandit's glee—echo a widespread ambivalence of feeling to memories of the Second World War, to Japanese atrocities in particular. Its questioning of moral certitudes sets up a connection with the existentialist scepticism of the West. Not since Eisenstein has so taut an energy found its expression in such

Akira Kurosawa: filming at the studio-constructed Rasho gate.

timing, editing (as in its use of hard-edged wipes) and ferociously heightened atmospheres. Kurosawa's response to events is kinaesthetic. He feels the juxtaposition of his images physiologically, and he encourages a corresponding physicality in his actors—as when he asked Toshiro Mifune to model his performance as the bandit on the study of a lion in a Martin Johnson travelogue. Against this physicality he pits the mystery of the rape and death in the forest, bringing together animality and the imponderable in a complex sensation for which he has often created an emblem in his samurai sword fights— where a tense pause, in which the contestants virtually hypnotize each other while trying to understand each other's intentions, will anticipate the timing of sharp, murderous lunges.

Rashomon depends on a tradition, or traditions, about which there is little knowledge. Most of the Japanese archives went up in flames during the blitz, and not much remains from the silent period. The American occupying forces destroyed 225 out of the 554 films made during the war. Any reconstruction of this history, therefore, is a hazardous undertaking. But apparently the Japanese welcomed the Lumière cameramen with enthusiasm; members of all classes became filmgoers; and stage actors willingly appeared on the screen. By 1921, if the Shochiku production *Souls on the Road* is anything to go by, the Japanese cinema had reached a maturity of expression as advanced as anything in the West. Minoru Murata, the twenty-seven-year-old director of *Souls on the Road*, had previously run his own theatrical company. He knew a good deal about foreign literature and films, and his style reveals the influence of Griffith and Sjöström. Mikiko Hisamatsu, as his heroine Fumiko, has the impish grace of Mary Pickford. She

Akira Kurosawa: *Living.*

represents a typical figure in Japan at this time, the 'moga', or modern girl, who shocks conventional middle-aged people.

Fumiko's father refuses to have any dealings with his son, an unworldly violin-playing idealist who has married out of his class. The girl tries to reconcile them but fails, and eventually the son and his family uncomplainingly starve to death. Meanwhile, she and a youth she has brought into her father's employment (played by Murata himself) are drawn to each other. Murata registers the stress in these relationships but he does not over-define them or underline their source in class conflict. He describes the tyrannical depressed father with some sympathy and, like the violin-playing son, appears to find beauty in everything: in landscape, in the quaint architecture of the father's house by day and in the glowing jewel impression created by its blazing lights at night.

Murata conveys a sense of thwarted energies, some of which finds an outlet in his appreciation of beauty. He does not define these energies, though, by translating them into politics. The helplessness of his characters stands in marked contrast to the vibrancy of his images: an impressionism that won him many followers. Yasujiro Shimazu, who was his lighting cameraman, learned a great deal from him; and Shimazu was later to concern himself, as a director, with training younger talents. Kenji Mizoguchi, very much in his formative years, was also impressed by *Souls on the Road*, although he was perhaps more impressed by the work of Daisuke Ito.

Ito articulates far more directly than Murata the feelings of discontent, the 'melancholy madness', which troubled Japan in the late twenties and which was vented to some extent in the Manchurian campaign of 1931. Politically active, he converted Mizoguchi to socialism, and the result began rather palely to show in Mizoguchi's filming. ('Mizoguchi', said a friend of his, 'was for a time a *parlour pink*.')[2] Ito was the first director to use the popular samurai genre as a vehicle for satire and protest, and he has been variously described as the Japanese Eisenstein and the Japanese Pudovkin. All that remains of his work from the silent period is a series of sword-fights taken from different films and strung together by a collector. They owe something to Kabuki, the merchants' theatre, and to Douglas Fairbanks; and similar sequences in Tomiyasu Ikeda's protracted *Reverence for the Emperor and Expulsion of Foreigners* (1927) demonstrate that Ito had no patent on the audacious choreography of his fights and camera movements. Yet to watch a succession of his heroes take on hordes of ruffians single-handed and kill them by every opportunity that sword, fist and rope can provide is a disquieting experience as well as a humorous one. If Murata's capacity for evoking the beautiful looks exceptionally developed by European standards, so does Ito's sense of concentrated ferocity: an extreme contrast of the exquisite and the brutal that characterizes the Japanese cinema and can often be found side by side in the same film.

It would be possible to give some sort of historical justification for this contrast by pointing out how the subtle, peace-loving tenth-century Heian civilization had instilled a love of beauty and decorum into the Japanese character while the Kamakura shogunate, which supplanted it in the twelfth century, energized martial virtues and cruelties. However, this view of the nation's identity resembles Stendhal's idealization of the Italians – mainly derived from opera – as both blood-thirsty and sublime. Even the tourist would be dissatisfied by it if it had not been endorsed by many Japanese commentators. 'Scratch a Japanese and you will find a pirate,' states Komakichi Nohara, author of *The True Face of Japan.* 'If the Japanese were to be truly themselves,' says the director Keisuke Kinoshita, 'the consequences would be dreadful.'[3] Such reflections suggest in part a healthy respect for the cruelty in everyone, in part a wish to remove the offence in foreign caricatures by parodying them to the point of absurdity. (Mifune's bandits are far more frightening than any toothy Nippon peering out of the undergrowth in American wartime B features.) The industry has confirmed the idea that something nasty may be forever brewing in the national Id by its tide of spectacular and occult fables, monster movies, samurai blood-lettings and studies in recondite forms of eroticism – during the sixties the production of blue films, which the Japanese call pink, reached 500 a year. Japanese film critics tend to be apologetic about this tide, as though it were unique to their country. In extenuation they point to a more honourable tradition which goes back to the first sound pictures of 1931: that of a realism centred on the pieties and dependencies of family life.

But on a limited aquaintance with their output, it does seem that when Shimazu, Gosho or Naruse work this domestic vein they do not work it hard enough. Their careful observation has left a useful record of Japanese family life in the early thirties. In Shimazu's *A Brother and His Younger Sister* (1939), for instance, a wife so cossets her husband that she even puts the paste on his toothbrush. But on the whole they use domestic realism as a formula of a soap opera kind, even though many of their themes are sombre, touching as they do on family tensions, the disappointments of love and the drudgery of obligation. This last-named theme has many forms: a favourite one concerns the type of person who supports an ailing relative by taking on an unpleasant job. Ruth Benedict, who devotes several pages of *The Chrysanthemum and the Sword* to the subject of obligation, believes, somewhat debatably, that this sense of indebtedness demarcates Japanese culture from any other.

'The word for "obligations" which covers a person's indebtedness from greatest to least is *on*,' she writes. 'People do not like to shoulder casually the debt of gratitude which *on* implies . . . Casual favours from relative strangers are the ones most resented. The passivity of a street crowd in Japan when an accident occurs is not just a lack of initiative.'[4]

The need to discharge moral debts owed to ancestors and the State, however distasteful the means of discharging them, was probably one reason why many people, taking a self-immolating pleasure in deprivation, supported the tyranny of the 1930s Showa regime without overt criticism. But this kind of sacrifice was not peculiar to the Japanese. It has occurred in many societies dominated by the ideal of duty, ranging from ancient Rome to imperialist Britain. The domestic realists, though, do not use the theme of indebtedness to comment on the power of the militarist regime: they decline to see family relationships as a microcosm of the State. Their prattle and gentle humour insulate subject-matter from the principal social tensions of the thirties. But one of them was to be an exception. There is no need to know that during the occupation of Singapore Yasujiro Ozu daubed anti-Japanese slogans on its walls to recognize the stubborn quietist dignity and radiance that informs his family dramas.

The Japanese movie industry is no different from other forms of Japanese commerce. It soon developed into a few monopolies, conservative in policy and run on authoritarian lines. The Americans tried to reorganize the industry during the occupation, but by the mid-fifties the five main companies—Toho, Shochiku, Toei, Daiei and Nikkatsu—were very much in the same position as they had been in the thirties. They were to remain so, until the slump of the late sixties. (Nikkatsu ceased production in 1969, Daiei went bankrupt in 1970, most of the other companies were in difficulties.) By Western standards they have always badly paid their writers, directors and crews, who work long schedules without overtime. Studio equipment tends to be primitive. Yet in a country where obedience to authority comes as second nature, this authoritarianism has usually avoided tyranny. Many of the older directors have taken their paternalism seriously. They have tried to build up a family atmosphere in the studios and trained their assistants as directors: conditions that allow for a speed and accuracy of filming unobtainable elsewhere. They seldom shoot more than one take. Kon Ichikawa, for instance, aims at thirty cuts a day on average and completed shooting on his complex feature *An Actor's Revenge* in under six weeks. In spite of this speed and economy, Japanese film-making has an unrivalled reputation for technical excellence.

Some of the more talented directors, however, have bridled against this authority and at times tried to break away from it. On two occasions, a number of them have set up independent production companies. But the first and perhaps most important act of protest was less a break-away than a collusion within the studio system, when five directors—Yamanaka, Uchida, Itami, Mizoguchi and Ozu— determined to resist the pressures of the militarist ideology of the thirties. They went about it with deference; even so, it is remarkable that these, the most gifted men in the industry, should have been tolerated. But Sadao Yamanaka was to be an exception. Mizoguchi and Ozu, both of them men of genius, thought Yamanaka the most able member of their group, and Kurosawa, whose ideas about film were formed by him, was left inconsolable by his death.

Yamanaka took over Ito's device of using the samurai story as a vehicle for social protest. But he was too explicit in his criticism, and his *Humanity and Paper Balloons* (1937) so angered the government that it sent him to the front line, where he died in 1938 at the age of twenty-seven. His bitterness in *Humanity and Paper Balloons* is unmistakable. He describes the frustrations of repressive authority through a number of interlocking events set in a lower-class quarter of eighteenth-century Tokyo (then known as Edo). A ronin—a samurai, that is, in the ignominious position of being without a master—seeks employment from a Lord Mori who had formerly been helped by the samurai's family, but who does not even bother to read his letter of recommendation. The ronin trudges from door to door, continually rebuffed; in the end he and his wife commit suicide. The effects of tyranny are present everywhere: Lord Mori and his peers cheat shopkeepers, order thugs to beat up an outspoken intellectual, impose an appalling deference. Yet Yamanaka does not allow the mood of bitterness to become self-indulgent. His treatment is dry. He conceives of incidents as shrewdly observed parables, as in the scene where a blind beggar recognizes a thief who has stolen his pipe by the sound of his talking through clenched teeth. His concluding image, of paper balloons floating down the sewage trench in a street, astringently summarizes his theme. His control over intricate plots and intricate compositions—he frequently has large groups in small rooms and frequently changes the focus of attention from one group to another —would be impressive in a director with twice his experience. Kurosawa was presumably working towards this kind of clarity in *The Lower Depths* (1957), his most sustained achievement, closely adapted from Gorky's play.

The hint of luxury in Yamanaka's compositions suggests that the compact austerity of his style was less a consequence of his personality than of an art created under the threat of reprisal. Its obliquity conveys the pressure of the 1930s more clearly, perhaps, than the deliberate re-creation of it in Kimisaburo Yoshimura's *Cape Ashizuri*, made almost two decades later and released in 1954. Yoshimura, who had trained under Shimizu, discovered in his theme a freshness and depth of feeling usually more typical of a first feature: it comes as a surprise to learn that he already had numerous credits to his name. But he is selfconscious about the militarist era in a way that Yamanaka is not, and he tends to lapse into an excessive pathos. He reconstructs the past so as to have the spectator identify with his gentle student hero; yet his Chopinesque piano music and slow tracking shots down autumn lanes have an effect, contrary to the one presumably intended, of insulating the spectator from the past. Like Murata he summons up a kind of Chekhovian mood which Chekhov knew nothing of. The story implies that the only way to live during a time of oppression is to retreat into the family circle and to suffer quietly—which may have been the case for many people in Japan. But by withdrawing into a contemplation of the isolated sensibility, Yoshimura has to fall back onto a portentous symbolism to suggest the motives that brought about this retreat.

Perhaps Yamanaka was alone in his terseness. His contemporaries appear to have asserted their independence by other means. Tomu Uchida made *The Earth* (1939) against the wishes of the studio executives at Nikkatsu, and he worked on location in a clandestine fashion with film stock and equipment smuggled from authorized Nikkatsu productions. His treatment demonstrates the exigencies of living as a tenant farmer while avoiding the standard pastoral claims to sympathy by its eye for abstract kinds of composition, by the architectural emphasis it derives from faces in extreme close-up, and by its tender lighting of such frugal and much-loved possessions as eating bowls and carefully wrought pieces of timber. Uchida's powers of abstraction are just as evident in his sense of rhythm. He brings together the pulse of men at work, the clacking, beating and grinding noises made by instruments and utensils, with the cyclic changes of nature, the crescendo of a storm, the timelessness of drought, the patter of the first rain to melt the parched earth. The repetitions of labour and biology unite into a powerful impression of fatality. Nature rules over man the maker, always threatening to destroy the community and its achievements. But the fact that Uchida observes man in the process of creating his communities discourages the thought that he might be politically passive. If he dwells on moments of despair and impoverishment, he is no different from later film-makers who were more optimistic about mankind's gift for mastery. In certain scenes, as in the arrival of a sweet-seller, he prefigures Satyajit Ray's *Pather Panchali*; in certain other scenes, as when a boat pulls away from a bleak and windy river bank, he defines a mood of desolation typical of the Italian neo-realist film. His sympathy for a caste traditionally despised by the samurai does imply some hostility to the military ethos: in 1939 it must have appeared to challenge the views then in fashion about the nature of civilization and about the forces that had most dynamically contributed to the forming of civilization.

Kenji Mizoguchi also let his political views be known in this oblique way. During the early forties he took on the theme most loved by the Japanese public—and sometimes filmed twice a year—the story of the forty-seven ronin. He persuaded the censor that he would interpret the legend as a study in loyalty, then developed it as a study in injustice. The meaning of war—its destruction of art and human relationships—troubles most of his post-war plots. But such interests would have been impermissible in the thirties, and during that decade Mizoguchi directed his criticism against certain barbarous aspects of civilian life.

He was born in 1898 of a desperately poor family. During one financial crisis his father, a carpenter, had to put to auction the family home and its contents and to sell off his daughter as a geisha. After his mother's death, Mizoguchi used to stay with his younger sister who had become the mistress of a wealthy businessman and lived in a luxurious apartment. He had little formal schooling and he remained virtually illiterate throughout his life. But he studied painting and tried to become an actor. He casually joined Nikkatsu in the early twenties. After the Tokyo earthquake of 1923, he was sent to direct movies in Kyoto. He married; his wife later went insane. It was said of him that he worked in the film industry so as to have enough money to entertain the women of the Gion (the geisha district of Kyoto).

His work never really escapes from this unusual past. He is fascinated by demi-mondaines, the inhabitants of the so-called floating world. But his compassion for their often tragic fate has something suspect about it. Their vulnerability appears to bring out a feline cruelty in him, as when he lingers over a fight between prostitutes in *Women in the Night* (1948). In this, and in his lyricism and identification with the feminine, he resembles the composer Giacomo Puccini; and indeed *Madame Butterfly* would make an ideal Mizoguchi scenario. Perhaps his shuttling back and forth between his father's home and his sister's luxurious apartment heightened his awareness of social nuance, of the precarious difference between poverty and wealth, and the gnawing pain of those who lose status or who are treated as inferiors. Just as possibly, it motivated the contrasts between austerity and luxury that mark his style throughout his career. In many of his films social criticism plays a secondary role to the richness that his highly orchestrated camerawork brings to melodramatic plots. He is a poet of houses and rooms, of architectonics and space. He loads the air with sumptuousness. Every image adds to the richness. His flowing camera continually finds unexpected levels and perspectives. The pace of his editing sets up a musical structure in counterpoint to the architecture of his settings. Son of a carpenter, he was sensitive to the Japanese tradition of craftsmanship and brought to the construction of his *mise en scène* the care of a master cabinet-maker. He discovered new kinds of compositions and narrative rhythms, and he rifled ideas from the prints and paintings of the *ukiyo-e* (the art of the floating world), modelling his heroes on a conception of male virtue alien to the West. Dr Ivan Morris has argued that Prince Genji, *beau idéal* of the Heian period, was pasty-faced and stout. The plump effeminacy of Mizoguchi's heroes can be deceptive.

White Threads of Waterfall (1933), one of the two of his silent films still available—he had by then directed over forty of them— reveals how the contours of his style had already formed. A woman turns to prostitution to support her lover through his law studies. In time he becomes a judge and has to pass a death sentence on her for murder. He visits her in the death cell. Images of their grave faces separated by the bars of her cell characterize Mizoguchi's fascination as a film-maker: the currents of ambivalent feeling that swirl beneath a surface of serene visual beauty. We know that at least once, in 1929, he turned briefly from period subjects to contemporary themes. He was to make this transition once more in 1936 when he directed *Osaka Elegy* and *Sisters of the Gion*. His style became leaner; he was less

Kenji Mizoguchi: *Sisters of the Gion.*

sensuous and more critical in his response to his heroines. Incidents in these stories, scripted by Yoshikata Yoda, recall his upbringing: an auction sale, a geisha entertaining her impecunious lover, the social distress of the demi-mondaine. Yet he transforms these random, personal incidents into a statement about the condition of urban Japan, approaching the customs of Osaka and Kyoto with a historian's respect. As in his films about the remote past, he conveys the feeling that no assumption or image should pass unquestioned, as though he thought that the experience of living in the present had to be dismantled and then reconstructed before it could be believed in. He appears to have recognized that the need for money, a motive force in his own unusual upbringing, lay behind the distorted functionings of society in general. He tended at this time to describe most behaviour in terms of greed and profit, declining to take any character on his or her own self-evaluation.

The result is waspish comedy. In *Sisters of the Gion* he compares a courteous old-style geisha with her younger sister, a tough social climber. The younger sister ends up in a car crash, brought on by a jealous lover, but continues to believe she is right to exploit men rather than be exploited by them. She recognizes no other kind of relationship. In *Osaka Elegy* a somnolent, fat doctor with little sense of vocation listens to the breakfast bickering of a wealthy couple and agrees with both parties. Later he meets Ayako, who has married a rich man to pay off her father's debts and been to prison. He asks her why she is walking by the river at night. She says she feels like a dog without a master. She admits that she is probably ill and asks him if he can diagnose and cure her condition. He says non-committally that he does not know; and as she walks past the camera, the film ends abruptly. In the Japan Mizoguchi evokes with a minute sense of detail, few people are dependable and everyone is to some extent corrupt. In both films the beautiful Isuzu Yamada plays the central role (Kurosawa was to cast her as Lady Macbeth); in both films she falls in love with a young man who turns out to be unreliable.

Mizoguchi makes points, ends scenes on some pay-off line or gag, distils a kind of humour that owes something to *The Woman of Paris*. His style when dealing with historical subjects or legends is quite different. He develops his narratives in an allusive manner; it may recall the unfurling of a scroll. At times, as with the shot of a rowing-boat floating across a misty lake after the lovers' deaths in *Chikamatsu Monogatari* (1954), this unfurling can dissipate accumulated charges of emotion. But few such losses in concentration occur in *The Story of the Last Chrysanthemums*.

It was released in 1939 and, like *Les Enfants du paradis*, its excitement about the theatre and the theatre's power for creating illusion may have been intensified by its avoidance of wartime urgencies. Mizoguchi compares the events on the Kabuki stage with outside events that are almost as fantastic. He places his story at the end of the nineteenth century, well into the Meiji period, at a time when Japan was being rapidly modernized: actors riding in rickshaws wear deerstalkers with their kimonos. And he appropriates some of the angular rhythms as well as the motifs of Kabuki for his main action: long tracking shots as slow as the movement of a rickshaw, then the incisive, startling cut which sets up energy for the next sequence.

A copy of the film reached the United States. Its plot puzzled Ruth Benedict, who had been invited by the American government to prepare a wartime report on the psychology of the enemy. Kikunosuke, adopted into a family of wealthy actors, doubts his abilities as a female impersonator. He falls in love with Otuku, a wet nurse in the household, maybe because she is the only person to tell him that his acting is bad. Together they enter the wilderness of third-rate acting companies, and gradually his talent develops. He returns to Tokyo and enjoys a brilliant success; but Otuku, conscious of the caste difference between them, refuses to join him. She feels she has satisfied honour by doing all she could for him, and she dies. Ruth Benedict noted how this conclusion went against what she imagined to be the expectations of American audiences. 'If they must weep at the end of a play, it must be because there was a flaw in the hero's character or because he was victimised by a bad social order.' [5]

But Otuku's sacrifice will not surprise readers of the Victorian novel, though they may wonder how ironic Mizoguchi intended to be in his treatment of this improving relationship. Otuku is very much the wet-nurse to her lover, dressing him for the stage, delighting him with the gift of a make-up box and dying when he no longer needs her. Kabuki tensions, raised to the point of shrillness, carry the action over some of its awkward bridge passages, and remarkable editing creates a *tour de force* out of the potentially bathetic concluding scenes. Mizoguchi cuts back and forth from the deathbed to the carnival triumph on a river boat. Kikunosuke bows to the applauding crowd, and as he raises his head a flash of pain crosses his face, presumably an intuition of Otuku's death. The woman dies so as to give the female impersonator a soul. Perhaps Mizoguchi believed that by torturing and destroying his heroines he, too, could heighten his feminine sensibility.

Mizoguchi's work in the thirties lays the ground for his post-war achievements. The same is true of Yasujiro Ozu. Yet in other ways the interests of these two men diverge. Mizoguchi was the chronicler of the floating world, Ozu the poet of family life; Mizoguchi was restless in technique and changed genres and epochs with nearly every

Kenji Mizoguchi: *The Story of the Last Chrysanthemums;*
above, events on the Kabuki stage.
below, a modernized Japan.

film; Ozu preferred the simplest and most economic means and played variations on more or less the same theme and subject. When he touches on life in the theatre, and then only briefly, in his first version of *Floating Weeds* (1934), he remains unmoved by the possible glamour of illusion. His theatre is a barn with a leaking roof and his group of actors resembles a family; one of them visits his illegitimate child and understands the need to be more fatherly. Most important of all, Ozu's awareness of beauty differs from Mizoguchi's. In *The Brothers and Sisters of the Toda Family* (1941), a mirror reflects an empty room, and the serenity of this image appears to be in concord with the seemingly opposed theme that human desire is infinite.

On his grave at Kamakura there is one ideogram, the Japanese word for *nothing*. He was not a religious man in any practising or fervent sense. But he had an intuitive feeling for the Buddhist awareness of life as transient. He could have retreated into detachment or indifference. In fact, his passionate yearning for the world and its inhabitants put him in touch with a poignancy of such depth that he had to imagine some ideal of permanence: and he does so by contrasting the fret and smoulder of existence with the stillness of objects. He punctuates nearly every sequence with a landscape or a composition of household utensils, so arranged and lit that they take on a radiant intensity; it is typical of his humour that in his post-war films he can raise this intensity from an arrangement of brightly-coloured plastic buckets or boxes of detergents. Moreover, he tries to recognize those moments of stability in human experience when the self finds a harmony in itself and appears to enter timelessness. His respect for formality encourages him in this kind of insight.

Ozu was born in 1903. On leaving university in 1923, he entered Shochiku studios and directed his first film in 1927. He was probably the last major director to turn to the sound film, in 1936. Only half a dozen of his thirty-five silent films remain in existence. All of them are, on the surface, comedies. At least three of them—*Tokyo Chorus* (1931), *I was Born but* ... (1932) and *Passing Fancy* (1933)—are about the relationship between sons and fathers: the sons being naughty, sturdy boys, the fathers being young and under stress from overwork. The sons idealize their fathers; events disillusion them. Ozu describes these relationships so credibly and with so unsentimental an affection that the action has the ring of autobiography, as though the director was reporting ruefully on his own attempts to bring up children. In fact, he never married and never was a father. He lived most of his life in the company of his mother and died shortly after she did. His father had died when he was very young and it may be that the comedies project a situation which he himself had never known. It is remarkable, then, that he should have avoided idealization.

His career has some parallel with that of Heinsuke Gosho, though he does not fall into the marginality of Gosho's often beautiful ventures into domestic realism during the thirties, and does not force perception as Gosho did in his two important statements of 1954, *The Inn at Osaka* and *The Valley of Love and Death*. Gosho, it would appear, was working towards the kinds of sensation about urban life that Antonioni was shortly to define. But his realism begins with a thesis about society which he then illustrates: a cerebral approach that keeps theme and perception apart. Ozu neither lets his material run to triviality nor does he impose upon it. He has the miraculous gift of giving his families the right to take on an independent life. He creates a stability in them which reciprocally strengthens his talent and allows him in a non-compulsive manner – and in spite of studio pressure – to continue refining the same subject throughout his life. In other words, he is seldom tormented by their presence, as Mizoguchi was by his characters, and he does not seek to destroy them.

In the silent comedies freedom of presence allows for a childlike pleasure in gentle, unsophisticated jokes. The boy in *Passing Fancy* tells his father that he can polish his nails on the milled edge of a coin, and the father, verifying this piece of information, is delighted. If the companionship of a son can rejuvenate a father, then it is possible that a return to the naïve pleasures of the first movie-makers, as Ozu acknowledges, can recharge the energies of a more advanced kind of film thinking. Yet his pleasure in naïvety is qualified by his sensitivity to the feelings of his characters. There is always a hint of possible tragedy.

His refusal to be possessive is evident in his technique. In his last films especially, he seldom moves his camera. He does not try to conceal the self-contained entity of each shot. There is no attempt to fake narrative flow or to impose expressiveness. With sound, the tragic becomes explicit and his images begin to have the quality of arrested time and to raise a consciousness of time similar to the poetry in Vermeer's paintings. His style changes; it becomes formal and austere, restraining great intensities. In *The Only Son* (1936) a mother scrubs floors to pay for her only son's education. He becomes a teacher in overcrowded Tokyo. She visits him, and he confesses that his life has come to nothing. She goes home, puts on a good face with her friends at the factory, then walks out into a sunlit courtyard. A barred gate, a pile of baskets. She sits down and weeps; and only in this final moment is the pent-up energy of the story released.

The theme of self-sacrifice, which here appears in three different forms, was not only among the most popular in Japanese fiction, it was also among the most prone to sentimental treatment. Ozu may seem to have moved in this direction when he chose a melody based on the

Yasujiro Ozu: *Records of a Tenement Gentleman* (1947).

Yasujiro Ozu: *What Did the Lady Forget?* (1937).

Yasujiro Ozu: *The Only Son* (1936).

Yasujiro Ozu: *Early Summer* (1951).

Yasujiro Ozu: *An Inn in Tokyo* (1935).

Yasujiro Ozu: *Young Miss* (1930).

tune of *Poor Old Joe* for a musical refrain. But he resists this impulse. When the critic Tadao Sato visited him on set, he noticed how Ozu rehearsed his actors until they lost all spontaneity, so that they behaved before the camera with all the embarrassed formality of a host entertaining a guest for the first time. The mother continues to be reticent, however much she may suffer, and her condition appeals to our sympathy because she declines to impose it upon us. When she does eventually break down into tears, Ozu shoots the scene from a distance as though he wished to respect her privacy. The sunshine, baskets and barred gate all yield up symbolic meanings if we wish them to; at the same time, their quiddity asserts their otherness to the mother's grief. The world continues on its own way whatever we may think or feel. By avoiding expressionism and its insistence, Ozu allows the ramifications of a deeper response to grow in his audience.

Although formal, he avoids the hierarchic cramping that Bresson sometimes resorts to. He frequently places the camera only a few inches off the ground, so that we believe ourselves reduced once more to a child's height and able to enjoy the humorous and affectionate relationship that can spring up between adults and children: a spontaneity that touches even the sombre, masterly scene where the son confesses his failure to his mother, as they sit on a grass verge close to the chimneys of a sewage farm. The verticality of the chimneys contrasts with the soft round shapes of the seated figures, and the composition reminds us of a poise that the son in his un-happiness has lost. It may remind us, too, that the son's confession, however personal, constitutes a severe criticism of a society which can waste its more talented and hard-working citizens so freely. Ozu's disenchantment with Fascist planning extends beyond Japan; he in-cludes a number of barbed references to National Socialist culture, and the mother falls asleep while watching a schmaltzy UFA musical; its 'lyrical' camera movements and over-expressiveness must have been qualities that he felt most opposed to.

In the year of Pearl Harbor he directed one of his most complex studies of family life, *The Brothers and Sisters of the Toda Family*. A powerful industrialist dies. His wife and one of his daughters un-expectedly find themselves without means and have to endure the brusque hospitality of relatives. They react to contempt with a discreet sense of amusement; but Ozu, typically, never loses touch with the greater pain. A brother returns from Manchuria and trounces his patronizing relatives. In turn, this just avenger finds his equanimity disturbed when his sister tries to push him into marriage.

The story develops through a series of family meetings: the official photograph taken on the lawn, the gathering of relatives at the time of death, the tea party from which the mother and daughter

Yasujiro Ozu: *The Brothers and Sisters of the Toda Family.*

are snobbishly excluded. Ozu does not draw a historical allegory out of these ceremonies as Nagisa Oshima has done with a similar kind of plot. Nor is he primarily interested in discriminating between selfish and generous behaviour. His principal aim, it would appear, is to put the spectator in touch with the distress felt by the widow and her younger daughter, while at the same time acknowledging the fact that the spectator is a stranger to the household and must extrapolate long-standing intimacies from the evidence of photographs and other souvenirs. The industrialist's house, with its ornate and dark collection of furniture, is alien enough to be chilling; and this feeling of detachment is pointed up by the frequent and slightly comic sight of the plants and mina bird that the mother and daughter lug from dwelling to dwelling. As in *The Only Son*, Ozu brings us close to the grief of others without explicit reference to the mother's tragedy. His humour finds in her presence a suitable means of undermining the pretensions of the cold-hearted.

The return of the brother from Manchuria, presumably from war service, is the nearest Ozu comes to mentioning the war. It is improbable that we shall ever know whether his silence was unusual or not. Japanese commentators are extremely reluctant to talk about the war period. SCAP, the American agency in charge of the Japanese film industry from 1945 to 1953, destroyed many of the so-called war films and confiscated the rest. Their definition of a war film appears to have been a wide one, for it included *The Story of the Last Chrysanthe-mums*, only recently released by the Library of Congress. Apparently one group in SCAP wished to destroy all evidence of a Japanese film industry and to fill the cinemas with Hollywood productions, while another group wished to restart the industry on a more liberal basis. The second group, though soon disbanded, did have a beneficial in-fluence and by 1947 had encouraged a type of film-making with some affinity to Italian neo-realism, among its more notable productions being Kurosawa's *No Regrets for Our Youth* (1946), Kinoshita's *Morning with the Osone Family* (1946), Yamamoto's *War and Peace* (1947) and Gosho's *Once Again* (1947).

It is unlikely that many of the destroyed films were overt war propaganda. The Japanese people were too obedient to the Emperor's wishes to need that sort of encouragement, and there were other more effective ways of reminding them of their obligations. 'Throughout the war a part of each day in every Japanese school was devoted to a terrible litany. The Ethics teacher would call the boys to the front of the class and demand of them one by one what they would do if the Emperor commanded them to die. Shaking with fright, the child would answer: "I would die, Sir, I would rip open my belly and die."'[6] The Emperor's power was so great that when he announced the surrender in August 1945, and counselled that 'we must bear the un-bearable', his people laid down their arms and began to serve their conquerors.

The Industry of Japan (1942), a documentary intended for European distribution (the Cape Town authorities captured a copy being taken to Lisbon), makes a good deal of the paternalist organization of Japanese factories: in microcosm, it encourages us to believe, a form of welfare state. But its happy family mood is tinged with melancholy and certain shots of regimentation at the conveyor belt are about as appealing as the factory scenes in René Clair's *A Nous la liberté*. Surely this propaganda won over nobody, though its quietness of tone and poetic touches—such as the repeated image of a bird-cage overlooking the factory compound—suggest less the wish to convert than to reassure.

There is nothing of samurai belligerence about it. The same is true, even more oddly, of *Five Scouts*, a war film released in 1938, a year of military jubilation when Japan captured Suchow, Peking and Nanking. It gives a tendentious account of the war's beginning and, like *The Industry of Japan*, over-promotes the virtues of a paternalist organization. Yet it differs in strategy from Anglo-American propa-ganda. Teinosuke Tasaka, its director (who was in Hiroshima at the end of the war and suffered for years from the after-effects of radiation), emphasizes more than Vidor or Milestone ever did the atmosphere of camaraderie that exists among a contingent of soldiers encamped behind the lines in a ruined Manchurian fort. He shows how much time is spent in thinking about food. Someone steals a water-melon and a goose; someone else plays a tune through a strand of grass. The treatment is both droll and elegiac. Then five scouts are sent out on patrol and rapid flanking shots track them through marshlands —a contrast to the rural jog of the scenes in camp. One of the scouts fails to return. His comrades weep, and feelings of solidarity intensify. But he does return, much at the same time as a command arrives from HQ ordering the battalion to the front line. Tasaka's treatment from this moment on is most unlike Anglo-American propaganda. The men sing a joyful hymn at the thought of meeting an almost certain death.

In Japan suicides are frequent, murders unusual. Aggression in peacetime is turned in on the self. The effect of *Five Scouts* resembles Kumagai's *The Tragedy of the Abe Clan* (1938) or the often filmed legend of the forty-seven ronin, both of which end with mass suicides, and adds credibility to the report that at one time Japanese audiences measured the pathos of a story by its number of suicides. Anglo-American propaganda often derives its satisfactions from attacks on the enemy; *Five Scouts* offers the bitter-sweet prospect of dying with one's friends, a death especially pleasurable since it discharges the onerous obligation all good citizens must feel to the Emperor.

The elegiac tone of *Five Scouts*, made at a time of victory, is indistinguishable from the tone of *The Burmese Harp* (1955), which recalls the consequences of defeat. If put together, these two movies suggest that many Japanese found the experience of war secondary to some far more enduring ritual of atonement. Kon Ichikawa, who directed *The Burmese Harp*, manages to transpose the elliptical texture of Michio Takayama's novel to the screen and holds the delicate balance between its symbolic and naturalistic intentions. He follows Takayama in telling the story from the viewpoint of some soldiers stranded in Burma at the time of the surrender. One of them, Mizoshima, a corporal, cheers up the others by playing a Burmese harp and leading them in plangent sing-songs. They idolize him as a kind of angel and fall into despair when he fails to return from a mission. One day they pass a monk on a bridge who resembles him but who does not stay to greet them. Later, on board the ship taking them back to Japan, they read a letter in which he tells them why he has decided to remain in Burma. He had witnessed so many corpses on his mission that he had determined to give over his life to burying the dead of whatever nation.

Ichikawa has said that his talent was shaped by the experience of living in the ruins of Tokyo. He has also said that Walt Disney's skill in marrying sound to images formed his resolve to become a film director—and, indeed, he began his career in animation. Both these statements reflect the contradictory nature of his personality. His main concern is an adoration, as of a disciple or child, for the kind of person who recognizes, as did the Emperor, that the honourable course is to bear the unbearable: the loner who voluntarily joins the losers. In laying open his heart in this way he makes himself exceedingly vulnerable, and he partly defends his films and protects his own privacy by a taste for fantasies that border on the whimsical, a mild sense of irony and a tendency towards self-deprecation. It is typical of his respect that his camera should follow Mizoshima at a distance, typical also that he should save himself from the charge of being mawkish, or of allowing his hero to fall into stereotype, by a quizzical obliquity. His irony usually contains some element of ambivalence; and though it would be ungenerous to see Mizoshima's act of renunciation as a means of discharging guilty feelings of obligation to those who died, Ichikawa does direct the spectator's thoughts in this direction by his habit of planting the seed of negativism in most of his central characters. Renunciation becomes a gesture of defiance in *The Sin* (1961), of destruction in *Conflagration* (1958), of erotic self-destruction in *Odd Obsession* (1959) and of sheer spite in *The Heart* (1955). At times, this negativism looks particularly Japanese, especially when it is mingled with nuances about caste difference. His intricate fascination with wayward behaviour can diminish the urgency of his themes.

Kon Ichikawa: *Conflagration.*

If he is typically Japanese, he is so in a selfconscious way that affected few, if any, of his predecessors. Occasionally, for instance, he appears to play up alien traits to please the tourist. His documentary *Kyoto* (1968), sponsored by Olivetti, virtually reduces the sights of the city to its two most insular monuments, the Katsura villa and the Ryoanji temple. His beautiful use of close-up converts the austerity and abstraction of Japanese architecture into a quintessence of strangeness that these places hardly embody, and some of his whimsical touches, as in the telephoto shot of a red mini wobbling down a street, could be intended to tantalize the foreigner by confounding him.

Yet his awareness of post-war internationalism has a positive side to it. Mizoshima bridges the hostility between Burma and Japan when he dons the robes of a Buddhist monk. His fate demonstrates a humanism that transcends nationalist interests: a theme Ichikawa has enlarged on in *Alone on the Pacific* (1963) and in his most important film so far, *Tokyo Olympiad* (1965). Leni Riefenstahl, in *Olympia*, had extolled the harmony and integration of the human body and seen in the present a realization of some Hellenic ideal. Ichikawa, who has no liking for sport, discovers his ideals elsewhere: in the gathering together of so many human and therefore fallible beings from all over the globe; in the friendships that can emerge from a mutual tolerance of physical limitation. He observes the winners admiringly; whenever his cameras, that is, can tear themselves away from the irresistible attraction of following the losers. Throughout the second half of the sixties he directed no features, claiming that the styles of the young French film-makers, with their implicit erosion of traditional morality, had shaken his confidence.

He had also been unsettled by the collapse of the studio system. Like Kurosawa at Toho, he has needed Daiei to finance his expensive productions; and though Kurosawa and he have not had an easy relationship with the studio chiefs, it has been a productive one. By 28 April 1952, when the American occupation officially ceased, the five leading companies had gained a control over the means of production and first-cinema runs that was even tighter than it had been before the war. They imitated Hollywood, and not only in their business practice. In 1950, at the time of the Korean War, they instigated a purge against Communist employees. A number of these expelled producers and directors, led by Kaneto Shindo, founded Kindai Eikyo, an independent production company. In a few years the company had become responsible for over thirty films, including Shindo's *Children of Hiroshima* (1952) and *The Island* (1961), Imai's *And Yet We Live* (1951) and Satsuo Yamamoto's *Vacuum Zone* (1952). The political intention in many of these films was plain: they were the first in Japan to bring to the screen the brutality of the Japanese army during the war and the devastation that followed the nuclear attacks. But though the company has continued to exist, it has been unable to keep up its impetus and in the sixties, for instance, Shindo turned his hand to horror movies such as the skilfully executed, insubstantial *Onibaba* (1964) and *Kuroneko* (1967). Nagisa Oshima has said: 'There was little in the content of their films or in the way they were directed that distinguished them from the major companies. I even asked myself if these were really independent productions. In the first four or five years they made great progress. But their lack of *shutaisei* (subjectivity, originality, consistency) was the main reason for the deterioration of their standards.' [7]

Oshima belongs to a later, more radical generation and is the best-known representative of the Japanese cinema's third break away into independence. He was to leave Shochiku, which he had joined in 1954, to found his own company, Sozosha, at the beginning of the sixties after *Night and Fog in Japan* had been withdrawn from the circuits on political grounds. In 1962 he and a number of freelance directors, including Susumi Hani, Shohei Imamura, Hiroshi Teshigahara and Masahiro Shinoda, formed the Arts Theatre Guild to increase their powers of distribution. What is striking about this new generation of film-makers is its refusal to subscribe to the paternalism of the past and its hostility to its predecessors, especially Kurosawa. Although many of them are committed to an analysis of problems from a Marxist viewpoint, their commitment seldom exhibits much emotional involvement in their subject-matter. Perhaps they are opposed to the idea that style may emerge unselfconsciously from the stress of experience like lines on a face; certainly most of them chose styles as they might a new suit.

No different from other nations, Japan has its chameleon directors, the most gifted of them being Keisuke Kinoshita. In a long career modelled on the example of Duvivier, Kinoshita has traversed a wide range of themes without giving any evidence of having touched on any centrality in himself. But the younger generation has chosen a different path. Its members despise journeymen; many of them have been influenced by the work of Jean-Luc Godard; and they see the film-maker as an individualist making statements much as a novelist can do. But whereas Godard has personality enough to discover a coherence in the essayistic or epistolary technique which mixes all manner of genres, his Japanese followers tend to lapse into impersonality when they use this technique. Apart from Hani's *She and He* (1963), which operates successfully within a familiar convention, the alienating effects of these directors often have the effect of merely alienating. In Shinoda's *Double Suicide* (1969) Bunraku puppeteers change scenes and move about the actors: a complicated plot device that comes between the spectator and any meaning the love story might have had. In *The Adventures of Buraikan* (1970) Shinoda's uneasiness about his subject emerges as a belittling of any belief in its dignity. Whether this incapacity in feeling reflects a loss of nerve in a diminishing field of communication or a failure of wider social significance remains an open question. Yet in the sixties, it is true, facetiousness and mannerism touched more than the work of the younger generation. They marred, in particular, Ichikawa's *An Actor's Revenge* (1963). Directors seem to have found human relationships insuperably difficult to enact, and portentous symbolism often stood as a substitute for feeling. Teshigahara's *Woman of the Dunes* (1964) demonstrates this trend into abstraction most uncompromisingly. Son of a well-known flower arrangement artist and trained as a painter, Teshigahara had helped to make a couple of short films on the effect of nuclear fission; all these experiences lie behind his account of the woman and her trapped lover. He sees their movements primarily as contrasts in texture—mainly of flesh against sand—or as a bold black and white pattern-making reminiscent of Japanese calligraphy. By 1968 Teshigahara had veered so far into abstraction that certain passages in *The Man without a Map* (1968) consist of cryptic arpeggios in imagery disconnected from Kobo Abe's difficult enough novel and screenplay. However, he had changed direction by the time he came to make *Summer Soldiers* (1972), employing symbolism only to heighten the meaning of relationships. A young GI deserter from Vietnam is protected by members of the Japanese Peace Movement, who pass him from family to family. Teshigahara is accurate about both the differences and similarities between races. He doesn't fall back on the myth of oriental inscrutability. And his portrait of the deserter—vulnerable, brash and frightened—is so built up as to convey the feeling of the character without explaining him.

In his early work Nagisa Oshima appears to have been dazzled by film technique. Yet already he was beginning to respond distinctively to a question that fascinated many Japanese directors in the sixties: how does a child maintain its sanity when brought up in a corrupt environment or raised by corrupt parents? He does not fall into the easy negativism of Shindo's answer to this question in *Live Today, Die Tomorrow* (1970); and in *Boy* (1969) and *The Ceremony* (1971) he began to reveal an exceptional capacity for symbolizing conflict. The main idea in the plot of *Boy* was drawn from a newspaper story. A young father, mentally disturbed by war service, obtains money by having his wife and child risk their lives in faking car accidents: he then blackmails the drivers. The police track down the family, and it moves more and more northwards until it reaches the snowy further-

Nagisa Oshima: *Boy*.

most tip of Hokkaido. The boy, forced to disguise himself behind a
pair of damaging thick-lensed spectacles, remains impassive for most
of the story, yet Oshima finds ingenious ways of dramatizing his
feelings. In one of the final scenes the boy builds a large snowman
as a substitute for his inadequate parents and movingly realizes
through it his dream of 'a spaceman of justice from the Andromeda
galaxy'.

Oshima's capacity for symbolizing conflict had become so intricate
by the time he came to make *The Ceremony* that he sometimes
found it hard to give it form. Masuo travels with a female cousin
by steamer and rowing-boat across lakes to an island where another
cousin, he soon learns, has committed hara-kiri: the ultimate
ceremony, in the sense that, like all ceremonies, it binds the self to its
ancestors. On the journey he recalls his birth in war-divided Manchuria
and his upbringing in Tokyo under the supervision of his stern
grandfather. He remembers the past through its funerals and
weddings. Awesome relatives squat before altars as impassively as
Byzantine emperors, in rooms where luminous blues and yellows
predominate. But the child Masuo soon discovers that the judges
are war criminals or profiteers and the grandfather, who has sired
nearly everyone around the altar, the most corrupt of all. In *Boy*
Oshima had interpreted the intermittent consciousness of his central
character in terms of reportage. In *The Ceremony* he touches on a
deeper level of consciousness, raises larger inferences and proffers
no immediate solutions. Masuo puts an ear to the ground and listens

Nagisa Oshima: *The Ceremony.*

to the breathing of his dead infant brother. He understands the world as a succession of animistic mysteries. His aunt appears to him like a bright angel. But she dies horribly, perhaps murdered by the grandfather; the mystery is never solved. Masuo is baffled by the comings and goings of his seniors, the awkward silences, the sudden changes of subject. Oshima observes the scandals in kinship and raises a monstrous genealogy as distracting as a maze.

His ambitious desire to describe the psychic history of his race since the war is not unusual in the Japanese cinema, though it is unusual when looked at in an international context. Kinoshita's *A Japanese Tragedy* (1953) and Koyabashi's *The Human Condition* (1959–61), as well as other movies, demonstrate how a bewilderment about the nature of the national identity can impel the film-maker to take a synoptic view. In *Legend from a Southern Island* (1968) Shohei Imamura studies with an anthropologist's eye the modernization of a semi-tropical island: how the civilization of airports and Coca Cola can replace the power of legends and priests. His scriptwriter, Keiji Hasebe, is a surrealist. They refer explicitly to Buñuel's *Robinson Crusoe,* and indeed to the ancient island in Antonioni's *L'avventura.* But Imamura moves too far away from his source in observation to be able to probe incisively into the meaning of spiritual change. His ideas do not add to the models from which they are derived.

For all its hostility to the studio system, the younger generation has never approached the sustained studio output of 1952–6, golden years when Gosho, Mizoguchi, Ozu and Kurosawa directed one important film after another. A number of factors contributed to this upsurge in creativity: box-office confidence, overseas recognition, the ending of the American occupation. In the mirror of neo-realism and of foreign approval, Japanese directors began to recognize their national identity. Mizoguchi was especially fortunate. A former colleague, Masaichi Nagata, was to be in charge of production at Daiei and gave him a great deal of freedom. He found a sympathetic cameraman in Kazuo Miyagawa, who worked on all the films of his last period.

He and Ozu had now become masters, although as masters they were more visionary than Olympian. They drew their ideas from the residues of past experience and allowed their material to take on a pace that appeared languid in comparison with that of other contemporary films: a pace, however, that allowed the formal and imaginative qualities of their themes to reach fruition. In *An Autumn Afternoon* (1962), for instance, Ozu creates a time and place of the mind, present-day Tokyo only by token. It gathers in all the skills and wisdom acquired through a long career.

Mizoguchi also built autonomous structures and achieved a formal poise that at moments touches on the serene. He had his scriptwriters delve deep into the past: in *The Life of O-Haru* (1952) and *Chikamatsu*

Kenji Mizoguchi: *The Life of O-Haru.*

Monogatari (1954) to the late seventeenth century, in *Sansho Dayu* (1954) and *Shin Heike Monogatari* (1955) to the eleventh century, in *The Empress Yang Kwei-Fei* (1955) to China in the eighth century. No other director has shown so assured a familiarity with the remote past. He evokes an experience – presumably universal in the Middle Ages – of an uncharted world where brigands, pirates, war-lords and beautiful malignant ghosts roam with impunity: an agoraphobic vision, epitomized by the recurring image of a small boat bobbing on a vast lake, that perhaps relates to his memories of the traumatized and blitzed Japan of 1945. Few of his leading characters enjoy the security of palace or hut for long. War and abrupt changes in fortune drive them out into the wilderness. They move over an unending land: an exile and a voyage that last a lifetime. But they are also victims of an arbitrary caste system which divides them from their relatives and loved ones by distances that seem even greater. A son learns that his mother is an Emperor's courtesan. A mother reduced to poverty dares not approach her baby son raised to riches and carried past in a sedan chair. *Sansho Dayu* illuminates this vision most fully. The bailiff Sansho separates a brother and sister from their youthful mother and brings them up as slaves in a concentration camp. The boy, brutalized by this upbringing, regains some humanity when his sister sacrifices herself to help him escape. He seeks for his mother and learns to his horror that at one time she had become a prostitute. Eventually he finds her, a blind old woman who lives by picking seaweed off a lonely sea-shore.

Mizoguchi conveys the belief that both mother and son have been beaten down by their pilgrimage to each other, at the same time subordinating the pathos of their meeting to an awesome impression of the sea-shore that surrounds them. He is less concerned with the tragedy of individuals or of communities than of tragic figures set in remarkable landscapes. There is a distancing in his view of agony, comparable to Ozu's anti-expressionism, and a sense of proportion comparable to a Zen garden, where solitary rocks stranded in a sea of small white pebbles can mysteriously arouse sensations of peace. He summons up a feudal belief in hierarchies. The concluding image of *Ugetsu Monogatari*, a crane shot rising above peasants tilling a mountain field, embodies the feudal understanding of mankind's relatively lowly place in the chain of being.

Mizoguchi died in 1956 and did not have to face the studio crises of the next decade, or the public's loss of interest in humanist themes. Some directors like Shindo and Ichikawa were able to some extent to adapt themselves to changing circumstances. Others would not, or could not; the most notable of them being Akira Kurosawa. Between *Red Beard* (1964) and *Dodeska Den* (1970) Kurosawa was involved in various projects, none of which (so far as he was concerned) came to anything. He provided much of the financial support for *Dodeska Den* out of his own pocket: a deeply cherished work which many of his European admirers greeted with bewilderment. Passing time will alone show whether their disappointment was justified. At present it looks, perhaps deceptively, like an amalgam of de Sica's *Miracolo a Milano* with a Minnelli musical of the forties.

Kurosawa's commitment to neo-realism has been both faithful and complicated. If his long-standing partnership with the flamboyant Toshiro Mifune represents his interest in childlike characters who clumsily and with a sense of burlesque aspire to the samurai ideal, his even more long-standing partnership with Takashi Shimura marks his attraction to a more fatherly neo-realist figure: someone less egocentric than the Mifune characters and more capable of learning from defeat. If Mifune as a wild beast at bay startles us into recognizing the knife-edged distinction between life and death, Shimura, as Mr Watanabe in *Living* (1952), deliberating over the meaning of death as cancer spreads through his stomach, gives us a more tentative and constructive response to the inevitable. (He liberates himself from routine, in fact, and uses his powers as a petty bureaucrat to promote a children's park.) Kurosawa constructs the story either through direct observation or through the reports and rumours of subsidiary characters; and in this complex time scheme, which includes some reference to the theme of illusion and reality, he diverges from the Italian neo-realists. Yet he cannot resist over-selling his case in the same way as de Sica did in *Umberto D.* (Both films were released in the same year.) He and Shimura present the old man as an object of charity. In recoiling from this importunity, the spectator may re-member André Gide's remark that art and good intentions are seldom compatible.

Kurosawa's earnest naïvety can be strident. It is hard to share his enthusiasm for the clowning porter in *They Who Sleep on the Tiger's Tail* (1945) or for the two peasants in *The Hidden Fortress* (1958) whose grimacing often seems to imitate certain forms of insanity. Yet Japanese audiences welcomed the populist appeal of the two peasants, and in intention at least these clowns do bridge the gap between ordinary people and Kurosawa's aloof tyrants. In *Yojimbo* (1961) and *Sanjuro* (1962) he once more won public approval by parodying the Western to the point of ridicule. Sergio Leone's *A Fistful of Dollars* (1964), which began a cycle of Italian Westerns, imitated this strategy and indeed borrowed Kurosawa's plot.

But he can relieve this naïvety by narrative wit, evident especially in his editing, and by a wish—often a consequence of naïvety—to push insights to the point where they become painful. He would like to see man as a fallen angel; at the same time, he cannot avoid acknowledging him as the most aggressive of animals. *Red Beard*

Akira Kurosawa: *Red Beard*.

promises to be a pale carbon-copy of neo-realist good intentions, like the *Dr Kildare* TV series, but Kurosawa's disturbing, animal-like view of the doctor's patients—a consumptive bites the air like a hen, a woman on an operating table jerks like a beast dying in a slaughter-house, a rich lord wheezes like an overfed poodle—intimates how close much human behaviour may be to the appearance of schizo-phrenia. The doctor believes that medicines are at best placatory. He thinks that deprivation and heartbreak bring on illness; all he can do is wait for his patients to find relief in confession. Kurosawa shows these confessions in flashbacks and often accompanied by eerie snow-storms, earthquakes and glittering, unearthly fields. This view of mind and memory brings him near to Dostoyevsky's type of insight. At moments his naïvety shows itself to be inseparable from an ex-plorer's courage.

He often constructs his stories around an unworldly idea and de-velops it with such tenacity that it becomes a monumental, worldly statement about the human condition. In *Seven Samurai* (1954) he starts with a picture of virtue, described most clearly in the scene where Shimura, as Kambei, an ageing samurai, risks his life by rush-ing into a hut and seizing a baby from a bandit who holds it hostage. Kurosawa idealizes his unemployed mercenary soldiers (they might be called ronin) to the point where they become, like Robin Hood, the stuff of legend. He accepts unquestioningly as good their desire to defend some peasant farmers and their crops against the attack of bandits, however suicidal the cost, even though the militarist regime of the thirties might have commended this self-destructive kind of justice. Indeed, the regime did commend such an idea to the Kamikaze pilots who killed themselves to protect the homeland. It also insisted on obedience, an important tenet for Kurosawa: the farmers, he shows us, resist the bandits successfully because they are willing to obey the samurai and to work together as a team. Kurosawa, son of an instructor at a military academy, revives a military ethos which the militarists had favoured. At the same time, he boldly seeks to rehabilitate this ethos which the militarists, in fact, had contaminated.

He works this change in a number of ways. He modifies the meaning of the samurai vocation so as to give it dignity in the contemporary world. His samurai have, in a sense, lived through the disillusion of 1945 and only slightly resemble their predecessors. Kambei states that prisoners of war should not be killed: an anachronistic view that would have been greeted with incomprehension before 1945. His acceptance of defeat without any outward evidence of glory would not have been probable before the unheroic end to the war. He appears to have lost any belief in the sympathy or cohesion of the nation or community. He and his fellow samurai act together as a team, yet they remain lonely, isolated figures. Their relationship with the farmers is a bitter one. They despise the farmers who deceive and cheat them, much as a returning soldier might despise war profiteers. They continue somewhat rigidly to observe their code of honour, though their code has lost its paternalist justification.

Kurosawa modifies the militarist ethos most interestingly by building his plot around the presence of Kikuchiyo (Mifune), the one wholly successful clown in his canon. Kikuchiyo is the illegitimate son of a farmer; he aspires to be a samurai; and he wins the affection of both farmers and samurai by his habit of burlesquing the mannerisms of both of them. At the beginning of the action he appears drunk and helpless, seemingly caged by the wooden struts of a byre; yet of all the characters he is the only one to achieve freedom. He does not fear to lose face; he has a sense of humour. He does not deny his birthright, yet he wishes to live less pusillanimously than the farmers do. He bridges the gap between the castes, and between the feudal past and the more democratic present.

The violence in this story remains unexplored. We see little of the bandits and never learn whether their motives are primarily economic or sadistic. Kurosawa does not see them as representing a form of social protest; and the temper of his work suggests no sympathy for the flamboyant nihilism of the Sicilian bandit who said: 'Ah gentlemen, if I had been able to read and write, I'd have destroyed the

Akira Kurosawa : *The Seven Samurai.*

human race.'[8] Yet their violence is ferocious, and Kurosawa can
barely contain it within the Pandora's box of simplistic morality. It
issues forth in splendid set pieces, such as the final battle scene with
its swirl of horses' rumps and falling bodies in a greyness of blinding
rain and mud. He films death in slow motion: a device that Sam
Peckinpah has often imitated, most notably in *The Wild Bunch.* But
while Peckinpah tries to exorcise the inevitable by viewing violent
death as an aesthetic experience, Kurosawa sees it as a different kind
of mystery, as part of an archaic world touched by sacred forces,
where the thump of a mill-wheel measures out an old man's pro-
phecies and dust-winds howl about the graves of heroes.

Alain Jessua: *La Vie à l'envers.*

14. The New Wave

*The media are exactly the places where the deepest and most personal
sensitivities and confessions of reality are most prohibited, mocked, suppressed.*

ALLEN GINSBERG, *San Francisco Chronicle*, 29 July 1959

France

Françoise Giroud in *L'Express* called it the Nouvelle Vague or New
Wave: a phrase which some commentators dismissed as a confusing
journalists' label. Yet confusing though it was, it did define an exceptional event. Between 1958 and 1963 about 170 French directors
made their first features, at a time when the French cinema, like the
cinema elsewhere, was losing its audiences. (In 1963 attendance
figures had fallen to 290 million, a steady loss of 100 million on the
figure for 1957.) But by a strange contradiction, this decline in
audiences opened up a number of opportunities for the film-maker. In
the late fifties producers had begun to recognize that expensive productions by Claude Autant-Lara, for one, were insufficiently adventurous to take people away from their television sets, even though
at this time television had less of a hold on the public in France than
in the United States and Great Britain. Braunberger and Beauregard
were notable among these producers in thinking it a better investment to risk the cost of an Autant-Lara production on eight or nine
low-budget features in the expectation of making more than adequate
profits on at least a couple of them.

They were encouraged in this thought by two factors. One of them
was the *loi d'aide*, a quality film award introduced in 1948 in an
attempt to revive a moribund industry and since then twice redefined,
in 1955 and 1959. The *loi d'aide* really did help the bold film-maker.
Truffaut's short *Les Mistons*, which had cost five million francs, was
awarded four-and-a-half million, while Chabrol's *Le Beau Serge*, which
had cost forty-six million, was awarded thirty-five million. It is unlikely that Truffaut would have gone on at once to direct *Les Quatre
Cents Coups*, or Chabrol *Les Cousins*, without this financial incentive.

The producers were even more impressed by the need to employ young directors to capture the teenage market: youngsters who could not bear to stay at home in the evenings, loathed all that their parents admired and hungered for a less conventional kind of movie. In one sense, this feeling of dissent was bound up with the adolescent condition; in another sense, its long-lasting intensity implied the existence of genuine social grievances. It was no accident that the French New Wave and its imitators in other countries should have followed the Beat movement in the United States or that later it should have had some connection with the university revolts of 1968. But its origins were complex and it did not begin in politics. A cycle of American movies that described the adolescent crisis from a middle-aged viewpoint—a viewpoint not so much parental as that of a slightly corrupt uncle—was certainly one of its sources. The two most memorable films in this cycle were Nicholas Ray's *Rebel without a Cause* and Elia Kazan's *East of Eden*, both of them released in 1955 and starring

Elia Kazan: *East of Eden*. James Dean, Julie Harris.

James Dean. Acting out the fantasy of a shy, helpless youth seemingly emasculated by the presence of a stern father and sexually inviting mother, Dean was to become as much admired by his generation as Valentino had been thirty years before.

But French directors were only marginally interested in this conflict between puritanism and licence. They tried to appeal to the public by different means. Alexandre Astruc's *Les Mauvaises Rencontres* (1955) suggested one way. 'Two years before Françoise Sagan,' wrote Louis Marcorelles, 'Astruc showed up (in spite of himself) the vacuity of a world without solid foundations, deeply corrupt, but a world in which youth, through its very despair, takes on an extra quality of pathos.'[1] Moreover, French directors were more fascinated by sexually emancipated women than by discontented adolescent males. While young American audiences were offered James Dean, Marlon Brando and Marilyn Monroe, who presented themselves as self-pitying and somehow damaged, the young French were offered Brigitte Bardot, who appeared to go through the most harassing experiences unscathed—her lovers bore the scathing. Like Mae West, Bardot embodied the idea of free sex without guilt. She played the role of Rousseau's child of nature, responding with pagan indifference to puritan envy.

Roger Vadim, briefly her husband, brought her to international stardom with *And God Created Woman* (1956). Formerly a *Paris Match* photographer, Vadim gave his film the glossy flair of *Paris Match* journalism, and also a Gidean distrust for conventional views on

Roger Vadim: *And God Created Woman*. Jean-Louis Trintignant, Brigitte Bardot.

morality and art—he had at one time been André Gide's private secretary. Following Wilde, Gide had argued that morality and art were inseparable and that in the novel, especially, the questioning of certain moral assumptions of necessity raised doubts about traditional means of constructing narrative and character. He was most fully to realize this position in his novel *Les Caves du Vatican*, where Lafcadio, a bland young pagan, commits a murder without apparent motive. Gide believed that this murder illustrated his theory of the *acte gratuit*. When Vadim said of *And God Created Woman* that he had not tried to tell a story or to explain his characters, he was perhaps acknowledging his debt to Gide as well as establishing a tenet of New Wave thought.

In working with Bardot, Vadim established his reputation as a film director. Louis Malle was to achieve the same results with Jeanne Moreau, a gifted actress who had previously been type-cast in films as a prostitute. Malle gave her a leading part in *Lift to the Scaffold* (1957), while in *Les Amants* (1958) he completed her transition from whore to society woman. Like Buñuel's *Belle de jour* (1966), which has a society woman amuse herself by working in a brothel during the afternoons, the equation apparently flattered women of both kinds as well as teasing certain men; yet it did not need much insight to see that the apparent freedom from inhibition of the characters played by Jeanne Moreau was associated with an almost permanent expression of soured discontent on their faces and a shallowness of feeling that could not be concealed by protracted displays of voluptuary skill. *Les Amants* enjoyed a *succès de scandale* and was thought to have opened up new areas of sexual frankness. But those who complained of its frankness would have been on surer ground if they had complained less of its frankness than of its obvious contrivance. An actress in bed remains an actress in bed; and for all her protestations of sincerity, the Moreau character remained a cool performer. Malle tried to conceal this limitation with the trappings of High Culture, having Brahms's plangent string sextet played for all its worth.

One of the more striking facts about the New Wave directors is that few of them reacted on film to the national crisis that had erupted at the time when many of them were first given the chance to direct. At the beginning of 1958, France appeared to be moving steadily to-towards civil war over the Algerian question. The government had proved itself to be ineffectual; the military threatened to seize power. In May 1958 General de Gaulle managed to have himself elected president by a series of adroit manoeuvres. After two years in which the OAS terrorized France and Algeria, de Gaulle found a way to re-solve the crisis and for the next decade submitted his country to an autocratic rule that had many of the features of a dictatorship. For a long time, the New Wave directors appeared to be at a remove from these events. Jean-Luc Godard's second feature, *Le Petit Soldat* (1960), was banned for some time in metropolitan France, but it did no more than allude to the coercions of the OAS. Robert Enrico elegantly touched on the war in *La Belle Vie* (1965). Apart from one incident— the Algerian leader Ben Barka was kidnapped outside the Brasserie Lipp, where he was to have met Georges Franju to discuss a film about his life—French film-makers appear to have lived light years away from the war. Their reticence seems all the more surprising when compared to their subsequent hostility, ceaselessly expounded, to the American presence in Vietnam. It was left to an Italian, Gillo Pontecorvo, to attempt an analysis of the war in *The Battle of Algiers* (1968).

The first stage of the French New Wave had spent itself by 1963. Producers were no longer so eager to promote young talent. The slump in the film industry had grown too severe to take even small gambles, and the prevailing system of finance, by which producers based their salaries on a percentage of the budget, made shoestring economies hardly worth their while. And the public had grown tired of the publicity surrounding the young directors, many of whom had been admired for their youth alone, and many of whom had turned out to be less talented than had been expected. The negative reaction to François Truffaut's *La Peau douce* at the Cannes festival of 1963 marked this reversal in public favour. But it was not to be long-lasting. Truffaut and many other figures in the New Wave were to continue making films; and indeed what was to be remarkable about these young film-makers was not that so many of them were to fail but that so many were able to continue in their careers, and to mature as talents to an extent that their first films had given little promise of. (Malle, Rivette and Rohmer are cases in point.)

Most of these survivors had originally been associated with one of two groups. Godard, Chabrol, Truffaut, Rivette and Eric Rohmer were part-time critics who most evenings went to the Cinémathèque Française and in this way came to know each other. The other group, the so-called Left Bank group, consisting of Agnès Varda, Alain Resnais and Chris Marker, was older than the Cinémathèque regulars. The members of this second group were to be less narrowly committed to movies for their own sake. They were interested in politics and the arts in general and in relating movies to this context. The box-office success of Truffaut and Chabrol helped them to find backing for their own features. More or less on the outside of these two groups were Agnès Varda's husband, Jacques Demy, the surrealist Georges Franju and the documentarist Jean Rouch.

Alexander Werth has suggested in his biography of de Gaulle that the General's retreat into nationalism was partly based on a wish to extricate France from the Cold War deadlock. Many Frenchmen, wrote Louis Marcorelles, 'resented the absurdity of a modern world split between two warring ideologies. In France itself, there is a co-existence between a significant body of Communist voters (who are not generally speaking Party members, but who bear witness to the spread and attraction of Marxist ideas, particularly among the intellectuals) and a social framework which becomes steadily more Americanised.'[2] At a period when French anti-American feeling was at its most intense, Godard and Truffaut were writing about Hollywood B features with an enthusiasm that Chateaubriand had once shown for the Red Indians of North America. But it may be no coincidence that, at the time when de Gaulle was stirring the embers of French nationalism, the young film-makers began to subscribe to a new form of nationalistic romanticism, the political complexion of which was ambiguous. 'The political ideas of Brasillach were the same as Drieu la Rochelle's,' wrote Truffaut in *Cahiers du cinéma* of two Fascist collaborators. 'Ideas which result in their authors being sentenced to death are necessarily estimable.'[3] For all their interest in Hollywood, the young French film-makers were to be intensely proud of their own national identity. They attacked the older generation for producing international films· without this specific identity and praised Renoir, Bresson, Becker and Cocteau in part for their being so French in style. And they saw a model for their own careers in Jean-Pierre Melville, who had made some fine, low-budget and personal films outside the usual production channels.

They were also to admire foreign directors who had not worked in Hollywood, Rossellini being notable among them. But while they aspired to the neo-realist belief in the possible fraternity of mankind and the neo-realist wish to cleanse the eye of perception, they also subscribed to an extreme form of individualism: an egocentricity that produced manners of expression very far from the neo-realist assumption that truth in film usually has the impersonality of newsreel. In point of fact, they removed 'realism' from its high position among the vaguer terms of critical approbation and replaced it by the concept of authority, viewing the director as this ultimate authority and the sole arbiter of a film's meaning. What the spectator responded to, in this view, was the director's skill in conveying moments of revelation, his gift for releasing great energies. They believed that films should provide sensations of intense joy, of a kind that approached religious ecstasy.

They felt free to discard many former postulates of film criticism, for example that the value of a film lay in its charitable intentions or choice of an important or significant subject. (Stanley Kramer, especially, was anathema to them.) They saw no reason why a director should not mix genres, play havoc with narrative conventions or bring together the conflicting styles of animated cartoon, newsreel and musical; no reason why he should not plunder the complementary techniques of painting, dance, sculpture or typography, as Eisenstein and the other Soviet directors had done. They required one consistency only: that the director should have a strong personality and that he should be able to project his convictions. Godard reveal-ingly described himself as an essayist. Truffaut said that he planned out his sequences as though it were a circus programme in which it would be considered too taxing to place one elephant act after another. Both of them referred admiringly to Rousseau, Goethe and Balzac. Yet both of them were to evolve their ideas out of a tradition centred firmly on film and not literature.

Jean Rouch: *Chronique d'un été.*

One of the New Wave directors, Jean Rouch, looked for his model less to the neo-realists than to Dziga Vertov. He appropriated Vertov's slogan *kino-pravda,* which Georges Sadoul had translated in 1948 as *cinéma-vérité,* and began filming with a Vertovian freeness that stimulated film-makers in the United States as well as France—even though many of these film-makers were unaware that Rouch had used *cinéma-vérité* techniques as a means to help him in anthropological research. The development of lighter 16mm. cameras and faster film stock allowed them to use the hand-held camera technique in nearly every climate and location and for almost every kind of subject. But too many films with endless travelling shots and trembling camera movements brought *cinéma-vérité* into disrepute. Rouch had used the technique discriminatingly. He had been conscious of its history. He had recognized it as only one technique among many. In this perception, he and most of the New Wave directors differed from their imitators and indeed from most film-makers in the past.

They were the first student generation quickly to acquire a comprehensive idea of film history and to base their views on this knowledge.

One man had been responsible for this education. Henri Langlois had not only built up the precious archives at the Cinémathèque Française but had programmed his showing of films in such a way as to rid them of any suggestion of being museum objects. He would run two or three films every evening in unexpected yet revealing juxtapositions, placing an Eisenstein before a Raoul Walsh, or a Hitchcock after a Mizoguchi. Those who were regular members of his audience were among the first to have their sensibilities immersed in the history of images from the time of Muybridge and Marey onwards.

But in one way Langlois's programme planning could encourage a misapprehension. He divorced films from their context in culture or time and presented them as an ever unfolding tapestry, so that it was possible to see them as emanations from some single God-like mind (one reason, perhaps, why the Roman Catholic André Bazin and his *Cahiers du Cinéma* followers were inclined to think of the experience in religious terms). It did not matter if the radiance from one film carried over into another less brilliant one. Langlois, a one-time surrealist, was only marginally interested in evaluation as such or in the history of cultural development. He wanted to involve his audiences creatively in an idea of the cinema and to stimulate them into making their own mental films out of the fascinating bricolage of the past. It was an extension of André Malraux's insight into the nature of art in an age of photographic reproduction.

The question whether Rubens was admired because he proved himself Titian's equal in some of his less Flemish canvases loses much of its point when we examine an album containing Rubens' entire output—a complete world in itself . . . A true anthology is coming into being. For we now know that an artist's supreme work is not the one in best accord with any tradition—not even his most complete and 'finished' work—but his most personal work, the one from which he has stripped all that is not his own, and in which his style reaches its climax. [4]

What the New Wave directors did, in fact, was to realize on film their own museums without walls. Their films were to be self-reflexive and saturated with playful quotations : tributes that at their most trivial encouraged the spectator to become an armchair detective, tracking down iconographic clues at the expense of wider interests. But what this method also revealed was that these directors were less inclined to see technique as a vehicle for statement than as something that was meaningful in its own right. By taking up this position, moreover, they were following in a tradition of critical theory that had existed in France since at least the end of the war.

Jean-Paul Sartre's enthusiastic review of *Citizen Kane*, published in *L'Ecran français*, and Alexandre Astruc's 1948 article *The Birth of a New Avant-Garde: The Camera Stylo* had articulated this theory, if obscurely. 'The cinema,' wrote Astruc, 'will gradually break free from the tyranny of the visual, from the image for its own sake, from the immediate and concrete demands of narrative, to become a means of writing just as flexible and subtle as written language.' [5] From some of his statements, it would seem that Astruc was anticipating a cinema for myopic intellectuals, as when he argued that every film was a theorem, 'a series of images which, from one end to another, have an inexorable logic of their own', [6] or stated that if Descartes were living now he would be writing his philosophy on film. 'Problems such as the translation of verbal tenses and logical relationships interest us much more than the creation of the exclusively visual and static art dreamt of by the surrealist.' [7] Yet Astruc was less opposed to the visual appeal of the image than to the pictorialism of glossy photography or of picturesque compositions. He proposed in their place the notion of *mise en scène*, the ability certain directors have of bodying forth sensations and thoughts on film. 'All thought, like all feeling, is a relationship between one human being and another human being or of certain objects which form part of his universe.' [8]

He appears to have believed, in other words, that the experience of film was essentially corporeal, and that editing, camerawork and a dynamic relationship between the camera and the things it photographs can arouse in the spectator kinaesthetic sensations. None of this was new (see p. 30). What was new, however, was his interest in the ways in which images can convey meaning, an interest that associates him with other practitioners in the field of communication theory, especially with those concerned with the study of signs and meanings known as semiology.

In *Elements of Semiology* (1967) Roland Barthes, one of the leading practitioners in this field, proposed that the cinema, television and advertising were too complex in their effect to yield to his system of analysis, a system which distinguishes between an ideal structure (what he calls language or code) and the manner in which this structure is modified when put to use (what he calls speech or message). But some of Barthes's followers believed that the way in which he applied his system to clothes, cars, furniture and food did open up a possible way of interpreting the meaning of screen images. 'Menus, for instance, illustrate very well this relationship between language and speech: any menu is concocted with reference to structure (which is both national—or regional—and social); but this structure is filled differently according to the days and the users, just as linguistic "form" is filled by the free variations and combinations which a speaker needs for a particular message.' [9]

The primary value of this kind of analysis is that it may help to free the spectator from the tyranny of the stock response, as when the English critic Peter Wollen insists that the film image can be symbol, icon or index. 'More than anyone else, Godard has realised the fantastic possibilities of the cinema as a medium for communication and expression. In his hands, as in Pierce's perfect sign, the cinema has become an almost equal amalgam of the symbolic, the iconic and the indexical. His films have conceptual meaning, pictorial beauty and documentary truth.'[10] Yet to a greater degree than any other kind of criticism, this approach removes the spectator from Godard's criterion of joy as a guarantee of valuable filming.

In 1954 Agnès Varda had placed together two separate plots in *La Pointe courte*, in an imitation of William Faulkner's novel *The Wild Palms*; Alain Resnais, who edited *La Pointe courte*, was to develop this technique of parallelism further in his first feature, *Hiroshima mon amour* (1959); while Chris Marker, a friend of Varda and Resnais, was to disrupt the conventional grammar of film signs far more completely than they in a series of film letters, or essays, filmed in China, Israel, Cuba and Siberia.

But Marker's succinct wit in editing his rushes was to be less evident in *Le Joli Mai* (1962), his feature-length study of Paris during the May of 1961. While Ruttmann had seen Berlin as a kind of universal idea existing outside time, in which certain actions and gestures could be described as permanently typical, Marker sees Paris as taking on being in time alone. He emphasizes this sense of the momentary by a conscious use of the accidental – as when his camera observes a spider on the jacket of someone being interviewed – by recording twenty-four hours in the city at immense speed, or by contemplating panoramic views of the city with the pictorial gravity of a nineteenth-century photographer. He concerns himself with urban unhappiness and its 'cells of solitude', and in the second half of the film brings this theme to bear on the reactions of Parisians to the Algerian crisis. But for someone who believes that the fate of each of us is related to the other's – 'as long as prisons exist, you are not free' – he appears curiously unable to integrate his information. He is defeated, in part, by the limitations of the filmed image. Faces glimpsed in the street, or the speculations and prejudices of the passer-by, can provide no more than superficial information on the people of Paris.

But his feeling for the power of the image and his incantatory conception of form was to stand him in good stead when he came to direct his 'photo-roman' *La Jetée* (1963). As a child, the central character of *La Jetée* had witnessed the murder of a man on a pier, at Orly airport. A few years later, and some time in the future, a nuclear attack destroys Paris: and the enemy who take over the city submit

Chris Marker: *La Jetée.*

its few remaining citizens to experiments in time and memory, an often fatal kind of torture that takes place in the basement of the Palais de Chaillot, where formerly the Cinémathèque Française had existed. The central character, included among these victims, is forced to travel through seas of time and to relive an unhappily concluded love affair. He is finally destroyed by the emotional cost of these journeys. As he dies, he realizes that the man he had seen murdered at Orly had been himself.

Like the plot of Resnais's *Last Year at Marienbad* (1961), this idea appears absurd when thought about, yet utterly enthralling when realized on the screen. The paradox that memory of its essence exists in the present moment fascinates Marker, and he implies that the very fact that memory exists should induce an awe of religious depth. For all his Marxism, he sets weight on the notion of an atemporal *promesse de bonheur*. He associates the murder at Orly with the sacramental (the interior of a cathedral and the chant of a choir), in turn relating these experiences to the destruction of Paris. He comes close to the insight that Jacques Rivette had formulated in *Paris nous appartient*: that if Paris belongs to us then in a sense we must be responsible for its lives and deaths.

But these voyages through time also evoke those sensations that Louis Delluc had called photogenic. Apart from one shot of a woman opening her eyes as she awakens from sleep, Marker compiles his images from still photographs. Clearly he did so to avoid the expense of constructing a blitzed Paris; but more positively he needed the isolated yet resonant photogenic image. He had been limited in *Le Joli Mai* by shots of faces that gave up little meaning in spite of their suggestibility. In *La Jetée* he was able through editing to use suggestibility for a precise end.

If Marker achieves an atmosphere of metaphysical reverie in *La Jetée* more characteristic of his friend Alain Resnais—and indeed Resnais was to deal with an almost identical subject in his over-explicit *Je t'aime, je t'aime* (1968)—it is worth-while observing that Resnais is just as politically committed a film-maker as Marker. The first reviewers of *Hiroshima mon amour* (1959) tended to praise Resnais's editing at the expense of obscuring his political interests. Since that time, his technique has so often been imitated—the ease with which he manages to weave together the lives of his two lovers through undemonstrative flashbacks—that it no longer attracts the same admiration. But if his political interests have become more noticeable, so too have certain failings in Marguerite Duras's screenplay, such as the way in which she relates the two lovers (Emmanuele Riva and Eiji Okada) to their native towns of Nevers and Hiroshima, as though they were delegates wearing name-tags at some UNESCO conference. The French woman, an actress working on a pacifist film in Hiroshima, is awoken from a condition of emotional numbness through an affair with a Japanese architect, an affair which frees her from the grief and rage she feels over the death of a German soldier she had once loved, a member of the forces occupying Nevers during the war.

In *Night and Fog* Resnais had tried to film the virtually unfilmable experience of the concentration camps. In *Hiroshima mon amour* he was to engage with the nuclear destruction of Hiroshima. He demonstrates how this nuclear experience has modified the sensibility of all of us. *Hiroshima mon amour* is not only about a disorientation that

Alain Resnais: *Hiroshima mon amour*. Eiji Okada, Emmanuele Riva.

Resnais and Duras think to be widespread but it also shows how this state of disorientation affects perception and feeling. In Stanley Kramer's *On the Beach* (1959), one of the survivors of a nuclear war walks in a diving suit through a deserted industrial town, through a dehumanized yet man-made world which conveys the impression of some extra-terrestrial civilization. In this one sequence Kramer allows sensibility to communicate his theme. He then loses its effect by submitting his actors to vague discussions on the fate of the world. Resnais and Duras do not entirely avoid this temptation, but Resnais at least often allows his sensibility to work for him without forcing the meaning of his subject. Marker had invoked awe at the sight of a ruined Paris. Resnais orchestrates his images and deploys his actors so as to achieve the gravity of grand opera.

He was to aim for the same gravity in *Last Year at Marienbad* (1961), where his actors move through Alain Robbe-Grillet's convoluted story with the deportment of models posing for a photograph in some Edwardian fashion magazine. He communicates this style with such authority that it takes some time for the thought to occur that content is virtually non-existent. To see it as a Bergsonian essay in time and memory, as some critics have done, lends it an excessive distinction; for in fact it celebrates little more than Resnais's gift for *mise en scène*, being a semi-abstract exercise in which camera movements and editing conspire to create a splendid mystification. Resnais was to find more substance for his intricate techniques in Jean Cayrol's screenplay for *Muriel* (1963), which centres on Hélène Aughian, an antique dealer whose apartment contains furniture for sale. Hélène's bewilderment about her past and present lovers is similar to her absent-mindedness about a Boulogne where buildings are raised and demolished so rapidly that the town seldom appears to be the same place. But then everything is transient in this comedy, and nearly everyone at cross-purposes with each other, either in pursuit or in flight. Although Resnais underplays one of the subplots, the one concerning the guilt and resentment of Hélène's son Bernard,

Alain Resnais: *Muriel*. Delphine Seyrig.

who has tortured a girl named Muriel while on military service in Algeria, his skill in dovetailing the numerous incidents in Cayrol's screenplay—at that time the most thorough fragmentation of straightforward narrative imaginable—is assured enough to adjust the spectator to a new form of coherence.

L'Écran français ceased publication in March 1952. But Astruc's theory of écriture was to be taken up by the critics of Cahiers du cinéma, a magazine which had come into being in April 1951. At first sight oddly, the Cahiers critics applied the theory to some of the most streamlined and least cerebral productions available (most of them emerging from a Hollywood that was by then in its death-throes), arguing that Hollywood's way of tailoring subjects to suit the consumer established sets of expectation against which any divergence could be measured. They categorized types of film, and film cycles, into genres with the decorum of seventeenth-century neo-classical theoreticians; and they allowed directors capable of realizing some personal accent within this rigid formalism to enter into the pantheon of those who practised la politique des auteurs. In this way the snobbery Langlois had tried to banish from film appreciation re-entered by another door. The pantheon included Rossellini, Welles, Renoir, Lang and Mizoguchi admittedly, but it also included, among others, Don Siegel, Budd Boetticher, Robert Aldrich and Samuel Fuller, whose careers had previously been neglected by the art houses and whose reputations the Cahiers critics defended with all the inflexibility of the art house snob.

In England, readers of Sight and Sound greeted news of this pantheon with some bewilderment, and Richard Roud had to explain to them that 'the Western and the film noir are perhaps the best test of the film critic because their value is so often a matter of form, technique and iconography; all the elements which separate the cinema from literature.'[11] The case for some of the pantheon directors has never been argued convincingly; yet one reason why they were admired—their ability to project a tough and energetic picture of life in the United States—can be deduced from the first films of Truffaut and Godard, although the charm of these first films largely depends on their characters and stories being as close to the real thing as little boys playing at cops and robbers. 'I do like A Bout de souffle very much,' said Godard, 'but now I see where it belongs—along with Alice in Wonderland. I used to think of it as Scarface.'[12]

A Bout de souffle was based on a fifteen-page scenario by Truffaut. It described the adventures of Antoine Doinel, Truffaut's surrogate, four years after his escape from a reformatory at the end of Les Quatre Cents Coups; and although much changed by its director, it still conveyed something of Truffaut's fascination with the ways in which experience can qualify desires and his interest in timid men who are attracted to formidable women. Truffaut the scenario writer is consistent with Truffaut the director. He joins Chaplin in being among the more self-absorbed of artists, a condition intensified, perhaps, by a deprived childhood and an early fame that recalls, in a less extreme form, Chaplin's career. But it would be inaccurate to describe his work—as one might Chaplin's films—as a hall of mirrors reflecting one figure. To look at a series of photographs of Jean-Pierre Léaud playing Antoine Doinel in a number of films and growing from boyhood to manhood suggests, rather, the poignancy of a Muybridge photo-sequence. Truffaut is very conscious of the transitory nature of things. He frequently observes happenings obliquely, as though out of the corner of his eye, as though the world contained too many changes for him to observe them all directly. In *Baisers volés* (1968), a detective dies while taking a phone call, an event almost unremarked in the hubbub of other events.

Although he was one of the *Cahiers* critics to observe most rigidly the tenets of genre criticism, he was to fly in the face of this decorum when he turned film-maker. He has tried to achieve, as he has said, 'a new blend of existing elements'. Admittedly, his films suggest that he enjoys both social conventions at their most elaborate and highly patterned plots: his adaptations of Henri-Pierre Roché's novels, *Jules et Jim* (1961) and *Les Deux Anglaises et le continent/Anne and Muriel* (1971) are based on a system of contrasts, parallels and symmetries.

François Truffaut: *Anne and Muriel*. Kika Markham, Jean-Pierre Léaud.

But he sets up this contrivance only to disrupt it. He shows how the passing of time, and those events that emphasize the ravages of time— such as passion and death—can destroy everything. The tidy plots and courtesies of high bourgeois art cannot contain these disruptions, and the guiding figure of Goethe must give way to Emily Brontë— much alluded to in *Anne and Muriel*—or to his lifelong hero, Balzac.

His talent is inward-looking. Psychologically observant, his perceptions are not directed to informing the spectator on how society is organized or nature composed. (But then, why should they be?) He is a lyricist whose art depends for its success or failure on his ability to invoke memories of intense feeling in his audience: of falling in love, or of being betrayed in love. At times his insistence on jealousy and grief does convey the impression that he has no belief in stable or abiding relationships. All of which would be unremarkable, if he did not have an exceptional gift for embodying these sensations within contemporary myths. He can take an American novel—by David Goodis or William Irish, say—and in *Shoot the Pianist* (1960), *The Bride Wore Black* (1968) and *La Sirène du Mississippi* (1969) enrich it with the most intimate feeling. Through the power of personality alone, he can make fantastic relationships, inconsequential acts and coincidences suddenly ring true. His myths would be hard to believe in without this intensity. But his intensity would appear aimless, and possibly insane, if it did not have as its object the incongruities of certain myths.

A number of his films embody journeys into the unknown, even journeys into a void. Two of them end in a snow landscape where an apprehension of beauty and a dread of death can combine. His sense of how ordinary happenings can acquire the resonance of myth owes something to the way in which Renoir develops his story in *La Grande Illusion* and something to the techniques used by Hitchcock at his less naturalistic. 'As I see it, Mr Hitchcock, emptiness has a magnetic appeal for you,' said Truffaut in a marathon interview later published as a book. 'You see film as a receptacle to be filled to the brim with cinematic ideas or, in your own terms, to be "charged with emotion".'[13] Shortly after this discussion had taken place, Truffaut tried to put this idea into practice in *The Bride Wore Black*. Julie Kohler (Jeanne Moreau) sets out to destroy five men who have taken part in the accidental shooting of her husband. She seems to emerge from nowhere and to kill without apparent purpose, presenting herself as a cypher into whom men can read their desires. And similarly, Truffaut creates a kind of type character and abstracted imagery into which he invites the spectator to project his secret hopes and fears.

His involvement in the tension that can exist between passion and decorum is complicated by his fascination with the idea of self-education, a fascination so earnest that it gives even his present-day stories a nineteenth-century tone. He has said of his fictional *alter ego*, Antoine Doinel, that in spite of his liking for other people he is basic- cally anti-social. At first sight the way in which he presents Doinel in *Baisers volés* as a gravely courteous youth in a sports-jacket would seem, deceptively, to place him as the good son of a bourgeois family; just as deceptively, he later implies that Doinel's bookishness and erratic behaviour give him a certain affinity to the dispossessed students, frenzied solitaries and tramps that he meets on his adven- tures. But Doinel clearly does not belong to any defined group or class. His closest kinship is with certain unworldly figures who existed — at least in fiction — before the great divide of the First World War: with Flaubert's Bouvard and Pécuchet, or with their successors, Roche's Jules and Jim, who are peevishly distracted from their con- templation of the ideal by the pressures of sex. Doinel's inability to be part of any community would suggest that he has never outgrown the boyhood shock and estrangement shown in *Les Quatre Cents Coups*: his appalling night spent in prison in a cage with pimps and prostitutes, and his journey through the empty glittering streets of Paris, seen through tears and from behind iron bars, as a police van takes him to the reformatory.

Truffaut's sympathy with the isolated auto-didact has never been more plain than in the way he filmed the ending to Ray Bradbury's *Fahrenheit 451* (1966), in which the Bookmen wander about like ghosts from Dante's *Inferno*, each reciting the one book he has com- mitted to heart as a last attempt to save culture from the vandalism of the Firemen.

It is possible to say that he aspires to be a Goethe, yet temperament- ally is much closer to Jean-Jacques Rousseau. He extrapolated the re- lationships of *L'Enfant sauvage* (1970) from reports made by a certain Dr Itard in 1801 and 1806 to the Academy of Medicine and to the French government on the means Itard had used to educate a twelve- year-old boy who had grown up as an animal in the forests; perhaps he was attracted to this subject because it recalled his own adoption by André Bazin. He seems to have believed that Dr Itard was right in carrying out this manner of education, and the fact that he himself acts the part of Dr Itard, and employs a Bressonian gravity of style that Dr Itard might have approved of, adds weight to this belief. But the effect of his film leaves the spectator far from convinced. Itard's tutelage may be preferable in certain ways to the wildness of the forest: yet his instruction is chastening and he and his housekeeper make a joyless pair. Shades of the prison-house do close upon this growing boy; and, whether intentionally or not, Truffaut does show the child's pleasure in nature to be more inviting than his lessons in the classroom. Yet to dwell on this contrast could be misleading. For Truffaut conceives of his narratives as a form of education and sees both passion and decorum as essential to this process of development. He cannot do without either. In the same way that Dr Itard's household would be a dull place without the eruptions of the child, so the child, if left to its own devices, would sink into a condition of monotonous disorder. Neither prospect in itself would provide the stimulus for a Truffaut film.

If Truffaut resembles a Jean-Jacques Rousseau who aspires to be a Goethe, then glibly one might say that his one-time friend Jean-Luc Godard resembles a Goethe who would prefer to be a Rousseau. Godard is also fascinated by the theme of education and has quoted Rousseau's *Emile* at length in both *Weekend* (1967) and *Le Gai Savoir* (1968). But unlike Truffaut, who has portrayed the pursuit of knowledge as a hopeless struggle against the erosions of time, Godard would seem to view knowledge as scraps of learning easily acquired and easily paraded. He has increasingly presented his lore dogmatically. Yet even at his most omniscient, he can reveal a diffidence and sense of humour that suggest he might be aware of the absurdity of his position. In certain respects, he, rather than Truffaut, might be the model for Antoine Doinel. For he is unworldly and immersed in the atmosphere of fiction, an avid yet restless filmgoer and reader of novels, who likes to imitate his heroes. Although his role-playing is more aggressive than Truffaut's, if only because it is less touched by sentiment, it is also more ineffectual.

He is both the least and most pretentious of film-makers. He has completely changed the intentions of his craft, converting it into an intimate—and serious—game between himself and his audience, a game in which he invents the rules as he goes along, allowing himself the most outrageous behaviour, flouting the properties of technique, boasting, saying the first thing that comes into his head. Modest in reducing 'the art of film' to such a game and in declining to make Olympian statements, he is pretentious in the insistence with which he continues the game long after his audience has tired of it. Yet his remarkable gift for transforming almost any idea into an assured style and his flair in understanding the desires of student audiences in the mid-sixties has often allowed him to retrieve his more freewheeling passages from chaos. His talents and boldness are such that he has been a dangerous example to other, less gifted contemporaries.

He rests his first feature *A Bout de souffle* (1959) on the assumption that his audience will sympathize with the killer Michel Poiccard, alias Laszlo Kovacs (alias Jean-Paul Belmondo), to such an extent that it will identify with Poiccard in his disgust for his girl friend Patricia (Jean Seberg). Patricia informs on Kovacs because he has shot down a policeman; but Godard presents her motives as mysterious, seeing her as innately treacherous, as he seems to imagine all women to be. Later in the decade, Arthur Penn (in *Bonnie and Clyde*), Lindsay Anderson (in *If . . .*) and Stanley Kubrick (in *The Clockwork Orange*) would invite the spectator to identify with their leading characters on the sole ground that their characters wished to murder the people who maintain law and order. Godard does not take up this position in *A Bout de souffle*, but he does open the way to it by implying that Poiccard's murders are semi-fictional, occupying some halfway house between a wish and its fulfilment. He shows Poiccard's mind to be saturated with memories of Hollywood thrillers and pretending to be Muni, Bogart or Widmark, actors who had played the roles of killers in earnest. It is impossible to imagine Poiccard's murders as facts in the world. Belmondo's Poiccard is the circus come to town, the Lumière boy who blocks the hosepipe, all the Sennett clowns rolled into one as they commandeer the streets of Los Angeles. If he elicits feelings of pathos in the audience, he does so almost unintentionally by the way in which he reveals a difference between his actual state and his delusions. Patricia is haunted by a thought that describes his condition. 'When elephants feel unhappy, they vanish.'

But Godard does show Poiccard's actual state as well as his delusions, in the bed-sitter sequences where the image of the tough guy crumbles and the adolescent played by Belmondo (who is pretending to be Poiccard alias Kovacs) emerges in all his vulnerability. Poiccard nags at Patricia about her previous lovers when she refuses to sleep with him, and he constantly ascribes the worst motives to her. Godard does nothing to redress the balance in her favour. He loses his sense of humour. He leaves her motives unresolved so that she takes on an enigmatic and fragmented presence. A cry that mingles yearning and rage arrests all irony, all sense of game.

Contradictorily enough, this cry comes over in this context as insincere. But how can an uncontrolled expression of pain be thought insincere? And why, after all, need the concept of sincerity be brought into any discussion about films? Both these questions can be given the same answer.

Godard has always been concerned to remind the spectator that film-making has a history and has evolved through many conventions. He nearly always provides a debate on the power of film to create illusions and in doing so has shifted attention away from the charismatic power of the image to the mind responsible for the image's use. He has shown all film-making to be revelatory of its maker. In the sense that all films consist of contrived situations, it is plausible to see them as fictions of one kind or another. In the sense that all films are permanent, almost clinical records of these fictions—

records that reveal more about the people who made them than they, caught up in the fashions and ideologies of their time, were probably aware of—it is plausible to see them as documentaries. Godard has thrown into disrepute the kind of barnstorming tradition associated with Griffith and DeMille, in which artists imagine themselves to be magicians casting a spell over their public. His manner of working provides a commentary on the content of his films which deepens any intimacy that may exist between the director and his audience and to some extent renders content immaterial. At the same time, he has raised problems which Griffith and DeMille never had to face. He has to come out in the open; and it is significant that the admiration and hostility aroused by his films has usually been directed not at his characters or plots but at the director himself. He can no longer rely on story or mood to captivate his public. He has raised certain expectations that oblige him continually to criticize his own mannerisms or incantatory powers so as to retain the trust of his audience. He is forever obliged to disclose his own incoherences and discontinuities. He can only give up his role as commentator—on himself, on his audience and on the cultural shorthand through which they communicate—at the risk of being exposed as dishonest.

It is for this reason that his misogyny is so damaging to *A Bout de souffle*, since this misogyny is intended to be incantatory and not to provoke thought. He was to try and contain it in such later films as *Vivre sa vie* (1962), *Une Femme mariée* (1964) and *Deux ou trois choses que je sais d'elle* (1966), by looking closely at the imperative some males feel to reduce women to prostitutes. But he has seemed unable to investigate the compulsion in this wish, perhaps because the actresses he employed tended to be too willing to adapt themselves to male fantasy. Even so, the very fact that his casting decisions can be related to his psychopathology in this way shows how he has modified consciousness about film. In the twenties, Fritz Lang and Thea von Harbou created a surrogate for the film director in Dr Mabuse, who could hypnotize his audiences to see whatever he wished them to see on his white screen and who died mad, his cell littered with plans for world domination. But while Lang and von Harbou present Mabuse's career as a parable about film directors as well as about other kinds of demagogue, they remain distanced from their subject, as though it did not really apply to them. Godard has minimized this distance. According to his beliefs, honest film-makers should no longer try to hypnotize their audiences; they should present their plans for world domination as nothing more than plans, or signs that the semiologist may read.

He puts this idea into practice with *Les Carabiniers* (1963). Ostensibly about war, its opening quotation from Jorge Luis Borges ('I use the old metaphors') implies that its subject, however, is the rhetoric

Jean-Luc Godard: *Les Carabiniers*.

of war. At first sight, it seems to be a home-made movie shot on the outskirts of Paris, in a dreary hinterland that resembles the main location of *Los Olvidados*. Its actors play out a game of soldiers going to war, raping girls, pillaging and returning home, as though they were students half-heartedly putting on a satirical revue. But meanwhile, it proposes a commentary on the power of the screen image. When one of the soldiers, Michel-Ange, goes to the cinema for the first time, he covers his eyes as a train roars into a station and leaps through the screen when shown a woman taking a bath.

He and his friend Ulysse bring back a collection of photographs from their wanderings. Going through these photographs, they list the many wonders of the world, and, when they come to a photograph of the leaning tower of Pisa, cock their heads to one side to straighten the tower. DeMille, no doubt, would have missed no opportunity to dramatize their travels if he had been handling the subject, but Godard supplies the most perfunctory signs to represent the meaning of these journeys; and, in part to justify his technique, refers to the tradition from which it was derived. He recalls Apollinaire's inclination, when writing poems, to list names at length and to compile extracts from newspapers, conversations overheard in bars and other unmediated bits of actuality, as though he were a painter constructing a collage.

On another level, he has integrated into this structure a number of extracts from war documentaries, newsreels, some of Himmler's circulars, and letters written at the Russian front and during the Napoleonic Spanish campaigns. He works them in with skill. But anyone coming to the film in the hope that Godard will have edited it in such a way as to bring out the power of his images will be disappointed.

Godard uses his skill to rob the images of any power that they might have had. He appears to be Dadaist when he has Michel-Ange salute a Rembrandt self-portrait as though he were a de Gaulle standing before the grave of some unknown soldier. But far from supporting Dadaism, he is determined to undermine the anti-art cult of violence. He contrasts culture, or rather the debris of culture, with war in such a way as to minimize the spiritual significance often read into them both; and he puts together some of his more sensational shots of destruction as though he were an archivist from outer space who had never heard of war. Hitchcock, according to Truffaut, sees the screen as an emptiness to be charged with feeling. Godard reverses this process and empties the screen of any emotional content that its images might have had. In doing so, he forces his audience to recognize how easily it can be cheated into accepting the rhetoric of the war film.

This deflation could not be further from his desire, as a young critic, that films should celebrate moments of joy: a need that his own filming has often satisfied, and not only in such moments as Anna Karina's casually graceful dance in *Bande à part* (1964), the vision of burning cars in *Pierrot le fou* (1965) or of slowly swirling cream in a cup of coffee in *Deux ou trois choses que je sais d'elle*. He has often filmed the scintilla of urban sights, observing at motor-car speed the smear of neon signs by night, the typography of posters by day. Like some of the Pop artists, he tries to snatch some semblance of beauty from an environment ravaged by greed. The essence of his operation is haste: seizing upon everything, digesting nothing. He would seem to believe in the importance of moving fast, even though the self may be dying of hunger beneath a superfluity of sensuous temptations.

He was to be at his most wild in *Made in USA* (1966), and managed to be even more incomprehensible than Hawks had been in *The Big Sleep* (one of his sources), alluding to, among other things, Frank Tashlin's comedies, television commercials and every kind of tough guy manner. But his use of colour—mostly contrasts and variations on dark blue—helped him achieve a semi-abstract concentration, at its most genial in the sequence where he had Marianne Faithfull sing 'In the Evening of the Day'. But he was unable to sustain the intensity of *Made in USA*. Only his closest friends could say how far either personal factors or public events brought on his breakdown, and how far these two might be separated; but it should be observed that between 1959 and 1968 he completed fifteen feature-length movies and numerous brief projects. His manner of improvising his ideas from at best a few pages of notes must have increased the risks of his work as well as given it urgency. Perhaps he felt ideological pressures even more strongly. In *Pierrot le fou*, Ferdinand tries to escape from a life-style constricted by the rituals of advertising

Jean-Luc Godard: *Pierrot le fou.* Anna Karina.

into the delusive prospects offered by art, gangsterism, travel and a passionate love affair. Godard believes that this type of escape recalls *You Only Live Once, Le Jour se lève* and *Pépé le Moko,* in the sense that it can only end in self-destruction.

Images of lovers forever in flight through overwhelming land-scapes can give way to an intimation of classical repose: as in the long-held shot of a sparkling, placid sea in *Le Mépris* (1963). But Godard was obliged to realize that this aestheticism tended to be as inadequate a response to the problems of life as any advertiser's promise. His sense of disillusionment began to centre on Hollywood. 'My early period was my hippie period,' he has said. 'I was addicted to movies as hippies can be to marijuana. But I am now over the movie marijuana magic thing.' He read a political meaning into the way Hollywood addicted its audiences, seeing it as an exercise of power typical of American imperialism, as practised in American business and in the Vietnam war. Yet he was to find it hard to re-place his Hollywood-based fantasies. His students in *La Chinoise* (1967) argue themselves into a Maoist position, which he works hard to dramatize; but its rigidity fails to generate the imaginative con-trast that Hollywood had once done between an ineffectual actuality and the ideal.

The quandary he was in became clear when in the spring of 1968 he went on a tour of the United States to discuss *La Chinoise* at the universities. He disappointed many of the students by declining to play Lafayette and by responding sceptically to their enthusiasm for the new American cinema. He pointed out that nothing of value could come from so corrupt a society and instanced *Bonnie and Clyde* – then enjoying a vogue – as being lifeless in form. He also offended the campus revolutionaries, who wished to see films purely as instruments in the class struggle, by declining to become an activist. 'I don't have a gun,' he said, 'and I'm so short-sighted that I would probably kill all my friends.'[14]

In his distrust of the United States he might seem to have been a Gaullist. But his admiration for de Gaulle, at least in the person of his Minister of Culture, André Malraux, had been short-lived. He was soon to replace the compliments he had paid Malraux at the 1966 Lumière retrospective with abuse. He ominously began his letter on the banning of Jacques Rivette's *La Religieuse* by addressing it to the minister of 'Kultur'; and he was to play a vigorous part in the polemics surrounding the dismissal of Langlois from the Cinémathèque. His distrust of Gaullist France erupted in *Weekend* (1968). It began as

Jean-Luc Godard: *Weekend.*

a denunciation of the French bourgeoisie as road-hog, and included an eight-minute tracking shot past a traffic pile-up that owed more to Sennett than to the real world. Although he tried to set out some of the motives that underlie financial aggression, his improvisatory methods were of no help to him in developing this investigation. He lost control over his theme and began to fall back on to a favourite resort of his: intellectual juggling about the relationship of film to life.

He returned to this concern with *Le Gai Savoir* (1968), which French television had first commissioned and then rejected. Two young actors meet in a pool of light and propose to indoctrinate the audience in the joys of knowledge by bombarding it with a haphazard selection of images and sounds: views of Paris streets, sounds recorded at the time of the May revolution, scribbled-over photographs and magazine advertisements. 'Chance has a structure, like the unconscious.' Godard proposes that politics and sexuality are closely linked and that all the types of politics he disapproves of—practically everything west of Mongolia—enact perversions. Much of the verbal play has an affinity to schizophrenic thought.

No one since Griffith, Chaplin and Eisenstein has had such an influence over other film directors. If he was not the first to revive the Soviet techniques of montage, of kinds of editing that call attention to themselves, he was the first to relate them to interests that appealed to the young. In doing so, he has helped to promote a culture where, schizoid-fashion, signs have come to be confused with the things they represent and revolutionary gestures believed to be identical to revolution itself. Orson Welles is alleged to have said that the studio facilities at RKO were like the best train set any boy could wish for. Godard has not only taken pleasure in the power of the technology at his disposal but shown how far its power has stimulated the promiscuity of modern experience, as in the undifferentiated arrangement of television programmes and magazine layouts, where advertisements for perfume can lie side by side with photographs of starving children.

Yet there can be no doubt that he and his contemporaries were opposed to the anti-rational and anti-evaluatory trends of the mid and late sixties. They had looked for areas of sensation outside the traditional provinces of culture and found it in comic strips, Hollywood B features and pulp novels; but by the end of the decade it was clear how far their intention had been to filter and refine these sources. At the beginning of the sixties it had seemed faintly scandalous when Jacques Demy claimed that he had drawn the inspiration for *Lola* (1960), *La Baie des anges* (1962) and *Les Parapluies de Cherbourg* (1964) from Hollywood musicals by Vincente Minnelli and Gene Kelly, and admitted his infatuation with Hollywood show business. What is more obvious now is that his delicate Marivaux-like comedies based on chance and coincidence not only point up the crudities in forties musicals but also depend on a recall of enthusiasms that are both distanced and rendered more complex by the structure built out of them.

But if Demy contemplates a Hollywood as lost as the forties themselves, in much the same way as the ancient Romans had idealized
rural life, then—and such is the change in sensibility over so short a
time—Paul Morrissey and Andy Warhol regard one sector of Hollywood in *Heat* (1971) with the uncomprehending stare of barbarians
wandering among the ruins of a sacked Rome. At least, that would
seem to be the impression they wish to put over. But their Candide-
type hero is less than candid, as they are themselves, and their humour relies on the callous improbability that he can pass through a
series of loveless sex adventures as unscathed as a Bardot. Their
jaded, matter-of-fact tone knowingly sets up an unusual incongruity
in relation to their picture of psychotic behaviour, yet its blandness
cannot conceal their anxieties or hatreds, most evident in their
grotesque portraits of both the landlady and the middle-aged actress
who solicit their hero's favours.

Heat has been compared to *Sunset Boulevard;* and certainly Wilder's
sentimental belief that people turn to prostitution because of some
failing in the economic system is one of its assumptions also. But
Morrissey and Warhol go much further than Wilder in leaving undisclosed the motives of their characters. Truffaut and Godard have
shown how this blankness about motive can allow for a wide play of
irony. The most that Morrissey and Warhol can demonstrate is that
to feign dumbness is in itself a form of dumbness. They parade madness as a form of entertainment—surely one of the most primitive
ways of dealing with the fear of madness in oneself.

Their barbarism is a yardstick by which to measure the intentions
of a New Wave film-maker like Claude Chabrol, who, from his second
feature on, has devoted himself to thriller subjects that usually contain some criticism of the bourgeoisie. So many of his bourgeois characters are unpleasant that it is possible to infer that Chabrol may consider that their class interests stimulate their unpleasantness. But the
moral paradoxes that he raises from their behaviour are of a kind both
liable to flatter bourgeois audiences as well as depress them. His murderers seldom collapse after committing their crimes or show much
sign of guilt, and at least one of them, Popaul in *Le Boucher* (1968),
responds with uncommon tenderness to his victims.

By suggesting that certain people can murder with impunity,
Chabrol allows for two contradictory deductions: that he believes
revolution may be useful on therapeutic grounds, or that he sees his
killers as representing bourgeois ambition at its most complete. His
views on the psychology of murderers go against the evidence. And
his filming hardly makes their behaviour plausible. Perhaps he still
holds to the views of his 1957 monograph on Hitchcock (written in
association with Eric Rohmer), which made it clear that he was less
interested in the psychological value of Hitchcock's films than in their

implied theological symbolism. In *Ten Days' Wonder* (1971), his most explicit parable up to that time, Orson Welles appears as an American multi-millionaire resident in France, a latter-day *Citizen Kane* who manipulates others in such a random fashion that his acts can only be explained on the grounds that Chabrol sees him as a surrogate for some God who performs his wonders in a mysterious way.

The need to criticize middle-class values was an important strand in film-making during the sixties. But Chabrol differs from many of his contemporaries in levelling his criticisms with less a political programme in mind than a desire to give voice to both a sense of grievance and a glee in destruction. He is like a rebellious son, secure in the knowledge of his family's stability, who criticizes the bourgeoisie from within a bourgeois position and hopes to conceal this contradiction by shifting significance at critical moments onto a mystical level where nothing can be verified. Often glib, usually cold, he tries to compensate for his lack of feeling by directing his attention to problems of interior decoration and *haute cuisine*, those familiar bourgeois substitutes for human warmth.

He has been fairly consistent in his attitudes over a great number of films; yet the cultural upheavals of the sixties have been such that Chabrol, the young Turk of *Les Cousins* (1959), did not have to change his position to have become the defender of conventional morality by the end of the decade. By then he was to seem far more of a rebel than he had seemed to be formerly: after all, the best way to appear rebellious in an age of licence is to argue the case for restraint. Such would appear to be the intention also of Chabrol's co-author on the Hitchcock monograph, Eric Rohmer; although, perhaps, Rohmer's attempts to put over the importance of being earnest with arguments of an almost Wildean grace, in his *contes moraux*, is never wholly convincing. The main point about the three different protagonists of *Ma Nuit chez Maud* (1969), *Claire's Knee* (1970) and *Love in the Afternoon* (1973) is that the first does not sleep with Maud, the second claims to have satisfied his infatuation with Claire by rubbing her kneecap, while the third fails to make love in the afternoon. Although each of them rationalizes his hesitation with charm, Rohmer sides with them too easily. He does not adequately explore the motives for their behaviour and fails to explore the implicit cruelty of their refusals. Like Chabrol, he too often uses a considerable intelligence to keep feeling at a distance: he trifles with the idea of seriousness.

These elegant debates depend for their sharpness on the moral atmosphere in which they were made. They are very different from Chabrol's first feature, *Le Beau Serge* (1958), which substantiates allegory with a concern for character and setting that allows the film to stand as a felt experience in its own right. For once, Chabrol seemed willing to bear the pain implied by his subject, to suffer this

Claude Chabrol: *Le Beau Serge*. Gérard Blain, Jean-Claude Brialy.

pain and thereby to think through its imaginative consequences. François returns to his native village to recover from a breakdown: the same village, Sardent, where Chabrol himself had been brought up. He meets again his childhood friend Serge, now married and alcoholic; he tries to help Serge out of his depression, but only succeeds in deepening it. In the final scenes of the film he drags Serge through snow to attend his wife in childbirth and in doing so he damages his own health—scenes that tactfully represent his wish to pull Serge back into life. Chabrol not only evokes fully the desperate nature of a friendship which cannot find means to communicate and can only hurt, but also the atmosphere of a damp village in winter with its shop windows misted over by condensation. The conviction of this film depends on a meditated care for circumstance.

Chabrol had been one of the first New Wave directors to criticize Kramer's assumption that major themes are valuable in themselves, yet he clearly has been unable to sustain the courage needed to keep on making connections out of his own experience. In Alain Jessua's *La Vie à l'envers* (1963) a young man, Jacques, becomes fascinated by the mystery of objects: of chairs, wrought-iron table legs, a broken egg. By the end of the film he has been placed in an asylum. Antonioni was to interpret similar experiences as examples of Marxist alienation and Polanski (in *Repulsion*) to connect them with fetishism. But Jessua prefers to leave open the question of interpretation, and the spectator is free to see Jacques as mad or to think of him as having reached some Zen-like peace with the world about him.

Jacques Rivette: *Paris nous appartient.*

Admirable though Jessua's openness may be, it does take film-making to the verge of incoherence, to a succession of instances which in themselves can be as dehumanizing as those projects in which the director allows theory to control intuition. But one way in which ideology and introspection can be more usefully related is by seeing films as investigations into the nature of film form. In Jacques Rivette's *Paris nous appartient* (1960) the principal action consists of a search for a tape-recording of some music that may bring coherence to a stage production of *Pericles*, a search that imitates Rivette's own need to discover some sublime way of linking together his various plots. It could be argued that Rivette's fascination with persecutory feeling leads him to some far-fetched conclusions. In the case of both this film and *La Religieuse* (1965), he was to imply, for instance, that

Jacques Rivette: *La Religieuse*. Anna Karina.

the fragmentary nature of contemporary experience may derive from the conflict in almost everyone between a desire for power and a wish to live creatively. He filmed *Paris nous appartient* over a long period of time and conceived of it as a kind of diary whose form, self-defeatingly, would only emerge after its author's death. With *L'Amour fou* (1969) it had become apparent that he could only discover a form with this technique at the cost of defining his subject in terms of some ideology.

Yet Rivette's self-reflexive technique has a more immediate use. The New Wave directors were not only bookish; most of them were driven by the desire to educate themselves and others and to extend the realms of filmed knowledge. In the summer of 1960 the anthropologist Jean Rouch joined forces with the sociologist Edgar Morin to investigate the thoughts and feelings of a group of Parisians. Determined to involve themselves with this group in the same manner as Flaherty had with Nanook and his family, they interviewed members of the group and then in turn invited them to interview each other and to comment on the rushes. The technique produced some results. Their interview with a Renault car worker was the first time someone had talked freely about factory conditions on the French media; even more impressively, the meeting they arranged between the Renault factory worker and an African student allows the spectator to observe the melting of distrust as the two men talk together. There is also a meeting between a Jewish woman and the African student, who does not know why she has a number tattooed on her

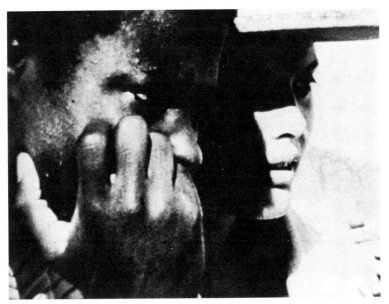

Jean Rouch: *Chronique d'un été.*

arm. Although some of these scenes are too contrived, their failings are raised as criticisms in the film and become part of the inquiry.

In its concluding scene, Rouch and Morin walk through the ethnography section of the Paris Museum of Mankind and admit to each other how surprised they were at the hostility certain members of the group had shown at the screenings. 'We wanted to make a film about love,' they say, 'but it turned out to be an impersonal sort of film.' In fact, *Chronique d'un été* contains a good deal of affection. It tries to set up connections between individuals and society at large and between Europeans and the peoples of the Third World. Admittedly, it ends on a disheartened note, touching on an unhappiness and a sense of failure that its directors had not predicted. And it leaves nearly all the questions it raises unanswered. But these failings, and the fact that they are conceded, are guarantees of its value. Unlike most films, which issue forth from the hands of their makers like divine injunctions and defy the spectator to find inadequacies in them, *Chronique d'un été* recognizes that it is impossible to be human without admitting to one's own limitations. It tries to see things as they are. Morin and Rouch decline to package the opinion of others to suit their own convenience, decline to use the camera as an instrument of tyranny. At a time when the media had begun to transform every subject, however serious, into a form of spectacle, they opened up a technique that could help to free the humanity in themselves and in anyone touched by their film.

Yet *Chronique d'un été* could not stem the process by which nearly every experience was turned into entertainment. Film-makers had not only received benefit from the invention of portable and quiet synchronized sound cameras, less heavy recording equipment and high-speed film stock to enter into situations that formerly had been barred to them, but were also under at least two pressures to carry out these intrusions. Television had exhausted a great number of themes and means of handling these themes, while film producers, faced by a chronic financial crisis, insisted on subjects being more and more sensational. The media both fed on anxieties about technology (the status of the individual in the computer age, etc.) as well as fed them, and confused the meaning of these anxieties by over-insisting on one of their marginal effects: the ways in which impersonal technology had sharpened the conflict between the generations.

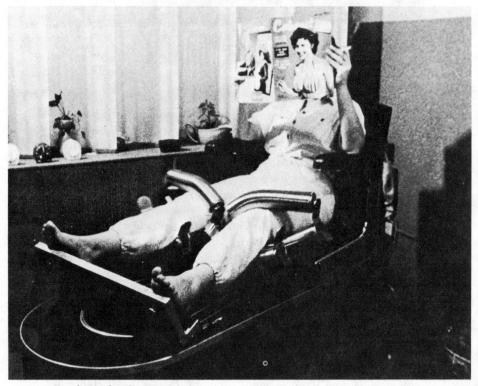

Joseph Strick: *The Savage Eye*.

United States

In 1953 D. A. Pennebaker bought 'a few rolls of drugstore Kodachrome' and in two or three days shot his five-minute documentary *Daybreak Express*, in which he observed New York as a constellation

of patterns and glowing colours from the window of an elevated railway carriage. He mostly edited the film within the camera; he had a
Duke Ellington record in mind while filming, and he later added it to
the sound-track. His delight in filters and a deep-focus lens, that seemingly brought the sun and buildings into distorted close-up, was
matched by his sense of pulse. Although his lyricism added little to
the opening sequence of Ruttmann's *Berlin* and had much in common with the dextrous juggling of sight and sound practised at this
time by Norman McLaren in Canada, Bert Haanstra in Holland (as in
his 1956 documentary *Glass*) and Francis Thompson's *NY.NY.*, on
which Pennebaker had worked, it did open up new directions.
Pennebaker not only used optics to transform an ugly urban scene
into a warmly felt impressionism, but through jazz was able to elicit
the city's idiom.

Jazz, movement and impressions of the city allowed him to evoke
an intimacy similar to the one that Godard was later to discover in
billboards and neon lights. Yet it in no way minimizes the importance
of the French New Wave to recognize that many of its interests had
been foreshadowed elsewhere or to recognize how reciprocal influences were to be. And if certain American directors were to look to
jazz as a model for new ways of thinking and feeling about film, they
were to do so in a spirit different from King Vidor's *Hallelujah*. They
did not think of jazz as a primitive folk art but as the liveliest element
in show business—and in a show business no longer confined to cel-
lars, night-clubs, recording studios and theatres.

The most obvious fact about Bert Stern's feature-length report on
the Newport Jazz Festival, *Jazz on a Summer's Day* (1961), is that it
reveals how jazz performers can merge into the holiday atmosphere of
sunlight and sea air, their music seeming to be an appropriate accompaniment to the movement of yacht sails, glittering water and the
contrasted faces of listeners. Like royalty or successful politicians,
Gerry Mulligan, Thelonious Monk and Anita O'Day look both distanced from their audience and yet relaxed enough to communicate
with it at ease. But Stern also demonstrated the extent to which the
styles of show business have filtered through American culture and
coloured the ways in which Americans see themselves and each other:
a permeation most complete in those areas of the culture which are
apparently dissociated from the pressures of business competition.

Although business has made huge profits from the wish many
people have to escape from the values engendered by business, it
may seem incongruous that the urbane Anita O'Day should be the
unseen star of Robert Frank's and Alfred Leslie's *Pull My Daisy* (1956)
—its effusion of zany pleasure largely relies on one of her recordings—
since this short movie was based on the third act of Jack Kerouac's
play *The Beat Generation* and seems to have been intended as a protest

against conventional styles; this incongruity resolves itself, however, when it is recalled that the Beats were among the first people actively to publicize their retreat from society and to profit financially from their rejection of commercialism.

Pennebaker, also, appears to have understood how far American culture had identified itself with the importance show business ascribes to the idea of success, and how the practice of such ambitions requires a feigning of those qualities, such as informality and intimacy, which ambition by its nature destroys. In his documentary *Jane* (1962) he studies Jane Fonda during a bleak period when she was working in a play that subsequently failed on Broadway. He took a theme familiar from countless American movies and filmed it in a rough, open-ended way that both gave it edge and suited his disinclination to probe into motives; and in doing so he raised doubts, which he never settles, about whether an actress ever stops acting before a camera. His *Don't Look Back* (1967) was to be even less forthcoming. Describing a Bob Dylan tour in which Dylan fended off interpretations of his behaviour and beliefs, it conveyed a sense of occasion without giving any clues as to the meaning of this occasion. The spectator was left to evolve his own speculations around the deadpan faces in Dylan's entourage.

Pennebaker had joined with Richard Leacock, Shirley Clarke and Willard Van Dyke in 1959 to found Film Makers, a cooperative which gave them the chance to share cutting-room facilities and equipment. Pennebaker and Leacock (with Terry Filgate and Al Maysles) had then been invited by Robert Drew, who worked for *Life* magazine and was intrigued by the problems of photojournalism, to take part in a Time-Life commission to produce television documentaries. Although *Primary* (1960), the first major film in this series and the first to use portable synchronized sound cameras, demonstrates the technical fluency documentary had acquired since the days of *March of Time*, its account of the Wisconsin primary, which John F. Kennedy won and Hubert Humphrey lost, plays up the drama of the conflict at the expense of the issues involved, much as *March of Time* might have done. In common with *Jane* and *Don't Look Back*, it compares backstage anxieties and fatigues with the glitter of public appearances. In one fine sequence the camera follows Kennedy through a double line of supporters and allows the spectator to identify with his sense of triumph as the admiring faces peel away from it; yet in spite of all its hovering and swooping, it can only give the illusion of intimacy; it never discloses what Kennedy feels or what his strategy might be. 'We know less about the Democrat Kennedy after seeing *Primary* than we do from reading Theodore White's book,'[15] said Jean-Luc Godard, perhaps expecting too much.

Its style gives an impression of spontaneity, like good jazz, and has the effect of favouring the more hip candidate. Indeed, John F. Kennedy comes over as a kind of Gerry Mulligan, cool in humour, relaxed and assured with women. He might have been tailored to suit photojournalism. Hubert Humphrey, on the other hand, resembles some DeMille tragi-comic clown. When he looks tired, as when he sleeps in his car to the sound of monotonously beating windscreen wipers, he looks worn out, like some trouper ready for retirement. But if *Primary* encourages its audience to see the candidates as entertainment personalities—and anticipates the tone of Norman Mailer's commentaries on later conventions—it does so because the candidates themselves were exercised by the need to sell themselves over television. It was this election, after all, which was decided by a Kennedy–Nixon broadcast that the public allegedly saw in terms of a Western.

A conflict of personalities brought Drew Productions to an end shortly after the filming of *Crisis* in 1963. Its documentaries had enjoyed little favour with American television programme planners, who thought them too liberal, and they were to be more widely appreciated by cinema audiences. They belong very much to an era when public figures could still seem to fall into the role of hero or villain; and *Crisis*, which reports on the means Robert Kennedy used to defeat Governor George Wallace in his stand against the desegregation of the Alabama schools, has been compared to a Howard Hawks adventure movie in its pathos and simplicities. But its climax is pre-Hawksian in its cross-cutting between Robert Kennedy on the phone and the Attorney-General moving up a school path to challenge the Governor. Although this Biograph parallel-editing sets up tension, it leaves the spectator little to consider once the film has ended.

In 1958 Allen Ginsberg had complained that the media tended either to prohibit or to mock the more personal sensitivities. By the mid-sixties, prohibitions had been diminished and the mockery grown more subtle. Two films by Shirley Clarke give some idea of this change. Her 1960 film version of Jack Gelber's off-Broadway play *The Connection* distinguished between the illusions and actualities experienced by a group of drug-takers. Although there was nothing especially unusual about this subject—Preminger's *The Man with the Golden Arm* (1955) and Zinnemann's screen version of Michael Gozzo's play *A Hatful of Rain* (1957) had already broken the media's silence over the problem of drug addiction—it was still thought to be faintly scandalous. A Charlie Parker recording not only gave the key to Shirley Clarke's style but also suggested its origins in 1940s hipsterism, a style to which John Cassavetes was to give the most complete expression in *Shadows* (1961): semi-improvised, cool, seldom disclosing motives, acutely aware of the race question.

But by the time she came to film *Jason* (1967), Shirley Clarke had
dropped all pretence of mediation between her subject and the audience. She discarded any semblance of plot and of reticence. For
twelve hours—cut down to 105 minutes of screen time—she allowed
her cameraman, Jeri Sapanan, to film the confessions of the Negro
Jason, which became increasingly perverse as he became more and
more drunk and drugged. How far does Jason tell the truth? Publicists
have evoked the name of Pirandello in relation to the film as they had
done for *The Connection*. Yet his confession has none of the moral
anguish that marks Pirandello's plays, nor does it raise the issue of
sincerity as Pennebaker's *Jane* had done. Jason is too far gone in his
illness for such notions as sincerity to have meaning. Indeed, the
spectator will probably be more intrigued by Shirley Clarke's motives
than by his: whether she thought him worthless, in which case he
may wonder why she wasted anybody's time over his confession, or
whether she saw some value in Jason, in which case he may wonder
why she risked disturbing the balance of Jason's mind further by
encouraging his exhibitionism.

She may have subscribed to arguments popular in the mid-sixties
that certain forms of insanity may be the truest reflections of an
alienated society, a belief that ignores the helplessness of the mad.
Warrendale (1966), a documentary produced by Allan King about a
residential treatment centre for disturbed children on the outskirts of
Toronto (later closed by the Canadian health authorities), reveals, perhaps unwittingly, how such arguments can often be practised at the

Allan King: *Warrendale*.

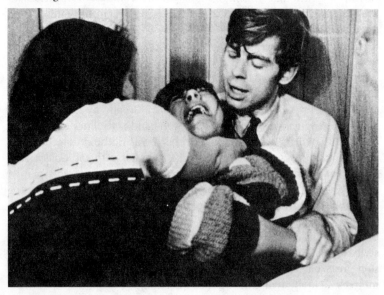

expense of the insane. One critic has described this documentary as 'shattering'. '*Warrendale* should be shown everywhere to give complacent audiences something to think about.' Yet those who are unaware of the suffering visible in every walk of life are unlikely to be 'shattered' by their exposure to such extreme forms of suffering on the screen. Their response is more likely to recall those visitors to Bedlam who ridiculed the mad.

The charge of complacency, on the contrary, might be more fairly levelled at Allan King and his associates. Not only does their wish to publicize the suffering of others fail to take into account the damage done by their filming for forty hours the struggles and fits of these children, but they also fail to demonstrate the value of the enterprise. They describe the Warrendale therapy without providing the kind of information needed to assess it, and they do not explain how the children might be helped by certain of its more brutal techniques, such as the technique of 'containment', in which one member of the staff crosses the arms of a violent child while another pins down its legs. Like Peter Weiss's play *Marat–Sade*, their film turns the experience of mental illness into *grand guignol*; and even the existentialist argument that it allows the audience to share in the strains of community life by demonstrating how its relationships are worked out cannot account for the arbitrary quality of judgements that must rely on nothing more than a (heavily-edited) succession of faces and gestures.

Godard, Truffaut, Pennebaker, Clarke, Cassavetes and King: all of them remind the spectator of the enigmatic nature of appearances; that faces and gestures in themselves can be interpreted in so many ways that they require the governing intelligence of an artist to give them a defined meaning. The camera used as an impersonal recording instrument cannot provide this discrimination. Allen Ginsberg wished for the media to do away with its prohibitions over 'personal sensitivities': yet the camera cannot make sense of the more intimate of human experiences; it registers the act of love, for instance, without the all-important feelings of the lovers; it cannot make the private public. A consciousness of this limitation informs Haskell Wexler's *Medium Cool* (1969), which comments on the way cameramen can be brutalized by their intrusions, while Jim McBride's spoof documentary, *David Holzman's Diary* (1967), shows up the falsity of Godard's belief that 'film is truth twenty-four times a second' by demonstrating how verisimilitude can be faked on the screen.

But to suggest that photography can degrade the more private of human activities may be to put the argument in a misleading way: for the issue to be decided, surely, is whether this degradation has been induced by technology or by certain attitudes long-established in Western culture. The ending of certain prohibitions in the media brought many implicit forms of cynicism into the open.

Alfred Hitchcock: *Psycho.*

Wilder's *The Apartment* and Hitchcock's *Psycho* were both released in 1960. In convention, one of them is a comedy, the other a horror film, although it is unlikely that Lubitsch or Murnau (let us say) would have thought of them as such. Wilder begins with a standard comedy subject — businessmen who keep call-girls on the side — but then feels free to investigate this subject with a candour previously denied him. In doing so, he uncovers the implicit cynicism of his subject (and of a culture which can find such a subject amusing) and touches on a depth of sadness that in all probability he had not intended. In the same way, Hitchcock transforms the conventions of Gothic romance by seeing his killer not as some cypher labelled as evil but as a psychotic; yet this attempt to disclose a human meaning in brutal murder has the effect of showing up the impersonality with which Hitchcock himself traps his characters in a web-like plot, the seemingly aimless movements of his camera being in fact as purposeful as a spider's spinning. Hitchcock made his attitude to this activity clear in one of his conversations with Truffaut, in which both men recall the screen murder of Janet Leigh—they give the name of the actress, not the role—in terms of technique alone.

It would be tempting to think that the cynicism that Wilder and Hitchcock have had to contend with was acquired during their years in Hollywood, but in fact it has been even more open among those

Billy Wilder: *The Apartment.* Jack Lemmon, Shirley MacLaine.

independent or 'underground' film-makers who feel themselves opposed to all that Hollywood has stood for. The origins of the term 'underground' are unexpected. In 1957 Manny Farber published an article entitled 'Underground Films', which was not about the avant-garde but about certain films, remarkable for their sense of observation and pace, by such Hollywood craftsmen as Hawks, Walsh, Wellman and Anthony Mann. Farber praised these movies and noted that not only did they tend to deal with the mean, gritty side to the metropolitan scene but they also practised their skills in a quiet underground way. He contrasted his pleasure in their often brutal action with his distaste for the cultivated, even self-conscious sensibility and 'liberal schmaltz'[16] of *The Best Years of Our Lives.*

Although some of the independent film-makers did not concern themselves with straight action or necessarily try to conceal their techniques, many of them did assume the qualities Farber had praised and like him were indifferent to the appeal of sensibility. Lionel Rogosin's *On the Bowery* (1957) and *Come Back Africa* (1959) were raw documentaries concerned with the meanness and grit of the metropolitan, while Irvin Kershner's *Stake Out on Dope Street* (1958), Alexander Singer's *A Cold Wind in August* (1962), and Terry and Denis Sanders's *Crime and Punishment USA* (1958), in which empty

Terry and Denis Sanders: *Crime and Punishment USA*. George Hamilton.

rococo fun-palaces and damp beach houses caught the mood of an off-season Santa Monica, all kept closely to the spirit of Mickey Spillane. In Joseph Strick's *The Savage Eye* (1959) a self-pitying divorcee surveys Los Angeles; and actuality shots of women convulsed at a faith-healing service, of crashes with their bleeding, stunned victims, and of jaded spectators at a striptease are offered up as a commentary on the affluent society. But Strick catalogues horrors with such an exuberance and edits them together so joltingly that he creates, much as Jacopetti did in *Mondo Cane* (1961), an effect as base as any of the witnessed degradations.

Strick and many of the other independents hoped their films would be shown on the circuits; and however much they may have distrusted Hollywood, they did subscribe to many of its ideas about the well-made film. By the end of the decade, their quirky way of looking at the individual in urban surroundings—Peter Bogdanovich's *Targets* being typical of the way in which this manner persisted throughout the sixties—had invaded Hollywood itself. Many of the studios had become no more than distribution agencies for the independent producer, and although the B feature category no longer had any meaning, its candour, rough-edged technique and low budget were now the prime ingredients in a selfconsciously new American style.

The genuine underground film-makers, however, claimed to be uninterested in commercial success and to have no competitive feelings towards Hollywood. Opposed to the Hollywood wish to flatter and placate, they tended to assault their audiences by riveting them into a condition of boredom, confusion or outrage. The moment at which the underground emerged out of the avant-garde experiments of the group centring on Maya Deren is uncertain, though Kenneth Anger's *Fireworks* (1947) signals many of its intentions. Anger had been brought up in Hollywood. At the age of four he had appeared in Reinhardt's *A Midsummer Night's Dream*, and in *Eaux d'artifice* (1953) it is possible to see how the style of this film has continued to influence him. Unlike other members of the underground, he is fascinated by Hollywood and its history; yet *Fireworks*, which he filmed at the age of seventeen, is as private as a diary written without thought for publication. It charts some of the masturbatory fantasies of bed-sitter existence and is indifferent to the guardians of morality. Stan Brakhage's *Flesh in the Morning* (1957) also moves outside any accepted notion of film construction and concerns itself with masturbatory fantasy, though with none of Anger's theatricality of style. In later films Brakhage has described lovemaking with his wife and the birth of their children. At a time when Hollywood was somewhat disapprovingly exploring the subject of teenage behaviour, Brakhage and his associates were recording the sensations of growing up without the slightest concern for social taboos. They have also challenged many preconceptions about the nature of good photography. 'By deliberately spitting on the lens or wrecking its focal intention,' writes Brakhage, 'one can achieve the early stages of impressionism . . . One may under- or over-expose the film. One may use the filters of the world, fog, downpours, unbalanced lights, neons with neurotic colour temperatures, glass which was never designed for a camera, or even glass which was, and can be used against specifications, or one may go into the night with a specific daylight film or vice versa.'[17]

The New American Cinema, as it is sometimes called, is uninterested in evaluation. Its supporters do not believe in using film for any other purpose than that of pleasing themselves. Anything goes; and does. Its imitators have been world-wide and any comment on them would have to be unjustly limited. Each spectator must decide on his own preferences. They cover a wide range of techniques and feelings, from the relaxed humour of Robert Nelson's *Oh Dem Watermelons* to the aggression of Bruce Conner's flickering white light. Most of them are interested in visual experiences that cannot be described verbally. The quietism of Bruce Baillie and Ron Rice reflects this bias. Baillie's *Castro Street* (1966)—its title is the nearest it comes to a political statement—is a fusion of railroad and street shots in colour with black and white superimpositions in negative. *Tung* has flowing images of hair and landscape, sun and moon. The enveloping power of these short films appears related to the tragedies of the drug addict. The work of Ron Rice, who died at the age of thirty-one, is also deliquescent. His *Senseless* (1962) consists of a miscellany of images taken from Mexican life—inexplicable, deeply sad and made with a certainty of touch that suggests that any failure of understanding must be ours—while his faintly orgiastic *Chumlum* (1964) is outstanding in its imaginative use of colour.

Ron Rice: *Chumlum*.

Intimate to the point of being intrusive, the New American Cinema was only marginally interested in politics (Bruce Conner's squibs being an exception). Yet in January 1968 it led to the formation of Newsreel, a group of radical film-makers backed by Jonas Mekas, a leading figure on the American avant-garde scene. Newsreel came into being during the month when the last of the official newsreel companies had closed, and it was fortunate enough to obtain from television, at no cost, 180,000 feet of unexposed black and white 16mm. film, adequate to produce about eighty-three hours of documentary. It wished to provide educational studies concerning those aspects of society which it believed its public might be misinformed or ignorant about; tactical exercises of immediate use on how to deal with the mounted police, the lay-out of the Pentagon and various protective devices; and a rapid coverage of events which it thought germinal to an understanding of change in the United States (such as the March on the Pentagon, the ghetto riots and the Vietnam draft issue).

Its films were short in length (about ten to fifteen minutes) and seldom, if ever, gave credits. Its strength lay in its flexibility and speed and the fact that it was not connected to any institution. It owed its inspiration to Vertov, Godard and to the radical spirit that became so dominant in the United States shortly after the assassination of John F. Kennedy. Newsreel had teams of cameramen stationed throughout the country, and its output consisted of about one film every fortnight. It was frank about being partisan and granted the viewer the distinction of having mind enough to form his own opinions; in this way it helped to counteract the despair and sense of isolation that 'balanced' television reporting can sometimes arouse in the spectator. It avoided the usual means of distribution and found ways to send film rapidly to clubs and university groups around the world.

Its lack of interest in the craft of film-making was plain. *No Games*, a test piece shot before the group had truly formed, covered the Pentagon demonstrations of October 1967. It was direct, but it was also badly structured, and it left no firm impression. *The Case against the Lincoln Center* set out to indict a 'sterile palace of culture', cutting between a Puerto Rican settlement, such as once had existed on the site, and the bland guests at the gala Lincoln Center first night. The fifty-minute *The Columbia Revolt* summons up the sudden and unexpected birth of a community inside the besieged university buildings, including an improvised wedding. The attack on the university gates, with helmeted police looking like an unending line of ants, creates an image of an Eisenstein-like memorability, while the blood-splattered walls of rooms ransacked by the police continue to haunt the mind long after the film has ended.

Newsreel's record of student agitation compares favourably with the treatment the mass media gave to it, latching on to the entertainment value of grievances and transforming protest movements into a national farce, though admittedly with the willing support of certain students. As John Searle has observed in *The Campus War* (1971):

When Jerry Rubin was to be subpoenaed by the House Un-American Activities Committee he arranged, with the co-operation of the Committee, to
have the whole scene televised on the Berkeley campus. He was not a student,
the Committee had nothing to do with the university, and the TV stations
are not under his direction. The case also illustrates a symbolic relationship
among the extreme right, the extreme left and the media—all at the expense
of the university—which we have seen over and over again in California. In
Rubin's career, this incident is only one among dozens; and indeed he and
Abbie Hoffman are the purest cases of radicalism as showbiz.

For sheer telegenic material, student unrest is hard to beat, and there is no
problem in getting the television crews to attend the demonstrations . . . An
event can be staged for the media which will then be reported as if it would
have occurred in precisely that form independently of the presence of the
media . . .[18]

Francesco Rosi: *Salvatore Giuliano.*

Italy

In Italy few of the more established directors were to be influenced by
the French or American New Wave and among the younger directors
the influence, though at one time intense, proved to be brief. Yet the
French were to help the Italian film industry, and Morando

Morandini was to write in *Sight and Sound* that in 1959 'Italian producers began, timidly enough, to embark on a slightly bolder policy largely as a result of the French example. This year films are being made in Italy which two or three years ago could not have been attempted. Fear of censorship is an excuse which no longer holds water; and film about Fascism can be made.'[19]

Few of these films actually dealt with the extreme right, but Morandini's allusion to Fascism has some point. Italian film-makers most differ from the French in their belief that culture should be aloof, distanced and faintly unappealing: a residue, possibly, of the Fascist attitude to the arts. When Visconti takes his themes from Thomas Mann, or Pasolini imitates the paintings of Mantegna or Antonioni the chic of *Vogue*, they appear to be reminding the spectator of their superior taste. Italian directors seldom achieve the unbuttoned gaiety of the French. Their humour tends to be puerile—as in Monicelli's *I soliti ignoti* (1958)—and their relationship with the audience formal.

Yet for all its occasional heaviness, their work can have an unusual breadth of feeling and intellectual interest. Many of them are masters of the grand style, of a majestic theatricality that arises in part from impressions of the architecture that surrounds them—the demonstrative façades and huge porticoes, evident in most of their cities, that evoke ancient Rome. As the Fascists knew, this style bears the imprint of authority; it does not equivocate; its assertions of imperial confidence cannot be avoided. Many of the more serious film-makers have realized that this style is now at best a vehicle for pathos; it points up the contrast between an assured past and the scepticism of the present-day world. They have an authoritarian impulse that cannot be satisfied, and an authoritarian style that cannot be justified. Many of them have made their awareness of this disparity into a theme.

Antonioni has defined it in terms of alienation, though this concept is too limiting when applied to the dissociation of men from the manner of their work and the things they make. It does not fully account for the tone that unites a remarkable body of work produced by the Italians during a brief period at the end of the fifties and the beginning of the sixties. The hallmark of all these films is a mood of desolation: Fellini appears to associate this mood with mountain communities, Antonioni and Pasolini with the outskirts of cities, Rosi with a battlefield after slaughter and Olmi with the monotony of an office in which the clerks behave like automata.

What does this mood signify? It recalls de Chirico's paintings of empty streets and piazzas and their atmosphere of cities that exist outside time—of a world constructed by men that no longer includes mankind. It recalls the neo-realists with their solitary figures stranded in marshlands suggesting the dawn of time. The final sequence in

Antonioni's *The Eclipse* (1962)—it consists of a series of urban views filmed at twilight with no more than a glimpse of people—captures this mood most completely. It is like the abandoned village in *L'avventura* (1959), or the island in the same film, so old that it has the effect of subduing confidence and arousing both irritation and awe in those who visit it.

The sense of the past is strong in these films, yet each of these directors has a different understanding of this past. For Antonioni it seems to be in some way related to mankind's present inability to adjust to technology. In broaching a problem that had once interested the Futurists, he provides a far more measured assessment of it than they had been capable of. Pasolini, however, believes that the example of the past may direct us away from the misconceptions of capitalism. Intrigued by those pagan customs that continue to influence the Italian mind in spite of centuries of Christianity, he claims that civilization has least affected the *lumpenproletariat*, who still have something of the pagan spirit—a spirit that may restore wholeness to the alienated self.

Fellini also appears to feel that a valuable part of ourselves is lodged, perhaps inaccessibly, in the remote past. In *La dolce vita* (1959) and his subsequent films about Rome, he has explored the tension that he feels exists between conventional morality, as embodied in Roman and Christian law, and his impulse to return—in imagination at least—to some older community which places its trust not in lawmakers but in some process of self-discovery through the senses. For more than sensationalist reasons, his commentator on ancient Rome has been the Petronius from whom he adapted *Satyricon* (1969) and not, say, Livy. Yet his understanding of the alienated self is more complicated than this account would suggest. He likes to rail against the moralists—usually they take the form of inquisitorial priests—for having stirred such feelings of guilt that they have distorted sensuous experience for nearly everyone. (In his confessional way he implies that above all he, Federico Fellini, has been incapacitated by such a guilt. And he may be right; for although he has touched on many forms of sexuality, he is among the least sensual of directors.) In spite of his resentment, though, he appears to have clung to Christian morality until late in his career. He has not hesitated to show those who have strayed from the fold, like the confidence trickster who dies on a mountainside in *Il bidone* (1955), as condemned to the hell of isolation. Yet the excommunication that he both desires and fears has a seriousness about it that involves more than his mixed feelings about the community. It may seem that his vision of the past, like those of his colleagues, half-admits to an even greater fear: that of a very negative vision of the future. For all their beauty, the streets of Milan at the end of *The Eclipse* or the ruins and catacombs of Fellini's *Roma*

(1972) anticipate a world in which mankind's presence has been annihilated by mankind itself. Such a fear is far more threatening than any awareness of industrial alienation. Pasolini's taste for pagan pleasures depends perhaps on the pagan fear that the world's end may be in sight, and such a fear may also partly account for Fellini's interest in the excesses of ancient Rome.

Many of these Italian directors would seem to be aware of the split that exists between their grand styles and the meanings it should convey, and some of them have relinquished any neo-realist impression of the actual world and moved into psychological exploration. Their filming has become uneasy, as when in *L'avventura* an elaborate camera choreography strains after the meaning of the events described without quite containing this meaning. Other directors have clearly not tried to adapt the grand style to the modern world. Giuseppe Patroni Griffi sets the present-day story of *Il mare* (1962) on a wintry off-season Capri that might be timeless. He describes the grandiose illusions of a young woman and her two male friends with considerable sympathy for their narcissism. His style is marble-cold, and at one moment alludes to Garbo's swaying movements around a tavern bedroom in *Queen Christina*. The boldness of his camera set-ups disrupts this hermeticism to some extent and dramatizes the physicality of the island; yet in an age suspicious of heroic gesture – the Italians have not forgotten Mussolini – audiences will find that his grand style provides little more than an exercise in heightened sensation within a luxurious setting.

The loss can be considerable; as when the Neapolitan director, Francesco Rosi, allows his taste for the grand style to overlay promising themes, as in his study of civic corruption, *Hands over the City* (1963), or of bull-fighting, *The Moment of Truth* (1964). In *Salvatore Giuliano* (1961), however, Rosi was able to use the grand style to illuminate the intricate hypocrisy that, he believes, pervades Italian public life at every level, from Mafia hirelings to Roman senators. He gives each of his characters a heroic cast; it is as though each of them were aggrandized by his belief in the bandit Salvatore Giuliano. He then undermines their pretensions by filming Giuliano either in long-shot or dead, so that each of them would appear to be responding to a void or legend of their own making. The absence of Giuliano as a presence in the film both undercuts their rhetoric and exposes one reason why the rhetoric exists; people need to see themselves in a dramatic light in order to avoid an awareness of the emptiness in their existence. One scene illustrates this point exactly: a group of Sicilian farmers stand with their backs to the camera before a row of arid mountains and listen while one of them intones a declamatory speech in praise of their country.

Men must live as best they can, and the stoic fatalism that Rosi portrays is touching as well as absurd. But he has no illusions about the baroque grandeur that this fatalism can induce. He shows how over the centuries the Sicilians have numbed themselves to the condition of their country at the cost of numbing themselves to the meaning of cruelty. He also shows how this fatalism, when it takes the form of baroque grandeur—as a way of cutting *una bella figura*—fits in too well with the ingenuity that comes so instinctively to Italians engaged in a vendetta. Other directors might have been tempted to underplay the poisoning of Salvatore's lieutenant, the cawing of a crow-like mother over Salvatore's corpse, or the massacre of the Communists, but Rosi describes them with all the callous flourish that baroque is capable of. Clear-sighted about the strain in the Italian temperament that most inseminated Jacobean tragedy, he recognizes how the grand style can both ennoble and render insensitive and how it can be a vehicle both for sensation and for a theatricality that can claim any sensation to be delusory. In his view of Italy, everyone manipulates everyone else, although the principal manipulator—perhaps some minister in Rome—remains undisclosed: a mystery that enlarges the sense of hollowness around which this film so dazzlingly extends its commentary.

The legacy of Fascism is nowhere so obvious as in the way Rosi confuses his distrust of rhetoric with his scepticism about whether heroism can exist in the present age. Yet such a heroism is all about us, as Roberto Rossellini, for one, has long pointed out. At the time when Rosi was filming *Salvatore Giuliano*, Rossellini had just completed *Viva l'Italia* (1960), a centenary tribute to the part played by Garibaldi in the unification of Italy, and the devious complications of one could not be more vividly contrasted than with the directness of the other. Although Rossellini notes the endearing vanity of Garibaldi's hats and his uncertainty when addressing the faithful thousand at Quarto, he declines to question the past with a present-day irony. His style has a candour that rises above changes in fashion, and his battle scenes are unsurpassed in the clarity with which they demonstrate strategy. No one has used the zoom shot less obtrusively, or used it to suggest that one of the battles might have been filmed from a balloon tacking over the field. Both here and in his television portraits of Louis XIV, Socrates, St Augustine and Cosimo de' Medici, he shows that the nature of heroism lies in the struggle to remain human while carrying out superhuman tasks.

One of his best studies in heroism is one of the earliest, *St Francis, Fool of God* (1950), which from the start demonstrates its origins in the neo-realist cult of the child. In its opening sequence St Francis and his monks are caught in a rainstorm. Some of the monks splash through a puddle, others dance with joy at being in the company of a saint. It could be a gauche scene, but Rossellini spares his audience's embarrassment by casting actual monks in these roles, whose radiant faces make their actions credible. He qualifies St Francis's sanctity by seeing him as an ambiguous figure, as much mentally retarded as blessed, and he does not try to conceal the sexuality of his companions. A thrill of pleasure overcomes them at the arrival of St Clare and her nuns, but they fail to understand the meaning of their excitement and kneel down in prayer with their visitors.

St Francis represents mankind before its experience of alienation. He is at one with the stony landscape. But he avoids the hardness of stone through his identification with the birds and gentler beasts. He resists the temptation to seek out physical comfort, and perhaps for someone so at home with this landscape, he does not feel the temptation too strongly. Rossellini evokes a spare, grey place that has some likeness to his blitzed Berlin. It is far from Giuliana's dream of a non-alienated world in Antonioni's *The Red Desert* (1964). Giuliana dreams of a blue lagoon and a coloured girl who bathes in its waters, of a mysterious schooner and a song that some siren might have sung, a Homeric vision translated into the imagery of a tourists' brochure.

But Antonioni, in all fairness to him, is concerned with problems of greater intricacy than this dream might imply. Rossellini's concern in describing the lives of heroes is bound up with the importance he sets on education; he follows Edison and Lumière in using the cinema as a means of investigation. Antonioni holds a more tentative view of knowledge. His male characters are frequently incapacitated by the scientific achievements most evident in the technology and architecture of the second machine age. They feel estranged from the language of action and will; they have retreated into sensibility; and the traditional forms of plot can no longer contain their sensations. Chris Marker had recalled (in *Le Joli Mai*) that the pursuit of happiness dates back no more than two centuries and that most men until recently would have scorned such a pursuit. Antonioni's men pursue happiness, and with some awareness that it will probably prove elusive. Most of them rely heavily on women, who respond far more fully than they do to the stress and promise of the modern world.

Antonioni has continued to remain fascinated by the hypothesis of a non-alienated world. Federico Fellini, on the other hand, has lost touch with it, even though he had helped to write the screenplay for *St Francis, Fool of God* (as well as for *Rome, Open City* and *Paisa*) and had, in *Il miracolo*—one of the two separate episodes in Rossellini's *Amore* (1947)—taken the part of the tramp who seduces a young woman by pretending to be a saint. While Antonioni evolved means by which to film some of the complexities of introspective

thought, Fellini has involved himself in the representation of obsessional fantasies. Often his powers of self-discovery appear to be
blocked by his pessimism. He seems unable to imagine an integrated
person who can stand up to stress, and he appears to believe that
the more admirable a person might be, the more vulnerable they are
to destruction.

Gelsomina in *La strada* (1954) is a variant on St Francis, a busker
and holy fool of God who communes with nature and at the moment
of her death is consoled by the touch of a pebble, as though the
pebble were an emblem of her faith. But Fellini mars this picture by
maintaining a position often ascribed to the Roman Catholic church:
that virtue and sexuality are of necessity opposed. He allows Gelsomina
to be reconciled with nature but not with herself. She serves another
busker, Zampanò, seen purely from her point of view as a caged wild
beast, or brutal phallic threat. Fellini never works through the meaning of this fantasy and presents Gelsomina very much as she sees herself, as someone whose innocence depends on her wits being dull.
He presumably wished to stir the same sort of admiration in his audience as Rossellini had done with St Francis, but in fact Gelsomina
behaves in a manner that at best arouses pity, and Giulietta Masina's
sly coquetry in the role underlines the similarity of this character to
Chaplin's tramp. Perhaps in spite of himself, Fellini cannot help showing her as degraded.

In *Juliet of the Spirits* (1965), Giulietta Masina appears as a later
development of this figure, a virtuous housewife who lives through a

Federico Fellini: *Juliet of the Spirits.*

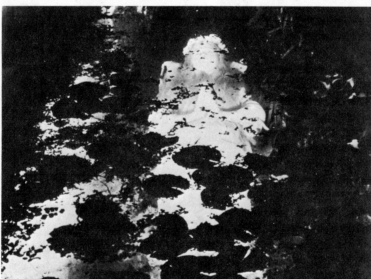

phantasmagoria. Fellini's ornate style includes motifs drawn from the statuary and votive offerings of Italian cemeteries, and he uses them to depict the sickening of a woman cut off from her desires. But he achieves a result that is closer to a case history than to his intended variation on the legend of St Anthony, and his implicit mockery of Juliet's ignorance—a mockery that appears as much directed at Giulietta Masina herself, who is Fellini's wife—robs his statement of any general significance.

But in mocking Juliet, Fellini would also appear to be mocking his own one-time provincial self. The scene in which Juliet visits a guru and fails to realize how far his religious rites are identical with certain forms of perversity (though Fellini is quite explicit about the equation) might be a commentary on the supposed innocence of Gelsomina. It is also possible to see the change in Fellini's attitudes to religion and sexuality as having some bearing on the changes that occurred in his style between the time of *La strada* and *Juliet of the Spirits*: a twin process of disillusionment and increasing elaboration of technique that can be traced through three films. At the end of *I vitelloni* (1953), the innocent Moraldo (Franco Interlenghi) leaves Viareggio to make a career in Rome, but by the time he appears in *La dolce vita* (1959), Moraldo—now played by Marcello Mastroianni—feels corrupted by the city and can no longer envisage it as either a worthy goal for his ambitions or as the city of God. He has lost his belief in innocence and in a God or Church that might underwrite the meaning of the universe: a despair that Fellini has admitted reflected his own loss of faith. In his subsequent film, *8½* (1963), he was to show that if Rome were to have a transcendental meaning it could only acquire this meaning as a presence in the mind.

The need to represent his thoughts in this way obliged him to evolve new techniques. In the carnival sequences of *I vitelloni* he was able to foreshadow the means by which he was to represent an ideal Rome, but he was still to contain these baroque effects within a neo-realist framework. In *La dolce vita* he had already moved towards a mobility of filming that resembles Roman baroque. He no longer used the grand style in a hesitant fashion: he himself would seem to have become that style.

It could be argued that this retreat into the fantastic marked a failure in his development as an artist, or that his insistent theatricality signalled some limitation of his talent; and both these cases could be argued with some force. Even so, his instinctive sympathy for the baroque has put him in touch with a striking aspect of the Italian way of life. Implicitly he recognizes that the outwardness of baroque has the contradictory effect of creating a sense of mysterious portent: that in Rome many buildings, or the crowds milling on the Via Veneto, show themselves off in a way that heightens their inac-

Federico Fellini: *8½*.

cessibility. These buildings and crowds would seem to imitate, in a secular fashion, the mysterious pomp of ecclesiastical ritual.

Most of Fellini's plots turn on a moment of disillusionment, when actors take off their make-up and costumes, as it were, and reveal themselves to be fallible human beings. In the 1960s Fellini was to apply this process of disclosure to some of his most cherished fantasies, as when, in *Satyricon*, he destroys the enchantment of his ideal Rome by revealing the often ugly motives that lie behind its pageantry. At the beginning of his career—as in *The White Sheik* (1952)—he had protected the Church from this kind of criticism by establishing two kinds of style, one of which—the ecclesiastical—was to be solemnly sustained, while the other—that of the music-hall—was to be seedily pretentious and vulnerable to his mockery.

By the time he came to direct *8½*, Fellini had begun to use a more personal iconography. Far from expecting to discover integration through the church, he had begun to think of its representatives as oppressors and hypocrites, who stunt the feelings of those in their care. And he concludes *8½* with a form of reconciliation, which may not be satisfactory, but which is far closer to him than the one offered by the Church. Its central character, a film director, imagines himself once more to be a child, leading those he loves and fears in a procession around a circus ring. Although the child does not abandon his desire for power over these figures—he controls them in much the same way as his adult self will control actors and will be unable to think of reconciliation in other than theatrical terms—the concluding image of this fantasy, of the solitary child playing a piccolo against

Federico Fellini: *8 ½*.

the encroaching darkness, formulates well the wish to take on responsibility for all that we might fear.

Fellini edits together fragments of dreams, recollections and immediate experiences into a narrative that, like all egotistic outpourings, pleads for approval. It is true that the quality of his fantasy, and the way he conceives of relationships, has a fluency and warmth absent from the *collages* of fantasy that Resnais puts together in *Last Year at Marienbad*, yet both he and Resnais appear to have recognized, at much the same time, that the public was now ready for a more reflective kind of film-making. The freedom of their editing has enough in common to support the view that a general change in consciousness was taking place.

Antonioni has contributed in a similar fashion to this particular development in film syntax, although in a manner less self-involved than Fellini, or less distanced than Resnais. In *The Red Desert*, Corrado lectures some workmen he has hired and finds his attention distracted by a blue line on the wall behind the men. The camera tracks the line along the wall, until it turns into a succession of coloured blobs and

Michelangelo Antonioni: *Cronaca di un amore.*

shapes, abstractions that in themselves have no conceptual meaning. Yet they make an appropriate accompaniment to the inadequacy aroused in Corrado by Giuliana's beauty and illness and also to the overriding mood of the film, an aimless despair that loses itself in abstraction. Antonioni does not imitate Corrado's musings so much as try to grasp at conjunctions that have become meaningful at a time when human consciousness would seem to be undergoing a change.

He directed his first feature, *Cronaca di un amore* (1950), at the age of thirty-eight, and his technique already suggested that he was dissatisfied with the available narrative conventions. In his next three features, and especially in *Le amiche* (1955), he evolved a type of plot that was more sensitive to the feelings of his characters. But the breakthrough was to come with *L'avventura* (1959). He began to hold his shots beyond the point where most directors would have cut, and he included scenes that added next to nothing to narrative momentum. By acknowledging events that were important in them-selves, though superfluous to his story-line, he began to release his characters from the usually deterministic sort of plot. They were no longer cogs in some narrative machine but beings to be observed and perhaps loved. His shot of Claudia in *L'avventura* running up and down a corridor adds nothing to the narrative, yet has the suggestion of a lover's memory; while the scene in which Claudia looks through a magazine while anxiously waiting for the arrival of Sandro, and then stands at a window in the dawn light, gives her existence a substance out of which later revelations arise naturally.

Michelangelo Antonioni: *The Red Desert*. Monica Vitti.

Antonioni sometimes has trouble in allowing his images to accrete meaning: as when he tries to force his male characters into being an alienated Everyman. Sandro's promiscuity in *L'avventura* is compulsive enough to make him into a text-book case, and though Antonioni may argue that the concept of psychopathology no longer has meaning in an age of total alienation, he hardly manages to show Sandro as typical of the middle-aged Italian. His failure to generalize experience was to be total in *La notte* (1960). Lacking any understanding of how writers think and feel, his portrait of the author, Giovanni Pontorno (Marcello Mastroianni), is so unconvincing that the spectator may be tempted to think that Giovanni's crisis of conscience is no more than a rationalization of his inability to escape from his wife's purse-strings. In *La notte*, Antonioni shows how difficult it is to dramatize the theory of alienation; he appears unable to see how the difference between the metaphysical pronouncements of his characters and their behaviour is often comic.

His feeling for women is less strained. Most of the sequences concerning Vittoria (Monica Vitti) in *The Eclipse* (1962) reveal her thought in an unforced symbolism, especially so in the scenes where she makes herself up as a black African or loses her black poodle or arrives

Michelangelo Antonioni: *The Eclipse*. Monica Vitti.

at Verona airport to find two Negroes standing by the airport bar, scenes that actualize a contrast between Italy in the age of technology and Africa as an imagined continent of the senses. But after directing *The Eclipse*, Antonioni appears to have lost interest in this introspective kind of thinking and would seem to have abandoned journeys through the landscape of the mind for actual travel. Yet not entirely. In *Blow Up* (1966), he invigorated a dull, inaccurate report on fashionable London by taking considerable technical risks in describing the consciousness of his central character, a photographer. His boldness was of a kind that would never have tempted Hitchcock, say, who had touched on a similar theme in *Rear Window* (1954).

Hitchcock's photographer is laid up with a broken leg and passes the time by spying on his neighbours and eventually coming across evidence of a murder. It is possible to understand *Rear Window* as a parable on the nature of the voyeurist, who usually manages to see the dirt that he wants to see, although Hitchcock never raises this possibility in his treatment. Antonioni, more aware of the psychological meaning of his stories, makes such a point about his photographer explicitly and comes close to Swift's observation in *Gulliver's Travels* that 'through a magnifying-glass, the smoothest and whitest skin looks rough and coarse and ill-coloured'. [20] He has one remarkable sequence in which his photographer prints enlargements of an increasing size of two lovers in a park, to the point where he sees what he presumably has been wishing to see. His subsequent madness would lend weight to the view that the photographs represented his jealous speculation about the lovers, although it must be admitted that Antonioni shows a corpse lying in the park in a shot unconnected with the photographer.

Throughout his career Antonioni has employed the most arresting of grand styles. In spite of his earnestness, he has consistently illu-

Michelangelo Antonioni: *Blow Up.*

minated modern man's relation to the eerie technological world that has grown up around him. His manner has been influential. It can be felt on Bernardo Bertolucci's second feature, *Before the Revolution* (1966), a present-day variation on Stendhal's *The Charterhouse of Parma* that manages however to lack Stendhal's sense of humour. Bertolucci is most Stendhalian in his ability to create impressions of generosity and the circumstances that can thwart such generosity. Some of his set pieces—the landowner's lament over the decline of his estate or the hero's meetings with his aunt—have a confidence and grandeur that would be remarkable achievements for any film-maker, let alone one aged twenty-five.

He was to be sardonic in *Partner* (1968), taking Jean-Luc Godard rather than Antonioni as his model. But he was unable to establish the sort of tone that gives an appearance of consistency to a fragmenting technique. In *The Conformist* (1970), based on a Moravia novel, he returned to the grand manner once more, though none too fortunately. Many of his inventions were as dehumanizing and pompous as the Fascist attitudes that Moravia had analysed. He was to be more perceptive in a television film made in the same year, *The Spider's Strategy*, tenuously drawn from a Jorge Luis Borges story but intended as a more general tribute to Borges's sense of irony and skill in handling complex time schemes. It brought out the deft as well as the grave side to his talent; and he was able to define some of the reasons why Fascism continues to appeal to certain sectors of the Italian public. But for all his gifts, he remains undefined in his interests and styles. *Last Tango in Paris* (1972), for instance, imitates Murnau's freedom in camera movement — Bertolucci has admitted to Murnau's influence — without any understanding of its significance. In his sensitivity to politics and to falsities in rhetoric, he seems to be aware of the neo-realist tradition, although he himself has often resorted to a sensationalism that the neo-realists would have despised.

Among Italian film-makers perhaps only Ermanno Olmi has resisted the desire to attract a dwindling audience sensationally and has kept close to the neo-realist intention. (Since 1965, though, he has been restricted to making films for Italian television.) He was to direct *Time Stood Still* (1959) and over thirty documentaries for Edison Volta before establishing an international reputation with *Il posto* (1961). A school-leaver applies for a job — the *posto* of the title; he is

Ermanno Olmi: *Il posto*.

taken on as a porter, and then graduates to being a clerk. It is implied that he will remain a clerk for the rest of his days. Olmi's gentle humour enlivens his description of the ways in which an office staff can be demoralized by its surroundings. He observes the irrationalities of solitary behaviour: the woman who drifts away from a group attending an interview to gaze at her reflection in a mirror, the silence that can descend on a packed room, the friendly glance that the atmosphere of the office almost wilts in mid-air. But beneath his droll sense of humour, Olmi's involvement in his subject is depressed.

His depression often takes the form of a chronic pessimism about the nature of human organizations. The Sicilian industrial complex in *I fidanzati* (1962), the Vatican in *A Man Named John* (1964) or the advertising business in *One Fine Day* (1969) seem to be so arranged as to destroy the spontaneity of those who work for them. Against these blighting communities he opposes the restoring powers of nature and comes close to setting up the traditional polarity of town and country. Yet memories of his upbringing on a farm near Brescia, and of the low standard of living provided by farming, have checked his idealization of the countryside. He has felt the experience of industrial alienation on the pulse. Compared to *I fidanzati*, Antonioni's *The Red Desert*, for one, looks no more than a blueprint for this theme. Antonioni deals with the anxieties of the managerial class, Olmi describes the helpless stoicism of a welder. His symbolism is unforced: the contrast in *I fidanzati* between the doll-like dancers of its opening sequence and the liberating, threatening storm at its conclusion is so felt that its meaning need only be alluded to. He has seen the darker side of the European economic miracle and in one or two images—a television set flickering in an empty room of a workers' hostel, a half-built factory glittering in the night like an ice palace— can say more about the experience of being a migrant worker than the whole of Visconti's *Rocco and His Brothers* put together. But the public preferred Visconti's theatricality and stayed away from Olmi's bleak vision. He had even less of a box-office attraction with Rod Steiger playing a former Pope, though *A Man Named John* is as illuminating a commentary as could be imagined on the worn and courageous face that appears in its final newsreel shots. Olmi sees John's virtue as embodying the grace of his rural upbringing and his anguish as originating in the education he received at the hands of an authoritarian priest. He shows how John's uncomplicated faith could withstand—at great cost to himself—the temptations of power, the mortifications of his often narrow-minded superiors and the meaningless cunning of diplomacy in post-war Paris. Overburdened by work, John can still berate himself for indolence as he watches night fishermen on the Bosphorus. Olmi's view of the Pope as a lonely prince estranged from the procedures of the church and capable of relating himself to the dispossessed fulfils the neo-realist wish to weave together some of the more important Christian and Marxist strands in current Italian thought.

He has not been alone in thinking Pope John a key figure in bringing about this synthesis. The Marxist Pier Paolo Pasolini was to dedicate *The Gospel According to St Matthew* (1964) to him, although

Pasolini's interpretation of Christ had none of the Pope's warmth. But then Pasolini has always been like some schoolmaster of perverse inclination, both in his choice of heroes and in his attitudes towards them. (In his first feature *Accattone* (1961), for instance, he saw a tragedy, deserving all the trappings of high culture, in a young man who decides that the only alternative to labour is a life of petty crime.) His Christ is a mean-faced intellectual who is most alive when rejecting his mother, or saying that he comes not in peace but with a sword. Pasolini presents him with all the distancing of a miracle play. He assumes a *faux-naïf* didacticism, and in certain scenes, such as when the virgin tells her bewildered husband of her pregnancy, or a severe child Salome dances, achieves a serenity that deliberately recalls the atmosphere of a Piero della Francesca painting. Yet both in this film and in his studies of Oedipus and Medea, Pasolini could not avoid the impression of a history book told in pictures.

The world-wide collapse of the film industry in 1963 did not exclude Italy. Panic set in with the closure of Titanus, a company that had backed *Il bidone*, *The Leopard*, *Altona*, *I fidanzati* — and Valerio Zurlini's sensitive *Cronaca familiare* (1962), which had won the Golden Lion award at Venice. Galatea, another company whose distinguished productions had included *Le mani sulla città* and Lina Wertmuller's *I basilischi* (1963), a languid variation on the theme of *I vitelloni*, was also forced to close down. Established directors—Fellini for one—had

Valerio Zurlini: *Cronaca familiare*.

difficulty in raising capital for their projects, while other careers were brought to an end. Yet Marco Bellocchio somehow managed to complete his ferocious *Pugni in Tasca* (1966) and Gillo Pontecorvo to achieve, in *The Battle of Algiers* (1966), the most lucid account on record of the Franco-Algerian war, told largely from an Algerian point of view, and limited only by the ease with which Pontecorvo underestimated the self-brutalizing price terrorists have to pay to carry out their humane ideals.

Milos Forman: *Taking Off*.

15. Radical Compromise

In the 1960s a great deal of film-making on both sides of the Atlantic committed itself to the promotion of radical politics, and with such a general consent from the industry and the critics that film directors were seldom taken seriously if their work did not reflect some disquiet about capitalism or some sense of grievance. Quite different in tone from the left-wing films of the 1920s and thirties, this professional radicalism had originated in the 1950s as an exploitation of the adolescent impulse to rebel against those in authority. Over a short period of time, however, it did take in such an issue as the mind's capacity to respond to urban and industrial stress. Godard found means to describe the fragmentary nature of perception, while Antonioni's extreme views on alienation—as in *The Red Desert*—anticipated the belief of other directors in madness as being the truest reflector of the modern condition. Even the act of film-making, which had become selfconscious and aspired to be a commentary on itself, was included within the compass of this estrangement. Traditional methods of narration now began to look out of keeping. At the beginning of the sixties a *Sight and Sound* international critics' poll on the ten best films of all time observed that *Bicycle Thieves* had lost its leading position in the poll held ten years previously—its transparency of style and type of plotting no longer, presumably, seemed meaningful—and that it had been replaced by *Citizen Kane*.

This social criticism had little political effect. It stimulated the underground cinema and cooperative groups, but brought about no change in the film industry, which appropriated the radical tone and remained much the same in its means of production and distribution. It had no measurable effect on politics in general either. By the end of the decade most electorates in the West had shifted to the right. It would be unfair to say that they were reacting against political trends in the movies, if only because, in the main, film-makers had been preaching to the converted. In the early 1930s educationalists had complained about the cinema's admiring view of the gangster and the call-girl. They had no reason to modify their views in the sixties; yet the intentions of the radical film-maker had changed since the time of the Depression. He now took an active pleasure in the idea of discontent, welcomed a well-heeled pessimism for its own sake and gave no sign of wishing for a new social order. Antonioni's melancholy, for one, appears inseparable from his talent.

Few imaginations were stirred to think of anything better than the acquisitive society. Happiness, though often referred to, was seldom realized convincingly. When Agnès Varda in *Cléo de 5 à 7* (1961) and *Le Bonheur* (1964), or Claude Lelouch in *Un Homme et une femme* (1966) and *Vivre pour vivre* (1967), or Mike Nichols in *The Graduate* (1967), tried to evoke it, they did so in the manner of television commercials with glowing colours, misted lenses and characters exhibiting an affluent style of living. They were not alone in confusing happiness with greed, one of the qualities they were most eager to deplore. It was often difficult to tell whether many directors set most store by writhing naked bodies, by luxurious surroundings or by preaching the gospel of freedom. Radicalism had become a commodity like any other. But a number of film-makers, including Bo Widerberg, one of the more talented of the younger Swedish generation, were aware of this trend. Widerberg has the painter's ability to evoke exquisite contrasts in colour, texture and shape. He is also attracted to grim themes. In *Elvira Madigan* (1967) he was unable to reconcile his interests— and he made a ravishing feast out of a double suicide. In *Adalen '31* (1969) he once more revealed an Impressionist's appetite for pretty washerwomen, the glint of a well-furnished table, the dapple of sunlight, the blaze of wild flowers. But how does a style that recalls Auguste Renoir relate to such a grave subject, the Adalen dock strike of 1931 which ended in bloodshed? It might be argued that a taut narrative would do more justice to starving men and stunted children. Widerberg raises this objection in the film and to some extent answers it by showing how he needs the idling richness of the Impressionist style to give an event in history all its fullness. In pulling together the various strands of his story, he demonstrates how this luxuriance adds conviction to his sense of outrage.

But if radical film-making in the capitalist West has on the whole been compromised by the techniques of advertising, what has been its condition in those countries, either underdeveloped or behind the Iron Curtain, where pressures have been of a different sort? In Cuba Fidel Castro recognized, as Lenin had done, the propaganda value of film, and after the 1959 revolution set up an Institute of Cinematographic Art and Industry. He appointed Santiago Alvarez, a documentary film-maker, as head of production. Alvarez's own output was to be astonishing—it averaged out at one newsreel a week for over a decade. His gifts as a propagandist were striking in *LBJ*, his eighteen-minute satire on American politics and the corrupting ethos of the Western. Put together out of brilliantly chosen photographs and extracts taken from Cinemascope features (eerily distorted to fit the 35mm. frame), it must rank with *74 Springs,* his portrait of Ho Chi Minh, as among the most virulently effective examples of compilation. Yet Alvarez's flair depends on his knowing use of the latest ideas in American graphics. He, too, is not immune from what Tom Wolfe has called Radical Chic.

Europeans may be disconcerted by the Cuban willingness to be influenced by the culture which, by its proximity and power, they have most reason to fear. Yet the dividing line between adventurous technique and fashionable mannerism is a narrow one. Manuel Octavio Gomez's ambitious reconstruction of the Cuban rising against Spanish rule in the 1860s, *The First Assault of the Machete* (1967), has harshly black and white images, and images flatly grey from over-exposure. Gomez uses the camera as an instrument of research: the leading participants in the action talk to it and try to explain their motives, *cinéma-vérité* style. Humberto Solas's *Lucia* (1968), on the

Humberto Solas: *Lucia.*

other hand, is as decorative as anything by Luchino Visconti, while carrying a certain insight and sympathy for the changing conditions of women. A surprising generosity can emerge from an industry so narrowly committed to revolution: Tomaas Gutierrez Alea's *Memories of Underdevelopment* (1969), for instance, tactfully delineates the doubts of a wealthy middle-class intellectual who decided to stay on in Cuba after 1959. But why should this industry be so tied to Hollywood in its working methods? Julio Garcia Espinosa, another Cuban director, has written in favour of an 'imperfect cinema'. He would replace the 'elitism' of the directors' cinema with a less controlled kind of production, one in which everyone on the studio floor could take a creative part. In common with most Latin American directors, Espinosa wishes to shake off the European heritage. 'When we look to Europe,' he writes, 'we give up. We see the old culture totally incapable of giving an answer to the problems of art.'[1] He and his contemporaries are in an uneasy position. In rejecting Roman Catholicism, they have been tempted to create a demonology out of the CIA; in forging a national idiom, they have been pushed back into accepting a Marxism still Europeanized; and in order to survive economically, they have been forced to seek distributors abroad, though they must have learnt from the increasingly baroque and flashy output of the Brazilian, Glauber Rocha, how foreign admirers can be among the most dangerous seducers.

At the same time, they do have a tradition of radical thought that to some extent protects them from the whims of fashion. In *The Modern Culture of Latin America*, Jean Franco has pointed out that Latin American artists have been concerned with the problem of national identity and the rejection of European styles since the mid-nineteenth century, while their commitment to the idea of revolution and their wish to terrorize the spectator date from an even earlier period. The present-day inheritors of this tradition are fascinated by passion and violent death. They are very much attracted to the necrophilic aspects of the society which they wish to destroy. Their cameras dwell on corpses, crucifixes and waxy statues of Christ. Sometimes this ambivalence can lead to a confusion of private and public events. In Miguel Lattin's *The Jackal of Nahueltoro* (1970), from Chile, a young director's interest in the details of a horrific murder almost submerges his theme, which is the State's power to change a man's personality. In the Cuban *Lucia*, bloody uprisings are so placed that they might be the erotic fantasies of two beautiful women.

Latin American films seem to elude the usual categories of experience. A European may be baffled by their strange pace and random prolixity, or by the fact that though they are coercive as propaganda, their narratives can be tentative to the point of seeming inept. Freewheeling camera movements, intended perhaps to extend the scope of perception, often leak away visual energy rather than intensifying it. But such an interpretation of their work depends on European assumptions about how films should be made—assumptions which many of them reject. Fernando Solanas's and Octavio Getino's *The Hour of the Furnaces* is a case in point. From a European viewpoint, this four-and-a-half-hour documentary on political oppression in Argentina seems both to overstate and to be obscure. Yet it is a landmark in the cinema of persuasion. Begun in 1965, it precedes Godard's agitational propaganda or the founding of militant cooperatives elsewhere. It was made by a group of people, not a single director, and this group decided to edit its rushes as little as possible, on the grounds that editing tends to impose a viewpoint on the spectator.

In Argentina *The Hour of the Furnaces* was thought to constitute a threat to the State, and the police raided even a private viewing of it. In Europe it appeared less striking than confused and touched by the depression that seems to colour Latin American protest films in general. For instance, a documentary like Humberto Ricos's *The Cry of the People* destroys any tourist's impression of Bolivian exoticism. It provides some statistics about the Bolivian tin-miners—how their expectation of life is about thirty years and few of them last more than five years in the mines—that become painfully credible as the camera explores the mines themselves and allows sensations of chill, damp and hopelessness to seep through. Poverty is omnipresent, and even the melancholic mountains and lakes outside the mines seem to reinforce the feeling that the miners may be stunned into a permanent despair. Rios appears to be as much caught up in the toils of futility as the people he describes: a state of mind that may account for both the incoherence and the indigenous strength of his statement.

Another Bolivian director, Jorge Sanjines, has dramatized the recent history of his country by more conventional means, at the cost, perhaps, of being more detached than Rios. Although he weakened his *Blood of the Condor* (1969) by an over-melodramatic plot, he also revealed an unusual gift for eliciting the seemingly irrelevant image that can pin a sequence in the memory. His second feature, *The Night of San Juan*, is comparable in the grandeur and irony of its set pieces to Rosi's *Salvatore Giuliano*.

The talent of film-makers in the Warsaw Pact countries has been shaped by different pressures. It would seem to be no coincidence that the Polish film industry took on life in 1953, the year of Stalin's death, or reverted to dullness once more with Gomulka's pronouncements against anti-populist art in 1964, or that the vitality of Czech film production during the Dubček administration should have been ended by the Soviet invasion of 1968. The thaws and freezes of Kremlin policy have determined nearly everything. But other factors have played some part: the foundation of some excellent film schools and the breakdown of the Polish film industry into small, fairly autonomous units in 1954 were both measures that stimulated talent. In common with the French under the German occupation, film-makers in the satellite countries have tended to work within the Romantic-Symbolist tradition. Censorship has obliged them to avoid topicality, or subjects rooted in any immediate context, although many of them have managed to work political or satirical references into their plots.

Certain Polish and Hungarian directors have asserted the theme of national identity to the point where it has become an implicit criticism of the Russian hegemony.

Few of them appear to be attracted to Socialist Realism. A wide variety of styles has been developed. For instance, a good deal of energy has been devoted to the puppet film and the animated cartoon, and with a freedom of invention that stands at the furthest remove from the tenets of Socialist Realism. In Yugoslavia the Zagreb School of Animation, opened in 1956, began by modelling its programme on UPA, but was soon to set new standards in the quality of its ideas and design. In Czechoslovakia the puppet films of Jiří Trnka (notably, *The Hand*) and Karel Zeman's feature cartoon *Baron Munchausen* (1961) were exceptional. In Poland Jan Lenica and Walerian Borowczyk (both of whom later emigrated to France) were to be outstanding in an industry where standards were already high.

Many directors working in the area of the feature film have tended to oppose populist trends and admire aristocratic virtues in a way that none of their contemporaries in the West would begin to think of doing. Andrzej Wajda's Polish trilogy *A Generation* (1954), *Kanal*

Andrzej Wajda: *A Generation.*

(1956) and *Ashes and Diamonds* (1958) relives the terrors of the last years of the war with little historical accuracy. In *Kanal* Wajda asserts that the Communist partisans took a leading part in the Warsaw uprising, which is untrue. He forbears to say, also, that the Russian army waited outside the city until the Home army had been annihilated. And he says nothing about Russian brutality or about the hostility many Poles felt to Communism. Less than informative as a historian, he does manage nonetheless to propagate a myth about the origins of the Polish socialist state that has power enough to give his trilogy stature. He is especially adroit at bringing together the ideal and the actual, as when in *A Generation* he contrasts the correct party hero Stach with the cowardly, sympathetic Jasio or when in *Ashes and Diamonds* he contrasts the dandified rebel Maciek with the buffoonish Drewnowski in such a way as to imply that while his heroes fulfil to some extent the Socialist Realist view of character, their *alter egos* register a more muddled and accurate state of affairs by their mistakes, panics and follies.

Like many of his characters, Wajda appears limited to an elegant stoicism and to a taste for mannerism and shock. Clearly uneasy about the Socialist Realist format of *A Generation*, which he took over from another director after shooting had begun, he is most involved in his filming whenever he has the opportunity to raise striking symbols for extreme conditions, as in the scene where Jasio commits murder or in the scene in which he is hounded to his death. Although he thinks of himself as one of Buñuel's followers, Wajda is much closer in his ideas and technique to the neo-expressionism of Marcel Carné.

His symbolism became more overt and his range of feeling more narrow as the trilogy progressed: a cerebral shorthand that won him acclaim during some of the bleaker years of the Cold War. With its parallels and coincidences, *Ashes and Diamonds* answered some public need in the fifties, being one of those self-enclosed and ornate structures, like *Rashomon, Wild Strawberries* or the melodramas of Torre Nilsson, that look back to the style of *Citizen Kane* and prefigure the sensibility of the mid-sixties, which was so influenced by Welles that it could be called the age of Kane. It also followed another trend of the fifties, in that its leading actor, Zbygniew Cybulski, imitated many of James Dean's mannerisms. But while Dean had represented one generation's idea of adolescent rebellion, Cybulski, as Maciek the Home army partisan, who stalks and kills an elderly Communist commissar, represents a more lethal and wide-ranging kind of response. At the moment of his death, the elderly Communist clutches at his killer, and a firework exploding in the sky is reflected in a puddle at their feet: an event so arranged that the two men together appear to represent extreme aspects of the Polish identity, briefly fused. But, like a short circuit, this fusion must destroy both of them and can only occur in a state of such bewilderment that sky and water become indistinguishable.

It is not surprising that so much Polish art should concern itself with the question of national identity. For the past two hundred years, Poland has been little more than a corridor through which hostile armies have swept. One of the first tasks the starving Poles addressed themselves to in 1945 was minutely to reconstruct Warsaw, which the Germans had razed to the ground. Wajda's wish that his plots should embody the conflicts of national identity seems inevitable, then, even though such a wish puts an insupportable strain on his plots and placed him at odds with government policy. At the end of *Ashes and Diamonds*, Maciek is seen to die on a rubbish dump, in a sequence that recalls the conclusion to *Los Olvidados*. As Maciek had been fighting the Communists, the Polish censors must have found his death justified. But as filmed, his death conveys a far less partisan significance and would appear to confirm the desperate stoicism that Maciek has professed throughout the film. Wajda presents him as a Polish Hamlet, who takes to action as purposefully as Fortinbras had done, but without Fortinbras's confidence in the value of action. He is less a stoic, perhaps, than someone numbed to feeling, who lives within a shadowy world of sentimental memories about the uprising, a sentimentality most plain in the scene where he and a friend light glasses of brandy as a tribute to their dead companions in arms. Wajda would seem not to have recognized the sentimentality of this scene. He refers to its nostalgia yearningly in *Everything for Sale* (1968), which re-enacts both this scene and the later actual death of Cybulski with an intricacy of structure that makes *Ashes and Diamonds* look a model of simplicity by comparison.

Maciek involves himself in a love affair that gives him some hope that existence may be more than automatic and futile. But Wajda does not seem to lay much credence on any belief in human potentiality. He begins discordantly the sequence in which an epicene count leads some of the people who have met Maciek during the last twenty-four hours of his life in a procession, and then suffuses it with a slow-motion enchantment. In doing so, he implies that members of the Polish gentry have debased Poland's former glory, while at the same time continuing to nourish some dream of this glory. This sequence resembles the ending to Fellini's $8\frac{1}{2}$, but Wajda's mixture of nostalgia and mockery has none of Fellini's (albeit slight) hopefulness. It relies on a pessimism about both the past and the present which his later films have not modified. His portrait of the defensive young lovers in *Innocent Sorcerers* (1960) brought him closest to a belief in the potentiality of human beings—a film that brought him into conflict with the Polish authorities. His father had been an army officer; and it might have seemed probable that the subject of *Lotna* (1959), which covers the Polish cavalry's tragic last stand against the German tank attacks, would have fired him to a treatment more heartfelt than the facetious elaboration which in fact characterizes it. A spear catches on some blood-red berries, a coffin reveals some ripe red apples, a wedding veil clings to the coffin lid: *Lotna* abounds with bright ideas, almost metaphysical conceits, that fail to take on life.

Andrzej Wajda: *The Birch Wood*.

He has allowed his feelings to engage with certain themes since then, as in *Samson* (1961) and *Landscape after Battle* (1970), but on the whole he has remained aloof. For all their skill, *Siberian Lady Macbeth* (1961), *Ashes* (1966) and *The Birch Wood* (1970) seem to be little more than exercises in style. In *Ashes*, especially, he appears to assume that the past can be so divorced from the present that, to all intents and purposes, it might have taken place on another planet and with a different species of being. But Polish film-making in the 1960s has generally been inclined to regress into mindless spectaculars; and a sequence in *Everything for Sale*, in which a film director visits a unit filming an absurd historical epic, does intimate that Wajda is aware of the bitter irony in these misuses of the past. He is only one among a number of talents who have been wasted in this way. Wojcieck J. Has directed the fascinating *Farewells* (1958), which

Wojcieck J. Has: *Farewells*.

has the whole repertoire of romantic effect—brief encounters, uncanny coincidences, young lovers surrounded by older people lost in
strange, private worlds—but also a strong feeling for passing time
and a sense of how war can change everything. But Has since then
has moved on into the deliberate bathos of a shaggy-dog story to end
all shaggy-dog stories, *The Saragossa Manuscript* (1964), and the hollow elegance of his lengthy historical reconstruction *The Doll* (1969).
The Poles have tried to win a place in the blockbuster market, and in
Aleksander Ford's *Knights of the Teutonic Order* (1960) and Jerzy
Kawalerowicz's *Mother Joan of the Angels* (1961) to escape from the
brittle optimism entailed by the doctrines of Socialist Realism. But
their policy has been a far from effective one.

Among the younger generation, Roman Polanski and Jerzy Skolimowski have both been attracted to work abroad. Polanski's first
feature, *Knife in the Water* (1962), in which a young man joins
a bureaucrat and his wife on a yachting weekend and upsets their
already edgy marriage, revealed an almost effortless gift for composition and timing, qualities that have characterized Polanski's later
work. But two earlier shorts, the surreal and prize-winning *Two Men
and a Wardrobe* (1958) and *The Fat and the Thin* (1963), a parable
in the manner of Samuel Beckett, throw more light on his later interests. He appears never to have escaped from the experience of an
appalling childhood in wartime Poland. His craving for the horrific is
barely contained by his deliberate technique. It tends to overwhelm a
childlike side to his talent that enjoys the playful element in fairy-
tales, perhaps most evident in *Dance of the Vampires* (1967). He has
often taken on tragic themes and, denying their tragic meaning, reduced them to grotesque black comedies. His brilliance can sometimes
lead to a callous aridity, as in *Cul de Sac* (1966), but it can sometimes
be perceptive about the nature of urban fantasies. In *Repulsion* (1965),
he described the thoughts and deeds of a young woman who goes
insane, carefully deriving the symbolism for her madness out of her
surroundings. Gil Taylor's camera stared coldly at objects most people
would prefer to turn away from, and by its steadiness transformed
the spectator's possible distaste at face packs, a skinned rabbit or
shadows falling across a chimney-piece into a state of fascination. In
common with Franju, Polanski is able to discover beauty in what
would usually be considered repulsive. He was to work the same
transformation in *Rosemary's Baby* (1968), creating a disturbing
effect by having Rosemary's New York apartment resemble a bright
fashion magazine photograph in all but one or two details. He generated tension in the main by cutting on a moving shot and ending
scenes abruptly. Although his adaptation of Ira Levin's novel was
faithful, he brought a humour to it that helped to suspend disbelief

Roman Polanski filming *Repulsion*.

in the idea that Rosemary had been possessed by the Devil, so that her fate became an apt metaphor for certain specifically metropolitan fears.

His friend Jerzy Skolimowski has not yet aroused the public interest that his talents deserve. Skolimowski tends to approach his subjects so obliquely that he often fails to convey even his enthusiasms: as for boxing—with himself as one of the boxers—in *Walkover* (1965), car rallies in *Le Départ* (1967) and swimming in *Deep End* (1970). At the same time, he has developed, in an intriguing manner, a type of editing that Godard had first explored in the early sixties. He began *Barrier* (1966) with a series of inconsequential shots that seem to make no narrative sense at all, and then had the camera pull back to disclose how the previously random-seeming images fitted together

Jerzy Skolimowski: *Le Départ.*

as parts of a credible situation. His flair for making far-reaching connections is considerable. But he has left it to others to develop the more meaningful Godardian type of link that brings together either widely different images or different conventions – fiction, say, with the documentary.

The most able practitioner in this field has been the Yugoslav director Dušan Makavejev, whose second feature, *The Switchboard Operator* (1967), revealed how fragments of newsreel, a fictional story, a documentary and two straightforward lectures could be related to each other in such a way as to set up metaphors of consider-

Dušan Makavejev: *The Switchboard Operator.*

able power. Like Godard, Makavejev is fascinated by the social determinants of eroticism, but he is also more in touch with the processes that constitute sexuality than Godard seems to be, and his supposedly free associations are less cerebral. And yet there is nothing dream-like or surreal about *The Switchboard Operator*. With little respect for chronology, Makavejev tells a love story that ends with a *crime passionel*, in which jealous Ahmed, the rat-catcher, drowns Isabela, the switchboard operator, in a Roman well. He cuts into this story extracts from two lectures: one of them given by a sexologist who believes that man is losing his genital powers, the other by a criminologist who believes that the perfect murder is possible. By implication, the sexologist's lecture is intended to comment on the lovers' behaviour, though in fact their behaviour has the effect of showing up his detached account of sex as amusingly irrelevant. Makavejev is less detached; and in one sequence of lyrical and startling images he shows how Isabela's beauty affects her lover.

The criminologist's lecture opens up another line of thought. He describes and illustrates some of the ways in which the police use clinical investigations to help them track down criminals and he refers to a post-mortem on a fine corpse found in a Roman well. (At this point in the narrative Isabela's death has not been disclosed.) Makavejev cuts back and forth between the post-mortem and the first raptures of the lovers: a contrast that should be incongruous, but in practice neutralizes feeling. This is how things are. His editing not only revitalizes tired insights concerning the evanescence of beauty, but also allows the spectator to compare an institutional account of feeling with the fury of Ahmed's breakdown after Isabela's death.

None of these responses cancels the others out; each of them contains a portion of the truth. Makavejev expects his audience to keep in mind a wide variety of cross-connections: the form of his film, appropriately, resembles a telephone switchboard. A scene showing Ahmed at his rat-catching leads on to a documentary about how the inexhaustibly fertile grey rats defeat the black rats. Some political reference is presumably intended—to the conflict between Communists and capitalists, the proletariat and their oppressors. Makavejev also cuts in old newsreel clips, mostly of events connected with the Russian Revolution. Do the excesses of the revolution seem ridiculous when compared to the lovers' intimacy or is revolutionary triumph to be related in some way to their conquest of inhibition? Makavejev remains impersonal, putting together his montages without overt comment. Sometimes his technique can misfire, as in *Innocence Unprotected* (1968), where his far-reaching connections were clever and no more, while in *W.R.: Mysteries of the Organism* (1971) he weakened the power of these connections by leaving the spectator uncertain as to whether he thought his central character, the psychiatrist

Wilhelm Reich, a liberationist hero or a crank, and by committing himself to a voyeuristic kind of filming that went against the spirit of Reich's activist ideas about sex.

But on the whole, East European film-makers have developed Godard's ideas more imaginatively than their contemporaries in the West, who either tend to imitate his techniques without understanding their meaning or enter into obscurity. On the one hand, Jean-Marie Straub, a Frenchman working in Germany, appears to do the second. In *Machorka-Muff* (1963) and *Unreconciled* (1965), his camera movements and editing appear to be motivated by no apparent logic, and his *Chronicle of Anna Magdalena Bach* (1967) adds little either to the chronicle or to Bach's music. His admirers think otherwise. On the other hand, Alexander Kluge could move from the Godard imitation of *Yesterday Girl* (1966) to an understanding of how Godard's techniques can be used in an exploratory manner. The central metaphor of *Artists at the Top of the Big Top: Disorientated* (1968) is of a circus where men often die in their attempt to transcend human limitation. It ends with a frightened impresario talking about *Il Trovatore*, so absurd in its plot, so sublime in its effect. Kluge intimates that genuine art courts ridicule by its necessary emotionalism. His disjointed tale recalls Goethe's *Wilhelm Meister*, with its contrast between the cautious bourgeoisie and playful actors, but it also comments on the possible riches to be entered into by adventurous Godardian filming. Kluge thinks it worth remembering that the circus came into being at the time of the French Revolution, and that the circus artist, like the singer of Verdi's music, reawakens an awareness of mankind's potentialities. But the liberating power of such skills can at times lead to the wrong sort of exhilaration, when men begin to think of themselves as supermen. Kluge brings together circus pageantry with newsreel of a Hitler mass rally. At the same time he does not forgo the sensuous and unique qualities of his particular circus: the seedy magnificence of the big top, the soulful elephants, the drab bravery of lion-tamers and snake-charmers. 'The clowns have lost their honour,' says someone. The connection between the circus and politics has been fairly enough worked out for this remark not to sound whimsical.

Certain Czech film-makers were to show the same freedom of invention, having been encouraged by the Party Congress of 1962 – which invited artists to 'show the dynamism and inner richness of life' – by the lively policies of the Prague Film School (FAMU), founded in 1946 and from which all of them were to graduate, and by the influence of Kafka's writings. Věra Chytilová, whose first feature *Ceilings* dates from 1962, began this movement. Her *Daisies* (1966) concerns two women, Marie I and Marie II, who are possibly aspects

Alexander Kluge: *Artists at the Top of the Big Top: Disorientated.*

of the same woman. She describes the way in which their inclination to destroy everything can be tempered by moments of caprice, wonder and depression—with great insight into the psychology of little girls.

One of her assistants had been Jiří Menzel (born 1938), who worked with her from 1962 to 1964 after a period at FAMU and was later to win an Academy award with an adaptation of a Bohumil Hrabal novel, *Closely Observed Trains* (1966). An unusual political twist is given to the old tale of a young man seeking sexual initia-

Jiří Menzel: *Closely Observed Trains.*

tion. The time is 1944, and the lovely partisan who claims to lead Miloš into manhood also leads him into heroism, for she brings a box of dynamite with her that will destroy him as he blows up a German freight-train. His death is one of the two startling moments in this story, an earlier one being when a Nazi collaborator turns to the camera and snarls: 'All Czechs are laughing hyenas.' The laughing hyenas, however, are seen to bite their masters.

Miloš works for the staff of a small, rural railway station. His mother dresses him ceremoniously for his first day's work; and Menzel perhaps overplays this scene as though it were a coronation. Menzel suggests that sexual behaviour and the social condition are somehow related, but only brings out this theme after Miloš has been seen wandering around asking men if their wives would kindly cure him of *ejaculatio praecox*. Although his filming lacks Olmi's tautness, Menzel resembles the Italian director in his low-keyed humour (and his Miloš, played by the Czech pop star Václav Neckář, has been compared to the hero of *Il posto*). It is interesting that both these film-makers should create an image of spiritual isolation out of a multiplicity of minutely recorded details, as though the meaning of the world had somehow been withdrawn from it, leaving it as no more than a husk of textures and shapes. Their mode of perception has some kinship to the novels of Kafka, whose manner of visualizing events permanently in close-up has the effect of depriving the reader of any sense of perspective. It is a manner of perception hard to dissociate from feelings of despair, and there are Czech films, like Pavel Juráček's *Josef Kilián* (1963) and Jan Němec's *The Party and the Guests* (1966), which are Kafkaesque in this regard. But there is at least one Czech director, Miloš Forman, who seems able to bear this split between events and their meaning without, on the whole, lapsing into pessimism, sentimentality or grotesque observation.

Forman has usually been attracted to the theme of young love and its effect on older generations, and he tends to construct his sequences out of a host of semi-improvised events. Although his sense of humour and areas of concern are similar to Olmi's, any comparison between the dancehall scenes in *A Blonde in Love* (1965) and *I fidanzati* soon shows how different their intentions are. Forman takes a benign pleasure in recognizing the likeness in human beings; he is aware that everybody has more or less the same problems in growing up and growing old. He neither denies nor deplores the timidity, craftiness or greed of his characters. Relaxed, undeceived, he is a Schweik who enjoys the Schweik in everyone. He has none of Olmi's metaphysical longing.

The bitter-sweet tone of *Peter and Pavla* (1964) and *A Blonde in Love* gave way to the cruel-sweet tone of *The Firemen's Ball* (1967); yet it would be wrong to say that his view of the firemen who arrange the ball is contemptuous, since he is perceptive enough to discover a boyish shyness in the most bloated face, or an owlish sense of humour beneath the most authoritarian mask. He raises a lengthy and only deceptively unkind gag out of the firemen's wish to present their retiring president with a tiny gold hatchet. The sweet old man wants to relieve his bladder, but a friend tells him to wait as the presentation is about to take place. The hours pass, and the president twice misses his cue and has to be turned back at the platform in full view of the audience. Finally, after most of the guests have left, he receives the gift, makes his carefully prepared speech and then opens the presentation box to find that the gold hatchet has been stolen; tactfully, he looks up at the other firemen in gratitude. Forman is reluctant to treat the misfortunes of the old with especial reverence and appears to argue that the elderly have to face ignominies like everyone else. He certainly does not spare the young from such ignominies, as when the firemen hold a beauty competition and line up some unpromising girls. The effect should be distressing, but Forman evidently enjoys any departure from conventional beauty and discovers grace in the gawkiness of a Miss Maypole and a handsome matron in a blowzy, soft girl.

After the Russian invasion of Czechoslovakia in 1968, he went briefly to the United States and directed *Taking Off* (1971) on location in New York, developing the idea of a beauty competition into one of his finest sequences: a marvellously edited audition in which he cuts from girl to girl on each line of a song and then ends the sequence on a compilation of their mistimings and fluffs. It adds up to a tribute to the likeability of American girls, yet by his casting he manages to make them all look Czech. His American parents respond to their eccentric children in an aghast, deadpan way, like the parents in *A Blonde in Love*; yet thanks in part to Buck Henry's screenplay and performance in the leading role, Forman also captures the feeling of New York humour.

Nearly all Czech films have something of Forman's sociability; even the nightmarish *The Party and Its Guests* depends for its effect on some suggestion of a warmth that once had been shared. But Hungarian films, and those of Miklós Jancsó in particular, seem to be divorced from any such community of feeling.

For the Western filmgoer, knowledge of Jancsó's career begins with his fourth feature, *My Way Home* (1964). Although more picaresque and lyrical than his later work, its central image—of figures wandering or riding, singly or in groups, on the airless, endless Hungarian plains—is one that he has only once abandoned in later years, in his Italian production *The Pacifist* (1971). It follows a vagrant student through his various meetings with the inhabitants of the plains, leaving uncertain who those people might be, and where they might be coming from or going to. The student says little, and his friendship with a boyish Russian prisoner of war (the time is 1945) adds up to a meagre intimacy. They shoot frogs together, jest or gorge on the roasted side of a bull; yet they remain isolated from each other, the soldier dying of some wound in the belly, the student uncommunicative. Then the soldier dies and the student begins to cry, but his grief is quickly suppressed and he is later beaten up for having been friendly to a foreigner. Jancsó's vision is a reductive one; like certain Czech directors, he isolates events from their possible meanings. A biplane, that unexpectedly fails to strafe the wanderers, keeps circling overhead. In terms of plot coherence, it links together the action. Yet its purpose, both as part of the narrative and formally, remains unexplained. It would be misleading to think of its presence as symbolic of something, since the point of *My Way Home* is to strip away such kinds of meaning. The biplane, we are made to feel, is just there.

Although the firing squad, the torture of naked women and the unprotestingly accepted degradations of war are all present in *My Way Home*, Jancsó was only fully to work out these motifs with *The Round Up* (1965). A militia, representing the Hapsburg authorities, arrests a group of peasants, which may include certain revolutionaries,

Miklós Jancsó: *The Round Up.*

and then by various means isolates the revolutionaries from the group and destroys them. Jancsó seems less interested in the meaning of this story than in patterning the behaviour of his inquisitors and their victims with a chess-like rigour. The skill of his semi-abstract compositions—figures and horses on the plains, a white wall with a row of doors in it—matches Dreyer's *The Passion of Joan of Arc*, though in one respect these two films are very different. Dreyer's close-ups bring out the spirituality, or lack of it, in faces. Jancsó relies on long or middle distance shots and only once, when soldiers whip a naked woman, invites audience identification.

His impassivity has become more and more suspect with each successive film, if only because it appears to be so easily obtained. He would seem to structure the relationships of his characters on some monotonous sado-masochistic model and then to deny these relationships any effect. When Robert Bresson, for one, abstracts his themes from some novel or play, he does so to isolate its human content. Jancsó shows no such concern in his need to abstract. The ironies he sets up in *The Red and the White* (1967) are mechanical, and its repeated acts—such as the stripping off of clothing—disclose nothing. His mind concentrates on technical virtuosity; and by the time he came to direct *Silence and Cry* (1968), he had begun to hold his shots for an unusual length of time and to achieve a choreography between his camera and actors of an exceptional complexity.

Usually this choreography is limited, to the point of being rigid, to a certain composition on three levels: in the foreground, taking up a minimal amount of space, will be one or two characters crucial to the scene, in the background the luminous plains and in the middle distance some figure, irrelevant to the immediate action, who gyrates or drifts, distracting the spectator's attention at the expense of the story. At one time his formalism had appeared to heighten the callous nature of his oppressors and the stoicism of their victims, but by now it was no more than a mannerism. With *Agnus Dei* (1971) and *Red Psalm* (1972), he completed the process of simplifying the Hungarian past into a series of mindless purges, gearing his imagery to tantalize every kind of erotic taste and comforting the censor by larding the action with Communist slogans. At the end of *Red Psalm*, a girl who might have stepped out of the pages of *Vogue* raises her manicured hands and asks that she and all other exploited manual workers should be liberated. Jancsó's influence over other Hungarian directors has been considerable and, in the case of András Kovács's *Cold Days* (1966) and István Gaál's *The Falcons* (1970), it has been largely benign.

Among these film-makers of the Warsaw Pact countries, one important Polish director has been deliberately left unmentioned so far.

Andrjez Munk died in a car accident in 1961. It is obviously impossible to know how he would have made out in the Poland of the 1960s, but during the previous decade his sardonic sense of irony, above all noticeable in *Eroica* (1957), set off admirably Wajda's more flamboyant interpretation of the war. At the time of his death, Munk had been working on *Passenger* (1961). Some of his associates compiled a film out of the material Munk had already shot: an experiment that happily complemented Munk's subject. A woman who had once been a concentration camp prisoner half-recognizes another female passenger on a holiday liner as having been one of the more brutal of the camp guards. Most of the narrative is concerned with memories of the camp; and this investigation into consciousness is an appropriate starting point for a film which is as much concerned with the process of creation, like an artist's notebook, as with telling a story. By chance, Munk and his associates discovered a way of assembling a film that opens up an entirely new convention.

The play of chance, or coincidence, also informs his earlier *Man on the Tracks* (1956), though in a different way. An engine-driver dies on the tracks. During a post-mortem investigation, some of his mates recall him, in flashback, as anti-social and spiteful; then other colleagues demonstrate more persuasively that he had been—in the way he died—a working-class hero. Munk's emphasis on class tension, his doctrinaire Marxism and the complicated yet stern way in which his post-mortem investigators search out the truth conflict with his evident distaste for the personality of the dead engine-driver; while his romantic attachment to the industrial landscape and to the idea of labour—as though the quintessence of reality were, in some unfixed and uncriticizable way, contained within them—also appears at odds with his disenchanted view of human beings. But what is most remarkable about *Man on the Tracks* is the fidelity with which it echoes the film-making traditions of a country remote in every possible way from Poland: for in its conception of reality it is identical with the attitudes that had informed the British GPO Film Unit of the thirties, the Crown Film Unit of the forties and the Free Cinema group of the fifties. What is hard to understand is why a dourness of Munk's kind, which can be accounted for in terms of the extremism and treacheries of Polish history over the past two hundred years, should have characterized the British documentary movement.

Lindsay Anderson, Karel Reisz and Tony Richardson, who were among the leading talents of the Free Cinema group, all appear to have been afflicted by the legacy of puritanism far more severely than British artists and thinkers working in other fields. Aware that Orwell and Jennings had reacted to popular culture with an ambivalence of feeling in which hostility was seldom repressed, they appear to have been hesitant about the possibilities of British socialism at its more creative. They seem to imitate the cultural poverty they wish to condemn, and their attempts to describe happiness have usually had the (perhaps unintended) effect of showing up happiness as either spurious or glib. They appear to have been mainly affected by the demotic, dramatic side to the resurgence of socialist humanism that occurred in the mid-fifties, at the time of the Suez invasion, the Aldermaston marches and the Soviet invasion of Hungary. None of them appears to have been influenced by the new directions opened up by Richard Hoggart's *The Uses of Literacy* (1957) and Raymond Williams's *Culture and Society* (1958) or by the first numbers of the magazine *New Left Review*, many of whose contributors wanted to reconceive politics as a means of developing an emotionally richer culture.

Hoggart's study of working-class customs was valuable in this respect. He wrote about areas of culture which tend to be invisible because they are too familiar. His curiosity, and his awareness that he was writing about his own upbringing, tempered his criticism. But little of his tact informed similar interests in the theatre or the cinema. The main appeal of John Osborne's *Look Back in Anger*, one of the two productions in George Devine's and Tony Richardson's opening season at the Royal Court Theatre in London, was that it centred on an articulate lower-middle-class character. It was thought to be a progressive play, yet Jimmy Porter's complaints were to be indistinguishable from the whimsical disgust of Osborne's writing at a later time, when he had taken up a position on the right.

John Braine, another left-wing writer who was soon to move to the right, was to be just as influential; and Jack Clayton's film of his novel *Room at the Top* (1958) was to be considered a landmark in the British cinema. Its love affair between a fairly young man and an older woman was intended to elicit 'mature' as a term of praise from the critics, which it did. Yet its mildly depressed tone and superficially tough relationships added nothing to a tone already established by the French *films noirs* of the thirties, while René Clément's London-based *Knave of Hearts* (1954) had portrayed the character of a philanderer more deftly. The leading performance in *Room at the Top* was given by a Frenchwoman, Simone Signoret, who brought a much-needed warmth to the film.

Clayton was not a polemicist. A charge that might be levelled at the Free Cinema group, on the other hand, was that too many of its members were over-anxious politically and forced experience to fit untested opinion. An article by Lindsay Anderson in favour of a committed, i.e. Marxist, kind of film-making, which was published in the *New Left Review* as well as in *Sight and Sound*, revealed a passion about film and a doctrinaire bluntness that readers had come to expect from *Sequence*, a magazine published from 1948 to 1952, which

Lindsay Anderson: *Every Day except Christmas* (1957).

Anderson had edited with Gavin Lambert. In common with Hoggart, the Free Cinema group investigated areas of British society previously little explored. But compared to their contemporaries on the other side of the Channel, they seemed unable to use Marxist insights in a heuristic way. Imitating Jennings's *Spare Time*, they gave a joyless impression of working-class pleasures, not only in their documentaries but also in their first features: Reisz's *Saturday Night and Sunday*

Richard Lester: *Petulia.* George C. Scott and Julie Christie facing each other.

Morning (1960), Richardson's screen versions of plays by Osborne and Delaney and of Alan Sillitoe's story *The Loneliness of the Long Distance Runner* (1962). Anderson went to a source of greater literary merit, David Storey's remarkable novel *This Sporting Life*. Although many of the characters in the film (1963) were deprived and their fate depressed, the intense involvement of both writer and director in their subject avoided paternalism. John Schlesinger's gifted *A Kind of Loving* (1962) was linked by the press to the Free Cinema group, if only because it, too, was suffused with melancholy at the pettiness of the lower middle class.

But these talented men were unable to adjust themselves to the social changes of the sixties and at best were to clutch at the straws of fashion. Yet some of these changes had had a direct bearing on their perhaps representative view of working-class culture. Far from being spiritually impoverished and down-trodden, this culture was to emerge with the Beatles in 1963 as a force of worldwide influence and to dominate the entertainment industry for nearly a decade. The Beatles owed a great deal to the style of American musicians and nothing to the British middle class. They were apolitical and indifferent to questions of class or public morality. American publicists welcomed their attitudes and, assisted by the British press, promoted the tourist fantasy of swinging London. A comparable change had occurred in the art world, though it took longer to become public. Pop art had originated with Richard Hamilton and Eduardo Paolozzi in the England of the late fifties; it had been taken up in the United States by Robert Rauschenberg, Jasper Johns, Roy Lichtenstein and others and then fed back into Britain with an added transatlantic prestige. Advertising, comic strips and Hollywood B features—all that educationalists had once denounced as corrupting—were now accepted as motifs for contemplation. Undergraduate filmgoers were to respond in a similar way to *Cahiers du cinéma*, even though *Cahiers* praised the kind of film that Seebohm Rowntree and G. R. Lavers had described in their social study *English Life and Leisure* (1951) as 'glorifying false values'.

Richard Lester was to glorify these values in the two films he directed for the Beatles, *A Hard Day's Night* (1964) and *Help!* (1965). An expatriate from Philadelphia, Lester recognized that there was much in British culture that had never reached the screen, and blended a surrealist knowingness with a type of humour derived from radio's The Goons. He also combined the technical freedom of Godard with the pace of television commercials. Yet for all his allusions, he was an observer in an alien land, and his work was only to take on some emotional depth when he returned to the United States, to San Francisco, to film *Petulia* (1968). He was only one among many foreign directors to benefit from American financial backing of the British film industry during the sixties. But two other expatriates had come to England under less pleasant circumstances: both Carl Foreman and Joseph Losey had been on the Hollywood black-list and both of them were to continue to bear openly the scars of McCarthyism. Foreman's need to moralize was to dissipate a good deal of the zest in his boyish adventure stories (*The Guns of Navarone*, *The Victors*, *Young Winston*), while Losey, as sensitive to injustice as any Englishman, and just as much preoccupied by questions of class, seemed incapable of grasping the various idioms of the English social structure; and his misunderstandings of its tensions usually led to caricature. *The Servant* (1963), for instance, was as uninforming about the Chelsea rich as *The Criminal* (1960) had been about the prison system. Although he has done more than anyone else to bring Hollywood expertise to British films—his long professional association with Richard MacDonald, the production designer, has transformed the quality of British set design—his elaborate taste in camera movements has often been practised at the expense of his subject-matter. *King and Country* (1964), which had been moving as a television play, became all fuss and vain striving in his hands. *Accident* (1967) was not only unconvincing as a portrait of Oxford town and gown, but imitated Resnais's *Muriel* to the point of mannerism. Losey is most at ease when he is most consciously romantic—as in his fantastic melodrama *Secret Ceremony* (1968)—or when he evokes the never-never Edwardian England of *The Go-Between* (1971).

During the American boom a large number of foreign directors worked in Britain: among others, Wilder, Hitchcock, Zinnemann, Wyler, Peckinpah, Lumet, Strick, Polanski, Antonioni, Godard, Skolimowski and Truffaut. Hampered in part by the labour practices of British studios and by the strange complexities of the society they were trying to describe, few of them managed to reach their usually high standards. Stanley Donen, who was resident in London at this time, tried to break away from his reputation as a maker of musicals, but was to achieve little more than the pictorial distinction that comes naturally to him. Yet one American director was to put British technical expertise to an imaginative use: Stanley Kubrick, who had moved to England in 1961.

Kubrick had been a photographer on *Look* and had directed a few documentaries and the feature-length *Fear and Desire* (1953) before establishing a foothold in the industry with an uneven thriller, *Killer's Kiss* (1955). His promise was to be realized with *The Killing* (1965), while *Paths of Glory* (1957), a *film à thèse*, won him an art-house reputation. Although he declines to see any meaningful connection between his projects, his unusual personality gives them all a distinctive colouring. He is an auto-didact and intellectual, fascinated by the sense of omnipotent control that computers and all kinds of photographic and recording equipment can provide. He seems to be aware, though, that these devices are fairly hopeless defences against insecurity. In *The Killers*, he places a perfectly planned racecourse robbery against the anguish of an uncertain marriage, which indirectly brings about the failure of the robbery: a strategy that recalls the conflict in Fritz Lang's German films between events arranged to the point where they are overwrought and a fate that can disrupt them. Kubrick resembles Lang in a number of ways, not least in his fascination with those areas of experience out of which the Nazi ideology arose. The influence of *Metropolis* on *Spartacus* (1960) is overt. Kubrick thinks little of this epic—he took over its direction from Anthony Mann—for the same reasons that Arthur Penn was later to disclaim *The Chase*; and yet in spite of production difficulties, both these films are among the most revealing of their directors' methods.

In *Lolita* (1962) and *Dr Strangelove, or How I Learned to Stop Worrying and Love the Bomb* (1963), Kubrick began to respect the variety of meanings contained within his anxiety about chance: how this anxiety could include a fear of the emotional chaos that may result when erotic or authoritarian obsessions remain unchecked, and how, at its core, lay a sense of terror at the prospect of death. In *Dr Strangelove* he undertook a critique of his kind of Germanic, death-laden romanticism by creating a gallery of monsters—General Jack D. Ripper (Sterling Hayden), General 'Buck' Turgidson (George C. Scott), Major Guano (Keenan Wynn) and Dr Strangelove himself (Peter Sellers)—each of whom represents, in caricature, different aspects of the obsessional personality. Kubrick allows these self-proclaimed guardians and apostles of a hygienic civilization to become responsible for the operation of a nuclear-control system that mirrors their compulsions. He then has one of them (by reason of his obsessions) trigger off this system, and the others (equally by reason of their obsessions) unable to control it once it has been set in motion. Kubrick seems to be aware that his wish for a perfect system is like the desire for perfection in art, in the sense that both aspirations imply a craving for the finality of death. In *Dr Strangelove* he evokes a fantasy of the all-powerful Daddy in a grotesque form, by having the President of the United States turn for help, just before the *Götterdämmerung* of a nuclear holocaust, to a crippled ex-member of the Nazi party.

He had earlier presented this fantasy in a less hedged manner. In *Killer's Kiss*, an unattractive, middle-aged night-club owner tries to destroy a muscular boxer whom he both admires and envies. Kubrick seems to feel sympathy for this night-club owner. He has often presented comic-strip muscle-men in his films, and with a lingering over their strength that discounts any possibility of his wishing to satirize the American tough-guy dream. He also appears to believe that he

can only imitate the potency of these figures by assuming the omnipotence that technology can confer. In *Dr Strangelove* he arranged
that an art of the machine should tick over faultlessly, and that Gil
Taylor's photography, Ken Adam's art direction and indeed every department in his production team should contribute a technique so
precise that it was freezing: a cold beauty underlined by the snowy
arctic wastes over which the death-planes pass.

He seems to have always found it difficult to balance his liking for
closely knit plots—for ironies as systematic in procedure as the plans
these ironies undermine—with his Renaissance taste for grandeur in
mise en scène: a feeling for architecture and space, in which his
muscular Siegfrieds might look at home. In *2001: A Space Odyssey*
(1968), he jeopardized his $12m budget by discarding any conven-
tional idea of a story. Yet with hindsight, it is possible to see that
this decision had to be made. He had worked out his production on
a visionary scale, and any type of neat plot would have appeared
shrunken and trite within its perspective. A spaceship drifts across the
infinite, as delicately complicated as a Leonardo drawing, as vast as a
skyscraper. Although his *adagio* ballets of docking and release may
seem to be pointless, in the same way that certain of the more
mystical ideas in Arthur C. Clarke's screenplay—monoliths that trans-
mit messages from Jupiter over the centuries, the giant embryo child
that returns to earth—may seem to be highflown nonsense, they have
an important function. They allow him to engage, far more directly
than ever before, with problems that have long exercised him: the
ways in which machines can be both beautiful and repugnant, or the
ways in which a foolproof plan can be disrupted by some incalculable factor; as when the computer HAL goes berserk and kills off
those whom it should protect. But most urgently of all, it allows him
to face a theme that has long haunted him but which he has always
been defensive about: that of his own death. He will be seventy-two
in 2001, and his journey into outer space is also very much a journey
into the self's awareness of its own annihilation. The last surviving
astronaut faces a prospect of streaming lights and dissonant colours
as he enters the field of Jupiter: a sequence which obliges Kubrick
to abandon his usual architectonic control over space. An opening
episode to the film, in which he relates man back to the ancestral
ape, allows him to span great tracts of time as well as space and
to raise an interesting proposal concerning the mystery of human
aggression: only by accepting the inevitably of death, he would
appear to suggest, will mankind be able to come to terms with its
inherited impulse to destroy.

He had hoped to follow *2001* with a film biography of Napoleon,
but the industry's financial crisis obliged him to postpone this project. He turned instead to Anthony Burgess's novel *A Clockwork Orange,*

Stanley Kubrick: *The Killing (top)* and *A Clockwork Orange*.

which predicts the future in a manner that complements the mysticism of *2001*. Bringing a Renaissance grandeur to a working-class subject, he shows how the ideals of the Renaissance, though corrupted, continue to linger on. His use of Walter Carlos's electronic distortion of Purcell's *Queen Mary* dirge and the way in which he films the brutal architecture of Thamesmead carry the implication of a fallen greatness. He demonstrates that a mean subject and an unpromising, setting need not presuppose a thinness of treatment; at the same time, he does not escape the taint of British puritanism. His investigation into hoodlum violence is coloured by sanctimony, especially obvious when Alex's victims take revenge on him. It could be argued, maybe, that he wishes to show how certain forms of moralizing are identical with the psychopath's desire for talion punishment, but he fails to make this case convincing. Alex's punishment fits in too well with Alex's conception of the adult world and appears to confirm his view that everyone must be as psychotic as himself.

In his interests, Kubrick is a solitary figure on the British scene and, perhaps, should be thought of as an internationalist. Yet it would be wrong to suppose that British film-makers are so committed to moral preaching that they are indifferent to the problems of craft. On the contrary, during the sixties many of them became over-preoccupied with questions of style. Actors turned director—Bryan Forbes and Richard Attenborough especially—appear to have conceived of style as a form of decoration or blandishment. Another actor turned director, Ken Russell, also lays on style as though with a trowel: yet in other ways Russell is unlike his contemporaries. A former television documentarist, he entered the film industry with a considerable reputation. After two less than auspicious features, he directed *Women in Love* (1969), which combined an infectious showmanship with a sympathy for the genteel Bohemianism of D. H. Lawrence's lovers. Very much pop culture's delegate to high culture, his taste could not be less like Humphrey Jennings's authoritarian respect for artists of secure reputation. He shatters preconceptions about the arts with the gusto of a Sennett comedian and then tries to create a bizarre reflection of himself out of the fragments. His good-humoured hostility is principally directed at those who wish to cloak the adventure of art in a pall of bureaucratic propriety. He has dedicated himself to a Romantic view of the artist, of so intense a kind that it often takes him beyond the bounds of judgement. But he is a genuine film talent, not least in his excesses.

The success of British pop culture has had some surprising side-effects. It stimulated an inventive feature-length cartoon about the Beatles, *The Yellow Submarine* (1968), directed by the Canadian animator George Dunning; while a pop group subject, *Catch Us If You Can* (1965), brought the director John Boorman out of television into the cinema. On the whole, Boorman's brilliant powers of visualization have been ill-served by his choice of themes. *Point Blank* (1967) has some claim to be the first non-figurative thriller, for long sections bordering on the incoherent, perhaps deliberately so. *Hell in the Pacific* (1968) traded in some heavy symbolism, yet still managed to deal

George Dunning: *The Yellow Submarine.*

with the man-as-animal issue tritely. Boorman has continued in this way. In *Leo the Last* (1970) he conceived of the colour problem in London almost entirely in aesthetic terms and in *Deliverance* (1972) considered man's relationship to nature as little more than a pretext for spectacular effects.

Boorman thinks of himself as an internationalist, as much at home in Los Angeles as in Notting Hill Gate. He has none of the moral abrasion that the Free Cinema group once displayed. In this he differs from many of the younger British directors, who feel indebted to the Free Cinema group and see it as having an integrity, however thorny, that has helped to save British film-making from the blandishments of advertising styles. Of these directors, Albert Finney with his *Charlie Bubbles* (1967), Ken Loach—especially his *Kes* (1969)—Barney Platts Mills and Bill Douglas have responded to working-class life with an intimacy that the Free Cinema group mostly lacked; although they probably would have been unable to achieve this distinction without the pioneering efforts of their predecessors. One other name needs to be mentioned: Kevin Brownlow, who avoids prevailing

Ken Loach: *Kes*.

fashions in the cinema and so far has had none of his projects backed by the industry. Raising a hypothesis of some magnitude in his privately financed feature *It Happened Here* (1964)—he supposed that the Germans had effectively invaded Britain in 1940 and tried to imagine how the British would have reacted to this occupation—he was able, by the sheer power of his editing and care for the most minute period detail, to suggest a treatment of epic proportions.

His career illustrates in an extreme form some of the hazards British film-makers have had to face in order to work within one of the most conformist film industries in the world. Even so, battles have been won and achievements realized by both the older and younger generations. In a review of J. Lee Thompson's *Woman in a Dressing Gown*, Jean-Luc Godard had lamented: 'One really has to rack one's brains to find anything to say about the British film.'[2] But the talent and enthusiasm of many British film-makers in the late sixties began to raise hopes that this situation might change.

Twentieth Century-Fox's failure to control the production costs on its blockbuster *Cleopatra* (1963) dramatized in the most public manner imaginable the economic disarray of Hollywood in the early sixties. The Press had at first mocked this waste, and then tempered its mockery with awe as the company, seemingly indifferent to criticism, continued to throw good money after bad. Hollywood, it was recalled, had never observed the practices of ordinary business; it had consolidated its power in the age of ballyhoo; it had always thrived in a lunatic atmosphere. And in fact, with typical Hollywood illogicality, the profligacy surrounding Cleopatra was an excellent advertisement, and the film actually made a profit. Not that this development did much to raise the spirits of the despondent Fox stock-holders, who deposed their president, Spyros P. Skouras, and induced his successor, Darryl F. Zanuck, to reorganize the studio on regimental lines.

The problems *Cleopatra* had raised were similar to those the newly formed MGM had faced in 1924, when it had taken over Metro's chaotically organized *Ben Hur*. Louis B. Mayer had summoned back the *Ben Hur* units from Italy, imposed a strict scrutiny on every department at Culver City and had perfected the Hollywood system with an authority that won the admiration of both Dr Goebbels and Joseph Stalin. Like *Ben Hur*, *Cleopatra* had been shot on location, partly in England and partly in Italy. It could be said to have marked the beginning of a process by which the history of Hollywood seemed to move into reverse; so that by the end of the decade, American films had recovered something of the spirit of film-making in 1915. For at the same time as young Americans in all walks of life were rejecting the middle-class ethos and joining communities that resembled the Nonconformist sects and Indian tribes of over a hundred years before, so professional freelance film directors (and not necessarily members of the underground) began to move away from the blandly presented, general themes characteristic of Hollywood in the thirties towards a raw-edged type of filming that Griffith and Ince would have recognized: rural in setting, frontier-minded and engaged with the problem of the individual and the law. Although some of these directors continued to be haunted by the technical efficiency of Hollywood at its prime, they tended to end up with a caricature when they tried to imitate this quality. Whether intentionally or not, *The Dirty Dozen* (1967) looked like a parody of the Hollywood war film, as *Bullitt* (1968) did of the forties thriller or *What's Up Doc?* (1971) did of the mid-thirties comedy.

Encouraged by the success of *Easy Rider* (1969), which grossed $30m for Columbia on a $40,000 outlay, the Hollywood studios were to be drawn more and more to the model of the off-beat independent movie. At first they imitated *Easy Rider* and *Bonnie and Clyde*. Most of these imitations flopped. Apart from the *Planet of the Apes* series, the Gordon Douglas thrillers or the Disney productions, they could discover no consistent money-making policy. They had tried to attract the family audience with the blockbuster movie, even though early on in the decade *Hollywood Reporter* had called this type of investment insane. A blockbuster has to earn two-and-a-half times its original cost to move into profit—so that *Cleopatra*, which had cost $40m, had to earn Twentieth-Century Fox a very large sum before it could break even. *The Sound of Music* may have earned over $100m, but many blockbusters had failed even to cover their costs. Yet producers found it hard to abandon this policy: they still hoped against hope to win the interest of all age groups. In 1967, Twentieth Century-Fox had $50m tied up in *Star!*, *Hello Dolly!* and *Dr Dolittle*. Bank charges alone were appalling, and Darryl F. Zanuck swore that the company could not bear this kind of outlay, even though it had the earnings of *The Sound of Music* behind it. Yet two years later it had the same amount of money tied up in *Hello Dolly!*, *Patton* and *Tora, Tora, Tora*. By the end of the decade his son, Richard Zanuck, was to state that nearly all budgets in the future would have a ceiling of two million dollars.

Without a workable policy and a steady output, the studios had lost their function. In 1969 five of the seven major studios announced losses of $110m. Fox, Paramount and Warner Brothers closed down many of their facilities and cut back on their staff. At MGM a new president, James Aubrey, sold off studios at home and abroad, reduced the labour force by forty per cent and auctioned off MGM's wardrobe, set departments and stock footage library. But the studios had been shaken by crises throughout the sixties. From 1960, when Fox sold off 256 acres of land to the Aluminum Company of America for $43m, to 1971, when Warner Brothers and Columbia decided to work on the Warner Brothers lot alone, nearly all of them had been obliged to diminish their holdings. Only the MCA-backed Universal, with its popular tours, and Disney Inc. did not have to retreat in this way. All the studios diversified into merchandise unconnected with film, and most of them were in part taken over by companies outside the film industry.

'Ironically,' wrote Axel Madsen in *Sight and Sound*,

the reasons for the sell-outs in the late 1960s were less mismanagement than the innate flimsiness of movies as negotiable goods, combined with the deeper involvement in European production which kept demanding heavier outlays in cash. Paramount Pictures became a division of Gulf and Western, a vastly diversified insurance company trust; United Artists sold out to Transamerica, a holding company originating in the Bank of America; Warner Brothers, after merging with the largely Canadian holding of Seven Arts, became in its turn a daughter company of Kinney National (parking lots, funeral-parlours, auto-rentals and *Mad* Magazine), and Joseph E. Levine's lively Embassy Pictures came under the Avco umbrella (military and space hardware, banking, credit cards); leaving Twentieth-Century Fox, Columbia Pictures and the family-owned and now vastly diversified Disney organisation the only moviemakers still in control. After three years of proxy battles, MGM went through three management changes in one year. Kirk Kerkorian took command by purchasing 40 per cent of MGM for 80 million dollars. He put former network boss James Aubrey in as president and began unloading much of Metro's real estate. [3]

In spite of these upheavals, Hollywood's world-wide earnings in 1969 were three billion dollars. US filmgoers paid more than one billion dollars at the box-office, the highest figure in seven years and two-thirds of the 1946 takings.

Television had played some part in this upheaval; yet television had also trained new talent to enter the film industry, and at least three directors schooled in television were to achieve a considerable distinction in the cinema. Of these three, Martin Ritt has been the most uneven. He can be too didactic, as in *Edge of the City* (1956), or too given to attitudinizing, as in *The Spy Who Came in from the Cold* (1965) or too ponderous, as in *The Molly Maguires* (1969). Yet in *Hud* (1963) he was to catch and hold a rueful mood similar to the one John Huston had failed to sustain in *The Misfits* (1961): the sense of small-minded

Martin Ritt: *Hud*. Paul Newman, Melvyn Douglas, Brandon de Wilde.

John Huston: *The Misfits*.

men only capable of destroying the half-tamed landscape around them. Although Ritt was more fortunate than Huston in having a tighter screenplay and a cast in neater trim—Patricia Neal, Melvyn Douglas and Paul Newman as the egocentric Hud—both he and Huston were admirably served by their cameramen, respectively James Wong Howe and Russell Metty.

Robert Mulligan, who also came from television, has directed a succession of intelligent movies, all of them worth seeing, all of them flawed by a complacent humanism. In common with Ritt, Mulligan is liable to fudge his liberal conclusions. He is at his sharpest when he keeps away from public themes, as when he evokes the secret games played by the children in *To Kill a Mockingbird* (1962) or when he wrily portrays the two lovers in *Love with a Proper Stranger* as wanting sex without involvement. But *Up the Down Staircase* (1967), though more perceptive than *The Blackboard Jungle*, handled the problem of overcrowded schools with less urgency, while *Summer of '42* (1971), a vapid recall of wartime childhood memories, showed him at his most self-indulgent. As insulated as his recall of 1942, his liberal imagination seems to have been unaffected by the social upheavals of the sixties.

John Frankenheimer, the most brilliant of the directors to emerge from television, began in films by contributing to the teenage cycle of the mid-fifties. Wooing an adolescent audience, he presented the self-pitying story of *The Young Stranger* (1957) without a trace of irony. The son of a rich film executive punches a cinema manager as a gesture of defiance against authority, especially the authority of his father, whom he believes misunderstands his good intentions. In *All Fall Down* (1961) he seemed to be in two minds about this kind of adolescent self-pity. His screenplay, by William Inge, was derived from a novel by James Leo Herlihy, who wrote the equally soft-

John Frankenheimer: *All Fall Down*.
Brandon de Wilde, Warren Beatty.

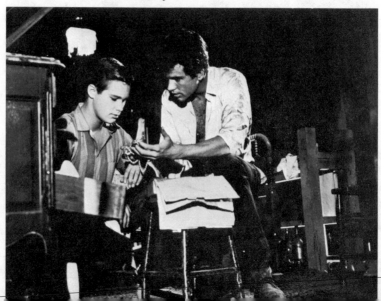

centred *Midnight Cowboy*, and charts an adolescent's disillusionment with his older brother, Clinton (Warren Beatty), whom he at first sees as the all-American hero, almost magical in his attraction. But Clinton, obtuse and frightened, precipitates the suicide of a young woman whimsically named Echo. How far Clinton and Echo should be thought of as responsible for their actions is left uncertain. But Frankenheimer's wit in sketching in atmosphere, moods and the oddities of this family allows him to raise a quirky filmic narrative out of this sentimentally motivated story.

In *The Birdman of Alcatraz* (1962) and *The Fixer* (1968) he presented both his central characters with equal sympathy, though one of them happened to be a murderer of genius while the other was innocent of any crime. He tended to underplay the importance of individual motive: yet by displacing responsibility from the individual onto parents, society or fate, he perhaps denied his characters the right of choice. For all his progressive stance, he temperamentally has something in common with such doom-laden myth-makers as Fritz Lang and Stanley Kubrick.

It was fortunate that he should have had the opportunity to film Richard Condon's novel *The Manchurian Candidate* (1962), which parodies this kind of myth-making. Although his film did badly at the box-office and satirized a hysteria more typical of the earlier McCarthyite period, it was a key document of the early sixties, especially in the way it pointed up the possible connections between private madness and public events. Egregious Raymond returns from a Korean prisoner-of-war camp, reputedly a hero—or so his fellow POWs claim—and the President awards him a Congressional medal. But then his fellow POWs begin to have nightmares that belie their memories, and it soon emerges that the Communists have brainwashed the platoon and programmed Raymond to kill a presidential

John Frankenheimer: *The Manchurian Candidate*.
Angela Lansbury, Laurence Harvey.

candidate. It also emerges that Raymond's tyrannical mother, a leading figure in right-wing politics, has been in league with the Communists to carry out this plot. George Axelrod's screenplay and Frankenheimer's direction caricature the popular view, which at other times Frankenheimer has appeared to concur with, that parents can in some way control their children's behaviour. According to this view, adolescents may see their parents as both all-powerful oppressors and ridiculous impostors: a contradiction that *The Manchurian Candidate* pushes to an extreme. For at the same time as it describes a nightmare in which Raymond and his fellow POWs are sleepwalkers guided by an alien power, it sets up a comedy built on the traditional contrast of illusion and reality, in which figures of authority and national emblems are never what they would seem to be. At a fancy-dress ball, Raymond's step-father, a right-wing senator in the pay of the Communists, dresses as Abraham Lincoln.

This mingling of nightmare and comedy, of Marx qualified by Freud, had been largely absent from political movies of the past. Mr Smith may have exposed the corruption of Washington senators, but his own integrity, and the integrity of democratic process, remained unassailed; while in Sturges's *Hail the Conquering Hero* and Welles's *Citizen Kane*, although the pressures of unconscious motive undermined public pretence, the mythologies of hero and state continued to be promoted. Frankenheimer's *mise en scène* owes something to Welles and possibly something to Sturges; but he goes beyond them in his matter-of-fact proposal that irrational behaviour is normal in politics and that myth-making is part of this irrationality. While all the assured characters in the film tend to be impostors—the insignia of power, with which they deck themselves out, being part of this pretence—most of the honourable characters acknowledge themselves to be under threat, not necessarily from some foreign enemy but from areas in their own minds over which they have, at best, a partial control. *The Manchurian Candidate* contains an attack on the electorate's trust in its politicians; and the value of this criticism has been confirmed by the mystery that still surrounds the assassination of John F. Kennedy, or the revelations of the Pentagon Papers and the Watergate affair. But, just as importantly, its debunking typified a distrust of politicians that the old Hollywood would never have allowed, an awareness of how inadequate human beings may well be in controlling the technological power that Kubrick was to play with in *Dr Strangelove* and Sidney Lumet to embroider on more solemnly in *Fail Safe* (1963), where a terrible dream about nuclear destruction is acted out in reality. Its assumptions underlie Franklin J. Schaffner's *The Best Man* (1964), based on Gore Vidal's play, and Theodore Flicker's more light-hearted *The President's Analyst* (1967).

Frankenheimer was to pursue this nervy speculative vein further in *Seven Days in May* (1964), a thriller which stressed, in the manner of Fritz Lang, the present-day technological aspect of politics, and in *Seconds* (1966), which satirized chillingly the omnipotence of

John Frankenheimer: *Seconds.*

American business corporations: of a corporation, in particular, that promises to rejuvenate middle-aged men at the cost of buying their souls. Frankenheimer was to elicit a fine performance from Will Geer as the folksy Mephistophelean president of the company and some subtle black and white photography from James Wong Howe. Covering the same ground as Kazan in *A Face in the Crowd* (1957), he translated its theme – the misuse of modern kinds of power – into a science-fiction fable; as though he believed that American desires needed the structure of fable and the techniques of surrealism to do justice to their many irrational ramifications. He has since turned to more respectable subjects, concerning the nature of civic dignity, and to the thrills and spills of professional sportsmen; and, at least temporarily, his career has entered a decline.

As the novels of Nathanael West have demonstrated, and as Leslie A. Fiedler was to point out in *Love and Death in the American Novel*, a lengthy critical survey which aroused considerable attention in 1960 (in part, perhaps, because it anticipated a major shift in public taste), American writers have long been attracted to Gothic incongruities and perversities. The strangeness of politics in the sixties appeared to sanction this pursuit of the grotesque and so, on a more frivolous level, did the influence of French film criticism. *Cahiers du cinéma* reviewed the B features of Don Siegel, Samuel Fuller and Robert Aldrich as though they were superior works of art, and although Siegel and Fuller were unaffected by this admiration and continued to manufacture brisk thrillers, Aldrich was impressed by it and addressed himself to more ambitious themes. But he had none of Godard's tact and in *Whatever Happened to Baby Jane?* (1962) and *The Killing of Sister George* (1968) responded to incongruity with a bar-room clumsiness that ill suited the craftsman who had been so reticent in *Sodom and Gomorrah* (1962).

A puritan distaste for the erotic, which assumed the form of an obsessive concern with sexuality and the wish to show sexuality as ugly and brutal, characterized this Gothic trend, and not only in the United States. Film directors everywhere found means to mutilate Terry Southern's novels, for instance; and as films, his *Candy* (1968) misfired just as badly as did his *The Magic Christian* (1969). Impressed by the popularity of flippant horror movies, producers thought that Gothic facetiousness was a box-office draw in its own right, even though a number of commercial setbacks should have warned them that ghoulish humour usually tends to wilt when transplanted from Transylvania. Yet clearly there was some impulse to relate Gothic romance to the sensations of contemporary life. Roger Corman, who has been prolific as a manufacturer of horror movies, was to turn without difficulty from Edgar Allan Poe to the elation of the Hell's Angels in *The Wild Angels* (1966) and to the drug phantasmagoria of *The Trip* (1967). The taste for Gothic romance seemed part of a general enchantment with the idea of madness.

But this enchantment found a more satisfactory outlet in the subject of war. Joseph Heller's novel *Catch-22*, and Mike Nichols's film of the novel (1970), resembled Kubrick's *Dr Strangelove* in imagining an insane system of ideas that appears irrefutable to those trapped inside it. However, the filmgoing public were to be less attracted to *Catch-22* than to Robert Altman's *M*A*S*H*, which preceded it by a few months. Set at the time of the Korean war, yet plainly alluding to the conflict in Vietnam, *M*A*S*H* relied for its interest on the contradiction it sets up between the behaviour and the actions of two army surgeons

(Donald Sutherland and Elliott Gould). In behaviour they are facetious, often maliciously so, and hostile to bureaucrats and prigs. In action they tend to be brave and kind, often operating under appalling conditions. Altman never explains why these two impassive hipsters should be so willing to engage with death or to relieve others of pain; but he implies by his contradiction that their courage sanctions this cool style and may in some way be derived from it.

In this, he appears to subscribe to a belief that was widespread among film-makers in the sixties. The argument that lay behind this belief proposed that once a person finds himself trapped in some lunatic social organization he can no longer appeal to justice or to any other principle, but must evolve a style, or silhouette, which will save him from being destroyed by his society. When Belmondo in *A Bout de souffle* imitated Bogart, he did not do so through some identification with Bogart's qualities but as a mimicry intended to preserve his sanity. He seemed to have thought that appearances alone could induce courage. The two army surgeons in *M*A*S*H* behave in the same way. But they would have appeared implausible if television had not at this time publicized a figure remarkably like them: the hippie campus hero (cf. p. 568). Altman reduces character to a kind of play-acting. He acknowledges a change in public consciousness about the nature of morality, character and plot, yet in doing so evades some of the central problems raised by this change—problems that Robert Rossen, with his feeling for the moral density of experience, had tried to engage with in his last two films.

In the same way that Rossen's *Body and Soul* had transposed the Group Theatre attitudes of the thirties into a manner more appropriate to the forties, so *The Hustler* (1963) transforms the preoccupations of *Body and Soul* into those of the early sixties. Eddie Felsen (Paul Newman), the hustler, is a sportsman like Charley Davis in *Body and Soul*, but differs from him in being neither a family man nor worried by ethnic problems. Indifferent to his surroundings—the all-night cafeterias and third-rate hotel rooms he stays in when away from the pool-table—he seems unaffected by loneliness. He represents an unexpected kind of hero in the American cinema, in his play-acting as well as in his unselfconscious isolation; for his role as a pool-player is bound up with his role as a con-man.

While *Body and Soul* had broached the question of social goals, and the American fascination with 'success', in terms of winning and losing at boxing, *The Hustler* tests the concepts of winning and losing far more critically. None of its characters shows much concern for material possessions—a state of affairs that would have been thought unusual in the forties—and Rossen appears to have come to the view that losers are the salt of the earth. Eddie takes on 'character' after he has mourned the death of his girl-friend Sarah. He no longer feels

Robert Rossen: *The Hustler*. Jackie Gleason, Paul Newman.

Robert Rossen: *Lilith*. Jean Seberg.

triumph in winning at pool and no longer plays guilefully. His rivalry with Minnesota Fats (Jackie Gleason), at first marked by contempt, becomes tempered by admiration. In one sense, *The Hustler* is far more depressed than *Body and Soul*, which is sombre enough: Eddie is surrounded by elderly men with worn faces and, it is implied, he will soon enough be like them. At the same time, it does raise the prospect of hope. After twenty-five hours of play, Minnesota Fats can return to the table as refreshed as 'a baby, all pink and powdered'. And Eddie, too, has the power to recuperate (as after his accident). He can be restored, above all, by his passion for the game, especially by his pleasure in its physicality, a pleasure reflected in the physicality of Rossen's filming: the extraordinary tension he sets up between his actors, or in his editing. Losing for Rossen is to abandon dreams of superiority and transcendence. He would appear to have recognized, as did Malamud in his baseball novel *The Natural*, that certain physical activities contain within them the promised grace of learning and bear a complex moral symbolism.

If *The Hustler* recalls *Body and Soul*, *Lilith* (1963) harks back to Litvak's *The Snake Pit*, even though it raises some fashionable doubts about the distinction between sanity and madness that would have been considered nonsensical in the forties. Its story, derived from J. R. Salamanca's novel, is unconvincing on at least two counts: no hospital administrator would allow someone as disturbed as Lilith (Jean Seberg) so much freedom, or put her in the charge of an attendant (Warren Beatty) so evidently unbalanced. Rossen's intentions, though, make these implausibilities seem marginal. He is less concerned with actual events than with moods. He creates the sensations of an inner landscape, and in this comes close to Corman's *The Trip* without participating in Corman's expressionism. Yet Lilith herself might be a Corman character: the mysterious girl who lives on the right side of the tracks and who turns out to be a vampire of sorts. As on *The Hustler*, Rossen's lighting photographer was Eugen Shüfftan, a leading cameraman in the German cinema of the twenties. Together they elicit feelings of the uncanny from natural images, from the swirl of water, say, or the shape of a branch.

The Broadway theatre has been as useful as the French and Italian New Wave in helping American directors to discover the contemporary spirit of the United States. In the same way that Rossen had continued to respect his kinship with Odets and the Group Theatre, so Arthur Penn, for all his work in television, has been most indebted to his training at the Actors' Studio and as a director on and off Broadway. He also appears to have been influenced by his professional association with the playwright William Gibson. Robert Hughes's documentary *Arthur Penn: Themes and Variations* (1969) brings out the importance for both Penn and Gibson of Erik H. Erikson's researches into the identity crises of adolescents. But although Erikson has provided Penn's ideas with some sort of structure, his vague use of 'identity' as a concept may account for the ease with which Penn idealizes the two psychopaths Bonnie and Clyde, to such an extent that he was able to tell Hughes that he thought of them as 'unconscious revolutionaries'. If his work in the theatre and his ability to respond to actors underlie his Rossen-like feeling for the physicality in behaviour, it is also responsible, perhaps, for a certain facility.

His first feature, *The Left-Handed Gun* (1958), revealed more of his defects than his strengths. Heavily knowing in a psychiatric way, he presents Billy the Kid as a kind of lunatic Huckleberry Finn and bathes relationships in a theatrical atmosphere. But his screen version of Gibson's *The Miracle Worker* (1962), which he had directed on Broadway, was to mark him out as being almost alone with Ingmar Bergman in his gift for isolating theatrical effects so clinically that they take on a cinematic verve. He was able to recognize how the tautness of a stage silence could be increased by exact editing. He was to see how the camera, when put to the service of a selective realism, could distil the gravity of objects—a water pump, a bunch of keys, tables, doors and windows—or the violently physical processes of education by which Annie Sullivan teaches her blind deaf-mute charge, Helen Keller, to speak. In common with Bergman, Penn has enough trust in his actors—in Ann Bancroft as Annie and Patty Duke as Helen—to risk lengthy close-ups and middle-distance shots, so that the belligerence and passion on Annie's face, or the disconnected intelligence of Helen's expression, combining brutality and a blank form of radiance, can dominate the action. His audience may resent his assault on its feelings and recall Truffaut's restraint with a similar theme in *L'Enfant sauvage*. But Penn's technique also has its value, in the sense that it overwhelms the spectator to such an extent that he is drawn into the cross-fire of emotion.

His *Mickey One* (1965) was a random attempt to marry Kafka, James Bond and the wilder styles of Orson Welles: an experiment that fizzled out inconsequentially. Compared to it, his control over the complicated plot of *The Chase* (1966) is all the more impressive. He was later to complain of interference, yet at the outset he and his colleagues appear to have worked in harmony. To its producer Sam Spiegel, who had recognized the box-office value of violent wide-scale themes at this time (and was to go over the edge of credibility in the next year with *The Night of the Generals*), the appeal of Horton Foote's novel and play is evident, and so too is its attraction for Lillian Hellman, whose screenplay elaborates on the corruptions exposed in *The Little Foxes*, but with a far deeper distrust of human nature. Penn has his admirably cast actors play hypocrites, power-hungry executives, coldly lecherous wives and self-deceivers with a force that seldom lapses into over-emphasis. His control is especially noticeable in the various degrading party sequences and in the climactic set piece at a burning car dump.

But once more in common with Bergman, he appears unable to discriminate between suffering and voluptuously received pain, between tragedy and *grand guignol*. As Sheriff Calder, the good man who stands up against injustice, Marlon Brando still seemed to be enthralled by the final scene in *On the Waterfront* and by the idea of the hero as sacrificial victim, bloodily staggering to some self-appointed Golgotha. Brando had given this masochistic fantasy uninhibited release in *One-Eyed Jacks* (1961), which he had directed himself, and it looks as though Penn was unable to restrain him in *The Chase*. The sequence

Marlon Brando, 'the hero as sacrificial victim'. Arthur Penn: *The Chase*.

in which some of the townsfolk beat up the sheriff takes violence into caricature, however true such an assault, and the breaking down of connections which it entails, may have been to the American imagination at that time.

Bonnie and Clyde (1967) discloses another side to this violence. David Newman and Robert Benton had submitted their screenplay to Godard and then to Truffaut, each of whom had suggested improvements. When both of them, in turn, had decided against directing it, Warren Beatty had taken up the option and pleaded with Warner Brothers to accept the package of Penn as director and himself as Clyde Barrow. Although it was a Warner Brothers' subject, it turned out to be quite unlike a Warner Brothers' gangster movie of the thirties, or even like Lang's *You Only Live Once*, from which it was derived. And not only in mood. In describing the journeys of his small-time robbers and killers as they move through rural America, Penn follows Godard and Truffaut, with their taste for unfolding vistas seen from a car-window, and allows landscape to enter into his narrative in a way that would have been inconceivable in the thirties.

Penn's awareness of the variety and immensity of the United States was to become a salient trait in the New American Cinema. Yet he overdoes it. Allowing his cameraman, Burnett Guffey, to be too obtrusive in his high-speed colour photography, he lapses into the modishly picturesque. He brings an unwarranted glamour to a country in the throes of a Depression: a prettiness that cannot be justified by the argument that he wished to make the sort of film that the actual Bonnie and Clyde might have wanted him to make. The result appears to have dissatisfied David Newman and Robert Benton, who directed as well as wrote a later variation on its main theme, *Bad Company* (1971). Depending far less on production values—though like Penn they look to transatlantic models for their style, to Jancsó and Truffaut in particular—they work for a simplicity of presentation that reveals how far certain American film-makers needed the stimulus of the European New Wave to help them recover some of the more cherished qualities of Griffith's *The Birth of a Nation*.

Penn is surest in his account of a rural America now irretrievably lost, in his choice of hillbilly music and in his vignettes of the secondary characters; he is at his least effective when he declines to face up to the motives of his killers and presumes that if Bonnie (Faye Dunaway) should find a stable relationship and Clyde work through his impotence, they would both be sane adults. On the slightest evidence, he shows them reach this kind of fulfilment and then undermines any hope this fulfilment may raise by linking it—if only by association—with their deaths; so that they seem to die because they have become capable of love. It is as though he believed that it is necessary to die, if only in spirit, in order to reach the adult state.

David Newman and Robert Benton: *Bad Company*.

A similar thought underlies *Easy Rider* (1969), whose box-office returns were to be as astounding as those of *Bonnie and Clyde*. Its two leading characters maintain a paradisal innocence by displacing their aggression onto the adult world; but eventually their aggression homes in on them. Captain America (Peter Fonda) and Billy (Dennis Hopper) are drug peddlers without the slightest guilt, who decide to ride on their motorcycles from Southern California to New Orleans for the Mardi Gras celebrations. They seek for ecstasy and perhaps for something more. Although they take food from various agrarian com-

Dennis Hopper: *Easy Rider*.

munities they meet on the way, and are willing to patronize members of these communities, they show no interest in joining them. Their transcontinental trip has the timeless quality of a drug trip, echoing American history and myth in a manner that underlines the futility of the present. Captain America tends to be narcissistic and Billy aimlessly purposeful, a Huckleberry Finn and Tom Sawyer who take no delight in their adventures.

But they do not feign the Warhol–Morrissey kind of obtuseness; neither does the film. Dennis Hopper's direction and his screenplay (written in association with Terry Southern) signal an awareness of the meaning of its themes and of its relationship to Whitman's poetry and to Kerouac's novel *On the Road*. The ride across the States is like a demonic parody of a pioneers' trek, a trip that can only lead to incarceration and death. Captain America and Billy remain glum, even when they reach New Orleans. They visit a brothel as though it were a dentist's waiting room and they make love to some girls in a cemetery. 'This used to be a hell of a good country,' says one of their friends. But in their numbed condition, Billy and Captain America are unable to respond to the passing landscape, however beautiful or despoiled.

This numbness, which reflects the tone of the film, seems to be merely one aspect of the persecutory feelings they entertain for their fellow countrymen. Their belief that everything may be trembling on the edge of apocalypse is confirmed by the people they meet. George Hanson (Jack Nicholson), a lawyer they pick up, who is presently murdered, broods over stories about mysterious flying objects in space, possibly enemy invaders; other strangers tend to be menacing. The final shot of the film shows their motorcycles blazing by the roadside. They can only maintain an illusion of innocence by projecting their aggression outwards so vehemently that it threatens to annihilate the very land over which they ride so easily.

The bafflement and confusion provoked by the conflict in Vietnam has reverberated through the New American cinema. If *Bonnie and Clyde* falls into the heroics of children imitating the Vietcong guerrillas in a fight against overwhelming forces, Sam Peckinpah's *The Wild Bunch* (released in 1969, the year of the Pinkville massacre) sides with the might of the oppressor. It tries to justify this position by imagining violence as omnipresent and by presenting this violence in voluptuously appealing imagery. Peckinpah may not be as openly belligerent as John Wayne was when he directed *The Green Berets* (1968), a tribute to John F. Kennedy's crack force in Vietnam: but from the child who feeds at the breast of a mother wearing a belt of bullets, through the cruel games boys play with scorpions, to the butchery, torture and kinds of killing practised by adults, Peckinpah seems capable of only one affirmation: the defiant laughter of the dying man. His filming of acts of aggression, and the way in which these acts may splinter perception, has been likened in style to Eisenstein, Kurosawa and Buñuel, but his imitation is purely a matter of style. In a way, he resembles Arthur Penn. For both he and Penn identify with the oppressor or the oppressed in an ambivalent manner. Both of them resort to slow-motion photography during scenes of violence, as though such moments provided relief from any form of responsibility.

Yet Peckinpah is most convincing when he bears witness to responsibility, as in certain moments of *Guns in the Afternoon* (1962) and *Straw Dogs* (1971), when jealous husbands begin to recognize how violently they feel about their wives. One of the more promising aspects of the New American Cinema, as the Vietnam war came to an end, was the willingness of its film-makers to be held accountable for their statements. Modelling themselves on Godard and Truffaut, they seem to have moved away from genre filming. Even an epic like Franklin J. Schaffner's *Patton* (1970)—which raises an unnecessary mystification about Patton's personality, rather in the manner of David Lean's *Lawrence of Arabia*, while remaining blank about Patton's genius as a tactician—managed to establish a rapport with its audience of a more personal kind than is usual with the blockbuster. In the late sixties many directors wished to suggest that the events they were describing had been coloured by their own experience. Francis Ford Coppola's *The Rain People* (1969), Bob Rafelson's *Five Easy Pieces* (1970), Irvin Kreshner's *Loving* (1970), Peter Bogdanovich's *The Last Picture Show* (1971) and Alan Pakula's *Klute* (1971) all had in common a sensitivity to changes in mood, an openness to the imponderable. All of them depended for their effect on an intimate tone of voice. Blockbusters like *The Godfather* (1972) or conventional romances like *Love Story* (1971) would continue to attract wide audiences, but it appeared that the main sources of energy in film-making of the seventies would emerge when the director spoke most directly to his public, unprotected by conventions of style or genre.

Francis Ford Coppola: *The Rain People.*

Notes

References have been abbreviated to author and date in cases where full publication details are given in the equivalent chapter entries in the bibliography.

CHAPTER 1: Inventions and Discoveries (*pages 3–27*)

1. Edison, Thomas Alva, *The Diary and Sundry Observations of Thomas Alva Edison*, New York, 1948, p. 83.
2. Geduld, 1970, Lumière's interview with Georges Sadoul, p. 39.
3. Josephson, 1961, p. 437.
4. Boring, 1929, p. 36.
5. Newhall, 1938, p. 14.
6. Gombrich, E. H., *Art and Illusion*, London, 1962, p. 34.
7. Ibid.
8. Scharf, 1968, p. 179.
9. Ibid., pp. 69, 73.
10. Ibid., p. 110.
11. Ibid., pp. 173–4.
12. Sadoul, Georges, *Louis Lumière*, Paris, 1966, p. 24.
13. Ceram, 1965, p. 149.
14. Sadoul, op. cit., p. 31.
15. Muybridge, 1899, p. 5.
16. Marey, E. J., *La Méthode graphique dans les sciences expérimentales*, Paris, 1885; supplement on photography, p. 3.
17. Freud, Sigmund, Standard Edition, London, 1953–74, vol. 4, 1953, p. xiv.
18. Josephson, 1961, p. 133.
19. Geduld, 1970, p. 42.
20. Münsterberg, Hugo, *Film: A Psychological Study*, New York, 1970, p. 74.
21. Ibid., p. 30.
22. Ibid., p. 39.
23. Ibid., p. 98. The moralist was 'a prominent criminologist'.

CHAPTER 2: Primitives (*pages 29–44*)

1. Morin, Edgar, *Le Cinéma ou l'homme imaginaire*, Paris, 1958, p. 43.
2. Ramsaye, T., *A Million and One Nights*, London, 1954, pp. 430–31.
3. Hampton, 1970, p. 122.
4. Eliot, T. S., *Collected Essays*, London, 1953, p. 458.
5. Lindsay, 1915, p. 88.
6. Ibid., pp. 261–2.
7. Jacobs, 1968, p. 57.
8. Vardac, A. Nicholas, *Stage to Screen*, Harvard, 1949, p. 67.
9. Patterson, Joseph Medill, 'The Nickelodeons: The Poor Man's Elementary Course in Drama', in the *Saturday Evening Post*, 23 November 1907. Reprinted in Pratt, 1973, p. 46.

CHAPTER 3: The Age of D. W. Griffith (*pages 45–75*)

1. Arvidson, 1969, p. 256.
2. Ibid., p. 55.
3. Wagenknecht, Edward, *The Movies in the Age of Innocence*, Oklahoma, 1962, p. 79.
'4. Gish, 1969, p. 99.
5. Brownlow, Kevin, *The Parade's Gone By*, London and New York, 1968, p. 90.
6. Goodman, Ezra, *The Fifty-Year Decline and Fall of Hollywood*, New York, 1961, p. 1.
7. Barry and Bowser, 1965, p. 47.
8. Mencken, H. L., *Americana 1925*, New York, 1925, p. vii.
9. Jarratt, Vernon, *The Italian Cinema*, London, 1951, p. 14.
10. Antongini, Tom, *D'Annunzio inconnu*, Paris, 1938, for D.Annunzio and the making of *Cabiria*.
11. Pratt, 1973, p. 144.
12. Fenin, George N., and Everson, William K., *The Western*, New York, 1973, p. 72.
13. Durgnat, 1969, p. 69.
14. Ibid., p. 73.
15. Cooke, 1940, p. 10.
16. Hampton, Benjamin B., *A History of the American Film Industry from Its Beginnings to 1931*, New York, 1971, p. 204.

CHAPTER 4: Aspects of the Soviet Cinema (*pages 79–116*)

1. Sachs, Hanns, *The Creative Unconscious*, Harvard, 1942, p. 116.
2. 'Horses on a cheek', from an Arts Council pamphlet for *Futurismo 1909–1919*, an exhibition of Italian Futurism, 1972, p. 30.
3. 'brilliant-hued motor buses': from an interview in the *Evening News*, 4 March 1912.
4. Cinema Manifesto in Marinetti, 1971, pp. 130–34.
5. Ibid.
6. Ibid.
7. Trotsky, 1925, p. 159.
8. Leyda, 1960, p. 413.
9. Pasternak, Boris, *Safe Conduct*, London, 1959, p. 272.
10. Pasternak, Boris, *An Essay in Autobiography*, London and New York, 1959, p. 94.
11. Leyda, 1960, p. 134.
12. Ibid., p. 161. From a letter written by Lunacharsky, dated 9 January 1925.
13. Blake, Patricia, introduction to 'The Bed Bug' by Vladimir Mayakovsky, in *Three Soviet Plays*, ed. Michael Glenny, Harmondsworth, 1966, p. 32.
14. Babel, Isaac, *The Collected Stories*, London, 1957, pp. 72–3.
15. Gray, 1962, p. 190.
16. Warshow, Robert, *The Immediate Experience*, New York, 1964, p. 202.
17. Pudovkin, V., *Film Technique*, London, 1968, p. 14.
18. Dickinson and De la Roche, 1948, p. 12.
19. Kuleshov, Lev, *The Art of the Cinema*, Moscow, 1929, quoted in Leyda, 1960, p. 165.
20. Review by Kh. Khersonski, *Izvestia*, 1924 (from programme note N.F.T. on film).
21. Kuleshov, 1929, quoted in Leyda, 1960, p. 174.
22. Kozintsev, Grigori, 'A Child of the Revolution', in Schnitzer, 1973, p. 100.
23. Ibid., p. 100.
24. Ibid., p. 106.
25. Leyda, 1960, p. 142.

26. 'Dickens, Griffith and the Film Today', in *Film Form*, New York, 1957, p. 244.
27. Trotsky, 1925, pp. 151–2.
28. Marinetti, 1971, p. 64.
29. Pudovkin, 1968, p. 143.
30. Nilsen, 1936, pp. 187–8.
31. Geduld, Harry M. (ed.), *Film Makers on Film Making*, Harmondsworth, 1970, pp. 95, 103.
32. Eisenstein, 1951, p. 43.
33. Leyda, 1960, p. 247.
34. Malevich, Kasimir, *The Non-Objective World*, Chicago, 1959, pp. 22–5.
35. Carr, E. H., *Socialism in One Country*, Harmondsworth, 1970, vol. 1, p. 136.
36. Dickinson and De la Roche, 1948, p. 13 f.n.

CHAPTER 5: The Influence of the French Avant-Garde (*pages 117–55*)

1. Diamant-Berger, Henri, *Le Film* (weekly magazine), 1917.
2. Moussinac, 1967, p. 238.
3. Arnoux, Alexandre, *Revue du cinéma*, May 1931.
4. Müsil, Robert, epigraph to *Young Törless*, source unknown.
5. Tariol, 1965, p. 168.
6. Delluc, Louis, *Cinéma et cie*, Paris, 1919, p. 17.
7. Tariol, 1965, p. 46.
8. Ibid., p. 37.
9. Delluc, Louis, *Charlie Chaplin*, trans. Hamish Miles, London, 1922, p. 13.
10. Leprohon, 1964, p. 36.
11. Renoir, Jean, *Premier Plan* anthology, Paris, 1962, p. 81.
12. Ibid., p. 61.
13. Brownlow, 1968, p. 542.
14. Dulac, Germaine, in *L'Art cinématographique*, vol. 2, Paris, 1927, p. 43.
15. Brownlow, 1968, p. 551.
16. Interview quoted by Georges Sadoul, *Le Cinéma français*, Paris, 1962, p. 47.
17. *La Révolution surréaliste*, no. 12, 15 December 1929. Quoted Kyrou, *Luis Buñuel*, Paris, 1962, pp. 18–19.

CHAPTER 6: Weimar and Scandinavia (*pages 157–215*)

1. From a letter by Lubitsch to Herman G. Weinberg, 10 July 1947, published in *Film Quarterly*, no. 25, Summer 1962, p. 39.
2. Kracauer, 1947, p. 74.
3. Willett, 1971, p. 160.
4. Taylor, A. J. P., *The Course of German History*, London, 1945, p. 194.
5. Gay, 1969, p. 75.
6. Phillips, 1971, p. 39. Full text of letter printed in Friedrich von Zglinicki, *Der Weg des Films*, Berlin, 1956.
7. Borde, R., Buache, F., and Courtade, F., *Le Cinéma-réaliste allemand*, Lyon, 1965, p. 18.
8. Willett, 1971, p. 190.
9. Amengual, 1966, p. 17.
10. Kracauer, 1947, p. 231.
11. Arendt, Hannah, *The Origins of Totalitarianism*, London, 1958, p. 215.
12. Mitry, vol. 2 (1915–25), 1969, p. 316.
13. Idestam Almquist, 1965.

CHAPTER 7: Hollywood in the Twenties (*pages 217–64*)

1. Mencken, H. L., *Americana 1925*, New York, 1925, p. 288.

2. Simpson, Louis, 'To the Western World', in *Selected Poems*, Oxford, 1966, p. 46.
3. Schlesinger, vol. 1, 1957, p. 48.
4. Ibid., pp. 68–9.
5. Ibid., p. 69.
6. Allen, 1931, p. 81.
7. Schlesinger, vol. 1, 1957, p. 64.
8. Hampton, 1931, p. 283.
9. Walker, 1970, p. 128.
10. Ibid., p. 129.
11. Banham, Harmondsworth, 1971, p. 25.
12. Glyn, 1955, p. 279.
13. Glyn, Elinor, *It and Other Stories*, London, 1927. Cf. Glyn, 1955, p. 301.
14. Brownlow, 1968, p. 427.
15. Boorstin, vol. 2, Harmondsworth, 1969, p. 109.
16. Calder-Marshall, London, 1963, p. 151.
17. Ibid., p. 95.
18. Grierson, John, *On Documentary*, London, 1966, p. 13.
19. Bowser, 1969, p. 35.
20. Panofsky, Erwin, *Renaissance and Renascences in Western Art*, London, 1970, p. 113.
21. Klingender and Legg, 1937, p. 69.

CHAPTER 8: Adapting to Sound (*pages 267–82*)

1. Empson, William, *Some Versions of Pastoral*, London, 1935; 1950 ed., pp. 114–15.
2. Stern, Seymour, 'The Bankruptcy of Cinema as Art', in *The Movies on Trial*, ed. William J. Perlman, New York, 1936, p. 125.
3. Antongini, Tom, *D'Annunzio inconnu*, Paris, 1938, for D'Annunzio and the making of *Cabiria*.
4. Vidor, King, *A Tree is a Tree*, New York, 1952, p. 175.

CHAPTER 9: The Depression: The Media and Social Conscience (*pages 285–332*)

1. Malraux, 1946, p. 26.
2. Grierson, John, *On Documentary*, London, 1966, p. 202.
3. Grierson, John, *Sight and Sound*, Winter, 1933–4.
4. Grierson, John, *On Documentary*, London, 1966, p. 54.
5. Ibid., p. 95.
6. Rotha, Paul, *The Film Till Now*, London, 1930, pp. 227–8.
7. Orwell, George, *The Road to Wigan Pier*, London, 1937, p. 21.
8. Kempton, Murray, *Part of Our Time: Some Ruins and Memorials of the Thirties*, New York, 1955, pp. 195–6.
9. Rosten, 1941, p. 160.
10. Report, *The Film in National Life*, London, 1932.
11. Forman, Henry J., *Our Movie-Made Children*, New York, 1935, p. 232.
12. Ibid., p. 45.
13. Orwell, op. cit., pp. 88–90.
14. Sarris, Andrew, *The Films of Josef von Sternberg*, New York, 1966, p. 15.
15. Green and Laurie, *Show Biz*, New York, 1951, p. 372.
16. Allen, 1940, p. 50.
17. Ibid., p. 47.
18. Bergman, Andrew, *We're in the Money*, New York, 1971, p. 49. Quoted from the *Literary Digest*, 9 January 1932.
19. Moussinac, Léon, *L'Age ingrat du cinéma*, Paris, 1967, p. 335.

20. Bazin, André, *Jean Renoir*, Paris, 1971, p. 42.
21. Schwob, 1929, pp. 243–4.

CHAPTER 10: Utopianism and Despair (*pages 335–66*)

1. Thorp, M. F., *America at the Movies*, Yale, 1939, pp. 213–14.
2. Randall, Richard S., *Censorship of the Movies*, Wisconsin, 1968, p. 194.
3. Ivens, 1969, p. 111.
4. Schickel, Richard, *The Disney Version*, New York, 1968, p. 167.
5. Ibid., p. 166.
6. Eisenstein, S. M., 'Mr Lincoln by Mr Ford', in *Film Essays*, ed. J. Leyda, London, 1968, p. 145.
7. Walker, Alexander, *Stardom*, London, 1970, p. 148.

CHAPTER 11: The Second World War (*pages 369–429*)

1. Morgan, 1948, pp. 69–70.
2. Powell, 1947, p. 39.
3. *Picturegoer*, 11 May 1940, p. 11.
4. Char, René, *Feuillets d'Hypnos*, Paris, 1946; 1962 ed., p. 102.
5. Morgan, 1948, p. 31.
6. See Graham, Peter, *The New Wave*, London and New York, 1968, for a translation of Bazin's essay.
7. 'Orson Welles in Oxford', interview with Derick Grigs, *Sight and Sound*, Spring, 1960.
8. Farber, 1971, p. 92.
9. Agee, 1958, p. 59.
10. Capra, Frank, *The Name above the Title*, New York, 1971, p. 326.
11. Leyda, Jay, *Kino: A History of the Russian and Soviet Cinema*, London, 1960, p. 371.
12. Schickel, Richard, *The Disney Version*, New York, 1968, p. 273.

CHAPTER 12: Neo-realism and the Cold War (*pages 431–79*)

1. Bentley, Eric (ed.), *Thirty Years of Treason*, New York, 1971, p. xxi.
2. Kyrou, *Luis Buñuel*, Paris, 1962, p. 97.
3. Agee, James, *Agee on Film*, New York, 1958, p. 194.
4. Zavattini, Cesare, *Sequences from a Cinematic Life*, trs. William Weaver, New York, 1959, p. 2.
5. The minister was named Ponti. See Borde, R., and Bouissy, A., *Le Néo-réalisme italien*, Lausanne, 1960, p. 70.
6. Agee, op. cit., p. 142.
7. Foreman, *Films and Filming*, September, 1963, p. 11.

CHAPTER 13: Internationalism (*pages 483–523*)

1. Radio broadcast, 28 September 1938. See David Thomson, *Europe since Napoleon*, Harmondsworth, 1966, p. 747.
2. Hisakazu Tsuji, in an interview with John Gillett and the author.
3. Remark made in a conversation with the author.
4. Benedict, 1967, pp. 99, 104.
5. Ibid., p. 192.
6. Oe, K., *A Personal Matter*, New York, 1969, p. viii.
7. Interview in *Japan Independent Film*, no. 1, Spring, 1970, p. 24.
8. He was Michele Caruso. See Hobsbawm, E. J., *Bandits*, London, 1969, p. 50.

CHAPTER 14: The New Wave (*pages 525–85*)

1. Marcorelles, Louis, *Sight and Sound*, Spring, 1958.
2. Ibid.
3. Truffaut, François, *Cahiers du cinéma*, no. 32, February 1954.
4. Malraux, André, *The Voices of Silence*, London, 1956, pp. 18–19.
5. Graham, London, 1968, pp. 17–23.
6. Ibid.
7. Ibid.
8. Ibid.
9. Barthes, London, 1967, p. 28.
10. Wollen, *Signs and Meaning in the Cinema*, London, 1969, p. 155.
11. Roud, Richard, *Sight and Sound*, Autumn, 1960.
12. Godard, 1972, p. 175.
13. Truffaut, London, 1968, p. 268.
14. Clouzot, 1968, p. 112.
15. Godard, 1972, p. 203.
16. Farber, Manny, *Negative Space*, London, 1971, p. 24.
17. Renen, Sheldon, 1968, p. 37.
18. Searle, John, *The Campus War*, Harmondsworth, 1972, p. 32.
19. Morandini, Morando, *Sight and Sound*, Summer, 1960.
20. Swift, Jonathan, *Gulliver's Travels*, Oxford, 1954, p. 105.

CHAPTER 15: Radical Compromise (*pages 587–633*)

1. Espinosa, Julio Garcia, *Afterimage*, Summer, 1971, pp. 56–67.
2. Godard, Jean-Luc, *Godard on Godard*, London, 1972, p. 85.
3. Madsen, Axel, *Sight and Sound*, Spring, 1970.

Bibliography

Unless otherwise stated, the dates given are those of first publication.

GENERAL HISTORIES

Griffith, Richard, and Mayer, Arthur, *The Movies*, New York, 1970.
  Helpfully categorizes certain cycles of the Hollywood film.
Jeanne, René, and Ford, Charles, *Histoire encyclopédique du cinéma*, Paris, 1947–68.
Knight, Arthur, *The Liveliest Art*, New York, 1957.
  A model of compression and readability.
Mitry, Jean, *Histoire du cinéma: art et industrie*, Paris, 1967–73.
  A three-volume account of the silent film.
Sadoul, Georges, *Histoire générale du cinéma*, Paris, 1946–54.
  This five-volume history was left incomplete at the time of the author's death. It is not always accurate, but is well-documented and does relate films to social trends in a stimulating manner.

WORKS OF GENERAL REFERENCE

Cawkwell, Tim, and Smith, John, *The World Encyclopedia of Film*, London and New York, 1972.
  A lengthy and (on the whole) reliable credit list for many of the principal contributors to films. Ample filmography.
Esnault, Philippe, *Chronologie du cinéma mondial des origines à nos jours*, Paris, 1963.
  Highly recommended.
Graham, Peter, *Dictionary of the Cinema*, London and New York, 1964.
Green, Abel, and Laurie, Joe, *Show Biz: From Vaudeville to Video*, New York, 1951.
  A useful half century of facts from the trade paper *Variety*.
Halliwell, Leslie, *The Filmgoer's Companion*, London and New York, 1965.
Manvell, Roger (ed.), *The International Encyclopedia of Film*, London, 1972.
  An excellent bibliography and some fine articles, notably on colour processes and the development of the cinema in various countries.

CHAPTER 1 : INVENTIONS AND DISCOVERIES

Benjamin, Walter, 'A Short History of Photography', *Screen*, Spring 1972.
Boring, E. G., *Sensation and Perception in the History of Experimental Psychology*, New York, 1929.
  An indispensable background text on physiological optics.
Ceram, C. W., *Archaeology of the Cinema*, London, 1965.
Cook, Olive, *Movement in Two Dimensions*, London, 1963.
  Both these are handsome picture-books, whose illustrations bring alive the world of the inventors and their primitive equipment.

Deslandes, Jacques, *Historie comparée du cinéma*, Tournai, 1966.

Geduld, Harry M. (ed.), *Film Makers on Film Making*, Bloomington, 1967; Harmondsworth, 1970.

Josephson, Mathew, *Edison*, London, 1961.

Marey, E. J., *La Développement de la méthode graphique par la photographie*, 1885. —*Movement* (in an English translation), London, 1895.

Morin, Edgar, *Le Cinéma ou l'homme imaginaire*, Paris, 1958.

Muybridge, Eadweard, *Animals in Motion*, London, 1899; New York, 1950.

Newhall, Beaumont, *The History of Photography from 1839 to the Present Day*, New York, 1937; 1938 ed.

Ramsaye, Terry, *Million and One Nights: A History of the Motion Picture*, New York, 1926; London, 1964.
   A fascinating and largely first-hand account of the early days of American cinema.

Robinson, David, *World Cinema*, London and New York, 1973.

Shattuck, Roger, *The Banquet Years*, New York, 1955.

Scharf, Aaron, *Art and Photography*, London and New York, 1968.
   An exceptionally valuable book which opens up a whole new field of cultural study.

Von Helmholtz, H., *A Treatise on Physiological Optics* (English translation), New York ed., 1962.

CHAPTER 2: PRIMITIVES

Balshoffer, Fred J., and Miller, Arthur C., *One Reel a Week*, Berkeley, California, and Cambridge, 1967.

Benjamin, Walter, 'The Work of Art in the Age of Mechanical Reproduction' in *Illuminations* (English translation), New York, 1968; London, 1970.

Brownlow, Kevin, *The Parade's Gone By*, London and New York, 1968.

Fenin, George N., and Everson, William K., *The Western from Silents to Cinerama*, New York, 1962.

Fescourt, Henri, *La Foi et les montagnes*, Paris, 1959.
   An account of the French 'primitives' by a film director who joined Gaumont well before the First World War.

French, Philip, *The Movie Moguls*, London, 1969; Chicago, 1971.

Hampton, Benjamin B., *A History of the American Film Industry from its Beginnings to 1931*, New York, 1931; 1970 ed.

Jacobs, Lewis, *The Rise of the American Film*, New York, 1939; 1968 ed.
   Both these are essential commentaries on the early American cinema; although neither of them (obviously) takes into account more recent research.

Jarratt, Vernon, *The Italian Cinema*, London, 1951; New York, 1972.

Lindsay, Vachel, *The Art of the Moving Pictures*, New York, 1915.

Leprohon, Pierre, *Italian Cinema* (English translation), London and New York, 1972.

Mitry, Jean, *Primitifs et précurseurs*, vol. 3, Paris, 1964.

Niver, Kemp R., *The First Twenty Years*, Los Angeles, 1968.

Paolella, Roberto, *Storia del cinema muto*, Naples, 1956.

Pratt, George C., *Spellbound in Darkness*, Rochester, 1966; New York ed., 1973.

Vardac, A. Nicholas, *Stage and Screen*, Harvard, 1949.

Wagenknecht, Edward, *The Movies in the Age of Innocence*, Oklahoma, 1962.
   A well written recollection of how the early American movies and their stars impressed a young filmgoer.

CHAPTER 3: THE AGE OF D. W. GRIFFITH

Agee, James, *Agee on Film*, New York, 1958; London, 1963.

Arvidson, Linda (Mrs D. W. Griffith), *When the Movies Were Young*, New York, 1925; 1969 ed.

Barry, Iris, and Bowser, Eileen, *D. W. Griffith: American Film Master*, New York, 1965.

Brown, Karl, *Adventures with D. W. Griffith*, London, 1973.

Chaplin, Charles, *My Autobiography*, London, 1964; New York, 1966.

Cooke, Alistair, *Douglas Fairbanks: The Making of a Screen Character*, New York, 1940.

Durgnat, Raymond, *The Crazy Mirror*, London, 1969.

Eisenstein, S. M., 'Dickens, Griffith and the Film Today', in *Film Form*, ed. Jay Leyda (English translation), New York, 1957.

Gish, Lillian, and Pinchot, Anne, *Lillian Gish*, Englewood Cliffs, New Jersey, and London, 1969.

Huff, Theodore, *Charlie Chaplin*, New York, 1951; London, 1952.

Pratt, George C., *Spellbound in Darkness*, Rochester, 1966; New York ed., 1973.

Sennett, Mack, *King of Comedy*, New York, 1954.

CHAPTER 4: ASPECTS OF THE SOVIET CINEMA

Arts Council of Great Britain, *Art in Revolution*, exhibition catalogue, 1971.

Banham, Reyner, *Theory and Design in the First Machine Age*, New York, 1960; London, 1970.

Bryher, *Film Problems of Soviet Russia*, Territet, 1929.

Carr, E. H., *A History of Soviet Russia*, 7 vols, New York and London, 1950. For the general background.

Conquest, Robert, *The Great Terror*, London and New York, 1968.

Dickinson, Thorold, and De la Roche, Catherine, *Soviet Cinema*, London, 1948; New York, 1972.

Eisenstein, Sergei M., *Film Form* (English translation), New York, 1949; London, 1951.

—*Notes of a Film Director* (English translation), New York, 1959.

—*The Film Sense* (English translation), London, 1943.

Gray, Camilla, *The Great Experiment: Russian Art, 1863–1922*, London, 1962.

Kirby, Michael, *Futurist Performance*, New York, 1971.

Leyda, Jay, *Kino: A History of the Russian and Soviet Cinema*, London and New York, 1960.

The key text. Leyda is discursive; he is starry-eyed about the revolution; and he respects old friendships too much to evaluate the films with any detachment. Yet he does bring the whole subject alive informatively.

Markov, Vladimir, *Russian Futurism*, Berkeley, California, 1968; London, 1969.

Marinetti, F. T., *Selected Futurism*, Berkeley, California, 1968; London, 1969.

Marinetti, F. T., *Selected Writings*, ed. R. W. Flint, New York, 1971; London, 1972.

Martin, Marianne, *Futurist Art and Theory, 1909–15*, Oxford and New York, 1968.

Nilsen, V., *The Cinema as Graphic Art*, London, 1936.

Pasternak, Boris, *Safe Conduct*, New York, 1958.

Evokes the intellectual climate of early revolutionary Russia.

Pudovkin, V., *Film Technique and Film Acting*. Joint editions with Introduction by Ivor Montagu, London, 1968; New York, 1970.

Sadoul, Georges, *Dziga Vertov*, Paris, 1971.

Schnitzer, Jean and Luda, *Dovjenko*, Paris, 1966.

Schnitzer, Jean and Luda (ed.), *Cinema in Revolution*, Paris, 1966; London, 1973.

Seton, Marie, *Sergei M. Eisenstein*, London, 1952; New York, 1960.
Trotsky, Leon, *Literature and Revolution*, 1925; Michigan, 1960.

CHAPTER 5: THE INFLUENCE OF THE FRENCH AVANT-GARDE
Arnoux, Alexandre, *Du Muet au parlant*, Paris, 1929, revised 1946.
L'Art cinématographique, Paris, 1927–30.
 A collection of essays which includes useful statements by Germaine Dulac
 and Abel Gance.
Bazin, André, *Jean Renoir*, Paris, 1971; (English translation) London, 1974.
Brownlow, Kevin, *The Parade's Gone By*, London and New York, 1968.
 For the chapter on Abel Gance.
Burch, Noël, *L'Herbier*, Paris, 1973.
Cobban, Alfred, *A History of Modern France*, vol. 3, 1871–1963, London,
 1965; New York, 1966.
 A useful introduction to the political background of the period.
Delluc, Louis, *Cinéma et cie*, Paris, 1919.
 —*Photogénie*, Paris, 1920.
 —*Charlot*, Paris, 1921.
Desnos, Robert, *Cinéma*, Paris, 1966.
 Interesting on surrealist hostility to the symbolist approach.
Fescourt, Henri, *La Foi et les montagnes*, Paris, 1959.
Francis, Eve, *Temps héroïques*, Paris, 1949.
 The memoirs of Delluc's wife.
Jeanne, René, and Ford, Charles, *Histoire encyclopédique du cinéma*, Paris,
 1947–68.
Lacassin, Francis, *Louis Feuillade*, Paris, 1964.
Leprohon, Pierre, *Jean Epstein*, Paris, 1964.
Muzhukin, Ivan, *Quand j'étais Michel Strogoff*, Paris, 1927.
 An autobiography; yet shrewd as criticism; cf. Muzhukin's views on
 Eisenstein and Keaton.
Moussinac, Léon, *Naissance du cinéma*, Paris, 1925. Included in the E. F. R.
 paperback of his writings, *L'Age ingrat du cinéma*, Paris, 1967.
Pathé, Charles, *Souvenirs et conseils d'un parvenu*, Paris, 1926.
 —*De Pathé frères à Pathé cinéma*, Lyons, 1940.
Tariol, Marcel, *Louis Delluc*, Paris, 1965.

CHAPTER 6: WEIMAR AND SCANDINAVIA
Amengual, Barthélemy, *G. W. Pabst*, Paris, 1966.
Beranger, Jean, *La grande aventure du cinéma suédois*, Paris, 1960.
Eisner, Lotte H., *The Haunted Screen*, Berkeley, California, and London, 1969.
 The best introduction to the Weimar cinema.
 —*F. W. Murnau*, Paris, 1964; London ed., 1972.
Gay, Peter, *Weimar Culture*, London and New York, 1969.
Huaco, George A., *The Sociology of Film Art*, New York, 1965.
Hull, David Stewart, *Film in the Third Reich*, Berkeley and Los Angeles, 1969.
Idestam-Almquist, Bengt, *Victor Sjöström*, Paris, 1965.
Kracauer, Siegfried, *From Caligari to Hitler*, Princeton and London, 1947.
 Tendentious and inaccurate, this book has influenced a whole generation of
 film writers; perhaps because it raised a powerful myth about the origins
 of Nazism that many readers found satisfying in the immediate post-war
 years. Indeed it still has power as an interpretation and should be read as a
 pioneer attempt at film sociology.
Mitry, Jean, *Historie du cinéma: art et industrie*, Paris, 1967–73.
 Useful on the early Swedish cinema.

Phillips, M. S., 'The Nazi Control of the German Film Industry', *Journal of European Film Studies*, 1971.

Rhode, Eric, *The Tower of Babel*, London, 1966.
For its essay on Fritz Lang in the 1920s.

Taylor, A. J. P., *The Course of German History*, London, 1945; New York, 1962.

Werner, Gösta, *Mauritz Stiller and His Films: 1912–1916*, Stockholm, 1969.

Wollenberg, H. H., *Fifty Years of German Film*, London, 1948; New York, 1972.

CHAPTER 7: HOLLYWOOD IN THE TWENTIES

Allen, F. L., *Only Yesterday: An Informal History of the Nineteen Twenties*, New York and London, 1931, revised 1957.

Banham, Reyner, *Los Angeles*, London and New York, 1971.

Baxter, John, *The Cinema of Josef von Sternberg*, New York, 1971.

Blesh, Rudi, *Keaton*, New York, 1966; London, 1967.

Boorstin, Daniel J., *The Americans*, 3 vols, New York, 1958–74; Vol. 1, Harmondsworth, 1965.

Bowser, Eileen (ed.), *Film Notes*, New York, 1969.

Brownlow, Kevin, *The Parade's Gone By*, London and New York, 1968.
See the section on William Wellman.

Calder-Marshall, Arthur, *The Innocent Eye: The Life of Robert J. Flaherty*, London, 1963; New York, 1966.

Crowther, Bosley, *The Lion's Share*, New York, 1957.
A history of MGM.

DeMille, Cecil B., *The Autobiography of Cecil B. DeMille*, New York, 1959; London, 1960.

Finler, Joel, *Stroheim*, London, 1967; Berkeley, California, 1968.

Glyn, Antony, *Elinor Glyn*, London, 1955.

Gordon, Jan and Cora, *Stardust in Hollywood*, London, 1930.
Good on the atmosphere at Paramount, and particularly evocative when describing Sternberg at work on *The Docks of New York*.

Hampton, Benjamin B., *A History of the American Film Industry from its Beginnings to 1931*, New York, 1931; 1970 ed.

Klingender, F. D., and Legg, Stuart, *Money Behind the Screen*, London, 1937.

Lasky, Jesse L., *I Blow My Own Horn*, New York and London, 1957.

Miller, William, *A New History of the United States*, New York, 1958; revised 1969.

Robinson, David, *Hollywood in the Twenties*, London and New York, 1968.
——*Buster Keaton*, London and Bloomington, Indiana, 1969.

Sarris, Andrew, *The Films of Josef von Sternberg*, New York, 1966.

Schlesinger Jr., A. M., *The Age of Roosevelt: The Crisis of the Old Order*, New York, 1957.

Sinclair, Upton, *Upton Sinclair Presents William Fox*, Los Angeles, 1933.

Stearns, Harold E., *Liberalism in America*, New York, 1919.

Von Sternberg, Josef, *Fun in A Chinese Laundry*, New York, 1965; London, 1966.

Walker, Alexander, *Stardom*, London and New York, 1970.

Weinberg, Herman G., *The Lubitsch Touch*, New York, 1968.

Zukor, Adolph, *The Public is Never Wrong: The Autobiography of Adolph Zukor*, New York, 1953.

CHAPTER 8: ADAPTING TO SOUND

Bergman, Andrew, *We're in the Money*, New York, 1971.
A study of the movies and the Depression.

Jeanne, René, and Ford, Charles, *Histoire encyclopédique du cinéma*, Paris, 1947–68.
> See the section in Volume IV on how the French adapted to the talkies.

Malraux, André, 'Equisse d'une psychologie du cinéma', in *Formes et Couleurs*, number 6, Paris, 1946.

Moussinac, Léon, *Panoramique du cinéma*, Paris, 1929, included in a paperback of his collected writings, *L'Age ingrat du cinema*, Paris, 1967.

Perlman, William, *The Movies on Trial*, New York, 1936.

Rosten, Leo C., *Hollywood: The Movie Colony, the Movie Makers*, New York, 1941.

Schickel, Richard, *The Disney Version*, New York 1968; also titled *Walt Disney*, London, 1968.

Shipman, David, *The Great Movie Stars: The Golden Age*, London, 1970.

Thorp, M. F., *America at the Movies*, Yale, 1939; London, 1946.
> A delightful sociological report on Hollywood during this decade.

CHAPTER 9: THE DEPRESSION: THE MEDIA AND SOCIAL CONSCIENCE

Allen, F. L., *Since Yesterday*, New York, 1940.
> A portrait of the Depression.

Agee, James, *Let Us Now Praise Famous Men*, New York, 1941; London, 1965.
> A study of the dust-bowl tragedy, with some remarkable photographs by Walker Evans.

Barnouw, Erik, *A History of Broadcasting in the United States*, volume 1: *A Tower in Babel*, New York, 1966.

Bogdanovich, Peter, *Fritz Lang in America*, London, 1968; New York, 1969.

Capra, Frank, *The Name above the Title*, New York, 1971.

Hardy, Forsyth (ed.), *Grierson on Documentary*, London, 1946.

Kael, Pauline, *The Citizen Kane Book*, New York, 1971; London, 1972.

Kempton, Murray, *Part of Our Time: Some Monuments and Ruins of the Thirties*, New York, 1955.

Lovell, Alan, and Hillier, Jim, *Studies in Documentary*, London and New York, 1972.

Paulen, Flavia, in *Twenty Years of Cinema in Venice*, edited by A. Petrucci, Rome, 1952.

Payne Fund Studies, *Motion Pictures and Youth*, New York, 1933–7.

Rosten, Leo C., *Hollywood: The Movie Colony, the Movie Makers*, New York, 1941.

Rotha, Paul, *et al.*, *Documentary Film*, London, 1936; New York, 1964.

Sales Gomes, P. E., *Jean Vigo*, Paris, 1957; English ed., London, 1971.

Schwob, René, *Une Mélodie silencieuse*, Paris, 1929.

Terkel, Studs, *Hard Times*, London and New York, 1970.

Wright, Basil, *The Long View*, London, 1974.
> For a favourable account of work at the G.P.O. film unit.

CHAPTER 10: UTOPIANISM AND DESPAIR

See the general portraits of Hollywood in the 1930s listed under Chapter 8.

Bazin, André, *Jean Renoir*, Paris, 1971.

Braudy, Leo, *Jean Renoir*, New York, 1972.

Ivens, Joris, *The Camera and I*, New York, 1969.

Snyder, Robert L., *Pare Lorentz and the Documentary Film*, Oklahoma, 1968.

CHAPTER 11: THE SECOND WORLD WAR

Agee, James, *Agee on Film*, New York, 1958; London, 1963.

Bazin, André, *Qu'est-ce que le cinéma?*, Paris, 1958–62; English translation, *What is Cinema?* Berkeley, California, 1967–72.

Bogdanovich, Peter, *John Ford*, New York and London, 1968.

Bost, Jacques Laurent, 'Four Years of French Cinema Under the Occupation', in *Cine Technician*, January/February 1945.

Calder, Angus, *The People's War: Britain, 1939–45*, London and New York, 1969.

Collier, Basil, *Short History of the Second World War*, London and New York, 1967.

Eisinger, Chester E., *The Nineteen Forties: Profile of a Nation in Crisis*, New York, 1969.

Erikson, Erik H., *Childhood and Society*, revised edition, London and New York, 1964.

See his essay on Donskoi's *My Childhood*.

Farber, Manny, *Negative Space*, New York and London, 1971.

Hackett, Hazel, *Sight and Sound*, Spring and Summer 1946.

For two articles on '*The French Cinema during the Occupation*'.

Longmate, Norman, *How We Lived Then*, London, 1971.

Morgan, Guy, *Red Roses Every Night*, London, 1948.

Polenberg, Richard (ed), *America at War*, New York, 1968.

Powell, Dilys, *Films Since 1939*, London, 1947.

Sadoul, Georges, *Histoire générale du cinéma*, Paris, 1946–54.

Tyler, Parker, *Magic and Myth of the Movies*, New York and London, 1971.

Wood, Alan, *Mr Rank*, London, 1952

CHAPTER 12: NEO-REALISM AND THE COLD WAR

Aranda, Francisco, *Luis Buñuel: A Critical Biography*, Barcelona, 1969; London, 1975.

Armes, Roy, *Patterns of Realism: a Study of Italian Neorealist Cinema*, London and New York, 1972.

Balcon, Michael, *Michael Balcon Presents*, London, 1969.

Bianco e Nero, the monthly cinema magazine published in Rome, contains numerous articles on the Italian neo-realist cinema.

Buache, Freddy, *Luis Buñuel*, London and Berkeley, California, 1967.

Esteve, Michel, *Robert Bresson*, Paris, 1962.

French, Philip, *Westerns*, London, 1973.

Amply makes up for my relative neglect of this genre in its later developments.

Guarnier, Jose Luis, *Roberto Rossellini* (translated by Elisabeth Cameron), London and New York, 1970.

Houston, Penelope, *The Contemporary Cinema*, Harmondsworth and New York, 1963.

—*Sight and Sound*, Summer and Autumn 1952, Two articles on 'Kramer & Co'.

Hovald, P-G., *Néoréalisme*, Paris, 1959.

Huaco, George A., *The Sociology of Film Art*, New York and London, 1965.

Kitses, Jim, *Horizons West*, London, 1969; Bloomington, Indiana, 1970.

Leprohon, Pierre, *Italian Cinema* (English translation), London and New York, 1972.

Sémolué, Jean, *Bresson*, Paris, 1959.

Steegmuller, Francis, *Cocteau*, London, 1970.

Warshow, Robert, *The Immediate Experience*, New York, 1962.

A collection of essays that conveys something of the Cold War tension, as well as being excellent in its own right.

Zavattini, Cesare, *Zavattini: Scenes from a Cinematic Life*, English translation by William Weaver, Englewood Cliffs, New Jersey, 1970.

A diary revealing how a key figure in the neo-realist movement was uninhibited by any narrow definition of its aims.

CHAPTER 13 : INTERNATIONALISM

Anderson, Joseph L., and Richie, Donald, *The Japanese Film: Art and Industry*, Rutland, Vermont and Tokyo, 1959.
  The standard book on the subject, though often inaccurate and curious in judgement.

Barnouw, Erik, and Krishnaswamy, S., *Indian Film*, New York, 1963.

Benedict, Ruth, *The Chrysanthemum and the Sword*, London and New York, 1967.

Iwazaki, Akira, *Kenji Mizoguchi* (French ed.), Paris, 1967.

Milne, Tom, 'Flavour of Green Tea Over Rice', in *Sight and Sound*, Autumn, 1963.

Morris, Ivan, *The World of the Shining Prince*, Oxford, 1964; New York, 1969.

Rhode, Eric, *Tower of Babel*, London and New York, 1966.
  For a portrait of Satyajit Ray.

Richie, Donald, *The Japanese Movie*, London and Tokyo, 1965.
  —*The Films of Akira Kurosawa*, Berkeley, California, 1965.
  —*Ozu*, Berkeley, California, 1974.

Sato, Tadao, *The Art of Yasajiro Ozu*, Tokyo, 1974.

Seton, Marie, *Portrait of a Director: Satyajit Ray*, London, 1971.

Simon, John, *Ingmar Bergman Directs*, New York, 1972; London, 1973.

Storry, Richard, *A History of Modern Japan*, New York, 1960; Harmondsworth, 1969.

Svensson, Arne, *Japan*, London and New York, 1971.
  A useful filmography.

Young, Vernon, *Cinema Borealis*, New York, 1971.
  An outstanding portrait of Ingmar Bergman.

CHAPTER 14 : THE NEW WAVE

Afterimage, Number 3, Summer 1971.
  On South American cinema.

Barthes, Roland, *Elements of Semiology*, London, 1967; New York, 1968.

Cameron, Ian, and Wood, Robin, *Antonioni*, London, 1968; New York, 1969.

Clouzot, Claire, 'Godard in the U.S.', in *Sight and Sound*, Summer, 1968.

Crisp, C. G., *François Truffaut*, London and New York, 1972.

Durgnat, Raymond, *Franju*, London, 1968; Berkeley, California, 1969.

Godard, Jean-Luc, *Jean-Luc Godard par Jean-Luc Godard*, Paris, 1968; English edition annotated by Tom Milne and Jean Norton, London, 1972.

Graham, Peter, *The New Wave*, London and New York, 1968.
  A key anthology of New Wave criticism.

Greenspun, Roger, 'Through the Looking Glass', in *Focus on Shoot the Pianist*, edited by Leo Braudy, Englewood Cliffs, New Jersey, 1972.

Jacob, Gilles, 'The New Wave', in *Sight and Sound*, Winter 1964.

Lane, John Francis, 'Italy', in Manvell, Roger, *The International Encyclopaedia of Film*, London, 1972.

Mamber, Stephen, *Cinéma-vérité in America*, Cambridge, Massachusetts, and London, 1974.

Mekas, Jonas, 'New York Letter', in *Sight and Sound*, Summer and Autumn 1959.
  —*Movie Journal*, New York, 1972.

Nogueira, Rui, *Melville*, London, 1971.

Pearson, Gabriel, and Rhode, Eric, 'Cinema of Appearance', in *Focus on Shoot the Pianist*, edited by Leo Braudy, Englewood Cliffs, New Jersey, 1972.

Renan, Sheldon, *An Introduction to the American Underground Film*, New York, 1967; as *The Underground Film*, London, 1968.

Roud, Richard, *Jean-Luc Godard*, London, 1967; New York, 1969.

Sarris, Andrew, *The American Cinema*, New York, 1968.

Siclier, Jacques, *Nouvelle Vague*, Paris, 1961.

Stack, Oswald, *Pasolini*, London, 1969; Bloomington, Indiana, 1970.

Truffaut, François, *Hitchcock* (English translation by Helen Scott), London and New York, 1968.

Tyler, Parker, *Underground Film*, New York, 1969; London, 1971.

Wollen, Peter, *Signs and Meaning in the Cinema*, London, 1969.

CHAPTER 15: RADICAL COMPROMISE

Baxter, John, *Hollywood in the Sixties*, London and New York, 1972.

Dunne, John Gregory, *The Studio*, New York, 1969; London, 1970.

Durgnat, Raymond, *A Mirror for England*, London, 1970; New York, 1971.

Franco, Jean, *The Modern Culture of Latin America*, Harmondsworth and New York, 1970.

Manvell, Roger, *New Cinema in Britain*, London and New York, 1969.

Searle, John, *The Campus War*, Harmondsworth, 1972.

Sussex, Elizabeth, *Lindsay Anderson*, London, 1969; New York, 1970.

Third World Cinema Festival, Part I: Latin America, 10–26 April 1971, NFT/ The Other Cinema, *Programme Notes*.

Toeplitz, Jerzy, *Hollywood and After*, London, 1973.

Walker, Alexander, *Hollywood, England*, London, 1974.

—*Stanley Kubrick Directs*, London and New York, 1971.

Acknowledgements

Without the help of the following it would have been impossible to write this book. My thanks to all of them.

The British Film Institute and the National Film Archive, London; the Cinémathèque Française; the Imperial War Museum; the Japan Film Library, Tokyo; the State Film Archives of the DDR; and the Swedish Film Archives.

Brian Baxter, Lutz Becker, Jeremy Boulton, Kevin Brownlow, M. and Mme René Charles, Wendy Cheshire, Clive Coultass, Brenda Davis, Sybille de Luze, Lotte H. Eisner, Colin Ford, René and Hiroko Govaers, John Gillett, Gillian Hartnoll, Mamoun Hassan, Philip Jenkinson, Vanda Jones, Mrs K. Kawakita, Caradoc King, Fritz Lang, Lilly Latté, Henri Langlois, Manfred Lichtenstein, Colin McArthur, David Meeker, Mrs Mary Meerson, Eugene McCreary, Nicky North, Marcus Phillips, Tadao Sato, A. Shimizu, Sheila Whiticker and Anna-Lina Wibom.

Index

A bout de souffle, 442, 538, 542–4, 625
A nous la liberté, 327–8, 510
A propos de Nice, 153, 330–31
Abbas, K. A., 487
Abe, Kobo, 515
Abraham, Karl, 192
Abraham Lincoln, 51
Abyss, The, see *Afgrunden*
Accatone, 442, 584
Accident, 610
ACE, 423
Ace in the Hole, 478
Action in the North Atlantic, 412–13
Actor's Revenge, An, 496, 515
Adam's Rib (1922), 224
Admirable Crichton, The 224
Adrian, Gilbert, 230, 259
Adventures of Buraikan, The, 515
Adventures of Oktyabrina, 92
Adversary, The, 487
Aelita, 115–16
Affaire est dans le sac, L', 324
Afgrunden, 157–8, 160
Against the Law, 90
Age d'or, L', 123, 152–5, 324, 451
Agee, James, 63, 393, 412, 418, 473
Agnus, Dei, 605
Aherne, Brian, 359
Air pur, 423
Aitken, Harry E., 45
Akutagawa, Ryunosuke, 491
Aldrich, Robert, 538, 624
Alea, Tomaas Gutierrez, 589
Algeier, Sepp, 196
All About Eve, 437
All Fall Down, 620–21
All Quiet on the Western Front, 255, 314
All the King's Men, 476
Allégret, Marc, 280
Allo Berlin, ici Paris, 344
Almquist, Bengt Idestam, 213
Alone on the Pacific, 513
Altman, Robert, 624–5
Alvarez, Santiago, 588–9
Amants, Les, 528
Ambler, Eric, 383
America, 46
America, America, 475

American Madness, 321–2
American Mutoscope and Biograph
    Company, *see* Biograph Company
American Telephone and Telegraph
    Company (AT & T), 262, 264, 285
American Tragedy, An, 299–300, 302
Amiche, Le, 578
Amis de Spartacus, Les, 124
Amore, 573
Amos 'n Andy, 285
Amour fou, L', 554
Amphytrion, 176
And God Created Woman, 527–8
And Yet We Live, 513
Anderson, G. M. (Broncho Billy), 39
Anderson, Lindsay, 543, 606–7, 609
Andreotti, Giulio, 472
Andreyev, Andrei, 199
Angels with Dirty Faces, 306, 323
Anger, Kenneth, 218, 565
Anges du péché, Les, 428
Anne and Muriel, see *Deux Anglaises et le
    continent, Les*
Année dernière à Marienbad, L', see
    Last Year at Marienbad
Anstey, Edgar, 289–90
Anti-Nazi League, 293
Antoine, 37, 129
Antonioni, Michelangelo, 422, 449,
    464, 472, 488, 553, 569–70, 573,
    577–81, 583, 587–8
Aparajito, 487
Apartment, The, 562
Apollinaire, Guillaume, 18, 118
Applause, 277
Apur Sansar, 487, 490
Aragon, Louis, 118
Arbuckle, Roscoe ('Fatty'), 223
Argent, L', 138–9
Arianne, 194
Arletty, 428
Arliss, Leslie, 382
Armat, Thomas, 39
Army Film Unit, 374, 379
Arne's Treasure, 210
Arnheim, Rudolf, 26
Arrangement, The, 475
Arrival of a Train, The, 19–20

Arroseur arrosé, L', see *Watering the Gardener*
Arsenal, 112–13, 353
Art in the Commune, 81
Artaud, Antonin, 127
Arthur Penn: Themes and Variations, 627–8
Artists at the Top of the Big Top: Disorientated, 600
Arts Theatre Guild (Japan), 514
Arvidson, Linda, 45
Ashes, 595
Ashes and Diamonds, 442, 593–4
Asphalt Jungle, The, 478
Asquith, Anthony, 383
Assassinat du Duc de Guise, L', 38, 52
Astaire, Fred, 304
Astruc, Alexandre, 526–7, 533
AT & T, *see* American Telephone and Telegraph Company
Atalante, L', 149, 329–30
Atlantic, 185
Atlantide, L', 149
Attenborough, Richard, 614
Aubrey, James, 618
Autant-Lara, Claude, 135, 425, 437, 525
Autumn Afternoon, An, 518
Avventura, L', 517, 570–71, 578–9
Axelrod, George, 622

Bacall, Lauren, 436
Back Stairs, see *Hintertreppe*
Bacon, Lloyd, 310
Bad Company, 630
Badger, Clarence, 228
Baie des anges, 549
Baillie, Bruce, 566
Baisers volés, 539, 541
Balcon, Michael, 350, 379
Balla, Giacomo, 80
Ballet mécanique, 114, 153
Balzac, Honoré de, 540
Bande à part, 546
Banton, Travis, 259
Baptism of Fire, 373
Bara, Theda, 72
Baranovskaya, Vera, 101
Bardem, Juan-Antonio, 483
Bardot, Brigitte, 527–8
Barka, Ben, 528
Barker, Reginald, 58
Baron Munchausen (1961), 592
Barrault, Jean-Louis, 428
Barrès, Maurice, 20
Barrie, James M., 224, 228, 238
Barrier, 597
Barry, Iris, 267
Barrymore, John, 335
Barthelmess, Richard, 75, 241

Bartholomew, Freddie, 439
Basilischi, I, 584
Bataille du rail, La, 445
Bath House, The, 85
Battle of Algiers, The, 529, 585
Battle of Russia, The, 414
Battle of San Pietro, 416
Battle of the Midway, The, 418
Battleship Potemkin, The, 84, 86, 97, 99, 103, 124, 324, 456
Baudelaire, Charles, 79–80
Bauman, Charles, 45, 58, 59
Bayard, Hippolyte, 4
Bazar de la Charité, 19
Bazin, André, 346, 387, 420, 467, 532, 541
Beat Generation, The, 557–8
Beatty, Warren, 630
Beau Serge, Le, 525, 551–2
Beauregard, Georges de, 535
Becker, Jacques, 428, 437, 530
Becky Sharp, 311
Bed and Sofa, 107
Bed Bug, The, 85
Beddington, Jack, 371
Before the Revolution, 581
Beggar's Opera, The, 441
Bell, Alexander Graham, 25
Bell, Charles, 5
Bell for Adano, A, 412
Belle de jour, 528
Belle et la bête, La, 130, 426
Belle Nivernaise, La, 130
Belle Vie, La, 528
Bellocchio, Marco, 585
Ben Hur (1907), 38
Ben Hur (1926), 230, 617
Benedek, Laslo, 476
Benjamin, Walter, 41
Benny, Jack, 286
Benton, Robert, 630
Berg-Ejvind och Hans Hustru, 208
Bergman, Ingmar, 206, 483–7
Bergner, Elisabeth, 193–4
Bergson, Henri, 328
Berkeley, Busby, 319–20, 401–2
Berlanga, Luis, 483
Berlin Alexanderplatz, 201
Berlin: Symphony of a Great City, 179–80, 202, 557
Bernanos, Georges, 454
Bernhardt, Sarah, 38
Berry, Jules, 325
Bertolucci, Bernardo, 581–2
Best Man, The, 622
Best Years of Our Lives, The, 421–2, 436, 563
Bezhin Meadow, 108
Bianco e Nero, 295, 472
Bicycle Thieves, 440–41, 443, 487, 587

Bidone, Il, 570
Big Blockade, The, 379–80
Big Parade, The, 254–5
Big Sleep, The, 436
Biograph Company, 38, 44–5, 65
Birch Wood, The, 595
Birdman of Alcatraz, The, 621
Birth of a Nation, The, 45–6, 48–51, 53, 251, 297
Bitter Tea of General Yen, The, 413
Bitzer, Billy, 53
Blackboard Jungle, The, 478, 620
Blackmail, 306
Blackton, J. Stuart, 39
Blair, Betsy, 478
Blesh, Rudi, 244
Blind Husbands, 229
Blithe Spirit, 462
Blockade, 336
Blonde in Love, A, 602
Blood Money, 310
Blood of the Condor, 591
Blow Up, 580–81
Blue Angel, The (1930), 134, 204–6, 313
Blue Dahlia, The, 436
Blue Light, The, 198
Blum, Léon, 437
Boccioni, Umberto, 80
Body and Soul, 476, 625
Boetticher, Budd, 538
Bogart Humphrey, 348–9, 394, 436
Bogdanovich, Peter, 565, 633
Bonheur, Le, 588
Bonnie and Clyde, 103, 475, 543, 548, 617, 627, 630–32
Boomerang, 473
Boorman, John, 467, 614–15
Boorstin, Daniel J., 355
Borgnine, Ernest, 478
Borinage, The, 291
Borowczyk, Walerian, 592
Borzage, Frank, 58, 228, 330
Boucher, Le, 550
Boudu sauvé des eaux, 329, 360
Boulting, John, 375
Boulting, Roy, 374–6
Bourgeois, Gérard, 37–8
Bourguignon, Serge, 467
Bow, Clara, 228
Boy, 515–16
Boy's Town, 317
Bragaglia, Anton Giulio, 81
Bragaglia, Arturo, 81
Braine, John, 607
Brakhage, Stan, 565
Brando, Marlon, 442, 629–30
Braque, Georges, 18
Brasier ardent, Le, 139–40
Brasseur, Pierre, 428
Braunberger, Pierre, 525

Bread, Love and Dreams, 472
Brecht, Bertolt, 169, 198–200, 441
Breen, Joseph I., 336
Brent, Evelyn, 220
Bresson, Robert, 428–9, 451, 453, 455, 471, 530, 605
Breton, André, 118, 127, 396
Brick Foxhole, The, 436
Bride Wore Black, The, 540
Brief Encounter, 410–12
Brik, Osip, 104
Bringing Up Baby, 311
Britannicus, 38
British Film Institute, 295
British Gaumont, 264
British National, 382
Brooks, Louise, 192
Brooks, Richard, 436, 478
Broken Blossoms, 46–7, 73–5
Brontë, Emily, 540
Brother and His Younger Sister, A, 495
Brothers and Sisters of the Toda Family, The, 504, 508
Brothers Karamazov, The (1931), 91
Brown, Clarence, 447–9
Brown, Roland V., 310
Browning, Tod, 313
Brownlow, Kevin, 615–16
Buckland, Wilfred, 224
Bullitt, 617
Bunny, John, 63
Buñuel, Luis, 152–5, 324, 450–53, 467, 471, 479, 483
Burlick, David, 81
Burlick, Nicolai, 81
Burma Victory, 376
Burmese Harp, The, 511–13
Burns, Robert Elliott, 316
Busch, Ernst, 200

Cabin in the Cotton, The, 322–3
Cabinet of Dr Caligari, The, 124, 165, 167–8
Cabiria (1913), 53
Cacoyannis, Michael, 483
Cagney, James, 304, 308, 348, 394, 400, 442
Cahiers du Cinéma (periodical), 122, 532, 538, 609, 624
Cain, James M., 406, 469
Calmettes, André, 38
Camera Lucida, 8
Campbell, Alan, 435
Candy, 624
Cannes Film Festival, 294, 529
Cantor, Eddie, 286
Canudo, Ricciotto, 123
Cape Ashizuri, 497–8
Capellani, Albert, 37
Capra, Frank, 321–2, 339–42, 413–15, 445

Caprelles, 128–9
Carabiniers, Les, 460, 544–6
Card Game, The, 23
Cardiff, Jack, 374
Carlos, Walter, 613
Carmen (1926), 149–50, 343
Carné, Marcel, 343, 345–6, 426–8, 437
Carnet de bal, Un, 310, 344
Carrie, 422
Casablanca, 370, 409–10, 434
Casanova (1927), 139
Casarès, Maria, 428–9, 463–4
Case Against the Lincoln Center, The, 567
Caserini, Mario, 53
Casque d'or, 428
Cassavetes, John, 464, 559
Cassirer, Ernst, 176
Castro, Fidel, 588
Castro Street, 566
Catch 22, 624
Catch Us If You Can, 614
Catelain, Jacque, 137
Caught, 456
Cavalcanti, Alberto, 134–5, 179, 290–91, 371, 479–80
Caves du Vatican, Les, 527–8
Cayrol, Jean, 466, 537
Cendrars, Blaise, 18
Central Casting Agency, 223
Centro Sperimentale di Cinematografia, 295
Cercle du Cinéma, 295
Ceremony, The, 515–17
César, 280
Chabrol, Claude, 525, 550–53
Chambers, Jack, 379
Champ, The, 439
Champion, 476
Champion, The, 64
Chandler, Raymond, 406, 436
Chang, 250
Chapeau de paille d'Italie, Un, 143
Chaplin, Charles, 45, 62–5, 73, 233–8, 259, 326–8, 330, 443–4, 539
Charleston, 134
Charlie Bubbles, 615
Charterhouse of Parma, The, 581
Charulata, 487
Chase, The, 611, 628–30
Chayevsky, Paddy, 478
Cheat, The, 121
Chess Fever, 90
Chevalier, Maurice, 276
Chiarini, Luigi, 472
Chien andalou, Un, 123, 148, 153–4
Chienne, La, 325, 328–9
Chikamatsu Monogatari, 501, 518–19
Children are Watching Us, The, 439–40, 442–3

Children of Hiroshima, 513
Chinoise, La, 107, 547
Christmas in July, 390
Chronicle of Anna Magdalena Bach, 600
Chronik von Grieshuus, Die, 167
Chronique d'un été, 554–5
Chronophotography, 4, 13
Chumlum, 566
Chute de la Maison Usher, La, 130
Chytilova, Vera, 600–601
Cinderella (1899), 36
Ciné Clubs de France, 123
CinemaScope, 439
Cinémathèque Française, 295, 532
Cinématographe, 15–16
Circular Panorama of Electric Tower, 40
Circus, The, 237
Citizen Kane, 286, 311, 385–9, 533, 587, 593, 622
City Girl, 257
City Lights, 259
Civilisation, 58
Clair, René, 141–3, 280–81, 327–8, 471
Claire's Knee, 551
Clark, Kenneth, 371, 379
Clarke, Arthur C., 612
Clarke, Shirley, 558–60
Clarke, T. E. B., 460
Clayton, Jack, 607
Clément, René, 445–6, 588, 607
Cléo 5 à 7, 588
Cleopatra (1963), 616–17
Clockwork Orange, A, 543, 612–14
Closely Observed Trains, 601–2
Close-Up (periodical), 490
Clouzot, Henri-Georges, 445
Club des Amis du Septième Art (CASA), 123
Coalface, 290–91
Cocoanuts, The, 282
Cocteau, Jean, 130, 425–6, 428, 463–4, 530
Coeur fidèle, 129–30
Cohn, Harry, 413
Colbert, Claudette, 403
Cold Days, 605
Cold Wind in August, A, 564
Collins, Ray, 286
Columbia Pictures, 618
Columbia Revolt, The, 567
Come Back Africa, 564
Comandon, Dr, 128
Comédie Française, 38
Comité d'Organisation de l'Industrie Cinématographique, 423
Communicants, The, see Winter Light
Company Limited, 487
Condamné à mort s'est échappé, Un, 454
Conflagration, 512
Conformist, The, 581

Connection, The, 559–60
Connor, Bruce, 566
Conrad in Quest of His Youth, 238
Contemporary Historians, 338
Cooke, Alistair, 70, 288, 295, 432
Coon Town Suffragettes, 49
Cooper, Gary, 255, 340
Cooper, Merian C., 249, 311–12
Copeau, Jacques, 123
Coppola, Francis Ford, 633
Corbeau, Le, 424
Corman, Roger, 624, 627
Coronation of Edward VII, The, 36
Costello, Maurice, 206
Cousins, Les, 551
Covered Wagon, The, 249–50
Coward, Noel, 373, 383, 410
Crainquebille, 150
Crawford, Joan, 407, 434
Creighton, Walter, 287–8
Cries and Whispers, 486
Crichton, Charles, 460–62
Crime and Punishment USA, 564
Crime de Monsieur Lange, Le, 141,
    325–6
Criminal, The, 610
Crisis (1945), 485
Crisis (1963), 559
Crisp, Donald, 74
Cromwell, John, 403
Cronaca di un amore, 472, 578
Cronaca familiare, 584
Crosby, Bing, 286
Crosby, Floyd, 339
Crossfire, 436
Crossways, 490–91
Crowd, The, 244, 277–8
Cruze, James, 249–50, 252–3
Cry of the People, The, 591
Cukor, George, 339, 358, 435
Cul de Sac, 596
Cure, The, 64
Curtiz, Michael, 301, 322–3, 400,
    405–10, 434
Custer's Last Stand, 58–9
Cybulski, Zbygniew, 593–4
Czinner, Paul, 193–5

Daddy Long Legs (1919), 68
Daedelum, 6
Daguerre, Louis-Jacques-Mandé, 3–4,
    7, 122
Daguerreotype, 4, 7, 9
Daiei, 513
Daisies, 600–601
Dali, Salvador, 436
Dalrymple, Ian, 371
Dames du Bois de Boulogne, Les, 428–9
Dance of the Vampires, The, 596
Dancigers, Oscar, 450

d'Annunzio, Gabriele, 53
Dante's Inferno (1909), 36
Daphnie, La, 128–9
Daquin, Louis, 424
d'Arrast, Harry d'Abbadie, 238–9
Darro, Frankie, 315
Date with a Tank, A, 379
David Holzman's Diary, 561
Davidson, Paul, 160–61, 170
Davies, Marion, 223
Davis, Bette, 323, 357, 403–4
Davis, Harry, 43
Day of Wrath, 215
Daybreak Express, 556–7
Days and Nights in the Forest, 488–90
de Forest, Lee, 260
de Robertis, Francesco, 456
de Rochement, Louis, 286–7, 473
de Seta, Vittorio, 472
de Seversky, Alexander, 415–16
De Sica, Vittorio, 387, 439–43, 445,
    472, 520
Dead End, 306
Dead of Night, 381
Dean, James, 442, 526, 593
Death in Venice, 471
Death Ray, The, 90
December 7th, 418
Decla-Bioscop, 170
Deep End, 497
Defeated People, A, 379
Degas, Edgar, 9–10
Déjeuner sur l'herbe, Le, 325
Del Guidice, Filippo, 373
Del Riccio, Lorenzo, 260
Delannoy, Jean, 425
Delaunay, Robert, 80
Deliverance, 615
Delluc, Louis, 120–26, 208, 289, 330
Demény, Georges, 15
DeMille, Cecil B., 72, 121, 223–6,
    260–62, 292
DeMille, William, 238
Dempster, Carol, 48
Demy, Jacques, 529, 549
Départ, Le, 497
Deren, Maya, 397–8, 565
Desert Victory, 370, 374–5
Deserto Rosso, see Red Desert, The
Desire, 339
Desnos, Robert, 141
Desperate Hours, The, 419–20
Deutsche Wochenschau, 423
Deutsches Theatre, 160
Deux Anglaises et le continent, Les,
    539–40
Deux ou trois choses que je sais d'elle,
    544, 546
Deux Timides, Les, 143
Devigny, André, 454

Devine, George, 607
Dewey, Thomas, 287
Diaboliques, Les, 445
Diary for Timothy, 377, 379, 461
Diary of a Country Priest, The, see
    Journal d'un curé de campagne, Le
Diary of a Lost Girl, 192
Dickens, Charles, 341, 462
Dickinson, Thorold, 379–80
Dickson, W. K. L., 3, 39
Dies, Martin, 293, 336
Dieterle, William, 359
Dietrich, Dr, 423–4
Dietrich, Marlene, 299, 358
Diorama, 7–8
Dirty Dozen, The, 617
Discreet Charm of the Bourgeoisie, The,
    155
Disney, Walt, 260, 272–4, 320, 395,
    415–16, 511, 617–18
Distant Thunder, 487
Dmytryk, Edward, 395, 436
Dr Jekyll and Mr Hyde (1931), 311
Dr Mabuse, the Gambler, 89, 174, 203,
    544
Dr Strangelove, 373, 611, 622, 624
Dr Zhivago, 412
Dodeska Den, 519–20
Dog's Life, A, 234
Dolce Vita, La, 570, 575
Doll, The (1919), 163–5
Doll, The (1969), 596
Don Juan, 160
Donen, Stanley, 471, 610
Donskoy, Mark, 416, 439
Don't Look Back, 558–9
Dos Passos, John, 338
Double Indemnity, 390, 406–7, 469
Double Suicide, 514–15
Douce, 425
Douglas, Bill, 615
Douglas, Gordon, 617
Douglas, Kirk, 476
Dovzhenko, Alexander, 111–14
Drama of the Futurist Cabaret No 13, 81
Dream Street, 160
Dreaming Lips (1937), 194
Dreams That Money Can Buy, 397
Dreier, Hans, 259
Drew, Robert, 558
Drew Productions, 558–9
Dreyer, Carl, 213–15, 268
Drifters, 188–9
Drôle de drame, 345
Duchamp, Marcel, 14
Dudow, Slatan, 200
Duel in the Sun, 435–6
Dulac, Germaine, 126–7
Dunning, George, 614
Dupont, E. A., 184

Durand, Jean, 38, 152
Duras, Marguerite, 536
Durbin, Deanna, 343
Duvivier, Julien, 310, 343–4
Dwan, Allan, 58, 71
Dylan, Bob, 558

Eady, Wilfred, 437
Ealing Studios, 460–61
Earth, 111, 113–14
Earth, The, 498
Earth Spirit, 188
East of Eden, 475, 526
Eastman, George, 3, 25
Easy Rider, 617, 631–2
Easy Street, 64
Eau d'artifice, 565
Eclipse, The, 105, 488, 569–70, 579
Ecran francaise, L', 538
Edge of the City, 619
Edison, Thomas Alva, 3, 4, 7, 10, 22,
    25, 36–9, 43
Edison Company, 44
Edouard et Caroline, 428
8½, 576–7, 594
Eisenstein, Sergei Mikhailovich, 41, 47,
    57, 86, 89, 92–100, 104–5,
    108–9, 210, 233, 289–90, 299
Eisler, Hans, 200, 466
Eisner, Lotte H., 160, 201
Ekk, Nicolai, 91, 316
El Lissitzky, Eleazar, 87
Eliot, T. S., 377
Elton, Arthur, 289
Eluard, Paul, 118
Elvira Madigan, 588
Emak Bakia, 152–3
Emerson, John, 70
Empire Marketing Board, 287–8
Empress Yang Kwei-Fei, see Yang
    Kwei-Fei
Empson, William, 342
Enfant sauvage, L', 541–2, 628
Enfants du paradis, Les, 424, 426–8
Engelein, 160
Enrico, Robert, 528
Enterprise Pictures, 476
Enthusiasm, 91
Entr'acte, 142, 152–3
Epstein, Jean, 124, 128–30, 152,
    425–6
Erikson, Erik H., 439, 628
Eroica, 606
Erotikon, 210
Espinosa, Julio Garcia, 589–90
Espoir, L', 336–7, 378
Essanay Company, 39
Eternel retour, L', 424–5
Etoile de mer, L', 152–3
Evans, Walker, 418

Everything for Sale, 594
Evrard, Blanquet, 5
Ewers, Hans Heinz, 166
Ex-Convict, The, 42
Extraordinary Adventures of Mr West in the Land of the Bolsheviks, The, 89–90

Face in the Crowd, A, 623
Face of Britain, The, 291
Fahrenheit 451, 541
Fail Safe, 622
Fairbanks, Douglas, 45, 69–71
Falcons, The, 605
Fall of the Romanov Dynasty, 89
Fall of Troy, The, 53
Fallen Idol, The, 442
Famous Players Film Company, 41, 65, 72
Famous Players-Lasky Corporation, 72–3
FAMU, 600–601
Fanck, Arnold, 187, 196–8
Fanny (1932), 280
Fantasia, 273
Fantômas, 118
Faraday's Wheel, 6
Faragoh, Francis, 305
Farber, Manny, 390, 563
Farewell My Lovely, see *Murder My Sweet*
Farewells, 595–6
Farrebique, 186, 447
Fat and the Thin, The, 596
Faulkner, William, 596
Faust, 186–7
Fear and Desire, 610
Feature Players, 72
FEKS, 91–2
Fellini, Federico, 443, 447, 464, 472, 569–71, 573–7, 584, 594
Femme de nulle part, La, 124, 208
Femme douce, Une, 455
Femme du boulanger, La, 280
Femme mariée, Une, 544
Fête espagnole, La, 126
Feu Mathias Pascal, 138
Feuillade, Louis, 38, 118–20
Feyder, Jacques, 143, 149–51, 343, 359
Fidanzati, I, 583, 602
Fiedler, Leslie A., 624
Fighting Lady, The, 421
Figueroa, Gabriel, 450
Filgate, Terry, 558
Fille de l'eau, La, 133–4, 193
Film d'Art, 267
Film Makers, 558
Finis terrae, 130, 132
Finney, Albert, 615
Firemen's Ball, The, 602–3

Fires Were Started, 379
Fireworks, 565
First Assault of the Machete, 589
First Days, The, 378
First National Company, 73
First of the Few, The, 380
First Writers' Congress (1934), 85
Fischer, Gunnar, 485
Fistful of Dollars, A, 520
Fists in the Pocket, see *Pugni in tasca*
Fitts, Burton, 293
Five Easy Pieces, 633
Five Scouts, 456, 491, 510–11
Fixer, The, 621
Flaherty, Robert, 246–9, 418, 448–9, 471
Flaubert, Gustave, 325
Fleischer, Richard, 476
Fleming, Victor, 358
Flesh and the Devil, 358
Flesh in the Morning, 565
Flicker, Theodore, 622
Floating Weeds, 504
Folsey, George, 402
Fonda, Jane, 558
Fool There Was, A, 72
Foolish Wives, 229
Footlight Parade, 320, 335
For Me and My Gal, 400–401
Forbes, Bryan, 614
Ford, Francis, 58, 250
Ford, John, 51, 250–54, 301–2, 353–6, 416–19, 471, 473
Foreman, Carl, 476–7, 610
Foreman Went to France, The, 379–80
Forman, Henry James, 296–8
Forman, Milos, 602–3
Forster, E. M., 377
Forster, Rudolf, 200
Forty-Five Minutes in Hollywood, 286
42nd Street, 318–19
Four Devils, 257
Four Horsemen of the Apocalypse, The (1921), 226
Four Hundred Blows, The, see *Quatres Cents Coups, Les*
Four Men and a Prayer, 353
Fox, William, 39, 44, 72, 257, 259–60, 264
Fox Company, 73, 310
Fox Movietone News, 260
Francis, Eve, 80, 120, 124–5
Franco, Jean, 590
Franju, Georges, 119–20, 528–9, 596
Frank, Robert, 557
Frankenheimer, John, 620–24
Frankenstein, 311
Freaks, 313
Fred Ott's Sneeze, 24–5
Free Cinema, 606–8, 615

Freed, Arthur, 275
French Can Can, 471
Frend, Charles, 379–80
Frenzy (1944), 206, 483
Fresnay, Pierre, 278–80
Freud, Sigmund, 24, 376
Freund, Karl, 167, 179, 184
Friese-Greene, William, 25
Frohman, Charles, 228
Front Page, The (1931), 314
Fuller, Samuel, 538, 624
Fury, 347–8

Gaal, Istvan, 605
Gabin, Jean, 344, 347
Gable, Clark, 442
Gad, Peter Urban, 157–8, 160
Gai Savoir, Le, 542, 548
Galeen, Henrik, 166
Galton, Francis, 13
Gance, Abel, 144, 146–9
Gang in die Nacht, Der, 181–2
Gang's All Here, The, 401–2
Garbo, Greta, 192, 213, 358–9
Gardiens de phare, 132
Garfield, John, 292
Garland, Judy, 343, 402, 439
Garmes, Lee, 299, 313
Gas Masks, 93
Gasnier, Louis, 37
Gates of Hell, 491
Gaucho, The, 71
Gaudio, Tony, 359
Gaumont Studios, 38, 267, 278
Gaumont, Léon, 37, 149
Gay Shoe Clerk, 40
Geer, Will, 625
General, The, 242–3
General Died at Dawn, The, 292, 315
General Electric, 285
General Film Company, 43–4
General Line, The, 109
General Post Office, see GPO
Generale della Rovere, Il, 472
Generation, A, 593
Genou de Claire, Le, see Claire's Knee
Gentleman of Paris, A, 238
Gentlemen's Agreement, 473
Gerlach, Arthur von, 167
Germania, anno zero, 460, 462, 468
Gertrud, 213
Getino, Octavio, 590–91
Gibbons, Cedric, 230, 259
Gibson, William, 627
Gide, André, 520, 527–8
Gilda, 434
Gilliatt, Sidney, 383
Ginna, Arnaldo, 80–81
Ginsberg, Allen, 559, 561
Girl Who Stayed Home, The, 46
Giroud, Françoise, 525

Gish, Lillian, 48, 56, 75
Glace à trois faces, La, 129
Glass, George, 477
Glass, 457
Glass Key, The, 394
Glyn, Elinor, 228–9
Go-Between, The, 610
Godard, Jean-Luc, 458, 460, 467,
    528–31, 534, 538, 544–9, 581,
    587, 590, 599–600, 630
Godfather, The, 633
Godsol, Frank, 229
Goebbels, Josef, 171
Gogol, Nicolai Vasilyevich, 86
Going My Way, 412
Gold Diggers of 1933, 318–20
Gold Rush, The, 237
Golden Coach, The, 364, 471
Goldwyn, Samuel, 72–3, 229, 306
Golem, The (1920), 166–7
Gomez, Octavio, 589
Goncharova, Natalia, 81
Gone with the Wind, 349, 357–8, 369,
    435
Good Earth, The, 230
Goodness Has Nothing to Do with It, 319
Goodwin, Hannibal, 3
Gordon, Jan and Cora, 217
Gosho, Heinsuke, 505
Gospel According to St Matthew, The
    459, 583–5
Gosta Berling's Saga, 211
Goupi Mains-Rouge, 428
GPO Film Unit, 285–9, 371, 378, 606
Graduate, The, 588
Grand Société Cinématographique des
    Auteurs et Gens de Lettres, 38
Grande Illusion, La, 294, 311, 360–61,
    363, 540
Grant, Cary, 432–3
Granton Trawler, 289–90
Grapes of Wrath, The, 356, 416–18,
    447
Grass, 249–50
Great Adventure, The, 449
Great Dictator, The, 328
Great Expectations, 462
Great Gatsby, The (book), 304
Great K & A Train Robbery, The, 254
Great Train Robbery, The (1903), 40–43
Greed, 229–33
Green Berets, The, 632
Greene, Graham, 442, 463
Greenstreet, Sidney, 392, 395
Greer, Howard, 259
Grémillon, Jean, 131–3, 424–5, 437
Gridoux, Lucas, 344
Grierson, John, 110, 246, 287–9, 371
Griffith, David Wark, 31–2, 41, 45–60,
    73–5, 90–91, 93–4, 101, 226, 232,
    251, 267, 447

Gropius, Walter 174–5
Guadalcanal Diary, 412
Guazzoni, Enrico, 53
Guernica, 465
Guffey, Burnett, 253
Guinée, Jean, 329
Gunnar Hedes Saga, 211–12
Guns in the Afternoon, 633
Guy-Blaché, Alice, 38, 118

Haanstra, Bert, 557
Hackett, Hazel, 424
Hail the Conquering Hero, 622
Hallelujah, 277, 557
Hallelujah I'm a Bum, 314
Halsey, Stuart & Co., 264
Hamer, Robert, 381, 462
Hamilton, Richard, 103, 609
Hammett, Dashiell, 293
Hammid, Alexander, 397
Hand, The, 592
Hands over the City, 571, 584
Hani, Susumi, 514
Hanson, Lars, 213
Harbou, Thea von, 172, 544
Hard Day's Night, A, 609
Hard to Handle, 317–18
Harlow, Jean, 308
Harris, John P., 43
Harron, Robert, 56
Hart, William S., 59, 250
Hartlaub, G. F., 181
Has, Wojcieck J., 595–6
Hassebe, Kenji, 517
Hatful of Rain, A, 559
Hawks, Howard, 308–9, 311, 314, 436
Hayakawa, Sessue, 121
Hays, Will H., 223, 280
Hays Office Code (1930), 223, 335
Hayworth, Rita, 369
Head, Edith, 259
Hearst, William Randolph, 37, 223
Heart, The, 512
Hearts of the World, 46
Heat, 550
Hecht, Ben, 298
Hell in the Pacific, 614–15
Hellman, Lillian, 538, 628
Hell's Angels, 256
Hellzapoppin, 396
Helm, Brigitte, 138, 192
Helmholtz, Hermann von, 25
Help, 609
Hemingway, Ernest, 290, 338
Henry, Buck, 603
Hepburn, Katharine, 442
Hergesheimer, Joseph, 240
Herlihy, James Leo, 620–21
Hepworth, Cecil, 26
Herlth, Robert, 183

Herschel, John, 5
Hidden Fortress, The, 520
High Noon, 476
Hillyer, Lambert, 58
Hi⁻tertreppe, 178
Hippocampe, L', 128
Hired Man, The (1919), 252
Hiroshima mon amour, 465–7, 534, 536–7
His Girl Friday, 314, 390
Hisamatsu, Mikiko, 493–4
Hitchcock, Alfred, 306, 325, 350–53,
    374, 432–4, 436, 546, 562–3, 580
Hitlerjunge Quex, 201
Hodgkinson, W. W., 73
Hoggart, Richard, 607–8
Hollywood Babylon, 218
Hollywood Revue of 1929, 275
Holm, Celeste, 473
Homme et une femme, Un, 588
Hope, Bob, 286
Hopper, Dennis, 632
Horse Feathers, 282
Hôtel du Nord, 346
Hour of the Wolf, 486
Hours of the Furnaces, The, 590–91
House of Wax (1953), 438
House Un-American Activities
    Committee, 422, 432, 474
Houston, Penelope, 471
How Green Is My Valley, 356
Howard, Leslie, 348–9, 380
Howard, Trevor, 411
Howe, James Wong, 620, 623
Hud, 619–20
Hue and Cry, 460–62
Hugenberg, Alfred, 170–71
Hughes, Howard, 369
Hughes, Robert, 627–8
Hulme, T. E., 377
Human Condition, The, 517
Humanity and Paper Balloons, 497
Humoresque, 434–5
Humphrey, Hubert, 559
Hurdes, Las, see *Land without Bread*
Hurwitz, Leo, 339
Husband or Lover, see *Nju*
Hustler, The, 476, 625, 627
Huston, John, 357, 392–4, 416, 463,
    478, 619–20
Huysman, Joris-Karl, 20, 79

I am a Fugitive from a Chain Gang,
    316–17
I Was Born But . . . (1932), 504
ICAIC, see Institute of Cinematographic
    Art and Industry
Ichikawa, Kon, 496, 511–13, 515, 519
IDHEC, see Institut des Hautes Etudes
    Cinématographiques
If . . ., 543

Ikeda, Tomiyasu, 494
I'm No Angel, 319
Imamura, Shohei, 514, 517
In Slavery Days, 49
In Which We Serve, 373, 383
Ince, Thomas H., 45, 57–9, 250–51, 303
Inconnus dans la Maison, Les, 424
India, 458
Indiarubber Head, The, 35
Industry of Japan, The, 510
Informer, The, 353
Inge, William, 620
Ingeborg Holm, 206–8
Ingram, Rex, 226
Inhumaine, L', 135–7
Inn at Osaka, The, 505
Innocence Unprotected, 499
Innocent Sorcerers, 594
Inondation, L', 124–5
Institut des Hautes Etudes
    Cinématographiques (IDHEC), 135
Institute of Cinematographic Art and
    Industry (ICAIC), 588
Intolerance, 41, 45, 47, 52–4, 88, 94, 125
Intruder in the Dust, 448
Invasion of the Body Snatchers, 431
Iron Curtain, The, 316, 431
Iron Horse, The, 250, 252–3
Iron Mask, The, 71
Isaacs, John, 10
Island, The, 513
Island of Lost Souls, The, 312–13
Isn't Life Wonderful? (1924), 46
It, 228
It Happened Here, 616
It Happened One Night, 339, 414
Italian Straw Hat, An, see Chapeau de
    paille d'Italie, Un
Itami, Mansaku, 497
Itard, Dr, 541
Ito, Daisuke, 494
It's a Wonderful Life, 445
Ivan the Terrible, 93, 210
Ivens, Joris, 291–2, 315, 337–8

J'accuse (1919), 144, 146
Jack and the Beanstalk (1902), 40
Jackal of Nahueltoro, The, 590
Jackson, Pat, 373–4
Jacob, Max, 118
Jacobs, Lewis, 60
Jacopetti, Gualtiero, 564
Jaenson, Henrik, 206
Jaenson, Hugo, 206
Jaenson, Julius, 206, 209
Jalsaghar, 487
Jancsó, Miklós, 464, 603–5
Jane, 558–560

Jannings, Emil, 163, 184–6
Janowitz, Hans, 168, 177
Janssen, Jules, 14
Japanese Tragedy, 517
Jarrel, Stig, 484
Jarry, Alfred, 20, 309
Jason, 560
Jasset, Victorin, 38
Jazz on a Summer's Day, 557
Jazz Singer, The, 260–61
Je t'aime, je t'aime, 536
Jeanson, Henri, 310, 346
Jehanne, Edith, 192
Jenkins, C. Francis, 39
Jennings, Humphrey, 371, 376–9, 460
Jenny, 345
Jenseits der Strasse, 201
Jessner, Leopold, 178
Jessua, Alain, 553
Jetée, La, 534–6
Jeux interdits, 445–6
Jezebel, 357
John, Pope, 583–4
Johnny Belinda, 447
Johnson, Celia, 412
Johnson, Martin, 249–50
Johnson, Nunnally, 417
Joli Mai, Le, 534, 536
Jolson, Al, 262, 277, 301
Jones, Jennifer, 403
Joseph Kilian, 602
Jour se lève, Le, 346
Journal d'un curé de campagne, Le, 454
Jouvet, Louis, 346
Joyless Street, 191
Juarez, 359
Judex, 119–20
Judith of Bethulia (1913), 32, 45, 48, 52
Jules et Jim, 539
Juliet of the Spirits, 574–5
Juráček, Pavel, 602
Just Pals, 252
Jutzi, Piel, 201

Kachenjunga, 487
Kafka, Franz, 602
Kalem Company, 39, 44
Kalmus, Herbert, 260
Kaltenhorn, H. V., 285
Kamenka, Alexander, 115, 139
Kammerspiele, Die, 161
Kanal, 592–3
Kanin, Garson, 383–4
Karin Ingmarsdotter, 208–9
Kaufman, Boris, 104, 331
Kaufman, Dennis, see Vertov, Dziga
Kaufman, Mikhail, 289
Kazan, Elia, 473–6
Kean, 147

Keaton, Buster, 141, 230, 241–4
Kelly, Gene, 471, 549
Kennedy, John F., 559
Kennedy, Joseph P., 230, 263
Kennel Murder Case, The, 322
Kermesse heroïque, La, 359
Kerouac, Jack, 557–8
Kershner, Irving, 564, 633
Kes, 615
Kessel, Adam, 45, 58, 59
Key, The, see *Odd Obsession*
Keystone Studios, 61
Kid, The, 177, 233–6
Kid Auto Races at Venice, California, 62
Killer's Kiss, 610–11
Killing, The, 610–11
Killing of Sister George, The, 624
Kind Hearts and Coronets, 462
Kind of Loving, A, 609
Kindo Eikyo, 513–14
Kinetoscope, 3, 15, 38
King, Allen, 560–61
King, Henry, 240–41
King and Country, 610
King Kong, 249, 311–12
King of Jazz, The, 274–5
Kino Nedelya, 87
Kino Pravda, 87
Kinoshita, Keisuke, 514, 517
Kinugasa, Teinsuke, 490–91
Kipling, Rudyard, 287–8
Kirsanov, Dmitri, 140
Kiss Me Deadly, 431
Kiss of Judas, The, 38
Kleine, George, 39
Kleptomaniac, The, 42
Kluge, Alexander, 600
Klute, 633
Knave of Hearts, 607
Knife in the Water, 596
Knight, Arthur, 304
Knights of the Teutonic Order, 596
Knoblock, Edward, 228
Kobayashi, Masaki, 517
Koch, Howard, 408–9
Kohlhiesal's Daughter, 165
Korkarlen, see *Phantom Carriage, The*
Kovacs, Andreas, 605
Kozintsev, Grigori, 91–2
Kramer, Stanley, 476–8, 530, 537
Krauss, Werner, 177
Ku Klux Klan, 49–50
Kubin, Alfred, 168
Kubrick, Stanley, 373, 543, 610–14
Kuhle Wampe, 200
Kumagai, Hisatora, 511
Kuroneko, 514
Kurosawa, Akira, 490–93, 497,
    513–14, 519–23
Kyoto, 513

La Guardia, Fiorello, 287
Lablanc, Georgette, 137
Labourdette, Elina, 429
Ladd, Alan, 394
Lady Eve, The, 390–91
Lady for a Day, 321–2
Lady in the Dark, 404–5
Lady Vanishes, The, 351, 353
Laemmle, Carl, 39, 65, 229, 264, 419
Lafitte brothers, 38
Lagerlöf, Selma, 209
Lamb, The, 70
Lambert, Gavin, 608
Lampe Institute, 298
Land, The, 246, 418
Land without Bread, 324, 450
Landscape after Battle, 595
Lang, Fritz, 169, 172–4, 202–4,
    347–8, 398–9, 538, 544, 611
Langdon, Harry, 321
Langlois, Henri, 20, 267, 295, 532,
    538, 548
Larionov, Mikhail, 81
Larsen, Roy, 286
Lasker, Albert D., 286
Lasky, Jesse, 72, 228, 248–9, 311
Last Command, The, 218–21
Last Days of Pompeii (1913), 53
Last Laugh, The, 183–4, 219
Last Picture Show, The, 633
Last Tango in Paris, 582
Last Year at Marienbad, 535, 537, 577
Latham, Woodville, 25
Lattin, Miguel, 590
Lattuada, Alberto, 472
Launder, Frank, 383
Laura, 436–7
Lavender Hill Mob, The, 462
Lavers, G. R., 609
Lawrence, Florence, 31
Lawrence of Arabia, 412, 633
Lawson, John Howard, 292, 412
Lawson, Wilfred, 375
Lazybones, 252
LBJ, 588
Le Prince, Louis, 25
Leacock, Richard, 558
Lean, David, 410–12, 462
Léaud, Jean-Pierre, 539
Lee, Roland, V., 313
Lef, 82, 104
Left-Handed Gun, The, 628
Legend of a Southern Island, 517
Léger, Fernand, 135, 386
Lehrman, Henry 'Pathé', 61
Leisen, Mitchell, 405
Lejeune, C. A., 295
Lelouch, Claude, 558
Leni, Paul, 172
Lenica, Jan, 592

Lenin, Vladimir Illich, 83, 94, 105
Lenya, Lotte, 200
Leo the Last, 615
Leonardo da Vinci, 93
Leone, Sergio, 520
LeRoy, Jean, 25
LeRoy, Mervyn, 268–9, 305, 308, 316–19
Leslie, Alfred, 557
Lesson in Love, A, 485
Lester, Richard, 609
Let There Be Light, 416
Letter from an Unknown Woman, 455
Letter to Three Wives, A, 437
Lévi-Strauss, Claude, 89
Lewis, John L., 287
L'Herbier, Marcel, 135–8
Liberty Films, 415
Liebelei, 194–6, 455–6
Life and Death of Colonel Blimp, The, 383
Life of an American Fireman, The, 41
Life of Emile Zola, The, 359
Life of O-Haru, The, 518–19
Lifeboat, 374
Lift to the Scaffold, 528
Lights of New York, 262
Lilith, 627
Linder, Max, 63
Lindsay, Vachel, 32–3
Listen to Britain, 378–9
Little Caesar, 269, 304–5, 317
Little Foxes, The, 386, 419–20
Litvac, Anatol, 414–15, 478
Live Today, Die Tomorrow, 515
Living, 520
Lloyd, Harold, 90, 244–5
Loach, Ken, 615
Lods, Jean, 331
Loew, Marcus, 39, 229, 264
Loew Inc., 310
Lola, 549
Lola Montès (1955), 456
Lolita, 611
London Films, 349–50
Loneliness of a Long Distance Runner, The, 609
Long, Huey, 287
Long, Samuel, 39
Loos, Anita, 70–71
Lord, Father, 335
Lorentz, Pare, 338–9
Lorre, Peter, 395
Losey, Joseph, 610
Lost Horizon (1937), 341
Lost Weekend, The, 407
Lotna, 594
Louis B. Mayer Pictures, 229
Louisiana Story, 249, 448
Love Finds Andy Hardy, 343
Love in the Afternoon (1973), 551

Love of Jeanne Ney, The, 189–90
Love Parade, The, 276
Love Story, 633
Love with the Proper Stranger, 620
Loved One, The (novel), 349
Loving, 633
Lower Depths, The (1957), 497
Loyal Forty-Seven Ronin, The (1941), 499
Lubin, Sigmund, 39, 49
Lubitsch, Ernst, 161–5, 210, 239, 276, 399
Lucia, 589–90
Luciano Serra, Airman, 294
Ludendorff, General, 170
Lukács, Georg, 100, 488
Lumet, Sidney, 478, 622
Lumière, Antoine, 15
Lumière, Auguste, 15
Lumière, Louis, 15, 19–21, 23–5, 267, 294
Lumière d'été, 424–5
Lunacharsky, Anatoli, 83, 85, 103
Lux Radio Theater, 286
Lye, Len, 288

M (1931), 202–3, 399
Ma nuit chez Maud, 551
McBride, Jim, 561
MacDonald, David, 374
MacDonald, Jeanette, 276
MacDonald, Richard, 610
Mace, Fred, 61
Mach, Ernst, 13
Machorka-Muff, 600
Mackenzie, William, 246
McLaren, Norman, 15, 557
MacPherson, Aimee Semple, 226
Madame Bovary (1924), 471
Madame de . . ., 456
Madame Dubarry, 162–3
Made in USA, 546
Maeterlinck, Maurice, 120, 228
Magendie, Francois, 5
Magic and Myth of the Movies (book), 398
Magic Christian, The, 624
Magnificent Ambersons, The, 357, 386–7, 389
Magnusson, Charles, 206, 213
Magritte, René, 119
Mahanghar, 488–9
Maisons de la misère, Les, 291, 324
Makavejev, Dusan, 498–9
Making a Living, 62
Malamud, Bernard, 627
Maldone, 131–2
Male and Female, 223–4
Malevich, Kasimir, 87, 108, 114
Malinowsky, Bronislaw Kaspar, 376–7
Malle, Louis, 458, 528–9

Mallet-Stevens, Robert, 135
Malraux, André, 336–7, 548
Maltese Falcon, The (1941), 390, 392–3
Maltz, Albert, 292, 415
Mammy, 301–2
Mamoulian, Rouben, 277, 311, 358–9, 436
Man Escaped, A, see *Condamné à mort s'est échappé, Un*
Man in Grey, The, 370, 382–3
Man Named John, A, 459, 583
Man of Aran, 249
Man on the Tracks, 606
Man Who Knew Too Much, The (1934), 350–53
Man Who Shot Liberty Valence, The, 471
Man with a Golden Arm, The, 559
Man with a Movie Camera, The, 105–7
Man without a Map, 515
Manchurian Candidate, The, 621–2
Manhattan Melodrama, 303
Mani sulla città, Le, see *Hands over the City*
Mankiewicz, Herman J., 385
Mankiewicz, Joseph L., 437
Mann, Anthony, 611
Mann, Delbert, 478
Mann, Thomas, 169, 486
Manon (1949), 445
Maraini, Antonio, 292–4
March of Time, 286, 291, 396
Mare, Il, 571
Marey, E. J., 4, 13–15, 22, 80
Marinetti, F. T., 79–81, 92
Marion, Frances, 68
Marion, Frank, 39
Marius, 278–80
Mark, Mitchell L., 72
Mark of Zorro, The (1920), 71
Marker, Chris, 529, 534–6, 573
Marseillaise, La, 310, 325
Marty, 478
Marvin, Henry H., 39
Marx Brothers, 230, 281–2, 320
M*A*S*H, 624–5
Masina, Giulietta, 574–5
Mask of Demetrios, The, 395
Mass Observation, 376–8
Maté, Rudolf, 214
Mathis, June, 226
Matter of Life and Death, A, 350
Maudits, Les, 445
Maugham, Somerset, 228
Mauvaises Rencontres, Les, 527
Max Factor, 259
May, Joe, 170, 172
Mayakovsky, Vladimir, 81–5, 87, 95, 100, 104
Mayer, Carl, 167–8, 177–9, 180–84, 257

Mayer, Louis B., 229, 343, 348, 358, 471, 617
Mayo, Archie, 348
Maysles, Al, 558
Mechanism of the Brain, The, 100, 192
Medium Cool, 501
Meerson, Lazare, 143
Meet Me in St Louis, 401
Mekas, Jonas, 566
Méliès, Georges, 33–8, 40
Méliès, Gaston, 38
Méliès Company, 44
Mélodie silencieuse, Une, 326–7
Melody of the World, 180, 413
Melville, Jean-Pierre, 530
Memories of Underdevelopment, 589
Memphis Belle, 421
Men, The, 422
Menilmontant, 140
Menjou, Adolphe, 236
Menschen am Sonntag, 202
Menzel, Jirí, 601–2
Menzies, William Cameron, 259, 272, 350
Mépris, Le, 547
Merry-Go-Round, 229
Merry Widow, The, (1925), 230
Mesguich, Félix, 115
Meshes in the Afternoon, 397
Messter, Oskar, 170
Metro-Goldwyn-Mayer, 58, 229–30, 244, 286, 293, 618
Metropolis, 204, 350, 611
Metty, Russell, 620
Metzner, Ernö, 201–2
Meyerhold, Vsevolod, 81, 90–91, 93
Michel Strogoff, 138
Mickey Mouse, 272, 343
Midsummer Night's Dream, A, (1935), 185, 565
Mifune, Toshiro, 493, 495, 520
Mildred Pierce, 405–6, 469
Milestone, Lewis, 314–15, 476
Milhaud, Darius, 337
Milky Way, The, 451
Million, Le, 143, 280–81
Millions Like Us, 383
Mills, Barney Platt, 615
Ministry of Information, 371, 383
Minnelli, Vincente, 402, 549
Miracle in Milan, 443, 445
Miracle Worker, The, 628
Miracolo, Il, 573
Miranda, Carmen, 369
Misfits, The, 416, 619–20
Miss Julie (1951), 484
Mission to Moscow, 408–9
Mr Blandings Builds His Dream House, 432
Mr Deeds Goes to Town, 339–42

Mr Smith Goes to Washington, 339, 341–42, 413, 622
Mistons, Les, 525
Mrs Miniver, 420–21
Mitry, Jean, 210
Mittler, Leo, 201
Mix, Tom, 254
Mizoguchi, Kenji, 456, 491, 494, 497, 499–502, 504–5, 518–19, 538
MGM, *see* Metro-Goldwyn-Mayer
Moana, 246, 248–9
Moby Dick (1956), 416
Modern Hero, A, 321
Modern Times, 328
Modot, Gaston, 152
Molander, Gustav, 484–5
Molly Maguires, The, 619
Moment of Truth, The, 571
Mondo Cane, 564
Monet, Claude, 9
Monk, Thelonious, 557
Monroe, Marilyn, 442
Monsieur Verdoux, 236, 328, 444
Montagu, Ivor, 350
Montesquiou, Robert de, 20
Moorhead, Agnes, 286
Moreau, Jeanne, 528
Morgenrot, 456
Morin, Edgar, 22, 122, 554–5
Morning with the Osone Family, A, 510
Morrissey, Paul, 550
Mort du Soleil, La, 127
Moscow State School of Cinematography, 88
Moscow Strikes Back, 414–15
Mother, 101–2
Mother Joan of the Angels, 596
Mother Krausen's Journey to Happiness, 201
Motion Picture Artists Committee, 293
Motion Picture Producers and Distributors of America Inc., 223, 336
Motion Picture Research Council of America, 295–8
Mouchette, 455
Moulin Rouge, 416
Moussinac, Léon, 120, 123–4, 438
Much Simplicity in Every Wise Man, 93
Müde Tod, Der, 139, 152, 172, 399
Mulligan, Gerry, 557
Mulligan, Robert, 620
Muni, Paul, 230, 309, 317, 359
Munk, Andrjez, 606
Münsterberg, Hugo, 26
Murata, Minoru, 493–5, 498
Muriel, 537–8
Murder My Sweet, 395
Murnau, Friedrich W., 161, 181–7, 204, 210, 257–9, 350, 422, 582

Mussolini, Benito, 293
Mussolini, Vittorio, 293–4
Mutual Company, 31, 45, 65
Muybridge, Eadweard, 4, 10, 14, 22, 25
Muzhukin, Ivan, 115, 138–40
My Childhood, 417, 439
My Darling Clementine, 253, 355, 471
My Home is Copacabana, 449
My Night with Maud, see Ma Nuit chez Maud
My Son John, 431
My Way Home, 603–4
Myra Breckinridge (novel), 398
Mystery at the Wax Museum, The (1933), 322

Nagata, Masaichi, 518
Nalpas, Louis, 139
Nana (1926), 134
Nanook of the North, 246–9, 448
Napoléon (1927), 148–9
Natan, Bernard, 278
National Film Board of Canada, 288
National Film Finance Corporation, 437
National Legion of Decency, 335–6
Nave bianca, La, 456–7, 459
Navigator, The, 242
Nazarin, 452
Nazi Strike, The, 413–14
Neckář, Vaclev, 602
Negri, Pola, 161–3
Negulesco, Jean, 434–5
Neher, Carola, 200
Neilan, Marshall, 68
Nelson, Robert, 566
Němec, Jan, 602
New Babylon, 92
New Earth, 292
New Left Review, 607
Newman, David, 630
Newsreel, 103, 566–7
Next of Kin, 379
Nibelungen, Die, 172–4
Nichols, Dudley, 293, 355
Nichols, Mike, 588, 624
Nicht Versöhnt, see Unreconciled
Nielsen, Asta, 115, 157–8, 160, 192
Night and Fog, see Nuit et brouillard
Night and Fog in Japan, 514
Night at the Opera, A, 281–2
Night Mail, 290
Night of San Juan, The, 591
Night of the Generals, 628
Night Shift, 379
Nikkatsu, 498–9
Nju, 193–4
No Games, 567
No Regrets for Our Youth, 510
Noailles, Vicomte de, 153

Nogent, Eldorado du dimanche, 345
Nordisk, 157, 170
Normand, Mabel, 61, 63
North Sea, 371
Nosferatu, 182–3, 204
Not as a Stranger, 478
Nothing Sacred, 315
Notorious, 432–3
Notte, La, 579
Nounez, J.–L., 329, 331
Nous les gosses, 424
Nouveaux Messieurs, Les, 143, 150–51
Novy Lef, 82
Now Voyager, 403–4
Nuit et brouillard, 465–6, 536
NY.NY., 557
Nykvist, Sven, 485

O'Brien, Willis, 312
October, 41, 98–9
O'Day, Anita, 557
Odd Man Out, 462–3
Odd Obsession, 512
Odets, Clifford, 292, 315
Oedipus Rex (1908), 38
Oh Dem Watermelons, 566
Old and the New, The, see General Line,
   The
Oliver Twist, 462
Olmi, Ermanno, 328, 459, 472, 569,
   582–3, 602
Olsen, Ole, 157
Olvidados, Los, 450–53
Olympiad, 176, 180, 294, 513
On the Beach, 537
On the Bowery, 564
On the Waterfront, 629
Once Again, 510
One Fine Day, 583
One of Our Aircraft Is Missing, 370, 383
One-Eyed Jacks, 629–30
Onibaba, 514
Only Angels Have Wings, 311
Only Son, The, 505, 508–9
Ophüls, Max, 194–6, 455–6
Orphée, 397, 463–4
Osaka Elegy, 500–501
Osborne, John, 607
Oshima, Nagisa, 509, 514–17
Ossessione, 469–70
Otto e mezzo, see 8½
Our Daily Bread, 320–21
Our Hospitality, 241–2
Our Russian Front, 315
Outlaw, The, 369
Outsider, The, 471
Overcoat, The, 92
Oyster Princess, The, 163
Ozep, Fyodor, 91
Ozu, Yasujiro, 491, 496–7, 502,
   504–9, 518

Pabst, G. W., 169, 181, 187–93,
   198–200, 321, 394
Pacifist, The, 603
Page of Madness, A, 491
Pagnol, Marcel, 278–80, 328
Painlevé, Jean, 128–9, 139, 331
Paisà, 412, 469, 573
Pakula, Alan, 633
Palm Beach Story, The, 390
Palmer, A. Mitchell, 221
Pandora's Box, 188–90
Panic in the Streets, 473–4
Paolozzi, Eduardo, 609
Paracelsus, 187
Paramount, 73, 224, 228, 310, 349,
   390, 618
Parapluies de Cherbourg, Les, 549
Paris International Exposition 1900, 19
Paris 1900, 465
Paris nous appartient, 535, 553–4
Paris qui dort, 141
Parker, Clifton, 374
Parker, Dorothy, 338, 435
Parson's Widow, The, 213
Partie de campagne, Une, 364, 470
Partner, 581
Party and the Guests, The, 602–3
Pas de deux, 15
Pasolini, Pier Paolo, 459, 569–71,
   583–4
Passenger (1961), 606
Passing Fancy, 504–5
Passion, see Madame Dubarry
Passion of Joan of Arc, The, 214, 605
Pastor Hall, 375
Pastrone, Giovanni, 53
Pathé, Charles, 19, 117–18, 138
Pathé, Léon, 37–8
Pathé, Frères, 117, 267, 278
Pather Panchali, 487, 490
Paths of Glory, 610
Patroni Griffi, Giuseppe, 571
Patton, 633
Paul, R. W., 26, 37
Pavlov, Ivan Petrovich, 100
Pawnbroker, The (1917), 64
Pawnbroker, The (1963), 336
Payne Fund, 295–8
Payne Report of 1933, 50, 295–8, 301
Peau douce, La, 529
Peckinpah, Sam, 523, 632–3
Penn, Arthur, 475, 611, 627–31, 633
Pennebaker, D. A., 556, 558–9
Pepé le Moko, 310, 344
Père Ubu, 20, 309
Perfido incanto, Il, 81
Perils of Pauline, The (1914), 37
Perier, François, 464
Périnal, Georges, 349
Perret, Léonce, 38
Persona, 485

Pétain, Marshal, 424
Peter and Pavla, 602
Petit Soldat, Le, 528
Petrified Forest, The, 348–9
Petrograd Film Studios, 88
Petulia, 609
Phantom Carriage, The, 209
Phenakistoscope, 4, 7
Philadelphia Story, The, 339
Phonograph, 4
Photoplay (periodical), 286
Picabia, Francis, 142
Picasso, Pablo, 18, 40, 118
Pick, Lupu, 177, 183
Pickford, Mary, 45, 65–9, 72, 223
Pickpocket, 455
Pierrot le fou, 546–7
Pilgrimage, 301–2
Pilota ritorna, Un, 450
Pink String and Sealing Wax, 381
Pinky, 473
Pirandello, Luigi, 72, 138, 560
Place in the Sun, A, 300
Plaisir, Le, 456
Planet of the Apes, 617
Plateau, J. A. F., 4, 7
Plow that Broke the Plains, The, 338–9
Poelzig, Hans, 167
Poil de carotte, 344
Point Blank, 614
Pointe courte, La, 534
Polanski, Roman, 553, 596–7
Polizeibericht: Ueberfall, 201–2
Pollyanna (1920), 65, 67
Pommer, Erich, 167–8, 170
Pontecorvo, Gillo, 529, 585
Poor Little Rich Girl, The, 65
Port of Call, 485
Porten, Henny, 165
Porter, Edwin S., 39–43
Postman Always Rings Twice, The, 469
Posto, Il, 328, 442, 582–3
Potamkin, Harry Alan, 317
Powell, Michael, 350, 383
Power, Tyrone, 286
Power and Glory, 311
Prampolini, Enrico, 81
Prelude to War, 413–14
Preminger, Otto, 436
President Vanishes, The, 315–16
President's Analyst, The, 622
Pressburger, Emeric, 383
Prévert, Jacques, 141–2, 245–6,
   324–5, 424, 426–8
Prévert, Pierre, 324
Pride of the Race, The, 59
Priestley, J. B., 380
Primary, 558–9
Prise du pouvoir de Louis XIV, La, 456
Prison, 485

Prisoner of Shark Island, 354
Private Life of Don Juan, The, 71
Private Life of Henry VIII, The, 349
Production Code, see Hays Office Code
Protazanov, Jacob, 115–16
Proust, Marcel, 20, 22–3
Psycho, 562–3
Public Enemy, The, 305–8
Pudovkin, Vselovod Illianarovich, 87–9,
   91, 100–103, 240, 314
Pugni in tasca, 585
Pull My Daisy, 557–8

Quai des brumes, 345–6
Quatorze Juillet, Le, 280–81
Quatres cents coups, Les, 468, 541
Quatres nuits d'un rêveur, 454
Que Viva Mexico, 108, 289
Queen Christina, 358–9, 571
Queen Elizabeth, 31, 72
Queen Kelly, 230–31
Quick Millions, 310
Quigley, Martin, 335
Quo Vadis? (1912), 53

Racket, The, 314
Radek, Karl, 85
Radio Corporation of America, 285
Radio-Keith-Orpheum, see RKO
Rafelson, Bob, 633
Raff and Gammon, 16
Raimu, 278–9
Rain People, The, 633
Rainer, Luise, 230
Rains, Claude, 342, 404
Random Harvest, 370, 404
Rango, 250
Rank, J. Arthur, 381–2
Rank Organisation, 381–3, 437
Rapper, Irving, 404
Rapt, 140
Rashomon, 490–93, 593
Rasp, Fritz, 200
Rattigan, Terence, 383
Ray, Charles, 239–40
Ray, Nicholas, 348, 442
Ray, Satyajit, 483, 487–90
RCA Photophone, 262, 264
Rear Window, 325, 580
Rebecca, 385
Rebecca of Sunnybrooke Farm (1917), 67
Rebel without a Cause, 526
Rector, Enoch, 39
Red and the White, The, 605
Red Badge of Courage, The, 416
Red Beard, 519–21
Red Danube, The, 431
Red Desert, The, 573, 577–8, 583, 587
Red Psalm, 605
Reed, Carol, 383–4, 462–3

Règle du jeu, La, 361–6
Régnier, Henri de, 20
Reich, Wilhelm, 599–600
Reid, Wallace, 223
Reimann, Walter, 168
Reinhardt, Max, 160–61, 185
Reisz, Karel, 606–8
Réjane, 38
Religieuse, La, 548, 553–4
Remorques, 423
Renoir, Auguste, 267, 325
Renoir, Jean, 23, 133–4, 192, 280,
    310, 325–6, 329, 360–66, 447,
    457, 467, 469–71, 487, 530, 538,
    540
Renoir, Pierre, 325
Report on the Aleutians, 416
Repulsion, 596
Resnais, Alain, 137, 398, 465–8, 529,
    534, 536–8, 577
Reverence for the Emperor and
    Expulsion of Foreigners, 494
Revolving Table, The, 26
' Reynaud, Emile, 25
Rice, Ron, 566
Richardson, Tony, 606–7, 609
Richer, Hans, 397
Rico, Humberto, 591
Ride the High Country, see Guns in the
    Afternoon
Riefenstahl, Leni, 176, 196–8, 293,
    342, 513
Rein que les heures, 134
Riera, Alberto, 329
Rimbaud, Arthur, 79
Riskin, Robert, 321, 339–41
Ritt, Martin, 619–20
River, The (1937), 339
River, The (1951), 487
Rivette, Jacques, 458, 529, 535,
    553–4
RKO, 264, 310
Roach, Hal, 244
Road to Life, The, 91, 316
Roaring Twenties, The, 269–70
Robbe-Grillet, Alain, 537
Robe, The, 439
Robert-Houdin Theatre, 38
Robin Hood (1922), 71
Robinson, Arthur, 167
Robinson, Edward G., 305, 348, 415
Robinson Crusoe, 479, 517
Rocco and His Brothers, 470, 583
Rodchenko, Alexander, 87
Rodin, Auguste, 10, 13
Rogosin, Lionel, 564
Rohmer, Eric, 529, 551
Röhrig, Walter, 168, 183
Roma, 570–71
Roman d'une pauvre fille, Le, 38

Rome, Open City, 372, 434, 457–60,
    472, 573
Ronde, La (1950), 456
Room, Abram, 107
Room at the Top, 607
Rooney, Mickey, 315, 343, 439
Roosevelt, Franklin D., 338
Roosevelt Year: 1933, The, 338
Rose, Reginald, 478
Rosemary's Baby, 596–7
Rosher, Charles, 68, 257
Rosi, Francesco, 569, 571–2
Rossellini, Roberto, 412, 456–60, 462,
    469, 472, 530, 538, 572–3
Rossen, Robert, 476, 625, 627
Rotha, Paul, 289, 291
Rothapfel, Sam, 260
Rouch, Jean, 247, 458, 529, 531,
    554–5
Roue, La, 117, 146–8
Round Up, The, 604–5
Rouquier, Georges, 386, 447
Rowntree, Seebohm, 609
Roxy Cinema, New York, 259–60
Roy, Bimal, 487
Ruskin, John, 100
Russell, Jane, 369
Russell, Harold, 422
Russell, Ken, 614
Russian Miracle, The, 95
Russolo, Luigi, 80
Ruttmann, Walter, 179–80, 413, 534
Ryan's Daughter, 412
Rye, Stellan, 166

Sachs, Hanns, 97–8
Sadoul, Georges, 15, 117
St Francis, Fool of God, 459, 572–3
St Louis Blues, 262
Salaire de la peur, La, see Wages of Fear
Salmonova, Lyda, 166
Salvatore Guiliano, 571–2
Samson, 595
Sanders, Denis, 564
Sang d'un poète, Le, 123, 148, 320, 324
Sanjines, Jorge, 591
Sanjuro, 520
Sansho Dayu, 519
Sapène, Jean, 138–9
Saragossa Manuscript, The, 596
Sartre, Jean-Paul, 324, 533
Sato, Tadao, 508
Saturday Night and Sunday Morning, 608
Satyricon, 570, 575
Savage Eye, The, 564
SCAP, 509–10
Scarface, 304, 308–9, 538
Scenes from True Life, 206
Schaffner, Franklin, 622, 633
Schary, Dore, 474

Schatten, 167
Schatz, Der, 190
Schenk, Nicholas M., 229
Schenk, Joseph, 244
Scherben, 177
Schertzinger, Victor, 139–40
Schlesinger, John, 609
Schneiderman, George, 253
Schoesdsack, Ernest, 249, 311
Schüfftan, Eugen, 202, 627
Schult, J. H., 5
Schwob, René, 326–7
Screen Actor's Guild, 293
Screen Writers' Guild, 293
Screenplays Incorporated, 476
Seashells and the Clergyman, The, 127
Seconds, 623
Secret Ceremony, 610
Secrets of a Soul, 192
Seeber, Guido, 167
Seiler, Lewis, 412
Selig, William, 44
Selznick, David O., 358, 402–3, 435
Sennett, Mack, 45, 59–64
Senseless, 566
Senso, 468
Sequence, 607–8
Sergeant York, 255
Servant, The, 610
Seven Days in May, 623
Seven Days to Noon, 375
Seven Samurai, 521–3
Seventh Heaven (1927), 228, 330
Seventh Seal, The, 431, 485
74 Springs, 589
Seymour, Clarine, 46
Shadow of a Doubt, 463
Shadows, 559
Shame, 486
Shanghai Gesture, The, 396
She and He, 514
She Done Him Wrong, 319
She Wore a Yellow Ribbon, 418
Sherlock Junior, 141, 243–4
Sherwood, Robert, E., 422
Shimazu, Yasujiro, 494–5, 497
Shimura, Takashi, 520
Shin Heike Monogatari, 519
Shindo, Kaneto, 513–14, 519
Shinoda, Masahiro, 514–15
Shochiku, 493, 504, 514
Shoeshine, 387, 443, 450
Shoot the Pianist, 540
Shub, Esther, 89
Siberian Lady Macbeth, 595
Sibirskaya, Nadia, 140
Siegel, Don, 538, 624
Sight and Sound (periodical), 295, 371,
    538, 587, 607
Signoret, Simone, 607

Silence, The (1920), 124
Silence, The (1963), 486
Silence and Cry, 605
Silence est d'or, Le, 471
Simon, Michel, 138, 328–9
Simon of the Desert, 451
Sin, The, 512
Since You Went Away, 402–3
Sinclair, Upton, 264, 286, 293
Singer, Alexander, 564
Singin' in the Rain, 471
Singing Fool, The, 310
Siodmak, Robert, 202, 398
Sir Arne's Treasure, see Arne's
    Treasure
Sirène du Mississippi, La, 540
Sisters of the Gion, 500–501
Sjöberg, Alf, 483–4
Sjöström, Victor, 206–10, 213–14
Skeleton Dance, The, 273
Skolimowski, Jerzy, 596–8
Skouras, Spyros P., 617
Sleeping Tiger, The, 477
Smiles of a Summer Night, 210, 485
Smith, Albert E., 39
Smith, Bessie, 262
Smith, G. A., 37
Smith, Gerald L. K., 287
Smith, Percy, 128
Snake Pit, The, 478, 627
So This is Paris, 239
Société Albatros, 115, 139–40
Société de Ciné-Romans, 139
Société du Film D'Art, 38
Socrate, 456
Sodom and Gomorrah, 624
Solana, Fernando, 590–91
Solas, Humberto, 589
Song of Bernadette, The, 403
Song of Ceylon, The, 190
Souls on the Road, 493–4
Sound of Music, The, 617
Soupault, Philippe, 118
Souriante Madame Beudet, La, 126–7
Sous les toits de Paris, 280–81
Southern, Terry, 624, 632
Southerner, The, 447, 476
Sovkino, 84
Sozosha, 514
Spaak, Charles, 310
Spanish Earth, The, 290, 337–8
Spare Time, 378, 608
Spartacus, 611
Speer, Albert, 176
Spellbound, 436
Spider's Strategy, The, 581–2
Spiegel, Sam, 628
Spione, 203–4
Splendour in the Grass, 476
Spoor, George, 39

Spring, 289
Spy Who Came in from the Cold,
   The, 619
Squadron 992, 372
Stagecoach (1939), 355–6, 417
Stake Out on Dope Street, 564
Stalin, Joseph, 88
Stalingrad, 415
Stampfer, Simon von, 4
Stand Up and Cheer, 334
Standard Oil Company (NJ), 448
Stanford, Leland, 10
Star Is Born, A, 435
State of the Union, 415
Steamboat Bill Junior, 242
Steamboat Round the Bend, 355
Steamboat Willie, 272
Steinbeck, John, 416–18
Steiner, Ralph, 339
Stendhal, 581
Sterling, Ford, 61
Stern, Bert, 557
Sternberg, Josef von, 204–6, 218–21,
   259, 298–300, 302, 313, 358, 396
Stevens, George, 300, 415, 421
Stewart, Donald Ogden, 293
Stewart, James, 342
Stiller, Mauritz, 206, 209–14, 358
Storck, Henri, 291, 324, 331
Storey, David, 609
Storm over Asia, 102–3
Story of the Last Chrysanthemums,
   501–2, 510
Strada, La, 574
Straight Shooting, 251, 356
Strand, Paul, 339
Strand Theatre, New York, 72, 260
Strange Love of Martha Ivers, The, 476
Stranger, The, 463
Straub, Jean-Marie, 600
Straw Dogs, 633
Streetcar Named Desire, A, 474–5
Strick, Joseph, 564
Strike, 95–6, 99
Stroboscope, 4, 6
Stroheim, Erich von, 47, 229–33, 443
Strong Man, The, 321
Stronger, The, 483
Student of Prague, The (1913), 165
Student of Prague, The (1926), 166
Studio des Ursulines, 123–4
Studio 28, 123
Sturges, Preston, 311, 389–92, 622
Sucksdorff, Arne, 449
Sullivan's Travels, 391–2
Sulley, Mounet, 38
Summer of '42, 620
Summer Soldiers, 515
Summer with Monica, 485
Sunrise, 257–9, 321

Sunset Boulevard, 471, 550
Suspicion, 432
Svensk Filmindustri, 213, 485
Svenska-Bio, 206
Swanson, Gloria, 223, 230
Sweet, Blanche, 48
Switchboard Operator, The, 498–9
Sylvester, 177

Tabu, 187, 249, 257
Takayama, Michio, 511
Taking Off, 603
Talbot, William Henry Fox, 4, 9
Tallents, Stephen G., 287
Target for Tonight, 370, 372–3
Targets, 565
Tartuffe, 184–5
Tasaka, Teinosuke, 491, 510–11
Tatlin, Vladimir, 87
Taurog, Norman, 315
Taylor, Gil, 596, 612
Taylor, William Desmond, 223
Technicolor Motion Picture
   Corporation, 260
Temple, Shirley, 343, 439
Ten Commandments, The (1923), 224–6
Ten Day's Wonder, 551
Tennyson, Pen, 379
Terje Vigen, 208
Terra trema, La, 469–70
Teshigahara, Hiroshi, 467, 514–15
Testament of Dr Mabuse, The, 204
Thais, 81
Thalberg, Irving, 229–30, 244, 249,
   255
That Certain Thing, 321
Thaumotrope, 6
Thérèse Raquin (1928), 149–50, 343
They Live by Night, 442
They Shoot Horses, Don't They?, 318
They Were Expendable, 252, 419
They Who Step on the Tiger's Tail, 520
Things to Come, 350
Third Man, The, 442, 463
Thirst, 485
Thirty-Nine Steps, The (1935), 353
This Sporting Life, 609
Thomas Graal's Best Film, 209–10
Thompson, Francis, 557
Thomson, Virgil, 339
Thorp, Margaret F., 356
Three Ages, 243
Three Bad Men (1926), 251
Three Caballeros, The, 395
Three Little Pigs, 335
Three on a Match, 268–9
Threepenny Opera, The, 198–200
Three Smart Girls, 343
Three Songs of Lenin, 165
Through a Glass Darkly, 486

Through the Back Door, 67
Tierney, Gene, 436
Time Stood Still, 582
Tisse, Edward, 84
Titanus, 584
To Kill a Mockingbird, 620
Tobis, 423
Toho, 490–91
Tokyo Chorus, 504
Tokyo Olympiad, 513
Tol'able David, 240–41, 447
Toland, Gregg, 386, 417–18
Toni, 280, 325
Topaze (1933), 328
Torre Nilsson, Leopold, 483, 593
Tosca, La (1908), 38
Tour, La, 153
Tourjansky, Victor, 139
Tourneur, Maurice, 68
Town, The, 396, 402
Tracy, Spencer, 315, 442
Traffic in Souls, 61
Tragedy of the Abe Clan, The, 511
Trauberg, Leonid, 91–2
Trauner, Alexander, 143
Treasure of the Sierra Madre, The, 394
Tree, Herbert Beerbohm, 31
Tree Grows in Brooklyn, A, 473
Trail, The, 463
Triangle Corporation, 45, 57, 59
Trip, The, 624, 627
Triumph of the Will, 378–9, 413
Trnka, Jiri, 592
Trotsky, Leon, 82–3, 85, 100
Trou, Le, 428
True Glory, The, 376, 383–4
True-Heart Susie, 46–7, 239
True Story of Jesse James, The, 348
Truffaut, François, 353, 458, 467,
    525, 529–31, 538–42, 628, 630
Tugwell, Rexford, 338
Tung, 566
Tunisian Victory, 375–6
Turin, Victor, 109–10
Turksib, 109–10
Turner, Otis, 49
Twelve Angry Men, 478
Twentieth Century, 211
Twentieth Century-Fox, 310, 398,
    439, 616–18
20,000 Years in Sing Sing, 323
Two Down and One to Go, 415
Two Men and a Wardrobe, 596
2001: a Space Odyssey, 612
Tyler, Parker, 398

Uchida, Tamu, 497–8
Udet, Ernst, 198
UFA, 170–71
Ugetsu Monogatari, 519
Ulmer, Edgar G., 202

Umberto D., 443–4, 520
Underworld, 298–9, 353
Unforgiven, The, 416
United Artists, 45
Universal Pictures, 229, 618
Unreconciled, 600
Unsuspected, The, 434
Uomo della Croce, L', 456
Up the Down Staircase, 620
UPA, 592
Upton, Francis R., 25
Urban, Joseph, 223
Ustinov, Peter, 383

Vacuum Zone, 513, 527–8
Vadim, Roger, 527–8
Valentino, Rudolf, 226
Vallee, Rudy, 286
Valley of Love and Death, The, 505
Van Dongen, Helen, 448
Van Dyke, Willard, 558
Van Gogh, 465
van Voorhis, Westbrook, 287
Varda, Agnès, 529, 534, 488
Variety (periodical), 184–5
Varlamov, Leonid, 415
Védrès, Nicole, 465
Venice Film Festival, 293–4
Verne, Jules, 79
Vertov, Dziga, 82, 84, 87, 91, 93, 95,
    104–7, 247, 331, 457, 531
Victimes de l'alcoolisme, Les, 38
Victory through Air Power, 415–16
Vidal, Gore, 398
Vidor, King, 344, 254–5, 277–8,
    320–21, 439, 533
Vie à l'envers, La, 553
Vie est à vous, La, 424
Vieux-Colombier cinema, 123
Vigo, Jean, 148, 201, 316, 326,
    329–32, 467
Virginian, The, 340
Viridiana, 452
Visages d'enfants, 150
Visconti, Luchino, 468–71, 569, 583
Visiteurs du soir, Les, 424, 426
Vita futurista, 80–81
Vitagraph Company, 39
Vitascope, 39
Vitelloni, I, 442, 575
Viva l'Italia, 572
Vivre pour vivre, 588
Vogel, Vladimir, 90
Voie Lactée, see *Milky Way, The*
Volkov, Alexander, 139, 147
Volpi, Count, 293
von Sternberg, Josef, see Sternberg,
    Josef von
von Stroheim, Erich, see Stroheim,
    Erich von
Voyage imaginaire, Le, 141, 148

Voyage surprise, 324

W.R.: Mysteries of the Organism, 599–600
Wages of Fear, The, 445
Wagner, Fritz Arno, 182
Wagner, Senator, 306
Wagonmaster, 355
Wajda, Andrzej, 592–5
Walk in the Sun, A, 476
Walkevitch, Georges, 426
Walking down Broadway, 230–31
Walkover, 597
Wallace, Edgar, 311
Walsh, Raoul, 269–70
Wanger, Walter, 336
War Activities Committee – Motion Picture Industry, 385
War and Peace (1947), 510
War and Peace (1956), 378
War Begins at Home, 378
Warhol, Andy, 398, 550
Warm, Hermann, 168
Warner Brothers, 260–61, 302, 310, 316–17, 348, 438, 618, 630
Warning Shadows see Schatten
Warrendale, 560–61
Warrens of Virginia, The, 224
Watering the Gardener, 25, 63
Watt, Harry, 290, 371–3
Waxworks, 172
Way Ahead, The, 370, 383
Way down East, 46, 101
Way to the Stars, The, 383
Wayne, John, 632
We Dive at Dawn, 383
Weavers, The, 200–201
Wedding March, 230
Wedgwood, Tom, 5
Wee Willie Winkie, 353
Weekend, 542, 548–9
Wegener, Paul, 165–7
Well Washed House, The, 62–3
Welles, Orson, 286, 338, 385–9, 392, 463, 470, 538, 549, 593, 622
Wellman, William, 225–6, 306–7, 315–16, 435
Wells, H. G., 350
Went the Day Well?, 381
Wertmuller, Lina, 584
West, Mae, 228, 308, 319, 527
West, Nathanael, 317, 624
West, Raymond B., 58
Western Approaches, 373–4
Western Electric, 262, 285
Wexler, Haskell, 561
Wexley, John, 292, 323
Whale, James, 311
Whatever Happened to Baby Jane?, 624
What's Up Doc?, 617

White Hell of Pitz Plau, The, 196–8
White Nights (1957), 471
White Sheik, The, 472, 575
White Threads of Waterfall, 500
Why We Fight, 413–15
Why Worry?, 245
Widerberg, Bo, 588
Wild Angels, The, 624
Wild Boys of the Road, 315–16
Wild Bunch, The, 103, 523, 632
Wild Palms, The (novel), 534
Wild River, 476
Wild Strawberries, 485, 593
Wilder, Billy, 202, 398, 406–7, 471, 478, 550, 562–3
Wilder, Thornton, 463
Williams, Raymond, 607
Wilson, Harold, 437
Wings, 255–6
Winter Light, 486
Woman in the Window, The, 399
Woman of Affairs, A, 358
Woman of Paris, A, 235–8, 501
Woman of the Dunes, 515
Woman without a Face, The, 484–5
Women in Love, 614
Women of the Night, 499–500
Wood, Sam, 358
Wright, Basil, 290, 371
Wuthering Heights, 385
Wyler, William, 357, 386–7, 419–22, 436

Yamada, Isuzu, 501
Yamanaka, Sadao, 490, 497–8
Yang Kwei-Fei, 519
Yankee Doodle Dandy, 400
Yearling, The, 447–8
Yellow Submarine, The, 614
Yesterday Girl, 600
Yoda, Yoshikata, 501
Yojimbo, 520
Yoshimura, Kimisaburo, 497–8
You Only Live Once, 347–8
Young Mr Lincoln, 353–5
Young Stranger, The, 620
Yule, Lady, 382
Yutkevich, Serge, 91–2

Zagreb School of Animation, 592
Zanuck, Darryl F., 285–6, 385, 617–18
Zanuck, Richard, 618
Zavattini, Cesare, 386–9, 439–43, 464, 468
Zéro de conduite, 149, 316, 324, 330–32, 439
Zecca, Ferdinand, 37, 62–3
Zelnick, Friedrich, 200–201
Zeman, Karel, 592
Zhadnov, Andre, 85

Ziegfeld, Florenz, 369
Ziegfeld Follies, 369
Zinnemann, Fred, 422, 476
Zola, Emile, 325
Zoo in Budapest, 313

Zoöpraxiscope, 4
Zukor, Adolph, 31, 39, 45, 65, 72–3,
  224, 228, 438
Zurlini, Valerio, 472, 594
Zvenigora, 111–12